ISOMETRIC GAME PROGRAMMING WITH DIRECTX 7.0

Check the Web for Updates!

To check for updates or corrections relevant to this book and/or CD-ROM visit our updates page on the Web at **http://www.prima-tech.com/updates.**

Send Us Your Comments!

To comment on this book or any other PRIMA TECH title, visit our reader response page on the Web at **http://www.prima-tech.com/comments.**

How to Order!

For information on quantity discounts, contact the publisher: Prima Publishing, P.O. Box 1260BK, Rocklin, CA 95677-1260; (916) 787-7000. On your letterhead, include information concerning the intended use of the books and the number of books you want to purchase.

ISOMETRIC GAME PROGRAMMING WITH DIRECTX 7.0

Ernest Pazera

Series Editor
André LaMothe
CEO Xtreme Games LLC

PRIMA TECH

A Division of Prima Publishing

Prima Publishing and colophon are registered trademarks of Prima Communications, Inc. PRIMA TECH is a trademark of Prima Communications, Inc., Roseville, California 95661.

Publisher: Stacy L. Hiquet

Associate Marketing Manager: Jennifer Breece

Managing Editor: Sandy Doell

Acquisitions Editor: Jody Kennen

Project Editor: Estelle Manticas

Technical Reviewer: Mason McCuskey

Copy Editor: Gayle Johnson

Interior Layout: LJ Graphics: Susan Honeywell, Julia Grosch, Patrick Cunningham

Cover Design: Prima Design Team

Indexer: Sharon Hilgenberg

ISBN: 0-7615-3089-4

Library of Congress Catalog Card Number: 00-107339

Printed in the United States of America

01 02 03 04 BB 10 9 8 7 6 5 4 3 2

For my mother

Acknowledgments

First and foremost, I'd like to thank Andre LaMothe for giving me a shot. I would also like to thank all the people at Prima who were on my project, including Kim Spilker, Jody Kennen, and Estelle Manticas.

Furthermore, I want to thank the following people for various things: Dave Astle and Kevin Hawkins (for testing my example programs), Mason McCuskey (my technical editor), Chris Ravens (my life mate), Diana Gruber (for the nice review on amazon and dirty jokes), Mary Jo Beall (my mom), and my sippy-bottle (filled with Pepsi—it helped me through).

Thanks also to the iso-people, as I've come to think of them: Jim Adams, Dino Gambone, Yanni Deliyannis, and the rest.

Also, all of the guys who submitted something for the CD: Joseph Farrell, Everett Bell, Andy Pullis, Octav, and others. Thanks.

And anyone else I've forgotten: just write your name into the space below, and thank you, too.

About the Author

Ernest S. Pazera started programming on a TRS-80 Color Computer 2 in 1986; he switched to PC permanently in 1990. He doesn't have a computer science degree, just a high school diploma. Ernest served in the United States Navy from 1993 until 1996 but never forgot his first love, which was game programming.

In 1995, Ernest picked up a copy of Sid Meier's *Civilization II*, which, in his estimation, is one of the greatest games of all times. By studying this game he discovered how isometric views worked, and he subsequently wrote a few articles on the subject. His interest in isometric game programming lead him to become part of a group that would eventually create GameDev.net, LLC (http://www.gamedev.net), and his involvement with that group lead him to become the author of this book.

In addition to book authorship and his involvement in GameDev.net, Ernest owns two companies: DTM Software, which has done contract work on two commercial games, and C&M Tax, where he prepares personal income tax returns (thus keeping him from starving while writing games as an independent operator).

Ernest goes by the name TANSTAAFL in #gamedev on afternet in IRC, and can be reached at tanstaafl@gamedev.net

Contents at a Glance

CONTENTS

Letter from the Series Editor

Dear Reader,

First off I would like to thank the author of this book, Mr. Ernest Pazera, for writing it. Now the pressure is off me to cover ISO Game Programming once and for all - thanks Ernest!

If you've picked up this book then you must have an interest in creating Isometric games. You have come to the right place. Isometric game programming is not the trivial task many 3D programmers think it is—in fact, Isometric rendering methods are not trivial, nor are they obvious. Moreover, the optimizations are very subtle. To date, no author has ever tried to write a book on the subject, since not only is the material complex, but it is in many cases a bit secret.

Luckily for us, Mr. Pazera has put down in these pages an unbelievable amount of information on every single topic of Isometric graphics and game programming. As I read the text I caught myself thinking, "So that's how they do it!" more than once.

The bottom line is, if you want to learn Isometric game programming then you need this book—it's the only book that will fill the order. I happen to know that Ernest is obsessed with ISO game programming, and that both his attention to detail and his high standards of perfection are illustrated in this work.

Andre' LaMothe

March 2001

Introduction

Thank you for buying my book. I really appreciate it.

Isometric games have been with us since the golden age of arcade machines, with games like *Zaxxon* and *Q-Bert*. They are still with us today—witness games like *Nox* and *Age of Kings*—and they are as popular as ever. Yet there has never been a book on making isometric games. That is the void I am seeking to fill with *Isometric Game Programming with DirectX*.

This Introduction will give you an overview of both the book itself and an introduction to the chapter structure contained herein. Over the course of this book you will go from isometric programming novice to expert. Okay, maybe novice to intermediate. You can't quite get to expert in just a single book!

What's in This Book?

This book, as you are no doubt aware, is a book about programming games—how to do so, specifically—and it emphasizes use of the isometric view. This means that the program examples are mainly concerned with the graphical aspect of game programming.

Contained herein is also quite a bit of information on the algorithms behind tile-based games. Isometric games tend to be tile-based. If you wanted to make overhead view tile-based games, the same algorithms apply.

Why did I write this book, you ask? Because isometric game programming, and isometric algorithms, have been largely ignored by other game programming books. Sure, you can find plenty of books on how to program 3D games, and there are plenty of books on 2D games, but none of the in-between stuff, like isometric games.

You will find the program examples (and there are a ton of them) that go along with the text on the CD in the back of the book; you will find instructions on how to load and run those examples in Appendix A. It is a good idea to turn to that appendix first, even before you start reading. That way, when the first mention of an example is made, you'll be ready to go.

Who Should Read This Book?

You are a programmer who has a reasonable amount of skill in C/C++ (you don't have to be an expert—I made my code as easy to follow as possible). You must also be interested in making isometric games. You very likely play strategy games (either real time or turn-based), computer role playing games, or puzzle games (all of these genres make use of the isometric view quite heavily).

Naturally, your goal is to make the greatest game of all time, and become filthy rich and buy a Corvette. Yeah, that's my goal too—it hasn't happened quite yet, but I'm patient. As with all things in life, we must walk before we can run, and before we can walk, we must crawl.

I won't tell you that immediately after reading this book you'll be able to go and make a wonderful game with the isometric view that will sell millions of copies. I *will* tell you, however, that this book will help you build a foundation of knowledge and algorithms that will make you a more valuable programmer.

How This Book is Organized

The four parts contained in this book—and the topics they cover—are as follows:

- **Part I: The Basics.** Introduces the world of tile-based isometric game programming and discusses topics common to all isometric games.
- **Part II: Isometric Fundamentals**. Delves into different ways of adding realism to isometric tile-based games.
- **Part III: Isometric Methodology**. Explores user interaction with isometric games and sheds light on more rendering topics.
- **Part IV: Advanced Topics.** Introduces a final ingredient, artificial intelligence, and fits it together with what you've learned previously.
- **Part V: Appendices.** Shows you how to load the example files into your compiler, and offers resaources for learning more about isometric game programming.

Chapter Structure

The chapters are similar in structure, though the topics vary widely. Each chapter contains all or most of the following elements:

- **Overview**. Each chapter starts with a brief overview, in which I give a brief rundown of the topics that will be discussed in that chapter, as well as a breakdown the chapter's topic headings.
- **Terminology**. When a new concept is introduced and a lot of new terms are thrown at you, there is a terminology section early in the chapter. This does not apply to all the chapters, and many of the chapters in Part 0 do not have them.
- **How-to Information.** Most of the content of each chapter contains information on how to accomplish the tasks that are covered in that chapter. Usually, a lot of code accompanies the text, and most of the time one or more sample programs are supplied for you to load, run, and modify to more fully explore the concepts put forth.
- **Libraries and Classes.** Some chapters have code libraries that I have written to help you with the tasks you perform in that chapter. These libraries or classes simplify some otherwise complicated coding topics. After a library is used in one chapter, most of the rest of the chapters will use it also.
- **Empowering the User**. Some chapters have a small section called "Empowering the User." This little section has some tips on how to not alienate your users and keep them playing your games. Most of the information is common sense, but many games and game developers have failed for the simple reason that they don't give the player enough control over his or her game experience. Perhaps an alternative name for the "Empowering the User" section would be "How to Not Tick off the User."
- **Summary**. The final part of the chapter consists of the summary. I review the topics we've discussed, and I often list things you should remember. The summary brings a sense of closure to the chapter.

Conventions Used in This Book

NOTE

Notes provide additional information about a feature, or extend an idea about how to do something.

CAUTION

Cautions warn you about potential problems and tell you what *not* to do.

What's on the CD?

The CD that accompanies this book doesn't autorun and doesn't have a setup program. It just has a number of folders for you to browse through.

- **DirectX.** In this folder, you'll find everything you need to install the DirectX 8.0 SDK.
- **Source.** The Source directory contains a folder for each chapter that has a programming example. Each folder is named Chapter*X*, where *X* is the chapter in question.

  Within each ChapterX folder are subfolders for each of the sample programs in the book. These contain the source code, the resources (such as bitmaps), and a precompiled executable.

  Keep in mind that when you copy files from a CD to a hard drive, they are often marked as read-only, so you need to right-click on them and unset that flag before modifying them.
- **Extras.** This folder contains, well, extras. Most of them are in zip files, so you'll need WinZip (which you can download for free at www.winzip.com) to extract them. Some of the extras are written by me, but most are contributions from others.

And We're off...

(Psst... This is the summary.)

All right. You've turned to Appendix A and learned how to load a project, right? No? Well go ahead and do so. That's about all you'll need to get started. This first part of the book goes a little fast, from zero to DirectX in less than 200 pages. I hope you're ready!

Engage, Mr. Paris!

Part I

The Basics

CHAPTER 1

Introduction to Win32 Programming

- Conceptual Overview of Windows Programs
- Of HWNDs and HINSTANCEs
- The WinMain Function
- Creating a Window

The Windows platform, no matter what you think of it, is the most viable platform on which to program for the home computer market. It has its weaknesses, yes, but you gotta love the market share! Think of it: you can write programs that will run on Windows 95, 98, NT, 2000, Millennium, CE, and the XBox, and it only takes a modest amount of work to convert them.

This chapter is a bare-bones introduction to WIN32 programming. If you've already got a solid footing feel free to skip it, but be sure to look at IsoHex1_1.cpp, located on the CD-ROM. IsoHex1_1.cpp is my basic WIN32 shell program; all future programs will be based on this foundation.

If you're still here, I'll try to be as brief while remaining complete and understandable. I'm not one for spouting a bunch of theory—I prefer practical applications. I will assume that you have a solid base in C and at least a familiarity with C++. I will make use of classes a bit later (but I swear unto you by all that is holy that there will be no MFC). Before you start pulling at your hair and shouting incoherently, I assure you I won't get too wacky. I won't force class hierarchies and virtual functions on you—just a few little utility classes to make our jobs a bit easier.

No matter what your personal feelings about the Windows OS, the fact that it is truly easy to use—its main selling point—is undeniable. This is a double-edged sword, of course. Because so much work went into making the OS easy to use, it is proportionally more difficult to program for. DOS, which was very hard to use, was easy to program for. So it goes.

Luckily, there is only a small amount of Windows-specific stuff that you absolutely have to know in order to program for Windows (*and there was much rejoicing*). This chapter is here to get you up to speed on those things. The programs we'll be doing won't be very complicated or functional, but they will provide a good base on which to get flying!

Conceptual Overview of Windows Programs

Windows (including 95, 98, NT, and 2000) is a multitasking, multithreaded operating system. You've heard that line before, I'm sure. *Multitasking* means that the computer can run more than one program at a time. The *multithreaded* part means that more than one thread (short for "thread of execution") can exist within a program. Each program has at least one thread in it.

But, if you have just a single processor, doing more than one thing at a time is impossible, right? Technically that's correct, but you can make it *seem* like two or more things are happening simultaneously by dividing time between the different programs and threads within programs.

With a a fast-enough processor, the computer can do some of one thing and some of another thing, switching back and forth between the two, and you, as a human being, cannot tell whether the tasks are being done simultaneously or not. Neat, huh?

For instance, say you had two applications, Walk.exe and ChewGum.exe. If you ran both of these, Walk.exe would operate for a millisecond or so, and then the computer would switch to ChewGum.exe for a millisecond, and then it would switch again, repeating until the applications end, as illustrated in Figure 1.1.

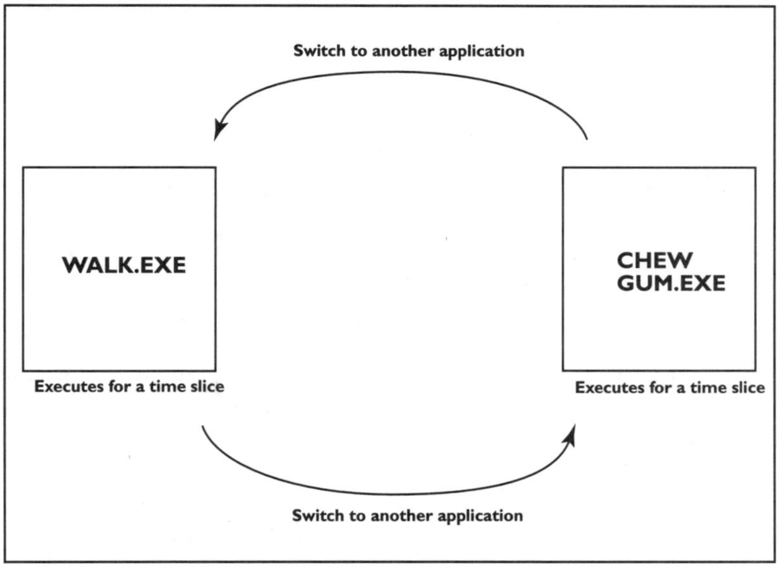

Figure 1.1

The computer walking and chewing gum at the same time

We human beings aren't set up with the proper hardware to perceive the passing of milliseconds, so to us, it appears that the computer is indeed walking and chewing gum at the same time.

You could also have a program called WalkAndChewGum.exe, and it would create one thread that walks and another that chews gum. The computer again would switch between the two threads, and the same effect is achieved within a single program.

The apparently simultaneous effect is based on idle time in the computer. As you add more and more applications and threads within those applications, more of the computer's time is taken up. At some

NOTE

I use the term *milliseconds* in this example. In reality, the amount of time an application executes a given application before switching to another one depends on a number of things and is most likely a unit of time other than a millisecond. My use of millisecond is my attempt to make the example seem more concrete. A more accurate term is *time slice*.

point, depending on your processor (how many you have, how fast they are), you reach a threshold where the simultaneous appearance is gone, and you start to notice some lag in the applications. So how does this concern us as game programmers?

Game programs are more demanding on the operating system and the hardware then any other type of program. Sloppy design and/or sloppy programming cause the game program to reach the nonsimultaneous threshold all on its own, without any other applications running. This is a bad thing.

None of the programs that you will write in this book will be multithreaded (it becomes confusing and gives me a headache). Also, none of them will be as optimized as they could be (the code is instructional—optimized code is by its nature rather cryptic, so it would defeat our purpose).

That's quite enough about multithreading and multitasking. Let's dive in, shall we?

Of HWNDs and HINSTANCEs

Much of what we do in Windows involves handles—most notably, window handles (`HWND`). So what are these handles all about, anyway?

Handles are pointers to pointers—sort of. They are a pre-OOP (object-oriented programming) method of keeping track of data in a completely dynamic operating system (namely, Windows). At any moment, an application's code can be moved from regular memory into virtual memory (that is, saved to disk in a temporary swap file). A handle ensures that no matter where something is, you can still talk to it by passing the handle into a function. Keeping track otherwise would be a nightmare!

Just treat handles as ordinary variables; you don't really care all that much about their implementation. Trust the operating system to keep track of windows and other things that use handles.

The three main types of handles that you will be using are `HINSTANCE`, `HWND`, and plain old vanilla-flavored `HANDLE`, which you will use to access disk files.

- `HINSTANCE` is a handle to the current instance of an application. (Yes, I know it's a circular definition, but I got it right out of MSDN.) Windows internally manages all running applications, and `HINSTANCE` is just a way to keep track of which application owns which windows and which resources.
- `HWND` is a handle to a window. It allows us to set the size, shape, and a variety of other aspects about a window. The operating system manages these windows and determines which are visible, the order in which to draw them, and the manner in which input (such as keystrokes and mouse movements) is directed.
- `HANDLE` is what you will use to access files; I'll get to it in Chapter 8. A normal old `HANDLE` is pretty generic.

There will be more handle types in the next chapter, so consider yourself warned. They are used quite a bit with graphical objects in Windows.

Life in an Event-Driven Operating System

Windows is actually a very simple mechanism. Whenever something happens—a mouse moves, a key is pressed, a certain amount of time elapses—Windows records it. It records what happened, when it happened, and which window (and thus which application) it happened to, packs the information into a little bundle, and sends it to that application's message queue. A message queue is nothing more than a list of messages that have been received by Windows but have not yet been processed by the application (much like huge lines to get on roller coasters). Figure 1.2 shows how the event-driven Windows operating system works internally. Keep in mind that this diagram is rather simplified.

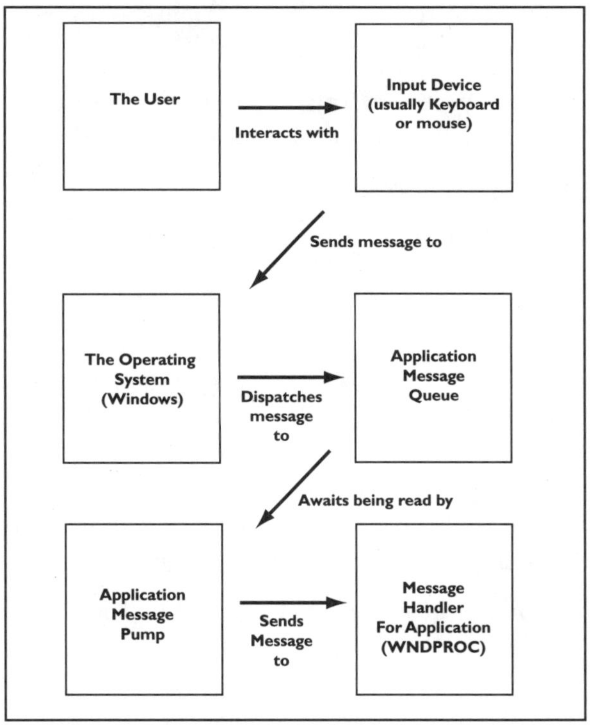

Figure 1.2

Simplified schematic of the inner workings of Windows

The following messages are stored in the MSG structure:

```
typedef struct tagMSG {
    HWND   hwnd;
    UINT   message;
    WPARAM wParam;
    LPARAM lParam;
    DWORD  time;
    POINT  pt;
} MSG, *PMSG;
```

The members of the MSG structure are explained in Table 1.1.

Table 1.1 MSG Members

Member	Purpose
hwnd	The window handle corresponding to the window that is to receive the message
message	The type of message received (WM_*)
wParam	One of the parameters for the message. It is context-sensitive. Each WM_ message has a different meaning for wParam.
lParam	One of the parameters for the message. It is context-sensitive. Each WM_ message has a different meaning for lParam.
time	Time when this message occurred
pt	Cursor coordinate at time of the message, specified in screen coordinates

Window Procedures

Each Windows application is responsible for checking its message queue for waiting messages. If there are any, it must either process them or pass them along to the default processing function. If this is not done, the messages will just pile up, your application will stop responding, and you might lock up the system.

Handle messages by using a window procedure. Here's what one looks like:

```
LRESULT CALLBACK WindowProc(
  HWND hwnd,       // handle to window
  UINT uMsg,       // message identifier
  WPARAM wParam,  // first message parameter
  LPARAM lParam   // second message parameter
);
```

This returns a value dependent on the message received (usually 0). Table 1.2 explains the purpose of the parameters.

Table 1.2 WindowProc Parameters

WindowProc Parameter	Purpose
`hwnd`	The window for which the message is bound (`msg.hwnd`)
`uMsg`	The type of message (`msg.message`)
`wParam`	A parameter of the message (`msg.wParam`)
`lParam`	A parameter of the message (`msg.lParam`)

NOTE

Your window procedure will not be named `WindowProc`. You can name it anything you wish, as long as it has the same parameter list and returns an `LRESULT` and is a `CALLBACK` function. Later, you will see that I have given my window procedure the cunning name `TheWindowProc`, so named because I only ever deal with a single window.

Got all that? It's time to start coding!

The WinMain Function

To explain the basic Windows stuff, we'll be using IsoHex1_1.cpp. Start a WIN32 application workspace, and add IsoHex1_1.cpp into it. It is the only file required for this example. Take a few moments to peruse the code. There isn't much, so it shouldn't take long.

NOTE

As much as I don't want this book to be nothing more than a code dump, I'm including the full listing for IsoHex1_1.cpp here. This will be one of the only dumps—I promise.

```
/*****************************************************************************
IsoHex1_1.cpp
Ernest S. Pazera
08APR2000
Start a WIN32 Application Workspace, add in this file
No other libs are required
*****************************************************************************/

////////////////////////////////////////////////////////////////////////////////
//INCLUDES
////////////////////////////////////////////////////////////////////////////////
#define WIN32_LEAN_AND_MEAN

#include <windows.h>

////////////////////////////////////////////////////////////////////////////////
//DEFINES
////////////////////////////////////////////////////////////////////////////////
//name for our window class
#define WINDOWCLASS "ISOHEX1"
//title of the application
#define WINDOWTITLE "IsoHex 1-1"

////////////////////////////////////////////////////////////////////////////////
//PROTOTYPES
////////////////////////////////////////////////////////////////////////////////
bool Prog_Init();//game data initializer
void Prog_Loop();//main game loop
void Prog_Done();//game cleanup

////////////////////////////////////////////////////////////////////////////////
//GLOBALS
////////////////////////////////////////////////////////////////////////////////
HINSTANCE hInstMain=NULL;//main application handle
HWND hWndMain=NULL;//handle to our main window

////////////////////////////////////////////////////////////////////////////////
//WINDOWPROC
////////////////////////////////////////////////////////////////////////////////
LRESULT CALLBACK TheWindowProc(HWND hwnd,UINT uMsg,WPARAM wParam,LPARAM lParam)
{
      //which message did we get?
```

```
	switch(uMsg)
	{
	case WM_DESTROY://the window is being destroyed
		{

			//tell the application we are quitting
			PostQuitMessage(0);

			//handled message, so return 0
			return(0);

		}break;
	case WM_PAINT://the window needs repainting
		{
			//a variable needed for painting information
			PAINTSTRUCT ps;

			//start painting
			HDC hdc=BeginPaint(hwnd,&ps);

			//////////////////////////////
			//painting code would go here
			//////////////////////////////

			//end painting
			EndPaint(hwnd,&ps);

			//handled message, so return 0
			return(0);
		}break;
	}

	//pass along any other message to default message handler
	return(DefWindowProc(hwnd,uMsg,wParam,lParam));
}

////////////////////////////////////////////////////////////////////////////////
//WINMAIN
////////////////////////////////////////////////////////////////////////////////
int WINAPI WinMain(HINSTANCE hInstance,HINSTANCE hPrevInstance,LPSTR
lpCmdLine,int nShowCmd)
{
```

```
//assign instance to global variable
hInstMain=hInstance;

//create window class
WNDCLASSEX wcx;

//set the size of the structure
wcx.cbSize=sizeof(WNDCLASSEX);

//class style
wcx.style=CS_OWNDC | CS_HREDRAW | CS_VREDRAW | CS_DBLCLKS;

//window procedure
wcx.lpfnWndProc=TheWindowProc;

//class extra
wcx.cbClsExtra=0;

//window extra
wcx.cbWndExtra=0;

//application handle
wcx.hInstance=hInstMain;

//icon
wcx.hIcon=LoadIcon(NULL,IDI_APPLICATION);

//cursor
wcx.hCursor=LoadCursor(NULL,IDC_ARROW);

//background color
wcx.hbrBackground=(HBRUSH)GetStockObject(BLACK_BRUSH);

//menu
wcx.lpszMenuName=NULL;

//class name
wcx.lpszClassName=WINDOWCLASS;

//small icon
wcx.hIconSm=NULL;
```

```
	//register the window class, return 0 if not successful
	if(!RegisterClassEx(&wcx)) return(0);

	//create main window
	hWndMain=CreateWindowEx(0,WINDOWCLASS,WINDOWTITLE, WS_BORDER | WS_SYSMENU
| WS_VISIBLE,0,0,320,240,NULL,NULL,hInstMain,NULL);

	//error check
	if(!hWndMain) return(0);

	//if program initialization failed, return with 0
	if(!Prog_Init()) return(0);

	//message structure
	MSG msg;

	//message pump
	for(;;)
	{
		//look for a message
		if(PeekMessage(&msg,NULL,0,0,PM_REMOVE))
		{
			//there is a message

			//check that we aren't quitting
			if(msg.message==WM_QUIT) break;

			//translate message
			TranslateMessage(&msg);

			//dispatch message
			DispatchMessage(&msg);
		}

		//run main game loop
		Prog_Loop();
	}

	//clean up program data
	Prog_Done();
```

```
        //return the wparam from the WM_QUIT message
        return(msg.wParam);
}

//////////////////////////////////////////////////////////////////////////////
//INITIALIZATION
//////////////////////////////////////////////////////////////////////////////
bool Prog_Init()
{
        ////////////////////////////////////
        //your initialization code goes here
        ////////////////////////////////////

        return(true);//return success
}

//////////////////////////////////////////////////////////////////////////////
//CLEANUP
//////////////////////////////////////////////////////////////////////////////
void Prog_Done()
{
        //////////////////////////
        //cleanup code goes here
        //////////////////////////
}

//////////////////////////////////////////////////////////////////////////////
//MAIN GAME LOOP
//////////////////////////////////////////////////////////////////////////////
void Prog_Loop()
{
        ///////////////////////////
        //main game logic goes here
        ///////////////////////////
}
```

Figure 1.3 shows what IsoHex1_1 looks like when it is running.

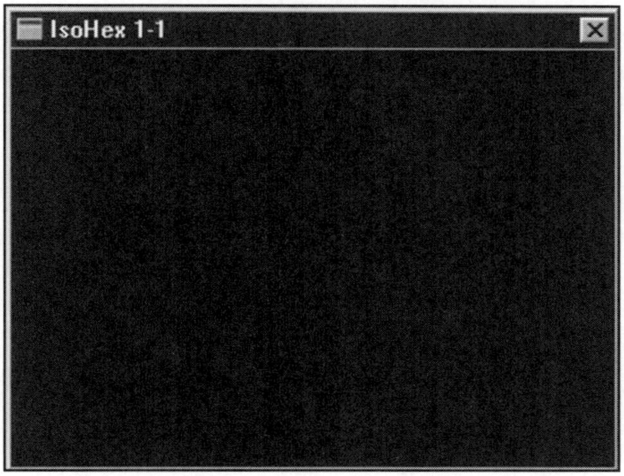

Figure 1.3

IsoHex1_1's output. Not much to look at, is it?

When talking about Windows programming, we always start with `WinMain`. On other platforms, the entry point for a program is the `main()` function. Not so in WIN32. Instead, we have a `WinMain` function, and the declaration looks like this:

```
int WINAPI WinMain(
  HINSTANCE hInstance,      // handle to current instance
  HINSTANCE hPrevInstance,  // handle to previous instance
  LPSTR lpCmdLine,          // command line
  int nCmdShow              // show state
);
```

This returns an exit code for the application (0 is the normal termination). Table 1.3 explains the parameter list.

Table 1.3 WinMain Parameters

WinMain Parameter	Purpose
`hInstance`	Handle to the current instance
`hPrevInstance`	Obsolete
`lpCmdLine`	String containing parameters passed on the command line. We will not be using this.
`nCmdShow`	Integer stating how the main window should be shown. We will be ignoring this also.

NOTE

Unlike window procedures, our `WinMain` function will always be named `WinMain`.

hInstance

For our purposes, the only parameter of any significance is hInstance. In IsoHex1_1.cpp, you will see that I took the value of hInstance and assigned it to a global variable called hInstMain:

```
//copy instance handle into global variable
hInstMain=hInstance;
```

We can write programs so that doing this is unnecessary, where WinMain passes the value of hInstance to whatever function needs it (many times, hInstance is never used for anything). However, most game code that I've written or seen written has placed hInstance's value into a global variable, whether it is used or not.

Window Class

Creating a window class is the next task that the program undertakes. A window class is nothing more than a structure that describes a type of window. You need one if you want to make your own types of windows.

```
typedef struct _WNDCLASSEX {
     UINT        cbSize;
     UINT        style;
     WNDPROC     lpfnWndProc;
     int         cbClsExtra;
     int         cbWndExtra;
     HINSTANCE  hInstance;
     HICON       hIcon;
     HCURSOR     hCursor;
     HBRUSH      hbrBackground;
     LPCTSTR     lpszMenuName;
     LPCTSTR     lpszClassName;
     HICON       hIconSm;
} WNDCLASSEX, *PWNDCLASSEX;
```

Okay...there's a lot of stuff in this structure, and not much of it is very intuitive. A breakdown of `WNDCLASSEX`'s members can be found in Table 1.4.

Table 1.4 WNDCLASSEX Members

WNDCLASSEX Member	Purpose
`cbSize`	The size of the WNDCLASSEX structure
`style`	Class styles (described in text below)
`lpfnWndProc`	Pointer to a `windowproc`, the function that we use to process window messages
`cbClsExtra`	Extra bytes to allocate for the class structure
`cbWndExtra`	Extra bytes to allocate for the window
`hInstance`	Application handle
`hIcon`	Icon to show in the upper-left corner
`hCursor`	Mouse cursor to use
`hbrBackground`	Brush to use for background color
`lpszMenuName`	The menu to use for this window class
`lpszClassName`	Name of the class
`hIconSm`	Small icon to associate with the class

Following is the code you will use to set up your window class:

```
//create window class
WNDCLASSEX wcx;
//set the size of the structure
wcx.cbSize=sizeof(WNDCLASSEX);
//class style
wcx.style=CS_OWNDC | CS_HREDRAW | CS_VREDRAW | CS_DBLCLKS;
//window procedure
wcx.lpfnWndProc=TheWindowProc;
//class extra
wcx.cbClsExtra=0;
//window extra
```

```
wcx.cbWndExtra=0;
//application handle
wcx.hInstance=hInstMain;
//application icon
wcx.hIcon=LoadIcon(NULL,IDI_APPLICATION);
//cursor
wcx.hCursor=LoadCursor(NULL,IDC_ARROW);
//background brush
wcx.hbrBackground=(HBRUSH)GetStockObject(BLACK_BRUSH);
//menu
wcx.lpszMenuName=NULL;
//class name
wcx.lpszClassName=WINDOWCLASS;
//small icon
wcx.hIconSm=NULL;
```

Several of the values, like `cbSize`, `hInstance`, and so on, are self-explanatory. I'll explain those that are less so.

wcx.style

This is the window class style. It's a series of flags that start with `CS_` values, combined using the bitwise `OR` operator (|).

- `CS_OWNDC` tells Windows that windows of this class will each have their own device context (DC). DCs will be explained in more detail in the next chapter.
- `CS_HREDRAW` and `CS_VREDRAW` tells Windows that if the windows created with this class are resized vertically or horizontally, the window must be repainted.
- `CS_DBLCLKS` tells Windows that you want the window to respond to double-clicks.

wcx.lpfnWndProc

This value is a pointer to a window procedure (which I mentioned briefly a little earlier). This member has been assigned to `TheWindowProc`, which is a function that you write to handle all the messages your window will receive.

wcx.hIcon

I promised I wouldn't add any new handle types until the next chapter. I lied. This is a handle to an icon, which I'm sure you're familiar with. If you have a normal-looking window, with a border and a system menu and so on, this is shown in the upper-left corner and on the Taskbar. We use `LoadIcon` to load `IDI_APPLICATION`, which is a system icon.

wcx.hCursor

This is another handle type—this time, to a mouse cursor. In this case, `LoadCursor` is used to load `IDC_ARROW`, which is the customary arrow that you find every day.

wcx.hBackground

This is yet another handle type—this time, a brush. Briefly, a brush is used to fill in areas with solid colors or patterns. `GetStockObject` is used to specify a black brush. The `(HBRUSH)` typecast is necessary because `GetStockObject` returns `void*`.

wcx.lpszClassName

This is the name of the window class. If you take a peek up near the top of IsoHex1_1.cpp, you will see the following lines:

```
#define WINDOWCLASS "IsoHex1"
#define WINDOWTITLE "IsoHex Example 1-1"
```

I don't usually use `#define` much (I prefer `const`). Since `WINDOWCLASS` is used in only two places, I didn't really see a need to use `const`. `WINDOWTITLE` is used only once (when we create our window later), so I felt that `#define` was adequate for our needs.

After you have filled out the window class struct, you use the `RegisterClassEx` function to register it with Windows. There is a small amount of error checking with the code. If the function returns `NULL`, you were unable to register the class, and you return 0 from `WinMain`, terminating the application.

Notice that `wcx` is not a global variable. You don't really need to worry about it after you have set it up and registered it, because you can just use the class's name.

Once you have registered a window class, you are ready to make a window and start processing messages.

The Message Pump

I'll show you the remainder of `WinMain` all at once, and then I'll take apart the pieces. Figure 1.4 is a flowchart of the process.

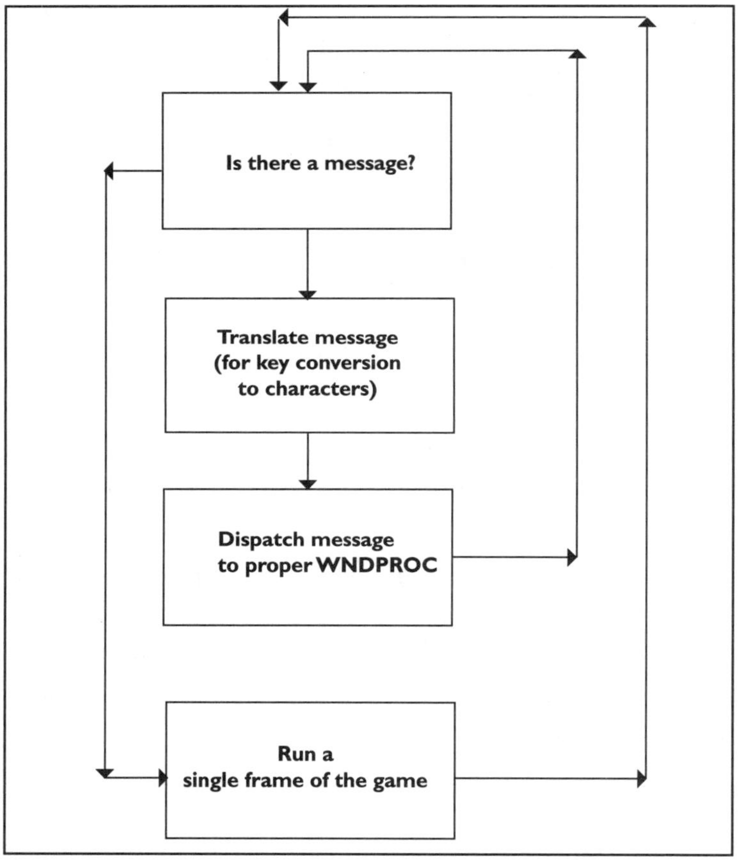

Figure 1.4

Flowchart of the message pump

```
//create main window
hWndMain=CreateWindowEx(0,WINDOWCLASS,WINDOWTITLE,
       WS_SYSMENU| WS_CAPTION | WS_VISIBLE,0,0,320,240,
       NULL,NULL,hInstMain,NULL);
if(!hWndMain) return(0);//error check
if(!Prog_Init()) return(0);//if program initialization failed, then return with 0
MSG msg;//message structure
for(;;)       //message pump
{
       if(PeekMessage(&msg,NULL,0,0,PM_REMOVE))
       {
```

```
if(msg.message==WM_QUIT) break;
                TranslateMessage(&msg);
                DispatchMessage(&msg);
        }
        else
        {
                Prog_Loop();
        }
}
Prog_Done();
return(msg.wParam);
```

NOTE

Some of the lines are broken into two. This is because the book format isn't wide enough to contain them. Just keep in mind that these lines actually exist as only one line in the real code.

Creating a Window

The first line of this segment of code creates your main window by calling `CreateWindowEx`:

```
HWND CreateWindowEx(
  DWORD dwExStyle,       // extended window style
  LPCTSTR lpClassName,   // registered class name
  LPCTSTR lpWindowName, // window name
  DWORD dwStyle,         // window style
  int x,                  // horizontal position of win-
dow
  int y,                  // vertical position of window
  int nWidth,            // window width
  int nHeight,           // window height
  HWND hWndParent,       // handle to parent or owner
window
  HMENU hMenu,           // menu handle or child identifi-
er
  HINSTANCE hInstance,  // handle to application instance
  LPVOID lpParam         // window-creation data
);
```

NOTE

Other books tend to use the `CreateWindow` function rather than `CreateWindowEx`. The only difference between `CreateWindow` and `CreateWindowEx` is that `CreateWindow` lacks a `dwExStyle` function.

This returns a handle to the newly created window.

dwExStyle

This parameter specifies the extended window style. I have placed 0 here because extended styles aren't needed for such a simple application. The help files have a comprehensive list of these flags under the entry for `CreateWindowEx`.

lpClassName

This parameter specifies the name of the window class to which this window belongs. In our case, this is WINDOWCLASS.

lpWindowName

This parameter specifies the text that will be displayed in the title of the window (if it has one) and also in the Taskbar. We are using WINDOWTITLE.

dwStyle

This parameter contains one or more WS_* flags, which are listed next. These flags (or combinations thereof) change the appearance of your window. Some flags also change the way a window behaves.

- **WS_BORDER** Creates a window with a thin line border.
- **WS_CAPTION** Creates a window with a title bar and a thin line border.
- **WS_CHILD** Creates a child window. Cannot be a pop-up. Cannot have a menu bar.
- **WS_CHILDWINDOW** See WS_CHILD.
- **WS_HSCROLL** Creates a window with a horizontal scroll bar.
- **WS_ICONIC** Creates a window that is initially minimized.
- **WS_MAXIMIZE** Creates a window that is initially maximized.
- **WS_MAXIMIZEBOX** Creates a window with a maximize button.
- **WS_MINIMIZE** See WS_ICONIC.
- **WS_MINIMIZEBOX** Creates a window that is initially minimized.
- **WS_OVERLAPPED** Creates a window that has a border and title bar.
- **WS_OVERLAPPEDWINDOW** Combines WS_OVERLAPPED, WS_CAPTION, WS_SYSMENU, WS_THICKFRAME, WS_MINIMIZEBOX, and WS_MAXIMIZEBOX.
- **WS_POPUP** Creates a pop-up window.
- **WS_POPUPWINDOW** Combines WS_BORDER, WS_POPUP, and WS_SYSMENU.
- **WS_SIZEBOX** Creates a window that has a sizing border.
- **WS_SYSMENU** Creates a window with a window menu on its title bar.
- **WS_THICKFRAME** See WS_SIZEBOX.
- **WS_TILED** See WS_OVERLAPPED.
- **WS_TILEDWINDOW** See WS_OVERLAPPEDWINDOW.
- **WS_VISIBLE** Creates an initially visible window.
- **WS_VSCROLL** Creates a window with a vertical scrollbar.

IsoHex1_1.cpp uses WS_CAPTION, WS_SYSMENU, and WS_VISIBLE. In the future, WS_POPUP and WS_VISIBLE will be used.

x, y

These parameters contain the upper-left corner of the window. You are using 0,0.

nWidth, nHeight

These parameters contain the width and height of the window. You are using 320,240.

hWndParent

Windows can be children of other windows (using the `WS_CHILD` window style), or they can be "owned" by other windows. The owner of either of these types of windows is called a *parent*. You are using `NULL` because this window has no parent.

hMenu

Most types of windows can make use of menus. In your case, you aren't using a menu, so pass `NULL`.

hInstance

The application instance that owns the window (such as `hInstMain`).

lpParam

Extra creation data. You don't have any, so pass `NULL`.

After we call `CreateWindowEx`, check to make sure that you window actually exists by checking that it is not `NULL`. If it is `NULL`, the program exits immediately, without even whimpering. (Theoretically speaking, if it does fail, you want to give the users of the application a nice message box containing the reason why the program halted so abruptly. Traditionally, these error messages are as cryptic as you can make them.)

Other Initialization

Next, call `Prog_Init()`, which is your user-supplied bit of initialization code. Later, you'll be initializing DirectDraw, Loading Bitmaps, and a number of other things, all in this function. For now, the function simply returns true, which is good, because if it returned false, the program would terminate.

On the next line is the declaration of a variable named `msg`, which is of type `MSG`. This variable will be what you use to look for, grab, translate, and dispatch Windows messages. I'll cover Windows messages later in this chapter. You've already seen the `MSG` struct, but here it is again:

```
typedef struct tagMSG {
    HWND   hwnd;
    UINT   message;
    WPARAM wParam;
    LPARAM lParam;
    DWORD  time;
    POINT  pt;
} MSG, *PMSG;
```

If you skip down to later in the code, you'll see that it checks the `message` member against `WM_QUIT` to determine whether or not to exit, but other than that, you just send a pointer to `msg` to functions. Windows handles the rest, and thank goodness! (I once developed a messages-based event queue for DOS by trapping interrupts, and it was a nightmare.)

Now comes the message pump itself—the most important but least interesting part of `WinMain`. It's the part that does the repetitive task of talking to Windows. It is contained in a `for` loop that never ends (well, theoretically never ends).

The message pump does the following (refer to Figure 1.4 for a graphical view):

1. Checks for a message.
2. If there is a message, processes that message.
3. If there is no message, runs a single frame of the game.

Checking for Messages

To check for a message, use `PeekMessage`. This is a departure from normal Windows programming. Most applications use `GetMessage`, because nongame applications do very little except in response to user input. A game, on the other hand, even if it is turn-based, still has tasks to perform when there are no messages.

```
BOOL PeekMessage(
  LPMSG lpMsg,          // message information
  HWND hWnd,            // handle to window
  UINT wMsgFilterMin,  // first message
  UINT wMsgFilterMax,  // last message
  UINT wRemoveMsg       // removal options
);
```

This returns 0 if there is no message and nonzero if a message is found. Table 1.5 explains the parameter list.

Table 1.5 PeekMessage Parameters

PeekMessage Parameter	Purpose
`lpMsg`	Pointer to a `MSG` structure that will be filled with message information if there is one available
`hWnd`	Specifies the handle of the window for which we are looking for messages. Passing `NULL` will get messages from any window in the application.
`wMsgFilterMin`	Lowest value of messages we are looking for
`wMsgFilterMax`	Highest value of messages we are looking for. Specifying 0 in both `wMsgFilterMin` and `wMsgFilterMax` will look for any message.
`wRemoveMsg`	Either the value `PM_REMOVE` or `PM_NOREMOVE`. Tells the function to remove or not remove the message from the message queue.

Processing Messages

You must do three things in order to process a message. First, check to see if the `msg.message` is a `WM_QUIT`. If it is, break out of the infinite `for` loop.

Next, call `TranslateMessage`:

```
BOOL TranslateMessage(
  CONST MSG *lpMsg    // message information
);
```

This function takes `WM_KEYDOWN` and `WM_KEYUP` messages and translates them into `WM_CHAR` messages. (It also translates `WM_SYSKEYDOWN` and `WM_SYSKEYUP` into `WM_SYSCHAR`.) The only parameter is an `LPMSG`. It returns 0 if the message is not translated and nonzero if it is. Either way, you don't really care. If there is translation to be done, you just want it done.

Finally, call DispatchMessage:

```
LRESULT DispatchMessage(
  CONST MSG *lpmsg    // message information
);
```

This function takes an LPMSG, just like TranslateMessage does, and it calls the appropriate message handler (usually a window procedure). The return value of DispatchMessage depends on what value is returned by the message handler it calls.

Running a Single Frame of the Game

If there is no message, call Prog_Loop(), which runs a single frame of your game. Currently, there is nothing in Prog_Loop.

Cleanup and Exit

After the infinite for loop has been exited, there are just two more lines, and my explanation of WinMain is done.

The next-to-last thing is calling Prog_Done(), which is the user-defined function that contains any cleanup code that you need.

And finally, you return the value of msg's wparam. This specifies your application's exit code. If the program ends as a result of PostQuitMessage, the value passed to that function will be in msg.wparam. Zero indicates normal termination.

I know I've gone rather quickly through this introductory stuff, and maybe, if you're new to the concept of WIN32 programming, I left you hanging just a little. I ask you to bear with me, because my goal is to get to the good stuff as quickly as possible. For more information on any of the functions I've listed here, take a look at the MSDN documentation (the help files). It has more information than you really want or need on how everything works. The WinMain function is rather dull; it's almost always written exactly the same way.

The Window Procedure

Here's the minimal windowproc that is used in IsoHex1_1:

```
LRESULT CALLBACK TheWindowProc(HWND hwnd,UINT uMsg,WPARAM wParam,LPARAM lParam)
{
      switch(uMsg)
      {
      case WM_DESTROY://the window is being destroyed
            {
```

```
                PostQuitMessage(0);//tell the application we are quitting
                return(0);//handled message, so return 0
            }break;
        case WM_PAINT://the window needs repainting
            {
                PAINTSTRUCT ps;
                HDC hdc=BeginPaint(hwnd,&ps);//start painting
                //painting code would go here
                EndPaint(hwnd,&ps);//end painting
                return(0);//handled message, so return 0
            }break;
    }
    return(DefWindowProc(hwnd,uMsg,wParam,lParam));
}
```

The skinny of the whole thing is this: depending on what message you are handling (such as the contents of the uMsg parameter), you execute different code; thus you have the switch. If you handle a message, you have to return 0. If you don't handle the message, you pass the parameters on to the default message procedure (DefWindowProc), which handles the rest of our messages.

The two messages that need to be taken care of are WM_DESTROY and WM_PAINT. There are a number of WM_* messages, everything from key presses and key releases to mouse movement and mouse button state changes to timers and so on. Some of them are cryptic, and you won't be using very many.

WM_DESTROY is sent when the window is being destroyed. It's there to allow you to clean up anything you might be doing specific to the window. All your data is elsewhere, so you don't have to do much. You just have to tell the application that you are quitting, with PostQuitMessage(0). The parameter for PostQuitMessage is an error code, and 0 specifies normal termination.

```
VOID PostQuitMessage(
  int nExitCode   // exit code
);
```

This function returns no value, and it takes as a parameter the exit code for the application.

WM_PAINT is sent whenever a window needs to be repainted. Usually this is when a minimized window is restored or a background application is brought to the front, if there were overlapping areas.

In order to repaint as little as possible, Windows uses a struct called PAINTSTRUCT, which contains information about what part of the window is to be redrawn:

```
typedef struct tagPAINTSTRUCT {
  HDC  hdc;
  BOOL fErase;
  RECT rcPaint;
```

```
  BOOL fRestore;
  BOOL fIncUpdate;
  BYTE rgbReserved[32];
} PAINTSTRUCT, *PPAINTSTRUCT;
```

I'm not going to go too much into this, because you don't use PAINTSTRUCT outside of your handling of a WM_PAINT message, and even in that, you'll never have much more code than what you've already got.

So, in the WM_PAINT handler, you declare a PAINTSTRUCT variable and then call BeginPaint, passing the parameters of the window handle (hwnd) and a pointer to your PAINTSTRUCT. The return value you assign to a new HDC variable called hdc. Don't worry about what an HDC is right now. All will be explained in Chapter 2.

```
HDC BeginPaint(
  HWND hwnd,             // handle to window
  LPPAINTSTRUCT lpPaint // paint information
);
```

Now you'd presumably do something with the hdc. Right now, there isn't anything that needs doing (hey, how hard can it be to manage a black rectangle?)

Finally, you call EndPaint, passing hwnd and a pointer to your PAINTSTRUCT again. This lets Windows know that you've done your job of repainting. Then 0 is returned.

```
BOOL EndPaint(
  HWND hWnd,                   // handle to window
  CONST PAINTSTRUCT *lpPaint  // paint data
);
```

Why must you do all this? Well, if you don't, Windows will whine, "PAINT YOUR WINDOW! PAINT YOUR WINDOW!" This BeginPaint/EndPaint stuff is there for no other reason than to shut Windows up and have it leave you in peace—a noble goal.

Sending Messages to a Window

To send a window message, you just need to use the function SendMessage:

```
LRESULT SendMessage(
  HWND hWnd,      // handle to destination window
  UINT Msg,       // message
  WPARAM wParam,  // first message parameter
  LPARAM lParam   // second message parameter
);
```

The return value depends on what is returned from the `windowproc` that is called. Table 1.6 explains the parameters.

Table 1.6 SendMessage Parameters

SendMessage Parameter	Purpose
`hWnd`	Window handle to which that you are sending the message
`Msg`	The message you are sending (`WM_*`)
`wParam`	First parameter of the message
`lParam`	Second parameter of the message

There is also a function called `PostMessage`. It does the same thing, sort of. `SendMessage` sends the message immediately to the window, where it will be processed and then returned, whereas `Postmessage` just adds the message to the list of events that the window has yet to handle. `PostMessage` has the same parameter list as `SendMessage`, but its return type is `BOOL`, and it is nonzero on success and 0 on failure.

Using Window Messages to Process Input

You'll use messages to process any input your window receives. If you're about to ask why I'm not using `DirectInput`, I ask you to check how thick this book is already and then factor in a chapter on DI. Also, for our purposes, window messages will suffice.

Keyboard Messages

You'll use three messages for the keyboard. There are many more than this, but you won't need them. Table 1.7 shows the meaning of `wParam` and `lParam` for these messages.

Table 1.7 WM_KEY* Messages

Keyboard Message	Meaning of wParam	Meaning of lParam
`WM_KEYDOWN`	Virtual key code (`VK_*`)	Shifts state/repeat count/flags
`WM_KEYUP`	Virtual key code (`VK_*`)	Shifts state/repeat count/flags
`WM_CHAR`	Character code (ASCII)	Shifts state/repeat count/flags

WM_KEYUP/WM_KEYDOWN

WM_KEYDOWN and WM_KEYUP are very similar in their use but are called at separate times. WM_KEYDOWN is called when a key is pressed, and WM_KEYUP is called when a key is released. (This ain't rocket science, I know.)

Table 1.8 lists some VK constants and their values.

> **NOTE**
>
> **Not all keys have a VK_* constant associated with them. The most noticeable lack is the alphabetic and non-numpad number keys. The constants VK_0 through VK_9 have the same values as 0 through 9, and VK_A through VK_Z have the values A through Z. None of the VK_* constants for numbers or letters actually exist.**

Table 1.8 VK_* Constants and Their Values

VK_BACK	0x08	VK_RWIN	0x5C	VK_F5	0x74
VK_TAB	0x09	VK_APPS	0x5D	VK_F6	0x75
VK_RETURN	0x0D	VK_NUMPAD0	0x60	VK_F7	0x76
VK_SHIFT	0x10	VK_NUMPAD1	0x61	VK_F8	0x77
VK_CONTROL	0x11	VK_NUMPAD2	0x62	VK_F9	0x78
VK_MENU	0x12	VK_NUMPAD3	0x63	VK_F10	0x79
VK_PAUSE	0x13	VK_NUMPAD4	0x64	VK_F11	0x7A
VK_ESCAPE	0x1B	VK_NUMPAD5	0x65	VK_F12	0x7B
VK_SPACE	0x20	VK_NUMPAD6	0x66	VK_F13	0x7C
VK_PRIOR	0x21	VK_NUMPAD7	0x67	VK_F14	0x7D
VK_NEXT	0x22	VK_NUMPAD8	0x68	VK_F15	0x7E
VK_END	0x23	VK_NUMPAD9	0x69	VK_F16	0x7F
VK_HOME	0x24	VK_MULTIPLY	0x6A	VK_F17	0x80
VK_LEFT	0x25	VK_ADD	0x6B	VK_F18	0x81
VK_UP	0x26	VK_SEPARATOR	0x6C	VK_F19	0x82
VK_RIGHT	0x27	VK_SUBTRACT	0x6D	VK_F20	0x83
VK_DOWN	0x28	VK_DECIMAL	0x6E	VK_F21	0x84
VK_SELECT	0x29	VK_DIVIDE	0x6F	VK_F22	0x85
VK_PRINT	0x2A	VK_F1	0x70	VK_F23	0x86
VK_INSERT	0x2D	VK_F2	0x71	VK_F24	0x87
VK_DELETE	0x2E	VK_F3	0x72	VK_NUMLOCK	0x90
VK_LWIN	0x5B	VK_F4	0x73	VK_SCROLL	0x91

For example, if you wanted to write a handler that closed the main window in response to the user's pressing the Esc key, you would write the message handler like so:

```
case WM_KEYDOWN:
{
	if(wParam==VK_ESCAPE)
	{
		DestroyWindow(hWndMain);//destroy main window
	}
	return(0);//we handled the message
}break;
```

WM_CHAR

WM_CHAR, on the other hand, responds to characters that the keyboard driver has translated into actual characters. The contents of wParam are the ASCII values, such as a, b, c, and so forth. In many cases, you don't care about what the key's ASCII code is (you only care if a key is down or not), so you'll use this message only when you are inputting strings.

The last word on keyboard input has nothing to do with messages. Responding to WM_KEYDOWN and WM_KEYUP usually gets you where you want to go, but not always. It's absolutely *awful* for just seeing if a key is down or not, especially if the user switches applications between the calls of WM_KEYDOWN and WM_KEYUP. To fix this, in those cases where you only care whether a key is up or not (to move a unit or character or something), you use GetAsyncKeyState:

```
SHORT GetAsyncKeyState(
  int vKey   // virtual-key code
);
```

vKey represents the virtual key for which you are trying to read the state. In the return value, the most significant bit will be 1 if the key is down or 0 if the key is up. Because the return value is a SHORT (a signed type), you can check to see if a key is down by checking to see if the return value is negative:

```
if(GetAsyncKeyState(VK_ESCAPE)<0)
{
	//stuff to do if the escape key is down
}
```

There are a few extra VK_* constants that only GetAsyncKeyState recognizes. These are listed in Table 1.9.

Table 1.9 VK_* Constants that Work Only with GetAsyncKeyState

VK_* Code	Hex Value
VK_LSHIFT	0xA0
VK_RSHIFT	0xA1
VK_LCONTROL	0xA2
VK_RCONTROL	0xA3
VK_LMENU	0xA4
VK_RMENU	0xA5

NOTE

You cannot use the values listed in Table 1.9 with any of the WM_KEY* messages. They just won't work.

Mouse Messages

There are a bunch of these, but you need only about a handful. Luckily, they are all formatted the same as far as the information passed in wParam and lParam. Table 1.10 lists the WM_* messages you will be concerned with.

Table 1.10 Mouse Messages

Message	When It Happens
WM_MOUSEMOVE	The mouse has been moved.
WM_LBUTTONDOWN	The left mouse button has been pressed.
WM_LBUTTONUP	The left mouse button has been released.
WM_RBUTTONDOWN	The right mouse button has been pressed.
WM_RBUTTONUP	The right mouse button has been released.

Its important to note here that "left" and "right" have some subjective meanings. For example, if you reverse your mouse buttons under your Windows settings, the buttons will be swapped as far as which messages they generate (as shown in Figure 1.5). In my opinion, this is one of the good features of Windows. We don't want to alienate the lefties!

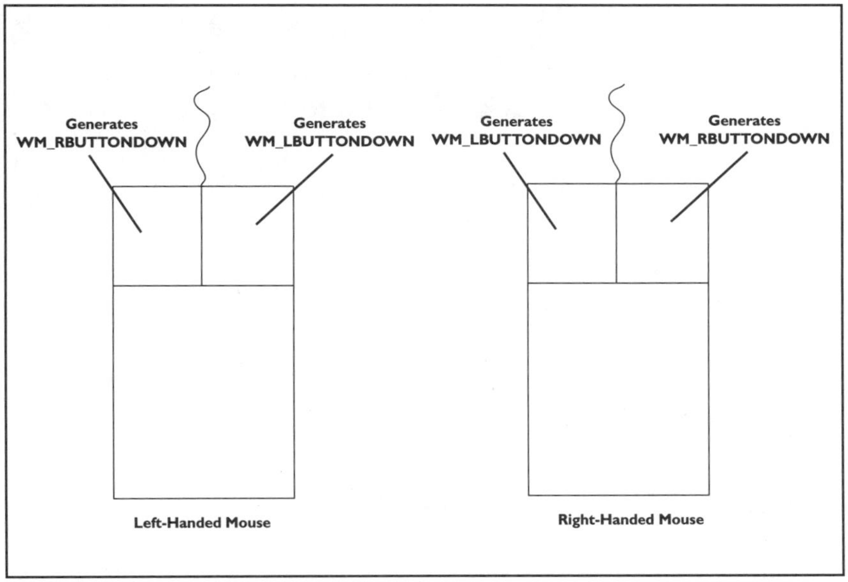

Figure 1.5

Reversed mouse buttons

The contents of `wParam` for a mouse message consist of a number of flags, covering stuff like the state of the Shift and Ctrl keys to the state of the mouse buttons. Table 1.11 is a breakdown of these flags.

Table 1.11 wParam Flags for Mouse Buttons and Shift States

Mouse Flag	Meaning
`MK_CONTROL`	The Ctrl key is down.
`MK_LBUTTON`	The left mouse button is down.
`MK_MBUTTON`	The middle mouse button is down.
`MK_RBUTTON`	The right mouse button is down.
`MK_SHIFT`	The Shift key is down.

If you want to check to see if the left mouse button is down in your message handler (for example, during a WM_MOUSEMOVE), do this:

```
//check for left button down
if(wParam&MK_LBUTTON)
 {
      //do something
}
```

> **NOTE**
> **You can also check the state of the mouse buttons using GetAsyncKeyState. However, this will not be correct for users who reverse the mouse buttons.**

lParam contains the x and y position of the mouse cursor. To retrieve these values, use something similar to the following code:

```
int x=LOWORD(lParam);//x is contained in the lower 16 bits
int y=HIWORD(lParam);//y is contained in the upper 16 bits
```

The documentation states that you should use the GET_X_LPARAM and GET_Y_LPARAM macros rather than the LOWORD and HIWORD macros. Personally, I've not seen a difference.

Other Window Messages

There seem to be thousands of window messages you could respond to. If you want to look at the list, load up MSDN (the help files should have come with your VC++ compiler). Go to the index tab, type in WM_, and look aghast at the long, long list of messages. Many or most of them are of limited use. On the MSDN CDs, the messages are pretty well documented, and the meanings of wParam and lParam are made pretty clear.

It seems kind of bizarre that out of hundreds of window messages, we'll only be using about a dozen, but that's just Windows.

There is just one miscellaneous message that I should cover WM_ACTIVATEAPP. We'll be using it later.

WM_ACTIVATEAPP

WM_ACTIVATEAPP is sent to an application when it is activated (if another application was the currently active one) and when it is deactivated (when the user switches to another application). wParam contains a boolean variable that specifies whether or not the current application is the one being activated (a nonzero value) or deactivated (a value of 0).

When your application is deactivated, especially when you are using DirectX in full-screen mode, you will want to put the application into some sort of "paused" state. It's not a bad idea to do so even when you're not in full screen, because if the application isn't active, you don't want to continue executing the game until the user reactivates it.

We'll handle activation with a global variable called `bActive`:

```
bool bActive=false;//start as non-active
```

Somewhere in the `Prog_Init()` function, you'll set `bActive` to true.

During `Prog_Loop()`, you check `bActive`. If it's false, you just return from the function without doing anything.

```
if(!bActive) return;
```

Finally, you respond to the `WM_ACTIVATEAPP` message:

```
case WM_ACTIVATEAPP:
{
	bActive=(bool)wParam;
	if(bActive)
	{
		//activation code
	}
	else
	{
		//deactivation code
	}
}break;
```

Managing Your Windows

There are a number of functions for managing windows that you'll probably at least want to be familiar with. Some of these functions—`SetWindowPos`, `MoveWindow`, and `GetWindowInfo`—concern themselves with a window's size and position. The rest of them—`SetWindowText`, `GetWindowText`, and `GetWindowTextLength`—concern themselves with the text displayed in the title bar and on the Taskbar.

SetWindowPos

```
BOOL SetWindowPos(
  HWND hWnd,              // handle to window
  HWND hWndInsertAfter,   // placement-order handle
  int X,                  // horizontal position
  int Y,                  // vertical position
  int cx,                 // width
  int cy,                 // height
  UINT uFlags             // window-positioning options
);
```

`SetWindowPos` returns nonzero on success and 0 on failure. Table 1.12 lists the parameters and their purposes.

Table 1.12 SetWindowPos Parameters

SetWindowPos Parameter	Purpose
`hWnd`	Handle to the window you want to reposition
`hWndInsertAfter`	This is a z-order thing. It's the handle to another window in your application that you want your window to be behind. Can also take some constants.
`int X`	The desired horizontal position of the left edge of the window
`int Y`	The desired vertical position of the top edge of the window
`int cx`	The desired width of the window
`int cy`	The desired height of the window
`uFlags`	Flags (see below under "Flags")

`SetWindowPos` can optionally change the z-order, position, and size of a window, depending on the parameters you give it.

Z-Order

If you had more than one window, you could set which one was on top of the others by calling `SetWindowPos` and specifying this. Besides window handles, `SetWindowPos` also takes a number of constants in this parameter:

- `HWND_BOTTOM` Places the window at the bottom of the z-order.
- `HWND_NOTOPMOST` Makes the window a non-topmost window and places it above all other non-topmost windows.
- `HWND_TOP` Places the window at the top of the z-order.
- `HWND_TOPMOST` Makes the window a topmost window and places it at the top of the topmost z-order.

Some of those explanations sound like gibberish, I know, especially when I'm talking about topmost. Topmost windows are windows that are always on top. They sort of have their own z-order. The Taskbar is one of these.

Flags

SetWindowPos responds to a number of flags, which can optionally turn the various other parameters on and off:

- **SWP_NOACTIVATE** Tells SetWindowPos not to activate this window when changing it.
- **SWP_NOCOPYBITS** Tells SetWindowPos not to copy the contents of the client area.
- **SWP_NOMOVE** Tells SetWindowPos to ignore X and Y.
- **SWP_NOSIZE** Tells SetWindowPos to ignore cx and cy.
- **SWP_NOZORDER** Tells SetWindowPos to ignore hWndInsertAfter.

MoveWindow

```
BOOL MoveWindow(
  HWND hWnd,       // handle to window
  int X,           // horizontal position
  int Y,           // vertical position
  int nWidth,      // width
  int nHeight,     // height
  BOOL bRepaint    // repaint option
);
```

Returns nonzero on success or 0 on failure. Table 1.13 explains the parameter usage.

Table 1.13 MoveWindow Parameters

MoveWindow Parameter	Purpose
hWnd	Handle to the window you are moving
X	The desired horizontal coordinate for the left edge of the window
Y	The desired vertical coordinate for the top edge of the window
nWidth	The desired width of the window
nHeight	The desired height of the window
bRepaint	Specifies whether or not you want the window to be repainted.

MoveWindow does much the same thing that SetWindowPos does, minus the window position in the z-order.

```
//resize the window to be 640x480
MoveWindow(hWndMain,0,0,640,480);
```

GetWindowInfo

```
BOOL GetWindowInfo(
  HWND hwnd,        // handle to window
  PWINDOWINFO pwi   // window information
);
```

This function fetches information about a given window (hwnd) in a WINDOWINFO structure. It returns nonzero on success and 0 on failure.

The WINDOWINFO structure looks like this:

```
typedef struct tagWINDOWINFO {
    DWORD cbSize;
    RECT  rcWindow;
    RECT  rcClient;
    DWORD dwStyle;
    DWORD dwExStyle;
    DWORD dwWindowStatus;
    UINT  cxWindowBorders;
    UINT  cyWindowBorders;
    ATOM  atomWindowType;
    WORD  wCreatorVersion;
} WINDOWINFO, *PWINDOWINFO, *LPWINDOWINFO;
```

Table 1.14 explains the members of `WINDOWINFO`.

Table 1.14 Members of WINDOWINFO

WINDOWINFO Member	Purpose
`cbSize`	The size of this structure
`rcWindow`	A `RECT` (more on these in Chapter 2) describing the area taken up by the window
`rcClient`	A `RECT` describing the area taken up by the client area of the window
`dwStyle`	The window's styles (`WS_*`)
`dwExStyle`	The window's extended styles (`WS_EX_*`)
`dwWindowStatus`	Whether or not the window is active. 0 means not active.
`cxWindowBorders`	Width of the window's border
`cyWindowBorders`	Height of the window's border
`atomWindowType`	Atom corresponding to the window class to which this window belongs
`wCreatorVersion`	Version that created this window

GetWindowText and GetWindowTextLength

```
int GetWindowText(
  HWND hWnd,          // handle to window or control
  LPTSTR lpString,   // text buffer
  int nMaxCount      // maximum number of characters to copy
);
```

Retrieves a copy of the window's title in `lpString`. `nMaxCount` is the string length to retrieve. Returns the number of characters actually read.

```
int GetWindowTextLength(
  HWND hWnd    // handle to window or control
);
```

Returns the length of the window's (hWnd's) title.

These two functions are best used together, like so:

```
//retrieve the length of the window title
int nTitleLength=GetWindowTextLength(hWndMain);
//allocate a buffer to the proper size
char* buffer=new char[nTitleLength];
GetWindowText(hWndMain,buffer,nTitleLength);
```

SetWindowText

```
BOOL SetWindowText(
  HWND hWnd,          // handle to window or control
  LPCTSTR lpString    // title or text
);
```

Sets the title of the specified window (hWnd) to the string supplied (lpString).

System Metrics

A system metric is a system-wide measurement usually concerning the height or width of something on the desktop. It also contains the existence of certain devices on the machine.

The function needed to retrieve one of these metrics is GetSystemMetrics.

```
int GetSystemMetrics(
  int nIndex    // system metric or configuration setting
);
```

Table 1.15 lists some of the possible `nIndex` values. There are more than just this, of course, but these are the ones you are most likely to use with any sort of frequency.

Table 1.15 Values for nIndex

Index	Return Value
SM_CMOUSEBUTTONS	The number of mouse buttons present
SM_CXBORDER, SM_CYBORDER	The width and height of a window border
SM_CXCURSOR, SM_CYCURSOR	The width and height of a cursor
SM_CXEDGE, SM_CYEDGE	The width and height of a 3D window edge
SM_CXSCREEN, SM_CYSCREEN	The width and height of the screen
SM_MOUSEPRESENT	TRUE if the mouse is connected, or FALSE if not
SM_SLOWMACHINE	TRUE if the machine is slow, or FALSE if not
SM_SWAPBUTTON	TRUE if the user setting swaps mouse buttons, or FALSE if not

Summary

We've gone through quite a bit in this first chapter, yet we still have only scratched the surface as far as WIN32 programming is concerned. I can't show you everything in just a few pages, even though I'd like to.

We've gone through basic window management, window messages, and the fundamental way Windows works. That's a lot to absorb in a single chapter. Even if you're one of those "I'll only be making full-screen games, anyway" folks, I ask that you consider the following: yes, most modern games are made full-screen—at least, the big titles are. However, that doesn't render this basic WIN32 stuff useless. For example, you'll need a regular window for some sort of configuration, or for the splash screen that commonly comes up whenever the CD autoruns (you know—the window with the Install, Play, Configure, and Quit buttons on it?).

CHAPTER 2

The World of GDI and Windows Graphics

- RECT and POINT
- Anatomy of a Window
- Device Contexts
- Pixel Plotting with GDI

Windows is a graphical operating system, with the emphasis on *graphical*. Windows achieves graphics through a subsystem called the Graphical Device Interface (GDI). With GDI, it doesn't matter what you are drawing on—the screen, system memory, a printer, a plotter, or any other graphical device—because GDI does most of the work for you.

Unfortunately, in many cases the performance of GDI isn't as good as you might want. Games are graphics hogs, and they cannot sacrifice speed. That's why DirectX was created; I'll cover it in Chapter 4, "DirectX at a Glance." But first I want to delve into GDI, because even when you get into using DirectX, some GDI will still be used, especially in the loading of bitmaps.

RECT and POINT

Before getting into the objects used by GDI, we first have to explore the use of two very useful structures—POINT and RECT—and the functions that manipulate them. RECT is also used quite a bit in DirectDraw (discussed in Chapter 5), so this won't be the only time you'll see them.

Before exploring the functions that deal with them, we first have to explore what POINT and RECT look like.

The POINT Structure

```
typedef struct tagPOINT {
  LONG x;
  LONG y;
} POINT, *PPOINT;
```

The POINT structure isn't all that complicated. It just contains an x,y pair of integers.

The RECT Structure

```
typedef struct _RECT {
  LONG left;
  LONG top;
  LONG right;
  LONG bottom;
} RECT, *PRECT;
```

RECT describes four points—(left,top), (right,top), (left,bottom) and (right,bottom). These four points represent a rectangular area.

NOTE

Something threw me for a while when I was first learning this stuff. The inside of a RECT is where x>=left and x<right and y>=top and y<bottom. In other words, the right and bottom edges of the RECT are not a part of the rectangle's interior.

Why? I've got a few guesses. My first guess is that Microsoft, when it decided how RECTs worked, said that a pixel is between two coordinate points (for example, pixel (100,100) is between x=100 and x=101 and y=100 and y=101). My second guess is that Microsoft did this so that the width of a rectangle is right-left and the height is bottom-top, thus minimizing the infamous "off by one" errors.

In either case, just keep in mind that the right and bottom are not in the RECT.

RECT and POINT Functions

I have these classified into three groups of related functions. Assignment functions deal with setting up the values of a RECT. Operation functions deal with manipulating RECTs. Testing functions deal with getting information about a RECT and how something interacts with it. Table 2.1 lists the various functions I cover and the classification into which I've put them.

Table 2.1 RECT and POINT Functions

Function	Category	Use
SetRect	Assignment	Sets a RECT's members to arbitrary values
SetRectEmpty	Assignment	Sets a RECT's members to all 0s
CopyRect	Assignment	Copies one RECT's members to another
IntersectRect	Operations	Finds the common area of two RECTs
UnionRect	Operations	Finds a RECT that contains both source RECTs
OffsetRect	Operations	Moves a RECT by an x and y offset
EqualRect	Testing	Finds if two RECTs have equal members
IsRectEmpty	Testing	Checks a RECT's members for all 0s
PtInRect	Testing	Checks whether a POINT is within the area of a RECT

Assignment RECT Functions

These functions either assign a RECT's values or copy one RECT into another.

SetRect

```
BOOL SetRect(
  LPRECT lprc, // rectangle
  int xLeft,   // left side
  int yTop,    // top side
  int xRight,  // right side
  int yBottom  // bottom side
);
```

This returns nonzero on success or 0 on failure. Table 2.2 explains the parameter list.

Table 2.2 SetRect Parameter List

SetRect Parameter	Purpose
lprc	Pointer to a RECT that will be filled with the values supplied in the other parameters
xLeft	Value to put in the RECT's left member
yTop	Value to put in the RECT's top member
xRight	Value to put in the RECT's right member
yBottom	Value to put in the RECT's bottom member

SetRect is equivalent to the following code:

```
//rc is a RECT
rc.left=xLeft;
rc.top=xTop;
rc.right=xRight;
rc.bottom=yBottom;
```

In my opinion, doing this in a single function call is much easier to read, and I think you'll agree.

SetRectEmpty

```
BOOL SetRectEmpty(
  LPRECT lprc    // rectangle
);
```

This returns nonzero on success or 0 on failure. The parameter `lprc` is a pointer to the `RECT` that you want to set to empty. An empty `RECT` has all members equal to 0.

`SetRectEmpty` is equivalent to this:

```
//rc is a RECT
SetRect(&rc,0,0,0,0);
```

It's a good idea to set any temporary `RECT` variable you aren't going to use for a while to empty. Following this practice will help minimize strange glitches.

CopyRect

```
BOOL CopyRect(
  LPRECT lprcDst,       // destination rectangle
  CONST RECT *lprcSrc   // source rectangle
);
```

This returns nonzero on success or 0 on failure. Copies the members pointed to by `lprcSrc` into the members pointed to by `lprcDst`.

It isn't absolutely necessary to use `CopyRect` to set one `RECT` equal to another. Indeed, you could just do the following:

```
//rc1 and rc2 are RECTs
rc2=rc1;
```

Doing this does the exact same thing as `CopyRect`. So why don't I suggest its use? Using `CopyRect` more accurately indicates the intended operation, and the equal sign does not.

Operation RECT Functions

These functions either combine or modify `RECT`s in some way.

OffsetRect

```
BOOL OffsetRect(
  LPRECT lprc,  // rectangle
  int dx,       // horizontal offset
  int dy        // vertical offset
);
```

This returns nonzero on success or 0 on failure. The left and right members pointed to by `lprc` are increased by `dx`, and the top and bottom members are increased by `dy`.

`OffsetRect` is equivalent to the following code:

```
//lprc is pointer to RECT
lprc->left+=dx;
lprc->top+=dy;
lprc->right+=dx;
lprc->bottom+=dy;
```

`OffsetRect` is quite handy when you want to have the same-sized `RECT` in a different location.

IntersectRect

```
BOOL IntersectRect(
  LPRECT lprcDst,          // intersection buffer
  CONST RECT *lprcSrc1,    // first rectangle
  CONST RECT *lprcSrc2     // second rectangle
);
```

If the `RECT`s pointed to by `lprcSrc1` and `lprcSrc2` intersect, this function returns nonzero. If they do not, it returns 0. `lprcDst` is filled with the intersecting `RECT`. Figure 2.1 illustrates the output of `IntersectRect`.

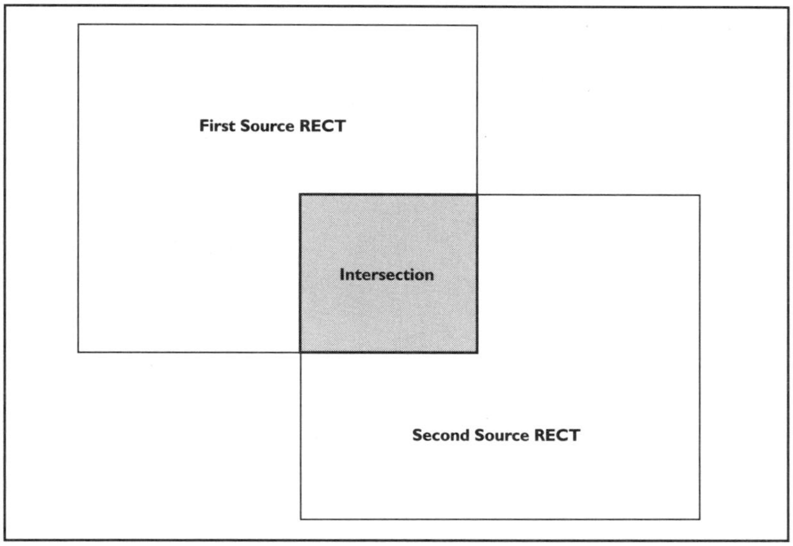

Figure 2.1

`IntersectRect` (the shaded area marks the intersection)

UnionRect

```
BOOL UnionRect(
  LPRECT lprcDst,          // destination rectangle
  CONST RECT *lprcSrc1,   // first rectangle
  CONST RECT *lprcSrc2    // second rectangle
);
```

This returns 0 if the resulting union (pointed to by `lprcDst`) is an empty `RECT`. It returns nonzero otherwise. The `RECT`s pointed to by `lprcSrc1` and `lprcSrc2` are combined to make the smallest `RECT` that could contain both, (see Figure 2.2).

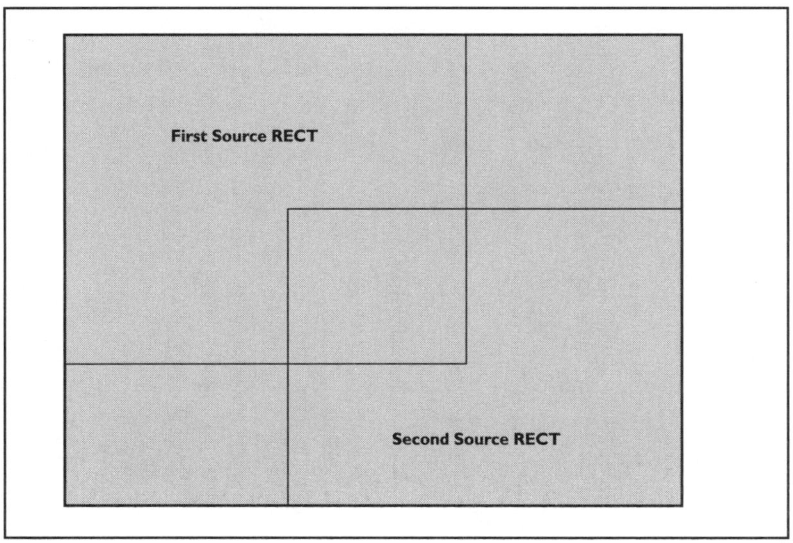

Figure 2.2

The shaded area shows the result of a call to `UnionRect`

Testing RECT Functions

The testing functions check the status of a RECT in relation to another RECT, in relation to itself, or in relation to a POINT.

EqualRect

```
BOOL EqualRect(
  CONST RECT *lprc1,  // first rectangle
  CONST RECT *lprc2   // second rectangle
);
```

This returns 0 if the two rectangles (pointed to by lprc1 and lprc2) are not equal, and nonzero if they are.

IsRectEmpty

```
BOOL IsRectEmpty(
  CONST RECT *lprc   // rectangle
);
```

This returns 0 if the rectangle pointed to by lprc is not empty, and nonzero if it is empty.

PtInRect

```
BOOL PtInRect(
  CONST RECT *lprc,  // rectangle
  POINT pt           // point
);
```

Checks to see if the POINT pt is within the RECT pointed to by lprc. This returns nonzero if it is, and 0 if it is not.

PtInRect is equivalent to the following code:

```
//lprc is pointer to RECT
BOOL ptinrect=((pt.x>=lprc->left) && (pt.x<lprc->right) && (pt.y>=lprc->top) &&
(pt.y<lprc->bottom));
```

There are a few more RECT functions, but they aren't very useful and so I didn't cover them. If you're curious, they are called InflateRect and SubtractRect, and they can be found in MSDN.

Anatomy of a Window

As you are well aware, a window consists of more than just an area on which you can draw. Depending on its use, a window contains minimize and maximize buttons, a title bar, a close button, a system menu, a sizable or nonsizeable border, scroll bars, and so on. The inclusion of these in your window depends on the style with which you create it. Windows takes care of making these look correct, so you can just concern yourself with drawing on the inside of the window.

The section upon which you can draw is called the *client area*. The rest of the window is the *nonclient area*. Figure 2.3 shows these two areas. When the client area needs repainting, you get `WM_PAINT` messages from Windows.

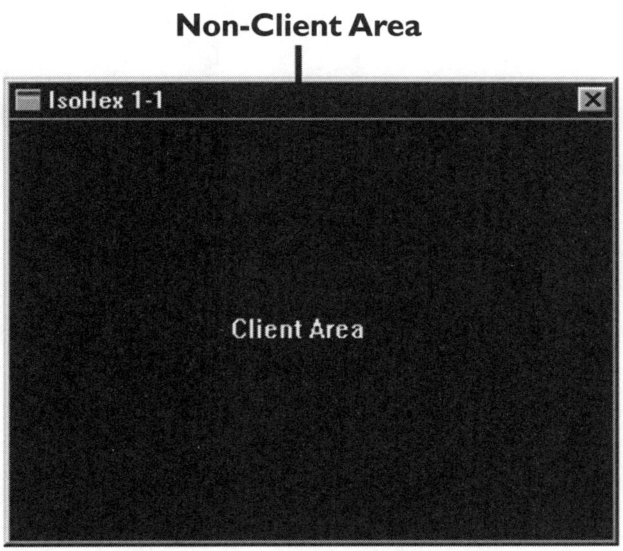

Figure 2.3

Client and nonclient areas of a window

> **NOTE**
>
> **If you want to, you can override the way Windows draws the nonclient area by responding to the `WM_NCPAINT` message.**

GetClientRect

The area contained in the client area can be retrieved with the function `GetClientRect`:

```
BOOL GetClientRect(
  HWND hWnd,       // handle to window
  LPRECT lpRect    // client coordinates
);
```

This returns nonzero on success or 0 on failure. Table 2.3 explains the parameter list.

Table 2.3 GetClientRect Parameter List

GetClientRect Parameter	Purpose
`hWnd`	Window for which you would like to retrieve the client area
`lpRect`	Pointer to a `RECT` into which the client area information is retrieved

The left and top members of the `RECT` are 0. The right and bottom contain the width and height.

GetWindowRect

The area that contains the entire window can be retrieved with the function `GetWindowRect`.

```
BOOL GetWindowRect(
  HWND hWnd,       // handle to window
  LPRECT lpRect    // window coordinates
);
```

This returns nonzero on success or 0 on failure. Table 2.4 explains the parameter list.

Table 2.4 GetWindowRect Parameter List

GetWindowRect Parameter	Purpose
`hWnd`	Window for which you would like to retrieve the client area
`lpRect`	Pointer to a `RECT` into which the client area information is retrieved

The coordinates returned in the RECT are screen coordinates, so this function yields different results when the window has been moved around.

Let's say that you are making a game that needs to have a play area that has certain dimensions (640×480, for example). You may want this application to be windowed, but it is nearly impossible to determine how big of a window you have to make, because user settings modify how large some types of windows are.

So, what to do?

AdjustWindowRect and AdjustWindowRectEx

Luckily, Win32 does have a couple of functions that help you in this area. They are AdjustWindowRect and AdjustWindowRectEx.

AdjustWindowRect

If you used CreateWindow to create your main window (or any window you might be adjusting), you would use AdjustWindowRect to modify the size of your client area.

```
BOOL AdjustWindowRect(
  LPRECT lpRect,  // client-rectangle structure
  DWORD dwStyle,  // window styles
  BOOL bMenu       // menu-present option
);
```

This returns nonzero on success or 0 on failure. Table 2.5 explains the parameter list.

Table 2.5 AdjustWindowRect Parameters

AdjustWindowRect Parameter	Purpose
lpRect	Pointer to a RECT that contains the desired client area on entry and the desired window RECT on exit
dwStyle	Style of the window (as sent to CreateWindow)
bMenu	TRUE or FALSE, depending on whether or not the window has a menu

AdjustWindowRectEx

If you used CreateWindowEx to create your window, use AdjustWindowRectEx to modify the size of your client area.

```
BOOL AdjustWindowRectEx(
  LPRECT lpRect,     // client-rectangle structure
  DWORD dwStyle,     // window styles
  BOOL bMenu,        // menu-present option
  DWORD dwExStyle    // extended window style
);
```

This returns nonzero on success or 0 on failure. Table 2.6 explains the parameter list.

Table 2.6 AdjustWindowRectEx Parameters

AdjustWindowRectEx Parameter	Purpose
lpRect	Pointer to a RECT that contains the desired client area on entry and the desired window RECT on exit
dwStyle	Style of the window (as sent to CreateWindowEx)
bMenu	TRUE or FALSE, depending on whether or not the window has a menu
dwExStyle	Extended style of the window (as sent to CreateWindowEx)

The choice of AdjustWindowRect versus AdjustWindowRectEx depends solely on whether or not CreateWindow or CreateWindowEx was used to create your window.

NOTE

Under WIN32, there is absolutely no functional difference between `CreateWindow` and `CreateWindowEx`, nor is there a difference between `AdjustWindowRect` and `AdjustWindowRectEx`. The `CreateWindow` function is not actually a function at all. It is a macro that calls `CreateWindowEx` and supplies the `dwExStyle` parameter with a 0. The same goes for `AdjustWindowRect`. It is always best to use the `Ex` version of the function.

Using AdjustWindowRectEx

Load IsoHex2_1.cpp into your compiler, and take a look at the `Prog_Init` function:

```
bool Prog_Init()
{
	//rectangle into which we will place the desired client RECT
	RECT rc;
	SetRect(&rc,0,0,640,480);
	//get the window rect based on our style and extended style
	AdjustWindowRectEx(&rc,WS_BORDER | WS_SYSMENU | WS_VISIBLE,FALSE,0);
	//use movewindow to resize the window
	MoveWindow(hWndMain,0,0,rc.right-rc.left,rc.bottom-rc.top,TRUE);
	return(true);//return success
}
```

In this function, you resize the window using `MoveWindow` so that you have a 640×480 client area.

Through my experience with using `AdjustWindowRectEx`, I have found that sometimes it just doesn't work, depending on the combination of style and extended style flags for the window. If you want to try using `AdjustWindowRectEx`, make sure you get the client `RECT` size you want. If you don't, all is not lost. You can manually get the proper window size by using `GetClientRect`, `GetWindowRect`, and `MoveWindow`, as shown in the following snippet of code:

```
//get the client rect
RECT rcClient;
GetClientRect(hWndMain,&rcClient);
//get the window rect
RECT rcWnd;
GetWindowRect(hWndMain,&rcWnd);
//make the window rect left and top be zero
```

```
OffsetRect(&rcWnd,-rcWnd.left,-rcWnd.top);
//get the difference in the width
int iWidthDelta=rcWnd.right-rcClient.right;
int iHeightDelta=rcWnd.bottom-rcClient.bottom;
//set up desired client rect
SetRect(&rcClient,0,0,640,480);//640 and 480 can be replaced with desired meas-
urements
//adjust the width of the desired client rect
rcClient.right+=iWidthDelta;
rcClient.botom+=iHeightDelta;
//use movewindow to set desired height and width
MoveWindow(hWnd,0,0,rcClient.right,rcClient.bottom,TRUE);
```

Up until now this chapter has been little more than a list of functions and parameters. Unfortunately, it has been necessary to make it so—there are a lot of things you have to know in order to use GDI effectively. Now that you've got the goods on `RECT`, `POINT`, and the client area, you can actually start doing something.

Device Contexts

Windows can draw to several different types of devices—monitors, printers, plotters, and system memory. Drawing to any of these devices is handled by the exact same mechanism—device contexts (DCs). A DC is an abstraction of something that can be drawn upon. Some devices have varying coordinate systems. For example, a printer might print at 600dpi, and your screen has 72dpi. DCs ensure that the proper transformations (scaling, stretching) can be performed, regardless of the coordinate system used internally by the device. This is a good thing, because it achieves device independence, and you have to deal with only a single set of functions instead of a billion different APIs, each for a different device.

Of course, device independence has its cost. Using device contexts is significantly slower than working directly with the hardware, since commands have to be filtered through several layers of abstraction before the operation is actually performed. You'll reduce this problem when you make the move to DirectX, which has a lower level of abstraction. (DirectX talks to hardware drivers, which is as close as you can get to bare metal in Windows.)

You had slight exposure to DCs in the preceding chapter, when you responded to the `WM_PAINT` message and used `BeginPaint` and `EndPaint`.

Obtaining Device Contexts

In `WM_PAINT`, you use `BeginPaint` and `EndPaint` to retrieve a DC, and you can then use that DC for drawing operations. This is one way to go about it. However, using `BeginPaint` and `EndPaint` is limited to times when areas of the client area have been invalidated (for example covered up by something else, like another window).

InvalidateRect

You can invalidate portions of the client area by using `InvalidateRect`.

```
BOOL InvalidateRect(
  HWND hWnd,            // handle to window
  CONST RECT *lpRect,  // rectangle coordinates
  BOOL bErase           // erase state
);
```

This returns nonzero on success or 0 on failure. The `hWnd` and `lpRect` parameters should be self-explanatory by now. `bErase` tells the application whether or not to erase the background during the next call to `BeginPaint`.

If you really want to, you can use this method. Call `InvalidateRect`, and wait for the `WM_PAINT` message to be processed. That would be very Windows-friendly of you. However, you are a game programmer, and games are rarely Windows-friendly.

GetDC

Most of the time, you'll grab a window's DC using `GetDC`.

```
HDC GetDC(
  HWND hWnd   // handle to window
);
```

This takes as a parameter the window for which you want the DC, and then it returns that DC. Keep in mind that Windows is letting you "borrow" this DC. You have to put it back later or suffer the consequences.

ReleaseDC

When you are done with the DC and it's time to give it back, you use `ReleaseDC`.

```
int ReleaseDC(
  HWND hWnd,  // handle to window
  HDC hDC     // handle to DC
);
```

> **CAUTION**
>
> **If you do not call `ReleaseDC` for every call to `GetDC`, very bad things will happen. You've been warned.**

So, if you want to perform some drawing operations on your main window, you do this:

```
//borrow the dc from the main window
HDC hdc=GetDC(hWndMain);
//draw stuff
//return the dc to the system
ReleaseDC(hWndMain,hdc);
```

Memory DCs

Not all the DCs you'll be working with will be borrowed from a window. For example, later you'll load images and place them into memory DCs. A memory DC is nothing more than a bit of your computer's memory that behaves as though it is a device upon which you can draw.

CreateCompatibleDC

The mechanism by which you will do this is `CreateCompatibleDC`.

```
HDC CreateCompatibleDC(
  HDC hdc   // handle to DC
);
```

This function creates a memory DC compatible with a supplied `hdc` and returns the created DC. If you pass `NULL`, the DC that is created is compatible with the screen.

DeleteDC

When you are done with a memory DC, you use `DeleteDC`.

```
BOOL DeleteDC(
  HDC hdc   // handle to DC
);
```

So, what is in these memory DCs after you create them? Not much, as it turns out. A memory DC contains a 1×1 monochrome bitmap. What good is that? Well, the 1×1 bitmap isn't really good for anything. However, there has to be something in a DC. Otherwise, it can't exist, and using the DCs in the functions that need them would cause errors.

GDI Objects

All this stuff about DCs is great, but we haven't actually covered what to do with them. That's where GDI objects come in. They aren't exactly objects in the object-oriented programming sense of the word. They are Windows objects, and you reference them by way of `HANDLE`s (I told you we'd be having more of them).

There are five types of GDI objects that you need to be concerned with: `HBITMAP`, `HBRUSH`, `HPEN`, `HFONT`, and `HRGN`:

- An `HBITMAP` consists of a two-dimensional graphic. In Windows, this usually comes from a .bmp file or is created to given dimensions on-the-fly.
- An `HBRUSH` consists of a colored fill pattern. It is used to fill in areas of a DC.
- An `HPEN` consists of a colored line style and width. It is used to draw primitives (lines, rectangles, ellipses) on a DC.
- An `HFONT` consists of a set of characters. It is used to print text on a DC.
- An `HRGN` represents a shape that can be used for clipping, drawing, framing, or filling. These regions can be rectangles, ellipses, polygons, or just about anything else you might imagine.

A DC can contain exactly one of each of these at any given time. This may seem a little backwards, but it's not. Consider a DC a mechanical device that draws. This machine can select a piece of paper (an `HBITMAP`) on which to draw, and it can pick a pen (`HPEN`) with which to draw, a brush (`HBRUSH`) with which to fill areas, a typeface (`HFONT`) with which to stamp letters, and an artist's template (`HRGN`) with which to draw shapes or draw on only a particular area.

SelectObject

In order to place a given object into a DC, you use `SelectObject`.

```
HGDIOBJ SelectObject(
  HDC hdc,           // handle to DC
  HGDIOBJ hgdiobj   // handle to object
);
```

This function places the desired GDI Object (`HBITMAP`, `HRGN`, `HFONT`, `HPEN`, or `HBRUSH`) into the DC, and it returns the GDI object that the new object has replaced (except in the case of `HRGN`—see Chapter 3, "Fonts, Bitmaps, and Regions").

CAUTION

We're about to have another "put your toys away" moment here. When you create a GDI object, no matter what kind, you have to later destroy it. Technically, in WIN32, you don't have to. WIN32 maintains a separate memory space for each application, and when the application terminates, all of that application's resources are released. Still, it's good programming practice to delete GDI objects when you're done with them.

So, if you wanted to bring a white brush into a DC and clean it up later, you'd do something like the following:

```
//create solid white brush
HBRUSH hbrNew=CreateSolidBrush(RGB(255,255,255));
//select the new brush into a dc and save the old one (note the typecast of the
return value)
HBRUSH hbrOld=(HBRUSH)SelectObject(hdc,hbrNew);
//use drawing functions that use the new brush
//return the old brush to the dc
SelectObject(hdc,hbrOld);
//delete the brush we no longer need
DeleteObject(hbrNew);
```

This is something of a pain, I know (*believe me*—I know).

Pixel Plotting with GDI

A *pixel* is a pictorial element. It is the smallest piece of graphics that you can manipulate. The number of pixels on the screen depends on your display settings. I run my machine at 1024×768 most of the time, so I have over 750,000 pixels on my screen.

Besides width and height, your screen also has color depth. Common color depths (measured in bits per pixel—bpp) range from 1 (which is monochrome) to 32 (true color with an extra byte). The most common color depths are 8, 16, 24, and 32. An 8-bit color depth requires a method of color abstraction known as color indirection and is handled by means of a palette. I won't be covering palettes.

For 16, 24, and 32 bits per pixel, there is an RGB representation for your pixels. This means that certain bits represent one of the three primary colors of light—red, green, or blue.

Pixel format will become more of a concern when you get to DirectDraw. In GDI, you get to pretend that everything is 24bpp, and Windows does all the conversions for you.

In GDI, all colors are represented by `COLORREF`s. A `COLORREF` is merely an `int`. It has 8 bits for each of red, green, and blue. Because each is 8 bits, you can have red, green, and blue values from 0 to 255. Since a `COLORREF` is 24 bits, it can be scaled down to 16 bits, and in 32-bit modes, the number of bits used per pixel for the color is still only 24.

The RGB Macro

To assign a color to a `COLORREF`, use the `RGB` macro:

```
#define RGB(r,g,b)
((COLORREF)(((BYTE)(r)|((WORD)((BYTE)(g))<<8))|(((DWORD)(BYTE)(b))<<16)))
```

Pixel Manipulation Functions

Essentially, there are three of these: `SetPixel`, `SetPixelV`, and `GetPixel`.

SetPixel

```
COLORREF SetPixel(
  HDC hdc,              // handle to DC
  int X,                // x-coordinate of pixel
  int Y,                // y-coordinate of pixel
  COLORREF crColor    // pixel color
);
```

`SetPixel` needs an `HDC`, an X,Y position, and a `COLORREF`. It does its best to plot the pixel to the given `HDC`. The return value contains the actual color that was plotted.

SetPixelV

```
BOOL SetPixelV(
  HDC hdc,              // handle to device context
  int X,                // x-coordinate of pixel
  int Y,                // y-coordinate of pixel
  COLORREF crColor    // new pixel color
);
```

Like SetPixel, SetPixelV needs an HDC, an X,Y position, and a COLORREF. Unlike SetPixel, this function does not return the color plotted. It returns 0 on failure or nonzero on success.

GetPixel

```
COLORREF GetPixel(
  HDC hdc,     // handle to DC
  int nXPos,   // x-coordinate of pixel
  int nYPos    // y-coordinate of pixel
);
```

GetPixel needs an HDC and an X,Y position. It returns the color of that position on the specified HDC.

A Pixel Plotting Example

Now that you can finally draw something (it's about time, I know), let's do so. Load up IsoHex2_2.cpp. The only difference between this program and IsoHex1_1.cpp is an added case in the window procedure:

```
        //the mouse moved
        case WM_MOUSEMOVE:
                {
                        //if the left button is down
                        if(wParam & MK_LBUTTON)
                        {
                                //extract x and y from lparam
                                int x=LOWORD(lParam);
                                int y=HIWORD(lParam);

                                //borrow the dc from the main window
                                HDC hdc=GetDC(hWndMain);

                                //plot the pixel
                                SetPixelV(hdc,x,y,RGB(255,255,255));

                                //return the dc to the system
                                ReleaseDC(hWndMain,hdc);
                        }

                        //handled, so return 0
                        return(0);
                }break;
```

In this little stretch of code, you respond to the `WM_MOUSEMOVE` message. First, you check to see if the left button is down. If it is, you borrow the DC from the main window, plot the pixel, and release the DC back to the system. With this relatively small change, you can now draw. Figure 2.4 demonstrates my lack of artistic ability.

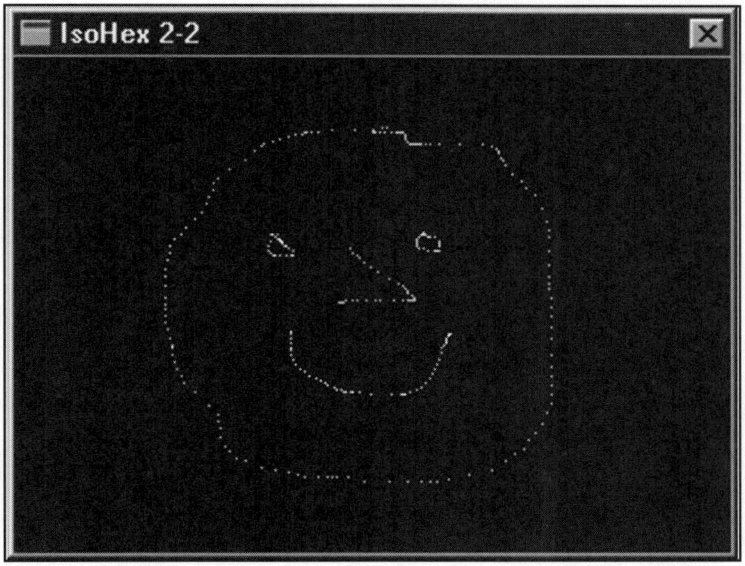

Figure 2.4

Pixel-plotting demo

OK, so it isn't Paint Shop Pro. Heck, it isn't even Microsoft Paint. But it is a step in the right direction, and that's all that counts.

NOTE

I'd like to point out something about this particular application, because it applies to most of the applications in the early part of this book. If you bring another application's window in front of it, and then bring it back in front, the part of the overlap will be erased. You'll read more about fixing this later.

Using Pens

Pixels are great, but dealing with just pixels for everything would become a nightmare, and game programming would stop being fun.

So, to draw lines and shapes and so on, you'll use HPENs and functions that use the pens in a DC.

CreatePen

Creating a pen is simple. The function that does so is named, of all things, CreatePen.

```
HPEN CreatePen(
  int fnPenStyle,     // pen style
  int nWidth,         // pen width
  COLORREF crColor    // pen color
);
```

This function returns a handle to a pen with the desired style, width, and color. Table 2.7 explains the parameter list.

Table 2.7 CreatePen Parameters

CreatePen Parameter	Purpose
fnPenStyle	The style of the pen (see the paragraph after this table)
nWidth	Desired width of the pen
crColor	Desired color of the pen

The fnPenStyle parameter can have a number of values:

- PS_SOLID A solid pen. May have any width.
- PS_DASH A dashed pen. Must have a width of 0 or 1.
- PS_DOT A dotted pen. Must have a width of 0 or 1.
- PS_DASHDOT A dash dot pen. Must have a width of 0 or 1.
- PS_DASHDOTDOT A dash dot dot pen. Must have a width of 0 or 1.
- PS_NULL An invisible pen

To use a pen, you simply select it into a device context using SelectObject, and you're ready to go.

Drawing Functions

Before we get to drawing functions themselves, let's take a moment to talk about the current position within a DC.

Internally, a DC maintains a current position. The current position is similar to a cursor in a way. It keeps track of where you left off when drawing. (In this way, you can draw continuous shapes without modifying more than one line of code.)

> **NOTE**
> Some drawing functions modify the current position, and others do not.

You can set or get the current position (CP) with the following two functions.

MoveToEx

```
BOOL MoveToEx(
  HDC hdc,           // handle to device context
  int X,             // x-coordinate of new current position
  int Y,             // y-coordinate of new current position
  LPPOINT lpPoint    // old current position
);
```

This returns nonzero on success and 0 on failure. Table 2.8 explains the parameter list.

Table 2.8 MoveToEx Parameters

MoveToEx Parameter	Purpose
`hdc`	Handle to the device context for which you are setting the CP
`X, Y`	The desired position of the CP
`lpPoint`	A pointer to a `POINT`. The former CP is placed here.

GetCurrentPositionEx

```
BOOL GetCurrentPositionEx(
  HDC hdc,         // handle to device context
  LPPOINT lpPoint // current position
);
```

This returns nonzero on success or 0 on failure. Table 2.9 explains the parameter list.

Table 2.9 GetCurrentPositionEx Parameters

GetCurrentPositionEx Parameter	Purpose
`hdc`	Handle to the device context for which you are getting the CP
`lpPoint`	Pointer to a `POINT` structure that will be filled with the CP

OK, so you can get and set the CP. So what? Seems sort of useless.

LineTo

Introducing the `LineTo` function. `LineTo` draws a line in the current pen from the CP to a specified point.

```
BOOL LineTo(
  HDC hdc,     // device context handle
  int nXEnd,   // x-coordinate of ending point
  int nYEnd    // y-coordinate of ending point
);
```

This returns nonzero on success or 0 on failure. It moves the CP to `nXEnd`, `nYEnd` in the given `hdc`. It draws a line as it does so.

A Line Drawing Example

Since we have a new toy (`LineTo`), let's play. Load up IsoHex2_3.cpp.

This program is similar to IsoHex2_2.cpp, but it gets a little more involved. First, you have to create a pen and select it into your window's DC, so you declare two global variables, `hpenNew` and `hpenOld`.

Here's the `Prog_Init` function:

```
bool Prog_Init()
{
	//create the new pen
	hpenNew=CreatePen(PS_SOLID,0,RGB(255,255,255));
	//borrow dc from main window
	HDC hdc=GetDC(hWndMain);
	//select new pen into dc
	hpenOld=(HPEN)SelectObject(hdc,hpenNew);
```

```
        //release dc to system
        ReleaseDC(hWndMain,hdc);
        return(true);//return success
}
```

Here you take care of creating the new pen (it's white) and putting it into the DC.

Now, here's `Prog_Done`, on the other end of the program:

```
void Prog_Done()
{
        //borrow dc from main window
        HDC hdc=GetDC(hWndMain);
        //restore old pen to dc
        SelectObject(hdc,hpenOld);
        //release dc to system
        ReleaseDC(hWndMain,hdc);
        //delete new pen
        DeleteObject(hpenNew);
}
```

Here you restore the old pen to the DC and delete the pen you created—you put your toys away after you are done playing with them.

Now that the pen is set up, you can take care of doing the real work. The main work in this case is done in two window message handlers, `WM_MOUSEMOVE` and `WM_LBUTTONDOWN`.

```
        case WM_LBUTTONDOWN:
                {
                        //extract x and y from lparam
                        int x=LOWORD(lParam);
                        int y=HIWORD(lParam);
                        //borrow the main window's DC
                        HDC hdc=GetDC(hWndMain);
                        //update the CP
                        MoveToEx(hdc,x,y,NULL);
                        //return the dc to the system
                        ReleaseDC(hWndMain,hdc);
                        //handled, return 0
                        return(0);
                }break;
```

In this handler, you must update the CP of the window's DC because if you just responded to movements of the mouse, you would get errors. (Try commenting out the MoveToEx line, and see what I mean.)

```
case WM_MOUSEMOVE:
        {
                //if left button is down
                if(wParam & MK_LBUTTON)
                {
                        //extract x and y from lparam
                        int x=LOWORD(lParam);
                        int y=HIWORD(lParam);

                        //borrow the main window's DC
                        HDC hdc=GetDC(hWndMain);

                        //line to the x,y position
                        LineTo(hdc,x,y);

                        //return the dc to the system
                        ReleaseDC(hWndMain,hdc);
                }

                //handled, return 0
                return(0);
        }break;
```

When the mouse is moved, and the left button is down, you draw a line to the mouse's position. Doing so updates the CP.

The resulting program doesn't do too much more than what IsoHex2_2 did, except that it isn't so...well, pixelated. Figure 2.5 shows the application's output.

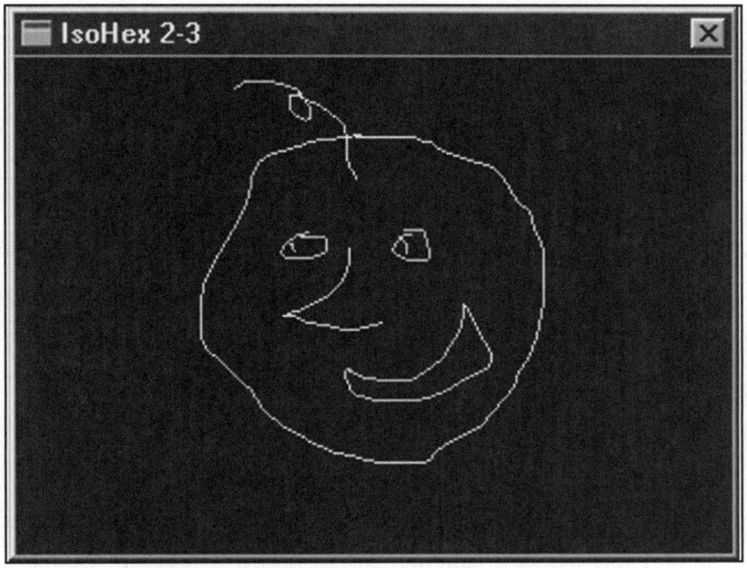

Figure 2.5

Once again, an artist I am not

> **NOTE**
> This program suffers from the same erasure problem that 2_2 did.

Play around with IsoHex2_3 a bit, changing the pen style and line width and color so that you can see the various effects that can be created. After you're done, we'll move on to brushes.

Brushes

In GDI, you use pens to draw, and you use brushes to fill. You can create brushes using a number of functions. The functions I'm going to cover here are the most commonly used: `CreateSolidBrush` and `CreateHatchBrush`.

Brush Creation

```
HBRUSH CreateSolidBrush(
  COLORREF crColor    // brush color value
);
```

`CreateSolidBrush` takes a color and returns a brush in that color.

```
HBRUSH CreateHatchBrush(
  int fnStyle,        // hatch style
  COLORREF clrref     // foreground color
);
```

`CreateHatchBrush` takes a style and a color and returns a brush with that color and style. Hatch brush styles are represented by HS_* constants like the following:

- `HS_BDIAGONAL` A 45-degree stripe that runs downward from left to right
- `HS_CROSS` A combination of horizontal and vertical stripes
- `HS_DIACROSS` A combination of the two diagonal stripes
- `HS_FDIAGONAL` A 45-degree stripe that runs upward from left to right
- `HS_HORIZONTAL` Horizontal stripes
- `HS_VERTICAL` Vertical stripes

To bring a brush into a device context, use `SelectObject` just like you do with pens. Always be sure to restore the old brush when you are done. Use `DeleteObject` to destroy brushes.

ExtFloodFill

To fill in a given area, use `ExtFloodFill`.

```
BOOL ExtFloodFill(
  HDC hdc,            // handle to DC
  int nXStart,        // starting x-coordinate
  int nYStart,        // starting y-coordinate
  COLORREF crColor, // fill color
  UINT fuFillType    // fill type
);
```

This returns nonzero on success or 0 on failure. Table 2.10 explains the parameter list.

Table 2.10 ExtFloodFill Parameters

ExtFloodFill Parameter	Purpose
hdc	Handle to a device context in which you would like the fill to occur
nXStart, nYStart	The coordinate at which to begin the fill
crColor	Depending on fuFillType, either the color at which to stop filling, or the color to fill over
fuFillStyle	Either the value FLOODFILLBORDER or FLOODFILLSURFACE. FLOODFILLBORDER fills until crColor is reached, and FLOODFILLSURFACE fills over any adjacent areas that are the same color as crColor.

A Brush Example

So, another example. Load up IsoHex2_4.cpp. IsoHex2_4.cpp is mostly just IsoHex2_3.cpp with an extra message handler, WM_RBUTTONDOWN.

```
case WM_RBUTTONDOWN:
        {
                        //extract x and y from lparam
                        int x=LOWORD(lParam);
                        int y=HIWORD(lParam);
                        //borrow the main window's DC
                        HDC hdc=GetDC(hWndMain);
                        //line to the x,y position
                        ExtFloodFill(hdc,x,y,RGB(255,255,255),FLOODFILLBORDER);
                //return the dc to the system
                        ReleaseDC(hWndMain,hdc);
        }break;
```

Figure 2.6 shows the output of this sample program.

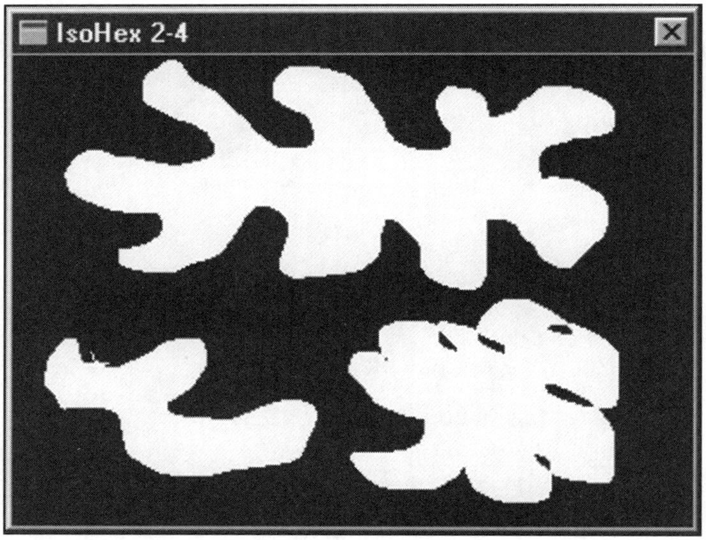

Figure 2.6

These are clouds. No, really.

In this app, you still draw lines with the left mouse button, and fill areas with the right.

Filling in Rectangular Areas

Possibly the most common brush operation you are likely to do is filling a rectangular area. This operation is done with the `FillRect` function.

```
int FillRect(
  HDC hDC,            // handle to DC
  CONST RECT *lprc,  // rectangle
  HBRUSH hbr          // handle to brush
);
```

On failure, this returns 0. On success, it returns nonzero. Table 2.11 explains the parameter list.

Table 2.11 FillRect Parameters

FillRect Parameter	Purpose
`hDC`	Handle to the device context for which you would like a rectangular area filled
`lprc`	A pointer to a rectangle describing the area you would like filled
`hbr`	The brush with which you would like the rectangular area of the DC filled

If you wanted, for example, to clear out the entire client area, this is what you would do:

```
//borrow dc from main window
HDC hdc=GetDC(hWndMain);
//set up rect to contain entire client area
RECT rc;
GetClientRect(&rc);
//fill in given rectangle with black brush
FillRect(hdc,&rc,(HBRUSH)GetStockObject(BLACK_BRUSH));
//return dc to system
ReleaseDC(hWndMain,hdc);
```

Pens and Brushes Together: Shape Functions

Now, being able to draw lines is great, and filling in bordered areas and rectangles is cool, too. However, in order to be a fully functional API, you have to have other primitives—circles, rectangles, polygons. GDI has these and more. I'm only going to cover `Ellipse`, `Rectangle`, `RoundRect`, and `Polygon`.

With all of these shapes, GDI outlines the shape with the current pen and fills it with the current brush.

Ellipse

```
BOOL Ellipse(
  HDC hdc,         // handle to DC
  int nLeftRect,  // x-coord of upper-left corner of rectangle
  int nTopRect,   // y-coord of upper-left corner of rectangle
  int nRightRect, // x-coord of lower-right corner of rectangle
  int nBottomRect // y-coord of lower-right corner of rectangle
);
```

This returns nonzero on success or 0 on failure. Table 2.12 explains the parameter list.

Table 2.12 Ellipse Parameters

Ellipse Parameter	Purpose
`hdc`	The `hdc` on which you want the ellipse to be drawn
`nLeftRect`	The left of the rectangle that bounds this ellipse
`nTopRect`	The top of the rectangle that bounds this ellipse
`nRightRect`	The right of the rectangle that bounds this ellipse
`nBottomRect`	The bottom of the rectangle that bounds this ellipse

With other graphical APIs, drawing an ellipse is done by specifying the center and then the x and y radii. In GDI, however, it is done by supplying the rectangle that bounds the ellipse.

> **NOTE**
>
> **The center of the ellipse is at** `x=(nLeftRect+nRightRect)/2` **and** `y=(nTopRect+nBottomRect)/2`**. The horizontal (x) radius is** `abs(nRightRect-nLeftRect)/2`**, and the vertical (y) radius is** `abs(nBottomRect-nTopRect)/2`**. The** `abs` **is in there because as far as** `Ellipse` **is concerned,** `nLeftRect` **does not have to be less than** `nRightRect`**, and** `nTopRect` **does not have to be less than** `nBottomRect`**.**

Rectangle

```
BOOL Rectangle(
  HDC hdc,          // handle to DC
  int nLeftRect,    // x-coord of upper-left corner of rectangle
  int nTopRect,     // y-coord of upper-left corner of rectangle
  int nRightRect,   // x-coord of lower-right corner of rectangle
  int nBottomRect   // y-coord of lower-right corner of rectangle
);
```

This returns nonzero on success or 0 on failure. Table 2.13 explains the parameter list.

Table 2.13 Rectangle Parameters

Rectangle Parameter	Purpose
`hdc`	The `hdc` on which you would like this rectangle drawn
`nLeftRect`	The left of the rectangle
`nTopRect`	The top of the rectangle
`nRightRect`	The right of the rectangle
`nBottomRect`	The bottom of the rectangle

`Rectangle` has the exact same parameters as `Ellipse`, only instead of drawing the ellipse bound by a rectangle, it draws and fills the rectangle.

RoundRect

```
BOOL RoundRect(
  HDC hdc,          // handle to DC
  int nLeftRect,    // x-coord of upper-left corner of rectangle
  int nTopRect,     // y-coord of upper-left corner of rectangle
  int nRightRect,   // x-coord of lower-right corner of rectangle
  int nBottomRect,  // y-coord of lower-right corner of rectangle
  int nWidth,       // width of ellipse
  int nHeight       // height of ellipse
);
```

This returns nonzero on success or 0 on failure. Table 2.14 explains the parameter list.

Table 2.14 RoundRect Parameters

RoundRect Parameter	Purpose
`hdc`	The `hdc` on which you would like this rounded rectangle drawn
`nLeftRect`	The left of the rounded rectangle
`nTopRect`	The top of the rounded rectangle
`nRightRect`	The right of the rounded rectangle
`nBottomRect`	The bottom of the rounded rectangle
`nWidth`	The width of the ellipse used for rounding the corners
`nHeight`	The height of the ellipse used for rounding the corners

I think that the `RoundRect` function is kind of cool. It can be used not only to draw rounded rectangles, but also plain rectangles (when `nWidth` and `nHeight` are both 0) or ellipses (when `nWidth` and `nHeight` equal the width and height of the rectangle itself).

Polygon

```
BOOL Polygon(
  HDC hdc,                  // handle to DC
  CONST POINT *lpPoints,   // polygon vertices
  int nCount                // count of polygon vertices
);
```

This returns nonzero on success or 0 on failure. Table 2.15 explains the parameter list.

Table 2.15 Polygon Parameters

Polygon Parameter	Purpose
`Hdc`	The `hdc` on which you want the polygon drawn
`LpPoints`	A pointer to an array of `POINT`s, containing the vertices of the polygon
`nCount`	The number of points pointed to by `lpPoints`

For the rest of your shape-drawing needs, you have `Polygon`. `lpPoints` must point to at least two vertices. The polygon drawn will automatically be closed (a line is drawn from the last point to the first point).

The manner in which your polygon is filled depends on two things. The first is whether you have any of the line segments of the polygon crossing, and the second is the polygon fill mode that you set for the `hdc` in question.

Polygon Fill Modes

You can manipulate the polygon fill mode with `SetPolyFillMode` and retrieve it with `GetPolyFillMode`.

SetPolyFillMode

```
int SetPolyFillMode(
  HDC hdc,             // handle to device context
  int iPolyFillMode   // polygon fill mode
);
```

This returns the previous fill mode for the given `hdc` and sets the new fill mode to `iPolyFillMode`.

GetPolyFillMode

```
int GetPolyFillMode(
  HDC hdc   // handle to device context
);
```

This returns the current fill mode for the given `hdc`.

There are two polygon fill modes—`ALTERNATE` and `WINDING`. Instead of explaining what they each mean (it's a confusing explanation), I'll just show you. Figure 2.7 illustrates the `ALTERNATE` polygon fill mode.

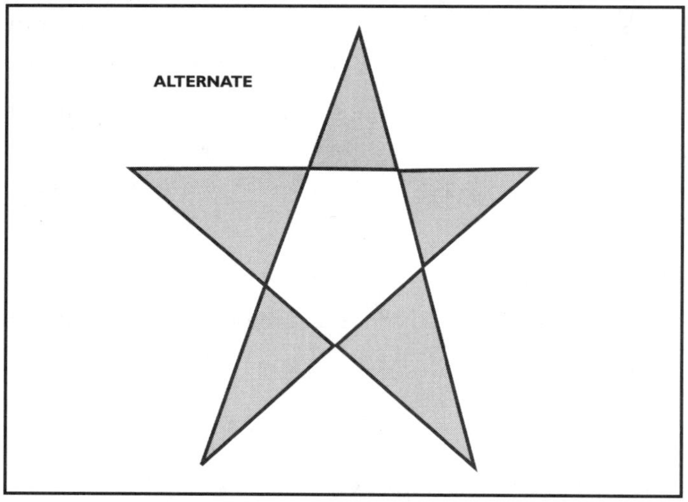

Figure 2.7

ALTERNATE PolyFillMode

In the ALTERNATE fill mode, a given pixel is filled if a horizontal line is sent in the positive x direction (to the right, that is) and if the number of line crossings is odd (1, 3, 5, and so on). If the number of crossings is even (0, 2, 4, and so on), no filling is done. I told you it was confusing. Figure 2.8 illustrates the WINDING fill mode.

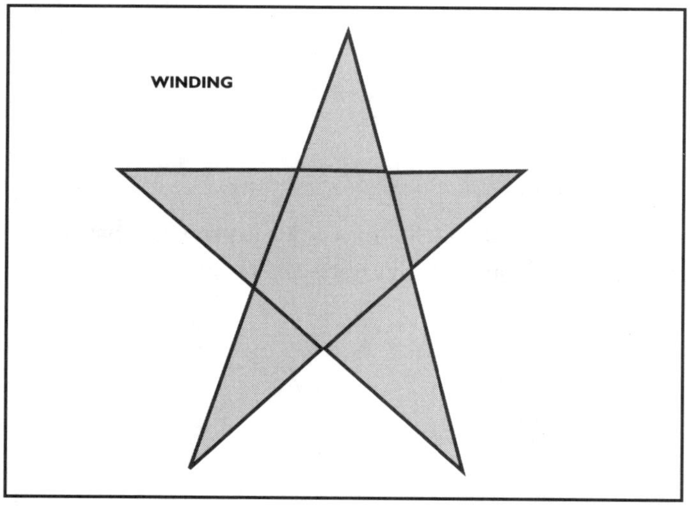

Figure 2.8

WINDING PolyFillMode

In the WINDING fill mode, a region is filled if it has a nonzero winding value. What the heck is a winding value, you ask? Let's see what MSDN Online (January 2000 edition) has to say about it: "This value is defined as the number of times a pen used to draw the polygon would go around the region. The direction of each edge of the polygon is important."

Confused? Me too. Using the WINDING polygon fill mode seems to fill in all of the nooks and crannies of a polygon, so let's just leave it at that.

Summary

This chapter inundated you with basic GDI; no, I won't pay for any therapy you may now need. We've gone through everything from Windows anatomy to graphical primitives. Much of this you won't be using too much, but it's good to know. The information you will be using from this chapter mainly consists of the RECT and POINT stuff, some of the brush stuff, and the device context stuff.

Most of what I've talked about so far has been listing functions and parameters. This will continue through at least the rest of this part of the book. Unfortunately, what I'm talking about requires a lot of knowledge, and I'm trying to get you just the important bits so that you can move on to the good stuff.

CHAPTER 3

Fonts, Bitmaps, and Regions

- Working with Fonts
- Creating and Using Regions
- Creating and Using Bitmaps

In the preceding chapter, we explored the basic use of GDI—namely, device contexts, pens, and brushes. This chapter builds on your knowledge of DCs, exploring the topics of fonts, bitmaps (including icons and cursors), and regions.

Working with Fonts

You know what a font is (at least, I hope you do). A font is a typeface, usually containing the alphabet, the numbers, and punctuation, but sometimes containing graphical characters (like the various wingding fonts). Various fonts are shown in Figure 3.1.

As a Windows programmer, you have the power to make use of any font installed on the system. There are even tools that allow you to create your own fonts. The key phrase is "any font installed on the system." If you develop your game to use some strange font that exists on only a few machines, you have to make sure you install the font as part of the installation for your game.

However, you may not want to require that a font be added to a user's machine—doing so makes the font available for use with other applications, but it also burdens your user's computer unnecessarily. If you were writing a word processing utility it would be appropriate, but you're writing *games!* So, when you want a font, you'll load it temporarily and unload it later.

AddFontResource

Loading a font temporarily into the system font table is pretty easy. You use `AddFontResource`:

```
int AddFontResource(
  LPCTSTR lpszFilename, // font file name
);
```

On failure, this function returns 0. On success, it returns the number of fonts added. Its parameter is described in Table 3.1.

Table 3.1 AddFontResource Parameter

AddFontResource Parameter	Purpose
lpszFilename	A string containing the file name from which to load the font into the system font table

When you are done with that font, you remove it from the system by using RemoveFontResource.

RemoveFontResource

```
BOOL RemoveFontResource(
  LPCTSTR lpFileName,  // name of font file
);
```

This returns nonzero on success or 0 on failure. This function has the exact same parameter list as AddFontResource.

CreateFont

Once you have a font resource loaded, you can create a font (HFONT) by using CreateFont.

```
HFONT CreateFont(
  int nHeight,              // height of font
  int nWidth,               // average character width
  int nEscapement,          // angle of escapement
  int nOrientation,         // baseline orientation angle
  int fnWeight,             // font weight
  DWORD fdwItalic,          // italic attribute option
```

```
  DWORD fdwUnderline,         // underline attribute option
  DWORD fdwStrikeOut,         // strikeout attribute option
  DWORD fdwCharSet,           // character set identifier
  DWORD fdwOutputPrecision,  // output precision
  DWORD fdwClipPrecision,    // clipping precision
  DWORD fdwQuality,           // output quality
  DWORD fdwPitchAndFamily,   // pitch and family
  LPCTSTR lpszFace            // typeface name
);
```

Scared yet? Yes, this function is a long one. Luckily, you usually won't need to worry about many of the parameters. Most of them are concerned with localization, and in those fields, you'll just pick whatever the default value is.

`CreateFont` returns an `HFONT` that is the closest match to what is described by all of the parameters. For the most part, the default value for these parameters is 0. Table 3.2 explains the parameter list.

Table 3.2 CreateFont Parameters

CreateFont Parameter	Purpose
`nHeight`	The desired average height of the font, in logical units
`nWidth`	The desired average width of the font, in logical units
`nEscapement`	The angle at which the font is to be drawn, in tenths of a degree
`nOrientation`	The angle at which the font's characters are to be drawn, in tenths of a degree
`fnWeight`	The boldness of the font
`fdwItalic`	`TRUE` for italic, `FALSE` for nonitalic
`fdwUnderline`	`TRUE` for underline, `FALSE` for nonunderline
`fdwStrikeOut`	`TRUE` for strikeout, `FALSE` for nonstrikeout
`fdwCharSet`	The type of character set you want
`fdwOutputPrecision`	The desired precision
`fdwQuality`	The desired quality
`fdwPitchAndFamily`	The family of the font and the pitch of the font
`lpszFace`	The typeface to use

CreateFont has lots of parameters, and most of them are used only when localization is an issue. (Localization is a vast topic, and I'm not going to explore it here. Just be aware that making your games easy to localize is a good idea, because people from many countries may want to play, and you can't always assume that they speak your language.)

With the exception of nHeight and lpszFace, you can get away with using all 0s in your calls to CreateFont. 0 loads the default font.

NOTE

You may have noticed that many of the CreateFont parameters speak of "logical units." In all of your cases, a logical unit is one pixel, because you use a mapping mode called MM_TEXT. There is more than just this one mapping mode. This is yet another part of GDI's device independence. You can specify arbitrary mapping modes for different devices. This is just an FYI. If you're curious about mapping modes, read about the SetMapMode function in the help files.

You can specify any value for nHeight. Inside GDI is a font mapper, and it will try its hardest to find a font that matches the height you ask for. Putting 0 in nHeight loads the default height.

lpszFace is the name of the font. If, for example, you wanted to use Tahoma, it would contain Tahoma.

Outputting with Fonts

In order to use a font in a given DC, you first have to bring it into the DC using SelectObject, which should be nothing new to you. Again, be sure to save the old font to restore it later. Also, when you are finished with a font (usually at the termination of a program), be sure to destroy it with a call to DeleteObject.

Next, you have to select a background mode and a text color. You do this with the SetBkMode and SetTextColor functions.

SetBkMode

```
int SetBkMode(
  HDC hdc,        // handle to DC
  int iBkMode     // background mode
);
```

On failure, this function returns 0. On success, it returns the previous background mode.

The hdc parameter is (of course) a handle to a device context for which you are setting the background mode. iBkMode is the new background mode, and it is either TRANSPARENT or OPAQUE. This is almost unnecessary to say, but TRANSPARENT will not write in the background color, and OPAQUE will.

SetTextColor

```
COLORREF SetTextColor(
  HDC hdc,            // handle to DC
  COLORREF crColor   // text color
);
```

This returns the previous text color or CLR_INVALID on failure. (In this case, returning 0 would be a valid color.)

The hdc parameter is the handle to the device context for which you are setting the text color, and crColor is the color itself.

TextOut

Finally, to actually get text on the screen, you use the TextOut function.

```
BOOL TextOut(
  HDC hdc,             // handle to DC
  int nXStart,        // x-coordinate of starting position
  int nYStart,        // y-coordinate of starting position
  LPCTSTR lpString,  // character string
  int cbString        // number of characters
);
```

This returns 0 on failure or nonzero on success. Table 3.3 explains the parameter list.

Table 3.3 TextOut Parameters

TextOut Parameter	Purpose
hdc	The handle to the device context on which you want to write characters
nXStart, nYStart	The x,y location for the start of the string
lpString	The text string to write
cbString	The number of characters to write

A TextOut Example

Let's do a little example. Load up IsoHex3_1.cpp, and be sure that Paganini.ttf is in the same folder as the project's workspace.

IsoHex3_1.cpp is a modification of IsoHex1_1.cpp. The main differences are two extra global variables and a modified `Prog_Init` and `Prog_Done`.

```
.
.
.
HFONT hfntNew=NULL;//paganini font
HFONT hfntOld=NULL;//store old font
.
.
.
bool Prog_Init()
{
	//add the paganini font to the system table
	AddFontResource("Paganini.ttf");

	//create a font that uses paganini
	hfntNew=CreateFont(-40,0,0,0,0,0,0,0,0,0,0,0,0,"Paganini");

	//borrow dc from main window
	HDC hdc=GetDC(hWndMain);

	//select new font into dc
	hfntOld=(HFONT)SelectObject(hdc,hfntNew);

	//set background mode to transparent
	SetBkMode(hdc,TRANSPARENT);

	//set text color to blue
	SetTextColor(hdc,RGB(0,0,255));

	//write text to dc
	TextOut(hdc,0,0,"Paganini",strlen("Paganini"));

	//release dc to system
	ReleaseDC(hWndMain,hdc);
```

```
	return(true);//return success
}
.
.
.
void Prog_Done()
{
	//borrow main window dc
	HDC hdc=GetDC(hWndMain);

	//restore original font
	SelectObject(hdc,hfntOld);

	//delete the new font
	DeleteObject(hfntNew);

	//return dc to system
	ReleaseDC(hWndMain,hdc);

	//remove the paganini font
	RemoveFontResource("Paganini.ttf");
}
```

The output looks like Figure 3.1.

Figure 3.1

TextOut

As you can see, the modifications are relatively minor. You just added some font-loading stuff and output the text to the window's DC.

Take a few moments with IsoHex3_1.cpp, and play with `SetBkMode`, `SetTextColor`, and the parameters for `CreateFont`. You might even go find a font somewhere and plug it into the program to see how it looks.

And that's the shortest way to get a font on the screen.

> **NOTE**
> `TextOut`, while useful, isn't very good at formatting text. I usually use it to display diagnostic information on-screen, like the mouse position or the frame rate.

DrawText

To do any real sort of application of fonts, you'll want to use `DrawText`.

```
int DrawText(
  HDC hDC,            // handle to DC
  LPCTSTR lpString,  // text to draw
  int nCount,         // text length
  LPRECT lpRect,      // formatting dimensions
  UINT uFormat        // text-drawing options
);
```

This usually returns the height of the text outputted, but it might differ depending on the `uFormat` parameter (see Table 3.5). Table 3.4 explains the parameter list.

Table 3.4 DrawText Parameters

DrawText Parameter	Purpose
`hDC`	The destination device context
`lpString`	The string of characters that you want to display
`nCount`	The number of characters to display. Can be -1 to detect the size of the string. In this case, `lpString` must be a null-terminated string.
`lpRect`	A pointer to the bounding `RECT`
`uFormat`	The format in which to show the text (see Table 3.5)

Most of these parameters match those of `TextOut`, except that positioning information is in `lpRect` and formatting options are in `uFormat`, as shown in Table 3.5.

Table 3.5 uFormat Values

uFormat Value	Meaning
DT_BOTTOM	Justifies text to the bottom of the rectangle. Must be used with DT_SINGLELINE.
DT_CENTER	Centers the text horizontally
DT_LEFT	Aligns text to the left
DT_NOCLIP	Does not perform clipping
DT_RIGHT	Aligns text to the right
DT_SINGLELINE	Displays the text on a single line only
DT_TOP	Justifies text to the top of the rectangle
DT_VCENTER	Centers text vertically. Use with DT_SINGLELINE.

This list is by no means exhaustive. These are just the most commonly used formatting options.

A DrawText Example

Another sample program? Sure, why not! IsoHex3_2.cpp (which is just a slightly modified IsoHex3_1.cpp) makes use of `DrawText`. The differences lie totally in `Prog_Init`.

```
{
	//retrieve the client rectangle
	RECT rcClient;
	GetClientRect(hWndMain,&rcClient);
	//add the paganini font to the system table
	AddFontResource("Paganini.ttf");
	//create a font that uses paganini
	hfntNew=CreateFont(-40,0,0,0,0,0,0,0,0,0,0,0,0,"Paganini");
	//borrow dc from main window
	HDC hdc=GetDC(hWndMain);
	//select new font into dc
	hfntOld=(HFONT)SelectObject(hdc,hfntNew);
```

```
        //set background mode to transparent
        SetBkMode(hdc,TRANSPARENT);
        //set text color to blue
        SetTextColor(hdc,RGB(0,0,255));
        //write text to dc
        DrawText(hdc,"Paganini",-1,&rcClient,DT_CENTER | DT_VCENTER | DT_SINGLE-
LINE);
        //release dc to system
        ReleaseDC(hWndMain,hdc);
        return(true);//return success
}
```

Figure 3.2 shows what it looks like.

Figure 3.2

`DrawText` demo

Again, play with IsoHex3_2.cpp using different combinations of the various `DT_*` constants and different `RECT`s. There is a lot of power in the GDI font system, and you'll be making use of it later in `DirectDraw`. Unfortunately, it's slower than a custom system you could design specifically for a game. If you want to further explore fonts, there's plenty of information about them in MSDN Online.

Creating and Using Regions

A region is a GDI object, just like a pen, brush, or font. Regions are very powerful and flexible tools with which to accomplish things that would otherwise be very difficult. However, because they are slow, they are practically ignored.

A region is nothing more than a shape—a rectangle, rounded rectangle, ellipse, polygon, or multiple polygons. You can do a number of things with a region. You can fill it (`FillRgn`), frame it (`FrameRgn`), or clip with it (by selecting it into a device context). You can use it to test whether or not a point is within a given nonrectangular shape.

Creating Regions

Regions, like any other GDI objects, are manipulated through the use of handles. In this case, the handle is `HRGN`. Table 3.6 lists several different types of regions and several different functions that create them.

Table 3.6 Region Creation Functions

Function	Type of Region Created
`CreateEllipticRgn`	An elliptical region
`CreatePolygonRgn`	A polygonal region
`CreateRectRgn`	A rectangular region
`CreateRoundRectRgn`	A rounded rectangular region

Most of these region creation functions mirror similar shape functions that use pens and brushes (minus the `HDC` parameter, of course).

CreateEllipticRgn

```
HRGN CreateEllipticRgn(
  int nLeftRect,    // x-coord of upper-left corner of rectangle
  int nTopRect,     // y-coord of upper-left corner of rectangle
  int nRightRect,   // x-coord of lower-right corner of rectangle
  int nBottomRect   // y-coord of lower-right corner of rectangle
);
```

CreateEllipticRgn returns a handle to an elliptical region. Table 3.7 explains the parameter list.

Table 3.7 CreateEllipticRgn Parameters

CreateEllipticRgn Parameter	Purpose
nLeftRect	The left x-coordinate of the bounding rectangle for the elliptical region
nTopRect	The top y-coordinate of the bounding rectangle for the elliptical region
nRightRect	The right x-coordinate of the bounding rectangle for the elliptical region
nBottomRect	The bottom y-coordinate of the bounding rectangle for the elliptical region

CreatePolygonRgn

```
HRGN CreatePolygonRgn(
  CONST POINT *lppt,  // array of points
  int cPoints,         // number of points in array
  int fnPolyFillMode  // polygon-filling mode
);
```

CreatePolygonRgn returns a handle to a polygon region. Table 3.8 explains the parameter list.

Table 3.8 CreatePolygonRgn Parameters

CreatePolygonRgn Parameter	Purpose
lppt	A pointer to an array of POINTs that contains the vertices of the polygon
cPoints	The number of points that are pointed to by lppt
fnPolyFillMode	Either ALTERNATE or WINDING. Specifies the desired fill mode.

CreateRectRgn

```
HRGN CreateRectRgn(
  int nLeftRect,   // x-coordinate of upper-left corner
  int nTopRect,    // y-coordinate of upper-left corner
  int nRightRect,  // x-coordinate of lower-right corner
  int nBottomRect  // y-coordinate of lower-right corner
);
```

This returns a handle to a rectangular region. Table 3.9 explains the parameter list.

Table 3.9 CreateRectRgn Parameters

CreateRectRgn Parameter	Purpose
`nLeftRect`	The left x-coordinate of the rectangle
`nTopRect`	The top y-coordinate of the rectangle
`nRightRect`	The right x-coordinate of the rectangle
`nBottomRect`	The bottom y-coordinate of the rectangle

CreateRoundRectRgn

```
HRGN CreateRoundRectRgn(
  int nLeftRect,       // x-coordinate of upper-left corner
  int nTopRect,        // y-coordinate of upper-left corner
  int nRightRect,      // x-coordinate of lower-right corner
  int nBottomRect,     // y-coordinate of lower-right corner
  int nWidthEllipse,  // height of ellipse
  int nHeightEllipse  // width of ellipse
);
```

This returns a handle to a rounded rectangular region. Table 3.10 explains the parameters.

Table 3.10 CreateRoundRectRgn Parameters

CreateRoundRectRgn Parameter	Purpose
`nLeftRect`	The left x-coordinate of the bounding rectangle
`nTopRect`	The top y-coordinate of the bounding rectangle
`nRightRect`	The right x-coordinate of the bounding rectangle
`nBottomRect`	The bottom y-coordinate of the bounding rectangle
`nWidthEllipse`	The width of the ellipse used to round the corners
`nHeightEllipse`	The height of the ellipse used to round the corners

Deleting a region is accomplished using `DeleteObject`, just like any other GDI object.

Using Regions

The most common use of a region is for clipping. *Clipping* is a method by which you draw on only a certain portion of your drawing area, similar to an artist's use of a graphical template (you know... the little plastic thingamajig with circles cut into it).

To use a region for clipping, you simply bring it into a device context using `SelectObject`. Unlike other types of GDI objects, `SelectObject` doesn't return the previously selected region for that device context. Instead, it returns one of the following values:

- `SIMPLEREGION` The region consists of a single rectangle
- `COMPLEXREGION` The region consists of more than one rectangle
- `NULLREGION` The region is empty

> **NOTE**
> Regions are the only GDI objects for which this strange behavior occurs.

Let's do a quick example to show you how to use regions for clipping. Load up IsoHex3_3.cpp.

This example has a few extra global variables:

```
//pens, old and new
HPEN hpenNew=NULL;
HPEN hpenOld=NULL;
//region
HRGN hrgnClip=NULL;
```

Also, `Prog_Init` and `Prog_Done` have been modified:

```
bool Prog_Init()
{
	//create a solid red pen
	hpenNew=CreatePen(PS_SOLID,0,RGB(255,0,0));

	//retrieve the client rectangle for the window
	RECT rcClient;
	GetClientRect(hWndMain,&rcClient);

	//create an elliptical region
	hrgnClip=CreateEllipticRgn(0,0,rcClient.right,rcClient.bottom);

	//borrow the dc from the main window
	HDC hdc=GetDC(hWndMain);

	//select the new pen into the dc, and keep the old one
	hpenOld=(HPEN)SelectObject(hdc,hpenNew);

	//select the clipping region into the dc
	SelectObject(hdc,hrgnClip);

	//make vertical stripes
	int nStripeX=rcClient.right/10;
	int nCount;

	//loop through and draw the stripes
	for(nCount=0;nCount<10;nCount++)
	{
		//move to the top of the client area
		MoveToEx(hdc,nStripeX*nCount,0,NULL);

		//line to the bottom of the client area
```

```
            LineTo(hdc,nStripeX*nCount,rcClient.bottom);
        }

        //make the horizontal stripes
        int nStripeY=rcClient.bottom/10;

        //loop through and draw the stripes
        for(nCount=0;nCount<10;nCount++)
        {
            //move to the left of the client area
            MoveToEx(hdc,0,nStripeY*nCount,NULL);

            //line to the right of the client area
            LineTo(hdc,rcClient.right,nStripeY*nCount);
        }

        //return the borrowed dc to the system
        ReleaseDC(hWndMain,hdc);

        return(true);//return success
}
.
.
.
void Prog_Done()
{
        //borrow the dc from the main window
        HDC hdc=GetDC(hWndMain);

        //restore the old pen
        SelectObject(hdc,hpenOld);

        //return the dc to the system
        ReleaseDC(hWndMain,hdc);

        //delete our gdi objects
        DeleteObject(hrgnClip);
        DeleteObject(hpenNew);
}
```

Without the region stuff, you'd get horizontal and vertical stripes (10 of each) running the length and width of your window's client area. With this example, you get the same effect, but the lines only get written to the elliptical area you have selected as the clipping region, as shown in Figure 3.3.

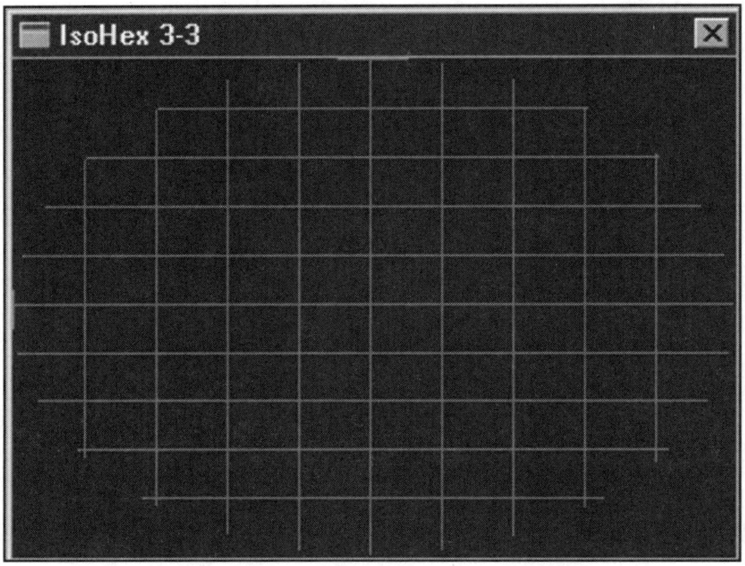

Figure 3.3

Elliptical region

For the moment, click on another window, obscuring this window, and then switch back to the first window. You might see something like Figure 3.4.

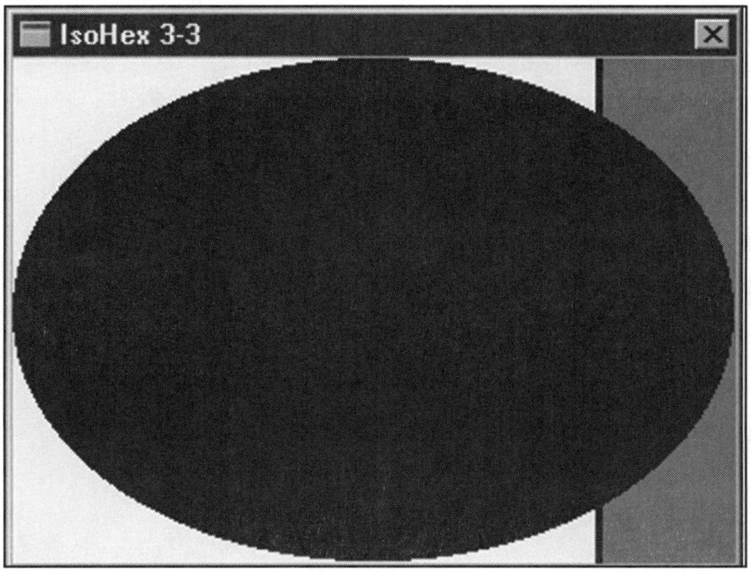

Figure 3.4

The dangers of using clipping regions

As you can see, Windows doesn't erase the part that lies outside of the clipping area. This is an important thing to think about when using regions. It's always best to keep a region that encompasses the entire client area that you select into the DC after you no longer need a DC that covers only a portion.

To see the differences between the various clipping areas you can have, let's modify IsoHex3_3.cpp slightly. Replace the line with `CreateEllipticRgn` in it with the following line:

```
hrgnClip=CreateRoundRectRgn(0,0,rcClient.right,rcClient.bottom,rcClient.right/2,r
cClient.bottom/2);
```

If you run this again, you'll see the same stripes, only now they are bounded by a rounded rectangle, as shown in Figure 3.5.

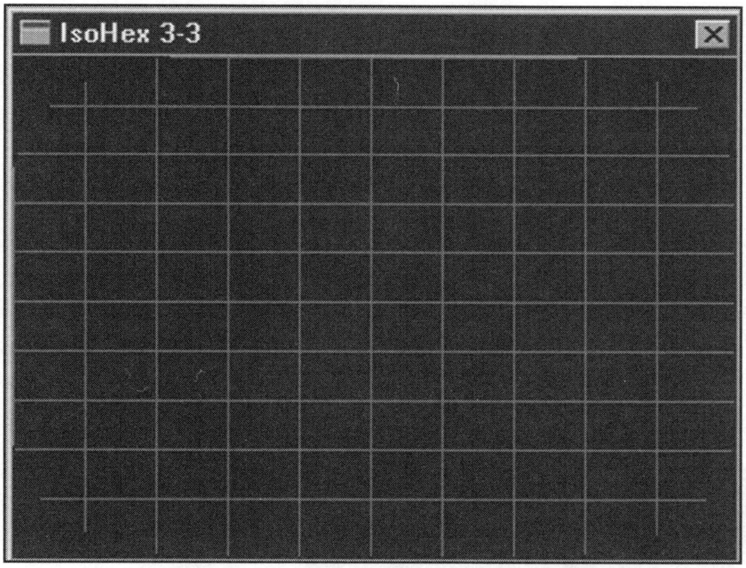

Figure 3.5

Rounded rectangle clipping region

Here's something you may have noticed: when you use these rounded regions, the program loads rather slowly; this is the main downfall of regions. Rectangular regions are much faster than curved ones.

NOTE

Why are nonrectangular regions slower than rectangular ones? The answer is that even a circular or elliptical region still consists of rectangles. Most of these rectangles are just a single pixel high. When you then take that region, select it in a device context, and use it to clip your output, each pixel drawn has to be compared to this gigantic list of rectangles to check whether or not the pixel is within the clipping area. As you might imagine, this can take quite a bit of time if the clipping region is oddly shaped. For this reason, when performance counts, use only rectangular regions, and use regions only if you absolutely must.

Change that line again to read as follows:

```
hrgnClip=CreateRectRgn(0,0,rcClient.right,rcClient.bottom);
```

When you compile and run this, it should come up a bit faster than the others did, because it's much easier to clip to a rectangle than an ellipse or a rounded rectangle (computers don't like doing curves).

We're going to do one more little modification, using a polygon region. Replace the region creation function with the following code:

```
POINT ptVertice[4];
ptVertice[0].x=rcClient.right/2;
ptVertice[0].y=0;
ptVertice[1].x=rcClient.right;
ptVertice[1].y=rcClient.bottom/2;
ptVertice[2].x=rcClient.right/2;
ptVertice[2].y=rcClient.bottom;
ptVertice[3].x=0;
ptVertice[3].y=rcClient.bottom/2;
hrngClip=CreatePolygonRgn(ptVertice,4,ALTERNATE);
```

This sets up a small array of points and creates a polygonal region based on them, using the `ALTERNATE` fill mode. (Refer to Chapter 2, "The World of GDI and Windows Graphics," for the different polygon fill modes.) Figure 3.6 shows what this region looks like.

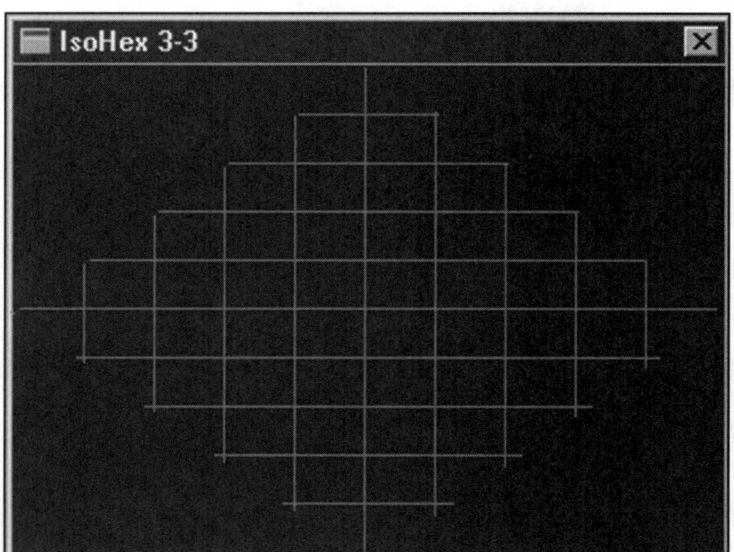

Figure 3.6

A polygon clipping region

You'll notice that this polygon region takes longer to run than a rectangular region but is not quite as slow as one of the curved regions. Clipping to arbitrary lines is still more difficult than a rectangle, but it's easier than clipping to curves.

Other Uses for Regions

While clipping is the most prevalent use for regions, it is not the only use. You can also use regions to fill in arbitrary shapes, as you would a rubber stamp on paper.

I won't spend too much time on this subject; I'll just list a few functions and leave you to experiment with them. You won't be seeing these functions again, but I didn't feel right leaving the topic of regions without at least showing them to you.

FillRgn

```
BOOL FillRgn(
  HDC hdc,     // handle to device context
  HRGN hrgn,   // handle to region to be filled
  HBRUSH hbr   // handle to brush used to fill the region
);
```

This returns nonzero on success or 0 on failure. Fills a shape (specified by `hrgn`) on `hdc` using a brush (`hbr`).

PaintRgn

```
BOOL PaintRgn(
  HDC hdc,     // handle to device context
  HRGN hrgn    // handle to region to be painted
);
```

This is similar to the `FillRgn` function, except that the brush used to fill the region is the one that is currently selected into the `hdc`.

FrameRgn

```
BOOL FrameRgn(
  HDC hdc,      // handle to device context
  HRGN hrgn,    // handle to region to be framed
  HBRUSH hbr,   // handle to brush used to draw border
  int nWidth,   // width of region frame
  int nHeight   // height of region frame
);
```

This returns nonzero on success or 0 on failure. It outlines the region with a brush. `nWidth` and `nHeight` are the width and height of the frame used to surround the region.

Take a breath. We're done with regions. That leaves only one GDI object to cover, easily the most important of all.

Creating and Using Bitmaps

And, at long last, bitmaps! In your games, bitmaps (in whatever form) will be your stock in trade. Your terrain, your units, and just about everything else will exist in the form of bitmaps that you will load into your program and use on-screen.

You'll be primarily concerned with two types of bitmaps: those that are blank, and those that you load from disk.

Creating a Blank Bitmap

To create a blank bitmap, use `CreateCompatibleBitmap`. A compatible bitmap has the same color format of a device context (you usually borrow the DC from the main window and make your blank bitmaps compatible with it).

```
HBITMAP CreateCompatibleBitmap(
  HDC hdc,          // handle to DC
  int nWidth,       // width of bitmap, in pixels
  int nHeight       // height of bitmap, in pixels
);
```

This returns a handle to the created bitmap. Table 3.11 explains the parameters.

Table 3.11 CreateCompatibleBitmap Parameters

CreateCompatibleBitmap Parameter	Purpose
`hdc`	The device context with which this bitmap is to be compatible
`nWidth`	The width of the bitmap
`nHeight`	The height of the bitmap

CAUTION

A bitmap created by a call to `CreateCompatibleBitmap` will contain garbage (whatever information was in that memory before the bitmap was created). In order to fix this, it must be selected into the DC and cleared out using `FillRect` or the like.

Loading a Bitmap from Disk

To load a bitmap from disk, use `LoadImage`. `LoadImage` is used not only for bitmaps, but also for icons and cursors. As a result, the return type has to be typecast.

```
HANDLE LoadImage(
  HINSTANCE hinst,    // handle to instance
  LPCTSTR lpszName,   // name or identifier of the image
  UINT uType,         // image type
  int cxDesired,      // desired width
  int cyDesired,      // desired height
  UINT fuLoad         // load options
);
```

This returns a generic handle, which must be typecast into the proper handle type. Table 3.12 explains the parameter list.

Table 3.12 LoadImage Parameters

LoadImage Parameter	Purpose
`hinst`	If this bitmap were a resource within the executable, this would be the application's handle. Since you are loading from disk, this can be `NULL`.
`lpszName`	The file name of the bitmap you want to load
`uType`	The type of image to load (one of `IMAGE_BITMAP`, `IMAGE_CURSOR`, or `IMAGE_ICON`)
`cxDesired`	The desired width of the bitmap (0 for the default width)
`cyDesired`	The desired height of the bitmap (0 for the default height)
`fuLoad`	Flags. When loading a bitmap, this should be `LR_LOADFROM-FILE`.

Using a Bitmap

In order to be of any use, a bitmap must be selected into a device context. Since you usually don't want bitmaps selected into your window's DC, you will create memory DCs.

Here are three code snippets. When you load bitmaps, create blank bitmaps, or get rid of a bitmap, these three code snippets are rather close to the actual code you will need.

Snippet 1: Creating a Blank Bitmap

In this first code snippet, you do all the work necessary to create a blank bitmap except for clearing it out with `FillRect`. By the end of this snippet, `hdcMem` is a memory DC, `hbmNew` contains a newly created bitmap, `hbmOld` contains the bitmap originally in `hdcMem`, and the new bitmap is selected into the new DC.

```
////////////////////////////////////////
//Creating a blank bitmap
////////////////////////////////////////
//borrow window's dc
HDC hdcCompatible=GetDC(hWndMain);
//hdcMem is an HDC global
hdcMem=CreateCompatibleDC(hdcCompatible);
//hbmNew is an HBITMAP global
hbmNew=CreateCompatibleBitmap(hdcCompatible,WIDTH,HEIGHT);
//return the borrowed dc to the system
ReleaseDC(hWndMain,hdcCompatible);
//hbmOld is an HBITMAP global
//select new bitmap into dc
hbmOld=(HBITMAP)SelectObject(hdcMem,hbmNew);
```

Snippet 2: Loading a Bitmap from Disk

You may notice that there is very little difference between the first snippet and the second. That's because the only difference is where you obtain the bitmap. In other words, you use `LoadImage` instead of `CreateCompatibleBitmap`.

```
////////////////////////////
//Loading a bitmap
////////////////////////////
//borrow window's dc
HDC hdcCompatible=GetDC(hWndMain);
//hdcMem is an HDC global
```

```
hdcMem=CreateCompatibleDC(hdcCompatible);
//return the borrowed dc to the system
ReleaseDC(hWndMain,hdcCompatible);
//hbmNew is an HBITMAP global
hbmNew=(HBITMAP)LoadImage(NULL,"FileName.bmp",IMAGE_BITMAP,0,0,LR_LOADFROMFILE);
//hbmOld is an HBITMAP global
//select new bitmap into dc
hbmOld=(HBITMAP)SelectObject(hdcMem,hbmNew);
```

Snippet 3: Cleaning Up

This final snippet returns the original bitmap into the memory device context and deletes the bitmap and the device context.

```
//////////////////////////
//Getting rid of a bitmap
//////////////////////////
//restore old bitmap to dc
SelectObject(hdcMem,hbmOld);
//delete bitmap
DeleteObject(hbmNew);
//delete dc
DeleteDC(hdcMem);
```

There: short, sweet, and for general use.

Consider the lengths of these code snippets. They aren't long, but if you had 100 bitmaps, they would add up quickly. Don't worry—later we'll develop a class to help wrap this up into a neat package. (Oh, don't groan like that. It'll be easy.)

BitBlt

Now comes the fun part—moving information from one device context to another. This is called *blitting*, and the primary function in GDI to do this task is called `BitBlt`. (`BitBlt` stands for "bit block transfer.")

```
BOOL BitBlt(
  HDC hdcDest, // handle to destination DC
  int nXDest,  // x-coord of destination upper-left corner
  int nYDest,  // y-coord of destination upper-left corner
  int nWidth,  // width of destination rectangle
  int nHeight, // height of destination rectangle
  HDC hdcSrc,  // handle to source DC
```

```
  int nXSrc,    // x-coordinate of source upper-left corner
  int nYSrc,    // y-coordinate of source upper-left corner
  DWORD dwRop  // raster operation code
);
```

This returns nonzero on success or 0 on failure. Table 3.13 explains the parameter list.

Table 3.13 BitBlt Parameters

BitBlt Parameter	Purpose
hdcDest	The destination device context
nXDest	The destination x-coordinate
nYDest	The destination y-coordinate
nWidth	The destination width
nHeight	The destination height
hdcSrc	The source device context
nXSrc	The source x-coordinate
nYSrc	The source y-coordinate
dwRop	The desired raster operation

`BitBlt` copies the contents of the source device context (`hdcSrc`), starting at `nXSrc,nYSrc` and copying a width of `nWidth` and a height of `nHeight` to the destination device context (`hdcDest`) at `nXDest,nYDest`. It combines the source with the destination, depending on the value of `dwRop`.

A Word About Raster Operations

Most of the parameters of `BitBlt` are self-explanatory; however, `dwRop` is not among them. A raster operation is just a manner in which the source and destination pixels in a blit are combined.

Table 3.14 lists some of the more commonly used raster ops.

Table 3.14 Raster Ops

Raster Operation Constant	Meaning
SRCCOPY	The source is copied to the destination with no regard for the contents of the destination.
SRCAND	The source and destination are combined using the AND operation. Useful for bitmasking.
SRCPAINT	The source and destination are combined using the OR operation. Useful for adding images while being nondestructive.
SRCINVERT	The source and destination are combined using the XOR operation. Blitting the same image to the same location twice using SRCINVERT restores the original contents of the destination. Useful for custom cursors.

Example time. Load up IsoHex3_4.cpp, and be sure to have IsoHex3_4.bmp in the same folder as the project.

In this example, clicking the mouse button blits a bitmap onto the window. In Prog_Init and Prog_Done, I simply modified the code snippets we covered a little earlier (so I won't repeat them here). The work is done by the WM_LBUTTONDOWN handler in TheWindowProc.

```
case WM_LBUTTONDOWN:
      {
            //borrow dc from main window
            HDC hdc=GetDC(hWndMain);
            //blit from the memory dc to the window's dc
            BitBlt(hdc,LOWORD(lParam)-BITMAPWIDTH/2,HIWORD(lParam)-
BITMAPHEIGHT/2,BITMAPWIDTH,BITMAPHEIGHT,hdcMem,0,0,SRCCOPY);
            //return the borrowed dc to the system
            ReleaseDC(hWndMain,hdc);
            //handled, so return 0
            return(0);
      }break;
```

`BITMAPWIDTH` and `BITMAPHEIGHT` are just constants that I added earlier in the application.

Figure 3.7 shows what this application looks like.

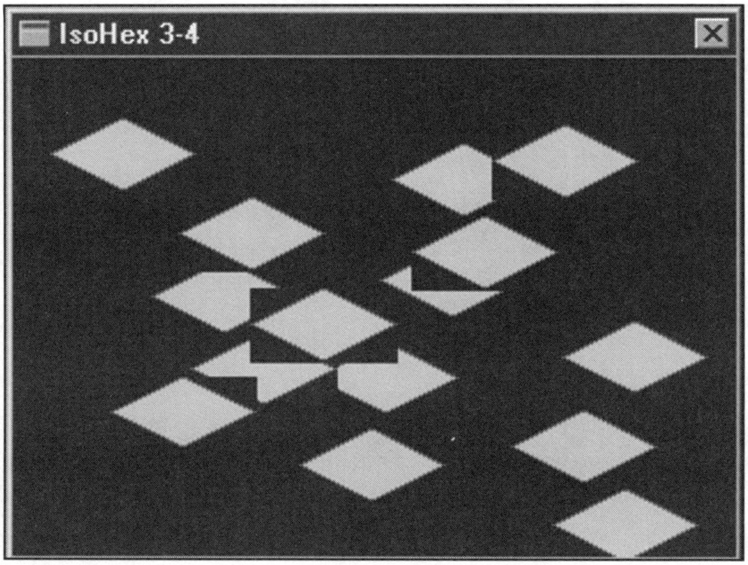

Figure 3.7

Blitting bits

You may notice that one image may overwrite part of another if they are too close together. This is because you are using `SRCCOPY`, which has no regard for the destination image.

Modify IsoHex3_4.cpp to use `SRCPAINT` instead, as shown in Figure 3.8.

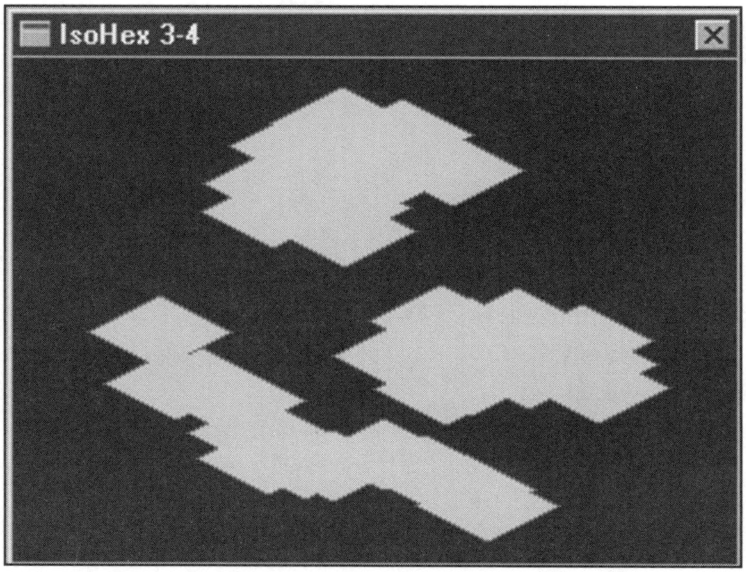

Figure 3.8

Demonstrating the `SRCPAINT` raster operation

Well, now you don't have the problem of the black corners obscuring the image below, but the images start to sort of merge, and it's hard to tell where each one is. The reason for this is that the image uses only three colors—black (RGB(0,0,0)), dark green (RGB(0,128,0)), and bright green (RGB(0,255,0)).

Table 3.15 specifies how each of these combine when using SRCPAINT.

Table 3.15 Color Combination Using SRCPAINT

		Source Pixel		
	SRCPAINT	Black RGB(0,0,0)	Dark Green RGB(0,128,0)	Bright Green RGB(0,255,0)
Destination Pixel	Black RGB(0,0,0)	Black RGB(0,0,0)	Dark Green RGB(0,128,0)	Bright Green RGB(0,255,0)
	Dark Green RGB(0,128,0)	Dark Green RGB(0,128,0)	Dark Green RGB(0,128,0)	Bright Green RGB(0,255,0)
	Bright Green RGB(0,255,0)	Bright Green RGB(0,255,0)	Bright Green RGB(0,255,0)	Bright Green RGB(0,255,0)

BITWISE OPERATOR REVIEW

If you're confused, I'm about to help. Let's review for a moment some of the bitwise operators—namely, AND, OR, and XOR. For a given combination of bits, you combine them in different ways. AND yields a TRUE (1) only if both source bits are true. OR yields a TRUE as long as at least one of the source bits is true. XOR yields TRUE only if one but not both of the source bits are true. Table 3.16 is a combined truth table for these operators.

Table 3.16 Truth Tables for AND, OR, and XOR

First Bit	Second Bit	First AND Second	First OR Second	First XOR Second
0	0	0	0	0
0	1	0	1	1
1	0	0	1	1
1	1	1	1	0

How Bitwise Operators Combine Colors

Now, let's examine two colors, bright red (RGB(255,0,0)) and bright blue (RGB(0,0,255)). First, you must convert these colors into their binary equivalents.

> **NOTE**
>
> **If you look back at the `RGB` macro in Chapter 2, you see that the green component gets shifted left by 8 bits and the blue component gets shifted by 16 bits, so the binary formats look something like this:**
>
> ```
> Bright Red =   00000000  00000000  11111111
> Bright Blue =  11111111  00000000  00000000
> ```

Next, combine the individual bits using the appropriate bitwise operator.

AND

```
00000000  00000000  11111111 (red)
11111111  00000000  00000000 (blue)
____________________________
00000000  00000000  00000000 (black)
```

The result is black (RGB(0,0,0)). When you `AND` red and blue, you get black, because red and blue have no bits in common.

OR

```
00000000  00000000  11111111 (red)
11111111  00000000  00000000 (blue)
____________________________
11111111  00000000  11111111 (magenta)
```

The result is magenta (RGB(255,0,255)). Since either or both bits can be set to yield a 1, you thus have a 1 for any column in which there is at least a single 1.

XOR

```
00000000  00000000  11111111 (red)
11111111  00000000  00000000 (blue)
________________________________
11111111  00000000  11111111 (magenta)
```

The result is magenta (RGB(255,0,255)), which is the same as the result from `OR`. Since the two colors have no bits in common, `XOR` combines to make the same result as an `OR`.

XOR, Take Two

Let's take the resulting value and `XOR` it with blue again.

```
11111111  00000000  11111111 (magenta)
11111111  00000000  00000000 (blue)
________________________________
00000000  00000000  11111111 (red)
```

You are left with red again, because both sets of bits have all blue bits set. This shows you that `XOR`ing the same thing twice leaves you with what you started out with.

Are you wondering what I'm up to, or have you figured it out already?

Raster Operation Example

Let's do another example. Load up IsoHex3_5.cpp.

This example looks a lot like IsoHex3_4.cpp. The main differences are the lack of a `WM_LBUTTONDOWN` message handler, the addition of a global variable and a function, and a modification of `Prog_Init`.

```
.
.
.
//cursor location
POINT ptCursor;
.
.
.
        case WM_MOUSEMOVE:
            {
                //extract x and y from lParam
                int x=LOWORD(lParam);
                int y=HIWORD(lParam);
                //borrow window's dc
```

```
                HDC hdc=GetDC(hWndMain);
                //write the cursor
                ShowTheCursor(hdc);
                //update the cursor position
                ptCursor.x=x;
                ptCursor.y=y;
                //write the cursor
                ShowTheCursor(hdc);
            //return dc to system
                ReleaseDC(hWndMain,hdc);
                //handled, so return 0
                return(0);
            }break;
.
.
.
bool Prog_Init()
{
    //borrow dc from main window
    HDC hdc=GetDC(hWndMain);
    //create a memory dc
    hdcMem=CreateCompatibleDC(hdc);
    //load in the bitmap
    hbmNew=(HBITMAP)LoadImage(NULL,"IsoHex3_5.bmp",IMAGE_BITMAP,0,0,LR_LOAD-
FROMFILE);
    //select bitmap into memory dc
    hbmOld=(HBITMAP)SelectObject(hdcMem,hbmNew);
    //set original cursor position
    ptCursor.x=0;
    ptCursor.y=0;
    //return dc to system
    ReleaseDC(hWndMain,hdc);
    return(true);//return success
}
.
.
.
//show the cursor
void ShowTheCursor(HDC hdc)
{
```

```
        BitBlt(hdc,ptCursor.x-BITMAPWIDTH/2,ptCursor.y-
BITMAPHEIGHT/2,BITMAPWIDTH,BITMAPHEIGHT,hdcMem,0,0,SRCINVERT);
}
```

The `ptCursor` variable is a `POINT`, and it keeps track of your "cursor" position. You load IsoHex3_5.bmp (it's a white diamond shape) and select it into `hdcMem`. In `Prog_Init`, you give this position an initial value of (0,0). It gets shown in the initial call to `WM_PAINT`.

During the `WM_MOUSEMOVE`, you call `ShowTheCursor` again. Since `ShowTheCursor` uses `SRCINVERT` to show the cursor (using the `XOR` operator), it erases the cursor currently showing. Then, you update the cursor position and show the cursor again. You have just a black background currently, so this doesn't look like a big deal. Later, when we get to double buffering, the uses of `ShowTheCursor` will become much more apparent. Figure 3.9 shows the output.

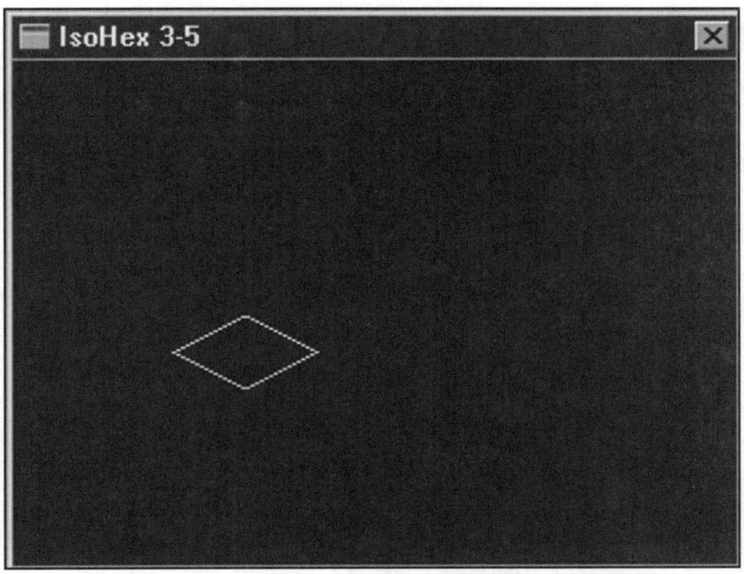

Figure 3.9

Cursor demo

An Application of Raster Operations: Bitmasking

Now that you've seen at least one application of raster operations, let's look at another—bitmasking. *Bitmasking* is a method of writing oddly-shaped graphics when you can only blit rectangles. It is one of several methods by which you can achieve transparency. For bitmasking to work you must rely on a few rules of bitwise operators.

First Rule of Bitwise Operators

Any bit, when you AND it with a 1, yields the bit's value.

```
0 AND 1=0
1 AND 1=1
```

Therefore, any color ANDed with white (11111111 11111111 11111111) gives you the original color.

Second Rule of Bitwise Operators

Any bit, when you AND it with 0, yields 0.

```
0 AND 0=0
1 AND 0=0
```

Therefore, any color ANDed with black (00000000 00000000 00000000) gives you black.

Third Rule of Bitwise Operators

Any bit ORed with 0 yields the bit's value.

```
0 OR 0=0
1 OR 0=1
```

So, using the preceding three rules, you can write any oddly-shaped graphic using BitBlt and the raster operations SRCAND and SRCPAINT.

Load up IsoHex3_6.cpp, and be sure to have IsoHex3_6-1.bmp and IsoHex3_6-2.bmp in the project folder. This example is pretty much just an enhanced IsoHex3_4.cpp. An extra bitmap is loaded, and during the WM_LBUTTONDOWN, there are two BitBlt calls instead of just one. I won't put the code here; you can take a look yourself. Figure 3.10 shows the output.

Figure 3.10

Bitmasks in action

Bitmasking is really important if you're going to use GDI to make isometric or hexagonal games (since iso-hex games tend not to use rectangular areas). Once you get into DirectDraw, you'll use transparency instead of bitmasking, but it's good to know about bitmasking, since you may still make your level editors and tools using GDI.

A Bitmap Management Class

As you've seen, the creation or loading of each bitmap, the selection of them into a device context, and the later destruction of them requires several lines of code, and with the more bitmaps and device contexts you add, the more code you get. Logically, you would wrap this activity, either in function form or class form. I'm something of an object-oriented nut, so I'm going to make a class. If you're a C person, I'll try to go easy on you.

First, our class (which I call `CGDICanvas`) has two purposes. One is to load a bitmap, and the other is to make a blank bitmap of an arbitrary size. You will make a member function for each of these. Also, our class must take care of deleting all the associated bitmaps and DCs, so there will be a member function for that as well.

The data logically contained in `CGDICanvas` consists of two handles to bitmaps and a handle to a DC. One last thing: I don't want to have to pull out a member each time in order to do a `BitBlt` using `CGDICanvas`, so I'm going to add a conversion operator.

Here's the declaration of `CGDICanvas` (which you can find in GDICanvas.h):

```
class CGDICanvas
{
private:
	//memory dc
	HDC hdcMem;
	//new bitmap
	HBITMAP hbmNew;
	//old bitmap
	HBITMAP hbmOld;
	//width and height
	int nWidth;
	int nHeight;
public:
	//constructor
	CGDICanvas();
	//loads bitmap from a file
	void Load(HDC hdcCompatible,LPCTSTR lpszFilename);
	//creates a blank bitmap
	void CreateBlank(HDC hdcCompatible, int width, int height);
```

```
        //destroys bitmap and dc
        void Destroy();
        //converts to HDC
        operator HDC();
        //return width
        int GetWidth();
        //return height
        int GetHeight();
        //destructor
        ~CGDICanvas();
};
```

Private means that you can't touch those members from outside of the class, and *public* means you can. It's a security thing. Allowing the user to play with `hdcMem` or `hbmNew` could be disastrous, so I made them private.

Something else that might be throwing you is the functions in the public section—especially the operator. The power of C++ classes is such that you can take what would normally be a struct (which is what the private part of the class looks like) and add functions that operate on that data.

Here are the equivalent C declarations to do the same thing:

```
struct GDICanvas
{
        //memory dc
        HDC hdcMem;
        //new bitmap
        HBITMAP hbmNew;
        //old bitmap
        HBITMAP hbmOld;
        //width and height
        int nWidth;
        int nHeight;
};
//loads bitmap from a file
void GDICanvas_Load(struct GDICanvas* pgdic,HDC hdcCompatible,LPCTSTR
lpszFilename);
//creates a blank bitmap
void GDICanvas_CreateBlank(struct GDICanvas* pgdic,HDC hdcCompatible, int width,
int height);
//destroys bitmap and dc
void GDICanvas_Destroy(struct GDICanvas* pgdic,);
```

And there would be nothing wrong with having these declarations. However, since the functions and the struct are tightly coupled (the functions are of no use except with the struct), it makes sense to make it a class.

You may have noticed that some of the functions were missing in the declarations for C. Getting the width, height, or `hdc` would just be done through the struct, so the extra functions were unnecessary. Also, the `CGDICanvas` and `~CGDICanvas` were missing (these are the constructor and destructor). In C++, the constructor is used to initialize the values of a class, and a destructor makes sure that the class cleans up after itself. You never call either of these functions.

You can take a look at the implementation of `CGDICanvas` on your own (it's in GDICanvas.cpp). There's not much to it, really. It just has the various code snippets for loading, making, and destroying bitmaps and DCs.

Loading Images with CGDICanvas

With `CGDICanvas`, loading images is much easier.

```
//declare a CGDICanvas variable
CGDICanvas gdicImage;
//borrow the window's dc
HDC hdc=GetDC(hWndMain);
//load the image
gdicImage.Load(hdc,"filename.bmp");
//release the window's dc
ReleaseDC(hWndMain,hdc);
```

Creating a Blank Bitmap with CGDICanvas

To create a blank bitmap instead, you can replace `gdicImage.Load` with this:

```
//create blank image
gdicImage.CreateBlank(hdc,100,100);
```

Do this to destroy it later:

```
gdicImage.Destroy();
```

You can see that this is a much more simplified process. `CGDICanvas` has a few other features of which you should be aware.

CGDICanvas Information Retrieval Functions

To retrieve the width or height of the image, you can use `GetWidth` or `GetHeight`.

```
//get width and height
int w=gdicImage.GetWidth();
int h=gdicImage.GetHeight();
```

Conversion to HDC

Also, because of the operator `HDC()`, you can use a `CGDICanvas` anywhere that an `HDC` is needed.

```
//blit from the image
BitBlt(hdcDst,0,0,gdicImage.GetWidth(),gdicImage.GetHeight(),gdicImage,0,0,SRC-
COPY);
```

You have now drastically simplified your life (at least in the loading and creating bitmaps area) with `CGDICanvas`.

A CGDICanvas Example

Load up IsoHex3_7.cpp. It requires the use of GDICanvas.h and GDICanvas.cpp, so be sure to have them in there. Also, be sure to have the IsoHex3_7 bitmaps in the project directory.

Compile and run IsoHex3_7.cpp. It does the exact same thing as IsoHex3_6.cpp, except that it uses `CGDICanvas`, which makes much of the initialization and cleanup code shorter. As you can see, `Prog_Init` is quite a bit shorter.

```
bool Prog_Init()
{
	//borrow dc from main window
	HDC hdc=GetDC(hWndMain);
	//load the images
	gdicTile.Load(hdc,"IsoHex3_7-1.bmp");
	gdicMask.Load(hdc,"IsoHex3_7-2.bmp");
	//return dc to system
	ReleaseDC(hWndMain,hdc);
	return(true);//return success
}
```

See how much easier it is?

You'll use `GDICanvas` quite a bit (which is why it doesn't have a normal IsoHex*X*_*Y* name). Even when you get into DirectDraw, you will still use `GDICanvas` to load your graphics.

Double Buffering with GDI

One thing that may be vexing you is that when you switch from one of the IsoHex examples and then switch back, most if not all of the content is erased by the windows that were in front. This is annoying in little sample cases like the ones we have been doing here, but it would be *disastrous* in any sort of real application (like a game). This content-erasure happens because Windows doesn't keep a copy of your client area, except on the screen, so if something draws over it you're out of luck.

> **NOTE**
>
> **This blank bitmap has to be large enough to contain the entire client area of your application. With the examples we've been doing, this isn't a difficult feat. Just make the blank bitmap the size of the client area after you have adjusted it. However, if you were making an application where the user can resize the border, you'd have to make the blank bitmap larger—say, the size of the entire screen (which you would retrieve by using `GetSystemMetrics`). Just something to think about.**

Not to worry, though: you can protect yourself against losing content by double buffering. A *Double buffer* is nothing more than an image stored elsewhere (that is, not on the screen) that is copied to the screen as it is needed. To double buffer, you need a blank bitmap selected into a DC, two Styrofoam cups, and a string. (Just kidding about the Styrofoam cups and string.)

And what you do with this blank bitmap is write to it instead of to the main window's DC. Doing so creates a problem, however: updating the window's client area. If you draw to your double buffer, you cannot see the double buffer unless you copy it onto your window; there are a few ways in which you can do so. One, you could blit the contents of the double buffer to the window every frame (in `Prog_Loop`). That's one solution, but not the one you want. Two, you could update only the regions that change. As a game programmer, you never want to draw anything you don't have to, and you especially never want to *redraw* anything you don't have to. So solution one is out, and two is in.

How to implement this fine idea? Use an update rectangle. Here's how it will work: if the update rectangle is an empty rectangle, you will do no drawing; if the update rectangle is not empty, you will copy the contents of the double buffer to the screen, but only from that rectangle. Now that you know how you'll be drawing with it, you also need to know how you'll determine the update rectangle.

When the update rectangle is empty, any rectangle added to it becomes the new update rectangle. When the update rectangle is not empty, any rectangle added to it is combined with the new rectangle using `UnionRect`. When `WM_PAINT` is called, you add a rectangle the size of the client area to the update rectangle.

Double Buffer Example

Load up IsoHex3_8.cpp. You'll need the IsoHex3_8 bitmaps, GDICanvas.h, and GDICanvas.cpp.

Again, this example looks exactly like IsoHex3_6 and IsoHex3_7. However, if you switch to another application and obscure some or all of the example, when you return, the contents of the client area remain because of the double buffer (`gdicBackbuffer` in the code).

Creating the Double Buffer

Creation of the double buffer consists of simply a few function calls:

```
//get the client rectangle
RECT rcClient;
GetClientRect(hWndMain,&rcClient);
//create a blank bitmap with the client area's dimensions
gdicBackbuffer.CreateBlank(hdc,rcClient.right,rcClient.bottom);
//clear out the blank bitmap
FillRect(gdicBackbuffer,&rcClient,(HBRUSH)GetStockObject(BLACK_BRUSH));
//clear the update region
ClearUpdate();
```

First, you get the client area so that you can create a double buffer of adequate size. Next, you clear out the double buffer with a black brush (a stock object). Finally, you clear out the update area (making sure that you initialize it properly).

The update rectangle itself is contained in a global variable called `rcUpdate`, declared near the top of the source file.

Update Rectangle Management

Management of the update rectangle is done by use of three functions: ClearUpdate, AddUpdate, and RenderUpdate.

ClearUpdate is rather simple. It just sets the update rectangle to empty.

```
//clears the update rectangle
void ClearUpdate()
{
	//set the update rect to empty
	SetRectEmpty(&rcUpdate);
}
```

AddUpdate does one of three things, depending on the current update rectangle and the rectangle being added.

- If you are attempting to add an empty rectangle, it returns immediately, because no real work needs to be done.
- If the current update rectangle is empty, it copies the added rectangle to the update rectangle.
- If the current update rectangle is not empty, AddUpdate uses UnionRect to combine the two rectangles and places that union into rcUpdate.

```
//adds the update rectangle
void AddUpdate(RECT* prcAdd)
{
	//if the new rectangle is empty, return without doing anything
	if(IsRectEmpty(prcAdd)) return;
	if(IsRectEmpty(&rcUpdate))
	{
		//if the rectangle is empty
		//copy the new rectangle to the update rectangle
		CopyRect(&rcUpdate,prcAdd);
	}
	else
	{
```

```
            //if the rectangle is not empty
            //create a temporary rectangle
            RECT rcTemp;
            //combine the new rectangle with the old rectangle in the temporary rect
            UnionRect(&rcTemp,&rcUpdate,prcAdd);
            //copy the temporary rectangle to the update rect
            CopyRect(&rcUpdate,&rcTemp);
      }
}
```

RenderUpdate does one of two things.

- If the update rectangle is empty, there is no need to render anything, so it returns immediately.
- If the update rectangle is not empty, it grabs the DC from the window supplied in hwndDst, copies over the part of hdcSrc corresponding to rcUpdate, and finally clears out the update rectangle.

```
//renders the update
void RenderUpdate(HWND hwndDst, HDC hdcSrc)
{
      //if the update rectangle is empty, return without doing anything
      if(IsRectEmpty(&rcUpdate)) return;
      //borrow the dc from the destination window
      HDC hdcDst=GetDC(hwndDst);
      //blit the update area
      BitBlt(hdcDst,rcUpdate.left,rcUpdate.top,rcUpdate.right-
rcUpdate.left,rcUpdate.bottom-rcUpdate.top,hdcSrc,rcUpdate.left,rcUpdate.top,SRC-
COPY);
      //return the destination dc to the system
      ReleaseDC(hwndDst,hdcDst);
      //clear the update area
      ClearUpdate();
}
```

Double buffering is a good tool for any application that has to live in a window. Redrawing all content each frame is a hassle, and it can kill performance. Using a double buffer and an update rectangle can streamline the process somewhat.

Summary

You thought I was going to go on forever about bitmaps, didn't you? Well, it was necessary. It's an important topic, and I'm still not entirely sure I gave it all the attention it deserves. In any case, I certainly hope I've given you enough GDI stuff to work with.

CHAPTER 4

DirectX at a Glance

- DirectX Components
- DirectX Configuration

Welcome to the wonderful world of DirectX! With it, you can grab control of your machine's capabilities and do a lot more a lot faster than with Windows. In the dark days before DirectX, taking full advantage of the enhanced capabilities of hardware was the domain of DOS applications. The first fledgling version of DirectX did little better. Now things are pretty darn good, and DirectX has become the norm for game programming for the Windows platform.

DirectX Components

DirectX 7 (which, because of backward compatability, is included with DirectX 8) has a number of components, of which you'll use only a scant few. The main components and their uses are as follows:

- **DirectDraw (DD).** The visible component of DirectX, DirectDraw encapsulates your video driver(s). With DirectDraw, you control the resolution of the screen, the system's cooperation with the windowed environment (either full-screen or windowed). You also control the use of display memory. DirectDraw allows you to program the machine independently for a variety of video cards.
- **Direct3D (D3D).** Direct3D is a cousin of DirectDraw. (In DirectX 8, DirectDraw and Direct3D will be combined.) It encapsulates a 3D hardware driver if one is present or emulates one if needed. Like DirectDraw, D3D achieves device independence. Hardware support in the driver allows the use of more of D3D's advanced features.
- **DirectSound (DS).** The audible component of DirectX, DirectSound encapsulates a computer's sound drivers. It is used to play digital sounds in a machine-independent manner.
- **DirectMusic (DM).** This is DirectSound's cousin. It allows an easy (well, not *easy*) way to play music on a variety of machines while still having it sound the same.
- **DirectInput (DI).** DirectInput encapsulates the drivers for various input devices, like keyboards, mice, joysticks, gamepads, flight-yokes, and a variety of specialized controllers.
- **DirectPlay (DP).** DP encapsulates network drivers, allowing an independent way to get information from one computer to another, making multiplayer games easier to create.
- **DirectSetup.** A minor component of DirectX, DirectSetup allows you to install the latest release of DirectX on a user's machine with a few simple function calls. In addition, it allows customization of the interface you present to the user during the setup process.

DirectX Configuration

Before you get flying, you need to get DirectX set up on your machine. The first step in doing so is installing the Software Developer's Kit (Installing the SDK is covered in Appendix A). Once you have the SDK installed, select Tools, Options, as shown in Figure 4.1.

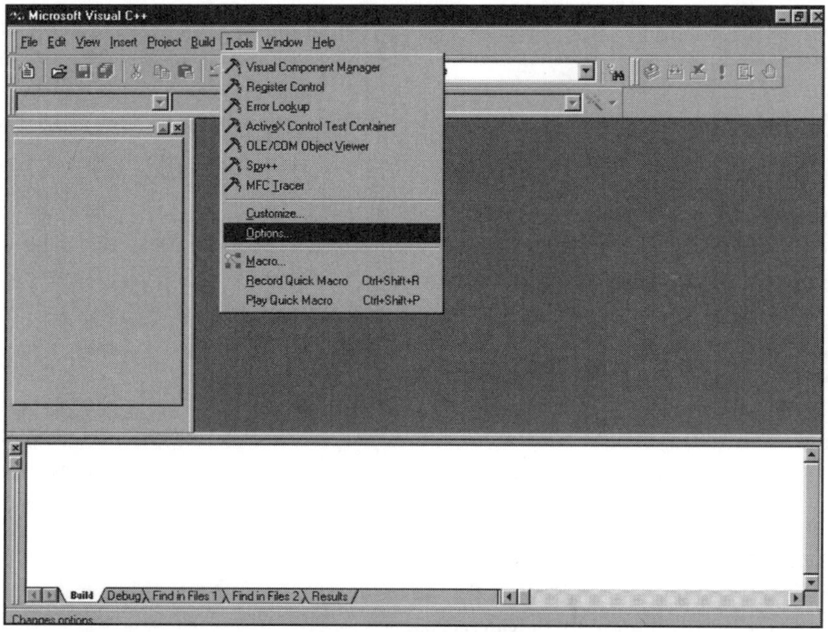

Figure 4.1

Selecting Tools, Options

You will see the Options dialog box, as shown in Figure 4.2. Click on the Directories tab, and make sure that the top two combo boxes read WIN32 and Include files.

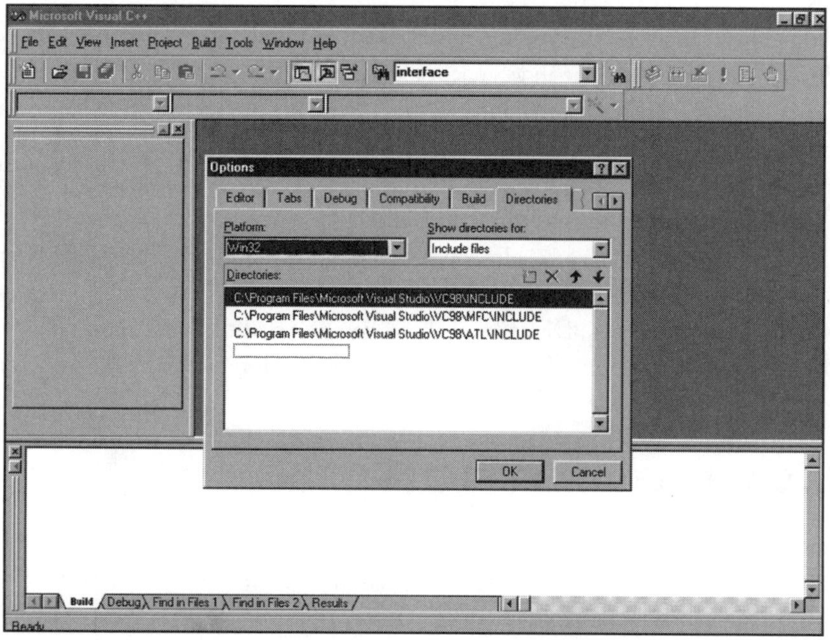

Figure 4.2

The Options dialog box

Click on the first empty line in the list box, and enter the path to the SDK's Include folder, or use the ellipsis button (...) to browse for it, as shown in Figure 4.3.

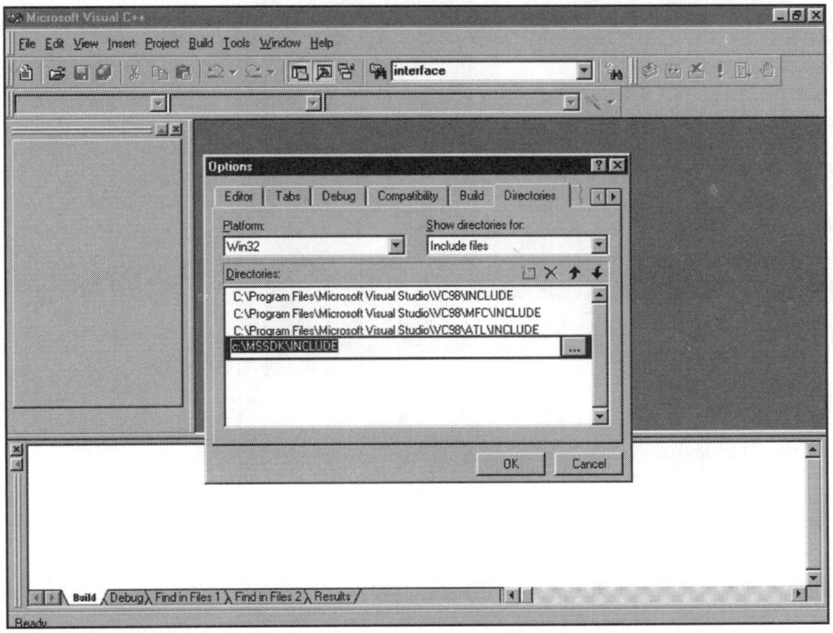

Figure 4.3

Adding a folder

Now, click on one of the other items to unselect that line, and use the up arrow button to move your new entry to the top of the list box. (See Figure 4.4.)

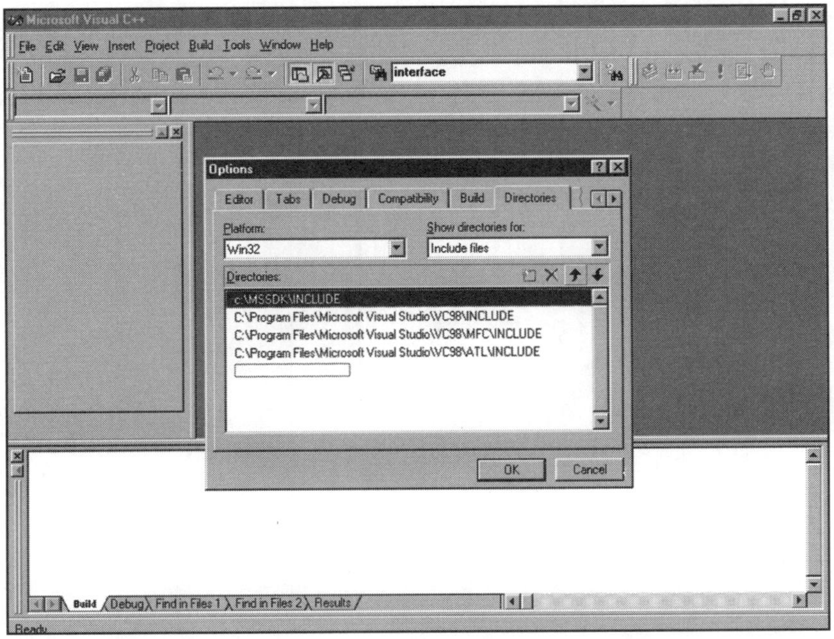

Figure 4.4

Bringing the new folder to the top of the list

Finally, do the same thing for the library files. The result is shown in Figure 4.5.

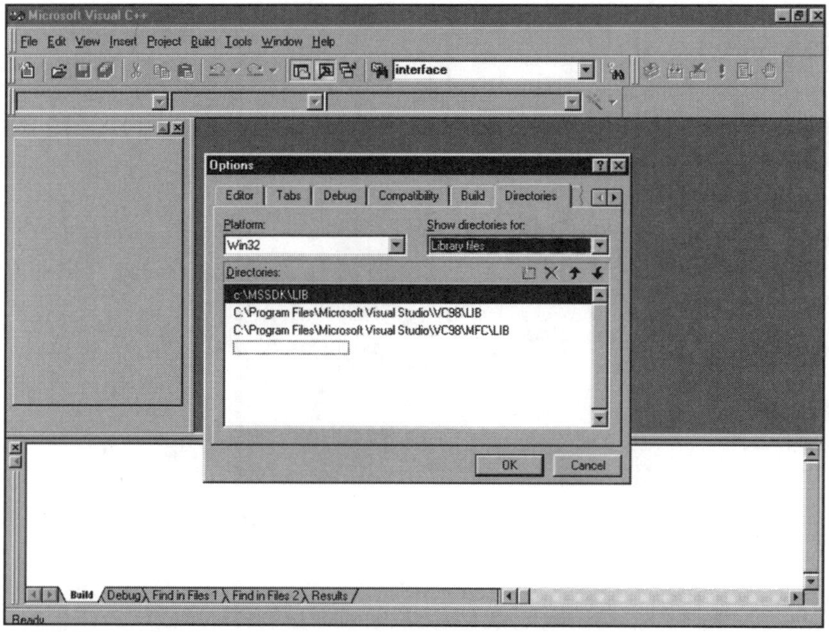

Figure 4.5

Library directories

Thankfully, you have to do this only once, and all the applications you write will have DirectX available to them.

Well, almost. There is one last thing you have to do for each application. When you are working on your application (and it's best to set this up somewhat early in the development so you won't forget and get a bazillion errors), select Project, Settings, as shown in Figure 4.6.

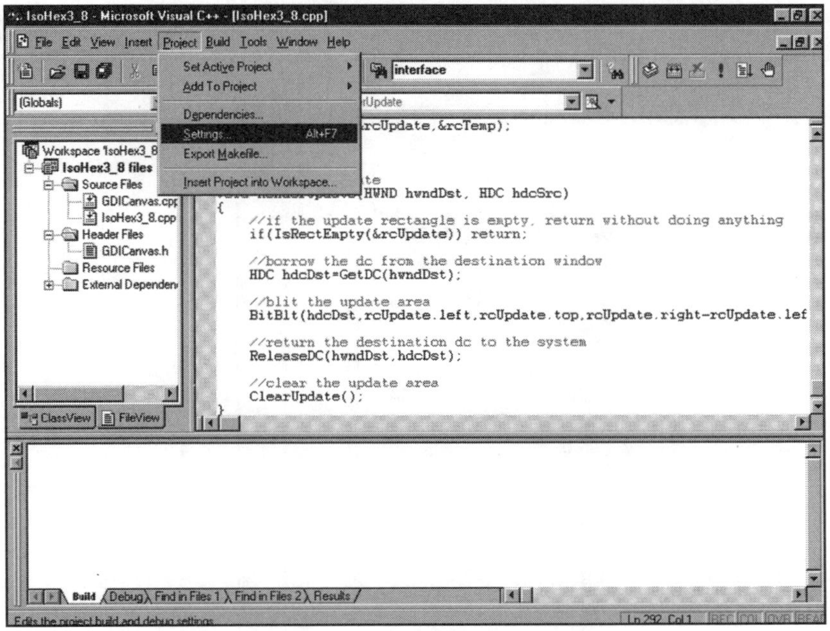

Figure 4.6

Project, Settings

Alternatively, you can press Alt+F7 to get to the same place.

After you have done either of these, you will be met with the dialog box shown in Figure 4.7.

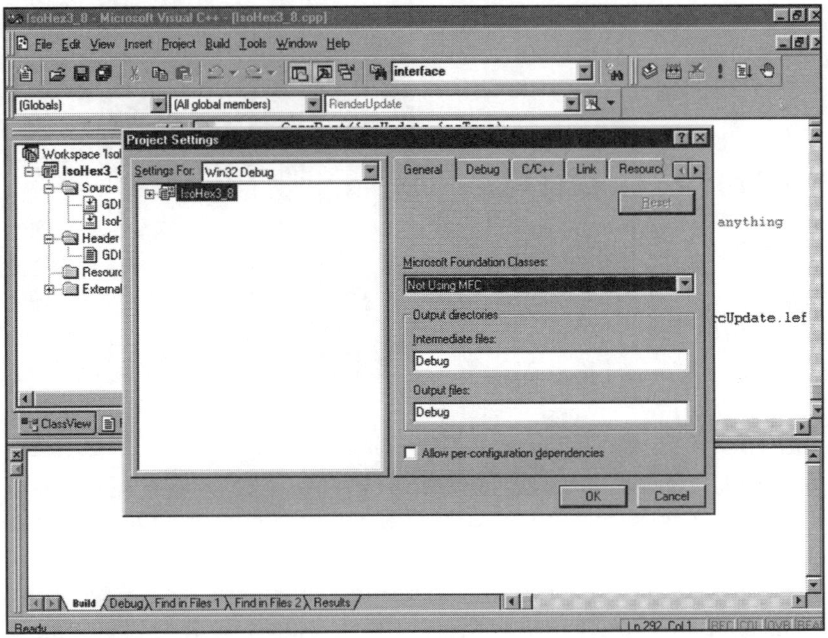

Figure 4.7

The Project Settings dialog box

Click on the Link tab, shown in Figure 4.8. In the Object/library modules text box, add any extra libs to which you want to link. In the case of DirectDraw, you'll want to put in ddraw.lib and dxguid.lib.

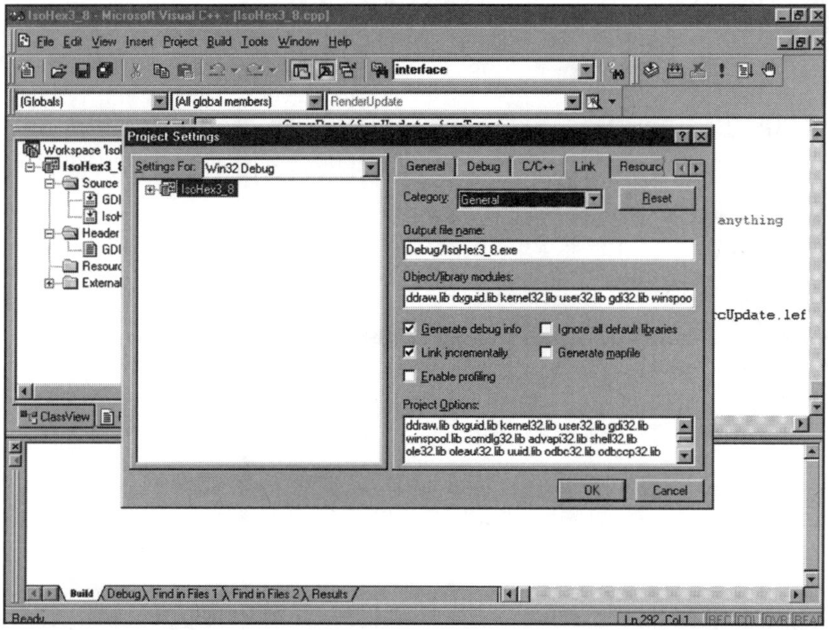

Figure 4.8

The Link tab

When you get to DirectSound a little later, you'll add dsound.lib and winmm.lib to this list as well.

That's all you need to do to set up your compiler to use DirectX.

> **NOTE**
>
> **When you're developing, you normally are in the Debug configuration. When it comes time to distribute your code, you'll switch to the Release configuration. When you do so, you'll have to select Projects, Settings because the libraries you link depend on what configuration you are in.**

Tradition and COM

In every book ever written about DirectX, the tradition is to spend some time talking about how DirectX works and how COM works. Who am I to break with tradition?

COM stands for Component Object Model. Hmm. You don't seem particularly impressed. OK. The why and wherefore of COM is pretty boring stuff anyway. Instead, let me tell you what COM can do for you, as far as DirectX programming is concerned. Number one: no matter what version of DirectX you use to write your game, it will run on any machine that has that version or later of the DirectX runtime installed on it. Number two: when you use DirectX objects, most of the housekeeping is done for you. You create your objects with the various `Create` functions and member functions, and you release them when you no longer need them. Each `Create` is paired with a `Release`, and that's all you have to do. COM and DirectX take care of the rest.

Version Control

First, let's address DirectX benefit number one, version control. You'll be using DirectX version 7. This version has a number of interfaces (an interface is just a set of functions used to access an object). These interfaces are `IDirectDraw7`, `IDirectDrawSurface7`, and `IDirectDrawClipper`. There are a few others that you won't be using.

In order for users to run your program, they must have DirectX 7 or later installed on their systems. However, what happens when later versions come out, and what happens if they drastically change the way things are done? Not a problem. `IDirectDraw7` and the rest will still be there, and new interfaces will have been made available to access the latest features.

Pretty cool. This means you can get a copy of some of the stuff I did using DirectX 5, and it'll still work. Backward compatibility is *good*.

Reference Counting

Now, DirectX benefit number two. As I said before, you'll be using a number of interfaces. I also explained that an interface is just a set of functions that allow you to talk to an object. In most cases in DirectX, the existence of one object depends on the existence of another object. Namely, an `IDirectDrawSurface7` object depends on an `IDirectDraw7` object to work properly. This could be disastrous if you deleted the `IDirectDraw7` object (by calling its `Release` function) before you were done using the `IDirectDrawSurface7` object.

That's where COM's reference counting comes in. When you create your `IDirectDraw7` object, its reference count becomes 1. When you use that object to create an `IDirectDrawSurface7` object, it is increased to 2. When the `IDirectDraw7` object is released, it drops to 1 again, but it is not deleted, because `IDirectDrawSurface7` still needs it. Only when `IDirectDrawSurface7`'s `Release` is called is the `IDirectDraw7` object deleted.

If you design a class or module that depends on one or more of DirectX's objects, you can also make use of reference counting. That is, if you design a class or module that needs an object, you can call `AddRef` to increment the reference count, and `Release` when you no longer need the object.

If you didn't get all of that in a single pass, don't worry. Suffice it to say that COM and DirectX protect you from yourself somewhat, but, of course, this doesn't give you a license to be sloppy.

Summary

This short chapter just showed you how to get DirectX up and running on your machine. We'll be getting into DirectDraw next, so be prepared.

CHAPTER 5

Using DirectDraw

- Creating the IDirectDraw7 Object
- Setting the Cooperative Level
- Enumerating Display Modes

DirectDraw (DD), along with its cousin, Direct3D (D3D), is the visible component of DirectX, and traditionally, it is always the first component a person new to DirectX learns. DD has one primary task, and that is granting you control over your video hardware—something that you wouldn't otherwise have under Windows. Or, at least, you couldn't control it very well or with any sort of good performance.

This chapter will get you up to speed on the component of DD that exerts your control over display resources, the `IDirectDraw7` interface. Chapter 6, "Surfaces," covers DD's stock in trade, `IDirectDrawSurface7` and `IDirectDrawClipper`.

Creating the IDirectDraw7 Object

All of the DirectX interfaces are used through the use of pointers, and each object has a special typed pointer that you use to talk to its interface. In the case of `IDirectDraw7`, this pointer type is `LPDIRECTDRAW7`. In a game or application, you need only one of these (unless you have a multiple-monitor system, in which case you could use two or more, but multimon systems are beyond the scope of what I'm showing you here).

So, when using DD, always declare a global variable that points to an `IDirectDraw7` interface:

```
//IDirectDraw7 pointer
LPDIRECTDRAW7 lpdd=NULL;
```

And somewhere early in your initialization (`Prog_Init`), create your object using `DirectDrawCreateEx`:

```
HRESULT WINAPI DirectDrawCreateEx(
  GUID FAR *lpGUID,
  LPVOID *lplpDD,
  REFIID iid,
  IUnknown FAR *pUnkOuter
);
```

This returns an HRESULT, which is DD_OK or some DDERR_* constant. The parameters are explained in Table 5.1.

Table 5.1 DirectDrawCreateEx Parameters

DirectDrawCreateEx Parameter	Purpose
lpGUID	A pointer to a GUID (globally unique identifier) that identifies the display drivers to use with the IDirectDraw7 object.
lplpDD	A pointer to your pointer to an IDirectDraw7 interface. Must typecast to void**.
iid	An object type identifier. Must be set to IID_IDirectDraw7.
pUnkOuter	COM aggregation stuff. Use NULL.

These parameters are pretty Greek, so I think I have some explaining to do. A GUID (globally unique identifier) is how Windows identifies everything. Your video card has one, as do most of the rest of the pieces of hardware in your machine. A GUID allows you to identify any piece of hardware with one simple (well, not exactly *simple*) numbering mechanism. You won't be doing too much with GUIDs, and you will be passing NULL when they are asked for.

The iid parameter is similar in function to a GUID—it's a class identifier. Each COM object (IDirectDraw7 included) has a class identifier; to make use of them, you must have dxguid.lib linked to your project under the Project, Settings tab.

Confused? I was when I first laid eyes on this COM stuff. Allow me to show you the code for creating your IDirectDraw7 object:

```
//create the direct draw interface
HRESULT hr=DirectDrawCreateEx(NULL,(void**)&lpdd,IID_IDirectDraw7,NULL);
```

Usually, the rule is as follows: if you don't know what the parameter is for or what its value should be, pass a NULL.

About HRESULT

I've mentioned HRESULTs twice up to this point—they're how DirectX returns error or success. Usually, when a function call returns and is successful, you get the value DD_OK. If it fails, you get one of the many DDERR_* constants, indicating both that it failed and why it failed.

To test for this condition, Microsoft has provided a macro called FAILED. To check for errors, you do something like the following:

```
//error check
if(FAILED(hr))
{
      //there was an error
}
```

> **NOTE**
> This type of error checking tends to clutter up source code. For this reason, I'll be leaving most of it out, using it only where absolutely necessary.

Setting the Cooperative Level

After you have created your IDirectDraw7 object, you need to specify the manner in which you want to use it. Essentially, there are two choices—windowed and full-screen.

Select the manner in which you will use IdirectDraw7 through IDirectDraw7's SetCooperativeLevel member function:

```
HRESULT SetCooperativeLevel(
  HWND hWnd,
  DWORD dwFlags
);
```

Like all other DirectX functions, this returns error or success in an HRESULT. The parameters are explained in Table 5.2.

Table 5.2 SetCooperativeLevel Parameters

SetCooperativeLevel Parameter	Purpose
hWnd	The top-level window that DirectDraw is to use
dwFlags	Cooperation flags (see Table 5.3)

There are only about a handful of flags that you'll use with any frequency. They are listed in Table 5.3. Most of the rest of the flags deal with multimon systems and Direct3D.

Table 5.3 SetCooperativeLevel Flags

SetCooperativeLevel Flag	Meaning
DDSCL_ALLOWREBOOT	Allows an end user to use Ctrl+Alt+Delete during a full-screen application. This is a *must* if you intend to make Windows-friendly games.
DDSCL_EXCLUSIVE	Specifies that you want exclusive control over the display hardware. You must use DDSCL_FULLSCREEN also.
DDSCL_FULLSCREEN	Specifies that you want a full-screen application. Must be used with DDSCL_EXCLUSIVE.
DDSCL_NORMAL	Specifies that you are making a windowed application with DirectDraw. Useful for debugging.

For the most part, you'll want to do full-screen, exclusive applications that have the ability to use Ctrl+Alt+Delete, so the code will look like this:

```
//set cooperative level-fullscreen-exclusive
hr=lpdd->SetCooperativeLevel(hWndMain,DDSCL_EXCLUSIVE | DDSCL_FULLSCREEN |
DDSCL_ALLOWREBOOT);
```

Now that you have grabbed full-screen access to your display, you might want to change the display mode. You can do one of two things: one, you can start picking display modes from the commonly available ones until one works, or until none of them work, in which case you'd be up a creek. Or two, you can enumerate the available display modes and then choose from that list. I prefer the latter method. Trial and error is not my style.

Enumerating Display Modes

Enumeration of any type is a bit confusing at first. I'm not going to do anything really weird here. I'm just going to put the display modes into a nice list that you can examine later in the code.

First, let's go over the function you'll be calling to actually do the enumeration, EnumDisplayModes:

```
HRESULT EnumDisplayModes(
  DWORD dwFlags,
  LPDDSURFACEDESC2 lpDDSurfaceDesc2,
  LPVOID lpContext,
  LPDDENUMMODESCALLBACK2 lpEnumModesCallback
);
```

This returns an `HRESULT` containing success or failure. Table 5.4 explains the parameter list.

Table 5.4 EnumDisplayModes Parameters

EnumDisplayModes Parameter	Purpose
`dwFlags`	Special flags telling DD what kind of enumeration you want
`lpDDSurfaceDesc2`	A description of the type of display mode you are looking for
`lpContext`	A user-defined context variable that gets passed to the callback function
`lpEnumModesCallback`	A pointer to the callback function

The `dwFlags` parameter has two special values: `DDEDM_REFRESHRATES`, which takes into account the refresh rate for the display mode, and `DDEDM_STANDARDVGAMODES`, which enumerates the normal old VGA 320×200×8 display mode. You won't use either of these flags; you will always pass 0.

`lpDDSurfaceDesc2` is a pointer to a `DDSURFACEDESC2` struct, which I will cover in more detail later in this chapter and in Chapter 6. If you were to set some of the members of a `DDSURFACEDESC2` and then call the enumeration, you could filter your search. For now, you'll just list all of the display modes, and to heck with limiting the search. (You can look through them later after you've listed them all.)

The final parameter, `lpEnumModesCallback`, is a user-defined callback function, one that looks similar to the following:

```
HRESULT WINAPI EnumModesCallback2(
  LPDDSURFACEDESC2 lpDDSurfaceDesc,
  LPVOID lpContext
);
```

This function will return one of two values: DDENUMRET_OK will continue enumeration, and DDENUMRET_CANCEL will stop it.

lpDDSurfaceDesc is another pointer to DDSURFACEDESC2, which contains information about the display mode being enumerated. lpContext contains the value you originally passed in the call to EnumDisplayModes.

There is a *lot* of information contained in a DDSURFACEDESC2 structure. Here's the definition:

```
typedef struct _DDSURFACEDESC2 {
    DWORD          dwSize;
    DWORD          dwFlags;
    DWORD          dwHeight;
    DWORD          dwWidth;
    union
    {
        LONG       lPitch;
        DWORD      dwLinearSize;
    } DUMMYUNIONNAMEN(1);
    DWORD          dwBackBufferCount;
    union
    {
        DWORD      dwMipMapCount;
        DWORD      dwRefreshRate;
    } DUMMYUNIONNAMEN(2);
    DWORD          dwAlphaBitDepth;
    DWORD          dwReserved;
    LPVOID         lpSurface;
    union
    {
        DDCOLORKEY    ddckCKDestOverlay;
        DWORD         dwEmptyFaceColor;
    } DUMMYUNIONNAMEN(3);
    DDCOLORKEY     ddckCKDestBlt;
    DDCOLORKEY     ddckCKSrcOverlay;
    DDCOLORKEY     ddckCKSrcBlt;
    DDPIXELFORMAT ddpfPixelFormat;
    DDSCAPS2       ddsCaps;
    DWORD          dwTextureStage;
} DDSURFACEDESC2, FAR* LPDDSURFACEDESC2;
```

As you can see, there's quite a bit here, and you will be using only a fraction of it. You'll be seeing DDSURFACEDESC2 in more detail in Chapter 6.

The information you care about for a display mode consists of three things: the width, the height, and the color depth. I explained a bit about color depth in Chapter 2, "The World of GDI and Windows Graphics," during the discussion on pixel plotting. Briefly, color depth specifies how many bits each pixel contains. It usually has a value of 8, 16, 24, or 32. In depths higher than 8, the bits correspond to some RGB (red, green, blue) value that describes a color.

In DDSURFACEDESC2, you can see the dwWidth and dwHeight members. These correspond to the size of the display mode (the resolution). Common values are 640×480, 800×600, and 1024×768. Some video cards can go even higher, and many video cards have more exotic display modes, like 400×300, 512×384, and so on.

The location of the bits per pixel is not quite as obvious in the DDSURFACEDESC2 structure, because it is part of the ddpfPixelFormat member, which is itself a DDPIXELFORMAT structure.

```
typedef struct _DDPIXELFORMAT{
    DWORD dwSize;
    DWORD dwFlags;
    DWORD dwFourCC;
    union
    {
        DWORD dwRGBBitCount;
        DWORD dwYUVBitCount;
        DWORD dwZBufferBitDepth;
        DWORD dwAlphaBitDepth;
        DWORD dwLuminanceBitCount;
        DWORD dwBumpBitCount;
    } DUMMYUNIONNAMEN(1);
    union
    {
        DWORD dwRBitMask;
        DWORD dwYBitMask;
        DWORD dwStencilBitDepth;
        DWORD dwLuminanceBitMask;
        DWORD dwBumpDuBitMask;
    } DUMMYUNIONNAMEN(2);
    union
    {
        DWORD dwGBitMask;
        DWORD dwUBitMask;
```

```
        DWORD dwZBitMask;
        DWORD dwBumpDvBitMask;
    } DUMMYUNIONNAMEN(3);
    union
    {
        DWORD dwBBitMask;
        DWORD dwVBitMask;
        DWORD dwStencilBitMask;
        DWORD dwBumpLuminanceBitMask;
    } DUMMYUNIONNAMEN(4);
    union
    {
        DWORD dwRGBAlphaBitMask;
        DWORD dwYUVAlphaBitMask;
        DWORD dwLuminanceAlphaBitMask;
        DWORD dwRGBZBitMask;
        DWORD dwYUVZBitMask;
    } DUMMYUNIONNAMEN(5);
} DDPIXELFORMAT, FAR* LPDDPIXELFORMAT;
```

This is another big structure with a lot of information (but most of it is in the form of unions). This is your first look at `DDPIXELFORMAT`. It will be explored in more detail in Chapter 6, when we'll take a look at converting from one pixel format to another. The member of `DDPIXELFORMAT` that concerns you is `dwRGBBitCount`, which contains the bit depth of the display mode. (Seems like a whole lot of structure for just three little `DWORD`s, doesn't it?)

Let's get enumerating, then. Enumerae twice: the first enumeration counts the display modes, and the second enumeration puts them into a list.

First, define a structure that contains all the applicable information about a display mode (at least, as far as you're concerned):

```
struct DisplayMode
{
      DWORD dwWidth;
      DWORD dwHeight;
      DWORD dwBPP;
};
```

Short and sweet, the way things should be. Next, add two global variables:

```
//the number of display modes will be kept here
DWORD dwDisplayModeCount=0;
//this will point to the list of display modes
DisplayMode* DisplayModeList=NULL;
```

The first enumeration function is quite simple, since it just counts the display modes:

```
HRESULT WINAPI EnumModesCallbackCount(
  LPDDSURFACEDESC2 lpDDSurfaceDesc,
  LPVOID lpContext
)
{
      //increment the count variable
      dwDisplayModeCount++;
      //continue the enumeration
      return(DDENUMRET_OK);
}
```

The second enumeration isn't much more difficult:

```
HRESULT WINAPI EnumModesCallbackList(
  LPDDSURFACEDESC2 lpDDSurfaceDesc,
  LPVOID lpContext
)
{
      //copy applicable information to the list
      DisplayModeList[dwDisplayModeCount].dwWidth=lpDDSurfaceDesc->dwWidth;
      DisplayModeList[dwDisplayModeCount].dwHeight=lpDDSurfaceDesc->dwHeight;
      DisplayModeList[dwDisplayModeCount].dwBPP=lpDDSurfaceDesc-
>ddpfPixelFormat.dwRGBBitCount;
      //increment the count variable
      dwDisplayModeCount++;
      //continue the enumeration
      return(DDENUMRET_OK);
}
```

Finally, put it all together to make the enumeration happen:

```
//clear the display mode count
dwDisplayModeCount=0;
//count display modes
lpdd->EnumDisplayModes(0,NULL,NULL,EnumModesCallbackCount);
//allocate space for the list
DisplayModeList=new DisplayMode[dwCount];
//reset the count
dwDisplayModeCount=0;
//list the display modes
lpdd->EnumDisplayModes(0,NULL, NULL,EnumModesCallbackList);
```

The `new` operator performs about the same function as `malloc`, only in a more typesafe way. The `malloc` equivalent would be:

```
DisplayModeList=(DisplayMode*)malloc(sizeof(DisplayMode)*dwDisplayModeCount);
```

When you are done with the list, use the following code to deallocate it:

```
//delete the display mode list
delete [] DisplayModeList;
DisplayModeList=NULL;
```

This is equivalent to using the `free` function that is normally used with `malloc`.

Now you have all the possible display modes in a list, and you can loop through that list and test to see which mode you want. Also, you can look through to see if a given mode is supported. If it isn't, you can settle for a less-ideal mode.

Let's do some code that checks for an 800×600×16 mode (almost universally available).

```
//set up the test mode
DisplayMode TestMode;
TestMode.dwWidth=800;
TestMode.dwHeight=600;
TestMode.dwBPP=16;
//our boolean test variable
bool found=false;
//our iterator
DWORD index;
//where we found it (all bits set means not found)
DWORD foundindex=0xFFFFFFFF;
for(index=0;(index<dwDisplayModeCount) && (!found);index++)
{
```

```
        if((DisplayModeList[index].dwWidth==TestMode.dwWidth) &&
            (DisplayModeList[index].dwHeight==TestMode.dwHeight) &&
            (DisplayModeList[index].dwBPP==TestMode.dwBPP))
        {
                foundindex=index;
                found=true;
}
}
```

Simple enough, right? You could perform a wide variety of tests on the display mode list, from finding the largest mode with a certain BPP to finding the greatest BPP for a given mode. Or, you might let the end user select what display mode he wants to run in, and save this value in a configuration file somewhere.

Now that you know what modes are available and what mode you want, you can use this information to set the display mode. (It's hard to believe that this topic took several pages to cover—the code gets executed in a fraction of a second.)

Setting the Display Mode

After enumerating the display modes, setting the display mode is easy. You set the display mode with the `SetDisplayMode` member function of `IDirectDraw7` (are you *really* surprised?).

```
HRESULT SetDisplayMode(
  DWORD dwWidth,
  DWORD dwHeight,
  DWORD dwBPP,
  DWORD dwRefreshRate,
  DWORD dwFlags
);
```

This returns an `HRESULT` again (by now you should be spotting a pattern), and the parameters look suspiciously like the members of `DisplayMode`, with the exception of `dwRefreshRate` (which you don't care about, so pass 0) and `dwFlags` (which you also don't care about, so pass 0).

Calling this function usually looks something like this:

```
//set the display mode
hr=lpdd->SetDisplayMode(800,600,16,0,0);
```

Of course, the 800, 600, and 16 are whatever display mode you want, or variables containing the values you want.

Retrieving the Current Display Mode

Of course, there may be times when you want to retrieve the current display mode. To do this, you use `GetDisplayMode`.

```
HRESULT GetDisplayMode(
  LPDDSURFACEDESC2 lpDDSurfaceDesc2
);
```

Look! It returns an `HRESULT`! (I'm not going to mention the return values for `DX` functions anymore. They are all `HRESULT`s and are all treated exactly the same way.)

The sole parameter of this function is `lpDDSurfaceDesc2`, which is a pointer to a `DDSURFACEDESC2`. Declare a variable of `DDSURFACEDESC2`, clean it out, and call the function. When it returns, your `DDSURFACEDESC2` contains the information describing the current display mode (similar to how it did when you enumerated display modes). But what do I mean by "cleaning out" a `DDSURFACEDESC2`? Well, in most cases, when you work with `DDSURFACEDESC2`s, or any other DirectX structure, you first have to initialize it (set all members to 0), and you have to set the `dwSize` member. This is how to do so:

```
//declare the variable
DDSURFACEDESC2 ddsd;
//initialize to all zeros
memset(&ddsd,0,sizeof(DDSURFACEDESC2));
//set the size
ddsd.dwSize=sizeof(DDSURFACEDESC2);
```

After it has been cleaned out, it is ready to use:

```
//retrieve the display mode
hr=lpdd->GetDisplayMode(&ddsd);
```

Just like within the enumeration function, the width and height of the display mode are stored in `ddsd.dwWidth` and `ddsd.dwHeight`, and the bits per pixel are stored in `ddsd.ddpfPixelFormat.dwRGBBitCount`.

A Final Thing: Releasing Objects

There is a certain way in which you delete almost all DirectX objects once you are done with them. For your `lpdd`, this is what it looks like:

```
if(lpdd)
{
        lpdd->Release();
        lpdd=NULL;
}
```

This exact same snippet, with just a different variable, will be used for most of your DirectX cleanup. Just as it was important during GDI to get rid of your object and DCs, it is also important to get rid of your DirectX object.

Check out IsoHex5_1.cpp (the *only* Chapter 5 example), and see in action what I have been talking about here. Don't expect much; you'll just end up with a black screen. However, now that you are into DirectX, that screen is *yours!*

Summary

This chapter has given you entry to the world of DirectDraw, but so far you've only got your foot in the door. Here are some key points to remember:

- The `IDirectDraw7` object controls display resources. It is the parent of all other `DirectDraw` objects. You create one with `DirectDrawCreateEx`.
- Depending on what you want to use the `IDirectDraw7` object for, you must set an appropriate cooperative level using `SetCooperativeLevel`.
- Although there are display modes that are widely supported on most video cards, it's still a good idea to enumerate the display modes before selecting the one you want to use.

CHAPTER 6

Surfaces

- What is a Surface?
- Creating a Surface
- Using Surfaces

Now we're getting into some cool stuff: DirectDraw surfaces (the `IDirectDrawSurface7` object). Surfaces are DirectDraw's stock in trade. They hold graphical images that you can display and manipulate, similar in function to memory device contexts but without all the abstraction inherent to GDI. Of course, you can still use GDI functions with your surfaces, as you'll see a little later. This is a big chapter, and we've got a lot of ground to cover, so let's get going.

What Is a Surface?

Quite simply, a *surface* is a block of memory (either on your video card or in system memory) that is managed by DirectDraw as though it were a rectangle, even though the memory itself is linear. Surfaces come in many types. The difference between these types lies in what each surface is capable of. The three types of surfaces that you will be concerned with at this point are primary surfaces, secondary surfaces (back buffers), and off-screen surfaces.

- **Primary Surface.** In any application, you will have only *one* primary surface for each DirectDraw object. (In a multiple-monitor system, with multiple DirectDraw interfaces, it is possible to have more than one.) The primary surface is the only surface in DirectDraw that is visible.
- **Secondary Surfaces.** A secondary surface, or back buffer, is not a surface all on its own. Not quite. Sure, you can still do all the things with a secondary surface that you can do with any other type of surface, but the existence of a secondary surface depends on other surfaces. It is attached to another surface and is part of what is called a *flipping chain*. More about this a little later.
- **Off-Screen Surfaces.** An off-screen surface is what you will use to store your bitmaps and other graphical data until it is needed. Quite often you'll have a large number of these, and many of them will be small in size. They serve about the same function as do memory DCs.

Now that you've been introduced to surfaces, let's start making them!

Creating a Surface

All surfaces (except secondary surfaces) start out their life with a call to `IDirectDraw7`'s `CreateSurface`.

```
HRESULT CreateSurface(
  LPDDSURFACEDESC2 lpDDSurfaceDesc2,
  LPDIRECTDRAWSURFACE7 FAR *lplpDDSurface,
  IUnknown FAR *pUnkOuter
);
```

On success, this returns DD_OK. Table 6.1 explains the parameter list.

Table 6.1 IDirectDraw7::CreateSurface Parameters

CreateSurface Parameter	Purpose
lpDDSurfaceDesc2	Pointer to a DDSURFACEDESC2 containing a description of the desired surface
lplpDDSurface	Pointer to an LPDIRECTDRAWSURFACE7 pointer that will be filled with a pointer to the new IDirectDrawSurface7 object
pUnkOuter	COM stuff. Use NULL.

DDSURFACEDESC2

Now I'm going to go into a little more detail about DDSURFACEDESC2, which was introduced in Chapter 5, "Using DirectDraw."

Here's the structure again, with the important fields highlighted in bold:

```
typedef struct _DDSURFACEDESC2 {
    DWORD           dwSize;
    DWORD           dwFlags;
    DWORD           dwHeight;
    DWORD           dwWidth;
    union
    {
        LONG        lPitch;
        DWORD       dwLinearSize;
    } DUMMYUNIONNAMEN(1);
    DWORD           dwBackBufferCount;
    union
    {
        DWORD       dwMipMapCount;
        DWORD       dwRefreshRate;
    } DUMMYUNIONNAMEN(2);
    DWORD           dwAlphaBitDepth;
```

```
    DWORD          dwReserved;
    LPVOID         lpSurface;
    union
    {
        DDCOLORKEY     ddckCKDestOverlay;
        DWORD          dwEmptyFaceColor;
    } DUMMYUNIONNAMEN(3);
    DDCOLORKEY     ddckCKDestBlt;
    DDCOLORKEY     ddckCKSrcOverlay;
    DDCOLORKEY     ddckCKSrcBlt;
    DDPIXELFORMAT ddpfPixelFormat;
    DDSCAPS2       ddsCaps;
    DWORD          dwTextureStage;
} DDSURFACEDESC2, FAR* LPDDSURFACEDESC2;
```

The highlighted fields are explained in Table 6.2.

Table 6.2 Meaningful Members of DDSUFACEDESC2

DDSURFACEDESC2 Member	Meaning
dwSize	The size of the DDSURFACEDESC2. Always set to sizeof(DDSURFACEDESC2).
dwFlags	Flags specifying which of the other members are meaningful (see the next section)
dwHeight	Height of a surface
dwWidth	Width of a surface
lPitch	The pitch of a surface (discussed later, in the section "The Nitty-Gritty: Lock and Unlock")
dwBackBufferCount	The number of back buffers that a surface has. Used when creating complex surfaces.
lpSurface	A pointer to the surface's memory (discussed in the section "The Nitty-Gritty: Lock and Unlock")
ddpfPixelFormat	The pixel format of the surface (discussed in more detail later)
ddsCaps	The capabilities of the surface (discussed in a moment)

Hopefully, this has made DDSURFACEDESC2 just a little less scary. Most of the rest of this stuff is for advanced use, and much of it isn't even implemented yet.

dwFlags

The dwFlags member specifies what other members are valid. Various flags are shown in Table 6.3.

Table 6.3 DDSURFACEDESC2 Flags

DDSURFACEDESC2 Flag	Member Validated
DDSD_HEIGHT	dwHeight
DDSD_WIDTH	dwWidth
DDSD_PITCH	lPitch
DDSD_BACKBUFFERCOUNT	dwBackBufferCount
DDSD_PIXELFORMAT	ddpfPixelFormat
DDSD_CAPS	ddsCaps

ddsCaps

When creating a surface, always use the ddsCaps member to specify what kind of surface you want. ddsCaps is in itself a structure, a DDSCAPS2.

```
typedef struct _DDSCAPS2 {
    DWORD     dwCaps;
    DWORD     dwCaps2;
    DWORD     dwCaps3;
    DWORD     dwCaps4;
} DDSCAPS2, FAR* LPDDSCAPS2;
```

All the members of this structure contain flags. Neither dwCaps3 nor dwCaps4 is currently used. The dwCaps2 member is for advanced stuff dealing with D3D, so the only one you need to be concerned with is dwCaps, which contains a number of flags that you will find useful. Some of these flags are listed in Table 6.4.

Table 6.4 Selected DDSCAPS2 Flags

dwCaps Flag	Use
DDSCAPS_BACKBUFFER	Creates a secondary surface
DDSCAPS_COMPLEX	Creates a primary surface that has a secondary surface attached
DDSCAPS_FLIP	Creates a primary surface that has a secondary surface attached
DDSCAPS_OFFSCREENPLAIN	Creates an off-screen surface
DDSCAPS_PRIMARYSURFACE	Creates a primary surface
DDSCAPS_SYSTEMMEMORY	Creates a surface in system memory
DDSCAPS_VIDEOMEMORY	Creates a surface in video memory

There are quite a few more flags, but you won't be using them.

Creating a Primary Surface

The first surface you create in a DirectDraw application is the primary surface. Then you fetch the back buffers (if any), and then you start making the off-screen surfaces.

At some point, usually in the globals section, you should declare a variable that will contain a pointer to the primary surface:

```
//primary surface
LPDIRECTDRAWSURFACE7 lpddsPrime=NULL;
```

NOTE

Your video card has only a limited amount of memory. The primary surface (and any back buffers for the primary) *must* be in video memory. Off-screen surfaces have greater performance if they are in video memory, but they can be in system memory as well—though you'll feel a performance hit.

Always create your surfaces in decreasing order of importance. If it is an oft-used surface—like the bitmap containing the main character—create it sooner than the surfaces that contain the graphics for the title screen (the title screen doesn't need to be as fast as the game itself).

First, set up your surface description:

```
//clean out surface description
DDSURFACEDESC2 ddsd;
memset(&ddsd,0,sizeof(DDSURFACEDESC2));
ddsd.dwSize=sizeof(DDSURFACEDESC2);
//set up the caps for the primary
ddsd.dwFlags=DDSD_CAPS;
ddsd.ddsCaps.dwCaps=DDSCAPS_PRIMARYSURFACE;
//finally, create the surface
lpdd->CreateSurface(&ddsd,&lpddsPrime,NULL);
```

And later, when you are closing the program and cleaning up, do a safe release of the primary surface (which looks almost exactly like the safe release of the `IDirectDraw7` object):

```
if(lpddsPrime)
{
        lpddsPrime->Release();
        lpddsPrime=NULL;
}
```

Creating a Secondary Surface/Back Buffer

Create back buffers, if you will have them, at the same time you create your primary surface. When you create your primary surface, specify that it is a complex surface that can be flipped, and specify how many back buffers it will have. (I'll discuss flipping in a moment.)

```
//surfaces
LPDIRECTDRAWSURFACE7 lpddsPrime=NULL;
LPDIRECTDRAWSURFACE7 lpddsBack=NULL;
//clean out surface description
DDSURFACEDESC2 ddsd;
memset(&ddsd,0,sizeof(DDSURFACEDESC2));
ddsd.dwSize=sizeof(DDSURFACEDESC2);
//set up the caps for the primary
ddsd.dwFlags=DDSD_CAPS | DDSD_BACKBUFFERCOUNT;
ddsd.dwBackBufferCount=1;
```

```
ddsd.ddsCaps.dwCaps=DDSCAPS_PRIMARYSURFACE | DDSCAPS_COMPLEX | DDSCAPS_FLIP;
//finally, create the surface
lpdd->CreateSurface(&ddsd,&lpddsPrime,NULL);
```

Now you've got the primary surface, which has the secondary surface attached to it. To retrieve this attached surface, use `GetAttachedSurface`:

```
HRESULT GetAttachedSurface(
  LPDDSCAPS2 lpDDSCaps,
  LPDIRECTDRAWSURFACE7 FAR *lplpDDAttachedSurface
);
```

This function takes a pointer to a `DDSCAPS2` structure, specifying the capabilities of the attached surface, and a pointer to an `LPDIRECTDRAWSURFACE7`, which will be filled with a pointer to the attached surface.

So, to retrieve the back buffer:

```
//clean out a DDSCAPS2
DDSCAPS2 ddsCaps;
memset(&ddsCaps,0,sizeof(DDSCAPS2));
//specify that we want a back buffer
ddsCaps.dwCaps=DDSCAPS_BACKBUFFER;
//retrieve the back buffer
lpddsPrime->GetAttachedSurface(&ddsCaps,&lpddsBack);
```

Why Use Back Buffers?

You *could* just write to the primary surface. You really could. However, there would be detrimental effects. The user would see items as they were being drawn to the screen, and if the drawing was not timed correctly, shearing would occur as the electron gun in the back of the monitor misses some of the information you placed on the primary surface. This creates a flickering effect, and in general is not considered good practice.

To make everything look as good as possible, it's a wise idea to make both a primary surface, which is shown to the user at all times, and attach to it a back buffer/secondary surface. Doing so makes the surfaces similar to a flip book; in fact, switching which surface is the primary and which is the back buffer is called *flipping*, and the two surfaces are called a *flipping chain*. You don't have to do anything special once you've flipped the primary surface. DirectDraw is smart enough to know how to exchange the memory of the two surfaces. You can do all your writing to a back buffer and then use `Flip`, which switches the memory from the back to the primary. DirectDraw takes care of timing it correctly. And miraculously, you will have no flicker.

Flipping

The Flip function looks like this:

```
HRESULT IDirectDrawSurface7::Flip(
  LPDIRECTDRAWSURFACE7 lpDDSurfaceTargetOverride,
  DWORD dwFlags
);
```

lpDDSurfaceTargetOverride is for use with advanced flipping chains, and you'll just pass NULL. The dwFlags parameter, however, can be useful. You will be placing the constant DDFLIP_WAIT into this parameter. This allows DirectDraw to time the transfer properly so that no flickering or shearing occurs.

One last thing about back buffers before we move on: you don't have to do a release of the back buffer—that's taken care of when the primary surface is released.

Off-Screen Surfaces

The final type of surface that you'll be dealing with (at least, until you get into D3D later in this book) is the off-screen surface. An off-screen surface can exist in either system memory or video memory. If you do not specify either of these in the ddsCaps member of DDSURFACEDESC2, DirectDraw will try to put it into video memory, and if that fails, it will place the surface in system memory.

Remember what I said earlier about the location of surfaces; make your most commonly used off-screen surfaces in video memory if you can, and resort to system memory if you have to.

Following is an example of creating an off-screen surface, trying first for video memory and then falling back to surface memory. Note that you set the dwWidth, dwHeight, and ddsCaps part of the DDSURFACEDESC2 structure.

```
//declaration (global)
LPDIRECTDRAWSURFACE7 lpddsOffScrn=NULL;
//set up the DDSURFACEDESC2
DDSURFACEDESC2 ddsd;
memset(&ddsd,0,sizeof(DDSURFACEDESC2));
ddsd.dwSize=sizeof(DDSURFACEDESC2);
//set flags... width, height, caps
ddsd.dwFlags=DDSD_WIDTH | DDSD_HEIGHT | DDSD_CAPS;
//attempt video memory
ddsd.ddsCaps.dwCaps=DDSCAPS_OFFSCREENPLAIN | DDSCAPS_VIDEOMEMORY;
//width and height=100x100
ddsd.dwWidth=100;
ddsd.dwHeight=100;
HRESULT hr=lpdd->CreateSurface(&ddsd,&lpddsOffScrn,NULL);
```

```
if(FAILED(hr))
{
	//not enough video memory, try system memory
	ddsd.ddsCaps.dwCaps=DDSCAPS_OFFSCREENPLAIN | DDSCAPS_SYSTEMMEMORY;
	//try again
	hr=lpdd->CreateSurface(&ddsd,&lpddsOffScrn,NULL);
	if(FAILED(hr))
	{
		//something still went wrong...
	}
}
```

Using Surfaces

Now that you know how to make surfaces, you can get down to the very serious business of using them. This section outlines the various ways in which you can write to and read from surfaces and copy them to one another.

GetDC/ReleaseDC, or Using GDI on Surfaces

Just because you are in DirectX doesn't mean that you have to leave GDI behind. Admittedly, using GDI in a time-critical section isn't the best idea, but for loading bitmaps and placing them on surfaces, GDI will do just fine.

In order to perform GDI functions on a surface, you need an `HDC`. Luckily, there is a function that does just that: `IDirectDrawSurface7::GetDC`.

```
HRESULT IDirectDrawSurface7::GetDC(
  HDC FAR *lphDC
);
```

To make use of this function, you send a pointer to an `HDC` to it, like so:

```
//grab the dc from the surface
HDC hdcSurf;
lpddsPrime->GetDC(&hdcSurf);
```

If successful, hdcSurf will now contain a GDI-compatible device context. Pretty cool.

When you are done using the DC, be sure to release it with IDirectDrawSurface7::ReleaseDC.

```
//release the dc
lpddsPrime->ReleaseDC(hdcSurf);
```

CAUTION

If you don't release the DC, your computer is very, very likely to lock up (and there's no Ctrl+Alt+Delete to save you). Also, between the calls to GetDC and ReleaseDC, your computer's display will be frozen, so don't keep the DC any longer than you have to. Just get in, get it done, and get out.

Enough of this talk! Let's do an example. Load up IsoHex6_1.cpp. You will also need your trusty GDICanvas.h and GDICanvas.cpp files, and IsoHex6_1.bmp.

IsoHex6_1.cpp was built from IsoHex5_1.cpp, with some extra stuff that we've covered this chapter. If you run it, you'll see a lazy ball that slowly meanders around the screen, bouncing off the walls, as shown in Figure 6.1.

Figure 6.1

The bouncing ball demo

You'll notice that the movement is slow, but smooth. This is partly because of GDI and partly because of my clearing the back buffer each time Prog_Loop is called.

Notice, though, in Prog_Loop, how I don't mess around too much between the calls to GetDC and ReleaseDC. I set up the filling RECT before I get there, and I take care of other stuff after I'm done.

```
void Prog_Loop()
{
	//set up rectangle for filling
	RECT rcFill;
	SetRect(&rcFill,0,0,dwDisplayWidth,dwDisplayHeight);
	//grab dc from back buffer
	HDC hdcSurf;
	lpddsBack->GetDC(&hdcSurf);
	//fill rectangle with black
	FillRect(hdcSurf,&rcFill,(HBRUSH)GetStockObject(BLACK_BRUSH));
	//show the ball

BitBlt(hdcSurf,ptBallPosition.x,ptBallPosition.y,gdicBall.GetWidth(),gdicBall.Get
Height(),gdicBall,0,0,SRCCOPY);
	//release dc
	lpddsBack->ReleaseDC(hdcSurf);
	//move the ball
	ptBallPosition.x+=ptBallVelocity.x;
	ptBallPosition.y+=ptBallVelocity.y;
	//bounds checking
	//left side
	if(ptBallPosition.x<=0) ptBallVelocity.x=abs(ptBallVelocity.x);
	//top side
	if(ptBallPosition.y<=0) ptBallVelocity.y=abs(ptBallVelocity.y);
	//right side
	if(ptBallPosition.x>=(int)dwDisplayWidth-gdicBall.GetWidth())
ptBallVelocity.x=-abs(ptBallVelocity.x);
	//bottom side
	if(ptBallPosition.y>=(int)dwDisplayHeight-gdicBall.GetHeight())
ptBallVelocity.y=-abs(ptBallVelocity.y);
	//flip surfaces
	lpddsPrime->Flip(NULL,DDFLIP_WAIT);
}
```

The code in bold is what is between `GetDC` and `ReleaseDC`, inclusive. I put absolutely *nothing* extraneous in that section. In reality, I shouldn't even have the function call to `GetStockObject` in there (heck, I even shouldn't be using GDI to do this, but this is an example).

So, we have now created a screen saver—a terribly slow screen saver. If you want to see why you should use back buffers, comment out the line with `Flip` in it, and then change `GetDC` and `ReleaseDC` to get and release from the primary surface. Or, if you're too lazy to do that, replace IsoHex6_1.cpp with IsoHex6_1A.cpp, where I did it for you. Running it again, you'll see how badly the ball flickers. Now imagine this happening with six or eight characters on the screen. Blech! And the defense rests. You're probably thinking that there has to be a better way, right? Of course there is.

Blt

The `IDirectDrawSurface7::Blt` function is the DirectDraw version of GDI's `BitBlt`, but it's faster. The reason it's faster is because DirectDraw doesn't give you a safety net like GDI does. In GDI, if one DC has a different pixel format than another, GDI converts it for you. This, of course, takes time, especially when the pixel formats are wildly different.

> **NOTE**
>
> **Technically, the statement about all surfaces' pixel formats being the same from a call to `CreateSurface` is not exactly true. However, for our purposes it is true enough, since we aren't dealing with any sort of specialized surface types.**

DirectDraw won't help you at all with pixel format conversion. It expects that both the source and destination have the same pixel format, and if they don't, you'll get garbage on the screen. Luckily, every surface created from a call to `IDirectDraw7::CreateSurface` has the same pixel format, so you only have to worry about pixel format conversion once, when you first load the bitmap onto a surface. In your case, this won't be too much of a problem because you'll use GDI to load the bitmap for you.

`Blt` also allows you to fill a rectangular area with a solid color, much in the same way `FillRect` does, but faster. You can stretch an image using `Blt`, and if the hardware acceleration is available you can even rotate it. You can also make use of a clipper when using `Blt`, but we'll get to clippers later.

For even less of a safety net, you can use `Blt`'s faster cousin, `BltFast`. `BltFast` is the fastest way that is supported by DirectDraw (it is possible to get faster using `Lock`/`Unlock`) to copy a rectangular image from one surface to another. No stretching, no clipping, no nothing. Any computations you need to do to make it work right are your problem.

Here's the `IDirectDrawSurface7::Blt` function:

```
HRESULT IDirectDrawSurface7::Blt(
  LPRECT lpDestRect,
  LPDIRECTDRAWSURFACE7 lpDDSrcSurface,
  LPRECT lpSrcRect,
  DWORD dwFlags,
  LPDDBLTFX lpDDBltFx
);
```

The parameters mirror somewhat the parameters of `BitBlt`. This returns `DD_OK` if successful. Table 6.5 explains the parameters.

Table 6.5 IDirectDrawSurface7::Blt Parameters

Blt Parameter	Purpose
`lpDestRect`	The destination rectangle. `NULL` is the entire surface.
`lpDDSrcSurface`	The source surface. `NULL` if not applicable.
`lpSrcRect`	The source rectangle. `NULL` if not applicable or the entire surface.
`dwFlags`	Flags specifying how you want the `Blt` to work
`lpDDBltFx`	A pointer to a `DDBLTFX` structure, with extra information about how the `Blt` is supposed to work. Used in conjunction with the `dwFlags` parameter.

Table 6.6 lists a handful of meaningful flags that can be passed in the `dwFlags` parameter—well, the flags that are meaningful to you, anyway.

Table 6.6 Selected Blt Flags

Blt Flag	Meaning
DDBLT_COLORFILL	This Blt is a color fill operation. This requries a non-null lpDDBltFx.
DDBLT_KEYSRC	This Blt is a partially transparent Blt (we'll check out color keys a bit later)
DDBLT_WAIT	The blitter (the hardware that performs blitting on the video card) must wait until the Blt is finished before returning
DDBLT_ROP	This Blt makes use of a raster operation (like SRCAND, SRCPAINT, and so on)

The DDBLTFX Structure

The DDBLTFX structure is another one that's like DDSURFACEDESC2, meaning it has a lot of useless members that either haven't been implemented yet or are never going to be implemented. Here's the structure, with the important members in bold:

```
typedef struct _DDBLTFX{
    DWORD dwSize;
    DWORD dwDDFX;
    DWORD dwROP;
    DWORD dwDDROP;
    DWORD dwRotationAngle;
    DWORD dwZBufferOpCode;
    DWORD dwZBufferLow;
    DWORD dwZBufferHigh;
    DWORD dwZBufferBaseDest;
    DWORD dwZDestConstBitDepth;
    union
    {
        DWORD                 dwZDestConst;
        LPDIRECTDRAWSURFACE lpDDSZBufferDest;
    } DUMMYUNIONNAMEN(1);
    DWORD dwZSrcConstBitDepth;
    union
    {
        DWORD                 dwZSrcConst;
        LPDIRECTDRAWSURFACE lpDDSZBufferSrc;
```

```
    } DUMMYUNIONNAMEN(2);
    DWORD dwAlphaEdgeBlendBitDepth;
    DWORD dwAlphaEdgeBlend;
    DWORD dwReserved;
    DWORD dwAlphaDestConstBitDepth;
    union
    {
        DWORD               dwAlphaDestConst;
        LPDIRECTDRAWSURFACE lpDDSAlphaDest;
    } DUMMYUNIONNAMEN(3);
    DWORD dwAlphaSrcConstBitDepth;
    union
    {
        DWORD               dwAlphaSrcConst;
        LPDIRECTDRAWSURFACE lpDDSAlphaSrc;
    } DUMMYUNIONNAMEN(4);
    union
    {
        DWORD               dwFillColor;
        DWORD               dwFillDepth;
        DWORD               dwFillPixel;
        LPDIRECTDRAWSURFACE lpDDSPattern;
    } DUMMYUNIONNAMEN(5);
    DDCOLORKEY ddckDestColorkey;
    DDCOLORKEY ddckSrcColorkey;
} DDBLTFX,FAR* LPDDBLTFX;
```

See what I mean? That's *huge!* And only three of the members have any meaning to you (not to say that none of the others are meaningful).

Making Use of a DDBLTFX

Much like a DDSURFACEDESC2, a DDBLTFX structure must first be cleared out, and the dwSize field has to be set, like so:

```
//clear our DDBLTFX
DDBLTFX ddbltfx;
memset(&ddbltfx,0,sizeof(DDBLTFX));
ddbltfx.dwSize=sizeof(DDBLTFX);
```

And to do a color fill, you set the dwFillColor field:

```
//set fill color
ddbltfx.dwFillColor=0;//zero is black
```

Now all you need is a destination rectangle, or can just use NULL if filling the entire surface.

```
RECT rcFill;
SetRect(0,0,dwDisplayWidth,dwDisplayHeight);
lpddsBack->Blt(&rcFill,NULL,NULL,DDBLT_WAIT | DDBLT_FILLCOLOR, &ddbltfx);
```

or

```
lpddsBack->Blt(NULL,NULL,NULL,DDBLT_WAIT | DDBLT_FILLCOLOR, &ddbltfx);
```

This solves your call to FillRect. You'll no longer need it.

Using Blt to Copy from Surface to Surface

Just doing a straight copy is no big deal. You don't need a DDBLTFX, and the only flag you need is DDBLT_WAIT. Other than that, it's just a matter of setting up the source and destination RECTs, like so:

```
RECT rcDst;
RECT rcSrc;
SetRect(&rcDst,DstX,DstY, DstX+DstWidth, DstY+DstHeight);
SetRect(&rcSrc,SrcX,SrcY, SrcX+SrcWidth, SrcY+SrcHeight);
```

Keep in mind, however, that if the RECTs have differing widths, you will have stretching, and unless there is hardware support for stretching, the software emulation won't be that great quality-wise.

Let's revise our little bouncing ball demo. Load up IsoHex6_2.cpp. The first thing I want to point out is that this example makes an additional surface, an off-screen surface called lpddsBall, onto which you load the picture of the ball.

```
//create an offscreen surface to contain the ball
//clear out ddsd
memset(&ddsd,0,sizeof(DDSURFACEDESC2));
ddsd.dwSize=sizeof(DDSURFACEDESC2);
//set ddsd flags
ddsd.dwFlags=DDSD_WIDTH | DDSD_HEIGHT | DDSD_CAPS;
//set width and height
ddsd.dwWidth=gdicBall.GetWidth();
ddsd.dwHeight=gdicBall.GetHeight();
//set caps
ddsd.ddsCaps.dwCaps=DDSCAPS_OFFSCREENPLAIN;
//create surface
```

```
lpdd->CreateSurface(&ddsd,&lpddsBall,NULL);
//grab dc from offscreen surface
HDC hdcSurf;
lpddsBall->GetDC(&hdcSurf);
//blit ball to surface
BitBlt(hdcSurf,0,0,gdicBall.GetWidth(),gdicBall.GetHeight(),gdicBall,0,0,SRC-
COPY);
//release dc
lpddsBall->ReleaseDC(hdcSurf);
```

Notice that you are still using `CGDICanvas` to load in your bitmap, and are using `GetDC/ReleaseDC` and `BitBlt` to get the image onto the surface.

Also, take note of the use of the `ptLastPosition` variable, an array of two `POINT`s. When moving the ball around in `Prog_Loop`, you clear out only the section of the screen that contained the ball two frames ago. Why two frames? Because there are two calls to `Flip` between the time a ball is shown and the time it is erased.

Confused? Let me explain. Let's say that the ball is moving 4 horizonal and 4 vertical pixels per frame. On the first frame (when there is still nothing on the primary surface), the ball's upper-left corner is at 0,0, where it gets drawn to the back buffer, and then the surfaces get flipped, and the ball shows up at 0,0 on the primary surface. Now the ball is at 4,4, gets drawn there, and gets flipped again. The ball image on the primary surface is at (4,4), and on the back buffer you have an image of the ball at (0,0)—the image of two frames ago. So, you erase the old image at (0,0) and draw a new one at (8,8) and flip it again. On the primary you now have it at (8,8) and on the back buffer at (4,4). See?

In a more complicated program (with a more complicated background, like a terrain map or something), you would probably be best served by copying the primary to the back buffer before restoring the old images (this way you'd have to keep track of only a single "last position"). For this example I wanted to make the program do as little work as possible.

Now that you are using `Blt`, the example is even smoother than the version that used GDI—so much smoother that I increased the speed by 4, and you don't even notice. If you look at the code, you'll see a lot of ugly stuff—all the clearings of `DDSURFACEDESC2`s and `DDBLTFX`s and the setting up of these structures. We're going to wrap these repetitive tasks into functions in just a bit.

Color Keying with Blt

One of the best parts of using `Blt` is the ability to make part of the image transparent by using a color key. To examine why having transparent pixels is important, take a look at IsoHex6_3.cpp. This example is an enhanced IsoHex6_2.cpp. The main difference is that there are now two balls instead of just one.

Watch closely as the program runs. When the balls are very close to one another, their rectangles overlap, as shown in Figure 6.2.

Figure 6.2

Overlapping rectangles; one ball erases part of another

This, as I'm sure you'll agree, is not good. In GDI you would use a bitmask, and you could do the same thing in DirectDraw, using the `dwRop` member of `DDBLTFX`. Support for `dwRop` is spotty, so we won't use it. However, DirectDraw gives us an easier solution.

There are two types of color keys—source and destination. With *source* color keying, you apply your key to the source, and then a color (or range of colors) of one surface is ignored when blitting to another surface. *Destination* color keying is different. It requires hardware support and is usually used only with video signals and the like, so I'm not going to cover it here.

To set a color key, you need to fill out a `DDCOLORKEY` structure:

```
typedef struct _DDCOLORKEY{
    DWORD dwColorSpaceLowValue;
    DWORD dwColorSpaceHighValue;
} DDCOLORKEY,FAR* LPDDCOLORKEY;
```

You may be pleasantly surprised to find DirectX has a structure that isn't as bloated as some others you've seen (like `DDSURFACEDESC2` and `DDBLTFX`).

There are two values in a `DDCOLORKEY`—a low and a high color value. This is in case you want to define a color space (a range of colors) and thus have more than one transparent color. Doing so requires hardware support, and the hardware support available for it is spotty, so try to get along with having only a single transparent color.

Setting up a DDCOLORKEY is pretty simple:

```
//set up a black color key
DDCOLORKEY ddck;
ddck.dwColorSpaceLowValue=0;
ddck.dwColorSpaceHighValue=0;
```

To set a surface's color key, you use IDirectDrawSurface7::SetColorKey:

```
HRESULT IDirectDrawSurface7::SetColorKey(
  DWORD dwFlags,
  LPDDCOLORKEY lpDDColorKey
);
```

The dwFlags parameter contains the type of color key you are assigning, which in this case will always be DDCKEY_SRCBLT. Other possible values include DDCKEY_DESTBLT, DDCKEY_SRCOVERLAY, DDCKEY_DESTOVERLAY, and combining any of these with DDCKEY_COLORSPACE (most of these require some sort of hardware support). So, setting the color key is pretty simple:

```
//assign color key
lpddsBall->SetColorKey(DDCKEY_SRCBLT,&ddck);
```

Finally, to make use of the color key, you add a DDBLT_KEYSRC to your Blt function:

```
lpddsBack->Blt(&rcDst,lpddsBall,&rcSrc,DDBLT_WAIT | DDBLT_KEYSRC, NULL);
```

The IsoHex6_3A.cpp example demonstrates this. Four lines of code were added, and one line of code was modified. The overlapping rectangle problem is gone, as you can see in Figure 6.3.

Figure 6.3

Source color keying

You could now have 100 balls on the screen bouncing around, and it would still be smooth and look right.

BltFast

Let me introduce you to `Blt`'s brother, `BltFast`. `BltFast` is in most cases a lot faster than `Blt`, because it doesn't do any range checking if there's a clipper involved. It also doesn't do stretching, color fills, or raster operations. In general, it doesn't give you any of the neat things that `Blt` can give you, except for transparency.

```
HRESULT IDirectDrawSurface7::BltFast(
  DWORD dwX,
  DWORD dwY,
  LPDIRECTDRAWSURFACE7 lpDDSrcSurface,
  LPRECT lpSrcRect,
  DWORD dwTrans
);
```

This returns `DD_OK` if successful. Table 6.7 explains the parameters.

Table 6.7 IDirectDrawSurface7::BltFast Parameters

BltFast Parameter	Purpose
`dwX`	Destination x-coordinate (upper-left)
`dwY`	Destination y-coordinate (upper-left)
`lpDDSrcSurface`	Source surface
`lpSrcRect`	Source rectangle
`dwTrans`	Type of transfer

Most of the parameters for `Blt` and `BltFast` are the same. There is only a single `RECT` parameter, however, because `BltFast` does not support scaling. Also, you'll note a lack of a `DDBLTFX` pointer. None of the special effects possible with `DDBLTFX` are available to you with `BltFast`.

The `dwTrans` parameter is similar to `Blt`'s `dwFlags` parameter, but with fewer options:

- DDBLTFAST_DESTCOLORKEY Uses the destination surface's destination color key
- DDBLTFAST_NOCOLORKEY Uses no color key
- DDBLTFAST_SRCCOLORKEY Uses the source surface's source color key
- DDBLTFAST_WAIT Waits until BltFast has finished before returning

These four options are the total of what is available to you with BltFast. It's not much, but speed comes at the price of flexibility.

Most of the examples will continue to use Blt rather than BltFast because of the capabilities it offers. However, don't be hesitant to use BltFast in a time-critical section of code. It can save you.

The Nitty-Gritty: Lock and Unlock

So far, I've presented the high-level ways to access a surface. Now we're going to explore the low-level way: using Lock and Unlock. When the speed of even the mighty BltFast just won't do, and you just *know* you can perform the operation faster, you can lock the surface memory and do the work yourself—doing so is the ultimate way of working without a net in DirectDraw.

Using IDirectDrawSurface7::Lock

Following is the function that locks the surface memory and fetches it for you so that you can do your own writing:

```
HRESULT IDirectDrawSurface7::Lock(
  LPRECT lpDestRect,
  LPDDSURFACEDESC2 lpDDSurfaceDesc,
  DWORD dwFlags,
  HANDLE hEvent
);
```

This returns DD_OK if successful. Table 6.8 explains the parameters.

Table 6.8 IDirectDrawSurface7::Lock Parameters

Lock Parameter	Purpose
lpDestRect	The rectangular area of the surface you want to lock
lpDDSurfaceDesc	A pointer to a DDSURFACEDESC2, which will be filled with the information you want
dwFlags	Flags specifying how to lock the surface
hEvent	Not supported. Use NULL.

You can lock different parts of the same surface, as long as the rectangles don't overlap. Some of the flags are shown in Table 6.9.

Table 6.9 Locking Flags

Flag	Meaning
DDLOCK_NOSYSLOCK	Tells DirectDraw not to do a WIN16 lock (which freezes the computer, making it impossible to get out other than by turning off the computer). Ignored if locking the primary surface.
DDLOCK_SURFACEMEMORYPTR	Tells DirectDraw that you want a pointer to the surface's memory.
DDLOCK_WAIT	Tells DirectDraw to wait for the lock to happen before returning. Useful if the surface is otherwise busy.
DDLOCK_WRITEONLY	Specifies that you only intend to write, not read, the surface.
DDLOCK_READONLY	Specifies that you only intend to read, not write, the surface.

Normally, the most useful combination is DDLOCK_SURFACEMEMORYPTR | DDLOCK_NOSYSLOCK | DDLOCK_WAIT, and to pass NULL as lpDestRect, thus locking the entire surface.

The lpDDSurfaceDesc parameter must simply be a clean DDSURFACEDESC2, with all 0s, and the dwSize parameter set.

Upon this function's return (assuming that it is successful), the specified area of the surface will be locked.

So, how do you write to the surface? The lpSurface and lPitch members of DDSURFACEDESC2 help you. lpSurface is the pointer to surface memory. Its original type is void*, so, depending on your bits per pixel, you need to cast it to some other type of pointer. On an 8-bit surface, you'd cast it to an unsigned char*. On a 16-bit surface, you'd use WORD*, and on a 32-bit surface, DWORD*. Since you primarily deal with 16-bit surfaces, your cast would look like this:

```
//cast the surface pointer
WORD* surfptr=(WORD*)ddsd.lpSurface;
```

The `lPitch` member contains a value indicating how many bytes make up a horizontal line on the surface. This is bytes, not pixels. To get the number of pixels per horizontal line, you have to divide `lPitch` by the number of bytes per pixel.

```
int pixelsperrow=ddsd.lPitch/(bitsperpix-
el/8);
```

After you have done this, you can plot to any part of the locked area:

```
surfptr[x+y*pixelsperrow]=0;//write a black
pixel at x,y
```

> **NOTE**
>
> **Logically, on an 800×600×16 surface, `lPitch` *should* be 1600 (800 pixels wide, 16 bits per pixel, and 8 bits per byte). This is not always so. Different video cards align their memory differently, so `lPitch` might extend past the surface a little. This is just something to keep in mind. Don't hardcode your surface pitches, because even though this may work on your machine, the image will likely look garbled if you take it to your friend's house to show him.**

Now that we're down to the pixel-plotting level, it's time to talk about pixel formats in more detail. The only real pixel format I've discussed so far is `COLORREF`, which you use the `RGB` macro to make. Each of the components (red, green, and blue) has 8 bits, for a total of 24 bits.

But what happens in a 16-bit surface like the ones you've been using? The image in the ball demo loaded up fine because you used GDI, which did the conversion for you. But now you're operating without any nets, using `Lock` to get the most direct access to your surface. What do you do? Well, you examine the surface's pixel format by using `IDirectDrawSurface7::GetPixelFormat`.

```
HRESULT GetPixelFormat(
  LPDDPIXELFORMAT lpDDPixelFormat
);
```

The `lpDDPixelFormat` parameter is simply a pointer to a `DDPIXELFORMAT` structure. You've seen this structure once before, when you were doing display mode enumeration.

```
typedef struct _DDPIXELFORMAT{
    DWORD dwSize;
    DWORD dwFlags;
    DWORD dwFourCC;
    union
    {
        DWORD dwRGBBitCount;
        DWORD dwYUVBitCount;
        DWORD dwZBufferBitDepth;
        DWORD dwAlphaBitDepth;
        DWORD dwLuminanceBitCount;
        DWORD dwBumpBitCount;
```

```
    } DUMMYUNIONNAMEN(1);
    union
    {
        DWORD dwRBitMask;
        DWORD dwYBitMask;
        DWORD dwStencilBitDepth;
        DWORD dwLuminanceBitMask;
        DWORD dwBumpDuBitMask;
    } DUMMYUNIONNAMEN(2);
    union
    {
        DWORD dwGBitMask;
        DWORD dwUBitMask;
        DWORD dwZBitMask;
        DWORD dwBumpDvBitMask;
    } DUMMYUNIONNAMEN(3);
    union
    {
        DWORD dwBBitMask;
        DWORD dwVBitMask;
        DWORD dwStencilBitMask;
        DWORD dwBumpLuminanceBitMask;
    } DUMMYUNIONNAMEN(4);
    union
    {
        DWORD dwRGBAlphaBitMask;
        DWORD dwYUVAlphaBitMask;
        DWORD dwLuminanceAlphaBitMask;
        DWORD dwRGBZBitMask;
        DWORD dwYUVZBitMask;
    } DUMMYUNIONNAMEN(5);
} DDPIXELFORMAT, FAR* LPDDPIXELFORMAT;
```

I've bolded the most important fields. When you retrieve the pixel format, you first have to clear out the DDPIXELFORMAT structure, just as you do with DDSURFACEDESC2 and DDBLTFX.

```
//clear out pixel format
DDPIXELFORMAT ddpf;
memset(&ddpf,0,sizeof(DDPIXELFORMAT));
ddpf.dwSize=sizeof(DDPIXELFORMAT);
//retrieve pixel format of primary surface
lpddsPrime->GetPixelFormat(&ddpf);
```

Once you have the surface's pixel format, you can use the members of DDPIXELFORMAT to help with your writing of pixels. The three members, dwRBitMask, dwGBitMask, and dwBBitMask, are binary representations of pure red, green, and blue for your surface. DDPIXELFORMAT also shows which bits are valid for each of the components.

For 16-bit surfaces, there are two common pixel formats. These formats are called RGB555 and RGB565, and they look something like the following:

RGB555

Red mask	0111110000000000
Green mask	0000001111100000
Blue mask	0000000000011111

RGB565

Red mask	1111100000000000
Green mask	0000011111100000
Blue mask	0000000000011111

The only real difference is the extra green bit in RGB565. Our eyes are more sensitive to green than to red or blue.

On certain odd video cards, you'll get a BGR instead of an RGB pixel format, meaning that the masks for red and blue are switched. These video cards are pretty rare, but they do exist. For this reason, you cannot make any assumptions about a pixel format, just as you can't make assumptions about a surface's pitch. Which raises the question, How can you plot pixels if you don't know the pixel format?

Since the pixel format of a surface is never guaranteed to be the same from one machine to the next, writing code to write pixels to a surface may seem impossible. Believe me, it's not. The trick is to use a known and stable pixel format that never changes (COLORREF) and to convert the values into the pixel format of the surface on which you are working, similar to what GDI does. If you have a limited number of colors that you work with a great deal, you can convert them all at once, keep them in a lookup table, and use them when you need them.

In a COLORREF, each of red, green, and blue are values from 0 to 255. 0 indicates that none of the component is present, and 255 indicates that 100% of the component is present. Logically, then, you could convert R, G, and B into values from 0.0 to 1.0 by dividing by 255 and storing them as a float. You can take this value and multiply it by the appropriate mask, such as ddpf.dwRBitMask for red, since the mask value indicated 100% of the color component present. Since a fractional component (extra bits that aren't in the mask) might be set by this multiplication, you can logically AND the mask on to the resulting value. Finally, after you do this for all the components and logically OR the three values together, you will achieve the pixel format conversion from COLORREF to native format.

Following are two functions that will allow you to convert back and forth from COLORREF to native DirectDraw pixel format. Keep in mind that they are not to be used in a time-critical section—there are too many multiplications and divisions to make it really efficient.

```
//from dd pixel to colorref
COLORREF ConvertDDColor(DWORD dwColor, DDPIXELFORMAT* pddpf)
{
	//extract color components
	DWORD dwRed=dwColor & pddpf->dwRBitMask;
	DWORD dwGreen=dwColor & pddpf->dwGBitMask;
	DWORD dwBlue=dwColor & pddpf->dwBBitMask;
	//multiply color components by max colorref value (255)
	dwRed*=255;
	dwGreen*=255;
	dwBlue*=255;
	//divide by masks
	dwRed/=pddpf->dwRBitMask;
	dwGreen/=pddpf->dwGBitMask;
	dwBlue/=pddpf->dwBBitMask;
	//return converted color
	return(RGB(dwRed,dwGreen,dwBlue));
}

//from colorref to dd pixel
DWORD ConvertColorRef(COLORREF crColor, DDPIXELFORMAT* pddpf)
{
	//extract color components
	DWORD dwRed=GetRValue(crColor);
	DWORD dwGreen=GetGValue(crColor);
	DWORD dwBlue=GetBValue(crColor);
	//multiply color components by max ddpixel value (the mask)
	dwRed*=pddpf->dwRBitMask;
	dwGreen*=pddpf->dwGBitMask;
	dwBlue*=pddpf->dwBBitMask;
	//divide by max colorref (255)
	dwRed/=255;
	dwGreen/=255;
	dwBlue/=255;
	//logical and with mask, to avoid fractions
	dwRed&=pddpf->dwRBitMask;
	dwGreen&=pddpf->dwGBitMask;
```

```
        dwBlue&=pddpf->dwBBitMask;
        //merge together, and return the result
        return(dwRed | dwGreen | dwBlue);
}
```

NOTE

Optimization nuts may be wondering why I divided by 255 instead of 256. If I were dividing by 256 I could use a bit-shifting operator, which would be much faster than doing the division myself. Point taken. However, I have tested doing it both ways, and I have found that dividing by 256 erroneously converts some of the values. Naturally, the errors aren't significant enough to make the image look very different, but if you are using a color key other than black, there can be problems when you use these functions to help set the color key.

OK, enough about pixel formats! Let's wrap up this part about locking the surface.

Finally, after you've locked the surface and done whatever you need to do to it, you have to unlock it.

```
HRESULT IDirectDrawSurface7::Unlock(
  LPRECT lpRect
);
```

The `lpRect` parameter specifies what area you are unlocking. (It's `NULL` if you originally locked the entire surface.) As when using `GetDC`/`ReleaseDC` on a surface, you should similarly not take too much time between calls to `Lock` and `Unlock`. I won't show any examples of using `Lock`/`Unlock` on surfaces—this will have to be one area you explore on your own. This type of low-level code tends to get convoluted and confusing, and my goal here is not to confuse, but to bring about understanding.

A DirectDraw Wrapper

Speaking of convoluted, have you noticed how much bulkier the DirectDraw examples have been compared to the examples of earlier chapters? Sheesh! All the `DDSURFACEDESC2`s and `DDBLTFX`s and so on...enough to really work your nerves, right?

I took the liberty of making a little group of functions to help you with these rather repetitive tasks. They are contained in DDFuncs.h and DDFuncs.cpp. The following sections contain a brief summary.

DDSURFACEDESC2 Functions

This first batch deals with setting up DDSURFACEDESC2 structures.

- **DDSD_Clear**
  ```
  void DDSD_Clear(DDSURFACEDESC2* pddsd);
  ```
  This function clears out the structure and sets the size. Beats the hell out of using memset all the time.
- **DDSD_PrimarySurface**
  ```
  void DDSD_PrimarySurface(DDSURFACEDESC2* pddsd);
  ```
  This function sets up a surface description for a primary surface, with no back buffer. It cleans out the surface description first, of course.
- **DDSD_PrimarySurfaceWBackBuffer**
  ```
  void DDSD_PrimarySurfaceWBackBuffer(DDSURFACEDESC2* pddsd, DWORD
  dwBackBufferCount);
  ```
  This function sets up a surface description for a primary surface *with* a back buffer.
- **DDSD_OffscreenSurface**
  ```
  void DDSD_OffscreenSurface(DDSURFACEDESC2* pddsd,DWORD dwWidth, DWORD
  dwHeight);
  ```
  This function sets up a surface description for an off-screen surface of a given width and height.

DDSCAPS2 Functions

This next group deals with DDSCAPS2 structures.

- **DDSCAPS_Clear**
  ```
  void DDSCAPS_Clear(DDSCAPS2* pddscaps);
  ```
  This function clears out a DDSCAPS2 structure. Yes, you could use memset, and you'd have the same number of lines. Shhh!
- **DDSCAPS_BackBuffer**
  ```
  void DDSCAPS_BackBuffer(DDSCAPS2* pddscaps);
  ```
  This function sets up a DDSCAPS2 structure for a back buffer.

DDBLTFX Functions

The DDBLTFX function group contains functions that manipulate DDBLTFX structures.

- **DDBLTFX_Clear**
  ```
  void DDBLTFX_Clear(DDBLTFX* pddbltfx);
  ```
- **DDBLTFX_ColorFill**
  ```
  void DDBLTFX_ColorFill(DDBLTFX* pddbltfx,DWORD dwColor);
  ```

Pixel Format Functions

Now, pixel formats.

- **DDPF_Clear**

  `void DDPF_Clear(DDPIXELFORMAT* pddpf);`

  This function clears out a `DDPIXELFORMAT` and sets the `dwSize` member.
- **ConvertDDColor**

  `COLORREF ConvertDDColor(DWORD dwColor, DDPIXELFORMAT* pddpf);`

  Converts from a native DirectDraw pixel to a `COLORREF` based on a pixel format.
- **ConvertColorRef**

  `DWORD ConvertColorRef(COLORREF crColor, DDPIXELFORMAT* pddpf);`

  Converts a `COLORREF` to a DirectDraw native pixel based on a pixel format

LPDIRECTDRAW7 Functions

Next are the functions for creating and releasing `IDirectDraw7` interfaces.

- **LPDD_Create**

  `LPDIRECTDRAW7 LPDD_Create(HWND hWnd,DWORD dwCoopLevel);`

  Creates an `IDirectDraw7` interface and sets a cooperative level.
- **LPDD_Release**

  `void LPDD_Release(LPDIRECTDRAW7* lplpdd);`

  Performs a safe release of an `IDirectDraw7`.

LPDIRECTDRAWSURFACE7 Functions

These are functions to replace the long and messy code required for surface creation.

- **LPDDS_CreatePrimary**

  ```
  LPDIRECTDRAWSURFACE7 LPDDS_CreatePrimary(LPDIRECTDRAW7 lpdd,DWORD
  dwBackBufferCount);
  ```

  Creates an `IDirectDrawSurface7` that will serve as the primary surface, with or without attached back buffers.
- **LPDDS_GetSecondary**

  `LPDIRECTDRAWSURFACE7 LPDDS_GetSecondary(LPDIRECTDRAWSURFACE7 lpdds);`

  Retrieves an attached surface (such as a back buffer).
- **LPDDS_CreateOffscreen**

  ```
  LPDIRECTDRAWSURFACE7 LPDDS_CreateOffscreen(LPDIRECTDRAW7 lpdd,DWORD
  dwWidth,DWORD dwHeight);
  ```

  Creates an off-screen surface with an arbitrary width and height.

- **LPDDS_LoadFromFile**
  `LPDIRECTDRAWSURFACE7 LPDDS_LoadFromFile(LPDIRECTDRAW7 lpdd,LPCTSTR lpszFileName);`
  Creates a new surface just large enough to load and hold the bitmap file.
- **LPDDS_ReloadFromFile**
  `void LPDDS_ReloadFromFile(LPDIRECTDRAWSURFACE7 lpdds, LPCTSTR lpszFileName);`
  Use this if you ever need to reload a bitmap onto a surface.
- **LPDDS_Release**
  `void LPDDS_Release(LPDIRECTDRAWSURFACE7* lplpdds);`
  Performs a safe release of an `IDirectDrawSurface7`.
- **LPDDS_SetSrcColorKey**
  `void LPDDS_SetSrcColorKey(LPDIRECTDRAWSURFACE7 lpdds,DWORD dwColor);`
  Sets a single source color key for a surface.

Tasks Not Included in the Wrapper

Please note that I do *not* have any functions in this little wrapper to do `Blt`, `BltFast`, `GetDC/ReleaseDC`, or `Lock/Unlock`. This is because making such functions would add unneeded overhead. Of course, you can still use some of the `DDBLTFX_*` functions to assist in your color fills and other special effects.

A wrapper should serve two purposes. First, it should make development faster. This it will do—instead of lines and lines of setting up your `DDSURFACEDESC2` structures, you can take care of this in a single function call. Second, a wrapper should aid in debugging. This is where my wrapper falls short. If you look through the code, there is absolutely *no* check of the return values from the DirectDraw calls. Naturally, when it comes time to make your own wrapper or engine, you will want to include these facilities.

That pretty much covers the basics of `IDirectDrawSurface7`, with the exception of one topic.

Empowering the User

You know that you can press Alt+Tab to switch between the calculator tool, paint program, sound recorder, and the bazillion other Windows applications that you may have open (I tend to have at least six open at a time). In a full-screen exclusive mode application, you have total control over video resources. In windowed mode, these same video resources have to be shared by all applications. When you hit Alt+Tab to switch from a full-screen exclusive mode application to a windowed application, you may lose some or all of the video resources you have been using if Windows needs them, whether you like it or not.

You could respond to the `WM_SYSCHAR` event (it's the window message that occurs when a system character—anything with an Alt+???—is pressed) and make sure that you can't switch out of the application. But you don't really want to do this, for a number of reasons. First, by doing so you defeat some of the Windows features that experienced users are used to. Second, if your application freezes, the user will be left with no alternative but to turn the machine off and then back on.

The other option is to let Windows seize the video resources when another application is activated and then seize them back when the user switches back. This is the most Windows friendly way to go. To do so, you need to respond to the `WM_ACTIVATEAPP` window message (see Chapter 1, "Introduction to WIN32 Programming," for a refresher). When `wParam` is nonzero, your application is the one being activated. When `wParam` is 0, it is being deactivated.

While deactivated, you don't want to do any rendering, so you should set some sort of "pause" state. When you are reactivated, you want to make sure that any of the surfaces in video memory are restored (since the video resources could have been preempted by Windows).

In older versions of DirectDraw, you had to check each surface to see if it was "lost" in this way, and then restore it if so. In DirectX 7, though, you can do all that with a single call to `IDirectDraw7::RestoreAllSurfaces`:

```
HRESULT IDirectDraw7::RestoreAllSurfaces();
```

`RestoreAllSurfaces` just reallocates the memory for a surface. It does not restore the contents. You have to do that yourself by reloading the images from disk. (The wrapper function `LPDDS_ReloadFromFile` is quite handy in this regard.)

IsoHex6_4.cpp is the final example in this chapter. It takes all that you have learned thus far and applies it to make your little bouncy-ball demo a solid DirectDraw application. The main source file is a bit shorter than IsoHex6_3A.cpp, although IsoHex6_4 is still over 400 lines long. (400 lines isn't very much, and for most of it, only one in three lines is an actual piece of code.) Four hundred lines, not counting the lines in GDICanvas.cpp or DDFuncs.cpp, and all you're doing is making a few balls bounce. No wonder a professional game usually has millions of lines of code!

Summary

In the end, it isn't the number of lines of code or the size of the executable that counts—it's performance. Hopefully I've given you enough to get started. We've gone over a lot of stuff in this chapter; here are a few things to keep in mind.

- An application has one primary surface and may or may not have back buffers.
- Off-screen surfaces can be used to store bitmaps until they are needed.
- You can use GDI with DirectDraw, but you should limit how often you do so.
- `Blt` is good for performing color fills and moving blocks from one surface to another.
- Color keys are a way to achieve transparency.
- `BltFast` is a faster way to move blocks of color from one surface to another.
- To work without a net, you can use `Lock`/`Unlock`.

CHAPTER 7

IDirectDrawClipper Objects and Windowed DirectDraw

- Using IDirectDrawClipper

I've talked quite a bit about DirectDraw surfaces and the capabilities of functions like `Blt`. In that discussion I mentioned briefly the ability to clip the output of `Blt` by use of a clipper. In this chapter we'll be covering just that. I'll also cover the (sort of) amazing world of DirectDraw in a windowed application. Oh, stop groaning! It'll be fun—I promise.

Using IDirectDrawClipper

A clipper in DirectDraw serves the same purpose as a region in GDI—it limits output to a certain area, as Figure 7.1 illustrates.

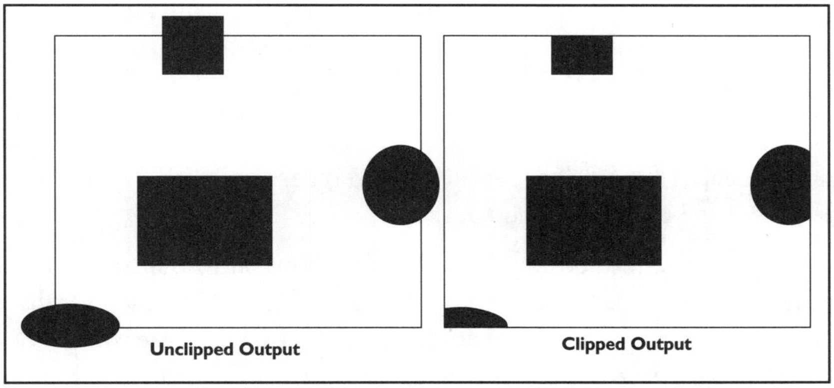

Figure 7.1

Clipped versus unclipped

This can be especially important when you're using the entire drawing area of a surface as the clipping region and blitting images that do not entirely fit in the display. In DirectDraw, drawing out of bounds usually doesn't draw anything unless you are making use of a clipper.

Here's something you should always keep in mind: `Blt` works with a clipper, but `BltFast` doesn't. Using a clipper is somewhat slower than not using one. However, when you're in a windowed environment (as you'll be in the second half of this chapter), a clipper is not only important, it's essential.

Creating Clippers

There are two ways to create a clipper—`DirectDrawCreateClipper` and `IDirectDraw7::CreateClipper`.

```
HRESULT WINAPI DirectDrawCreateClipper(
  DWORD dwFlags,
  LPDIRECTDRAWCLIPPER FAR *lplpDDClipper,
  IUnknown FAR *pUnkOuter
);
```

As with all other DirectDraw functions, this returns `DD_OK` if successful.

Of the three parameters for `DirectDrawCreateClipper`, only one of them is functional: `lplpDDClipper`. The other two, `dwFlags` and `pUnkOuter`, are not used, and they must be 0 and `NULL`, respectively. Hooray for unused parameters!

```
HRESULT IDirectDraw7::CreateClipper(
  DWORD dwFlags,
  LPDIRECTDRAWCLIPPER FAR *lplpDDClipper,
  IUnknown FAR *pUnkOuter
);
```

This returns `DD_OK` on success.

Hey, look! It got the exact same parameter list as `DirectDrawCreateClipper`, and the same rules apply…ignore `dwFlags` and `pUnkOuter` by placing 0 and `NULL`.

So, what is the difference between these two methods of clipper creation? Not much, as it turns out. `DirectDrawCreateClipper` creates a clipper that isn't "owned" by a DirectDraw object, meaning that it can be used by any surface, even those created with a different `IDirectDraw7` object. Since you will never have more than one `IDirectDraw7` object, it seems silly to use `DirectDrawCreateClipper`, so let's just go with using `IDirectDraw7::CreateClipper`.

As you have seen, there isn't much to the actual creation of a clipper—just the following code:

```
//globals
LPDIRECTDRAWCLIPPER lpddclip=NULL;
//create clipper (lpdd is our IDirectDraw7)
lpdd->CreateClipper(0,&lpddclip,NULL);
```

Setting up a Clipping Region

When you initially create a clipper, it contains nothing—a null clipping region, which is useless. In order for a clipper to be useful, you first must fill it with information that describes the clipping region.

You do this is by using IDirectDrawClipper::SetClipList:

```
HRESULT IDirectDrawClipper::SetClipList(
  LPRGNDATA lpClipList,
  DWORD dwFlags
);
```

This returns DD_OK if successful.

As with most of the clipper functions, dwFlags is not used and must be 0. The important parameter here is lpClipList, which is a pointer to a RGNDATA structure. A RGNDATA structure is a variable length type (which means you usually have to work with it through pointers, malloc, and memcpy).

```
typedef struct _RGNDATA {
    RGNDATAHEADER rdh;
    char          Buffer[1];
} RGNDATA, *PRGNDATA;
```

This contains two members—rdh (a RGNDATAHEADER) and a buffer of chars. The char buffer is where the variable length comes in. Starting at this location is RGNDATA's clip list. It can be as long or as short as needed to describe the clipping area.

Here is the RGNDATAHEADER structure:

```
typedef struct _RGNDATAHEADER {
    DWORD dwSize;
    DWORD iType;
    DWORD nCount;
    DWORD nRgnSize;
    RECT  rcBound;
} RGNDATAHEADER, *PRGNDATAHEADER;
```

The RGNDATAHEADER describes the clipping region overall—the type of clipping region (iType), the number of rectangles (nCount), and the bounding rectangle for all the rectangles in the clip list (rcBound). Set dwSize to sizeof(RGNDATAHEADER), and set nRgnSize to 0.

Does it sound like a real pain to work with these structures? It is. That's why you're not going to play with RGNDATA and RGNDATAHEADER. Instead, you're going to make your clippers by creating and combining GDI regions.

If you've spent any time working with RGNDATA, you know what kind of problems it has. After months of research (OK…only a few hours), I found out that instead of working with the clumsy structure, you can create HRGNs and extract the RGNDATA structure once you've let GDI make the clipping area you want.

Now for a brief review. Table 7.1 lists the functions most commonly used to create regions for GDI. For the most part, you'll want to try and stick to CreateRectRgn as much as possible, because it is the least slow of the regions as far as clipping is concerned. However, you can use any region you create with these functions, extract the rectangle list, and use it to set a DirectDrawClipper's clip list.

Table 7.1 Region Creation Functions

Function	Type of Region Created
CreateEllipticRgn	An elliptical region
CreatePolygonRgn	A polygonal region
CreateRectRgn	A rectangular region
CreateRoundRectRgn	A rounded rectangular region

After you use one of these functions to create a clipping region, you have to get it out into a RGNDATA structure, since that is what IDirectDrawClipper::SetClipList takes. To do this, you use the GetRegionData function:

```
DWORD GetRegionData(
  HRGN hRgn,              // handle to region
  DWORD dwCount,          // size of region data buffer
  LPRGNDATA lpRgnData     // region data buffer
);
```

Table 7.2 explains the parameter list.

Table 7.2 GetRegionData Parameters

GetRegionData Parameter	Purpose
hRgn	The region for which you are extracting the RGNDATA
dwCount	The size of the buffer that will receive the information
lpRgnData	A pointer to the buffer

This is one of Windows' many functions that retrieve data into a buffer, and it also serves as a function to retrieve the size required for the buffer by passing NULL as lpRgnData. So, your extraction is actually performed in a number of steps:

```
//retrieve buffer size
DWORD dwBufSize=GetRegionData(hrgn,0,NULL);
//allocate large enough buffer
LPRGNDATA lprd=(LPRGNDATA)malloc(dwBufSize);
//extract region data
GetRegionData(hrgn,dwBufSize,lprd);
//assign clip list to ddclip
lpddclip->SetClipList(lprd,0);
```

Assigning a Clipper to a Surface

Just as an HRGN by itself isn't very useful, an IDirectDrawClipper is of no use in a void. It has to be assigned to an IDirectDrawSurface7 by using IDirectDrawSurface7::SetClipper:

```
HRESULT SetClipper(
  LPDIRECTDRAWCLIPPER lpDDClipper
);
```

This returns DD_OK if successful.

At last! A function involving clippers that doesn't have a useless parameter in it. lpDDClipper is a pointer to the clipper that you are assigning to the surface. You can assign a clipper to more than one surface at the same time (usually, you'll only assign a clipper to the back buffer, but there are exceptions).

To remove a clipper from a surface, you can pass NULL in the call to IDirectDrawSurface7::SetClipper.

Let's do a quick example. Load up IsoHex7_1.cpp. This is based on IsoHex6_4.cpp. Two functions involving clippers have been added to DDFuncs.h and DDFuncs.cpp. Figure 7.2 shows the output.

Figure 7.2

IsoHex7_1.cpp output

By far the most common use of a clipper is to encompass the entire screen. However, in many games, this isn't always the best plan. You may have a playing area, a status bar on one side, a message bar on the top or bottom, etc., etc. In cases like these, writing only to the appropriate area takes some careful planning on your part. Clippers can help—you can make one clipper for the view area, one for the status bar, one for the message bar, and so on, and use `IDirectDrawSurface7::SetClipper` to switch between them as needed.

That's about all I have to say for now about clippers. They are a powerful tool when used correctly, but they are not always the best solution. In a game where speed really counts, you will want to use your own sort of clipping. We will visit clippers again briefly in a moment.

Windowed DirectDraw

You may be wondering why I'm covering windowed DirectDraw at all. DirectDraw games are all full-screen, right? Well, true... mostly. However, it is always a good thing to give your user the ability to choose whether to run full-screen or in a window. Empowering the user to do so is important, just like when giving the user the ability to switch display modes based on personal preferences.

Differences between Full-Screen and Windowed DirectDraw

There aren't actually that many differences between a full-screen DirectDraw application and a windowed one. However, the changes that do exist are important. They are summarized in Table 7.3.

Table 7.3 Full-Screen versus Windowed DirectDraw

Item	Full-Screen	Windowed
Flags sent to `IDirectDraw7::SetCooperativeLevel`	`DDSCL_FULLSCREEN | DDSCL_EXCLUSIVE | DDSCL_ALLOWREBOOT`	`DDSCL_NORMAL`
Call `IDirectDraw7::SetDisplayMode`	Yes	No
Create back buffers	Yes	No
Use a clipper	Optional	Strongly suggested

Display Modes

Since you can't call `SetDisplayMode`, you are stuck with whatever the user has currently set up. If the user is in an 8-bit mode, so are you. Being stuck in 8-bit mode will probably mean that your game will not look as good as it can, and it also means that if you want to support this mode, you'll have to make use of an `IDirectDrawPalette`.

First, you can't allow the program to run in an 8-bit mode. You can determine how many bits per pixel the display has by calling `IDirectDraw7::GetDisplayMode`:

```
HRESULT GetDisplayMode(
  LPDDSURFACEDESC2 lpDDSurfaceDesc2
);
```

This returns `DD_OK` if successful. `lpDDSurfaceDesc2` points to a `DDSURFACEDESC2`. Examine the pixel format to retrieve the bits per pixel. This way is not very empowering to your users, and it might completely alienate them. And if they don't play your game, they don't tell their friends to buy it, and you make less money (and you have to settle for a Neon instead of a Ferrari).

Second, you can detect the bits per pixel. If the current display mode set by the user shows that it's in an 8-bit mode or less, pop up a message box warning him that the display might not look correct in that mode and asking if he would like to continue (see Figure 7.3).

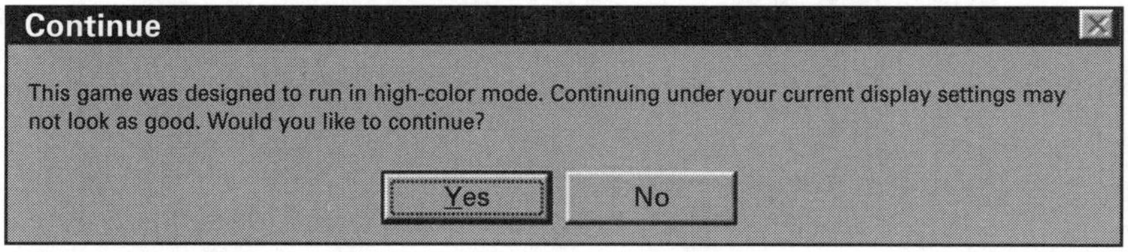

Figure 7.3

A friendly way to warn about 8-bit graphic performance

Now the user has been warned, and he is less likely to e-mail you telling you that your game sucks. Little touches like this will make your games seem more professional.

No Back Buffers

Another problem with windowed DirectDraw is that you can't make use of a back buffer, which means you can't use `Flip`. You can solve this problem by making an off-screen surface that is the exact size (or the maximum size) of the client area, and once per frame, blitting from this surface to the primary. In some cases, it won't be as smooth as when using a back buffer, but that's the price of being in a window.

Which brings me to the problem of the primary surface's coordinates. No matter whether you are full-screen or windowed, the primary surface takes up the entire area of the visible surface. This is significant. It means that (0,0) on the primary surface is (0,0) on the screen, and not (0,0) in your window's client area—unless your client area has (0,0) at screen (0,0). Luckily, Windows gives you the ability to convert between client coordinates and screen coordinates, with the `ClientToScreen` function:

```
BOOL ClientToScreen(
  HWND hWnd,        // handle to window
  LPPOINT lpPoint  // screen coordinates
);
```

This returns nonzero on success or 0 on failure. Table 7.4 explains the parameter list.

Table 7.4 ClientToScreen Parameters

ClientToScreen Parameter	Purpose
`hWnd`	Window from which you are converting client coordinates
`lpPoint`	On entry, the client coordinate; on exit, the screen coordinate (pointer)

When you want to blit to only the window, you just convert from the (0,0) client coordinate to whatever the screen coordinate is, like so:

```
//(0,0) client coordinate
POINT pt;
pt.x=0;
pt.y=0;
//convert to screen coordinate
ClientToScreen(hWndMain,&pt);
//pt now contains the screen coordinates
```

Simple, no?

You could convert the client to screen coordinates every frame, but you don't necessarily have to. You can just respond to the `WM_MOVE` window message, and keep the screen coordinates for the (0,0) client coordinate in a global somewhere.

Clippers in Windowed DirectDraw

In full-screen DirectDraw, clippers are optional and often aren't used. In windowed DirectDraw they are almost mandatory, because the viewable area of the primary screen through your window may change based on other windows in the system and the placement of your window. Fortunately, you don't have to do the clipping by yourself; you can have DirectDraw automatically do it by calling `IDirectDrawClipper:SetHWnd`:

```
HRESULT IDirectDrawClipper::SetHWnd(
  DWORD dwFlags,
  HWND hWnd
);
```

This returns DD_OK if successful. The dwFlags parameter must be 0. The hWnd parameter is a window handle from which the clipper obtains the clip list. Once you call this function and then call the primary surface's SetClipper function, that's it—DirectDraw takes care of the rest.

IsoHex7_2.cpp puts all this stuff about windowed DirectDraw into practice. Figure 7.4 shows the output.

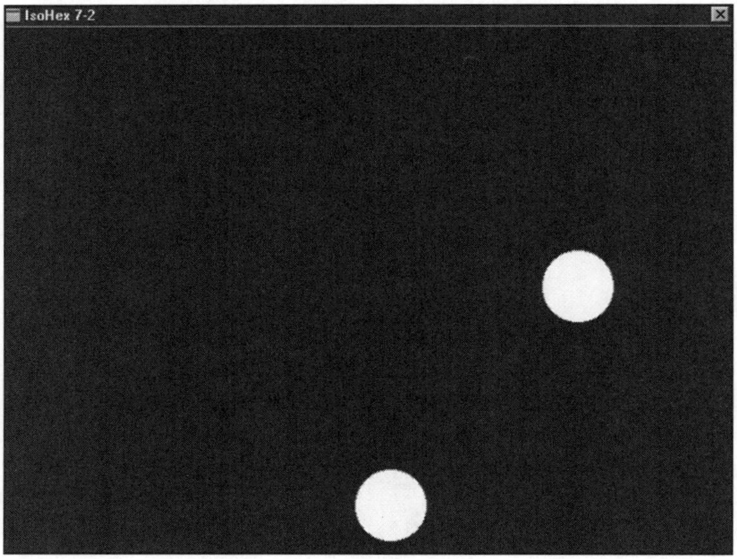

Figure 7.4

Balls bouncing in a window

The first thing you'll notice when running this program is that the balls seem to bounce around much more quickly. However, you should also notice that the smoothness is gone and the balls leave an afterimage.

The main differences between the full-screen bouncing ball demo and the windowed one are as follows:

- The IDirectDraw7 object has a cooperative mode of DDSCL_NORMAL.
- Modes are not enumerated.
- The primary surface has no back buffers.
- The "back buffer" that is created is in actuality an off-screen surface.
- A variable called ptPrimeBlt keeps track of the (0,0) client position in screen coordinates. It is first calculated in Prog_Init and is recalculated in response to WM_MOVE.
- Instead of two previous positions for the ball, you keep track of only one (since the contents of the "back buffer" and the primary do not get exchanged).
- Because your "back buffer" is not a true back buffer, you have to release it the same as any other surface.
- The demo checks to see that the bpp of the display mode is at least 16 and displays a warning message if it is not.

Summary

This finishes up all you really need to know about DirectDraw to get started. As you become more familiar with DirectDraw you'll naturally want to explore more. I regret that I cannot cover it in more detail, but I need to get on to the really fun stuff.

Here's what you have learned:

- You can clip output with `IDirectDrawClipper`.
- Empowering the user is important.
- Windowed DirectDraw is a pain in the rear.

CHAPTER 8

DirectSound

- The WIN32 Way to Play Sounds
- The IDirect Sound Object
- The IDirect Sound Buffer Object
- Using WAV Files

Just as you used DirectDraw to seize control of your display, you will use DirectSound to grab the resources of your sound card. DirectSound and DirectDraw have a lot in common as far as how things are set up, but we'll get to that in a moment.

First, a little history. Back in the Stone Age of about 5 years ago, using digital sound on the PC was a Herculean task. There were hundreds of sound card manufacturers, and each one had its quirks. If you wanted to write a game that used them, you had to choose which you were going to support and stay with it. It was indeed a dark day for the rebellion. After Windows 95 came out, there was only limited support for playing sounds, and there were problems with latency (the time between when you told a sound to play and when it actually started playing), so using digital sound in Windows 95 was something of a joke.

That was before DirectX came out. With DirectSound, you no longer have to worry about who the manufacturer of your sound card is. Most sound cards now have drivers that make them compatible with DirectSound, emulating features if needed. It's a beautiful thing.

Even though this book really isn't about sound programming, I felt a certain obligation to at least do the basics of DirectSound. Nowadays, any game written is required to have sound, and usually music as well.

The Nature of Sound

You may or may not have ever given thought to the nature or physics of sound. It's really a fascinating subject. Well, not as fascinating as game programming, of course, but it's still pretty darn neat!

How Our Ears Work (the Really Simplified Version)

Our ears are truly magnificent instruments. They allow us to interpret subtle changes in air pressure to gain clues about our environment. As I type this, I am listening to the blowing sound of my computer's power source fan and the clicks of my fingers on the keys. (I tend to work quite late at night, and I prefer quiet, unlike many of my colleagues, who listen to music while working.)

When I press a key on my keyboard, I displace air, which sends a shock wave through the atmosphere between my keyboard and my ears. These shock waves vibrate my eardrums, which moves tiny bones in my inner ear, which causes compression of some fluid in my cochlea, which sends electrical signals to my brain, which then realizes that it's hearing my keystrokes. It is a wondrous thing. The process is illustrated in Figure 8.1.

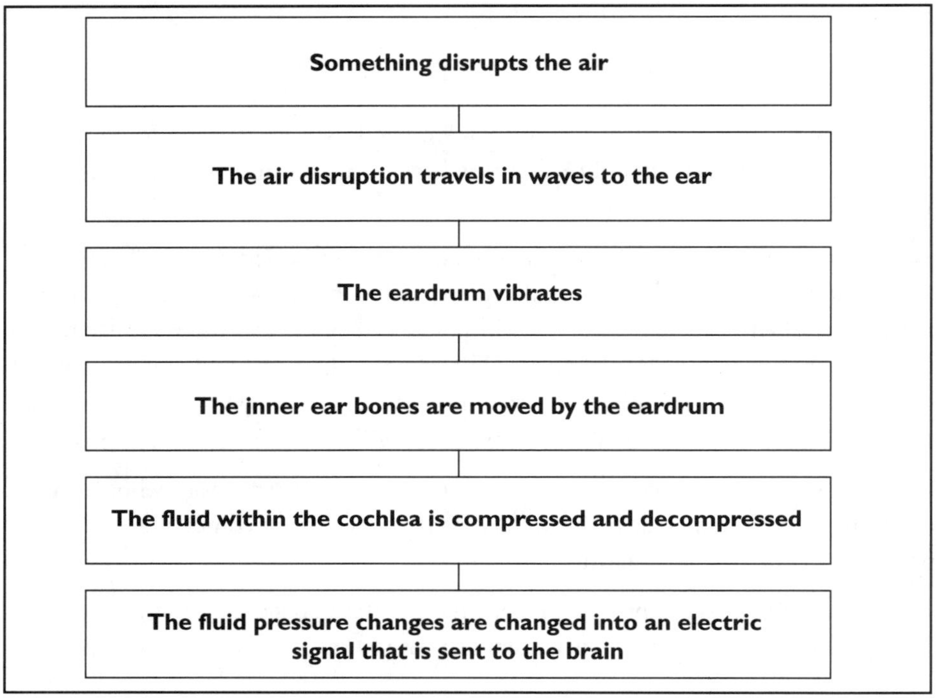

Figure 8.1

Rough sketch of how ears work

How Speakers Work

If our ears do nothing more than detect variations in air pressure, speakers must do nothing more than create variations in air pressure. In fact, a speaker is very much like the opposite of an ear (see Figure 8.2).

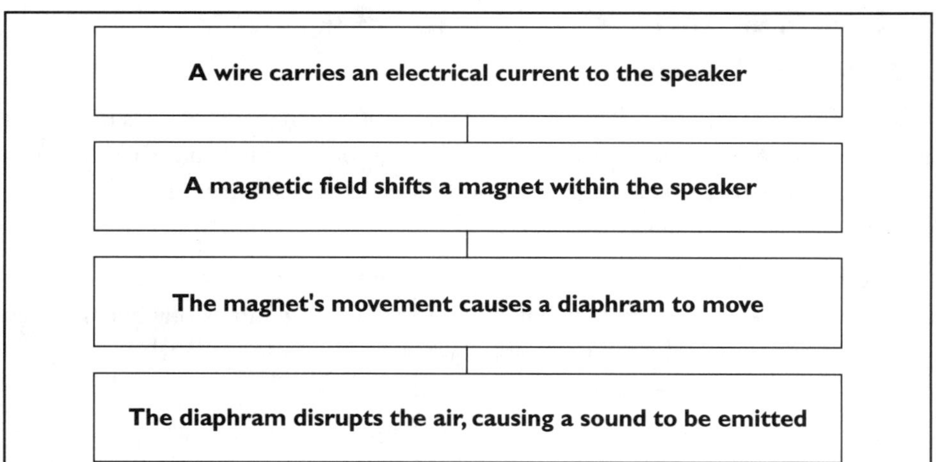

Figure 8.2

How speakers work

A speaker makes noise by moving a cardboard or paper membrane (kind of like an eardrum) back and forth, thus distorting air pressure. It does this by moving a little magnet back and forth (similar to but opposite in function from the tiny bones in the inner ear). This magnet is moved around by applying different magnetic fields, which are themselves created by electrical charges in wires.

How Sound Cards Work

In the speaker-to-ear comparison, a sound card performs approximately the same function as the cochlea. Much like the cochlea takes the vibration and converts it into a meaningful signal for the brain, the sound card takes a meaningful signal and translates it into an analog electrical current that is then applied to the speaker's magnet. This process is illustrated in Figure 8.3.

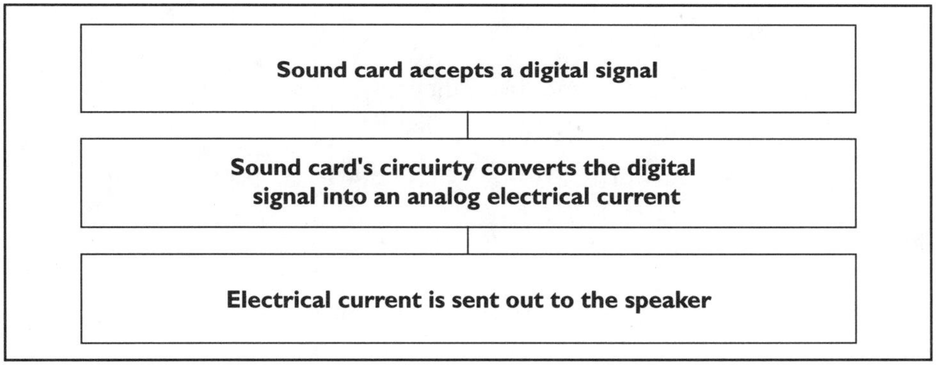

Figure 8.3

How sound cards work

On the flip side, the sound card can also convert the other way, through the microphone, where, instead of taking a digital signal and converting it into an analog current, it takes analog current and converts it into a digital signal.

The WIN32 Way to Play Sounds

Before we get into what DirectSound has to offer, let's take a moment to explore what WIN32 has to offer (it ain't much). By doing so, you may appreciate DirectSound more.

To make use of WIN32's sound capabilities, you must include mmsystem.h in your program, and you must link to the winmm.lib library. The sum total of the WIN32 support for playing digital sound files (WAV files) rests in the hands of a single function, `PlaySound`:

```
BOOL PlaySound(
  LPCSTR pszSound,
  HMODULE hmod,
  DWORD fdwSound
);
```

This returns nonzero on success. Table 8.1 explains the parameters.

Table 8.1 PlaySound Parameters

PlaySound Parameter	Purpose
`pszSound`	File name for the WAV file
`hmod`	Handle to the module containing the sound resource. Use `NULL`, because you are loading from a file.
`fdwSound`	Flags concerning how the sound is to be played or where it is from

A typical call to `PlaySound` looks like this:

```
//play the bounce sound
PlaySound("bounce.wav",NULL,SND_FILENAME | SND_ASYNC);
```

- `SND_FILENAME` and `SND_ASYNC` are a couple of the flags that can be passed. Here are some others, as well as their meanings:
- `SND_ASYNC` The sound will be played asynchronously (that is, the function returns immediately without waiting for the sound to be played)
- `SND_FILENAME` `pszSound` is a file name
- `SND_LOOP` The sound played loops over and over
- `SND_NOWAIT` If the sound driver is busy, returns `FALSE` and doesn't play the sound
- `SND_PURGE` Stops any sounds that are playing for the calling process
- `SND_SYNC` Waits until the sound is finished playing before returning

Most of the time, you will want `SND_ASYNC` and `SND_FILENAME`, as shown in the preceding code.

Load up IsoHex8_1.cpp. This is the same old bouncing ball demo that we've been working on for the last few chapters, only this time a sound will play each time a ball strikes the edge of the screen.

```
//bounds checking

//left side
if(ptBallPosition[index].x<=0)
{
	//change direction
	ptBallVelocity[index].x=abs(ptBallVelocity[index].x);
	//play sound
	PlaySound("bounce.wav",NULL,SND_FILENAME | SND_ASYNC);
}
//top side
if(ptBallPosition[index].y<=0)
{
	//change direction
	ptBallVelocity[index].y=abs(ptBallVelocity[index].y);
	//play sound
	PlaySound("bounce.wav",NULL,SND_FILENAME | SND_ASYNC);
}
//right side
if(ptBallPosition[index].x>=(int)dwDisplayWidth-gdicBall.GetWidth())
{
	//change direction
	ptBallVelocity[index].x=-abs(ptBallVelocity[index].x);
	//play sound
	PlaySound("bounce.wav",NULL,SND_FILENAME | SND_ASYNC);
}
//bottom side
if(ptBallPosition[index].y>=(int)dwDisplayHeight-gdicBall.GetHeight())
{
	//change direction
	ptBallVelocity[index].y=-abs(ptBallVelocity[index].y);
	//play sound
	PlaySound("bounce.wav",NULL,SND_FILENAME | SND_ASYNC);
}
```

If you run this, you'll see the full-screen bouncing ball demo and hear bouncing sounds. Despite the simplicity of the demo, you might actually begin to believe that, instead of little pictures of circles being erased and redrawn and digital sounds playing, there are little balls bouncing around inside your computer. That's what adding sound capabilities is all about... added realism.

PlaySound is fine if you don't need accurate timing. A larger sound takes longer to load, so the lag would be more noticeable than the lag with bounce.wav, which is such a small sound (3K) that you don't notice the latency (unless, of course, you are an android with superhuman hearing).

The IDirectSound Object

Just as DirectDraw has IDirectDraw7, DirectSound has IDirectSound, and for the exact same reason. IDirectSound abstracts the capabilities of sound hardware, in the same way that IDirectDraw7 abstracts display hardware. (There is no IDirectSound7, because there really hasn't been all that much revision in the way sound cards work; you just use the plain old IDirectSound interface.)

Creating the DirectSound Object

To create an IDirectSound object, use DirectSoundCreate.

```
HRESULT WINAPI DirectSoundCreate(
  LPCGUID lpcGuid,
  LPDIRECTSOUND * ppDS,
  LPUNKNOWN  pUnkOuter
);
```

This returns DS_OK if successful (it returns DD_OK for DirectDraw or DS_OK for DirectSound). Table 8.2 explains the parameters.

Table 8.2 DirectSoundCreate Parameters

DirectSoundCreate Parameter	Purpose
lpcGuid	The GUID of the sound drivers to use. (We will use NULL.)
ppDS	A pointer to an LPDIRECTSOUND variable that will be filled with a pointer to a new DirectSound object.
pUnkOuter	COM aggregation stuff. Use NULL.

This should look a little familiar, because it's a lot like the call to `DirectDrawCreateEx`.

The code required to create an `IDirectSound` object looks like the following:

```
//variable declaration(global)
LPDIRECTSOUND lpds=NULL;
//creating IDirectSound object (usually in Prog_Init)
DirectSoundCreate(NULL,&lpds,NULL);
//cleaning up IDirectSound(Prog_Done)
if(lpds)
{
      lpds->Release();
      lpds=NULL;
}
```

See? It's so much like DirectDraw, it's scary.

Setting the Cooperative Level

Another similarity between DirectDraw and DirectSound is the use of a cooperative level.

```
HRESULT IDirectSound::SetCooperativeLevel(
  HWND hwnd,
  DWORD dwLevel
);
```

This returns `DS_OK` if successful. Table 8.3 explains the parameter list.

Table 8.3 IDirectSound::SetCooperativeLevel Parameters

SetCooperativeLevel Parameter	Purpose
`hwnd`	The main window of the application that is using DirectSound
`dwLevel`	The cooperative level flags (discussed next)

The flags for DirectSound's cooperative levels are as follows:

- DSSCL_NORMAL The application plays well with others, but output is restricted
- DSSCL_PRIORITY The application can change the format of the output
- DSSCL_EXCLUSIVE DDSCL_PRIORITY, plus no other applications can play sounds
- DSSCL_WRITEPRIMARY Total control over the sound hardware, probably more than you want

For your purposes, DSSCL_NORMAL will suffice.

```
//set normal cooperative level
lpds->SetCooperativeLevel(hWndMain,DSSCL_NORMAL);
```

When in DSSCL_NORMAL, you are stuck with a 22KHz 8-bit stereo format. This isn't exactly the best sound format in the world, but it will suffice for your purposes. Exploring the other sound formats is an exercise I leave to you.

That's all you need to do to set up your IDirectSound object. If you were using a cooperative level other than DDSCL_NORMAL, there would be extra steps.

The IDirectSoundBuffer Object

Now that you've established contact with your sound card, you need to give it something to do. A sound card does one thing and does it well: it plays sounds. You keep these sounds (or, at least, binary representations of them) in buffers.

Creating Sound Buffers

Create sound buffers by using IDirectSound::CreateSoundBuffer:

```
HRESULT IDirectSound::CreateSoundBuffer(
  LPCDSBUFFERDESC lpcDSBufferDesc,
  LPLPDIRECTSOUNDBUFFER lplpDirectSoundBuffer,
  IUnknown FAR * pUnkOuter
);
```

This returns DS_OK if successful. Table 8.4 explains the parameters.

Table 8.4 IDirectSound::CreateSoundBuffer Parameters

CreateSoundBuffer Parameter	Purpose
lpcDSBufferDesc	Pointer to a DSBUFFERDESC (similar in purpose to a DDSURFACEDESC) that describes the buffer
lplpDirectSoundBuffer	Pointer to an LPDIRECTSOUNDBUFFER pointer that will be filled with a pointer to an IDirectSoundBuffer interface.
pUnkOuter	COM aggregate stuff. Use NULL.

The DSBUFFERDESC structure tells how a buffer is to be created.

```
typedef struct {
    DWORD           dwSize;
    DWORD           dwFlags;
    DWORD           dwBufferBytes;
    DWORD           dwReserved;
    LPWAVEFORMATEX  lpwfxFormat;
    GUID            guid3DAlgorithm;
} DSBUFFERDESC, *LPDSBUFFERDESC;
```

Table 8.5 shows the meaning of the various DSBUFFERDESC members.

Table 8.5 DSBUFFERDESC Members

DSBUFFERDESC **Member**	**Meaning**
dwSize	Size of this structure
dwFlags	Flags for how to create the buffer
dwBufferBytes	Number of bytes to allocate for the buffer
dwReserved	Reserved
lpwfxFormat	Pointer to a WAVEFORMATEX structure
guid3DAlgorithm	For 3D sound, which I will not cover

You must set the dwSize parameter to sizeof(DSBUFFERDESC).

Here are some possible flags for dwFlags:

- DSBCAPS_CTRLFREQUENCY Controls the frequency of the sound
- DSBCAPS_CTRLPAN Controls the panning (left-right position) of the sound
- DSBCAPS_CTRLVOLUME Controls the volume for this sound
- DSBCAPS_LOCHARDWARE The sound is stored in the sound card's hardware memory, and you can make use of hardware mixing (not necessarily available).
- DSBCAPS_LOCSOFTWARE The sound is stored in software (system memory).
- DSBCAPS_STATIC The buffer is intended to be loaded once and played many times, rather than used for streaming.

Here are a few words of advice concerning these flags:

- Don't use more than are necessary. If you want to control the volume, that's fine, but if you don't need something like frequency control, don't ask for it.
- If you attempt to use the DSBCAPS_LOCHARDWARE flag, be sure to have a fallback plan (for example, respond to a return code that is *not* DS_OK).
- Most of your sounds are likely to be static, so make good use of the DSBCAPS_STATIC flag.

I'll go into more detail on some of these flags later.

The WAVEFORMATEX Structure

Sounds come in many different formats—mono (single-channel), stereo (dual-channel), 8-bit, 16-bit, 11KHz, 22KHz, and 44KHz. As you can see, a sound file can have a number of properties, and these are specified in a WAVEFORMATEX structure:

```
typedef struct {
    WORD  wFormatTag;
    WORD  nChannels;
    DWORD nSamplesPerSec;
    DWORD nAvgBytesPerSec;
    WORD  nBlockAlign;
    WORD  wBitsPerSample;
    WORD  cbSize;
} WAVEFORMATEX;
```

Table 8.6 explains the members of WAVEFORMATEX.

Table 8.6 WAVEFORMATEX Members

WAVEFORMATEX Member	Meaning
wFormatTag	The waveform audio type (typically WAVE_FORMAT_PCM, which is used by WAV files)
nChannels	Either mono (1) or stereo (2)
nSamplesPerSec	The frequency of the sound, typically 11025, 22050, or 44100
nAvgBytesPerSec	The number of bytes per second
nBlockAlign	The number of bytes in a block (depends on wBitsPerSample and nChannels)
wBitsPerSample	8 or 16, specifying the size of a sample in bits
cbSize	Extra data; ignored when using WAVE_FORMAT_PCM

Is your head swimming with all of these audio terms? Don't worry about them too much. You don't actually care all that much about how sounds work; you just want to load them and play them.

The members of WAVEFORMATEX that you need to supply numbers for are wFormatTag, nChannels, nSamplesPerSec, and wBitsPerSample. You should always make cbSize equal to 0. The rest can be calculated:

```
nBlockAlign = nChannels * wBitsPerSample / 8;
nAvgBytesPerSec = nBlockAlign * nSamplesPerSec;
```

So, to create a sound buffer, do this:

```
//declare buffer (global)
LPDIRECTSOUNDBUFFER lpdsb;
//set up a buffer description
DSBUFFERDESC dsbd;
//code to fill out dsbd
//create buffer (initialization)
lpds->CreateBuffer(&dsbd,&lpdsb,NULL);
```

```
//safe release (cleanup)
if(lpdsb)
{
        lpdsb->Release();
        lpdsb=NULL;
}
```

Control Flags

There are a number of control flags that can be sent to DirectSound to specify how much and what sort of control you want for individual sounds. All of these control flags start with DSBCAPS_. There are more control flags than are described here; I'll just mention the commonly used ones.

Frequency

The frequency of a sound corresponds to the `nSamplesPerSec` member of `DSBUFFERDESC` and is typically 11025, 22050, or 44100. The higher the frequency, the more bytes per second (hence, a larger WAV file), and the better the sound quality.

You set the frequency of the sound when you create the buffer, but if you include a `DSBCAPS_CTRLFREQUENCY` flag in your buffer description, you can change it later with `IDirectSoundBuffer::SetFrequency`:

```
HRESULT IDirectSoundBuffer::SetFrequency(
  DWORD dwFrequency
);
```

This returns `DS_OK` on success. `dwFrequency` is the new frequency at which you want the sound to be played. This number can be in the range of `DSBFREQUENCY_MIN` to `DSBFREQUENCY_MAX`. Another constant, `DSBFREQUENCY_ORIGINAL`, reverts the sound to its original frequency.

When you change the frequency of a sound, both the length and the pitch change. If you put in a smaller number, the sound will be longer, and it will be lower in tone. If you put in a larger number, the sound will play more quickly, and it will sound higher (the chipmunk effect).

To retrieve the frequency of a sound, use `IDirectSoundBuffer:GetFrequency`:

```
HRESULT IDirectSoundBuffer::GetFrequency(
  LPDWORD lpdwFrequency
);
```

This returns DS_OK if successful. The lpdwFrequency parameter is a pointer to a DWORD that is filled with the sound's frequency.

Volume

If you use the DSBCAPS_CTRLVOLUME flag, you can make use of volume control for a sound. You might be surprised at how the volume controls in DirectSound work, because volume control is actually attenuation control. In other words, you don't actually set how loud a sound is; you set how muted it is. The second thing that might give you trouble is that attenuation is a logarithmic scale, specified in hundredths of a decibel (dB). Crazy, huh?

So, what the heck is a decibel? A decibel is one-tenth of a bel. (Not too helpful, I know.) A sound that is 2 bels (20 decibels) is 10 times louder than a sound that is 1 bel (10 decibels). To flip this around, a sound that is attenuated by 10 decibels is 10 times softer than a sound that is not attenuated at all. To specify attenuation, you use a minus sign. Because the units are in hundredths of a decibel, attenuating by 10 dB has a value of –10000. The maximum attenuation value for DirectSound is DSBVOLUME_MIN, which equals –100000, or –100 dB, which is 10 billion times softer than a nonattenuated sound—for all intents and purposes, silence. On the other end of the scale is DSBVOLUME_MAX, which is 0, meaning no attenuation.

Set the attenuation with a call to IDirectSoundBuffer:SetVolume:

```
HRESULT IDirectSoundBuffer::SetVolume(
  LONG lVolume
);
```

This returns DS_OK on success. The lVolume parameter specifies the attenuation value for this sound.

To retrieve the attenuation value, use IDirectSoundBuffer::GetVolume:

```
HRESULT IDirectSoundBuffer::GetVolume(
  LPLONG lplVolume
);
```

This returns DS_OK on success. The lplVolume parameter is a pointer to a LONG that is filled with the attenuation value.

Most of the time, you won't want to work with a logarithmic scale for setting volumes, and your users definitely won't. Usually, you'll want some nice scalar measure for volumes, like a percentage; one way to do it is to calculate the logarithmic values for the percentages from 0 to 100 and store them in a lookup table or just calculate them on-the-fly. To do this, just use the following equation.

> **CAUTION**
>
> **Be careful not to put a 0 into the `log` function, or you will cause an infinite feedback loop that will destroy all matter in the universe! Or you'll get a runtime error, which is much, much worse.**

```
//the log10 function requires the use of math.h
attenuation=log10(volume)*1000; //volume is a value between 0 and 1
```

Panning

Pan is similar in function to volume and works in a similar way. Pan sets the relative volume between the two speakers. The `DSBCAP_CTRLPAN` flag is required to change the pan.

Panning is accomplished by attenuating either the left or right speaker's output, similar to how volume attenuates both. This attenuation is in addition to the attenuation because of volume control. The units are the same—hundredths of a decibel. Positive values attenuate the left speaker, leaving the right speaker alone, and negative values attenuate the right speaker, leaving the left speaker alone. A value of 0 means no attenuation to either speaker.

To set the pan, use `IDirectSoundBuffer::SetPan`:

```
HRESULT IDirectSoundBuffer::SetPan(
  LONG lPan
);
```

This returns `DS_OK` if successful. `lPan` species how to pan the sound. (Noticing a pattern with these functions?)

There are a few constants that you can use with `SetPan`. `DSBPAN_LEFT` (equal to –10000) silences the right speaker, `DSBPAN_RIGHT` (equal to 10000) silences the left speaker, and `DSBPAN_CENTER` sets no attenuation for either speaker.

To retrieve the current panning for a sound, use `IDirectSoundBuffer::GetPan`:

```
HRESULT IDirectSoundBuffer::GetPan(
  LPLONG lplPan
);
```

This returns DS_OK if successful. The lplPan parameter is a pointer to a LONG that is filled with the current pan level.

Locking and Unlocking Sound Buffers

Before we actually get into locking and unlocking a sound buffer, we must first discuss the concept of a sound buffer. A DirectSound sound buffer is conceptually circular, allowing you to loop a buffer indefinitely, or even to have streaming content to a buffer (that is, writing to one section of the buffer while another section is playing). Because of this, when you lock a buffer, instead of just getting a single pointer to the memory contained in the buffer, you might get two pointers (because you might be playing the middle of the buffer while you are locking two of the ends). I won't cover streaming buffers, but I thought that you should be aware of them.

To lock the buffer, you use the IDirectSoundBuffer::Lock function:

```
HRESULT IDirectSoundBuffer::Lock(
  DWORD dwWriteCursor,
  DWORD dwWriteBytes,
  LPVOID lplpvAudioPtr1,
  LPDWORD lpdwAudioBytes1,
  LPVOID lplpvAudioPtr2,
  LPDWORD lpdwAudioBytes2,
  DWORD dwFlags
);
```

This returns DS_OK if successful. Table 8.7 explains the parameters.

Table 8.7 IDirectSoundBuffer::Lock Parameters

Lock Parameter	Purpose
dwWriteCursor	Offset from the start of the buffer (in bytes) where you want the lock to start
dwWriteBytes	Size, in bytes, of the portion you want to lock
lplpvAudioPtr1	Pointer to a pointer that will be filled with the memory location of the start of the locked portion
lpdwAudioBytes1	Number of bytes pointed to by what will be filled into lplpvAudioPtr1
lplpvAudioPtr2	If the buffer had to wrap around (go from the end to the beginning again), this is filled with the second pointer, so you can continue to write. If NULL, lplpvAudioPtr1 points to the entire locked area of the buffer.
lpdwAudioBytes2	The size in bytes of the area that starts at lplpvAudioPtr2
dwFlags	Flags specifying how you want to lock the buffer

Since you will be working with static buffers only, you can ignore lplpvAudioPtr2 and pass NULL. However, you still need to pass in a pointer to a DWORD for lpdwAudioBytes2, even though it will be filled with 0. Also, since you are dealing with static buffers, you pass DSBLOCK_ENTIREBUFFER, which means that dwWriteBytes is ignored and you can pass 0 there as well.

To lock a buffer, do the following:

```
//pointer to buffer (it is UCHAR* to work with 8 bit audio, if using 16 bit, you
should use USHORT*)
UCHAR* pBuffer;
//buffer sizes
DWORD dwBuf1;
DWORD dwBuf2;
//lock the buffer
lpdsb->Lock(0,0,(void**)&pBuffer,&dwBuf1,NULL,&dwBuf2,DSBLOCK_ENTIREBUFFER);
```

After locking the buffer, you can fill it with whatever data you want (usually by using memcpy). When you are all done, use IDirectSoundBuffer::Unlock:

```
HRESULT IDirectSoundBuffer::Unlock(
  LPVOID lpvAudioPtr1,
  DWORD dwAudioBytes1,
  LPVOID lpvAudioPtr2,
  DWORD dwAudioBytes2
);
```

This returns DS_OK on success. The parameters for Unlock should look familiar, because they are most of the parameters for Lock.

Do the following to unlock the buffer:

```
lpdsb->Unlock(pBuffer,dwBuf1,NULL,0);
```

Now you're ready to start using the sound.

Playing Sounds

Once you have your sound buffer created and filled with the proper data, it's time to put it to work by playing it. To do so, use IDirectSoundBuffer::Play:

```
HRESULT IDirectSoundBuffer::Play(
  DWORD dwReserved1,
  DWORD dwPriority,
  DWORD dwFlags
);
```

This returns DS_OK if successful. Table 8.8 explains the parameters.

Table 8.8 IDirectSoundBuffer::Play Parameters

Play Parameter	Purpose
dwReserved1	No purpose. Pass a 0.
dwPriority	Meaningless when using the DSSCL_NORMAL cooperative level. Pass a 0.
dwFlags	Pass 0 to play the sound once. Pass DSBPLAY_LOOPING to loop the sound repeatedly.

```
//play a sound once
lpdsb->Play(0,0,0);
//play a sound continuously
lpdsb->Play(0,0,DSBPLAY_LOOPING);
//stop a sound
lpdsb->Stop();
```

Duplicating Sound Buffers

The problem with DirectSound buffers is that, at any given time, only one copy can be playing. To play more than one copy of the same sound, you can do one of two things: you can load the sound into more than one sound buffer, or you can duplicate the sound buffer. The first method is wasteful, especially if you have a large number of sounds. Digital sounds can take up a lot of space—in some cases, more than graphics can.

Duplication is a good alternative. When you duplicate a sound buffer, you do not make an independent copy. A duplicated buffer points to the exact same memory that the original does, so if you lock the duplicate and modify the contents, you'll get the same change if the original is played. Right after duplication the new buffer has the same parameters (volume, pan, frequency) as the original. These parameters can be changed.

To duplicate a sound buffer, you use `IDirectSound::DuplicateBuffer`:

```
HRESULT IDirectSound::DuplicateSoundBuffer(
  LPDIRECTSOUNDBUFFER lpDsbOriginal,
  LPLPDIRECTSOUNDBUFFER lplpDsbDuplicate
);
```

This returns `DS_OK` if successful. This method increases the original buffer's reference count, so you can safely release it and rest assured that the duplicate will still function properly.

```
//duplicate buffer
lpds->DuplicateSoundBuffer(lpdsb,&lpdsbcopy);
```

You may wonder why in the world you would ever need more than a single copy of a sound. In many (or even most) cases, you probably don't. However, as with oft-repeated sounds such as a gun firing, you may want to have two copies or even more.

Using WAV Files

I've been talking about sound and WAV files the whole chapter long, and at last, I'm going to show you how to load them. WAV files are the final bridge between you and making your program come alive with digital sound! Before I discuss WAV files let's take a brief detour and explore how to open and read from files the WIN32 way (I'm not a big `fstream` fan).

Using HANDLEs to Do File Operations

We've spoken at length about the various types of `HANDLE`s prevalent in WIN32 programming. File access is also done using a `HANDLE`. In order to do any sort of sequential access of a file, you need to know only four functions: `CreateFile`, `WriteFile`, `ReadFile`, and `CloseHandle`

For your purposes (loading from a WAV file), these four functions will get the job done. Let's take a quick look at them.

CreateFile

Use `CreateFile` to either create a new file or open an existing one.

```
HANDLE CreateFile(
  LPCTSTR lpFileName,                          // file name
  DWORD dwDesiredAccess,                       // access mode
  DWORD dwShareMode,                           // share mode
  LPSECURITY_ATTRIBUTES lpSecurityAttributes, // SD
  DWORD dwCreationDisposition,                 // how to create
  DWORD dwFlagsAndAttributes,                  // file attributes
  HANDLE hTemplateFile                         // handle to template file
);
```

This returns a handle to the file. If the function fails, the return value is `INVALID_HANDLE_VALUE`. Table 8.9 explains the parameters.

Table 8.9 CreateFile Parameters

CreateFile Parameter	Purpose
lpFileName	The name of the file
dwDesiredAccess	Access mode desired (GENERIC_READ or GENERIC_WRITE)
dwShareMode	Share mode
lpSecurityAttributes	Pointer to security attributes
dwCreationDisposition	How the file is to be created
dwFlagsAndAttributes	File attributes
hTemplateFile	Template file

CreateFile has a bunch of parameters, most of which you won't use:

- **lpFileName** will contain a string with the name of the file and a relative path.
- **dwDesiredAccess** will be either GENERIC_READ or GENERIC_WRITE, depending on which you want to do.
- **dwShareMode** will be 0. You are greedy, and you don't want to share your sound files with anybody.
- **lpSecurityAttributes** points to security junk, which you don't care about, so you'll pass NULL.
- **dwCreationDistribution** will either be CREATE_ALWAYS (when making a new file) or OPEN_EXISTING (when opening an old one).
- **dwFlagsAndAttributes** should always be FILE_ATTRIBUTE_NORMAL.
- **hTemplateFile** we aren't discussing, so pass NULL.

WriteFile

This function is used to write data to the file.

```
BOOL WriteFile(
  HANDLE hFile,                    // handle to file
  LPCVOID lpBuffer,                // data buffer
  DWORD nNumberOfBytesToWrite,     // number of bytes to write
  LPDWORD lpNumberOfBytesWritten,  // number of bytes written
  LPOVERLAPPED lpOverlapped        // overlapped buffer
);
```

This returns nonzero on success. Table 8.10 explains the parameters.

Table 8.10 WriteFile Parameters

WriteFile Parameter	Purpose
`hFile`	Handle to the file to which you are writing
`lpBuffer`	A buffer that contains the contents to be written
`nNumberOfBytesToWrite`	The number of bytes in the buffer
`lpNumberOfBytesWritten`	A pointer to a `DWORD` that contains the number of bytes actually written
`lpOverlapped`	Ignore. Pass `NULL`.

It's important to check the value returned in `lpNumberOfBytesWritten` against the number that you told it to write in order to check for errors.

ReadFile

`ReadFile` is used to read data from a file. It looks quite a bit like `WriteFile`.

```
BOOL ReadFile(
  HANDLE hFile,                // handle to file
  LPVOID lpBuffer,             // data buffer
  DWORD nNumberOfBytesToRead,  // number of bytes to read
  LPDWORD lpNumberOfBytesRead, // number of bytes read
  LPOVERLAPPED lpOverlapped    // overlapped buffer
);
```

This returns nonzero on success. Table 8.11 explains the parameters.

Table 8.11 ReadFile Parameters

ReadFile Parameter	Purpose
`hFile`	Handle to the file from which you are reading
`lpBuffer`	Buffer into which data from the file will be stored
`nNumberOfBytesToRead`	Number of bytes in the buffer
`lpNumberOfBytesRead`	A pointer to a `DWORD` that will be filled with the actual number of bytes read
`lpOverlapped`	Ignore. Pass `NULL`.

As with `WriteFile`, be sure to check the value returned in `lpNumberOfBytesRead`.

CloseHandle

The simplest of them all, `CloseHandle` closes the file.

```
BOOL CloseHandle(
  HANDLE hObject    // handle to object
);
```

This returns nonzero on success. `hObject` is the file handle.

The Structure of a WAV File

Now that you can read data from a file, it's almost time to do so. But first (you saw that one coming), let's talk a little bit about the structure of a WAV file. Then, I promise we'll get to the actual loading of the file.

The WAV file format is based on the RIFF format, which was developed to allow many types of files to use the same format—even files with radically different purposes. Not surprisingly, the first four bytes of a WAV file contain the string `"RIFF"`. The next four bytes contain the length of the rest of the file. These eight bytes make up what is called the *RIFF header*. This is common to any file with the RIFF format.

Now we start getting into the particulars of the WAV file itself. The next four bytes contain the string `"WAVE."` This is what identifies the file as a WAV file. The remainder of the file consists of data "chunks." Figure 8.8 shows a graphical version of the contents of a chunk.

You are concerned with exactly two types of chunk: the "fmt" chunk (there is a space after the t) and the "data" chunk. The "fmt" chunk contains information about the format of the sound, and the fields correspond, for the most part, to the members of WAVEFORMATEX. The "data" chunk contains the raw audio data that you put into the buffer after you have locked it.

There are more than just these two chunks, but for the purpose of loading a WAV file, these are the only two that are of any use. In all of the WAV files I've ever worked with, the "fmt" chunk always comes first, and, in most cases, the "data" chunk comes immediately thereafter.

Loading a WAV File from Disk

As with the bitmap loader back in Chapter 3, I've written a class to do the WAV file loading:

```
//wave loader class
class CWAVLoader
{
private:
	//format
	LPWAVEFORMATEX lpWfx;
	//data chunk
	UCHAR* ucData;
	//length of the data chunk
	DWORD dwDataLength;
public:
	//constructor
	CWAVLoader();
	//destructor
	~CWAVLoader();
	//get data length
	DWORD GetLength();
	//get data pointer
	UCHAR* GetData();
	//get pointer to format
	LPWAVEFORMATEX GetFormat();
	//load from a file
	void Load(LPCTSTR lpszFilename);
	//destroy buffer
	void Destroy();
};
```

The constructor does very little—it simply makes sure that all of the data members are cleared out. The destructor just calls `Destroy`, which performs any necessary cleanup. The `Get` members retrieve the data stored in the class. The main job of the class is done by `Load`:

```
//load from a file
void CWAVLoader::Load(LPCTSTR lpszFilename)
{
	//destroy any old buffer
	Destroy();
	//four character buffer
	char Buffer[5];
	Buffer[4]=0;
	//read length
	DWORD dwNumRead;
	//length variable
	DWORD dwLength;

	//data buffer
	UCHAR* ucTemp;
	//open a handle to the file
	HANDLE hfile=CreateFile(lpszFilename,GENERIC_READ,
		FILE_SHARE_READ,NULL,OPEN_EXISTING,
		FILE_ATTRIBUTE_NORMAL,NULL);
	ReadFile(hfile,Buffer,4,&dwNumRead,NULL);//"RIFF"
	ReadFile(hfile,&dwLength,sizeof(dwLength),&dwNumRead,NULL);//length of file
	ReadFile(hfile,Buffer,4,&dwNumRead,NULL);//"WAVE"
	//chunks
	bool done=false;
	while(!done)
	{
		ReadFile(hfile,Buffer,4,&dwNumRead,NULL);//chunk header
		ReadFile(hfile,&dwLength,sizeof(dwLength),&dwNumRead,NULL);//length
of chunk
		ucTemp=new UCHAR[dwLength];
		ReadFile(hfile,ucTemp,dwLength,&dwNumRead,NULL);
		//depending on the chunk header, do something
		if(strcmp("fmt ",Buffer)==0)
		{
			//format chunk
			//allocate format
			lpWfx=new WAVEFORMATEX;
```

```
                //clear out format
                memset(lpWfx,0,sizeof(WAVEFORMATEX));
                //copy from buffer
                memcpy(lpWfx,ucTemp,dwLength);
            }
            if(strcmp("data",Buffer)==0)
            {
                //data chunk
                //allocate data buffer
                ucData=new UCHAR[dwLength];
                //copy length
                dwDataLength=dwLength;
                //copy buffer
                memcpy(ucData,ucTemp,dwDataLength);

                //we are done, and need no more chunks
                done=true;
            }
            delete ucTemp;
        }
        //close the file
        CloseHandle(hfile);
}
```

Using CWAVLoader to Load from a File to a DirectSoundBuffer

Load up IsoHex8_2.cpp. It's our favorite bouncing ball demo again! This time, though, we are using `IDirectSoundBuffer` and `CWAVLoader`.

```
//declarations (global)
//sound manager
LPDIRECTSOUND lpds;
//buffers
LPDIRECTSOUNDBUFFER lpdsb[2];
//setup (Prog_Init)
        //load wav file
        CWAVLoader wav;
        wav.Load("bounce.wav");
        //set up sounds
        DirectSoundCreate(NULL,&lpds,NULL);
```

```
        //set coop level
        lpds->SetCooperativeLevel(hWndMain,DSSCL_NORMAL);
        //set up buffer description
        DSBUFFERDESC dsbd;
        memset(&dsbd,0,sizeof(DSBUFFERDESC));
        //size
        dsbd.dwSize=sizeof(DSBUFFERDESC);

        //flags
        dsbd.dwFlags=DSBCAPS_LOCSOFTWARE;
        //length and sound format
        dsbd.dwBufferBytes=wav.GetLength();
        dsbd.lpwfxFormat=wav.GetFormat();
        //create buffer
        lpds->CreateSoundBuffer(&dsbd,&lpdsb[0],NULL);
        DWORD buflen,buflen2;
        void* bufptr;
        //lock entire buffer
        lpdsb[0]->Lock(0,0,&bufptr,&buflen,
NULL,&buflen2,DSBLOCK_ENTIREBUFFER);
        //copy from wave loader to sound buffer
        memcpy(bufptr,wav.GetData(),wav.GetLength());
        //unlock the buffer
        lpdsb[0]->Unlock(bufptr,buflen,NULL,buflen2);
        //duplicate the sound
        lpds->DuplicateSoundBuffer(lpdsb[0],&lpdsb[1]);
//clean up (Prog_Done)
        //clean up sounds
        if(lpdsb[1])
        {
              lpdsb[1]->Release();
              lpdsb[1]=NULL;
        }
        if(lpdsb[0])
        {
              lpdsb[0]->Release();
              lpdsb[0]=NULL;
        }
        //clean up sound manager
        if(lpds)
        {
```

```
            lpds->Release();
            lpds=NULL;
        }
//The "bounce" (Prog_Loop)
        //bounds checking
        //left side
        if(ptBallPosition[index].x<=0)
        {
            ptBallVelocity[index].x=abs(ptBallVelocity[index].x);
            lpdsb[index]->Play(0,0,0);
        }
        //top side
        if(ptBallPosition[index].y<=0)
        {
            ptBallVelocity[index].y=abs(ptBallVelocity[index].y);
            lpdsb[index]->Play(0,0,0);
        }
        //right side
        if(ptBallPosition[index].x>=(int)dwDisplayWidth-gdicBall.GetWidth())
        {
            ptBallVelocity[index].x=-abs(ptBallVelocity[index].x);
            lpdsb[index]->Play(0,0,0);
        }
        //bottom side
        if(ptBallPosition[index].y>=(int)dwDisplayHeight-gdicBall.GetHeight())
        {
            ptBallVelocity[index].y=-abs(ptBallVelocity[index].y);
            lpdsb[index]->Play(0,0,0);
        }
```

As you can see, two sound buffers are created, one for each ball. One is loaded from the WAV file, and the other is a duplicate. In reality, you would probably want to make more. Occasionally a ball will bounce off one wall and then almost immediately bounce off another wall. With only one buffer per ball, this would mean that only one bounce is heard if the time between bounces is shorter than the sound itself. Take into consideration situations like this when deciding how many copies of a sound to make—if you don't make the copies at design time, they will have to be added during development or even during beta.

The DSFuncs Library

Like the DDFuncs library I showed you in Chapter 6, the DSFuncs library is meant to help you avoid repetitive tasks necessary during the creation of sound buffers. There isn't much to this library.

LPDSB_LoadFromFile

```
LPDIRECTSOUNDBUFFER LPDSB_LoadFromFile(LPDIRECTSOUND lpds,LPCTSTR lpszFileName);
```

This returns a new sound buffer. `lpds` is a pointer to an `IDirectSound` object that is used to create the new buffer. `lpszFileName` is the file name of the WAV file that you want loaded into this buffer.

LPDSB_Release

```
void LPDSB_Release(LPDIRECTSOUNDBUFFER* lplpdsb);
```

This returns nothing. It performs a safe release on an `IDirectSoundBuffer`. `lplpdsb` is a pointer to `LPDIRECTSOUNDBUFFER`. Note that I didn't wrap up `DuplicateSoundBuffer` or the `SetVolume`, `SetPan`, or `SetFrequency` functions. They are simple enough in their current form.

Empowering the User

It may not seem that there too many places where you can empower the user as far as sound is concerned. The empowerment is not nearly as obvious as it is with DirectDraw. The most essential sound empowerment you can give your users is the ability to turn sound *off*. Yes, your sounds are spiffy and they really add to the flavor of the game, but face it: at some point, they *will* get repetitive and begin to annoy even the most insesitive user. So make at least a "sound off" option. By doing so, your users can play at work and get their coworkers addicted to your game.

The second user empowerment for sound is the ability to set the volume. Depending on the game, this may be one, two, or three different volumes. Usually, sound effects (SFX), voice (VOX), and music (MUS) have different volumes. If you have a sufficiently small number of sounds, you can get away with having only one or two of these. This empowerment isn't nearly as important as "sound off," but it is nonetheless important. It is a feature that your users will be expecting.

Summary

DS's capabilities far exceed what little we've covered here. Those capabilities include 3D sound, using notification, syncing sounds, and DirectMusic. I could never hope to do justice to all of these in a short introductory chapter.

Following are a few things to remember:

- To play sounds the WIN32 way, you use PlaySound.
- To use the capabilities of DirectSound, you create an `IDirectSound` object, much in the same way you created an `IDirectDraw` object in DirectDraw.
- Digital sounds are stored in `DirectSoundBuffers` and are created by using `IDirectSound::CreateSoundBuffer`.
- Depending on how you set it up, you can control a sound's volume, pan, or frequency to get various effects.
- If you need more than a single copy of a WAV file, it is best to use `DuplicateSoundBuffer` rather than loading the same sound multiple times.

CHAPTER 9

Game Design Theory

- The Intangible Nature of Games
- Designing a Game
- From Theory to Practice

This is the last chapter in Part I, but I think it is the most important. This chapter has nothing to do with WIN32, graphics, or sound. It has to do with the design of the game itself. Game design theory is one of my favorite topics; I could talk about it all day.

A Definition of Game

Let's start with a definition of what makes a game. A *game* is a structured activity not generally related to survival. This definition is a little vague, but it's the most concise I could come up with. Let's take it apart:

- **Structured.** The meaning of "structure" here denotes a set of formalized rules that are essential for a game's existence.
- **Activity.** In order to play a game you must be *doing* something.
- **Not generally related to survival.** Granted, Russian Roulette is related to survival, but most other games are not.

The Intangible Nature of Games

Please note that I speak of rules and activities, but I make no mention of boards, tokens, play money, or any other sort of marker whatsoever. These are not required to have a game. Some games, especially athletic ones, do indeed require the use of the equipment associated with them. Basketball needs a ball that can be bounced and something to serve as a net. Baseball needs a stick and a ball and four bases, but anything can serve as the bases (when I was a kid, we often used trees). Figure 9.1 shows some game-playing paraphernalia.

Figure 9.1

A variety of game equipment

So, the game is not the stuff with which you play the game; you may have balls and bats and hoops and chess pieces and a chessboard, but these things are not the game. The game is contained totally within your head. The pieces positioned on the board or the players positioned on the bases just keep track of the game's current state. When playing the game, you attempt to manipulate the game's state in your favor. The manner in which you manipulate the game's state is called a *game mechanic*.

The game mechanic is governed by the rules. The rules define the possible game states that are legal, as well as what game mechanics are available to you to manipulate the game state. When all of these possible game states are taken together, they are the *game state space* (that is, all possible moves after a given game state).

At the start of the game, the game state space can be very large (enormous, when playing games such as chess), or nearly impossible to determine in athletic games such as basketball or baseball. As play progresses, the game state space diminishes until the game reaches completion, at which time the game state space is empty. This is called the *final game state*, or the *end game*.

In some games, it is impossible to determine the end game until the absolute end of the game has been reached. Many games involving cards are this way, as are most games of chance. In most games, though, it becomes more and more evident how the game will end as the end approaches. Chess is a good example of this, as is backgammon. In no game is it ever certain from the beginning how the game will end up.

Why We Play

Games are played in every culture on earth; and if we should ever encounter an alien species, I expect them to bring some good games with them, or else they can just go home. The question of *why* we play games remains. Both you and I, as game programmers, play a lot of games. We would not have been interested in making them if we didn't like playing them. It sure isn't the game programming pay that motivates us!

I believe it's in our nature to be competitive with the other members of our species (but, paradoxically, cooperative at the same time). Ever since the days of cavemen, we've been competing for good hunting land, good shelter, and other natural resources.

In fact, it's easy to imagine the first game (or at least a candidate for the first game)—target practice. Throwing spears at trees to improve accuracy would help the ability to hunt, and thus would help the hunter and the clan survive. As technology improved, and people learned to raise crops and cultivate livestock, hunting for food became less important, so target practice with spears became non-survival-related. Perhaps people came up with a scoring system, using something similar to the archer's target. Target practice games survive to this day, in several forms. Darts, archery, lawn darts, and even horseshoes could date back to this game.

The target practice example doesn't explain our personal reasons for playing games, but it does illustrate how games can come about. Our reasons for playing games change as the game develops. The cavemen played a spear throwing game to hone their hunting skills. After hunting was no longer as important, the game continued because it was fun. It allowed people to compare skill levels.

So, there are several reasons that we play games—we develop skills, solve problems, enjoy the thrill of the unknown outcome, and test our mettle against another. Mainly, we play games because they are fun, and different games are fun for different reasons.

Computer Games

Computers have been used to play games almost since the moment of their inception. Now we have force-feedback joysticks, as well as graphical capabilities that in the coming years may even mimic real life, and sound capabilities that already do.

Computers are uniquely suited for playing games. With a computer to implement the rules and represent the game state on-screen, we don't have to have a board or tokens. As computers have gotten faster, more and more complex rules have been used; some or all of these rules can be cleverly hidden so that the player needs only a dim awareness of them. (Yes, in computer role-playing games, you know that when you try to hit a monster, there is some sort of randomized skill check. However, you don't actually care about the roll, just whether or not you hit. This is what I mean by rule hiding.) This is called *game mechanic encapsulation.* Most modern computer games would not be fun if they were played on a board with tokens and markers, because of the sheer number of game mechanics.

Game Analysis

In order to be a good game designer, you should have a solid grasp of how other games are designed. Good games are balanced, meaning that they are not unfair. Fairness in a game is hard to realize. In a computer role-playing game, as the characters that the player controls become more powerful, they should be met with more powerful foes. If the foes get too tough too quickly, the player will become frustrated and give up. If the foes do not become tougher quickly enough, the player will become bored and again will quit playing. Sustaining the challenge while still having a victory condition is important in these progressive types of games. Other games, like most board games and most sports, are not progressive. The challenge is the same throughout the game, and incremental difficulty is not required.

As an exercise, take your favorite sport or board game, and write down its rules. Write down these rules as though you were explaining them to someone who has never heard of this game and is from a totally different culture. Even in the most simplistic of games, a description like this can take up many pages. For example, if you were describing baseball, you would have to define the meaning of bases, baseballs, bats, and teams. Then you'd have to talk about innings and outs and balls and strikes, defining each as you went.

It would quickly become quite a large description, especially if you went into RBIs, batting averages, and so on.

You should do this kind of analysis on computer games as well. Many of the game mechanics are encapsulated, but you should be able to at least hazard a guess as to how they are accomplished.

Designing a Game

After you've analyzed a number of games (and you'll notice that when looking at a game analytically, it has a different feel than when you're just playing for fun), you can get down to the serious business of designing new ones.

A warning: there really aren't any "totally original" games any more. Most games these days are just variations on games of the past, or games from a different point of view, or an older game with a new twist. Game design in the modern world pretty much consists of variation on a theme. But don't be dismayed. You don't have to clone other games in order to be a game designer and game programmer.

During your game analysis, presumably you looked at several games from the same genre for which you want to write. You should have good data concerning how these games are put together and what their game mechanics are. You can now do a comparative analysis of what makes these games effective.

If you find an overwhelming commonality between the games you analyze, it probably means that the feature is expected for the genre. This doesn't mean you should automatically include it in your game. It does, however, mean that you should take it under most serious consideration. Is doing it this way the absolute way to do it, or is there another way, just as effective or even more effective? Be skeptical about everything, and question everything. This is not to say that you should reject everything that came before, but just to point out that institutions should always be scrutinized.

When you notice a feature that is included in some games you have analyzed but not in all of them, you should question whether the feature is appropriate to your game. It might help the game, it might do nothing for the game, or it might hurt the game. Trying to anticipate potential problems with a feature now, at design time, is much more productive than having to rip out code later.

If it hurts the game, definitely leave it out, unless you feel you can come up with a modification that fixes the problems. If a feature does nothing for your game either way, you have a few options. You can leave it out completely, or you can make it optional. Not all features can be made optional (a good example in strategy games is the ability to do tactical battle screens, or just let the computer auto-resolve them). You should never just "throw it in." By doing so, it is evident that you don't care about your game, and the users will see this.

If you find a feature that is in only a few or just one or two of the games you analyzed, you should seriously question whether or not to include it. Most times, this means that the feature was haphazardly done and probably isn't very good.

My main point here is that when designing a game, it is very important to think about the features you want. Beginning game developers tend to run into problems with their project getting too large, too fast, because they just started writing the game and adding features as they went. Most of the time, this winds up being a project that is never completed (as I well know...I've failed to complete hundreds of games).

At the end of analysis, you should have a good list of features that you want in your game, and a list that you definitely don't. You should keep both of these lists, because they will help you as you develop your initial concept and as you flesh out that concept.

Initial Concept

You have an idea for a game. Great! Actually, I'm about to show you that you don't have an idea for a game, you have a pre-idea.

Your idea can probably be stated in about one or two sentences, and maybe as much as a whole paragraph. Write it down. If anywhere in your game idea you have the words "like X," where X is the name of a game currently on the market, scratch out the idea and rewrite it so that it doesn't compare itself to another game. This is important. You are not a lemming! Your game will not be the other game, nor a clone of it. It will be a work that stands on its own! Oh, and did I forget to mention *have a good, positive attitude about yourself, your skills, and your idea*?

If applicable, you may want to develop a little bit of a back story. A *back story* is the reason that the game is being played (at least, the reason in the alternate universe within the computer). In strategy games, it tends to be an epic struggle between forces, or the fight of a small band of settlers to survive and grow. There is a story in there somewhere—find it. However, don't go into too much detail on the back story right now. Get the main ideas on paper, and flesh it out later. Sure, you could write a novel about the back story, but you'd never get your game done!

Fleshing It Out

Take your idea and apply the results of your comparative analysis to it. Pick which aspects will be included and which won't. Find features that fit with your game idea and your back story. Feel free to add more features that you think are needed, but remember to rigorously analyze their appropriateness later.

Once you have chosen which features you'll include, you should start drawing pictures (they don't have to be works of art...simple sketches will do) that are sort of a "story board" of your game. Put in as much descriptive detail about your game as possible. Explain how you will implement the various features that you have picked for your game.

Break it down, flesh it out, and put in as much detail as you can. When you have finished, congratulations! You have a design document.

From Theory to Practice

OK…so far I've been talking about vague theoretical concepts and using ambiguous terms like "feature." The difficulty with discussing game design is that it encompasses so many aspects, and various genres have different ways of dealing with them.

Let's pick some genres and look at them.

The Arcade/Action Genre

This genre includes such games as *Pac-Man, Space Invaders, Asteroids, Centipede, Joust, Gauntlet,* and many more too numerous to mention. Mainly, these games are concerned with wave upon wave (with incremental difficulty) of "bad guys" or obstacles. Table 9.1 outlines the main point in each of the games listed.

Table 9.1 Some Arcade Games and Their Underlying Ideas

Game	Idea
Pac-Man	Gobble all the dots and avoid ghosts
Space Invaders	Shoot all invaders before they land
Asteroids	Destroy all asteroids or ships before they destroy you
Centipede	Destroy a number of centipedes and other enemies before they kill you
Joust	Kill all enemies before they regenerate and before they kill you
Gauntlet	Kill enemies and collect power-ups while trying to find the exit

All of these games have "hostiles"—whether they be asteroids or invaders or ghosts. These must be avoided or killed, or they will kill you (whether consciously through an AI, or just by wandering around like the asteroids). Most of these games have some sort of power-up system. At the very least, at various score levels you gain an extra "life." In Pac-Man, the power pills turn the tables on the ghosts. In Gauntlet, keys and potions make your job easier.

These games also all have a "wave" or "level" structure to them. When one level is finished, the next level is loaded. *Centipede* is the only exception: the waves run right into one another without any sort of break (the colors just change).

Now that you have a few topics to analyze, let's take a closer look at them and ask the big questions.

Are Hostiles Necessary?

Hostiles are the primary motivator in all of these games. They provide the ability for the player to fail. Notice how most of these games cannot be "won"? This is so mainly to keep frantic teen-agers pumping quarters into the machines, but it also demonstrates that you don't have to be able to "win" for the game to be fun. Other rewards will suffice, such as getting to the next level, or getting a high score. If you wanted to replace hostiles in a game, you would have to provide a different way for the player to fail. Doing so would take you out of the arcade/action genre, so having a hostile is definitely a fundamental aspect of having a game of this genre.

Are Power-Ups Necessary?

All of these games (except *Gauntlet*) have at least one power-up—the extra life after so many waves or levels or after a certain score. Other power-ups, like *Pac-Man's* power pellet, or the potions and keys in *Gauntlet,* depend entirely on the specific game. Without the power pellets, *Pac-Man* would be a lot harder to play…maybe *too* hard. *Gauntlet* keys are absolutely essential, because part of the challenge is to find enough keys to get through all the doors. The potions in *Gauntlet* aren't absolutely necessary, but they relieve (for a moment) the stress of being embroiled in a battle, so they are appropriate to the game.

Are Waves or Levels Necessary?

Levels or waves help break up the play a little bit, but they aren't absolutely required. You can achieve incremental difficulty without having levels, but using levels makes implementing that incremental difficulty easier.

As you can see, we've pretty much nailed down the action/arcade genre. Waves, power-ups, and hostiles are key elements. If you were to design a game for this genre, you would want to carefully consider how you wanted to implement these things, or if you wanted to find an alternative.

Isometric Games

Isometric games usually fall into a few genres: computer role-playing games, turn-based strategy games, real-time strategy games and simulations, and board/puzzle games.

Let's take a look at the turn-based strategy game subgenre. (Turn-based strategy games still belong to the strategy game genre, but the implementation is much different from a real-time game or simulation.) A few of the games in this subgenre include *Civilization II, Civilization: Call to Power, Master of Orion II, Imperialism II,* and *Alpha Centauri.*

- In all of these games, you start out with a limited number of units (usually only one or two), and from this, you have to build a grand empire. Some games, however, have a "scenario" mode, in which a situation is set up for you, and you have certain objectives that you have to reach.
- In all of these games, the units available to you depend on what technologies you possess, and these games have ways to assign the technologies you are researching.
- These games, for the most part, have resources that you have to discover and exploit, and you have to improve the land or a city or colony to better make use of these resources.
- The goal of most of these games is to subdue all of your computerized opponents, either diplomatically, through military action, or by completion of a task before they complete it.

There's a lot more to turn-based strategy games, but this is a good sampling.

Is Starting Out the Player with Only a Few Units Necessary?

It's not necessary to start out everybody as a weakling. However, except where the player has selected the "impossible" option or has chosen to play a scenario, it is a good idea to start out all the players (human and computer) as approximately even. This is one of the important aspects of turn-based games. The player gets to take his single unit and create an empire with it.

Are Technology and Research Necessary?

Technology and research enhance the replay value. Without technology to research, all things are available to the player at the beginning. This might be what you want. However, including technology and research in the game promotes careful planning and forethought on the part of the player.

This is not to say that having technology and research in a game is essential to the genre. In fact, it seems that every game maker just throws them in. I remember playing the old Avalon Hill strategy board games (with the hex grids), and very few of them had technology and research.

What Sort of Win Conditions Are Necessary?

In most types of games, an absolute "win" condition is not necessary. In strategy games, however, some sort of win condition is necessary, whether it is the construction of some device before any of your opponents, the elimination of your opponents, or whatever. Commonly, strategy games have a scoring system based on any number of things—level of technology, size of army, population, and so on. This scoring system lets you rank players after they have quit the game, and you can then build a "hall of fame" list.

As you can see, quite a bit of thought goes into designing a game. You have to ask yourself the big questions. That's really what this chapter is about... thinking. Sure, you could just take a game you like and make something that looks and plays like it (and many beginners want to do just that). That's not necessarily a bad idea, but too close of a copy won't do much for your game programming image.

Empowering the User: Giving Thought to the User Interface

Throughout the game design process, you should keep user empowerment in mind. When designing screens with which the user will interact, you should strive to make the most intuitive interface you can. This means menus and buttons and other user interface components. It also means character selection, object manipulation, and just about everything that the user can do in the game. Putting a good deal of thought into this topic will be of great help later, when it comes time to actually make your game.

Also, you should determine which of your game's features are optional. Customizing game play is a great way to empower your users. I once played a game that had an option screen with exactly two options: music on/off and sound on/off. That was the total of the options (and yes, it was a full-screen option panel)! In my opinion, that is unacceptable.

If you plan to have your game sell in more than one language, you'll probably want to use icons on your buttons instead of text. Doing so is fine, but be sure to put some sort of textual tool tips on the screen if the mouse hovers over these icons for a few seconds.

This brings me to something else... your game's learning curve. When I buy a game, I want to plop the CD in the drive, close the door, install it, and play it. Note that I did not mention "read the manual" or "read the help file" anywhere in this process. I want to play, and I want to play *now!* Most game players are like this... many of them never read the manual. Not all games can accomplish the "just sit down and play" intuitiveness, however. *Imperialism II* by SSI is one of these. It's a turn-based strategy game that at first seems difficult to play, but playing the tutorials shows you that it's actually not so hard and, in reality, is a fun game. If you can avoid requiring tutorials or reading manuals or help files, though, do so.

On the other hand, I hate games without adequate documentation. You should have a good help system for your game, even if your player never uses it. You should have strategy tips of some kind if applicable. Don't give everything away, but do give a nudge in the right direction.

A Few Notes About Controls

If you use keyboard controls, use the arrow keys or the numeric keypad. If you use the keypad, try not to use the 5 key for anything. The Esc key is for canceling something or exiting something. The spacebar is a big key, and you can probably find a use for it. F1 is for help. If you have controls for a number of related purposes, try to use a row of keys rather than scattering about the keyboard.

When using mouse controls, the left button is for the primary action, and the right button is for the secondary action. Most of the time, the primary and secondary actions can be determined by what the mouse is currently pointing at. If it's pointing at a monster, attack. If it's pointing at an item, pick it up. If it's pointing at a door, open it.

Also, when the mouse is over something, provide a visual clue—a highlight, a different cursor, or just something that lets the user know that the mouse is over something that can be interacted with. It's also not a bad idea to have a tool tip or some text in a status bar when the mouse hovers over an object.

Finally, in games that take up more than the screen, it is traditional to scroll through the map when the mouse is on the edge of the screen. Also, there should probably be a mini-map of some sort, with a rectangle showing where the current view is.

Making a Real Game

I've included a sample game as IsoHex9_1.cpp. It incorporates most of what we have covered in this first part of the book.

The game is *Breakout,* something I'm sure you've played before. The idea is to use a paddle to bounce a ball and strike bricks. When all of the bricks from one level are destroyed, the game advances to the next level (which looks just like the first level). Figure 9.2 shows what this game looks like.

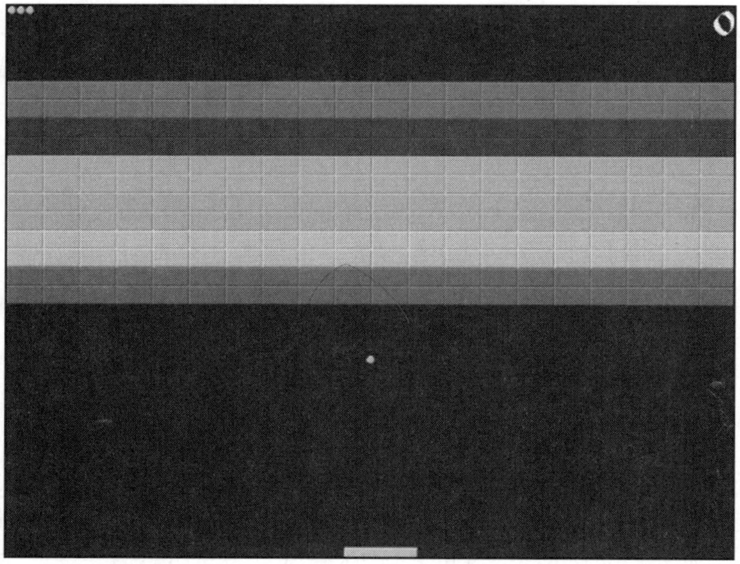

Figure 9.2

The look of IsoHex9_1.cpp

The graphics are less than dazzling, I know. (I spent about 15 minutes with Paint Shop Pro to make them.) The main reason for including this demo is to show you some of the basic ways you can accomplish tasks in a game program.

The controls are pretty simple: you move the paddle with the mouse, and a left-click starts things. There are no title screens or option screens. There is very little user empowerment (hey, it's just a sample). There are plenty of sounds—a bouncing noise (borrowed from the boucing ball demo), a different brick hit noise for each color of brick, a losing sound, a winning sound, and a few voice sounds for when you hit more than 10 bricks between paddle hits. These sounds all come from either my voice or my Yamaha keyboard.

Game State

IsoHex9_1.cpp has a number of global variables. The first of these is game state. While the game state is kept track of by all the variables in the program (score, paddle and ball positions, number of bricks left), there is a main game state—playing, waiting to play, game over, win, death, and so on.

I keep track of these using an `enum` and a variable.

```
//game states
enum GAMESTATE
{GS_START,GS_STARTWAIT,GS_PLAY,GS_DEAD,GS_RESET,GS_WINLEVEL,GS_LOSEGAME};
//main game state
GAMESTATE GameState=GS_START;
```

I also could have managed these with a number of `consts` or `#defines`, but in an `enum`, I know that I won't duplicate a number accidentally and have to track down a bug for five hours. It's mainly a matter of personal preference.

The `GameState` variable is processed in `Prog_Loop()`:

```
void Prog_Loop()
{
        switch(GameState)
        {
        case GS_START:
                {
                        dwScore=0;
                        dwLives=3;
                        SetUpGame();
                        GameState=GS_STARTWAIT;
                }break;
```

```
case GS_STARTWAIT:
        {
                ShowBoard();
                lpddsprime->Flip(NULL,DDFLIP_WAIT);
        }break;
case GS_PLAY:
        {
                //limit frame time
                DWORD dwTimeStart=GetTickCount();
                //move ball
                MoveBall();
                //show board
                ShowBoard();
                //show frame
                lpddsprime->Flip(NULL,DDFLIP_WAIT);

                //wait for 10 ms to elapse
                while(GetTickCount()-dwTimeStart<10);
        }break;
case GS_DEAD:
        {
                dwLives--;
                if(dwLives)
                {
                        GameState=GS_RESET;
                }
                else
                {
                        GameState=GS_LOSEGAME;
                }
        }break;
case GS_RESET:
        {
                ResetGame();
                GameState=GS_STARTWAIT;
        }break;
case GS_WINLEVEL:
        {
                SetUpGame();
                GameState=GS_STARTWAIT;
```

```
            }break;
        case GS_LOSEGAME:
            {
                GameState=GS_START;
            }break;
        }
}
```

Prog_Loop doesn't really do much. It manipulates game state variables (mainly GameState), and calls functions depending on the value of GameState. This use of a variable like GameState is pretty standard, but, of course, there are other, more efficient ways to implement it. For example, I could have created an array of pointers to functions that get called during each Prog_Loop. This would certainly be more efficient than the switch I currently have in there, but since the code is instructional in nature (and because the use of function pointers would have been confusing to read), I used the switch.

If you take a look at the const/#define section of the code, you'll see that most of the stuff in there is hardcoded (such as the widths and heights of various objects). I have told you not to do this, and then I went and did it. Feel free to yell "hypocrite!" if you wish. Because of this choice I made, changing the code would be more difficult and prone to errors. The reason I hardcoded is because it speeded up development. (It is only an example, after all.)

I want you to take a closer look at the code within the GS_PLAY game state:

```
//limit frame time
DWORD dwTimeStart=GetTickCount();
//move ball
MoveBall();
//show board
ShowBoard();
//show frame
lpddsprime->Flip(NULL,DDFLIP_WAIT);
//wait for 10 ms to elapse
while(GetTickCount()-dwTimeStart<10);
```

You'll notice the use of GetTickCount at either end of this game state. GetTickCount retrieves the number of milliseconds that have passed since you started your computer. As you enter this code, it sets dwTimeStart to the tick counter's current value. Later, the code spins a while until GetTickCount-dwTimeStart is no longer less than 10. This is called a frame rate lock. With this code, even on a superfast machine made at some future date, this game will not output more than 100 frames per second (1000 ms in a second, 10 seconds per frame).

IsoHex9_1 is done, but not finished. What is the difference? Well, when a game is "done," it is playable. You can play this game for hours and hours, but it doesn't include the amenities that come with other games. Here's a short list of features that IsoHex9_1 needs in order to be "finished":

- The ability to set volumes and mute sounds
- Title screen
- Top ten list
- Some sort of messages when you start, die, or lose the game
- Maybe some different types of levels
- The ability to play in a window

As you can see, IsoHex9_1 is far from finished. A lot of beginning game developers work on things like the title screen and other stuff before they work on the game itself. This is not a good practice. Often, you'll end up with 10 title screens and no games. I've seen many a beginning game developer pour several days into making a really good title screen and main menu, only to later abandon the project.

I left IsoHex9_1 unfinished on purpose. The reason? I want *you* to finish it. This game is by no means difficult to finish. It just takes time and commitment. Finishing a game is a true accomplishment. If you don't want to finish this game, make a smallish game like it and finish that. Feel free to send me a copy.

A Few Words about Finishing Games

The easiest thing in the world is to start a game project. The hardest thing is finishing it. Since we as game developers are at heart game players, our attention span isn't as long as it could be. We start out working on a game, and we work on it for three days straight, and then we get burned out and say "I'll get back to it later"—but we never do. It just sits there, until eventually we reformat the hard drive, and then it's gone forever. I know I must have done this about a thousand times. With several hundred thousand game programmers out there, that means that there are several hundred million unfinished games out there. *Several hundred million!*

Needless to say, you should finish a game you start. This isn't as easy as it sounds. Boredom, burnout, a new game you pick up at the store—these are all things that keep us from finishing our games. Don't let them.

A Few Tips for Finishing Games

Following are just a few gems of wisdom I've acquired over the years. They make game development more likely to wind up with an actual finished product, rather than a collection of abandoned partially finished games.

Tip #1: Pace Yourself

Don't work 24 hours a day on anything. Unless you have a publisher, you don't have any deadlines, and you can take as long as you like making the game. Try not to work more than eight hours a day on it. If you have other commitments (job, school, family), don't work more than three to six hours a day. As a corollary, just a single hour, or even two hours, won't work. You have to get into "the zone," which takes about an hour to an hour and a half to achieve.

Tip #2: Plan, Plan, Plan

Develop the game's design before you start working on it. Draw everything, from main game play down to the menus. The more you decide on during the design phase, the less you have to think about during development—you just have to take the concepts from paper to code. Write down all your neat ideas. Also, if you decide to redesign part of the game while in the middle of development, step away from the computer to do the redesign. Avoid designing on-the-fly as much as possible.

Tip #3: Know Your Limitations

Aim low. Yes, the sky's the limit, and you can do anything you put your mind to. Whatever. Aim low. By this, I mean that you should pick projects you know you can do. Not *think* you can do. Not something you *might* be able to do. Something you *can* do. Something you *can* do is more likely to be finished, as opposed to something where you first have to learn something. If you want to learn something, make a demo program that demonstrates how to use the new thing all by itself, not a game that uses it.

Tip #4: Wax On, Wax Off

Even when you think you're finished, you could probably add some more polish. On the other hand, there comes a time to declare things done. Usually, before you are finished with a project, you will hate working on it. This is the trial by fire of all programs, especially those where you aren't getting paid to make it. Push through that time, and finish.

Summary

I can't possibly hope to imbue you with all the stuff about game design I've absorbed over the years. Most of it has become so ingrained in my programming style that I don't think about it—it just happens. It takes time to develop game design skills. It can't happen overnight, or even over the course of a book.

This closes the chapter and this part of the book. Here are a few thoughts I want to leave you with before moving on to the next chapter:

- Design your game as fully as possible, and really think about the design.
- Work incrementally. Make small games as you start out and large ones later.
- Finish your games. The feeling of stepping back and looking at a finished piece of work is one of the best feelings in the world.

Part II

Isometric Fundamentals

CHAPTER 10

Tile-Based Fundamentals

- What Does "Tile-Based" mean?
- An Introduction to Rectangular tiles
- Managing Tile Sets
- Tile Map Basics

With this chapter, we break away from the introductory matter that filled Part 1 and start to move into the really cool stuff. Naturally, you aren't going to fly when you haven't walked yet. We will explore tile-based fundamentals, from both the management and user interface sides of the coin.

What Does "Tile-Based" Mean?

You've seen floor tiles, right? Sometimes, especially in older buildings or in malls, different tiles are combined into a pattern (sometimes very elaborate patterns). That's exactly what we'll be doing, but instead of using linoleum or porcelain, we'll be using graphic images.

This is where the comparison ends between tile-based games and floor tiles. When you make a tile-based game, each graphic tile has a different meaning. One might be the floor, and the other solid rock (representing a wall). In a tile-based game, some sort of "characters" or "units" usually occupy tiles, and are moved around by either the player or the computer's AI. These are called *agents* in AI terminology.

The rules of the game determine what happens to the agents as they occupy the various tiles of the game, and they also govern how the agents may move from one tile to another. In a strategy game, an agent may be able to move three tiles per turn. However, different tiles (such as grassland and hills) may have different "movement costs" associated with them. Grassland might only cost 1 to move, but a hill could easily cost 2 or 3. Further addition of things like roads or rivers may reduce these costs. It can all get very complicated very quickly.

Of course, the player isn't really thinking about all this. He just presses the up arrow to move to whatever square is there, and the computer takes care of movement cost. (Even though the player isn't consciously thinking about movement costs, he does know that it takes longer to traverse hills than it does to traverse plains.)

Myths about Tile-Based Games

The first myth about tile-based games is that they are dead. This is wholly untrue. Yes, the days of pure 2D tile-based games are over. These days you have to have 3D rendering to make a really hot game. However, even 3D games can be tile-based, and many are. This is where isometric games come in. I won't go into how isometric tiles work until chapter 11, but suffice it to say that isometric *is* 3D, even if it's done with just 2D rendering. Most real-time strategy games and turn-based strategy games are made using isometric tiles (although the days of pure 2D isometric tile-based games are drawing to a close as well).

The second myth is that no one will buy a tile-based game. Also untrue. In your local computer game store, see for yourself. The strategy genre is filled with tile-based games.

Tile-Based Terminology

While reading this section, keep in mind that these are mainly the terms I use. You might have different names for them. For the most part, these terms are standard.

- **Tile**. A graphic used to render a portion of the background. When using rectangular tiles, this usually means that the entire rectangular area is taken up by the tile. This is not always so, however. You might have "fringe" tiles to take care of coastlines or a transition from one type of terrain to another, in which case the tile may cover only a portion of the rectangular area.
- **Sprite**. An arbitrarily-sized graphic that is usually used for either agents or foreground objects. Really, everything that isn't a tile is a sprite. *Sprite* is just a generic term, like *tile*. You may decide to subclass them into units, buildings, and markers, depending on the type of game.
- **Tileset**. A set of tiles. It is inefficient to store each tile in a separate graphics file. It's easier to just take tiles and group them into logical sets and then place them all into a single graphics file that gets parsed later. A tileset might include sprites or might consist entirely of sprites.
- **Space**. Any arbitrarily-sized and shaped two-dimensional space. Usually a space is rectangular, but not in all cases. You tend to work with nonrectangular spaces using a bounding rectangle as well as whatever other structure describes them.
- **Screen space**. The space on the screen used for rendering the play area, not including any borders, status panels, menu bars, message bars, or any other nonplay area structures. In some cases, the entire display is the screen space. Often, it is not.
- **View space**. The same size as screen space, but the upper-left corner is always at (0,0) for view space. Many times, view space and screen space are the same. View space, in most cases, is purely abstract and plays no part in the rendering process.
- **Tile space**. The smallest space (usually rectangular) that is taken up by an individual tile. In rectangular tiles, this is often the entire rectangle. Tile space can also refer to the space taken up by a sprite.
- **World space**. The space that allows the display of an entire map of tiles and their associated object/agent sprites. In board games and puzzle games, world space may be equal to or smaller than screen space/view space. In larger games, world space might be hundreds of times larger. Figure 10.1 shows the relationship between the screen, view, and world spaces.

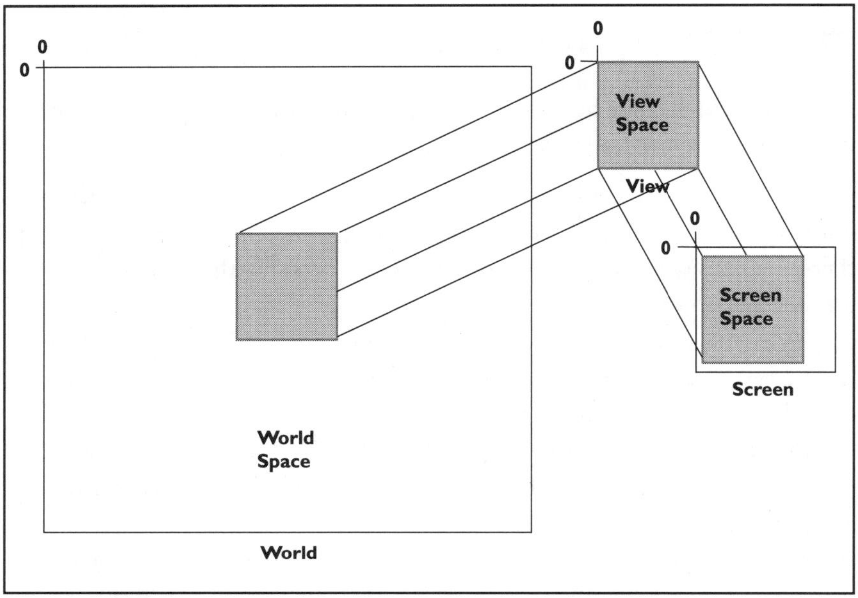

Figure 10.1

Screen, view, and world spaces and their relationship

- **Anchor**. A correlation of one point of a space (usually (0,0)) to another space. An example of this is a correlation of view space to screen space. If you had an 8-pixel border around the main viewing area, you would keep a point that kept track of the relationship from view space to screen space—namely, (8,8). This lets you know how to convert between screen space and view space. Another example would be an anchor that converts from view space to world space. In a scrolling tile engine (with a world space larger than the view space), this anchor helps determine which tiles have to be rendered by translating the tile's world space coordinates into view space coordinates. From there, you can translate them into screen space coordinates.
- ***Anchor space***. A space that defines legal values for the view-to-world anchor. Clipping your anchor point with anchor space lets you easily manage the view-to-world anchor and lets you keep the player from having an illegal view.
- ***Extent***. A rectangle relative to a point (usually an anchor), often with negative left and top values. We will get into this more when I talk about using templates to manage files.
- **Tilemap**. An array containing information about how the world looks—that is, which tiles are in what location. Tilemaps also contain information about objects and agents in the world, even though the structure that contains agents or objects may be a different array, or not even an array at all.
- **Agent**. Any sprite (or sequence of sprites used for animation) that moves, either by AI or by player action.
- **Object**. An unmoving graphic, representing such things as trees, rocks, or other items.

Hope I didn't lose you. If you're fuzzy on the real application of these terms, don't worry. I'll explore the meaning and uses of each as I go, and you will gain full understanding.

AN INTRODUCTION TO RECTANGULAR TILES

Rectangular tiles are the easiest of all to work with, because of their rectangular-ness. Most of the time, when working in rectangle land, you use square tiles. You can use other sizes, of course, but square seems to be a favorite. An example of a tile is shown in Figure 10.2.

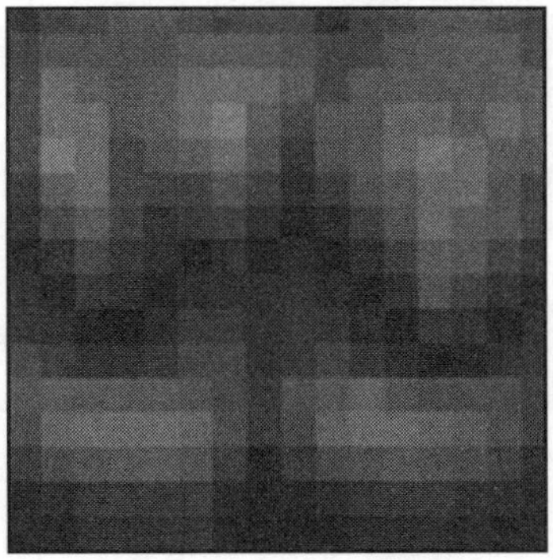

Figure 10.2

A square tile

The point of view for games with square tiles is usually *top down* or *overhead.* This just means that all your graphics must be drawn as though you are looking down on the object. Sometimes you can give your game a slightly angled view so that you are looking mostly down, but you can see some of the front or back, depending on how the agent is facing.

Another point of view for square tiles is the *side scroller* view, where you are looking at the world from its side. This was very popular among older action games like *Super Mario Bros* (Nintendo) and the original *Duke Nukem.*

With the advance of 3D display technology, both the top-down and side-scroller views have become nearly obsolete.

NOTE

Later, when we get to isometric tiles, you will use a view called "3/4," in which you render your agents and object as though you are looking straight at them. It gives the illusion of 3D without perspective correction. Luckily, the human eye is easy to fool, because it automatically corrects for the errors in the projection.

Normally, you will want to group your tiles and sprites into graphical files where more than one tile or sprite is in the file. Normally, you'll want one or two files with the graphics for the background, a file for objects, and then a number of files for the agents (one file to an agent, unless you don't have too many animation sequences).

The examples shown in Figures 10.3, 10.4, and 10.5 are from Ari Feldman's SpriteLib, which is a free graphics package that has been around for a few years. If you aren't graphically inclined (don't be ashamed…you're not alone), you may want to download it from http://www.arifeldman.com.

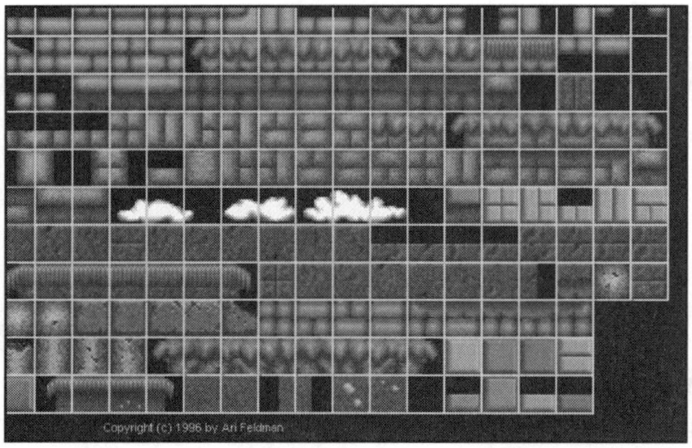

Figure 10.3

Background tiles

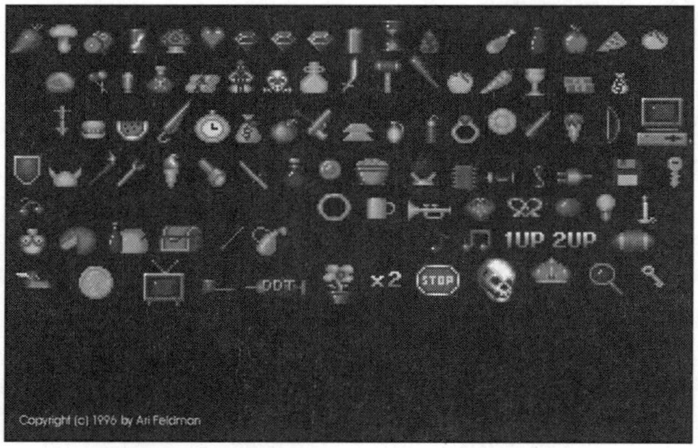

Figure 10.4

Object tiles

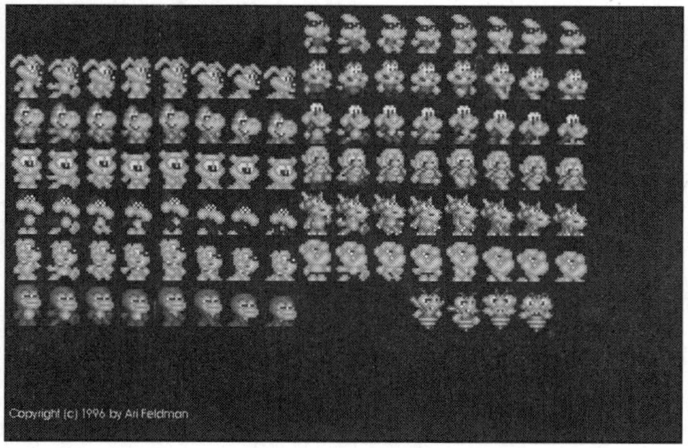

Figure 10.5

Character tiles

MANAGING TILESETS

The tilesets and sprite sets you just saw are great, but they aren't exactly in a form that is easy to work with for programmers like you and me. If you wanted to work with them, you'd have to store a bunch of rectangles in a text file or other configuration file, or (*gasp!*) you'd have to hardcode image rectangles. Later, if you decided to change the art, this would be a maintenance horror show. You'd have to go back and change around the rectangle lists. Of course you'd forget one, and naturally you wouldn't find out until one of your beta testers got really far into the game... well, I think you get the idea.

So, what's the solution to this dilemma? Templates. A template is used in the first example of a tileset—the one with the white boxes around it (Figure 10.3). That's one way to do a template. However, it's not the best way, because you still have to either hardcode or put into a configuration file the width and height of the template.

Load IsoHex10_1.bmp into your favorite graphics editing program. Figure 10.6 shows what it looks like.

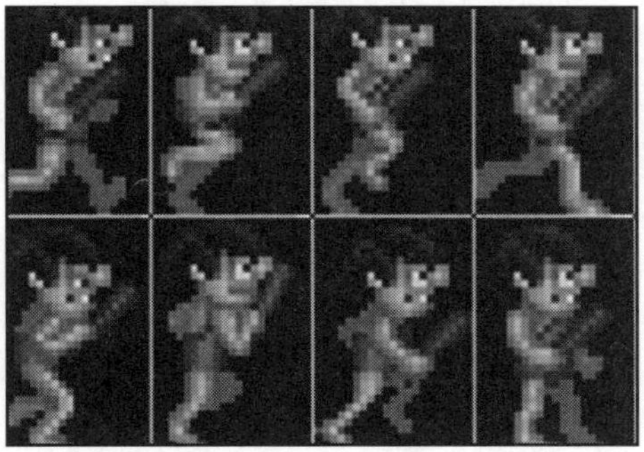

Figure 10.6

A sample tileset

You can see the border around each of the images. Unlike the tileset shown in Figure 10.3, the border is green instead of white. Or is it?

Take a really close look at the top cell (zoom in as far as the program will let you), shown in Figure 10.7.

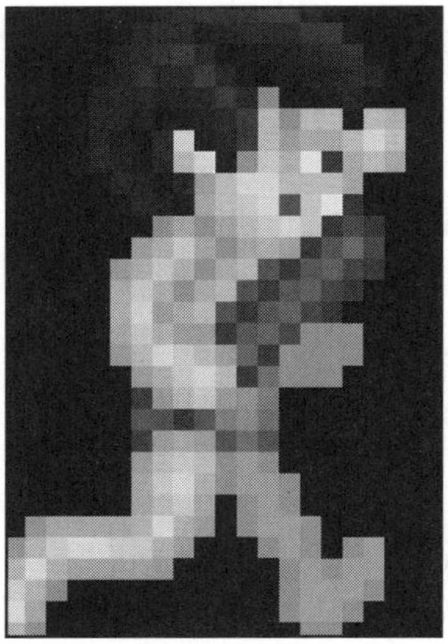

Figure 10.7

Zooming in on the caveman

There is more than just green... there is also white and cyan (you can't see it too well in the book, but you can see it just fine in a graphics program). As you might have guessed, each of the different colors means something. The green dots span the width and height of the image. White dots are part of the frame but outside of the image. The black dot in the corner is what designates the corner of a tile cell, and also the transparent color of the tileset. The cyan dot (or blue dot) designates a coordinate for the tile's anchor. (I use cyan when the anchor is within the bounds of the tile image itself. In other words, it would otherwise be a green dot, and blue when the anchor point would otherwise be white.)

Why these colors? Why not a completely different set of colors? Quite frankly, you *could* use a different set of colors, and this type of template supports just that. Take a look and zoom in on the upper-right corner of the tileset (shown in Figure 10.8).

Figure 10.8

The upper-right corner of the tileset, demonstrating control colors

There are five pixels in the rightmost column, in the following order: black, white, blue, green, and cyan. These specify corner, frame, anchor, inside, and inside anchor, respectively. If you wanted to, you could change one of these colors to red (for example), and put it in the proper control color position, and use it instead of the color used here.

Using an extended template like this gives you a great deal of freedom. You can make a template and later change the width or height of the cells, and it will still load the same way. The green and blue and cyan pixels let you calculate tile spaces, anchor points, and tile extents, which you can parse into arrays of rectangles and points. You can move an image's anchor point and have it show up in a different location. An extended template takes pressure off programmers and removes stress from artists, who, when using it, are less constrained by the normally tight restrictions for tile-based graphics.

Before you finish building your utopian society, though, you have to write code that will parse a graphics file into arrays of rectangles and points. Let's start by figuring out what information you need about each tile. Presumably, these templated graphics will be on an `IDirectDrawSurface7` somewhere, and you want to optimize your data structures for using `Blt` and `BltFast`. Since both of these use source rectangles, you'll definitely want to keep an array of `RECT`s for that. The coordinates held in these `RECT`s will be pixel coordinates measured from (0,0) in the tileset's image. Figure 10.9 shows what one of these `RECT`s might look like.

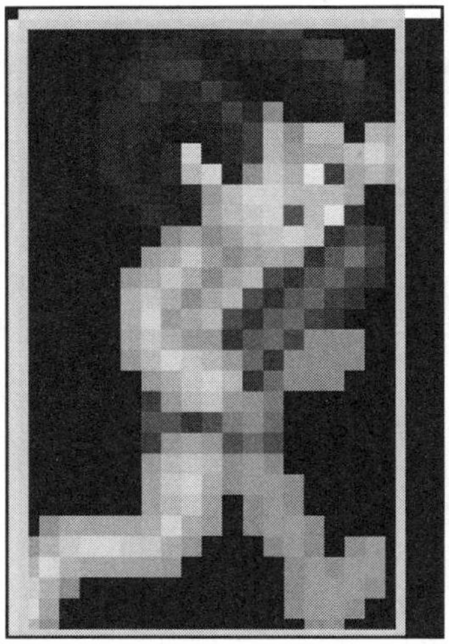

Figure 10.9

Source RECT

In Figure 10.9, the RECT has the coordinates (1,1)–(39,61). Remember that you have to add one to the bottom and right because of how RECTs work. Doing so gives you a resulting RECT of (1,1)–(40,62).

Because you might or might not be referencing off the upper-left of these source RECTs (the blue and cyan points might lie elsewhere), you need an array of POINTs to keep track of the tile anchors. Like the source rectangles, these POINTs contain coordinates into the tileset image, meaning that a tile with a rectangle of (100,100)–(200,200) has its anchor point within the x and y range of that RECT (rather than having the anchor point in reference to the tile cell's upper-left corner, which is another way you could have done this that would have added unnecessary computations). Figure 10.10 shows the anchor point.

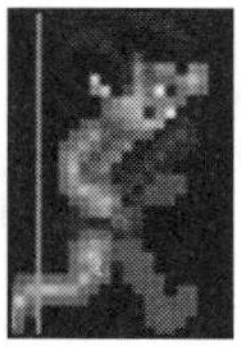

Figure 10.10

Anchor point

In Figure 10.10, the anchor point is (7,1), which is within the range of your source RECT, as I said it would be.

Finally, you add another array of RECTs to hold the tile extents. Extents can be calculated after the source RECT and anchor POINT have been determined, like so:

```
//copy source rect
CopyRect(&rcExtent,&rcSrc);
//offset by anchor point
OffsetRect(&rcExtent,-ptAnchor.x,-ptAnchor.y);
```

In this case, the extent is (–6,0)–(32,60). The derivation of these values is as follows:

Upper Left:
From source RECT (1,1)
Minus anchor point (7,1)
Combine coordinates (1–7,1–1)
Solve (–6,0)

Bottom Right:
From source RECT (40,62)
Minus anchor point (7,1)
Combine (40–7,62–1)
Solve (33,61)

Yes, there's a negative left coordinate; this is quite common for this type of tileset, where you might want to reference a tile from a point other than the upper left. It would not be a stretch to use the character's feet or center. Just use whatever works to give an animation continuity and smoothness. For this tileset, the horizontal aspect of the anchor lines up with the back of the caveman's hair.

The idea here is that you want to be able to simply specify a single (x,y) screen coordinate and tell it which tile to blit, and have it come out right. When blitting, the (x,y) point corresponds to the tile's anchor point. This means that if you tell this tile to blit to screen coordinate (100,100), you want screen coordinate (100,100) to correspond to the tileset image's coordinate (7,1).

You want the extent so that you can simplify the process of determining the coordinates of the destination RECT (or the destination (x,y) for BltFast). Taking the source RECT and subtracting the point gives you the extent. This way, based on a single set of coordinates (dstX and dstY), you can determine the proper destination rectangle. For example:

```
//for Blt
CopyRect(&rcDst,&rcExtent);
OffsetRect(&rcDst,dstX,dstY);
//perform the Blt

//for BltFast
dstX+=rcDst.left;
dstY+=rcDst.top;
//perform bltfast
```

If you didn't precalculate the extents, you would have to calculate them from the source rectangle, anchor point, and destination point each time you wanted to render the tile. Although doing so isn't too much more work (about a dozen add or subtract operations), it *is* work, and in game programming, you want to avoid any work that you can. Precalculating tile extents might give you just one extra frame per second or even only half a frame per second, which doesnt' sound like much, but if you have two optimizations that each give you an extra half-frame per second, you've just earned yourself another frame per second. Game programming is a game of inches.

A TileSet Class

So, now that you've decided what information you want, you just have to go in and get it. I made a class to work with these sorts of templates. It's called `CTileSet`, and you can find the code for it in TileSet.h and TileSet.cpp.

The Class Declaration

First, I designed a struct to contain important information about tiles, including source rectangle, anchor point, and destination extent. I put this information into `TILEINFO`.

```
//tileset information structure
struct TILEINFO
{
	RECT rcSrc;//source rectangle
	POINT ptAnchor;//anchoring point
	RECT rcDstExt;//destination extent
};
```

The members of TILEINFO are explained in Table 10.1.

Table 10.1 TILEINFO Members

TILEINFO Member	Meaning
rcSrc	Source RECT for the tile
ptAnchor	Anchor POINT for the tile
rcDstExt	Destination extent RECT for the tile

Next, here's the class itself:

```
class CTileSet
{
private:
	//number of tiles in tileset
	DWORD dwTileCount;
	//tile array
	TILEINFO*  ptiTileList;
	//filename from which to reload
	LPSTR lpszReload;
	//offscreen plain directdrawsurface7
	LPDIRECTDRAWSURFACE7 lpddsTileSet;
public:
	//constructor
	CTileSet();
	//destructor
	~CTileSet();
	//load (initializer)
	void Load(LPDIRECTDRAW7 lpdd,LPSTR lpszLoad);
	//reload (restore)
	void Reload();
	//unload (uninitializer)
	void Unload();
	//get number of tiles
	DWORD GetTileCount();
	//get tile list
```

```
        TILEINFO* GetTileList();
        //get surface
        LPDIRECTDRAWSURFACE7 GetDDS();
        //retrieve filename
        LPSTR GetFileName();
        //blit a tile
        void PutTile(LPDIRECTDRAWSURFACE7 lpddsDst,int xDst,int yDst,int
iTileNum);
};
```

The private members contain all of the information needed to process the tileset. These are listed in Table 10.2.

Table 10.2 CTileSet Private Members

CTileSet Private Member	Meaning
`dwTileCount`	The number of tiles contained in the tileset
`ptiTileList`	A pointer to an array of `TILEINFO` that describes each tile
`lpszReload`	The file name from which this tileset was loaded
`lpddsTileSet`	The `IDirectDrawSurface7` pointer that is the off-screen surface containing the tileset

The member functions in the public section perform all necessary operations on the tileset. Table 10.3 explains these member functions.

Table 10.3 CTileSet Public Member Functions

CTileSet Public Member Function	Purpose
`CTileSet`	Constructor that initializes all variables to 0 or `NULL`
`~CTileSet`	Destructor that calls `Unload`
`Load`	Loads and parses an image
`Reload`	Reloads the image (if for some reason the surface has been freed, such as resulting from an Alt+Tab)
`Unload`	Frees the resources associated with the tileset
`GetTileCount`	Returns the number of tiles
`GetTileList`	Returns the tile info pointer
`GetDDS`	Returns a pointer to the `IDirectDrawSurface7` containing the tileset
`GetFileName`	Returns the name of the file from which the tileset was loaded
`PutTile`	Puts a tile on a surface, given a coordinate and a tile number

The constructor and destructor don't do much and aren't very interesting, but the other functions are more important, so I'll explain them in more detail.

CTileSet::Load

This function loads a bitmap and places it onto a DirectDraw surface and also parses the image into its component tiles.

```
void CTileSet::Load(LPDIRECTDRAW7 lpdd,LPSTR lpszLoad);
```

The `lpdd` parameter is a pointer to an `IDirectDraw` object, which is used to initially create the tileset surface. The `lpszLoad` parameter is the name of the file to load that contains the image you want for this tileset.

This function is quite long, because of the image parsing. It performs the following tasks:

1. Loads the image.
2. Grabs the control colors from the upper-right corner.
3. Counts and measures the horizontal and vertical cells.
4. Allocates the tile list.
5. Scans each tile's left and top for anchor points and inside points (using default values if these control points are not specified).
6. Calculates destination tile extents.

All of the main work is done here, at load time, so that after a call to `Load`, you can immediately start using `PutTile`, and you never really have to worry about it ever again.

CTileSet::Reload

`CtileSet::Reload` reloads an image if and when it is lost due to a display mode change or Alt+Tab incident.

```
void CTileSet::Reload();
```

If, as a result of an Alt+Tab or other such misfortune, your tileset's surface is lost, a call to `IDirectDraw7::RestoreAllSurfaces` may be required. After that, you can call `CTileSet::Reload`, and the image will be reloaded (but not reparsed).

CTileSet::Unload

This frees all the resources used by the tileset. It is called during the destructor and whenever `Load` is called.

```
void CTileSet::Unload();
```

Very likely, you will never call this function directly, since it is taken care of in the destructor. Even if you wanted to load a different image into a tileset, you could just call `Load`. The only time you would ever want to call `Unload` is if you were trying to conserve video memory for other images. It is here mainly for completeness.

CTileSet::GetTileCount

This one's a no-brainer.

```
DWORD CTileSet::GetTileCount();
```

This function returns the number of tiles in the set.

CTileSet::GetTileList

This function gives you access to the tile information, which is very important if you want to implement clipping yourself rather than relying on a DirectDraw clipper and `CTileSet::PutTile`.

```
TILEINFO* CTileSet::GetTileList();
```

This function returns the pointer to the tile array. You can use the result of this function just as you would an array.

```
//make tileset
CTileSet tsExample;
tsExample.Load(lpdd,"Sample.bmp");
//retrieve the info about tile zero
TILEINFO ti=txExample.GetTileList()[0];
```

CTileSet::GetDDS

This function allows access to the DirectDraw surface on which dwell the tiles.

```
LPDIRECTDRAWSURFACE7 CTileSet::GetDDS();
```

This function returns the `IDirectDrawSurface7` pointer that contains the image of the tileset. If for some reason you wanted to modify or read from the surface, this would be the function you'd start with. Keep in mind that any changes you make to the surface will not survive a call to `CTileSet::Reload`. Also, if you want to keep a copy of the surface pointer for a long time, it might be best to use `AddRef` so that the surface isn't inadvertently deleted in the interim.

CTileSet::GetFileName

This function is pretty self-explanatory.

```
LPSTR CTileSet::GetFileName();
```

This returns a pointer to the file name that is used to reload the tileset.

CTileSet::PutTile

This function is the reason for the whole show. It's the workhorse of the `CTileSet` class.

```
void CTileSet::PutTile(LPDIRECTDRAWSURFACE7 lpddsDst,int xDst,int yDst,int
iTileNum);
```

This takes care of putting a tile onto a destination surface (`lpddsDst`), with `xDst,yDst` corresponding to the anchor point of the specified tile (`iTileNum`). Tiles are numbered starting with 0 and are ordered left to right, top to bottom.

An Animated Sprite Example

One of the many uses for a tileset is for an animated sprite sequence. Earlier in this chapter, I showed you a tileset consisting of some caveman images from spritelib, which is a good example of one such animation sequence. Load up IsoHex10_1.cpp, which makes use of `CTileset` (among other things; see the top of IsoHex10_1.cpp). If you load and run it, you will see the caveman running in place, as shown in Figure 10.11.

Figure 10.11

Animation demo

This example is based on IsoHex1_1.cpp, just like the rest of the examples. The main differences exist in `Prog_Init`, `Prog_Loop`, and `Prog_Done`.

Setting up

The `Prog_Init` does the required DirectDraw setup (creating the DirectDraw interface, creating the primary surface and the back buffer). It also loads the tileset into `tsCaveMan` (a global `CTileSet` variable).

```
bool Prog_Init()
{
	//create IDirectDraw7
	lpdd=LPDD_Create(hWndMain,DDSCL_FULLSCREEN | DDSCL_EXCLUSIVE |
DDSCL_ALLOWREBOOT);
	//set display mode
	lpdd->SetDisplayMode(800,600,16,0,0);
```

```
	//create primary surface
	lpddsMain=LPDDS_CreatePrimary(lpdd,1);
	//get back buffer
	lpddsBack=LPDDS_GetSecondary(lpddsMain);
	//clear out back buffer
	DDBLTFX ddbltfx;
	DDBLTFX_ColorFill(&ddbltfx,0);
	lpddsBack->Blt(NULL,NULL,NULL,DDBLT_WAIT | DDBLT_COLORFILL,&ddbltfx);
	//load in tileset
	tsCaveMan.Load(lpdd,"IsoHex10_1.bmp");
	return(true);//return success
}
```

The Main Loop

In Prog_Loop, three things happen. First, the back buffer is cleared out. Second, one of the cells of the tileset is written to the approximate middle of the screen. Third, the application is locked to 15 frames per second.

```
void Prog_Loop()
{
	//start timer
	DWORD dwTimeStart=GetTickCount();
	//clear out back buffer
	DDBLTFX ddbltfx;
	DDBLTFX_ColorFill(&ddbltfx,0);
	lpddsBack->Blt(NULL,NULL,NULL,DDBLT_WAIT | DDBLT_COLORFILL,&ddbltfx);
	//put the caveman
	tsCaveMan.PutTile(lpddsBack,400,300,dwCaveManFrame);
	//change the frame number
	dwCaveManFrame++;
	dwCaveManFrame%=8;
	//flip
	lpddsMain->Flip(NULL,DDFLIP_WAIT);
	//lock to 15 FPS
	while(GetTickCount()-dwTimeStart<66);
}
```

You can see that using CTileSet is a great deal easier than setting up RECTs and going down that path. The tileset makes sprite and tile management easy and doesn't add that much overhead.

Cleaning up

You don't have to call the Unload function, because CTileSet's destructor automatically does so, and you can essentially ignore your tileset in Prog_Done. You can just destroy the primary surface and the IDirectDraw and be done with it.

```
void Prog_Done()
{
        //destroy primary surface
        LPDDS_Release(&lpddsMain);
        //destroy IDirectDraw7
        LPDD_Release(&lpdd);
}
```

Taking Control

Although just watching a caveman run in place is fun, you'd probably rather control him. For this, I wrote IsoHex10_2.cpp. This example is mostly the same as IsoHex10_1, except that now you respond to the arrow keys and use that information to move the caveman back and forth across the screen. The major change happens in Prog_Loop.

```
void Prog_Loop()
{
        //start timer
        DWORD dwTimeStart=GetTickCount();
        //clear out back buffer
        DDBLTFX ddbltfx;
        DDBLTFX_ColorFill(&ddbltfx,0);
        lpddsBack->Blt(NULL,NULL,NULL,DDBLT_WAIT | DDBLT_COLORFILL,&ddbltfx);
        //put tile

tsCaveMan[dwCaveManFace].PutTile(lpddsBack,dwCaveManPosition,300,dwCaveManFrame);
        //move
        if(MoveLeft^MoveRight)
        {
                if(MoveLeft)
                {
                        //moving left
```

```
                dwCaveManFace=1;
                //update position
                dwCaveManPosition+=796;
                dwCaveManPosition%=800;
                //update animation frame
                dwCaveManFrame+=1;
                dwCaveManFrame%=7;
            }
            else
            {
                //moving right
                dwCaveManFace=0;
                //update position
                dwCaveManPosition+=4;
                dwCaveManPosition%=800;
                //update animation frame
                dwCaveManFrame+=1;
                dwCaveManFrame%=7;
            }
        }
        else
        {
            //standing
            dwCaveManFrame=7;
        }
        //flip
        lpddsMain->Flip(NULL,DDFLIP_WAIT);
        //lock to 15 FPS
        while(GetTickCount()-dwTimeStart<66);
}
```

The global variables named `MoveLeft` and `MoveRight` are bools, and you change their status in response to `WM_KEYUP` and `WM_KEYDOWN`.

```
        case WM_KEYDOWN:
            {
                //on escape, destroy main window
                if(wParam==VK_ESCAPE)
                {
                    DestroyWindow(hWndMain);
                }
                //movement keys
```

```
                if(wParam==VK_LEFT)
                {
                        MoveLeft=true;
                }
                if(wParam==VK_RIGHT)
                {
                        MoveRight=true;
                }
                return(0);//handled
        }break;
case WM_KEYUP:
        {
                //movement keys
                if(wParam==VK_LEFT)
                {
                        MoveLeft=false;
                }
                if(wParam==VK_RIGHT)
                {
                        MoveRight=false;
                }
                return(0);//handled
        }break;
```

In Prog_Loop, you can see that, depending on which key is being pressed, the facing (contained in dwCaveManFace), the position (dwCaveManPosition), and the animation frame (dwCaveManFrame) are updated. Nothing happens if both keys are pressed at the same time.

This is about it for your crash course in tile and sprite management. Throughout the rest of the book, you will make heavy use of CTileSet. I hope I've shown you that this stuff isn't so hard after all, as long as you have the proper tools and classes to help you.

NOTE

You may have noticed that no subtraction is done—only addition. This is because all the variables are DWORDs, or unsigned longs, which have no negative values. You can see that all the additions are shortly followed by a modulus (%) operation. Combining addition and modulus, you get a net subtraction.

Tilemap Basics

A single tile, or even a sequence of tiles depicting an animated character, isn't in itself very useful. In order to be useful, a variety of sprites and tiles must be used together. Now that you've seen how easy it is to manipulate tilesets, the time has come to get into tilemaps. When creating a tile-based world, you must have a way to represent it in your computer's memory. Usually, you do so with some sort of array, although there are other more complicated but more flexible solutions.

Since we are still in rectangle land, our tilemaps are more intuitive than they will be once we get into isometric and hexagonal tilemaps. They are simply two-dimensional arrays, like so:

```
int iTileMap[WIDTH][HEIGHT];
```

`WIDTH` and `HEIGHT` can be any old value—whatever you need to make your tilemap the proper size. In a chess or checkers game, `WIDTH` and `HEIGHT` would both have a value of 8. A side-scroller might have a `HEIGHT` equal to the screen height divided by the tile height, but the width of the map times the width of the tiles might be several times the width of the screen. The `WIDTH` and `HEIGHT` values depend entirely on what kind of game you are making.

The meaning of the numbers in this array remains in question. Intrinsically, they have none; the meaning of the numbers is entirely up to you. You may not even have ints in the array, but instead a completely different custom structure. Again, this is entirely game-dependent.

For example, in a checkers game, the board squares are alternately black and red, as shown in Figure 10.12. You might put this in the number as a bit flag (if bit 0 is set or not set, for example). On the other hand, you might decide that a board whose x and y add up to be an even number is black, and an odd number is red, like so:

```
if((tilex+tiley)&1)
{
	//red square
}
else
{
	//black square
}
```

Figure 10.12

A checkerboard

Figure 10.13 shows the calculations for (x+y) & 1 for the sample checkerboard.

0	1	0	1	0	1	0	1
1	0	1	0	1	0	1	0
0	1	0	1	0	1	0	1
1	0	1	0	1	0	1	0
0	1	0	1	0	1	0	1
1	0	1	0	1	0	1	0
0	1	0	1	0	1	0	1
1	0	1	0	1	0	1	0

Figure 10.13

Alternating odd/even checkerboard

You may want to only contain in your checkerboard's tile array which piece is or is not there. There are a total of five options: black piece, red piece, black king, red king, and empty; you might create an `enum` to keep track of them.

```
enum{EMPTY=0,BLACKPIECE=1,REDPIECE=-1,BLACKKING=2,REDKING=-2};
```

In this scheme, all black pieces are positive numbers, and all red pieces are negative. This provides an easy way to differentiate them and conveniently leaves 0 for representing empty. The starting board configuration tilemap values are shown in Figure 10.14.

Y↓ \ X→	0	1	2	3	4	5	6	7
0	1	0	1	0	1	0	1	0
1	0	1	0	1	0	1	0	1
2	1	0	1	0	1	0	1	0
3	0	0	0	0	0	0	0	0
4	0	0	0	0	0	0	0	0
5	0	-1	0	-1	0	-1	0	-1
6	-1	0	-1	0	-1	0	-1	0
7	0	-1	0	-1	0	-1	0	-1

Figure 10.14

Starting board configuration

More Complicated Tilemaps

Checkers is a good example of a game for which to use a very simple map structure. There isn't much variety in the tiles this map can hold. This is true of most board and puzzle games, like chess, Reversi, and so on. However, more complicated games like turn-based or real-time strategy games are more visually rich and thus have a more complicated map structure. Also, these types of maps tend to be layered.

For example, you might decide that your turn-based strategy game will have several different types of terrain: ocean, plains, forest, hills, and mountains. These would become your basic terrain types. In addition, you might want to have rivers and roads connecting various map squares. Roads and rivers would be contained in different layers. Also, you'll undoubtedly want to have cities and units on the map, and this can add even more layers. To accomplish all this layering, you might have a struct like the following to describe your tilemap areas:

```
struct TILEMAPSQUARE
{
	char BasicTerrain;//0=ocean;1=plains;2=forest;3=hills;4=mountains;
	unsigned char RoadFlags;//bit 0=north; bit 1=northeast; bit 2=east; etc.
	unsigned char RiverFlags;//bit 0=north;bit 1=east;bit2=south;bit3=west
	UNIT* Unit;//pointer to a unit
};
```

I think you get the idea. The more rich the world, the more complicated becomes the map structure. For now, we will stick with simplistic tilemaps. We'll get into more complicated structures in later chapters.

Rendering a Tilemap

Storing a tilemap somewhere in an array is important. Doing so allows you to persist a world without having to hardcode it. With such a tilemap, you can save to and load from disk, and create an editor that allows you to modify the map. Creating an editor is a great idea; you can distribute it with your game so that your players can create their own levels if they wish, thus enhancing the replay value of your game. Take, for example, the popularity of *Civilization II,* which was written several years ago but is still played heavily. Entire Web sites are dedicated to modified tilesets and scenarios that can be played within the game.

Having said that, let's talk about how to render a tilemap, and then we'll make a simple map editor that uses a tileset from spritelib. I'll bring up and talk about some of the terms I mentioned earlier in this chapter.

Screen Space

First, we'll talk about screen space in more depth. Screen space is nothing more than a rectangle describing the play area shown on-screen. This could be the entire screen, or it could be a smaller portion. Most modern games have some sort of status bar on the side or bottom of the screen, so quite often screen space is smaller than the entire screen.

For the editor that we will be making, let's use 800×600×16 mode. We will use a 600×600 area for editing the map on the left side of the screen, leaving 200×600 on the right for tile selection. The tiles we will be using are 32×32. The tileset is shown in Figure 10.15.

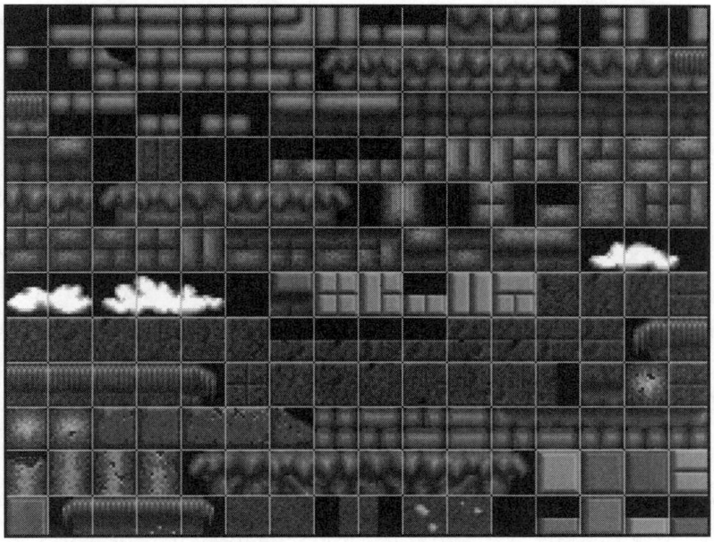

Figure 10.15

Tileset for the editor

Of course, neither 200 nor 600 is evenly divisible by 32. 200/32=6.25, and 600/32=18.75, leaving extra pixels. For this reason, there will be borders around both the editing panel and the tile selection panel, as shown in Figure 10.16. This makes the map panel 576×576 (or 18 tiles by 18 tiles), and the tile selection panel 192×576 (or 6 tiles by 18 tiles).

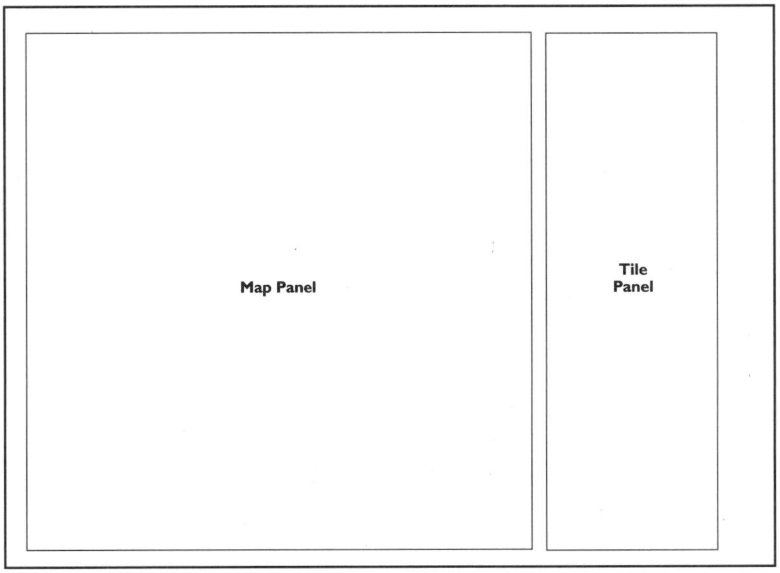

Figure 10.16

Layout of the map editor

You want your map panel centered within the 600×600 rectangle, and you want the tile selection panel centered within the 200×600 rectangle on the right. This will give your map panel RECT the value of (12,12)–(588,588) and your tile selection RECT the value of (12,604)–(796,588). This gives you not one, but two screen spaces. In the map panel, draw the current representation of the map based on your map array, which contains indices into the tileset (make the tilemap 18×18 so that it conveniently fits). In the tile selection panel, draw all the tiles, in order, and outline the one that is currently selected.

But now you have more tiles in the set than will fit in the tile selection box. You can fit 6×18 tiles (108 tiles), but you have 192. In order for the editor to be any good, you must either reduce the number of tiles in the set—something you don't want to do—or make it so that all the tiles can be selected by allowing some sort of scrolling mechanism. This is a better solution. You may, at some point, want to handle a variably-sized tileset, so not locking yourself into a fixed-size tileset is wise.

World Space and View Space

You have already decided to have an 18×18 tile grid, and this will be the total of your world space. Since each tile is 32*32, this makes the pixel measurement of world space 576×576. Since you are making world space 0-based, the world space RECT is (0,0)–(576,576).

Your view space is based on your screen space. Since screen space spans from (12,12)–(588,588), you simply must subtract (12,12) from each coordinate pair to determine your view space. This makes view space 0-based, which makes conversion from one space to another much easier. The point (12,12) is called the screen-to-view anchor.

Upper Left:
Screen coordinate (12,12)
Minus anchor (12,12)
Combine (12–12,12–12)
Solve (0,0)

Lower Right:
Screen coordinate (588,588)
Minus anchor (12,12)
Combine (588–12,588–12)
Solve (576,576)

Conveniently, your view space RECT works out to be (0,0)–(576,576), which is exactly the same as your world space RECT, meaning that no conversion is necessary to go from world to view space. So, to convert from world to screen space, simply add the coordinate (12,12). To do the reverse, subtract (12,12).

A Simple TileMap Editor

Load up IsoHex10_3.cpp. This example demonstrates what we've been talking about for the last several pages. It sets up a map panel and a tile panel. The map panel is your screen space for the tilemap. The tile panel shows the variety of tiles that you can place in the tilemap. Figure 10.17 shows sample output for this example.

Figure 10.17

A simple `TileMap` *editor*

The controls for this example are rather simple, and the features rather slim. Clicking anywhere in the map panel puts the selected tile there. Clicking in the tile panel selects a new tile. Clicking above or below the tile panel scrolls the tile panel up or down. All in all, this example is pretty spartan. It doesn't save, it doesn't load, it doesn't really do much except let you play with the tileset. Still, I think it's a pretty good example of what a tilemap editor looks like at its very core. Let's take a look at how it works.

Constants

First, I made a number of constants to keep track of the sizes in the editor. Quite a few of them are dependent on other constants.

```
//map and tile constants
const int TILEWIDTH=32;
const int TILEHEIGHT=32;
const int MAPWIDTH=18;
```

```
const int MAPHEIGHT=18;
//panels
const int MAPPANELX=12;
const int MAPPANELY=12;
const int MAPPANELWIDTH=MAPWIDTH*TILEWIDTH;
const int MAPPANELHEIGHT=MAPHEIGHT*TILEHEIGHT;
const int TILEPANELX=604;
const int TILEPANELY=12;
const int TILEPANELCOLUMNS=6;
const int TILEPANELROWS=18;
const int TILEPANELWIDTH=TILEPANELCOLUMNS*TILEWIDTH;
const int TILEPANELHEIGHT=TILEPANELROWS*TILEHEIGHT;
```

Globals

Besides our usual globals (window handle, our DirectDraw pointer, and our primary and back surfaces), there are a few extras with which to keep track of the state of the editor.

```
//tileset
CTileSet tsTileSet;
//tilemap
int iTileMap[MAPWIDTH][MAPHEIGHT];
//tile selection
int iTileTop=0;
int iTileSelected=0;
```

The `tsTileSet` variable contains the tileset you'll be using. `iTileMap` is the array in which you contain your tilemap. The `iTileTop` and `iTileSelected` variables are for managing the tile selection panel. `iTileSelected` keeps track of what tile is currently selected for drawing, and `iTileTop` tracks what tile is shown at the top of the tile selection panel.

Set up and Clean up

The changes to `Prog_Init` are minor. You set up DirectDraw, load your tileset, and clear out your tilemap. I won't list the function's contents here. In `Prog_Done`, there are effectively no changes, since you neither have to deallocate the tilemap nor destroy the tileset.

THE MAIN LOOP

The main loop itself (Prog_Loop) does virtually nothing. It delegates to ShowMapPanel and ShowTilePanel and then performs a flip.

ShowMapPanel

This function has no parameters, returns no value, and carries out two tasks. The first task is clearing out the entire map panel with black. The second is looping through all the tiles in the tilemap and putting them onto the map panel.

```
void ShowMapPanel()
{
	//clear out map panel
	//set up fill rect
	RECT rcFill;
	SetRect(&rcFill,MAPPANELX,MAPPANELY,MAPPANELX+MAPPANELWIDTH,MAPPANELY+MAP-
PANELHEIGHT);
	//set up ddbltfx
	DDBLTFX ddbltfx;
	DDBLTFX_ColorFill(&ddbltfx,0);
	lpddsBack->Blt(&rcFill,NULL,NULL,DDBLT_WAIT | DDBLT_COLORFILL,&ddbltfx);
	//loop through map
	for(int mapy=0;mapy<MAPHEIGHT;mapy++)
	{
		for(int mapx=0;mapx<MAPWIDTH;mapx++)
		{
			//put the tile
			tsTileSet.PutTile(lpddsBack,MAPPANELX+mapx*TILEWIDTH,
				MAPPANELY+mapy*TILEHEIGHT,iTileMap[mapx][mapy]);
		}
	}
}
```

ShowTilePanel

`ShowTilePanel` is responsible for displaying all of the tiles in the tile panel and for placing a white box around the currently selected tile.

```
void ShowTilePanel()
{
	//clear out map panel
	//set up fill rect
	RECT rcFill;
	SetRect(&rcFill,TILEPANELX,
TILEPANELY,TILEPANELX+
TILEPANELWIDTH,TILEPANELY+
TILEPANELHEIGHT);
	//set up ddbltfx
	DDBLTFX ddbltfx;
	DDBLTFX_ColorFill(&ddbltfx,0);
	lpddsBack->Blt(&rcFill,NULL,NULL,
DDBLT_WAIT | DDBLT_COLORFILL,&ddbltfx);
	//set tile counter to first tile
	int tilenum=iTileTop;
	//loop through columns and rows
	for(int tiley=0;tiley<TILEPANELROWS;tiley++)
	{
		for(int tilex=0;tilex<TILEPANELCOLUMNS;tilex++)
		{
			//check for tilenum's existence in tileset
			if(tilenum<tsTileSet.GetTileCount())
			{

tsTileSet.PutTile(lpddsBack,TILEPANELX+tilex*TILEWIDTH,TILEPANELY+tiley*TILE-
HEIGHT,tilenum);
				//check for selected tile
				if(tilenum==iTileSelected)
				{
					//grab the dc
					HDC hdc;
					lpddsBack->GetDC(&hdc);
					//calculate outline rect
					RECT rcOutline;
```

```
SetRect(&rcOutline,TILEPANELX+
tilex*TILEWIDTH,
TILEPANELY+
tiley*TILEHEIGHT,
TILEPANELX+
tilex*TILEWIDTH+
TILEWIDTH,
TILEPANELY+
tiley*TILEHEIGHT+
TILEHEIGHT);
                                //select a white pen into dc
                                SelectObject(hdc,
(HPEN)GetStockObject(WHITE_PEN));
                                //place selection rectangle
MoveToEx(hdc,rcOutline.left,
rcOutline.top,NULL);
                                LineTo(hdc,rcOutline.right-1,rcOutline.top);
                                LineTo(hdc,rcOutline.right-1,rcOutline.bottom-
1);
                                LineTo(hdc,rcOutline.left,rcOutline.bottom-1);
                                LineTo(hdc,rcOutline.left,rcOutline.top);

                                //release the dc
                                lpddsBack->ReleaseDC(hdc);
                        }
                }
                //increase tile counter
                tilenum++;
        }
    }
}
```

Accepting Input

The only topic left to cover is accepting input and making things happen. I'm only going to show the event handler for WM_LBUTTONDOWN, since the handler of WM_MOUSEMOVE is almost identical, and because of the sheer size of the handler.

In essence, the WM_LBUTTONDOWN handler takes the position of the mouse and places it in a POINT variable called ptMouse. Then it sets up a series of RECTs—one for the map panel, one for the tile panel, one for the area above the tile panel, and one for the area below the tile panel. It checks to see if the mouse is within these RECTs, and if it is, it carries out the appropriate action: place a tile if within the map panel, select a tile if within the tile panel, scroll the tile panel up if above or down if below.

WM_MOUSEMOVE does mostly the same thing, except for the scrolling of the tile panel if above or below.

```
case WM_LBUTTONDOWN:
	{
		//point to contain mouse coords
		POINT ptMouse;
		ptMouse.x=LOWORD(lParam);
		ptMouse.y=HIWORD(lParam);
		//RECT used for zone checking
		RECT rcZone;
		//other variables
		int mapx=0;
		int mapy=0;
		int tilex=0;
		int tiley=0;
		int tilenum=0;
		//check the map panel
	SetRect(&rcZone,MAPPANELX,MAPPANELY,
MAPPANELX+MAPPANELWIDTH,
MAPPANELY+MAPPANELHEIGHT);
		if(PtInRect(&rcZone,ptMouse))
		{
			//in map panel
			//calculate what tile mouse is on
			mapx=(ptMouse.x-MAPPANELX)/TILEWIDTH;
			mapy=(ptMouse.y-MAPPANELY)/TILEHEIGHT;
			//change map tile to currently selected tile
			iTileMap[mapx][mapy]=iTileSelected;
			return(0);//handled
		}
		//check the tile panel
		SetRect(&rcZone,TILEPANELX,TILEPANELY,
TILEPANELX+TILEPANELWIDTH,
TILEPANELY+TILEPANELHEIGHT);
		if(PtInRect(&rcZone,ptMouse))
		{
			//calculate which tile was selected
			tilex=(ptMouse.x-TILEPANELX)/TILEWIDTH;
			tiley=(ptMouse.y-TILEPANELY)/TILEHEIGHT;
```

```
                    tilenum=iTileTop+tilex+tiley*TILEPANELCOLUMNS;
                    //check for valid tile
                    if(tilenum<tsTileSet.GetTileCount())
                    {
                          //assign current tile
                          iTileSelected=tilenum;
                    }
                    return(0);//handled
              }
              //scroll tileset up
        SetRect(&rcZone,TILEPANELX,0,TILEPANELX+
TILEPANELWIDTH,TILEPANELY);
              if(PtInRect(&rcZone,ptMouse))
              {
                    //check if we can scroll up
                    if(iTileTop>0)
                    {
                          //scroll up
                          iTileTop-=TILEPANELCOLUMNS;
                    }
              }
              //scroll tileset down
              SetRect(&rcZone,TILEPANELX,TILEPANELY+
TILEPANELHEIGHT,TILEPANELX+
TILEPANELWIDTH,600);
              if(PtInRect(&rcZone,ptMouse))
              {
                    //check if we can scroll down
if((iTileTop+TILEPANELCOLUMNS)<
              tsTileSet.GetTileCount())
                    {
                          //scroll up
                          iTileTop+=TILEPANELCOLUMNS;
                    }
              }
              return(0);//handled
        }break;
```

A Few Words about the TileMap Editor

Even though the sample map editor doesn't do much, it does illustrate important points about all map editors. Just about every map editor I've made or used includes something similar to the map panel and something similar to the tile panel (although usually with a more obvious way of scrolling through the tileset).

A Tile-Based Example: Reversi

Now that we've delved a bit into the tile-based world, let's put this knowledge into practice. The first example I'd like to show you is a game called Reversi. (It's also called Othello, but Othello is trademarked by Milton Bradley, so we'll call ours Reversi.)

The basic idea of Reversi is pretty simple. In case you aren't familiar with the game or the rules, here's a brief breakdown: the game pieces are a board, divided into an 8×8 grid of 64 squares, and at least 64 two-sided pieces of contrasting color (usually black and white). At the beginning of the game, the center four squares are filled with pieces, two black and two white, as shown in Figure 10.18.

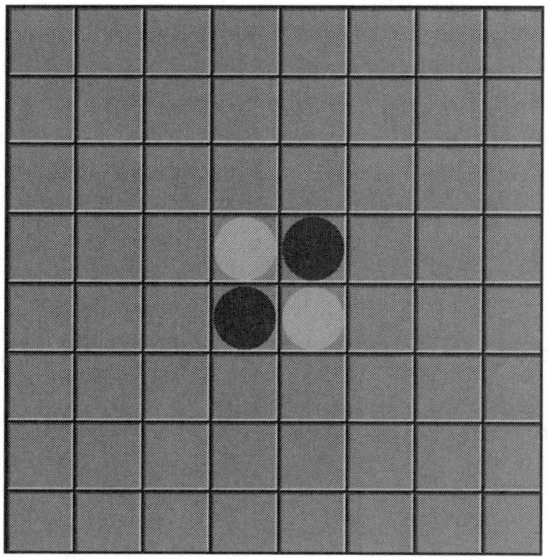

Figure 10.18

The Reversi board at the beginning of play

Two players alternate taking turns placing a single piece on the board and capturing any opposing pieces that they outflank. To outflank means to have one piece of your color on each end of a horizontal, vertical, or diagonal row of your opponent's pieces. You cannot outflank across your own pieces or across open squares. If on a player's turn there is no valid square on which he can play a piece and outflank his opponent, he forfeits that turn. Play progresses until no valid moves for either player are left (usually this happens when the board is full, although it can happen earlier).

Having said that, let's make the game.

Designing Reversi

I have Milton Bradley's Othello sitting on my game shelf, so I looked to that to model this game. The board is green with a black border separating the squares. Two cells in from the corners, there is a small square on the junction of the black lines, apparently to separate the sides and corners from the middle of the board. The pieces are double-sided and two-colored, with white on one side and black on the other.

I wanted to have some sort of method with which to highlight the possible squares to which the player can move on his turn, so I also made yellow versions. I wanted an animated "flipping over" of the pieces, so I made a sequence of ellipses to show that. Figure 10.19 shows the tileset I came up with for this game. You can also find it in the source code for this chapter, under the name IsoHex10_4.bmp. I used magenta instead of black as the transparent color. (Originally, I considered having a black piece instead of the dark gray that I later settled on.)

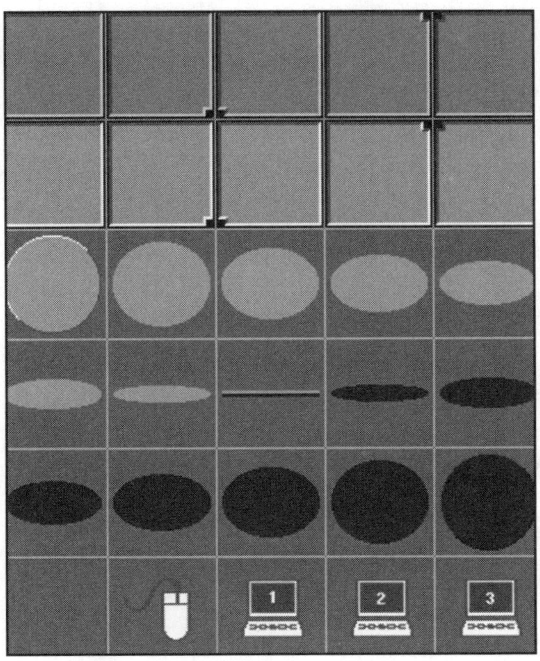

Figure 10.19

Tileset for Reversi

The first row of tiles is the nonhighlighted version of a board background tile. The second row is the highlighted version. Rows three through five are the animation sequence for the piece flip, with the actual pieces for both sides on opposite ends of the sequence. The last row consists of extra graphics I needed to finish up the UI. There is a red square to represent the last move made, and four icons to show the AI level chosen for the players.

AI Levels

I decided on four levels of AI for this example (none of them are very difficult to beat). These levels are represented by constants defined in the source.

```
//ai levels
const int AI_HUMAN=0;
const int AI_RANDOM=1;
const int AI_GREEDY=2;
const int AI_MISER=3;
const int AI_COUNT=4;
```

Table 10.4 explains these AI levels.

Table 10.4 AI Levels and Their Tactics

Level	Tactic
AI_HUMAN	None. Waits for input from the mouse.
AI_RANDOM	Picks a random valid move.
AI_GREEDY	Picks the valid move that will give it the greatest score.
AI_MISER	Picks the valid move that best limits the opponent's movement.

> **NOTE**
> AI_COUNT is not an AI level, but rather a constant to keep track of the number of levels that exist, in case you later want to add more AI levels.

Game States

As with all games, there are a number of major game states in which Reversi might dwell at any given time. I was able to reduce it to only five states.

```
//game states
const int GS_NONE=-1;
const int GS_WAITFORINPUT=0;
const int GS_NEWGAME=1;
const int GS_NEXTPLAYER=2;
const int GS_FLIP=3;
```

Table 10.5 explains these states.

Table 10.5 Reversi Game States

Game State	Meaning
GS_NONE	A neutral state. The board is drawn, but no other action takes place.
GS_WAITFORINPUT	If the current player is computer-controlled, a move will be made. Otherwise, it waits for mouse input.
GS_NEWGAME	Sets up a new game
GS_NEXTPLAYER	Checks for game over. If the game is not over, it selects the next player.
GS_FLIP	In this state, the pieces captured during this turn are taken through the animation sequence.

Tile Information Structure

Reversi may seem like a simple board game, but the struct that keeps track of the tile information is a little more complicated than just a simple array of integers.

```
//tile information structure
struct REVERSITILE
{
	int iTileNum;//base tile number for square
	bool bHilite;//hilited, or not hilited
	int iPiece;//piece occupying square
	bool bLastMove;//last move made
};
```

iTileNum

This member keeps track of the background and specifies one of the first five tiles of the tileset. Most squares contain tile zero, but a few contain the others. I could have easily just used tile zero for the entire board, but that would have been boring.

bHilite

When the current player can make a valid move on a given square, `bHilite` is true. If the square is not a valid move for the player, `hHilite` is false. `bHilite`, when used in conjunction with `iTileNum`, provides the background tile. When `bHilite` is true, 5 is added to `iTileNum`.

iPiece

This member has four meaningful values: `PIECEEMPTY(-1)`, `PIECEBLACK(0)`, `PIECEWHITE(1)`, and `PIECETRANSIT(2)`. The empty, black, and white are self-explanatory. The transit piece is for use with the `GS_FLIP` state. It specifies which pieces undergo the animation sequence.

bLastMove

Only one square at a time will ever have `bLastMove` set to `TRUE`. `bLastMove` specifies that the red rectangle (tile 25 of the tileset) is to be shown over the background, thus indicating that the square was the most recent move. Keeping track of this is not absolutely necessary, but I find it helpful when playing the game.

Score Indication

I wanted to have a score indication that did not require a font to implement. I could have used some extra tiles for the numerals 0 through 9 in the tileset, but I just didn't like that idea. Instead, I decided to use vertical stacks of the pieces alongside the board. Both stacks are on the left side of the board, so they can easily be compared to see who is winning.

AI Level Control

I didn't want to make a configuration screen, so I had to work in some sort of AI level control right on the screen itself. What I came up with was to put two of the colored pieces in the bottom-left corner (aligned with the score stacks), and I would blit icons representing what AI levels controlled which color. The icons are from the wingdings font, but I colored them in to make them look better.

IMPLEMENTATION OF REVERSI

With the design in mind, here's some of the implementation detail for Reversi. Because of space concerns, I can't get into every minute detail, but the full source code can be found in IsoHex10_4.cpp. I'm going to concentrate on the main game loop (`Prog_Loop`) and break it down by game state.

MAJOR GLOBAL VARIABLES

Reversi uses full-screen DirectDraw, set to an 800×600×16 resolution. The major global variables are shown next.

Your basic run-of-the-mill `IDirectDraw7` pointer:

```
//IDirectDraw7 Pointer
LPDIRECTDRAW7 lpdd=NULL;
```

A primary surface and the attached back buffer:

```
//surfaces
LPDIRECTDRAWSURFACE7 lpddsMain=NULL;
LPDIRECTDRAWSURFACE7 lpddsBack=NULL;
```

The main tileset to contain all of the graphics used:

```
//tileset
CTileSet tsReversi;
```

The main board and a temporary storage area:

```
//the board
REVERSITILE Board[8][8];
//backup board
REVERSITILE BackUpBoard[8][8];
```

A variable to keep track of the current player:

```
//current player
int iPlayer=0;
```

An animation counter for use during `GS_FLIP`:

```
//counter for animated "flipping" of pieces
int iAnimation=0;
```

An array to keep track of what AI controls each color:

```
//ai level for the players
int iAILevel[2];
```

The main game state:

```
//gamestate
int iGameState=GS_NONE;
```

All Game States

Regardless of game state, a certain amount of code runs each loop. This code prepares a new frame for the game and then displays it.

```
//clear out back buffer
DDBLTFX ddbltfx;
DDBLTFX_ColorFill(&ddbltfx,0);
lpddsBack->Blt(NULL,NULL,NULL,DDBLT_WAIT | DDBLT_COLORFILL,&ddbltfx);
//***OMITTED CODE***
//show the board
ShowBoard();
//show the scores
ShowScores();
//show players
ShowPlayers();
//flip
lpddsMain->Flip(NULL,DDFLIP_WAIT);
```

This bit is pretty simple. First, you clear out the back buffer, and then you draw the board, draw the scores, draw the AI levels, and finally flip the page. It's a pretty to-the-point snippet. You can take a look at the constituent functions in the source code if you're interested. The following sections offer a brief rundown of the major function calls.

ShowBoard

This function loops through all of the board squares and follows approximately these steps:

1. Based on `iTileNum` and `bHilite` for this board square, determine which tile to use as the background tile.
2. Determine what piece, if any, is resting on this square. If it is `PIECEBLACK` or `PIECEWHITE`, show the appropriate tiles. If it is `PIECETRANSIT`, determine what tile to show based on the global variable `iAnimation`.
3. If this square has `bLastMove` set, put the red square on top.

ShowScores

This function shows the scores for each color, representing the score with a vertical stack of pieces. For each piece on the board, `ShowScores` renders one piece. The first piece is rendered with the top of the piece at y=0, and y increases by 4 for each additional piece on the board. This allows a nice, easy way to tell who is winning while avoiding numerals.

ShowPlayers

This function shows the AI levels of both colors in the bottom-left corner of the screen. A black piece sits next to a white piece. On top of these pieces the function renders an icon that represents the AI level for that color. A mouse represents a human player, and computers with the numerals 1, 2, and 3 represent the three levels of computer AI.

GS_NONE

This game state does almost nothing. In fact, there is no case for it in the `iGameState` switch in `Prog_Loop`. Only in the `WM_LBUTTONUP` event handler does `GS_NONE` get a mention. If the board is clicked on while in `GS_NONE`, the game moves to `GS_NEWGAME`.

```
case WM_LBUTTONUP:
	{
		//grab mouse position
		POINT ptMouse;
		ptMouse.x=LOWORD(lParam);
		ptMouse.y=HIWORD(lParam);
		//test rectangle
		RECT rcTest;
		//get tile width and height
		int iTileWidth=tsReversi.GetTileList()[0].rcSrc.right-
			tsReversi.GetTileList()[0].rcSrc.left;
```

```
        int iTileHeight=tsReversi.GetTileList()[0].rcSrc.bottom-
              tsReversi.GetTileList()[0].rcSrc.top;
        //calc board rect
        SetRect(&rcTest,(400-iTileWidth*4),
              (300-iTileHeight*4),(400+iTileWidth*4),
              (300+iTileHeight*4));
              //point on board?
        if(PtInRect(&rcTest,ptMouse))
        {
        //***CODE OMITTED
              //if a game is over, start a new game by clicking on the
              board
              if(iGameState==GS_NONE)
              {
                    iGameState=GS_NEWGAME;
              }
        }
        //***CODE OMITTED***
  }break;
```

GS_NEWGAME

GS_NEWGAME starts a new game, and is actually one of the simpler game states. First, it makes a call to `SetUpBoard`, which does all of the reinitialization necessary to start out with a clean board. Then it sets the player to `PLAYERTWO` and sends the game into `GS_NEXTPLAYER`. I could have done this another way, by setting `iPlayer` to `PLAYERONE` and sending it into `GS_WAITFORINPUT`.

```
case GS_NEWGAME:
      {
            //clear the board
            SetUpBoard();
            //set player
            iPlayer=PLAYERTWO;
            //change game state
            iGameState=GS_NEXTPLAYER;
      }break;
```

GS_WAITFORINPUT

This game state is the central game state. All AI moves are done here. When the game first enters GS_WAITFORINPUT, it checks the current player's AI level. If AI_HUMAN is indicated, the game does nothing. If it is a computer AI (AI_RANDOM, AI_GREEDY, or AI_MISER), it calls the appropriate AI function.

```
case GS_WAITFORINPUT:
	{
		//make move appropriate to the AI
		switch(iAILevel[iPlayer])
		{
		case AI_RANDOM:
			{
				MakeRandomMove(iPlayer);
			}break;
		case AI_GREEDY:
			{
				MakeGreedyMove(iPlayer);
			}break;
		case AI_MISER:
			{
				MakeMiserMove(iPlayer);
			}break;
		}
	}break;
```

Note that the AI level of AI_HUMAN isn't even represented in this snippet. That is because all of the AI_HUMAN stuff for GS_WAITFORINPUT is handled in the WM_LBUTTONUP event handler. (AI and GS and WM... oh my!)

```
//***CODE OMITTED***
//point on board?
if(PtInRect(&rcTest,ptMouse))
{
	//if we are waiting for input and the ai is "human," check for inside the
board
	if((iGameState==GS_WAITFORINPUT) &&
		(iAILevel[iPlayer]==AI_HUMAN))
	{
		//find board position
		int BoardX=(ptMouse.x-rcTest.left)/iTileWidth;
		int BoardY=(ptMouse.y-rcTest.top)/iTileHeight;
```

```
            //check for a valid square
            if(ValidMove(iPlayer,BoardX,BoardY))
            {
            //make the move
                MakeMove(iPlayer,BoardX,BoardY);
                SetLastMove(BoardX,BoardY);
                iGameState=GS_FLIP;
            }
        }
        //***CODE OMITTED*** (the GS_NONE check)
}
//***CODE OMITTED***
```

GS_FLIP

After a move has been made, the newly captured pieces are not set to the color of the player who captured them. Instead, they are changed to PIECETRANSIT, and GS_FLIP is the game state responsible for making sure that the animation sequence for capturing these pieces is shown.

```
case GS_FLIP:
    {
        switch(iPlayer)
        {
        case PLAYERTWO:
            {
                if(iAnimation==0)
                {
                    FinishMove(iPlayer);
                    iGameState=GS_NEXTPLAYER;
                }
                else
                {
                    iAnimation-;
                }
            }break;
        case PLAYERONE:
            {
                if(iAnimation==14)
                {
                    FinishMove(iPlayer);
                    iGameState=GS_NEXTPLAYER;
```

```
                    }
                    else
                    {
                            iAnimation++;
                    }
                }break;
            }
        }break;
```

The main purpose of GS_FLIP is to modify iAnimation, which controls what part of the animation sequence you are on. When it is PLAYERONE's turn, iAnimation starts at 0 and is incremented until it hits 14, at which point the move finishes (by a call to FinishMove, which changes all PIECETRANSITs to a color's piece). Similarly, on PLAYERTWO's turn, iAnimation starts at 14 and moves backwards until it hits 0. In either case, after GS_FLIP is finished, the game moves into GS_NEXTPLAYER.

GS_NEXTPLAYER

After a move has been completed, this game state checks to see if the game is over or sets the next active player. If the game is over (there are no valid moves for either player), it sends the game into GS_NONE. If the game is not over, it checks to see if the opposing player has a valid move. If the opposing player does not have a valid move, it goes to GS_WAITFORINPUT without changing the player. If the opposing player does have a valid move, it sets the current player to the opposing player and moves into GS_WAITFORINPUT.

```
case GS_NEXTPLAYER:
        {
                //scan for moves
                ScanForMoves(iPlayer);
                //if no more valid moves, game over
                if((!AnyValidMoves(PLAYERTWO)) && (!AnyValidMoves(PLAYERONE)))
                {
                        iGameState=GS_NONE;
                }
                else
                {
                        //find if opponent has any moves
                        if(AnyValidMoves(1-iPlayer))
                        {
                                iPlayer=1-iPlayer;
                        }
```

```
                    //scan for moves by current player
                    ScanForMoves(iPlayer);

                    //get next move
                    iGameState=GS_WAITFORINPUT;
            }
    }break;
```

Miscellaneous Actions

Before we complete our treatment of Reversi, I have a few last things left that I want to point out.

- **Changing AI Levels.** During every loop, the current AI levels are shown at the bottom left of the screen. You can change the level by clicking on the indicators. Each time you click, you increase the AI level by 1. Clicking on the highest level brings you back to the lowest level (`AI_HUMAN`).
- **Keyboard Controls.** Esc exits the program, no matter what game state you are in. F2 starts a new game, no matter what game state you are in.

Final Words on Reversi

This simple little game of Reversi is far from complete. Yes, it is fully functional and playable, but it lacks any extras. Just like the Breakout game in the preceding chapter, I'm leaving it for you to finish. Here's a brief list of features I think it needs:

- A title screen
- Some sort of "bells and whistles" when you win
- Sound/music

And I'm sure you'll come up with 50 ways to improve the program. Have fun with it.

Summary

In this chapter, you took a step into a larger world. You explored the power that graphical tiles can give you. I went into great detail on the topic of tileset management, and for good reason. From here on out, just about everything you do will be done using the `CTileSet` class, in some fashion or another.

CHAPTER 11

Isometric/ Hexagonal Tile Overview

- Introduction to IsoHex
- IsoHex Tiles versus Rectangular Tiles
- IsoHex Engines versus Rectangualr Engines

This chapter marks a new beginning. All of the preparatory information and discussion is over, and it is at last time to sally forth into the wonderful world of isometric and hexagonal graphics. This is not to say that what we have discussed so far has been meaningless. To the contrary! All of the previous topics have been building up to this chapter and to the rest of this book.

This chapter takes you on a ride through isometric land. Mainly, I will talk about the special considerations you have to keep in mind when creating isometric or hexagonal tiles, rendering these tiles, and interacting with them on-screen.

Introduction to IsoHex

So, what is "IsoHex"? Simply, it's a word I made up. A couple of years ago, I was sitting around playing Sid Meier's *Civilization II* and generally being a nonfunctional human being. Of course, I'd been a game programmer for many years, but most of my stuff dealt with the normal top-down rectangular tiled methodology that was common in the waning days of DOS.

I was quite impressed with the look of *Civilization II*. It looked a heck of a lot better than the original. The isometric view gave it a semi-3D look. Naturally, I just *had* to know how it was done. So I looked through the directory in which *Civilization II* was installed, and I viewed the several GIF files that stored the images. Then I started playing around with similar tiles in my own experiments.

A friend of mine, Isaac Vanier, posted a question on a message board about how to take mouse input and determine what tile it was on in an isometric map. Having toyed with the idea of isometric tiles, I sent him an e-mail answering his question. Apparently, my little e-mail helped him out quite a bit, because he e-mailed me back, telling me that I should write an article about it.

I thought surely there must be resources on how to do this stuff, and that writing another article about it would be unnecessary. So I scoured the Internet for a trace of isometric tutorials, or at least *something* about them. Needless to say, there wasn't much out there. I saw bizarre linear algebra computations, and some pretty crazy and not-very-optimized ways to do isometric tiles. There was one exception—an article by Jim Adams called "Isometric Views," written in 1996 (keep in mind, I was doing this search in 1998). This article was originally a newsgroup post by Mr. Adams and had been "translated" into article form. It was just about the only isometric article you could find on the Net. The article had a bunch of god-awful ASCII art, and it didn't talk about mapping screen coordinates to tile coordinates. I decided to write my article after all.

Originally, I put my article on my Web page (you know. . . the Web space that your ISP gives you) and gave links to it from message boards. Eventually, a few people linked to it. Finally Matt Reiferson, the Webmaster of GPMega (the most popular amateur game programming site at that time) contacted me and asked if he could put the article on his site. I agreed. My little article (and a sequel that I wrote a while later) became quite popular. Eventually, some of the other guys who hung out in the GPMega chat room and I formed our own site, Sweet.Oblivion. Eventually Sweet.Oblivion joined with other sites to form GameDev.net. Throughout these events, this little article has followed me. Currently, it is the 27th most frequently accessed article on GameDev.net.

What does this have to do with the word "IsoHex"? Well, that little article first coined the term. That article is also the primary reason you are reading this book. Without that article, I would never have been asked to write this book. (I admit, it's more complicated than that, but it was a key component.)

So, the original question remains: what is IsoHex? IsoHex is, quite naturally, a combination of the words *isometric* and *hexagonal*. An isometric projection is a 3D projection that does not correct for distance (in other words, something 30 tiles away is just as big as something 10 tiles away). The isometric projection is one of a family of *axonometric* projections. (The meaning of axonometric isn't terribly important. It's an engineering term.) *Rhombuses*, or diamond shapes, are usually used to represent an isometric tiled world. Figure 11.1 shows a field of isometric tiles.

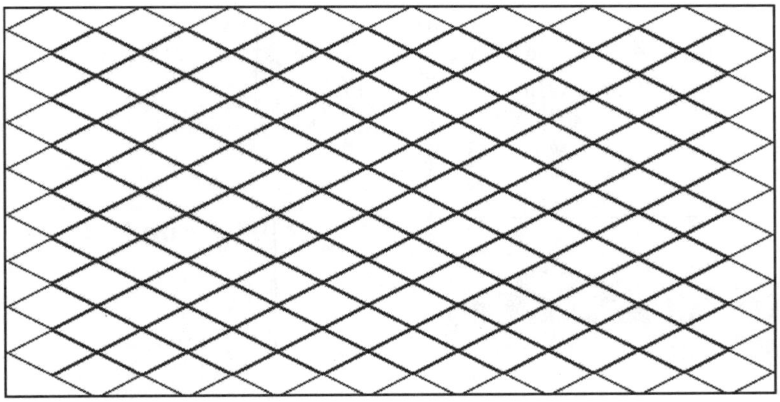

Figure 11.1

An isometric tile field

Hexagonal means six-sided. As far as tiled graphics go, there is almost no difference between an iso-tiled world and a hex-tiled world. The difference is all in connotation and convention (meaning that on a hex map, you can move in six directions instead of eight, as with iso). Hex maps are commonly used by paper-and-pencil RPGers and by strategy gamers, such as those who play *Battletech*. Figure 11.2 shows a hexagonal field.

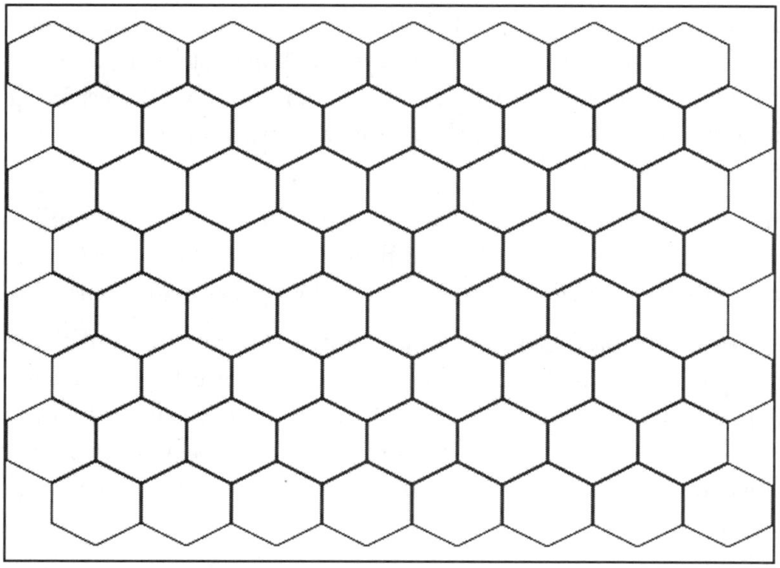

Figure 11.2

A hexagonal tile field

The main difference between an iso tile and a hex tile is that the two halves of an iso tile are split apart, and a rectangular area is inserted between them, as shown in Figure 11.3.

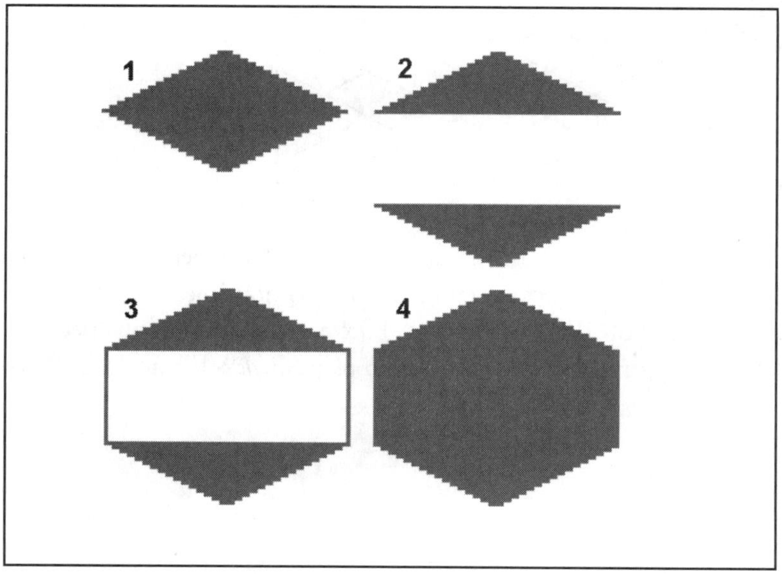

Figure 11.3

Iso to hex

There really is not much of a difference between iso and hex as far as programming goes. It is mainly a user interface issue. At this point, I think you've probably had more than you want to hear about IsoHex, and you would rather start doing stuff. I don't blame you, so let's get to it!

IsoHex Tiles versus Rectangular Tiles

So far, the tile-based examples have always used rectangular areas that contain the tiles; this is not going to change. What will change is how you will render them in relation to one another.

Take, for example, a 64×64 rectangular tile, like the ones used in the Reversi example in the preceding chapter. In order to blit these tiles onto a grid, you simply use multiples of 64, as shown in Figure 11.4.

Figure 11.4

Making rectangular tiles flush

IsoHex tiles can't do this (or, at least, most of them can't). Since only a portion of the rectangle is filled with the actual tile, the rectangles containing the tile have to overlap, both vertically and horizontally, as shown in Figure 11.5.

Figure 11.5

Making IsoHex tiles flush

As you can see, the IsoHex tiles have to be shifted over by half a tile on alternating rows, whereas no adjustment is necessary for rectangular tiles. This brings up another important point: blitting order. With rectangular tiles, you can blit in any order you want—left to right, right to left, top to bottom, bottom to top—and the map will look right no matter what, because none of the tiles overlap. IsoHex tiles, however, often have something "sticking up out of them," like a tree or a building or a unit. There are some important ramifications of this.

- **Rule 1**. IsoHex tiles must be blitted in a manner so that no tile is blitted after a tile that is "in front" of it. The methods of doing this are based on the type of tilemap used. I'll get into this later.
- **Rule 2**. If only a small portion of the screen has to be updated, you cannot just blit the tile that changed. You have to blit neighboring tiles as well, and you have to make certain that you follow Rule 1 while doing so. Clippers come in quite handy to help with this.
- **Rule 3**. Except for the diamond tilemap, you must avoid as much as possible showing the jagged edges of the tilemap (they are the most severe on staggered maps). This isn't really a rule; it's more a matter of aesthetics.

IsoHex Tilemaps versus Rectangular Tilemaps

Rectangular maps are maintained by a two-dimensional array in most cases. The same is true of IsoHex maps. However, the meaning of the x- and y-coordinates changes somewhat. In a rectangular map, increasing x moves east, and increasing y moves south. In an iso tilemap, depending on type, increasing x might mean moving southeast, and increasing y might mean moving southwest.

Why? Because of the overlap. Every other row or column has to be shifted half a tile—either right, left, up, or down—in order to make the tiles flush with one another. I showed you this in the preceding section. For this reason, increasing y by 1 almost never means to move south. However, in most cases, increasing x by 1 does mean to move east.

This makes navigating an IsoHex tilemap a bit more involved than navigating a simple rectangular map. You have to use a lookup table (and sometimes two) to get it right. Don't worry. I won't leave you hanging; I'll show you everything you need to know, when you need to know it.

Isometric Engines versus Rectangular Engines

There are several components to any good tile engine. If you want to make tile-based games, it's smart to have a good set of functions or classes to wrap up the tricky stuff for you. This is especially important in IsoHex, since the tilemaps are trickier than in normal rectangular tiles.

TilePlotter

A TilePlotter is used to convert map coordinates (indices into the tilemap array) into world space coordinates. In a rectangular engine, you simply multiply by the width and height of the tile, since x always goes east-west and y always goes north-south. In isometric engines, the meanings of x and y change, and at least one of them moves in a diagonal direction, which changes the equation. Once a TilePlotter has converted a map coordinate into a world coordinate, it can be from there translated into view and screen coordinates.

MouseMap

A MouseMap goes the opposite way of a TilePlotter. It takes a world coordinate and converts it into a map coordinate. A MouseMap is necessary because of the irregular (nonrectangular) shape of the isometric and hexagonal tiles. In a rectangular tile engine, a MouseMap is unnecessary, because all of the rectangles are already... well, rectangular.

In an iso or hex engine, you still need to check to see if the mouse is in rectangular areas, because of the fact that it is computationally inexpensive to do so. You could instead use equations or some other method to check for being within tiles, but the math is just too weird and too complicated, and MouseMaps make them unnecessary. The MouseMap itself is a second step in the world-to-map conversion. First, the x and y coordinates are divided by the MouseMap width and height, and then the remainders are fed into the MouseMap to determine which tile corresponds to the pixel coordinate.

So, why is this important component called a "MouseMap"? Although it has many uses as the reciprocal of the TilePlotter (which has a name befitting its function), the most important use for the MouseMap is taking a mouse's (or other pointing device's) screen coordinate and finding the corresponding map coordinate.

TileWalker

The TileWalker is absolutely necessary, although most iso folks wouldn't list it as a major component. In my opinion, it is just too darned important not to be all on its own. A TileWalker does just one thing: move from map coordinate to map coordinate. This might seem a pretty tame feature, but it is essential for using a MouseMap, moving units, and pathfinding.

Minimally, a TileWalker can consist of a single function that returns a `POINT` with the following parameters: a `POINT` specifying a map coordinate, an int specifying direction of movement, and another int stating how many map coordinates to move.

The Three Types of IsoHex Tilemaps

There are three types of IsoHex tilemaps: slide, staggered, and diamond. Each has its own set of quirks, its own methods of rendering, its own way of representing a tilemap, and its own method of navigating them. I will briefly introduce them here and then explore them more fully in the next three chapters.

As far as an iso tilemap is concerned, any of these types of map is usable, depending on what game you are making. For hex, however, staggered is the most commonly used map type, although I have seen a diamond map using hex tiles.

The explanation of each type of map briefly covers some of the problems you face in designing each of the core engine components.

Slide Maps

The slide tilemap is probably the easiest to render, navigate, and interact with. Unfortunately, it has limited uses. It's mainly used to scroll action games.

Usually, a slide map has a horizontal x axis and a diagonal y axis, although it is possible to have a vertical y axis and a diagonal x axis. Figure 11.6 shows a few samples of what slide maps can look like.

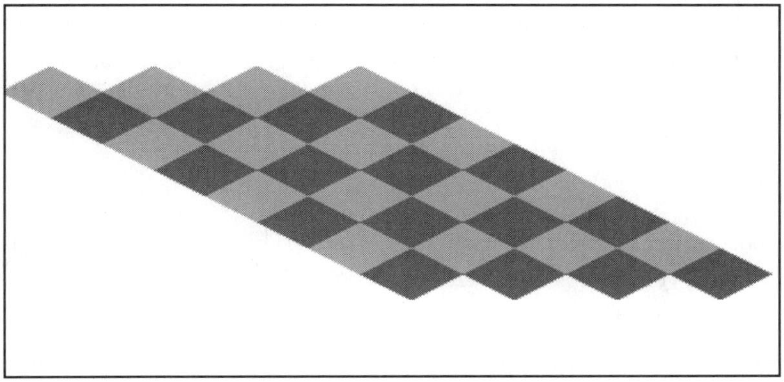

Figure 11.6

Slide maps

TilePlotting, MouseMapping, and TileWalking in a slide map are all very regular and consistent. The tiles are blitted in horizontal rows top to bottom.

Staggered Maps

For most serious isometric/hexagonal turn-based strategy games, the staggered map is king. Each new row is alternately shifted one-half of a tile left or right (certain hex maps turned on their sides shift up or down). This results in a zigzag pattern of tiles, as shown in Figure 11.7. The x-axis usually is horizontal (increasing to the east), and the y-coordinate is alternately southeast and southwest. Staggered maps are best suited for maps that wrap around (move from one edge to the other) and for times when you want to completely fill a rectangular area. This is also the most common type of hex map.

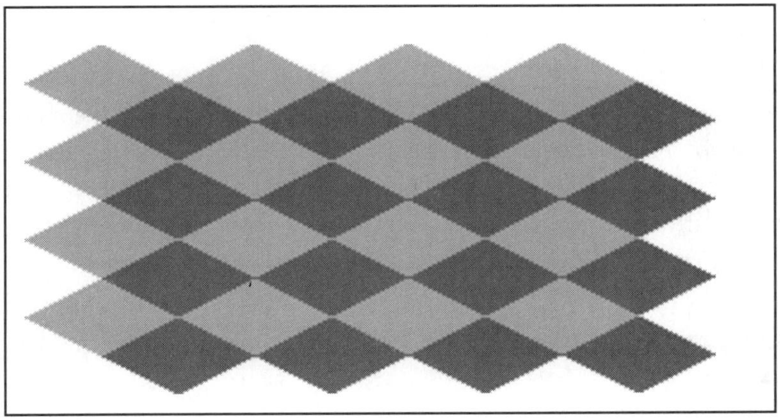

Figure 11.7

Staggered maps

Staggered maps are the most irregular of the three. TilePlotting, MouseMapping, and TileWalking are all slightly complicated due to the offset of every other row. The tiles are blitted in horizontal rows, top to bottom.

Diamond Maps

The diamond map is by far the most popular for real-time strategy games and "sims." The edges of this type of map are the least offensive. (Staggered maps have "tattered" edges, slide maps have "tattered" tops and bottoms, and diamond maps are smooth.)

Usually, the x-axis increases in the southeast direction, and the y-axis increases in the southwest direction, although this isn't absolutely necessary to follow my configuration exactly. In diamond maps, the only requirement is that both the x- and y-axis are diagonal. Figure 11.8 shows an example of a diamond map.

Figure 11.8

Diamond map

Based on the "turned on its side" nature of diamond maps, you would think that they were the most complicated to make. In reality, they are not, but the equations are a little weird for the TilePlotter (both the x and y of the map coordinate are used to calculate the tile's world coordinate). The TileWalker is completely regular, and the MouseMap is similarly quite normal. The only odd thing about the MouseMap is that often the world coordinates can be negative, and the divisions and remainders have to be adjusted for that.

IsoHex Tilesets and the Importance of Anchors

When making isometric games, you use tilesets just like when you make rectangular games. However, the tile anchors become much more important. In the rectangular example from the preceding chapter, you simply put the tile anchor at the upper-left corner of the tile, and you didn't have to worry about it.

Iso and hex games don't provide that luxury. You have to deal with countless objects, all of which are an odd shape. You have to ensure that when you have everything rendered, the images line up.

For the most part, I handle this by putting the anchor in the center of an iso or hex tile. Figure 11.9 shows what I mean. Using a centered tile anchor like this makes selecting anchors for nonbackground images (like trees or units) a lot easier, because you then have to put the x anchor at the horizontal center of the image and the y anchor somewhere near the base of the image. Figure 11.10 shows a suitable anchor for a unit tile, and Figure 11.11 shows what these two tiles look like when used together.

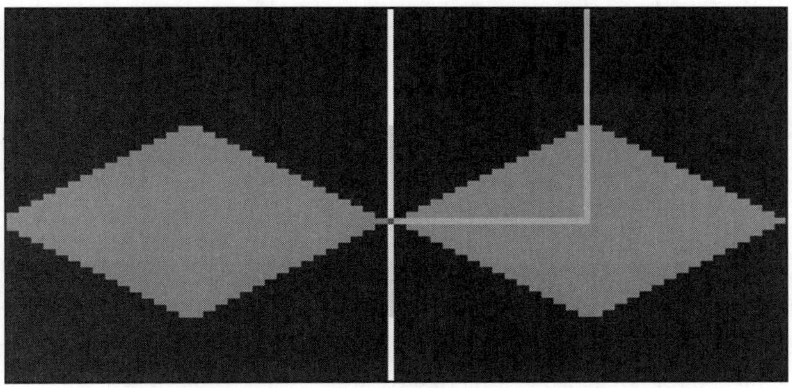

Figure 11.9

An isometric tile, with center anchor

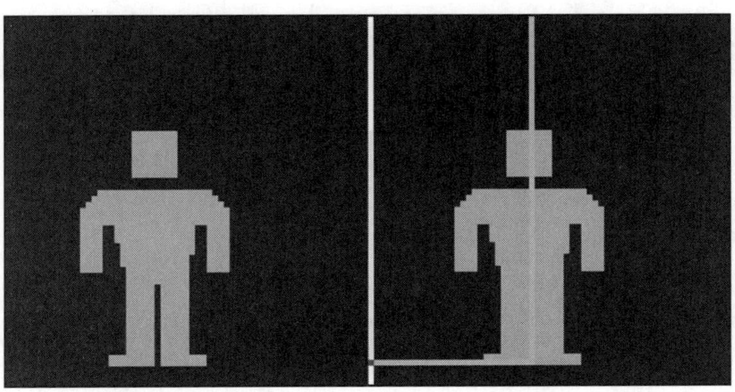

Figure 11.10

Foreground iso image

Figure 11.11

Background iso tile with foreground image added

Just keep in mind that you want a tile anchor scheme that is easy to manage and that doesn't complicate the core engine. The easier you make it on your artists, the less they will revolt. Oh, and be sure to throw them a Dr. Pepper once in a while, even if they don't really deserve it.

Summary

You are now ready for what lies ahead. The next few chapters explore the different types of iso tilemaps, and you'll make a few games along the way, too. Mainly, you will put down the foundations of an honest-to-goodness 2D iso tile engine. The tools to make awesome isometric games are just a few pages away!

CHAPTER 12

Slide Isometric Tilemaps

- Interlocking IsoHex Tiles
- Coordinate System
- Tile Plotting

This chapter begins the first of three chapters that cover the various types of IsoHex tilemaps. This chapter covers the simplest (and least commonly used) type: slide maps. Even if you don't like slide maps, you should probably read this chapter because it covers some of the explanations common to all types of IsoHex mapping techniques, including the basis for the three major components of an IsoHex tile engine, which I mentioned briefly in the preceding chapter.

The first question that might come to mind is why I'm calling this particular type of IsoHex tilemap a "slide map." When I was originally going through and classifying IsoHex items, I had to come up with terms for these maps. With slide maps, I noticed that while the x-axis was normal, the y-axis "slides" off to the side. Hence, I named them "slide maps." There really is no official term for them, so I made one up. Simple enough?

Interlocking IsoHex Tiles

You haven't really learned about interlocking IsoHex tiles yet. I told you that the rectangles containing IsoHex tiles overlapped, but not much more than that. Before you can proceed, you've got to be able to interlock the tiles—that is, make the diagonal edges match up with no missing pixels. To learn how to interlock the tiles, you first have to take a look back at how rectangular tiles work.

As you can see in Figure 12.1, the interlocking of rectangular tiles is quite simple. The colored pixels are in the upper-left corners to represent the anchors, which makes visualizing the interlocking easier. To move east (to the right of the screen), you simply add the width of the tile to the x-coordinate. To move south (down), you add the height of the tile to the y-coordinate. From these two calculations, you can infer that to move west (left), you simply subtract the width from x (moving west is the opposite of moving east). To move north, you simply subtract the height from y. As soon as you have the four cardinal directions (north, east, south, and west), you can construct the other four directions (northeast, southeast, southwest, and northwest) by combining the other directions. Table 12.1 shows the x and y modifications necessary for a rectangular tile system using `TileWidth*TileHeight` tiles.

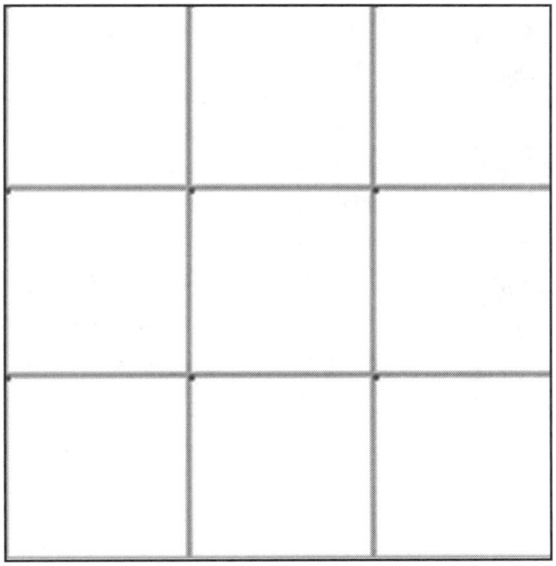

Figure 12.1

Rectangular tiles interlocking

Table 12.1 Rectangular Tile Plotting

Direction	Change x	Change y
North	0	`-TileHeight`
Northeast	`+TileWidth`	`-TileHeight`
East	`+TileWidth`	0
Southeast	`+TileWidth`	`+TileHeight`
South	0	`+TileHeight`
Southwest	`-TileWidth`	`+TileHeight`
West	`-TileWidth`	0
Northwest	`-TileWidth`	`-TileHeight`

> **NOTE**
>
> **I use compass directions (north, south, east, and west) rather than up, down, right, and left, not to confuse you, but rather to clearly indicate the absolute direction. The compass directions have absolute meanings, whereas left and right do not, since a character that is facing toward you has a different left and right than one facing away from you.**

Figure 12.2 is a more graphical representation of Table 12.1. I feel that a visual is much better at conveying this than just a simple table. It's the whole "a picture is worth a thousand words" idea. Based on this table, and based on the direction of the x- and y-axis (x increases to the east, and y increases to the south), you can come up with an equation to determine where to blit your rectangular tiles:

```
//TileX/TileY are the pixel positions (in world space) for the tile being blitted
//MapX/MapY are the map coordinates of the tile
TileX=MapX*TileWidth
TileY=MapY*TileHeight
```

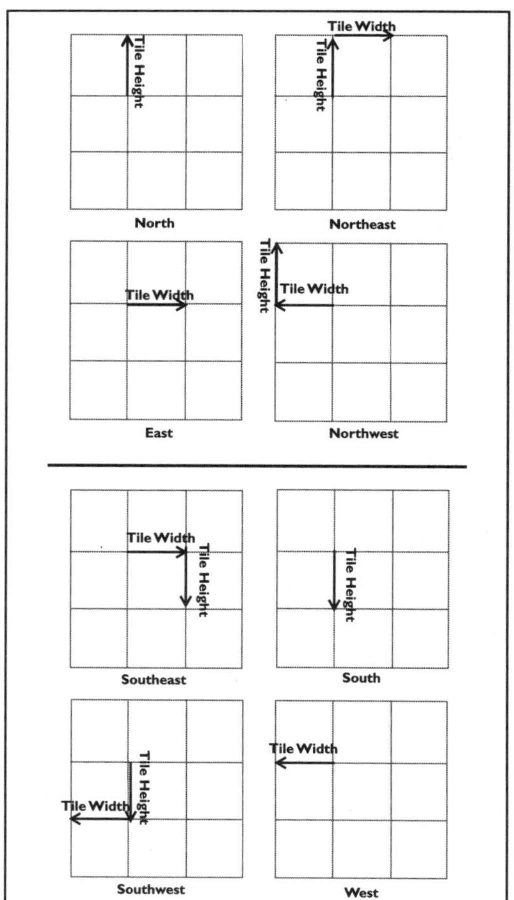

Figure 12.2

A graphical representation of Table 12.1

You have been using these calculations all along. You just haven't really done any sort of analysis as to why they work.

Now take a look at some standard iso and hex tiles and do some similar figuring for plotting adjacent tiles. Figure 12.3 shows some standard iso and hex tiles (*standard* meaning similar to what we will use in this book). The anchors are marked.

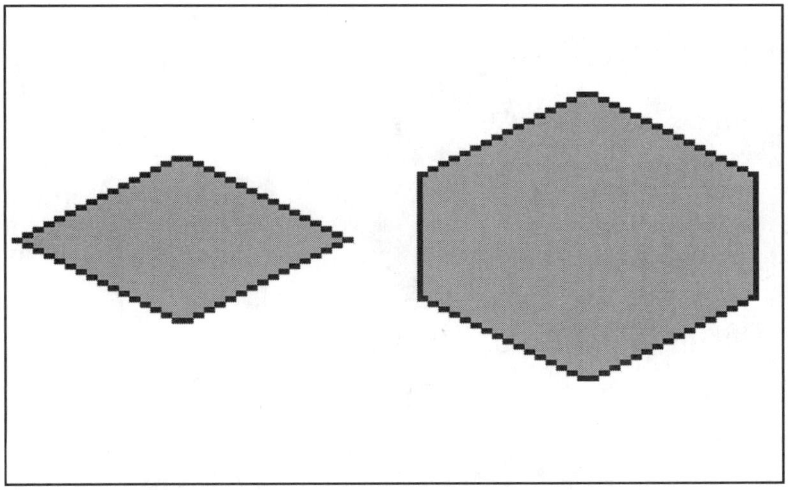

Figure 12.3

Standard iso and hex tiles

Figure 12.4 shows the iso and hex tiles grouped with others of the same kind. I will use these to show positional calculations between tiles, just like I did with rectangular tiles.

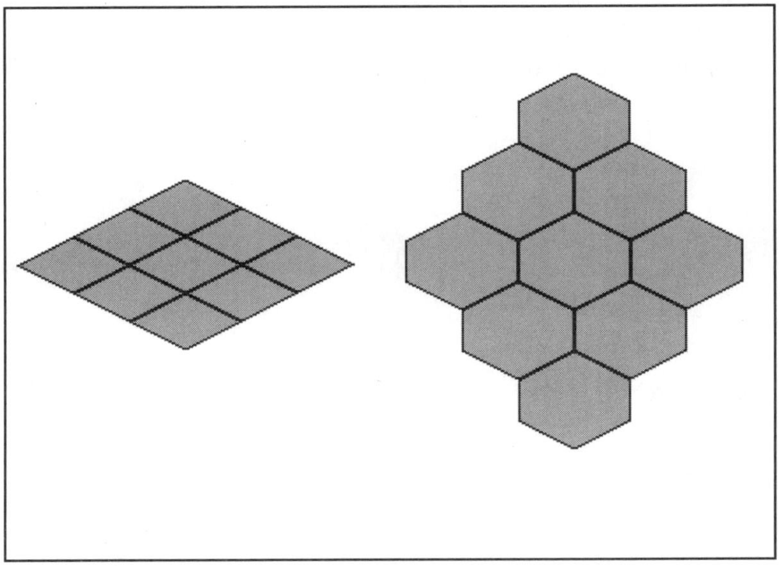

Figure 12.4

Iso and hex tiles together

In iso, moving east moves by the width of the tile. Similarly, moving south moves by the height of the tile (not exactly, but close enough). Thus, moving north or west is the opposite of these directions. However, if you look at moving in a diagonal direction, you can see that a tile is half of the width to one side horizontally and half of the height vertically offset. Table 12.2 shows the changes in x and y based on the direction traveled.

Table 12.2 Iso Tile Plotting

Direction	Change x	Change y
North	0	`-TileHeight`
Northeast	`+TileWidth/2`	`-TileHeight/2`
East	`+TileWidth`	0
Southeast	`+TileWidth/2`	`+TileHeight/2`
South	0	`+TileHeight`
Southwest	`-TileWidth/2`	`+TileHeight/2`
West	`-TileWidth`	0
Northwest	`-TileWidth/2`	`-TileHeight/2`

Figure 12.5 shows graphically what is contained in Table 12.2. Based on these calculations, it is obvious that at least one axis of the tilemap has to be on a diagonal. If not, the tiles positioned based on `TileWidth/2` and `TileHeight/2` would be skipped completely, leaving the map full of holes, as shown in Figure 12.6.

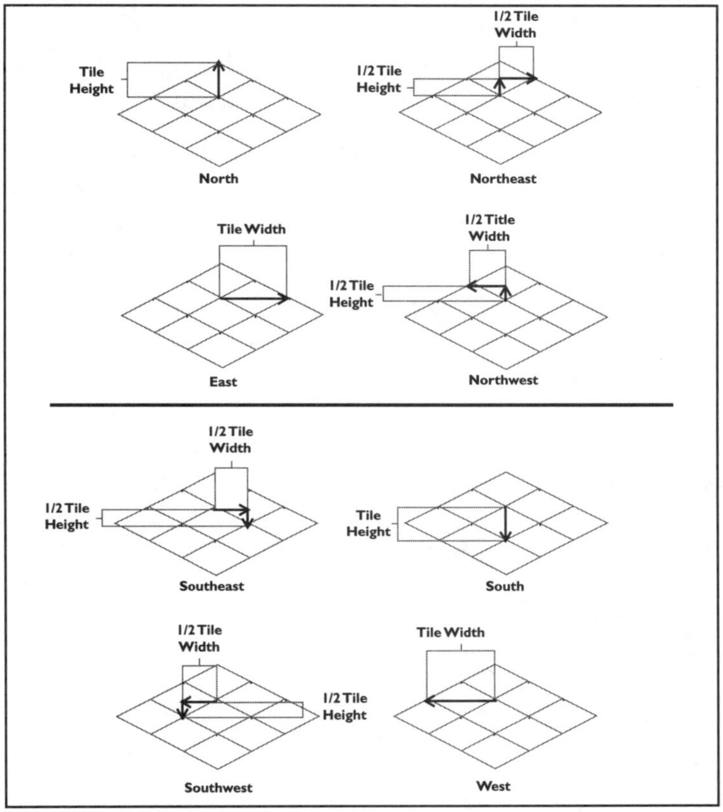

Figure 12.5

A graphical representation of Table 12.2

Figure 12.6

Holey map, Batman!

Hex tiles are very similar to iso tiles, with one major difference: Two directions of movement are disallowed—in this case, north and south. While reading this discussion on hex tiles, keep in mind that the tiles could easily be turned on their sides, and east-west movement disallowed instead.

The movement to the east is dependent on `TileWidth`, but the southeast movement is based on `TileWidth/2` for x and a y value that depends on the shape of the tile (mainly, the height of the vertical lines). For the time being, I will name this value `HexRowHeight`, since it has no particular relationship to the tile's height.

Table 12.3 is similar to Table 12.2, with the word `HexRowHeight` substituted for the word `TileHeight`. Also, north and south are missing. Table 12.3 shows plotting from tile to adjacent tile in a hex map.

Table 12.3 Hex Tile Plotting

Direction	Change x	Change y
Northeast	`+TileWidth/2`	`-HexRowHeight`
East	`+TileWidth`	0
Southeast	`+TileWidth/2`	`+HexRowHeight`
Southwest	`-TileWidth/2`	`+HexRowHeight`
West	`-TileWidth`	0
Northwest	`-TileWidth/2`	`-HexRowHeight`

Figure 12.7 shows the calculations in Table 12.3 in a more graphical and easy-to-understand manner. Turning the hex on its side is something I won't show here, since it is much the same as the hexes I've already shown, with some of the x and y changes flipped.

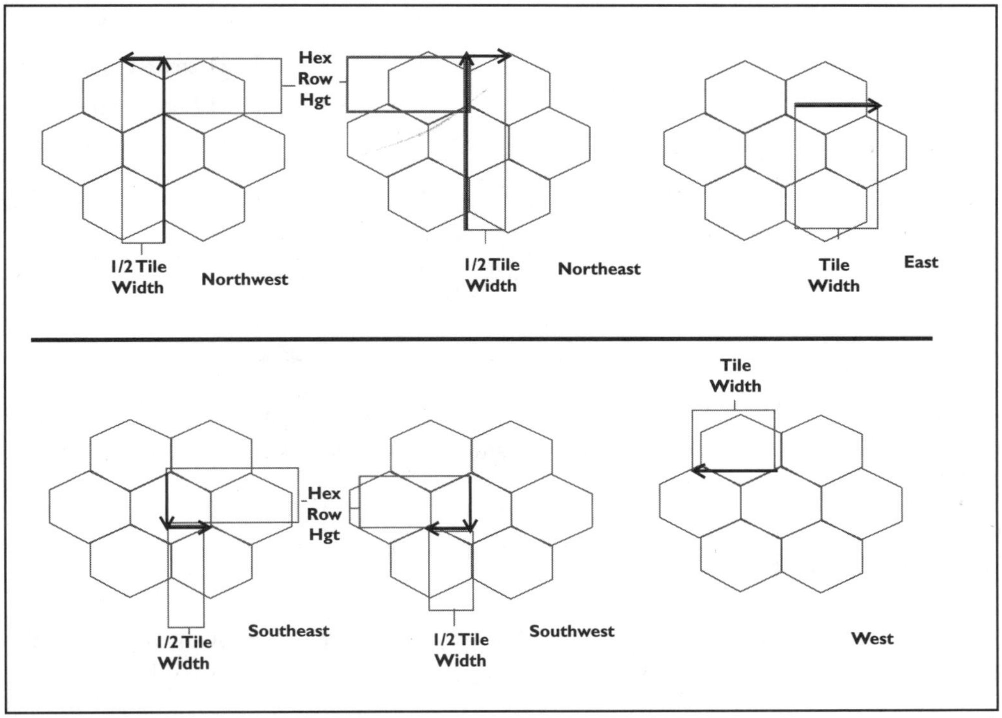

Figure 12.7

Graphical version of Table 12.3

All of the tables and figures I've shown in the last couple of pages are the most important calculations in IsoHex. They are the basis for all of the main engine parts.

Coordinate System

In the preceding chapter, I briefly touched on how slide maps are structured. Now you will take that information, add the calculations you did just a few pages ago, and move on to building a primitive version of an isometric engine.

A slide map—just like a rectangular map—consists of a two-dimensional array, usually of some sort of structure, but it can be as simple as just an int or a char. However, since you earlier determined that one isometric or hexagonal axis has to be diagonal, you have to take that into account for your slide map.

Theoretically, 32 variations of a slide map are possible. However, many of them look quite similar, so only four variations have any sort of distinction. These four variations are just reflections of the one variation that you will use, which is x increasing to the east and y increasing to the southeast, as shown in Figure 12.8.

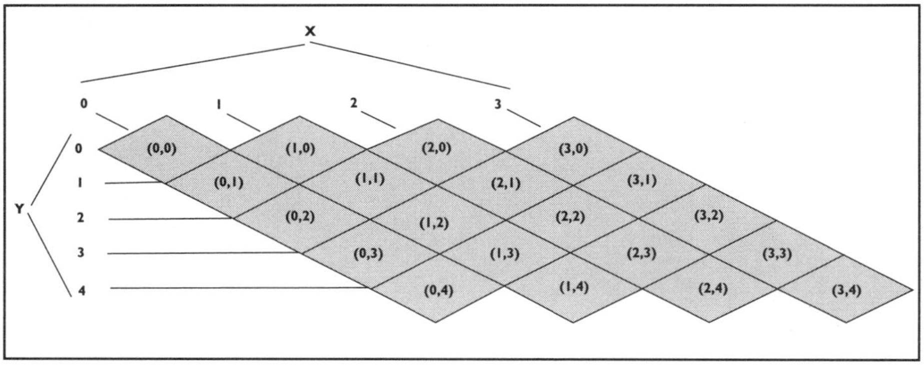

Figure 12.8

x increases to the east, and y increases to the southeast

Now that you've covered most of the bases for slide maps, it's time to start using your knowledge to make some practical applications. You will do this by making the main components of an IsoHex engine: the TilePlotter, the TileWalker, and the MouseMap.

Tile Plotting

Although all three components are essential for a proper IsoHex engine, the first component you will make is a TilePlotter, because you can immediately see the results of your labor with a quick example.

I've already discussed the axes of a slide map. x increases to the east, and y increases to the southeast. Assuming that you plot tile (0,0) at pixel position (0,0), you need to be able to calculate the pixel positions of other tiles based on their map coordinates.

The first part of the calculation affects the pixel coordinate based on the map's x value. Since x increases to the east, you can just look at Table 12.2 to see that the map's x increases the pixel's x by `+TileWidth`, and the map's x does not affect the pixel's y at all. However, the map's y affects both the pixel's x and y values, by `+TileWidth/2` and `+TileHeight/2`, respectively. Table 12.4 shows this, and derives the tile plotting equations.

Table 12.4 Slide Map Tile Plotting

Pixel Value	Increase in MapX	Increase in MapY	Equation
`PixelX`	`+TileWidth`	`+TileWidth/2`	`MapX*TileWidth+MapY*TileWidth/2`
`PixelY`	0	`+TileHeight/2`	`MapY*TileHeight/2a`

So, the tile plotting equation, in code form, looks like this:

```
//MapX,MapY are map coordinates
//TileX,TileY are world coordinates
TileX=MapX*TileWidth+MapY*TileWidth/2;
TileY=MapY*TileHeight/2;
```

And, believe it or not, you have a TilePlotter. Of course, you'd prefer to have a function that plots the tiles rather than having to do the equations yourself. The following is an example of such a function:

```
POINT SlideMap_TilePlotter(POINT ptMap,int iTileWidth,int iTileHeight)
{
	POINT ptReturn;
	ptReturn.x=ptMap.x*iTileWidth+ptMap.y*iTileWidth/2;
	ptReturn.y=ptMap.y*iTileHeight/2;
	return(ptReturn);
}
```

So you're sitting there screaming, "That's it?!" at the top of your lungs. Calm down. A great deal of the functionality of an IsoHex engine rests on just such a function.

For hex, there is just a slight modification to the function:

```
POINT SlideMap_TilePlotter(POINT ptMap,int iTileWidth,int iHexRowHgt)
{
	POINT ptReturn;
	ptReturn.x=ptMap.x*iTileWidth+ptMap.y*iTileWidth/2;
	ptReturn.y=ptMap.y*iHexRowHgt;
	return(ptReturn);
}
```

Now that you actually have some code, try an example. Load up IsoHex12_1.cpp; it uses the same plotting function that I showed you earlier. As currently written, it plots an eight-column by 20-row slide map, as shown in Figure 12.9. The main work is done by two functions: `SetUpMap` and `DrawMap`. The rest of the program is just your basic "set up DirectDraw" type of stuff.

Figure 12.9

The output of example IsoHex12_1.cpp

The SetUpMap function (shown next) loops though all the map squares, assigning each square to a random tile. (I have just a handful of tiles, all the same shape.) Notice that I base the random number on the number of tiles in the set. I could add as many tiles as I want and not have to recompile this code.

```
void SetUpMap()
{
	//randomly set up the map
	for(int x=0;x<MAPWIDTH;x++)
	{
		for(int y=0;y<MAPHEIGHT;y++)
		{
			iTileMap[x][y]=rand()%(tsIso.GetTileCount());
		}
	}
}
```

The DrawMap function loops through all the map squares and uses the plotter to plot them:

```
void DrawMap()
{
	POINT ptTile;//tile pixel coordinate
	POINT ptMap;//map coordinate
	//get tile width and height
```

```
	int iTileWidth=tsIso.GetTileList()[0].rcSrc.right-
tsIso.GetTileList()[0].rcSrc.left;
	int iTileHeight=tsIso.GetTileList()[0].rcSrc.bottom-
tsIso.GetTileList()[0].rcSrc.top;
	//the y loop is outside, because we must blit in horizontal rows
	for(int y=0;y<MAPHEIGHT;y++)
	{
		for(int x=0;x<MAPWIDTH;x++)
		{
			//get pixel coordinate for map position
			ptMap.x=x;
			ptMap.y=y;
			ptTile=SlideMap_TilePlotter(ptMap,iTileWidth,iTileHeight);
			//plot the tile
			tsIso.PutTile(lpddsBack,ptTile.x,ptTile.y,iTileMap[x][y]);
		}
	}
}
```

Now you can see one of the major downfalls of the slide map. I'm sure you noticed that most of the screen is blank, and only a portion of the corner is filled in with tiles. This is the biggest limitation of slide maps. You just can't make a map that fills up the entire screen unless you waste a considerable number of tiles doing so. For this reason, slide maps are unsuitable for many types of games.

However, in games that scroll, you can use slide maps to make the scrolling direction diagonal and give a nice illusion of 3D.

Scrolling

I covered the term *scrolling* in Chapter 10, "Tile-Based Fundamentals," and mentioned it several times since, but I haven't yet gone into what is involved. Your next task is to make a larger slide map (still with random tiles on it). You will scroll though it using the arrow keys. This will by no means be an optimized scroll; all tiles from the tilemap will be blitted each frame, and you will rely on the clipper to keep them out.

You will use the entire screen, so the screen space and view space are both (0,0)–(640,480). This will be the window into your little tile world, as shown in Figure 12.10.

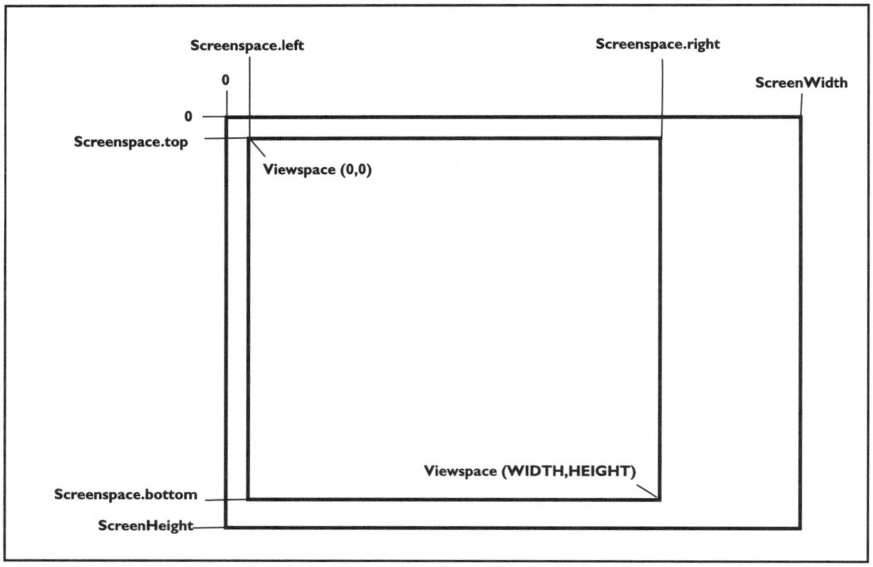

Figure 12.10

Screen space/view space

Calculating world space is quite simple. Simply take the world rectangles (which can be retrieved with the help of the TilePlotter) and use `UnionRect` to combine them all into one big rectangle, as shown in Figure 12.11. (In your case, you can cheat and just use the upper-right and bottom-left extent to make the world space rectangle.)

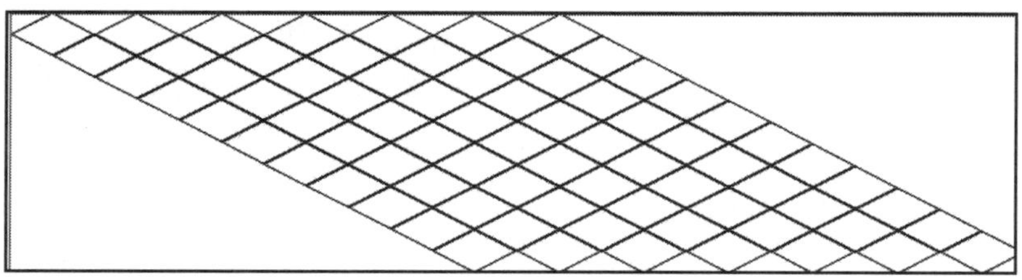

Figure 12.11

World space `RECT`

You'll use another type of anchor. This time, the anchor matches the screen space/view space coordinate (0,0) with a coordinate in the world space (that coordinate being the contents of the anchor). This anchor, when used with the output of the plotter, gives you the proper screen coordinate for the tile. Figure 12.12 shows such an anchor in action.

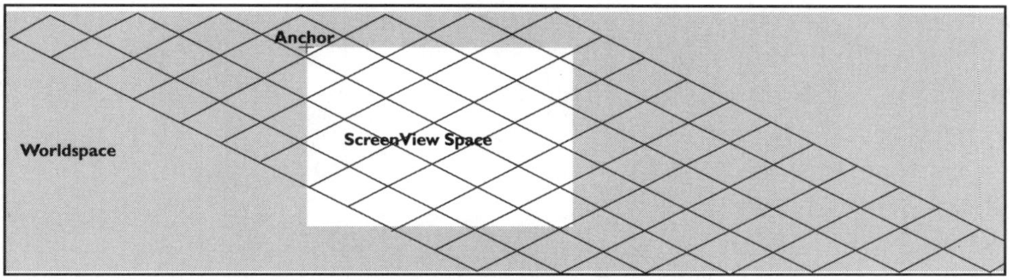

Figure 12.12

Screen anchor in the world space

Finally, you want to keep the anchor in values that are valid. That is, you don't want to allow scrolling too far away from the tilemap. So you need to create anchor space, the boundaries that clip the anchor. To do so, simply make a rectangle that starts at the upper left of the world space and has a width and height equal to the difference of world space width and screen space width. Figure 12.13 shows this idea graphically.

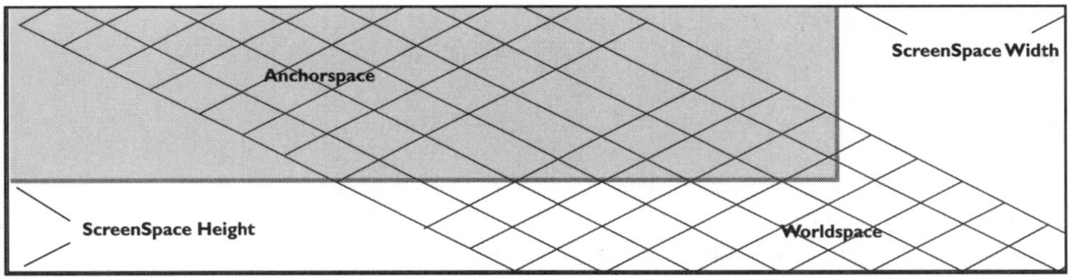

Figure 12.13

Anchor space

So, with all of this in mind, go back to the task of scrolling. Load up IsoHex12_2.cpp—your first little scrolling demo. For illustration purposes, I made a number of global variables to keep track of the various spaces.

```
//spaces
RECT rcWorldSpace;//world space
RECT rcScreenSpace;//screen space (also, view space)
RECT rcAnchorSpace;//anchor space
POINT ptScreenAnchor;//screen anchor
```

These spaces are set up or calculated within a function called `SetUpSpaces`. (I'm not one who gives my functions incredibly clever names, as you might have noticed!)

```
void SetUpSpaces()
{
       //set up screen space
       SetRect(&rcScreenSpace,0,0,640,480);
       //get a few metrics from the tileset
```

```
	int iTileWidth=tsIso.GetTileList()[0].rcDstExt.right-
tsIso.GetTileList()[0].rcDstExt.left;
	int iTileHeight=tsIso.GetTileList()[0].rcDstExt.bottom-
tsIso.GetTileList()[0].rcDstExt.top;
	//grab tile rectangle from tileset
	RECT rcTile1;
	RECT rcTile2;
	POINT ptPlot;
	POINT ptMap;
	//grab tiles from extents
	CopyRect(&rcTile1,&tsIso.GetTileList()[0].rcDstExt);
	CopyRect(&rcTile2,&tsIso.GetTileList()[0].rcDstExt);
	//move first tile to upper-left position
	ptMap.x=0;
	ptMap.y=0;
	ptPlot=SlideMap_TilePlotter(ptMap,iTileWidth,iTileHeight);
	OffsetRect(&rcTile1,ptPlot.x,ptPlot.y);
	//move first tile to lower-right position
	ptMap.x=MAPWIDTH-1;
	ptMap.y=MAPHEIGHT-1;
	ptPlot=SlideMap_TilePlotter(ptMap,iTileWidth,iTileHeight);
	OffsetRect(&rcTile2,ptPlot.x,ptPlot.y);
	//combine these two tiles into world space
	UnionRect(&rcWorldSpace,&rcTile1,&rcTile2);
	//copy world space to anchor space
	CopyRect(&rcAnchorSpace,&rcWorldSpace);
	//subtract screen space
	//adjust right edge
	rcAnchorSpace.right-=(rcScreenSpace.right-rcScreenSpace.left);
	//make sure right not less than left
	if(rcAnchorSpace.right<rcAnchorSpace.left)
rcAnchorSpace.right=rcAnchorSpace.left;
	//adjust bottom edge
	rcAnchorSpace.bottom-=(rcScreenSpace.bottom-rcScreenSpace.top);
	//make sure bottom not less than top
	if(rcAnchorSpace.bottom<rcAnchorSpace.top)
rcAnchorSpace.bottom=rcAnchorSpace.top;
	//initialize screen anchor
	ptScreenAnchor.x=0;
	ptScreenAnchor.y=0;
}
```

This is the longest function in the program, as it should be. All scrolling is based on the calculations here. After you have your variables set up, implementing scrolling becomes a simple matter. The `DrawMap` function is mostly the same as the one you saw in IsoHex12_1.cpp, with a minor change (which I have highlighted in bold) to include the use of the anchor.

```
void DrawMap()
{
	POINT ptTile;//tile pixel coordinate
	POINT ptMap;//map coordinate
	//get tile width and height
	int iTileWidth=tsIso.GetTileList()[0].rcSrc.right-
tsIso.GetTileList()[0].rcSrc.left;
	int iTileHeight=tsIso.GetTileList()[0].rcSrc.bottom-
tsIso.GetTileList()[0].rcSrc.top;
	//the y loop is outside, because we must blit in horizontal rows
	for(int y=0;y<MAPHEIGHT;y++)
	{
		for(int x=0;x<MAPWIDTH;x++)
		{
			//get pixel coordinate for map position
			ptMap.x=x;
			ptMap.y=y;
			ptTile=SlideMap_TilePlotter(ptMap,iTileWidth,iTileHeight);
			//plot the tile (adjust for anchor)
			tsIso.PutTile(lpddsBack,ptTile.x-ptScreenAnchor.x,
				ptTile.y-ptScreenAnchor.y,iTileMap[x][y]);
		}
	}
}
```

Finally, to make scrolling work with the arrow keys, I modified `Prog_Loop` to respond to the four arrows:

```
//check for keys, and adjust screen anchor
//up
if(GetAsyncKeyState(VK_UP)<0)
{
	if(ptScreenAnchor.y>rcAnchorSpace.top) ptScreenAnchor.y--;
}
//down
if(GetAsyncKeyState(VK_DOWN)<0)
{
```

```
        if(ptScreenAnchor.y<rcAnchorSpace.bottom) ptScreenAnchor.y++;
}
//right
if(GetAsyncKeyState(VK_RIGHT)<0)
{
        if(ptScreenAnchor.x<rcAnchorSpace.right) ptScreenAnchor.x++;
}
//left
if(GetAsyncKeyState(VK_LEFT)<0)
{
        if(ptScreenAnchor.x>rcAnchorSpace.left) ptScreenAnchor.x—;
}
```

With all of these working together, you can run the program and move the view around the map with the arrow keys. I've talked to a lot of folks about scrolling, and I've seen some pretty complicated methods of doing it—most of them either didn't work or worked very poorly. The method I presented here will work in all cases. If you want to make a rectangular map that works with a TilePlotter, it will work. It will also work with any of the other types of IsoHex tilemaps.

Naturally, you aren't totally finished with your treatment of scrolling, but you are finished for now. The method here works, even if it's not the most efficient. Depending on the size of your tilemap, many tiles can be blitted but completely clipped out by the clipper. As maps get bigger, it results in more of a performance hit. You'll return to scrolling and improve on this method in a later chapter.

Tile Walking

The next fundamental piece of an isometric engine is the TileWalker. A TileWalker does nothing more than move from one map location to an adjacent map location based on a direction traveled. Much like the TilePlotter, the TileWalker is a very easy-to-implement component.

Figure 12.14 shows the allowable directions of movement for iso and hex tiles. As you can see, iso allows eight directions and hex allows six. In a normal rectangular tilemap, tile walking is very easy because of how the tiles line up next to one another. Table 12.5 shows how the x and y coordinates change in a rectangular map.

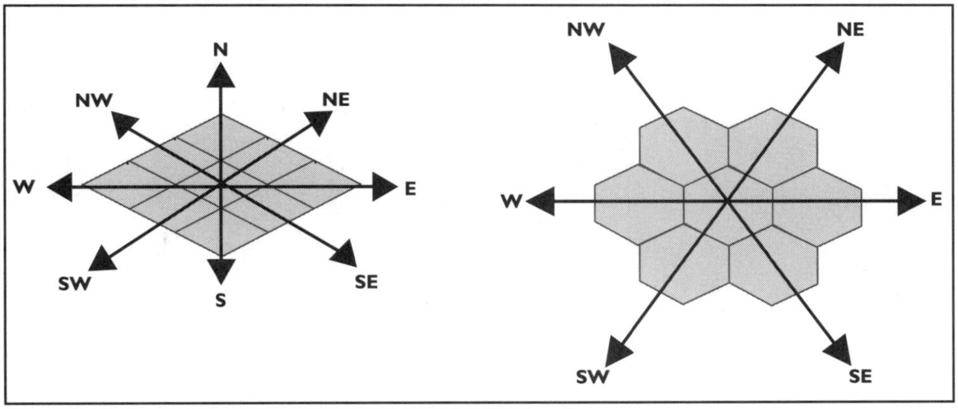

Figure 12.14

Directions of movement for iso and hex

Table 12.5 Rectangular Tile Walking

Direction	Change x	Change y
North	0	–1
Northeast	+1	–1
East	+1	0
Southeast	+1	+1
South	0	+1
Southwest	–1	+1
West	–1	0
Northwest	–1	–1

Figure 12.15 shows a graphical representation of Table 12.5. We used something of a TileWalker in the Reversi example in Chapter 10, "Tile-Based Fundamentals," in the form of the `DeltaX` and `DeltaY` functions. (Take a look back at IsoHex10_4.cpp if you want a refresher.) That is all a TileWalker is.

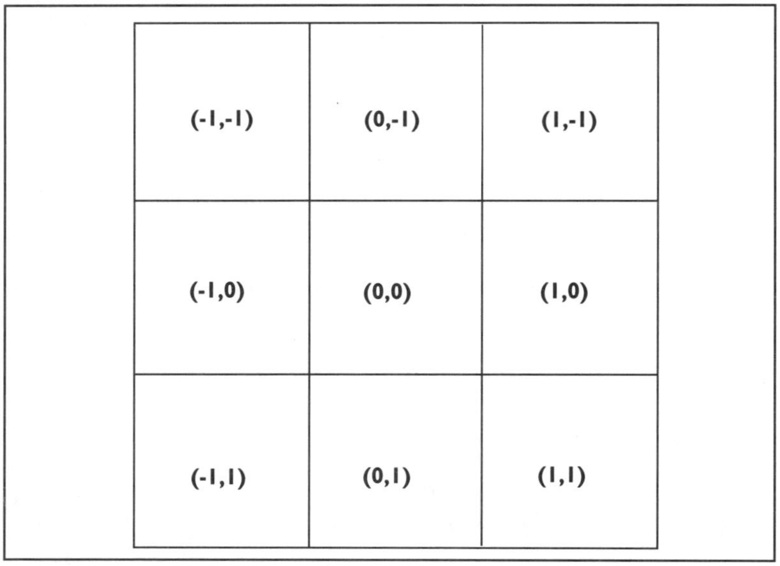

Figure 12.15

A graphical representation of Table 12.5

"Big deal," you say. Perhaps it's not a big deal, but it is fundamental for making any sort of tile-based engine work. In an isometric or hexagonal engine, the numbers become a little weird, so having the TileWalker in a nicely wrapped-up function is more important.

So, with the purpose of a TileWalker in mind, consider the slide map. From the get-go, you know that x increases in the east direction, so for eastward movement, you add 1 to x and leave y alone. Conversely, moving west has the opposite effect (subtract 1 from x and leave y alone). Also, you know that moving southeast increases y by 1 and leaves x alone, and conversely, moving to the northwest subtracts 1 from y and leaves x alone. So far, you have the information shown in Table 12.6.

Table 12.6 Slide Map TileWalker (So Far)

Direction	Change x	Change y
East	+1	0
Southeast	0	+1
West	–1	0
Northwest	0	–1

You have four of the eight directions, and you just have to derive the other directions based on what you already have. To do this, you simply make movements you know how to make in order to get to squares to which you have not yet gone. Take a look at the directions one by one.

North

To move north, you can move one square to the east, two squares to the northwest. The net change for x is +1(east) +0(northwest)+0(northwest)= +1. The net change for y is +0(east)–1(northwest) –1(northwest)= –2. A graphical representation of this derivation is shown in Figure 12.16.

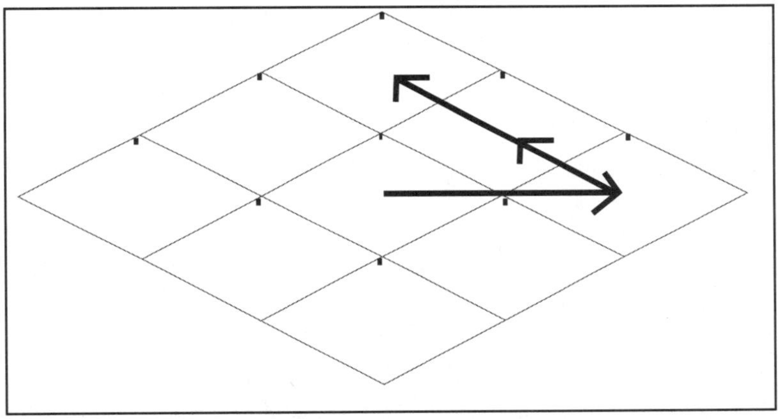

Figure 12.16

Moving north on a slide map

Northeast

To move northeast, you can move one square to the east and one square to the northwest. The net change for x is +1(east)+0(northwest)= +1. The net change for y is +0(east) –1(northwest)= –1. A graphical representation of this derivation is shown in Figure 12.17.

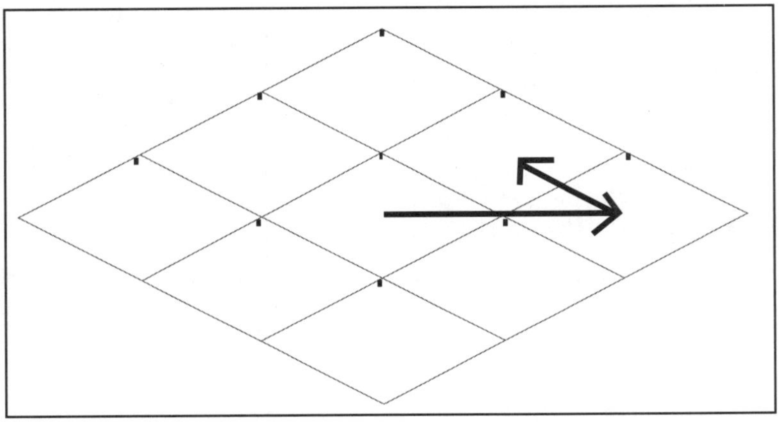

Figure 12.17

Moving northeast on a slide map

South

To move south, move one step west, two steps southeast. The net change for x is –1(west) +0(southeast)+0(southeast)= –1. The net change for y is +0(west)+1(southeast)+1(southeast)= +2. Figure 12.18 shows this derivation graphically.

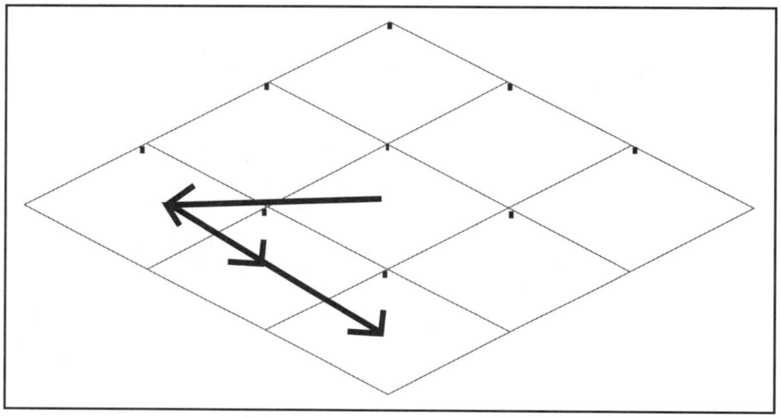

Figure 12.18

Moving south on a slide map

Southwest

To move southwest, move one step west, one step southeast. The net change for x is –1(west)+0(southeast)= –1. The net change for y is +0(west)+1(southeast)= +1. Figure 12.19 shows this graphically.

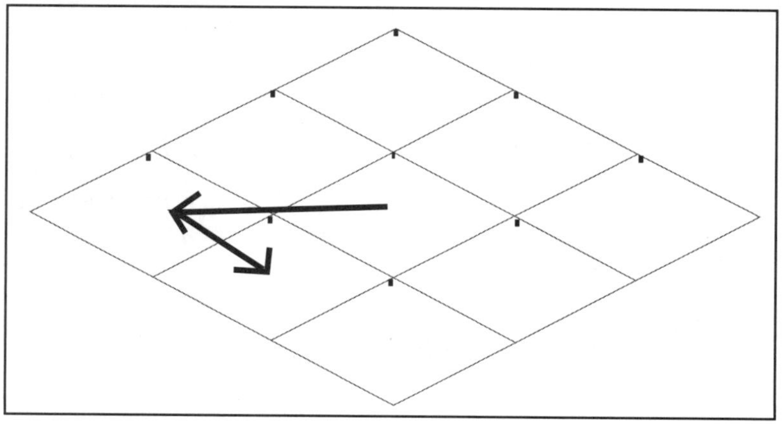

Figure 12.19

Moving southwest on a slide map

Finally, you have enough information to complete your tilewalking table for slide maps. Table 12.7 shows the information for moving all directions. For hex maps, eliminate two opposing directions, depending on the hexagon's orientation.

Table 12.7 Slide Map Tilewalking (Complete)

Direction	Change x	Change y
North	+1	–2
Northeast	+1	–1
East	+1	0
Southeast	0	+1
South	–1	+2
Southwest	–1	+1
West	–1	0
Northwest	0	–1

Now that you can walk from tile to tile, it is time to construct a suitable function to do so. In order to make it all work, you need to set up a few things. The first is some sort of enumeration for direction constants:

```
enum IsoDirection{
ISO_NORTH=0,
ISO_NORTHEAST=1,
ISO_EAST=2,
ISO_SOUTHEAST=3,
ISO_SOUTH=4,
ISO_SOUTHWEST=5,
ISO_WEST=6,
ISO_NORTHWEST=7
};
```

> **NOTE**
>
> **If you're interested in hexagonal (I know you're out there—I can hear you breathing), you simply leave out two directions from this enumeration and replace `ISO_` with `HEX_`.**

After you have the enumeration, you just have to build the function itself. As with the TilePlotter, you will have the TileWalker use `POINT`s:

```
POINT SlideMap_TileWalker(POINT ptStart, IsoDirection Dir)
{
	switch(Dir)
	{
	case ISO_NORTH:
		{
			ptStart.x++;
			ptStart.y-=2;
		}break;
	case ISO_NORTHEAST:
		{
			ptStart.x++;
			ptStart.y—;
		}break;
	case ISO_EAST:
		{
			ptStart.x++;
		}break;
	case ISO_SOUTHEAST:
		{
			ptStart.y++;
		}break;
	case ISO_SOUTH:
		{
			ptStart.x—;
			ptStart.y+=2;
		}break;
	case ISO_SOUTHWEST:
		{
			ptStart.x—;
			ptStart.y++;
		}break;
	case ISO_WEST:
		{
			ptStart.x—;
		}break;
	case ISO_NORTHWEST:
		{
```

```
                ptStart.y--;
            }break;
    }
    return(ptStart);
}
```

And you've got your TileWalker, which brings us to example time. Load up IsoHex12_3.cpp. Make sure you get both of the bitmaps and other necessary files. This example takes the previous scrolling example (IsoHex12_2.cpp) and puts in the TileWalker.

My basic goals for this example were to move the cursor around the tilemap using the numeric keypad and to keep the view centered on the cursor, or as centered as possible. The phrase "as centered as possible" might be a little confusing. What I mean by this is that when the current position is within the central part of the map, the cursor appears at the center of the screen. When the cursor is near the edges, it won't appear at the center of the screen (the anchor will remain bound by anchor space).

Figure 12.20 shows a centered cursor (it's somewhere in the middle of the tilemap). Figure 12.21 shows it on an edge (the cursor isn't centered). These figures demonstrate just how useful an anchor space can be. There are no special cases involved, just the adjustment of `ptScreenAnchor` to lie within the bounds of `rcAnchorSpace`.

Figure 12.20

IsoHex12_3 in the middle of the tilemap

The cursor is in the center of the screen.

Figure 12.21

IsoHex12_3 near the upper-left corner of the map

The cursor is not centered.

The Code for IsoHex12_3

You've already seen the TileWalker, and the `enum` for directions, so I won't repeat those here. The main changes from IsoHex12_2 to IsoHex12_3 are the addition of the cursor and the response of numeric keypad keys.

Showing the Cursor

The cursor is shown by calling `ShowIsoCursor`. The cursor itself is contained in a tileset (separate from the tiles that comprise the map) called `tsCursor`. The map position of the cursor is contained in the global variable `ptCursor`.

```
void ShowIsoCursor()
{
	//copy cursor position
	POINT ptMap=ptCursor;
	//get a few metrics from the tileset
	int iTileWidth=tsIso.GetTileList()[0].rcDstExt.right-
tsIso.GetTileList()[0].rcDstExt.left;
	int iTileHeight=tsIso.GetTileList()[0].rcDstExt.bottom-
tsIso.GetTileList()[0].rcDstExt.top;
	//plot cursor position
	POINT ptPlot=SlideMap_TilePlotter(ptMap,iTileWidth,iTileHeight);
	//put the cursor image
```

```
	tsCursor.PutTile(lpddsBack,ptPlot.x-ptScreenAnchor.x,ptPlot.y-
ptScreenAnchor.y,0);
}
```

`ShowIsoCursor` performs two major tasks. First, it finds where the cursor is supposed to go using the TilePlotter, and then it puts in the tile, adjusting for the screen anchor.

Moving the Cursor

This is where the TileWalker comes into play. During the program's response to `WM_KEYDOWN` events, the following has been added:

```
//move cursor
if(wParam==VK_NUMPAD8)
	MoveCursor(ISO_NORTH);
if(wParam==VK_NUMPAD9)
	MoveCursor(ISO_NORTHEAST);
if(wParam==VK_NUMPAD6)
	MoveCursor(ISO_EAST);
if(wParam==VK_NUMPAD3)
	MoveCursor(ISO_SOUTHEAST);
if(wParam==VK_NUMPAD2)
	MoveCursor(ISO_SOUTH);
if(wParam==VK_NUMPAD1)
	MoveCursor(ISO_SOUTHWEST);
if(wParam==VK_NUMPAD4)
	MoveCursor(ISO_WEST);
if(wParam==VK_NUMPAD7)
	MoveCursor(ISO_NORTHWEST);
```

Each key on the numeric keypad sends a command to the `MoveCursor` function, shown next. The `MoveCursor` function works in two phases. First, it tilewalks the cursor to a new position (it first checks to see that the move is valid). Second, it adjusts the anchor and clips the anchor to anchor space.

```
void MoveCursor(IsoDirection Dir)
{
	//move the cursor using the tilewalker
	POINT ptTemp=SlideMap_TileWalker(ptCursor,Dir);
	//get a few metrics from the tileset
	int iTileWidth=tsIso.GetTileList()[0].rcDstExt.right-
tsIso.GetTileList()[0].rcDstExt.left;
```

```
	int iTileHeight=tsIso.GetTileList()[0].rcDstExt.bottom-
tsIso.GetTileList()[0].rcDstExt.top;
	//bounds checking
	//x<0
	if(ptTemp.x<0) ptTemp=ptCursor;
	//y<0
	if(ptTemp.y<0) ptTemp=ptCursor;
	//x>MAPWIDTH-1
	if(ptTemp.x>(MAPWIDTH-1)) ptTemp=ptCursor;
	//y>MAPHEIGHT-1
	if(ptTemp.y>(MAPHEIGHT-1)) ptTemp=ptCursor;
	//assign new cursor position
	ptCursor=ptTemp;
	//do a test plot of the cursor (for centering)
	POINT ptPlot=SlideMap_TilePlotter(ptCursor,iTileWidth,iTileHeight);
	//center
	ptScreenAnchor.x=ptPlot.x-320+iTileWidth/2;
	ptScreenAnchor.y=ptPlot.y-240+iTileHeight/2;
	//bounds checking for anchor
	if(ptScreenAnchor.x<rcAnchorSpace.left)
ptScreenAnchor.x=rcAnchorSpace.left;
	if(ptScreenAnchor.y<rcAnchorSpace.top) ptScreenAnchor.y=rcAnchorSpace.top;
	if(ptScreenAnchor.x>rcAnchorSpace.right)
ptScreenAnchor.x=rcAnchorSpace.right;
	if(ptScreenAnchor.y>rcAnchorSpace.bottom)
ptScreenAnchor.y=rcAnchorSpace.bottom;
}
```

You may have a question about the centering segment, where I subtract 320 from the anchor's x and 240 from anchor's y, while adding half of the tile's width and height to x and y, respectively. The 320 and 240 are easy to explain away—they are half of the width and height of the screen. The tile's width and height modifications are because your tile anchors exist in the upper-left corner of the tile, and you must further adjust so that the cursor appears in the center of the screen. Later, a `ClipScreenAnchor` function will do this for you.

That's about all there is to the TileWalker. Just like the TilePlotter, it's a pretty simple concept. The TileWalker winds up an important part of the MouseMap, which you will get to next.

MOUSEMAPPING

The final core component of any isometric engine is the MouseMap. A MouseMap is used to convert world coordinates into map coordinates. Since the screen anchor lets you easily convert screen coordinates into world coordinates, the MouseMap is essential for finding out what tile the mouse or other pointing device is on (hence the name "MouseMap"). It has other uses as well, like streamlining which tiles must be blitted to fill up screen space without wasting too many trivially clipped tiles.

Determining on which tile the mouse rests is the most common dilemma for a lot of folks just beginning in IsoHex. The overlap makes it confusing, and I've seen plenty of ways to do it, including some requiring hard-to-understand equations. MouseMaps, once you have the basic idea down, are quite easy, and very effective. As you know, determining whether a `POINT` is within a `RECT` is quite easy—just use the `PtInRect` function! You could come up with many schemes for detecting whether a point is within a diamond or a hexagon. You might make polygon `RGN`s and use `PtInRgn`; this is a valid way to do it, and it would work. The problem is that this method would be slow, since when a region is created, it rips it into little rectangles and compares the `POINT` to all those rectangles to see if it is within the `RGN`.

Alternately, you can use the fact that determining whether a `POINT` is within a `RECT` is fast. You can divide your IsoHex maps into rectangular areas (as shown in Figures 12.22 and 12.23) and work from there. These rectangular areas reach from the top of one tile down to the top of the tile to the south, and from the left of the tile to the left of the tile to the east.

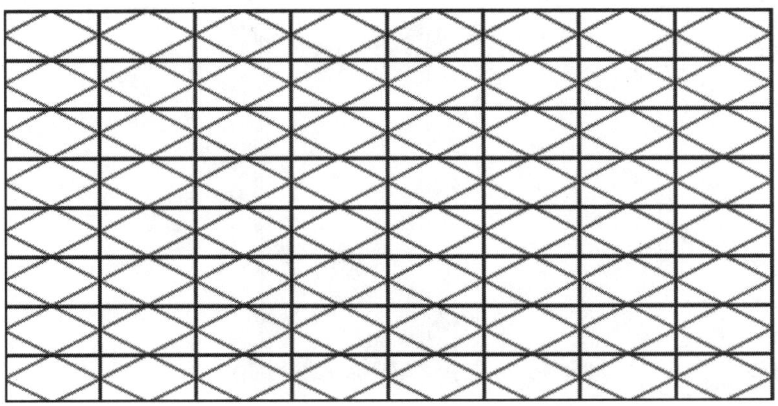

Figure 12.22

An iso map divided into rectangular zones

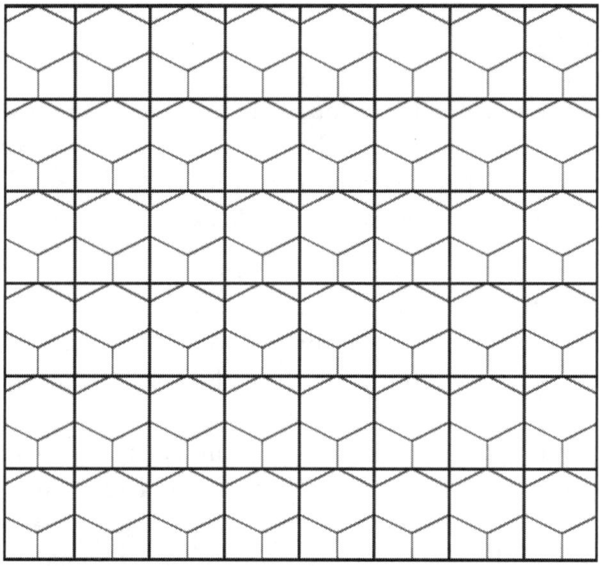

Figure 12.23

A hex map divided into rectangular zones

If you take just one of these rectangular areas and color each tile that has a portion within this area with a different color (as shown in Figures 12.24 and 12.25), you will have a MouseMap. Now you can do some serious work. Ready for the mental leap?

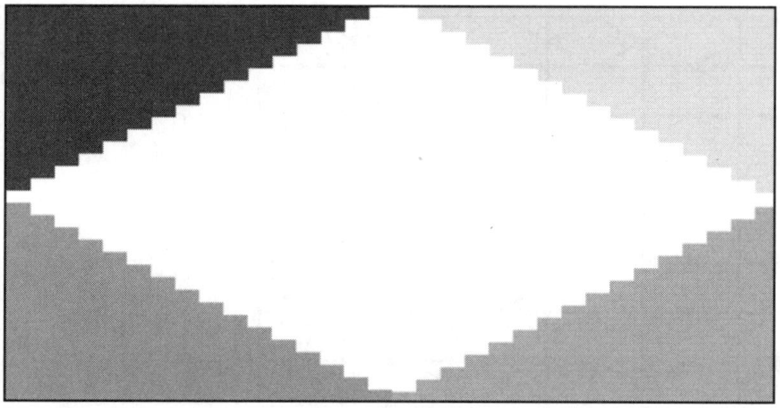

Figure 12.24

Iso MouseMap

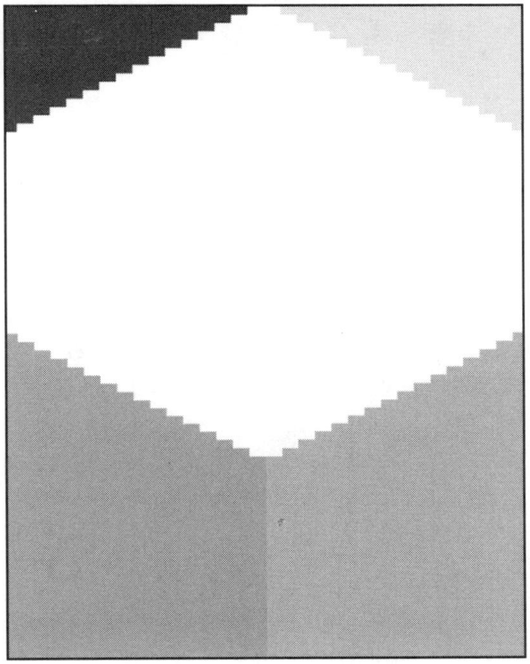

Figure 12.25

Hex MouseMap

Because you have divided your tilemap into rectangular areas, you can easily determine which rectangle you are in. After you know which rectangle you are in, you can calculate where you are within that rectangle. If you check the color at that position, you know which tile you are on.

> **NOTE**
>
> In reality, you don't want to leave your MouseMap as a bitmap, because you would then have to use GDI to get the pixel color. Later, you will create an array, scan the bitmap for the different colors, and just have numbers in a lookup table, but the bitmap example is much better for visualization.

Step-by-Step Mousemapping

This section goes through the entire process of mousemapping as it is usually performed—to take the position of the mouse and convert it into map coordinates. You start with a `POINT` called `ptMouse`, which contains the screen coordinates of the mouse.

Step #1: Convert Screen Coordinates to World Coordinates

This is a simple-enough step. Add the screen anchor to ptMouse.

```
//screen to world translation
ptMouse.x+=ptScreenAnchor.x;
ptMouse.y+=ptScreenAnchor.y
```

Step #2: Subtract World Coordinates for the Upper Left of the Map Position (0,0)

For this, you use the TilePlotter and make use of the tile extent for tile (0,0). In this case, the coordinate winds up being (0,0), but in cases where world space extends beyond the tilemap, or when tile anchors are not at the upper left of the tile, this becomes important.

```
//retrieve some tile metrics
int iTileWidth=tsIso.GetTileList()[0].rcDstExt.right-
tsIso.GetTileList()[0].rcDstExt.left;
int iTileHeight=tsIso.GetTileList()[0].rcDstExt.bottom-
tsIso.GetTileList()[0].rcDstExt.top;
//get map position 0,0
POINT ptMap;
ptMap.x=0;
ptMap.y=0;
//determine plot position
POINT ptPlot=SlideMap_TilePlotter(ptMap,iTileWidth,iTileHeight);
//adjust the plotted point for the tile's extent
ptPlot.x+=tsIso. GetTileList()[0].rcDstExt.left;
ptPlot.y+=tsIso. GetTileList()[0].rcDstExt.top;
//subtract ptPlot from ptMouse
ptMouse.x-=ptPlot.x;
ptMouse.y-=ptPlot.y;
```

Now ptMouse contains a coordinate relative to the upper left of the tile at map position (0,0). This is important, because the MouseMap is designed to be aligned with that tile.

Step #3: Determine MouseMap Coordinates

Now determine which rectangular area (which is the same size as the MouseMap) you're in by dividing `ptMouse` by the width and height of the MouseMap (which would be stored in global variables prior to using the MouseMap). These are the "coarse" MouseMap coordinates.

At the same time, you want to know where within the rectangular area `ptMouse` points. You will use the modulus operator (%) to get the remainder of the division. These are the "fine" MouseMap coordinates.

```
//find coarse coordinates
POINT ptMouseMapCoarse;
ptMouseMapCoarse.x=ptMouse.x/MouseMapWidth;
ptMouseMapCoarse.y=ptMouse.y/MouseMapHeight;
//find fine coordinates
POINT ptMouseMapFine;
ptMouseMapFine.x=ptMouse.x%MouseMapWidth;
ptMouseMapFine.y=ptMouse.y%MouseMapHeight;
//adjust for negative fine coordinates
if(ptMouseMapFine.x<0)
{
	ptMouseMapFine.x+=MouseMapWidth;
	ptMouseMapCoarse.x—;
}
if(ptMouseMapFine.y<0)
{
	ptMouseMapFine.y+=MouseMapHeight;
	ptMouseMapCoarse.y—;
}
```

Some explanation might be necessary for the segment on adjusting for negative fine coordinates. In slide maps, this adjustment is unnecessary, because all plotted tiles have a nonnegative coordinate for their upper-left corner. Later, when we get into diamond maps, this adjustment becomes necessary. I just wanted to bring it up here so that all the parts of mousemapping are explained in one spot.

Because of the way computers do integer arithmetic, using division on a negative number works differently than it does in mathematics. In mathematics, –32/64 would be –1 (the nearest integer *below* the actual answer). In a computer, however, –32/64 is 0 (the nearest integer closest to 0).

The modulus operator (%) is based on division. The calculation looks something like this:

```
Remainder=Dividend - [Dividend/Divisor] * Divisor
```

The [] means integer result.

In mathematics, the modulus always gives you a positive value. Take, for example, (–32)%64 and 32%64. (The first number is the dividend, and the second is the divisor.)

Computer

Remainder = –32–[–32/64]*64=–32–0*64=–32–0=–32
Remainder = 32–[32/64]*64=32–0*64=32–0=32

Mathematics

Remainder = –32–[–32/64]*64=–32–(–1)*64=–32+64=32
Remainder = 32–[32/64]*64=32+(0)*64=32+0=32

As you can see, mathematics always gives a nonnegative result, but with a computer, it depends. Luckily, computers do have the nice even steps, as long as the dividend and divisor are both positive.

So, when you come to a negative remainder on a computer, you simply add the divisor to it, subtract 1 from the calculated answer, and you're good to go. Pesky integer arithmetic will bother you no more.

Step #4: Perform a Coarse Tile Walk

Now you get to incorporate the TileWalker; both steps 4 and 5 make use of it. The first task is a coarse tile walk based on the `ptMouseMapCoarse` x and y. If `ptMouseMap.x` is greater than 0, take that many steps to the east. If x is negative, take that many steps to the west. Make similar north or south steps for negative or positive y values.

> **NOTE**
>
> **Hey, hex folks. No, I haven't forgotten you. You might be scratching your head at the coarse tile walk, because two of your directions don't exist. They are usually north and south or east and west. As applicable, you have to make double steps, like a northeast step plus a southeast step to make one eastward step if you can't go east.**

A coarse tile walk looks something like this:

```
//set up map coordinate
ptMap.x=0;
ptMap.y=0;
//north movement
while(ptMouseMapCoarse.y<0)
{
ptMap=SlideMap_TileWalker(ptMap,ISO_NORTH);
      ptMouseMapCoarse.y++;
}
//south movement
while(ptMouseMapCoarse.y>0)
{
ptMap=SlideMap_TileWalker(ptMap,ISO_SOUTH);
      ptMouseMapCoarse.y—;
}
//east movement
while(ptMouseMapCoarse.x<0)
{
```

```
        ptMap=SlideMap_TileWalker(ptMap,ISO_WEST);
        ptMouseMapCoarse.x++;
}
//west movement
while(ptMouseMapCoarse.x>0)
{
        ptMap=SlideMap_TileWalker(ptMap,ISO_EAST);
        ptMouseMapCoarse.x–;
}
```

Now you are pretty close to your real map coordinate—no more than a single tile away.

Step #5: Use the MouseMap Lookup Table

This is where the MouseMap comes in. Check the color of the map (or the value in the lookup table) corresponding to the coordinate within `ptMouseMapFine`. This will contain one of five values: `MM_CENTER`, `MM_NW`, `MM_NE`, `MM_SE`, or `MM_SW`. Each value tells you how to make your final tile walk onto the proper map position (`MM_CENTER` simply means no tile walk is necessary). For the purpose of illustration, you will make your MouseMap a 2D array of values.

```
//use mousemap lookup table
switch(MouseMapLookUp[ptMouseMapFine.x][ptMouseMapFine.y])
{
case MM_CENTER:
        {
                //no movement
        }break;
case MM_NE:
        {
                //move one to the northeast
                ptMap=SlideMap_TileWalker(ptMap,ISO_NORTHEAST);
        }break;
case MM_SE:
        {
                //move one to the southeast
                ptMap=SlideMap_TileWalker(ptMap,ISO_SOUTHEAST);
        }break;
case MM_SW:
        {
                //move one to the southwest
                ptMap=SlideMap_TileWalker(ptMap,ISO_SOUTHWEST);
```

```
        }break;
case MM_NW:
        {
                //move one to the northwest
                ptMap=SlideMap_TileWalker(ptMap,ISO_NORTHWEST);
        }break;
}
```

And you're done! The coordinate in ptMap is the map coordinate the mouse points to. Easy, right? I know it seems like a lot of code, but it's quite fast.

Now that you've got the basic algorithm down, you just need to wrap it. The first thing you need is a nice little structure to hold the lookup table and MouseMap dimensions (width and height). I suggest something like the following:

```
//enumeration type for mousemap directions
enum MouseMapDirection {MM_CENTER,MM_NE,MM_SE,MM_SW,MM_NW};
struct CMouseMap
{
        //x and y size of the mousemap
        POINT ptSize;
        //reference point for overlaying the mousemap on tile 0,0
        POINT ptRef;
        //lookup array
        MouseMapDirection* mmdLookUp;
};
```

The ptMouseMapSize member contains the width in x and the height in y. The world coordinate for tile (0,0) is stored in ptMouseMapRef. (This means you only have to calculate it once and can thereafter use it many times.) chMouseMapLookUp is a pointer that you allocate to store enough information for the entire map. It is a one-dimensional array that acts like a two-dimensional array.

Next, you need a function that loads in a MouseMap from a bitmap. To make it happen, use CGDICanvas:

```
void MouseMapLoad(CMouseMap* pmm,LPCTSTR lpszfilename)
{
        //create canvas
        CGDICanvas gdic;
        //load file
        gdic.Load(NULL,lpszfilename);
        //assign width/height
```

```
    pmm->ptSize.x=gdic.GetWidth();
    pmm->ptSize.y=gdic.GetHeight();
    //allocate space for the lookup table
    pmm->mmdLookUp= new
        MouseMapDirection[gdic.GetWidth()*gdic.GetHeight()];
    //colorref values for filling lookup
    COLORREF crNW=GetPixel(gdic,0,0);
    COLORREF crNE=GetPixel(gdic,gdic.GetWidth()-1,0);
    COLORREF crSW=GetPixel(gdic,0,gdic.GetHeight()-1);
    COLORREF crSE=GetPixel(gdic,gdic.GetWidth()-1, gdic.GetHeight()-1);
    //test pixel color
    COLORREF crTest;
    //scan convert bitmap into lookup values
    for(int y=0;y<gdic.GetHeight();y++)
    {
        for(int x=0;x<gdic.GetWidth();x++)
        {
            //grab test pixel
            crTest=GetPixel(gdic,x,y);
            //set lookup to default
            pmm->mmdLookUp[x+y*pmm->ptSize.x]=MM_CENTER;
            //check colors
            if(crTest==crNW)
            pmm->mmdLookUp[x+y*pmm->ptSize.x]=MM_NW;
            if(crTest==crNE)
            pmm->mmdLookUp[x+y*pmm->ptSize.x]=MM_NE;
            if(crTest==crSW)
            pmm->mmdLookUp[x+y*pmm->ptSize.x]=MM_SW;
            if(crTest==crSE)
            pmm->mmdLookUp[x+y*pmm->ptSize.x]=MM_SE;
        }
    }
}
```

This function does all the work to get a bitmap converted to a lookup table. However, it doesn't put in the reference point for tile (0,0). Also, the lookup table was dynamically allocated, so to avoid memory leakage it will have to be deallocated later with the following line:

```
//mm is a CMouseMap variable
delete [] mm->mmdLookUp;
```

A Mousemapping Example

Now you have all you need to implement a MouseMap in an IsoHex application. Load IsoHex12_4.cpp. This example is based on IsoHex12_3.cpp, but instead of keyboard control, you now have mouse control. The MouseMap setup and MouseMap functions are essentially the same as the code I showed you earlier, with the exception that now the tile (0,0) reference point is stored in the MouseMap structure and does not have to be calculated each time. Another difference (albeit a small one) is that all of the lines where `iTileWidth` and `iTileHeight` were calculated are gone; I'll talk more about that a little later.

One more enhancement I put into this example is scrolling by moving the mouse pointer near the edge of a screen. The closer it gets, the faster the scroll. The amount of scrolling is stored in a variable called `ptScreenAnchorScroll` (a `POINT`). The following is the snippet that does the scrolling itself:

```
//scroll the map
ptScreenAnchor.x+=ptScreenAnchorScroll.x;
ptScreenAnchor.y+=ptScreenAnchorScroll.y;
ClipScreenAnchor();
```

The `ClipScreenAnchor` function (shown next) simply ensures that the screen anchor doesn't wander out of anchor space; it's similar to what you did when you centered the cursor in IsoHex12_3.cpp.

```
void ClipScreenAnchor()
{
	//clip to left
	if(ptScreenAnchor.x<rcAnchorSpace.left)
ptScreenAnchor.x=rcAnchorSpace.left;
	//clip to top
	if(ptScreenAnchor.y<rcAnchorSpace.top) ptScreenAnchor.y=rcAnchorSpace.top;
	//clip to right
	if(ptScreenAnchor.x>rcAnchorSpace.right)
ptScreenAnchor.x=rcAnchorSpace.right;
	//clip to bottom
	if(ptScreenAnchor.y>rcAnchorSpace.bottom)
ptScreenAnchor.y=rcAnchorSpace.bottom;
}
```

This is a very simple but very effective scrolling scheme. It would not be possible without a screen anchor and anchor space rectangle. As you might have guessed, you can use this exact scrolling algorithm in any of your IsoHex games and demos. It just goes to show that you don't need especially complicated code to allow scrolling.

The main work of this example is done in the `WM_MOUSEMOVE` handler. The tasks are divided into three parts: mousemapping the cursor, clipping the cursor to a valid tile (that is, not allowing cursor locations outside the tilemap), and assigning the values of `ptScreenAnchorScroll` if the mouse is near one or more of the screen's edges.

```
case WM_MOUSEMOVE:
	{
		//grab mouse coordinate
		POINT ptMouse;
		ptMouse.x=LOWORD(lParam);
		ptMouse.y=HIWORD(lParam);
		//mousemap the mouse coordinates
		ptCursor=SlideMap_MouseMapper(ptMouse,&mmMouseMap);
		//clip cursor to tilemap
		if(ptCursor.x<0) ptCursor.x=0;
		if(ptCursor.y<0) ptCursor.y=0;
		if(ptCursor.x>MAPWIDTH-1) ptCursor.x=MAPWIDTH-1;
		if(ptCursor.y>MAPHEIGHT-1) ptCursor.y=MAPHEIGHT-1;
		//check for scrolling zones
		ptScreenAnchorScroll.x=0;
		ptScreenAnchorScroll.y=0;
		//top
		if(ptMouse.y<8)
			ptScreenAnchorScroll.y=-(8-ptMouse.y);
		//bottom
		if(ptMouse.y>472)
			ptScreenAnchorScroll.y=(ptMouse.y-472);
		//left
		if(ptMouse.x<8)
			ptScreenAnchorScroll.x=-(8-ptMouse.x);
		//right
		if(ptMouse.x>632)
			ptScreenAnchorScroll.x=(ptMouse.x-632);
		return(0);
	}break;
```

Figure 12.26 shows the output of IsoHex12_4.cpp. It looks quite a bit like the other examples in this chapter, except that the highlighted tile contains the mouse.

Figure 12.26

Output of IsoHex12_4.cpp

The mouse is contained in this tile.

As you've been going along here, you've probably noticed that you're are getting further and further away from code that actually manipulates the tilemap and the coordinates of the various tiles. Mostly, you rely on the three major iso components—the TilePlotter, the TileWalker, and the MouseMap. This is a good thing, because it frees you from special case code and from having to always think about the coordinate system while trying to add other features to your games.

That's it for mousemapping for now. You'll learn more about it later, when I will show you some extra and surprising uses of the MouseMap. Your fundamental slide map iso engine is complete, and the possibilities are now endless.

Summary

You've come quite a way from the rectangular tiles and tilemaps discussed in Chapter 10. I showed you that isometric tile-based algorithms are not nearly as complex as you might have thought. In fact, with the steps you've taken in this chapter, you might now think they're downright simple. You'd be right!

Also, the topic of scrolling, which befuddles and confuses most IsoHex beginners, has been demystified with the use of anchors and anchor space. You aren't done yet with scrolling. Later, you will make it more efficient, but the basic foundation is there.

You've got the goods on slide maps, which are great to bring out first because of their simpler structure, but we still have two more map types to discuss. However, don't discount the usefulness of slide maps. The very first isometric game that I know of (*Zaxxon*, Sega 1982) used something very similar to an iso slide map.

Also, you took a brief look at hex in this chapter, mainly to show you how similar iso and hex are. From here on out, however, you'll concentrate on iso. For the topics and specific concerns of hexagonal tile mapping, check out Appendix B, "Hexagonal Tile-Based Games."

Staggered maps, here we come!

CHAPTER 13

Staggered Tilemaps

- Coordinate System
- Tileplotting
- Tilewalking
- Mousemapping in Staggered Maps

The preceding chapter covered the basic groundwork for isometric engines while exploring the simplest of the iso tilemap types, the slide map. There's not much call for slide maps in computer games, but if you're creative enough, you can find a use for them.

This chapter focuses on one of the more commonly used map types—the staggered map. Many strategy games, past and present, use this type of map, games such as *Civilization II, Civilization: Call to Power, Imperialism II,* and *Alpha Centauri,* These are (or were) popular titles. (*Civ II,* several years old, does not show its age; its popularity continues. It is possibly one of the most heavily played strategy computer games ever.)

> **NOTE**
> **Be aware: Most of the fundamentals for IsoHex maps were covered in Chapter 12, "Slide Isometric Tilemaps." You might want to turn back at times for a quick refresher. This chapter is considerably shorter than Chapter 12, since in it I cover just algorithms specific to the staggered tilemaps.**

Coordinate System

Figure 13.1 is a graphical representation of a staggered tilemap. The x-axis increases to the east, just as it does in slide maps. The unusual part is the y-axis, which alternately moves southeast and southwest, depending on what tile row you are on, giving a somewhat zigzagging southern direction to the y-axis. The advantage of this is that you can more easily fill rectangular areas without encountering some of the difficulties you had with slide maps.

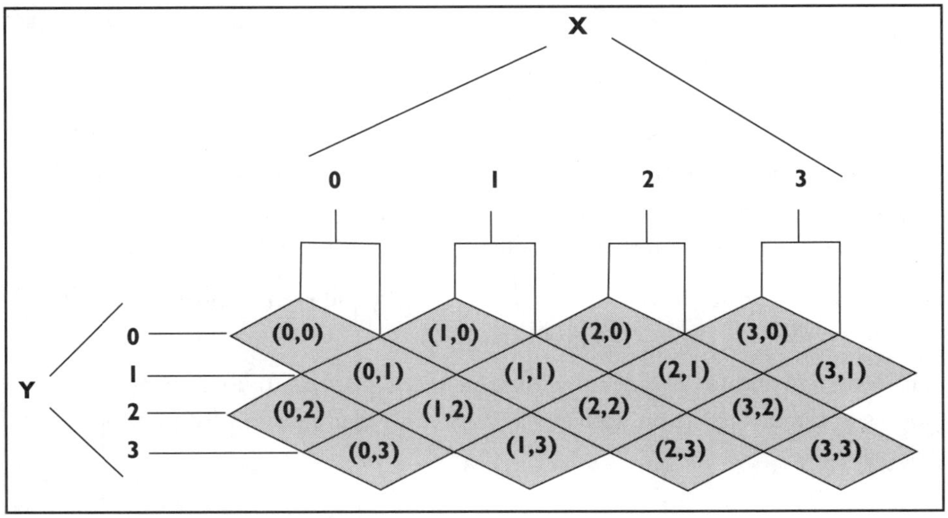

Figure 13.1

Staggered tilemap coordinate system

The best way to describe the coordinate system for staggered maps is not to speak of the strange behavior of the y-axis, but instead to say that even rows (y=0, 2, 4, and so on) are in a straight column, and odd rows (y=1, 3, 5, and so on) are shifted to the east by half a tile. Of course, you can shift to the west if you like, or you can even turn the map on its side and offset vertically instead of horizontally, but the examples in this chapter use the even/odd row scheme to plot your tiles.

Because of this different coordinate system, you will find some differences in the TilePlotter and TileWalker (especially the TileWalker). However, as you will see, the MouseMap is completely unaffected, because it relies on the other two components to work properly.

TilePlotting

Naturally, you will want to plot your staggered maps in horizontal rows, just as you did with your slide maps. This is easy to do because of the eastward direction of the x-axis. The y-axis may trip you up, but only a little.

At first glance, you might consider special cases for your TilePlotter, including a simple check to see if y is odd or even, as shown here:

```
//check for even y
if(y%2==0)
{
        //even
        //special case for even tiles here
}
else
{
        //odd
        //special case for odd tiles
}
```

This is a valid way to go about solving the problem, but I'm not particularly thrilled with it. The problem I have is that it includes special-case code, and experience has shown me that special-case code tends to break easier. Ideally, I would have a nice equation that works for all cases. Fortunately, I have one.

Besides checking `y%2` for an odd/even test, you can alternately use `y&1`. For all even numbers, `y&1` will yield 0, and for all odd numbers, `y&1` will yield 1. So, problem solved.

Now consider the coordinate system and we'll come up with some nice equations to use in your TilePlotter. The x-axis moves in the east direction, so here's a portion of your equation for plotting x:

```
//MapX is map coordinate, PlotX is world coordinate
PlotX=MapX*TileWidth;
```

That's not the end of the story, however. The odd rows (where `y&1` yields 1) are shifted east by half a tile (`+TileWidth/2`), so you modify the equation slightly:

```
//mapx, mapy are map coordinates, plotx is world coordinate
PlotX=MapX*TileWidth+(MapY&1)*(TileWidth/2);
```

The y-coordinate calculation is much simpler. The y-axis alternately moves southeast and southwest. Both of these directions affect the world y-coordinates by moving half of a `TileHeight` downward. So, the calculation for y is as follows:

```
//mapy is a map coordinate, ploty is a world coordinate
PlotY=MapY*(TileHeight/2);
```

And that's all there is to it! You just take these two calculations, slap them into a function, and you're off:

```
POINT StagMap_TilePlotter(POINT ptMap,int iTileWidth,int iTileHeight)
{
        POINT ptPlot;
        ptPlot.x=ptMap.x*iTileWidth+(ptMap.y & 1) * (iTileWidth/2);
        ptPlot.y=ptMap.y*(iTileHeight/2);
        return(ptPlot);
}
```

I bet you'd like an example, wouldn't you? Very well. Load up IsoHex13_1.cpp. The code suspiciously resembles that of IsoHex12_1.cpp, as well it should, since I copied the code into a new workspace, made about five minor changes, and recompiled it. Talk about a short development cycle!

Figure 13.2 shows the result of running IsoHex13_1.cpp. It is essentially the same code as in the preceding chapter, but with a drastically different look. The staggered map takes up more of a rectangular area, and if you can clip out the jagged edges, it fills up a rectangular viewport very nicely. This is a lot better result than you can achieve with a slide map, which tends to have large, ugly black areas.

Figure 13.2

Output of IsoHex13_1.cpp

It's astounding, really, that after exploring the basics so much in the last chapter, staggered maps are a breeze to learn. The TilePlotter is built, and you are one-third of the way to mastering the subtleties of staggered maps.

Tilewalking

The staggered map TileWalker will put to rest a few questions you might have had in Chapter 12. If you didn't immediately pick up on something a little strange with the slide map TileWalker, let me point it out.

As you recall, the slide map TileWalker looks like the following:

```
POINT SlideMap_TileWalker(POINT ptStart, IsoDirection Dir)
{
	//depending on direction, move the point
	switch(Dir)
	{
	case ISO_NORTH:
		{
			ptStart.x++;
			ptStart.y-=2;
		}break;
	case ISO_NORTHEAST:
		{
			ptStart.x++;
```

```
                        ptStart.y--;
                }break;
        case ISO_EAST:
                {
                        ptStart.x++;
                }break;
        case ISO_SOUTHEAST:
                {
                        ptStart.y++;
                }break;
        case ISO_SOUTH:
                {
                        ptStart.x--;
                        ptStart.y+=2;
                }break;
        case ISO_SOUTHWEST:
                {
                        ptStart.x--;
                        ptStart.y++;
                }break;
        case ISO_WEST:
                {
                        ptStart.x--;
                }break;
        case ISO_NORTHWEST:
                {
                        ptStart.y--;
                }break;
        }
        //return the point
        return(ptStart);
}
```

Still can't see it? Time's up! The problem with the slide map TileWalker is that it can take only a single step at a time. This seems silly, considering the regularity of the slide map, and it reduces the efficiency of the MouseMap, which uses the TileWalker to convert from MouseMap coordinates to map coordinates.

Why would I intentionally write inefficient code? Well it's not *terribly* inefficient. Incrementing and decrementing variables and passing eight bytes back from a function hardly affects anything, especially in simple examples like the ones you've been doing (rest assured that you'll have much better TileWalkers later).

So, I should have designed the slide map TileWalker according to how many steps you need to go in the given direction. The prototype would look something like this.

```
POINT SlideMap_TileWalker(POINT ptStart, IsoDirection Dir, int iSteps);
```

There are two reasons I didn't do this from the start. One, these examples are meant to educate, and being as efficient as possible isn't necessarily the best way to go about explaining something. Two, I wanted to have uniformity while explaining the three map types, and in staggered maps, tilewalking in multiple steps is more difficult.

What do I mean? Well, consider Figure 13.3, which illustrates two steps, both in the southeast direction, starting from map position (0,0). The first step moves from (0,0) to (0,1). The second step moves from (0,1) to (1,2). Take a closer look at these steps.

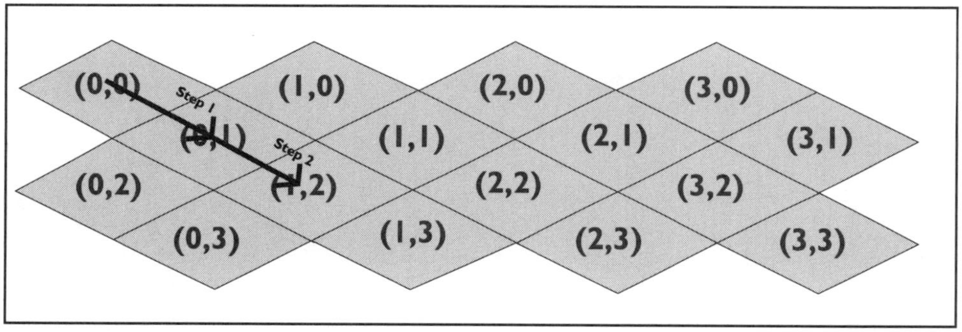

Figure 13.3

The TileWalker problem with staggered maps

Step 1:

Start	x=0	y=0	
End	x=0	y=1	
Difference		dx=0	dy=1

Step 2:

Start	x=0	y=1	
End	x=1	y=2	
Difference		dx=1	dy=1

As you can plainly see, the differences in these two steps change from one step to another. Both steps have a y difference of 1, but the x differences change between steps. This shows that multi-step tilewalking can be solved, with some difficulty. I'm not saying it's impossible, but the code is a bit confusing until you've got a solid grasp of what's going on. So, for now, at least, stick with single-step tilewalking.

For your staggered map TileWalker, you'll treat map coordinates as two special cases—one for an even y-coordinate, and one for an odd y-coordinate. You will later put them together in a single function.

Moving east or west is the same, no matter if y is odd or even. Moving east causes x to increase by 1, and moving west causes x to decrease by 1. The y is unaffected in either case.

Direction	Change x	Change y
East	1	0
West	-1	0

From an even y-coordinate, y increases to the southeast. From an odd y-coordinate, y increases to the southwest.

Direction	y Even/Odd	Change x	Change y
Southeast	Even	0	1
Southwest	Odd	0	1

Believe it or not, you now have enough information to derive the rest of the values for your TileWalker. I'll go over all of it, step by step, so that you can have a full understanding of how it works (it can seem really strange at first).

First, since you move x by 0 and y by 1 to move southeast from an even y position (which then leaves you at an odd y position), the opposite move (moving northwest from an odd y position) should change x by 0 and y by –1. Similarly, since moving from an odd y increases y to the southwest, moving northeast from an even y should change y by –1. Figure 13.4 demonstrates what I'm trying to say—in this case, words don't convey the idea nearly as well as a figure does. The directions you have so far are listed in Table 13.1.

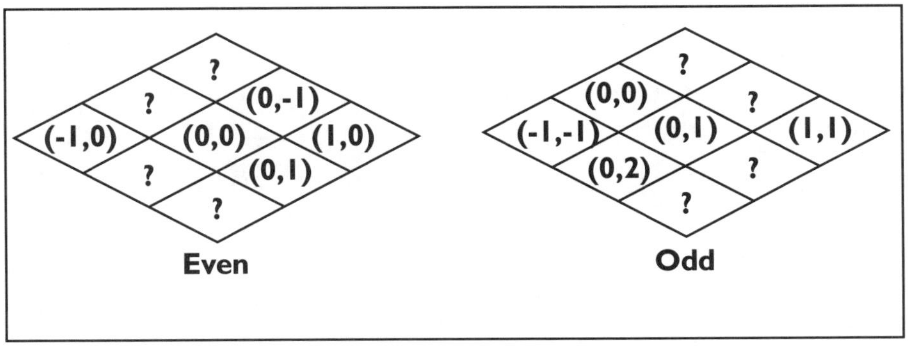

Figure 13.4

Deriving the staggered TileWalker

Table 13.1 Staggered TileWalker (Initial)

Direction	+/–x (Even y)	+/–y (Even y)	+/–x (Odd y)	+/–y (Odd y)
North	???	???	???	???
Northeast	0	–1	???	???
East	1	0	1	0
Southeast	0	1	???	???
South	???	???	???	???
Southwest	???	???	0	1
West	1	0	1	0
Northwest	???	???	0	–1

From this, you can easily derive the rest. Do them one at a time, starting with the even y directions.

Even Y Tilewalking

You are missing four directions: north, south, southwest, and northwest.

To move northwest, you can first move northeast and then move west. Moving northeast subtracts 1 from y (leaving you at an odd y position). Moving west subtracts 1 from x whether y is odd or even. So, moving northwest moves you to (x–1,y–1) if you start on an even y-coordinate.

To move southwest, you first move southeast to (x,y+1), an odd y-coordinate. From there, you move west by subtracting 1 from x, leaving you at (x–1,y+1).

To move north, you first move northeast to (x,y–1), an odd y-coordinate. Next, you move northwest, which subtracts 1 from y since you are on an odd y, giving you (x,y–2). To move south, you move southeast to (x,y+1) (odd), and then southwest to (x,y+2). Your even y TileWalker is complete, as shown in Table 13.2.

Table 13.2 Staggered TileWalker (Completed Even)

Direction	+/–x (Even y)	+/–y (Even y)	+/–x (Odd y)	+/–y (Odd y)
North	0	–2	???	???
Northeast	0	–1	???	???
East	1	0	1	0
Southeast	0	1	???	???
South	0	2	???	???
Southwest	–1	1	0	1
West	1	0	1	0
Northwest	–1	–1	0	–1

Odd Y Tilewalking

Again, you have four directions yet to figure out—north, northeast, southeast, and south. To move north and south, you can follow the crooked y-axis two steps, just as you did with the even y-coordinates. You will wind up with the same values—(0,–2) for north and (0,2) for south.

To move northeast, you first move northwest to (x,y–1) (even) and then move east to (x+1,y–1) (even). To move southeast, you first move southwest to (x,y+1) (even) and then move east to (x+1,y+1) (even).

Finally, your staggered TileWalker is complete, as shown in Table 13.3.

Table 13.3 Staggered TileWalker (Complete)

Direction	+/–x (Even y)	+/–y (Even y)	+/–x (Odd y)	+/–y (Odd y)
North	0	–2	0	–2
Northeast	0	–1	1	–1
East	1	0	1	0
Southeast	0	1	1	1
South	0	2	0	2
Southwest	–1	1	0	1
West	1	0	1	0
Northwest	–1	–1	0	–1

You could make a TileWalker for staggered maps from this table, but you aren't done just yet. You can streamline a few things about this table so that your TileWalker will be more concise (and you won't have to have a bunch of `if` statements to check for an even/odd y-coordinate).

The first thing you'll notice is that the cardinal directions (north, south, east, west) are the same for both even and odd y values, so you don't need to have a special case for them.

Also, the y changes for all the directions are the same for both even and odd y values, so you don't have to special-case those either. Once you take the cardinal directions and the +/–y columns out of the table, you are left with Table 13.4.

Table 13.4 Staggered TileWalker (Cardinal Direction and +/-Y Removed)

Direction	+/–x (Even y)	+/–x (Odd y)
Northeast	0	1
Southeast	0	1
Southwest	–1	0
Northwest	–1	0

Now you can observe the painfully obvious truth that was hidden when this data was strewn about the larger table. When y is odd, you add 1 to the +/–x value. This means you can use `y&1` to modify this value and create a TileWalker that will work in both cases, without any special-case code!

```
POINT StagMap_TileWalker(POINT ptStart,IsoDirection Dir)
{
        POINT ptDest=ptStart;
        switch(dir)
        {
        case ISO_NORTH:
        {
                ptDest.y-=2;
        }break;
        case ISO_NORTHEAST:
        {
                ptDest.y–;
                ptDest.x+=( ptStart.y&1);
        }break;
        case ISO_EAST:
        {
                ptDest.x++;
        }break;
        case ISO_SOUTHEAST:
        {
                ptDest.y++;
                ptDest.x+=( ptStart.y&1);
        }break;
        case ISO_SOUTH:
        {
                ptDest.y+=2;
        }break;
        case ISO_SOUTHWEST:
        {
                ptDest.y++;
                ptDest.x+=( ptStart.y&1-1);
        }break;
        case ISO_WEST:
        {
                ptDest.x++;
```

```
        }break;
        case ISO_NORTHWEST:
        {
                ptDest.y–;
                ptDest.x+=(ptStart.y&1-1);
        }break;
        }
        return(ptDest);
}
```

And there you have it—a reasonably concise staggered TileWalker, only one case for each direction, just like you had for the slide map TileWalker. And that means it's time for an example.

Load up IsoHex13_2.cpp. Other than a difference in the TilePlotter and TileWalker, this example uses the exact same code as IsoHex12_3.cpp, which illustrates just how similar staggered and slide maps really are, as far as plotting and walking. You'll see this code again in the next chapter.

Figure 13.5 shows the output of IsoHex13_2.cpp. The cursor is centered on the screen (except near the edges), and the numeric keypad is used to move around the tilemap. You use the exact same scroller that you used in Chapter 12, which I think is a very cool thing.

Figure 13.5

Output of IsoHex13_2.cpp

Mousemapping in Staggered Maps

I talked at great length about the MouseMap in the preceding chapter, but I won't have to here because the MouseMap is primarily based on the TilePlotter and the TileWalker. Because you've already changed these two components to accommodate your staggered map, you don't have to do anything to your MouseMap—it will still work just fine.

Load up IsoHex13_3.cpp. This example is based on IsoHex12_4.cpp. The only differences exist in the TilePlotter and TileWalker. The MouseMap code has not been touched. Figure 13.6 shows the output of IsoHex13_3.cpp.

Figure 13.6

Output of IsoHex13_3.cpp

Okay, I lied. I did change one other thing. I changed the `ClipScreenAnchor` function to a more accurate version. In the older one, the screen anchor could have an x value equal to the right of the anchor space, and as we discussed in Chapter 2, "The World of GDI and Windows Graphics," the right edge of the `RECT` is not inside the `RECT`.

```
void ClipScreenAnchor()
{
        //clip to left
        if(ptScreenAnchor.x<rcAnchorSpace.left)
ptScreenAnchor.x=rcAnchorSpace.left;
        //clip to top
        if(ptScreenAnchor.y<rcAnchorSpace.top) ptScreenAnchor.y=rcAnchorSpace.top;
        //clip to right
```

```
    if(ptScreenAnchor.x>=rcAnchorSpace.right)
        ptScreenAnchor.x=rcAnchorSpace.right-1;
    //clip to bottom
    if(ptScreenAnchor.y>=rcAnchorSpace.bottom)
        ptScreenAnchor.y=rcAnchorSpace.bottom-1;
}
```

This might seem like a minor change, but it is necessary, especially for what I'm about to show you.

Unique Properties of Staggered Maps

Unlike the slide map, which always has the problem of the big, ugly black areas no matter what you do, staggered maps are more "rectangular" and so are ideally suited for certain tasks. The first of these tasks is "no jaggies," or the elimination of the ugly black triangles on the edges, and the other task is "wrapping around," which is good for making cylindrical worlds. Both of these things can strongly enhance the look of your staggered map-based game.

No Jaggies

First, I want to show you how to eliminate the jaggies. Surprisingly, this has nothing to do with the tile's image or any of the iso engine components. It just has to do with the scroller. In IsoHex 13_4.cpp, the code is almost identical to IsoHex13_3.cpp, with the exception that I added and changed a few lines in `SetUpSpaces`.

```
void SetUpSpaces()
{
    //set up screen space
    SetRect(&rcScreenSpace,0,0,640,480);
    //grab tile rectangle from tileset
    RECT rcTile1;
    RECT rcTile2;
    POINT ptPlot;
    POINT ptMap;
    //grab tiles from extents
    CopyRect(&rcTile1,&tsIso.GetTileList()[0].rcDstExt);
    CopyRect(&rcTile2,&tsIso.GetTileList()[0].rcDstExt);
    //move first tile to upper-left position
    ptMap.x=0;
    ptMap.y=0;
    ptPlot=StagMap_TilePlotter(ptMap,mmMouseMap.ptSize.x,mmMouseMap.ptSize.y);
```

```
        OffsetRect(&rcTile1,ptPlot.x,ptPlot.y);
        //move first tile to lower-right position
        ptMap.x=MAPWIDTH-1;
        ptMap.y=MAPHEIGHT-1;
        ptPlot=StagMap_TilePlotter(ptMap,mmMouseMap.ptSize.x,mmMouseMap.ptSize.y);
        OffsetRect(&rcTile2,ptPlot.x,ptPlot.y);
        //combine these two tiles into world space
        UnionRect(&rcWorldSpace,&rcTile1,&rcTile2);
        //copy world space to anchor space
        CopyRect(&rcAnchorSpace,&rcWorldSpace);
        //subtract screenspace
        //adjust right edge
        rcAnchorSpace.right-=(rcScreenSpace.right-rcScreenSpace.left);
        //make sure right not less than left
        if(rcAnchorSpace.right<rcAnchorSpace.left)
rcAnchorSpace.right=rcAnchorSpace.left;
        //adjust bottom edge
        rcAnchorSpace.bottom-=(rcScreenSpace.bottom-rcScreenSpace.top);
        //make sure bottom not less than top
        if(rcAnchorSpace.bottom<rcAnchorSpace.top)
rcAnchorSpace.bottom=rcAnchorSpace.top;
        //adjust edges of anchorspace for "no jaggies"
        //add 1/2 height to top
        rcAnchorSpace.top+=(mmMouseMap.ptSize.y/2);
        //subtract 1/2 height from bottom
        rcAnchorSpace.bottom-=(mmMouseMap.ptSize.y/2);
        //add 1/2 width to left
        rcAnchorSpace.left+=(mmMouseMap.ptSize.x/2);
        //subtract 1/2 width from right
        rcAnchorSpace.right-=(mmMouseMap.ptSize.x/2);
        //initialize screen anchor
        ptScreenAnchor.x=rcAnchorSpace.left;
        ptScreenAnchor.y=rcAnchorSpace.top;
        //initialize cursor
        ptCursor.x=0;
        ptCursor.y=0;
}
```

As you can see, the changes are pretty minor. You simply reduce your anchor space by half a tile on each edge and initialize the screen anchor to the top left of the screen space, where before you initialized it to (0,0).

Figure 13.7 shows the output of this program. You'll notice that it's similar to most of the rest of the examples in the chapter, except it has no jaggies. Now that you have eliminated the jagged edges, you can certainly see how much more immersive the environment is. Those jagged edges weren't serving any useful purpose... they just distracted you.

Figure 13.7

Output of IsoHex13_4.cpp. No jaggies!

So, was that easy enough for you? Good. Now move on to cylindrical staggered maps.

Cylindrical Maps

When I say *cylindrical* maps, what I mean is that you can move from the left edge to the right edge, and vice versa. In cases like these, the map is called cylindrical because if you were to print the map and put the left and right edges together, you would make a cylindrical tube.

You can also make another type of map, one that not only moves continuously east and west, but also moves continuously moves north and south. These are called *torus* maps. If put into the real world, they would be doughnut-shaped. We won't be dealing with torus maps today, but after you've learned how to make maps cylindrical, it's just a matter of doing the same thing in another direction.

If you're sitting there clutching your heart, hyperventilating, and screaming, "But I'm not ready for this!", calm down. Relax, breathe deeply, and have some herbal tea. Like most of the topics we've covered in our isometric discussions, it's a lot easier than it sounds. In fact, it's really easy... forehead-slapping easy, even.

Since you aren't yet detecting which tiles absolutely must be blitted for each screen (which you will be doing later) you have to render each tile twice. The basic rendering loop will look something like this (this is psuedocode, y'all):

```
void RenderTiles()
{
        for(y=0;y<MAPHEIGHT;y++)
        {
                for(x=0;x<MAPWIDTH*2;x++)//the doubling takes place here
                {
                        MapX=x%MAPWIDTH;//grab the tile that is supposed to go here
                        PlotTile(x,y,TileMap[MapX][y]);
                }
        }
}
```

Why do you render twice? Well, in order to give the illusion of a continuous east-west edge, you have to write tiles "beyond the horizon," or past the right edge. You do not have to do this for the left edge. You don't actually have to write all the tiles twice. You could just do an extra screen width's worth, but since you currently have no particular relationship between screen and map, you must write all tiles twice. You might be saying, "But won't that decrease performance?" Yes, it certainly will. Right now, though, you're working on getting stuff done. Performance comes later.

Load up IsoHex13_5.cpp. Essentially, it is a modified IsoHex13_4, but now you can smoothly scroll left or right forever. Only a few tweaks are necessary to make this happen. First, you need to modify `DrawMap` in order to write each tile twice (as I demonstrated earlier). I have underlined the lines I had to change from the IsoHex13_4 version.

```
void DrawMap()
{
        POINT ptTile;//tile pixel coordinate
        POINT ptMap;//map coordinate
        //the y loop is outside, because we must blit in horizontal rows
        for(int y=0;y<MAPHEIGHT;y++)
        {
                for(int x=0;x<MAPWIDTH*2;x++)
                {
                        //get pixel coordinate for map position
                        ptMap.x=x;
                        ptMap.y=y;
```

```
ptTile=StagMap_TilePlotter(ptMap,mmMouseMap.ptSize.x,mmMouseMap.ptSize.y);
                        //plot the tile (adjust for anchor)
                        tsIso.PutTile(lpddsBack,ptTile.x-ptScreenAnchor.x,ptTile.y-
ptScreenAnchor.y,iTileMap[x%MAPWIDTH][y]);
                }
        }
}
```

Next, you have to modify the anchor space (in the `SetUpSpaces` function) to add a screen width to it. Since you are already subtracting a screen width from anchor space, you'll just remove that part. Also, you have to eliminate the right edge adjustment that you used in the "no jaggies" example. Here is the modified code, with underlined changes:

```
void SetUpSpaces()
{
        //set up screen space
        SetRect(&rcScreenSpace,0,0,640,480);
        //grab tile rectangle from tileset
        RECT rcTile1;
        RECT rcTile2;
        POINT ptPlot;
        POINT ptMap;
        //grab tiles from extents
        CopyRect(&rcTile1,&tsIso.GetTileList()[0].rcDstExt);
        CopyRect(&rcTile2,&tsIso.GetTileList()[0].rcDstExt);
        //move first tile to upper-left position
        ptMap.x=0;
        ptMap.y=0;
        ptPlot=StagMap_TilePlotter(ptMap,mmMouseMap.ptSize.x,mmMouseMap.ptSize.y);
        OffsetRect(&rcTile1,ptPlot.x,ptPlot.y);
        //move first tile to lower-right position
        ptMap.x=MAPWIDTH-1;
        ptMap.y=MAPHEIGHT-1;
        ptPlot=StagMap_TilePlotter(ptMap,mmMouseMap.ptSize.x,mmMouseMap.ptSize.y);
        OffsetRect(&rcTile2,ptPlot.x,ptPlot.y);
        //combine these two tiles into world space
        UnionRect(&rcWorldSpace,&rcTile1,&rcTile2);
        //copy world space to anchor space
        CopyRect(&rcAnchorSpace,&rcWorldSpace);
        //subtract screen space
        //adjust right edge (removed)
        //make sure right not less than left
```

```
	if(rcAnchorSpace.right<rcAnchorSpace.left)
rcAnchorSpace.right=rcAnchorSpace.left;
	//adjust bottom edge
	rcAnchorSpace.bottom-=(rcScreenSpace.bottom-rcScreenSpace.top);
	//make sure bottom not less than top
	if(rcAnchorSpace.bottom<rcAnchorSpace.top)
rcAnchorSpace.bottom=rcAnchorSpace.top;
	//adjust edges of anchorspace for "no jaggies"
	//add 1/2 height to top
	rcAnchorSpace.top+=(mmMouseMap.ptSize.y/2);
	//subtract 1/2 height from bottom
	rcAnchorSpace.bottom-=(mmMouseMap.ptSize.y/2);
	//add 1/2 width to left
	rcAnchorSpace.left+=(mmMouseMap.ptSize.x/2);
	//eliminate right edge adjustment
	//initialize screen anchor
	ptScreenAnchor.x=rcAnchorSpace.left;
	ptScreenAnchor.y=rcAnchorSpace.top;
	//initialize cursor
	ptCursor.x=0;
	ptCursor.y=0;
}
```

So, what's all this about? Well, in order to give the illusion of wrapping forever, you have to allow the screen to sweep past the right edge by an entire screen width. This is what you did by eliminating the subtraction of the screen width from the anchor space. Now, since the left edge has been adjusted by half a tile, you must do the same to the right edge (which you did before by subtracting half of the tile width, leaving you with a net zero change to the right edge), so that when you scroll from one edge to the other, there isn't a "skip" of anything, and the scrolling is nice and smooth.

Penultimately, you have to modify your `ClipScreenAnchor` function so that it moves cleanly from one horizontal edge to the other. This is done simply by checking to see whether the anchor has passed one of the edges, and adding or subtracting the width of the anchor space to bring it back into the proper range:

```
void ClipScreenAnchor()
{
	//wrap to left
	if(ptScreenAnchor.x<rcAnchorSpace.left)
ptScreenAnchor.x+=(rcAnchorSpace.right-rcAnchorSpace.left);
	//clip to top
	if(ptScreenAnchor.y<rcAnchorSpace.top) ptScreenAnchor.y=rcAnchorSpace.top;
	//wrap to right
```

```
	if(ptScreenAnchor.x>=rcAnchorSpace.right) ptScreenAnchor.x-
=(rcAnchorSpace.right-rcAnchorSpace.left);;
	//clip to bottom
	if(ptScreenAnchor.y>=rcAnchorSpace.bottom)
ptScreenAnchor.y=rcAnchorSpace.bottom-1;
}
```

Finally, you have to remove the restriction that the cursor cannot go beyond the right edge of the map, by eliminating a single line in your WM_MOUSEMOVE handler:

```
case WM_MOUSEMOVE:
	{
		//grab mouse coordinate
		POINT ptMouse;
		ptMouse.x=LOWORD(lParam);
		ptMouse.y=HIWORD(lParam);
		//mousemap the mouse coordinates
		ptCursor=StagMap_MouseMapper(ptMouse,&mmMouseMap);
		//clip cursor to tilemap
		if(ptCursor.x<0) ptCursor.x=0;
		if(ptCursor.y<0) ptCursor.y=0;
		//if(ptCursor.x>MAPWIDTH-1) ptCursor.x=MAPWIDTH-1;(eliminated)
		if(ptCursor.y>MAPHEIGHT-1) ptCursor.y=MAPHEIGHT-1;
/*REST OF CODE OMITTED FOR BREVITY*/
```

And that's it! You've got an east-west "scroll forever" staggered map. See how easy it was? Plus, now the world looks endless, even though you know it is of finite size.

Summary

In this chapter, you got into some pretty cool stuff. Granted, these examples are still rather elementary, but hopefully you're starting to feel comfortable with isometric graphics. As I've said several times, they really aren't as complicated as everyone seems to think.

CHAPTER 14

Diamond Maps

- Coordinate System
- Tileplotting
- Blitting Order
- Scrolling Revisited

This chapter presents the final type of isometric map—the diamond map. In the past, I've been known to call these "diagonal" maps because of the direction of both axes. This type of map is probably the most familiar and the most commonly used, mainly in the area of real-time strategy games like *Age of Empires/Age of Kingdoms, Sim City 2000/3000, Roller Coaster Tycoon,* and a wide variety of simulations. Diamond maps, it seems, are the perfect choice for real-time isometric games. Those are not the only uses, of course. The world of board games—chess, checkers, Reversi, and so on—can really benefit from these types of maps, since they look far superior to the boring top-down views of ages old.

Coordinate System

While there are several ways to go about using a diamond map, the simplest that I have found makes the top corner into map position (0,0). You could pick any corner you wanted, and do the TilePlotter and TileWalker figuring, and it would work just fine. In fact, I have in the past used the leftmost corner as (0,0), so it really doesn't matter.

The following basically describes the coordinate system of the diamond maps I present here:

- The origin is at the top corner of the map.
- The x-axis increases to the southeast.
- The y-axis increases to the southwest.

The coordinate system is shown in Figure 14.1.

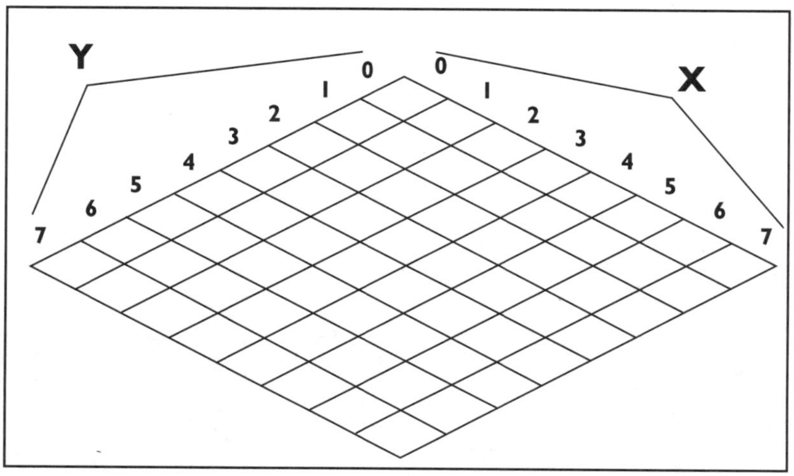

Figure 14.1

Coordinate system of diamond maps

The diamond map isn't by any means as tricky as staggered maps, but it is a bit more complex than the slide map. Its little quirks will become apparent as we move on.

Tileplotting

As usual, your first task in a new style of map is to be able to plot the tiles. In this area, the diamond map shows the first of its little quirks. Unlike both slide and staggered maps, which have the x-axis moving east-west, the diamond map has a diagonal axis. While this is odd, it doesn't hold you up for long, because you've already dealt with diagonal axes, mainly in the arena of the y-axis for the other types of map.

The x-axis increases to the southwest, just as the y-axis does in slide maps. In slide maps, you determined that to move southeast, you must move east half a tile and south half a tile. You will do the same thing here.

```
//MapX is a map coordinate, PlotX and PlotY are world coordinates
PlotX=MapX*TileWidth/2;
PlotY=MapX*TileHeight/2;
```

Of course, you still have the map's y-coordinate to take into account. Since y moves to the southwest, you must move half a tile to the west (multiply by `-TileWidth/2`) and half a tile to the south (multiply by `TileHeight/2`). From this value, modify `PlotX` and `PlotY`.

```
//MapY is a map coordinate, PlotX and PlotY are world coordinates
//from the last code snippet
PlotX+=(MapY*(-TileWidth/2));
PlotY+=(MapY*(TileHeight/2));
```

You would like to have the two parts of this tileplotting placed into fewer lines than this, so let's rewrite it:

```
//MapX,MapY=map coord; PlotX, PlotY=world coord
PlotX=MapX*TileWidth/2-MapY*TileWidth/2;
PlotY=MapX*TileHeight/2+MapY*TileHeight/2;
```

Or, you might like to have only one multiplication per line:

```
PlotX=(MapX-MapY)*TileWidth/2;
//you could further eliminate the /2 by using >>1 instead
PlotY=(MapX+MapY)*TileHeight/2;
```

Both map axes affect both world axes as far as tileplotting goes, which is something you haven't seen in the other map types. This seems like one of the more difficult parts of using diamond maps, but as you can see, it's not really hard at all.

The Tileplotting Function

You will base your TilePlotter on the TilePlotters of previous chapters, for consistency.

```
POINT DiamondMap_TilePlotter(POINT ptMap,int iTileWidth,int iTileHeight)
{
	POINT ptReturn;
	ptReturn.x=(ptMap.x-ptMap.y)*iTileWidth/2;
	ptReturn.y=(ptMap.x+ptMap.y)*iTileHeight/2;
	return(ptReturn);
}
```

Simple enough? Good. Time for an example? You betcha!

A Diamond Map Tileplotting Demo

Load up IsoHex14_1.cpp. It's the diamond map plotting demo, based mainly on code from IsoHex12_1, which was the slide map plotting demo. The main difference is the replacement of the TilePlotter.

You can see what this example looks like in Figure 14.2. IsoHex14_1.cpp reveals yet another quirk of the diamond map. Some of the map extends off the left side of the screen. Since you are not currently scrolling and are not using an anchor to correct your coordinates, this means that a diamond map extends into a negative-valued world coordinate—not really a big deal, because you already have compensation for this in your MouseMap (remember the "negative numbers" chat we had two chapters ago?)

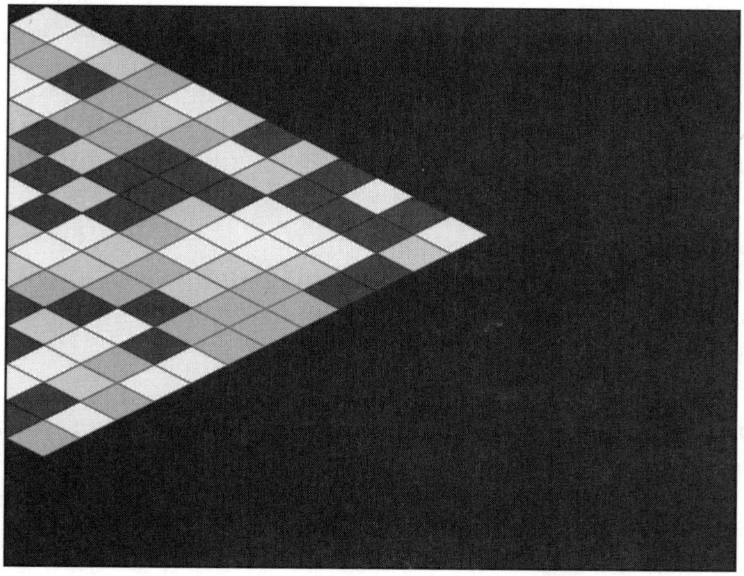

Figure 14.2

Output of IsoHex14_1.cpp

Blitting Order

One last topic I want to discuss, as far as diamond maps are concerned, is blitting order. I told you in the last two chapters that blitting should be done in horizontal rows if possible. There was no problem doing this with slide maps and staggered maps, because with both, the x-axis travels east-west.

However, diamond maps are a different story. Currently, without a TileWalker, you can't move east or west, and your axes travel in diagonal lines. This is one of the reasons I picked the topmost corner for tile (0,0): so that the rendering order is acceptable enough that you won't have to change the `DrawMap` function. You can simply iterate through map y values, and inside that loop have another loop that iterates through the map x values, and plot accordingly. In a later chapter, I will show you how to blit in horizontal rows, no matter what the map looks like.

Scrolling Revisited

Because of the strange orientation of diamond maps, I need to discuss scrolling, at least for a moment. Yet another quirk.

In slide and staggered maps, construction of the world space rectangle is rather straightforward. Simply take the extents from the upper-left and lower-right corner tiles and use `UnionRect` to combine them into a larger `RECT`.

If you did the same thing with a diamond map, where (0,0) is the topmost corner and (`MAPWIDTH-1,MAPHEIGHT-1`) is the bottommost corner, you would have a rather narrow strip for world space. Instead, you have to also bring the left and right corners into the union, like so:

```
//grab tile rectangle from tileset
RECT rcTile1;
RECT rcTile2;
RECT rcTile3;
RECT rcTile4;
POINT ptPlot;
POINT ptMap;
//grab tiles from extents
CopyRect(&rcTile1,&tsIso.GetTileList()[0].rcDstExt);
CopyRect(&rcTile2,&tsIso.GetTileList()[0].rcDstExt);
CopyRect(&rcTile3,&tsIso.GetTileList()[0].rcDstExt);
CopyRect(&rcTile4,&tsIso.GetTileList()[0].rcDstExt);
//move first tile to top corner
ptMap.x=0;
ptMap.y=0;
ptPlot=DiamondMap_TilePlotter(ptMap,iTileWidth,iTileHeight);
OffsetRect(&rcTile1,ptPlot.x,ptPlot.y);
```

```
//move to bottom corner
ptMap.x=MAPWIDTH-1;
ptMap.y=MAPHEIGHT-1;
ptPlot=DiamondMap_TilePlotter(ptMap,iTileWidth,iTileHeight);
OffsetRect(&rcTile2,ptPlot.x,ptPlot.y);
//move to left corner
ptMap.x=0;
ptMap.y=MAPHEIGHT-1;
ptPlot=DiamondMap_TilePlotter(ptMap,iTileWidth,iTileHeight);
OffsetRect(&rcTile3,ptPlot.x,ptPlot.y);
//move to right corner
ptMap.x=MAPWIDTH-1;
ptMap.y=0;
ptPlot=DiamondMap_TilePlotter(ptMap,iTileWidth,iTileHeight);
OffsetRect(&rcTile4,ptPlot.x,ptPlot.y);
//combine these four tiles into world space
UnionRect(&rcWorldSpace,&rcTile1,&rcTile2);
UnionRect(&rcWorldSpace,&rcWorldSpace,&rcTile3);
UnionRect(&rcWorldSpace,&rcWorldSpace,&rcTile4);
```

The rest of the spaces (screen space and anchor space) remain unaffected. Only the world space is changed.

A Diamond Map Scrolling Demo

It's time for me to show instead of tell. IsoHex14_2.cpp is the next example. It is patterned quite closely after IsoHex12_2.cpp. The differences are that this example uses the diamond map TilePlotter and implements the changes to the world space calculation. The actual code was changed slightly, since I didn't want to use a `UnionRect` call with the destination pointer also serving as a source pointer. (Doing stuff like that always makes me nervous.) You can see what this example looks like in Figure 14.3.

Use the arrow keys to scroll through the map. Pretty neat, huh? And to think that almost half of the world space has a negative x value, but our little plotter/scroller combination doesn't really care. That's part of the beauty of these engine components—they're like little black boxes that take your input and spew the proper output.

Figure 14.3

Output of IsoHex14_2.cpp

TILEWALKING

With the many other diamond map quirks, it would be reasonable to assume that tilewalking is quirky. This reasonable assumption would be wrong. Tilewalking in a diamond map is totally regular (unlike the staggered map), as you will see during its derivation.

You start with the knowledge of two things: x increases to the southeast, and y increases to the southwest. Let's start with Table 14.1.

Table 14.1 Diamond Tilewalking (Initial)

Direction	Change x	Change y
North	???	???
Northeast	???	???
East	???	???
Southeast	1	0
South	???	???
Southwest	0	1
West	???	???
Northwest	???	???

From this point, you can easily figure out the northeast and northwest directions. Because they are the opposites of southeast and southwest, they are located opposite them. Table 14.2 reflects this.

Table 14.2 Diamond Tilewalking (All Diagonals)

Direction	Change x	Change y
North	???	???
Northeast	0	–1
East	???	???
Southeast	1	0
South	???	???
Southwest	0	1
West	???	???
Northwest	–1	0

Hey! You're halfway done already. You've got all your diagonals, and deriving the cardinal directions will be easy. You'll just use the two-step method to figure them out.

To move north, you move one step northeast (0,-1) and one step northwest (–1,0), which gives you (–1,–1).

Step	Change x	Change y
Northeast	0	–1
Northwest	–1	0
Total	–1	–1

To move south, you move one step southeast (1,0) and one step southwest (0,1), which gives you (1,1).

Step	Change x	Change y
Southeast	1	0
Southwest	0	1
Total	1	1

To move east, you move one step southeast (1,0) and one step northeast (0,-1), which gives you (1,–1).

Step	Change x	Change y
Southeast	1	0
Northeast	0	–1
Total	1	–1

To move west, you move one step southwest (0,1) and one step northwest (–1,0), which gives you (–1,1).

Step	Change x	Change y
Southwest	0	1
Northwest	–1	0
Total	–1	1

Now you're done, and you can complete your table (see Table 14.3).

Table 14.3 Diamond Tilewalking (All Diagonals)

Direction	Change x	Change y
North	–1	–1
Northeast	0	–1
East	1	–1
Southeast	1	0
South	1	1
Southwest	0	1
West	–1	1
Northwest	–1	0

You finally have all the information you need to construct your TileWalker function. See how easy that was? Once you know one type of map, you know them all.

```
POINT DiamondMap_TileWalker(POINT ptStart,IsoDirection Dir)
{
	switch(dir)
	{
	case ISO_NORTH:
		{
			ptStart.x–;
			ptStart.y–;
		}break;
	case ISO_NORTHEAST:
		{
			ptStart.y–;
		}break;
	case ISO_EAST:
		{
			ptStart.x++;
			ptStart.y–;
		}break;
	case ISO_SOUTHEAST:
		{
			ptStart.x++;
		}break;
	case ISO_SOUTH:
		{
			ptStart.x++;
			ptStart.y++;
		}break;
	case ISO_SOUTHWEST:
		{
			ptStart.y++;
		}break;
	case ISO_WEST:
		{
			ptStart.x–;
			ptStart.y++;
		}break;
	case ISO_NORTHWEST:
		{
			ptStart.x–;
```

```
            }break;
        }
        return(ptStart);
}
```

The output of IsoHex14_3.cpp is shown in Figure 14.4.

Figure 14.4

Output of IsoHex14_3.cpp

It's time to put your new TileWalker into service. Load up IsoHex14_3.cpp, which looks suspiciously like IsoHex12_3.cpp, except for the change from slide to diamond. In this example, you can use the keyboard to move around the map, and the current cursor location will be centered as much as possible based on the anchor's position in anchor space. Near the corners, at least one direction will not be centered.

MouseMapping

Ah, the final component—the MouseMap. Like the TileWalker, the MouseMap ends up being not quirky at all, since you already learned how to handle a negative world coordinate back in Chapter 12, "Slide Isometric Tilemaps." Mouse mapping has been covered so well, in fact, that there is little to do now except plug it into the program. The exact same MouseMap that we used in Chapters 12 and 13 will work just fine.

So, without further ado, load up IsoHex14_4.cpp (again, it's based on IsoHex12_4.cpp). Like its predecessor, you can scroll about the map by putting the mouse pointer at one of the edges, and the cursor will be shown on the proper tile. Figure 14.5 shows what it looks like.

Figure 14.5

IsoHex14_4.cpp in action

I'd like to point out here that, for the examples in these chapters, it took me about 5 minutes to convert them from their Chapter 12 equivalents. I just had to replace the code in the various isometric engine components, and whammo, I was done. This goes a long way toward showing how universal these elements are.

Summary

This chapter might seem a little light compared to how much time we spent on the other two types of tilemaps. On the contrary. All of the discussion for the other types of maps made diamond maps need almost no explanation.

Now that I've introduced the three types of isometric maps, I hope you're starting to get some ideas as to how you want to use them to make games. And you're probably wondering about various issues, like how to put objects in an isometric map. Rest assured that all of your questions shall be answered.

You are now equipped with the basic idea of how IsoHex engines work fundamentally. You have been introduced to the TilePlotter, TileWalker, and MouseMap (as well as the Scroller, which is not in itself an IsoHex component). We will build on this foundation

CHAPTER 15

The IsoHexCore Engine

- Overview of IsoHexCore
- IsoDirection
- Using CTilePlotter
- Using CMouseMap

Good news: I have finally finished the introductory subject matter. . . well, almost. This chapter is the last bit. It introduces the IsoHexCore engine, which is essentially a small library of classes that wrap up everything I've talked about for the past three chapters.

Overview of IsoHexCore

A number of files are contained in the IsoHexCore engine: a main header file that includes all the components, a header file/source file pair for each of the four components, and finally a header file for the universal definitions required for an isometric engine.

Table 15.1 lists the files contained in IsoHexCore and briefly describes their contents.

Table 15.1 IsoHexCore Files

File	What It Contains
IsoHexDefs.h	Fundamental enumerations for other components
IsoTilePlotter.h	Declarations for the `CTilePlotter` class
IsoTilePlotter.cpp	Implementation for the `CTilePlotter` class
IsoTileWalker.h	Declarations for the `CTileWalker` class
IsoTileWalker.cpp	Implementation for the `CTileWalker` class
IsoScroller.h	Declarations for the `CScroller` class
IsoScroller.cpp	Implementation for the `CScroller` class
IsoMouseMap.h	Declarations for the `CMouseMap` class
IsoMouseMap.cpp	Implementation for the `CMouseMap` class
IsoHexCore.h	All other components in a single header

As you can see, the files mirror the fundamental components of any isometric engine: TilePlotter, TileWalker, MouseMap, and scroller. They are split into different files to make the engine a bit more manageable. The file listed last, IsoHexCore.h, brings all the headers together. It's the only file you need to include in your project.

> **NOTE**
>
> None of these components are what you'd call "game-worthy." That is, the code I present here is nowhere close to the performance you could get from a highly optimized isometric engine. The code is meant to be easily read and understood, not necessarily the fastest in the world. When it comes time to write real code for your own isometric engine, I expect you to write stuff that leaves this little engine in the dust!

One by one, in the same order as the table, I'll show you each of these components, explain how they were put together, and show how they are intended to be used.

IsoHexDefs.h

This file, the full contents of which are shown next, contains exactly two enumerations: one for the isometric directions (`ISODIRECTION`), and one for the different isometric map types (`ISOMAPTYPE`).

```
//the isometric directions
typedef enum
{
      ISO_NORTH=0,
      ISO_NORTHEAST=1,
      ISO_EAST=2,
      ISO_SOUTHEAST=3,
      ISO_SOUTH=4,
      ISO_SOUTHWEST=5,
      ISO_WEST=6,
      ISO_NORTHWEST=7
} ISODIRECTION;
//directional turning macros
#define ISO_TURNRIGHT(dir,turn) (ISODIRECTION)(((int)(dir)+(turn))&7)
#define ISO_TURNLEFT(dir,turn) (ISODIRECTION)(((int)(dir)+(turn)*7)&7)//iso
map types
typedef enum
{
      ISOMAP_SLIDE,
      ISOMAP_STAGGERED,
      ISOMAP_DIAMOND,
      ISOMAP_RECTANGULAR
} ISOMAPTYPE;
```

I'll spend some time explaining each of these enumerations and how they are used. They have widespread effects on the rest of IsoHexCore.

ISODIRECTION

`ISODIRECTION` was used before, in the TileWalkers and MouseMaps, and that is essentially what they are for now. However, those aren't the only use for this enumeration. You can also keep track of which way something is facing during your game and use the macros provided that allow turning. The enumeration constants and directions are shown in figure 15.1.

Each direction has an assigned number, which is unusual for any sort of enumeration. Most either don't specify values at all or just specify the value of the first identifier and let the compiler figure out the rest. I could have done either of these and come out with the same values I'm currently assigning. My reasons for assigning these numbers, and for employing the order that I do, is so that 0 means north and the rest of the directions are determined by slowly turning clockwise. This is what makes the turning macros (explained next) work.

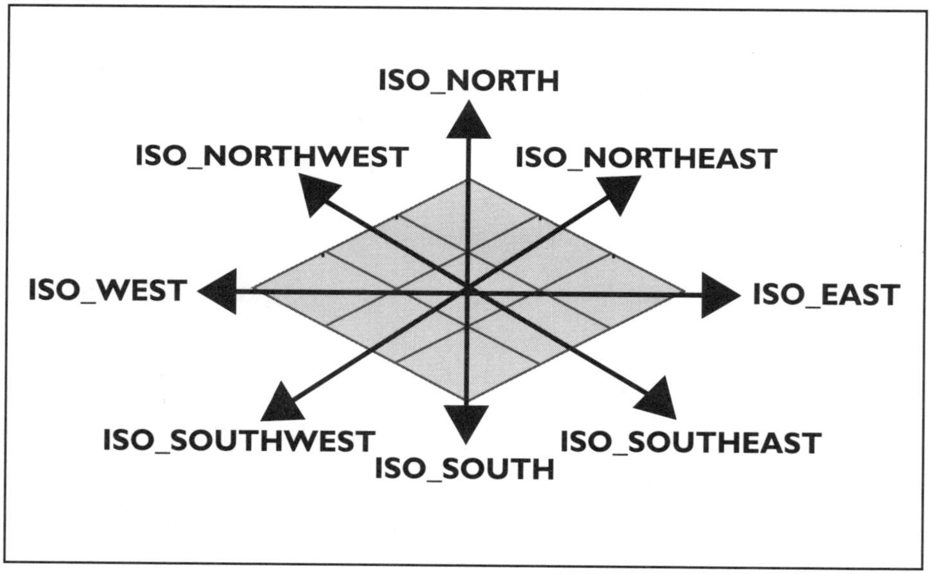

Figure 15.1

`ISODIRECTION` values

ISODIRECTION Macros

ISODIRECTION macros allow you to turn from one heading to another.

```
//directional turning macros
#define ISO_TURNRIGHT(dir,turn) (ISODIRECTION)(((int)(dir)+(turn))&7)
#define ISO_TURNLEFT(dir,turn) (ISODIRECTION)(((int)(dir)+(turn)*7)&7)
```

In each case, dir represents an initial direction, and turn represents the number of 45-degree turns to make. Hence, to turn 90 degrees left from north, you would use this:

```
ISODIRECTION Dir=ISO_TURNLEFT(ISO_NORTH,2);//assigns ISO_WEST to Dir
```

This expands to

```
ISODIRECTION Dir=(ISODIRECTION)(((int)(ISO_NORTH)+(2)*7)&7);
```

and is reduced to

```
ISODIRECTION Dir=(ISODIRECTION)((0+14)&7);
```

It is further reduced to

```
ISODIRECTION Dir=(ISODIRECTION)(14&7);
```

And again:

```
ISODIRECTION Dir=(ISODIRECTION)(6);
```

And 6 is the value of ISO_WEST, which is the correct answer. I am not a big fan of macros, but in simple cases like these, the extra overhead of a function is really unnecessary. I still don't advocate the heavy use of macros and #defines. They make debugging more difficult than it has to be.

ISOMAPTYPE

ISOMAPTYPE contains identifiers for the various styles of isometric maps. In its current state, IsoHexCore supports four map types: slide, staggered, diamond, and rectangular. Yes, it supports rectangular, mainly to show how similar rectangular tile-based games are to isometric tile-based games.

You don't really do much with the ISOMAPTYPE enumeration other than supply its values to your TilePlotter and TileWalker. Figure 15.2 shows the differences between the values of ISOMAPTYPE.

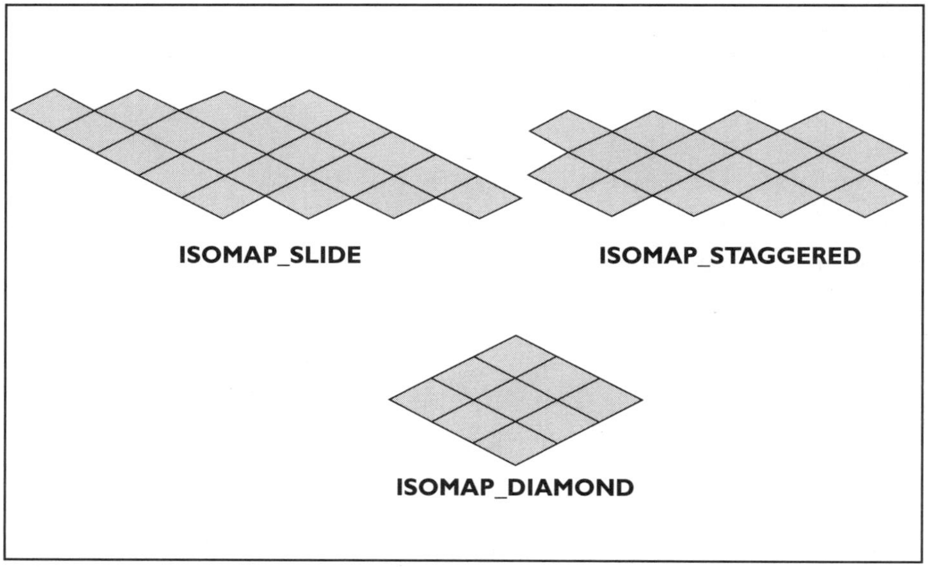

Figure 15.2

`ISOMAPTYPE` values and their meanings

IsoTilePlotter.h/IsoTilePlotter.cpp

Now that you've got the isometric fundamentals down, you can start to get serious. The IsoTilePlotter.h and IsoTilePlotter.cpp files contain the code necessary for the `CTilePlotter` class, the declaration of which is shown here:

```
////////////////////////////////////////////////////////////
//typedef for tile plotter function pointer type
////////////////////////////////////////////////////////////
typedef POINT (*ISOHEXTILEPLOTTERFN)(POINT ptMap,int iTileWidth,int iTileHeight);
////////////////////////////////////////////////////////////
//tile plotter class
////////////////////////////////////////////////////////////
class CTilePlotter
{
private:
	//type of map
	ISOMAPTYPE IsoMapType;
	//width and height of tiles
	int iTileWidth;
	int iTileHeight;
	//function called to calculate plotted tiles
	ISOHEXTILEPLOTTERFN IsoHexTilePlotterFn;
```

```
public:
	//constructor/destructor
	CTilePlotter();
	~CTilePlotter();
	//map type
	void SetMapType(ISOMAPTYPE IsoMapType);
	ISOMAPTYPE GetMapType();
	//tile size
	void SetTileSize(int iTileWidth,int iTileHeight);
	int GetTileWidth();
	int GetTileHeight();
	//plot a tile
	POINT PlotTile(POINT ptMap);
};
```

This component has two main parts: the `ISOHEXTILEPLOTTERFN` type and `CTilePlotter` itself.

ISOHEXTILEPLOTTERFN

The following ugly little declaration is the main reason that you can make a single `TilePlotter` class without having to incorporate any sort of inheritance or other object-oriented mechanism:

```
typedef POINT (*ISOHEXTILEPLOTTERFN)(POINT ptMap,int iTileWidth,int iTileHeight);
```

If you're confused, don't worry too much. This is how you declare a function pointer type. In C/C++, a function is really no different from a variable, except that it has parentheses afterwards. Take, for instance, the following two lines of code:

```
int x;//variable
int x();//function
```

See? The only difference is the `()` at the end of the second line. In all other ways, the declarations look identical. But if you wanted `x` to be a pointer to a function that takes no parameters, you would have to do this:

```
int (*x)();//ugly, ain't it?
```

"But wait!" you say. "Couldn't I just do this..."

```
int *x();
```

"...and accomplish the same thing?"

Sorry, but no. `int *x();` is a function that returns a pointer to an integer, not a variable that contains a pointer to a function that takes no parameters and returns an `int`. See the difference? That's why you have to put parentheses around the `*` and the variable name, because the makers/extenders of C/C++ haven't come up with a better way to swrite function pointer variables. Other languages, such as Pascal, have much better mechanisms.

So, back to the declaration. You already know how to declare pointers to function variables. The next task is to figure out what the type of the function pointer is. In the declaration `int x;` `x` is of type `int`, so you can conclude that taking the variable name and the semicolon out of the declaration will give you the type. Let's try it. If you remove `x` and `;` from `int (*x)();`, you are left with `int (*)()` as the type. Boy, this is getting uglier by the second. Luckily, you're almost done. Having icky definitions like `int (*)()` makes your code unsightly, so you want to avoid this as much as possible by using a `typedef`.

Normally, you do a `typedef` as follows:

```
typedef OriginalType TYPEALIAS;
```

Alas, function pointer types screw you up again, because of the backward way you have to declare them. You have to put the name of the type after the `*`, so if you want to have a type of function pointer that takes no parameters and returns an `int` called `INTFUNCPTR`, you have to have the following `typedef`:

```
typedef int (*INTFUNCPTR)();
```

Now the nightmare is over, and thank goodness! Now you can have some declarations like these:

```
int func();//function
INTFUNCPTR x;//variable that points to a function that takes no parameters and
returns an int
x=func;//no ( ) when assigning a function pointer to an existing function
int y=x();//call the function that x points to
```

Is your head swimming yet? Function pointers are about the most confusing aspect of the C/C++ language. The declarations are messy, but they can gain you a lot of power if used correctly.

Back to the `ISOHEXTILEPLOTTERFN` type. The way that this type is declared, a variable of this type can be assigned to any function that looks like the following:

```
POINT func(POINT pt,int i1,int i2);//the actual names of the parameters
                                                     //are unimportant.
Only the type matters.
ISOHEXTILEPLOTTERFN x=func;//assigns function's pointer to variable
POINT pt1=x(pt,i1,i2);//calls the function
```

Here's what makes this cool: IsoTilePlotter.cpp has four functions, which I've listed here:

```
//plotting function prototypes
POINT IsoHex_SlidePlotTile(POINT ptMap,int iTileWidth,int iTileHeight);
POINT IsoHex_StagPlotTile(POINT ptMap,int iTileWidth,int iTileHeight);
POINT IsoHex_DiamondPlotTile(POINT ptMap,int iTileWidth,int iTileHeight);
POINT IsoHex_RectPlotTile(POINT ptMap,int iTileWidth,int iTileHeight);
```

In case you didn't notice, all of these functions can have their pointers held by any variable of type ISO-HEXTILEPLOTTERFN. This means that you can just keep one of these function pointers somewhere and use it to call whatever function you need to in order to plot your tiles correctly. Also, you could add more functions and allow expansion into other types of tile-based games (there are more than just isometric, hexagonal, and rectangular, you know).

ISOHEXTILEPLOTTERFN is important to CTilePlotter, and a similar mechanism comes into play with CTileWalker to switch tilewalking functions.

CTilePlotter

After that too-long treatise on the why and wherefore of function pointers, I'm sure you want to take a break with something simpler, like how quantum mechanics affect the speed of light in a total vacuum. Well, that *is* a fascinating subject, and I'd love to pursue it with you sometime, but right now I'd rather talk about CTilePlotter. Hope you don't mind. Like all of my classes, CTilePlotter is divided into two parts: the private area that stores the data for the class, and the public area that has all of the functions that operate on the data.

Data Members

CTilePlotter has a modest number of data members—four in total. Table 15.2 lists them and explains their purposes.

Table 15.2 CTilePlotter Data Members

Member	Purpose
IsoMapType	Type of map with which this plotter is to be used
iTileWidth	Width of a tile. Used to calculate plotted tiles.
iTileHeight	Height of a tile. Used to calculate plotted tiles.
IsoHexTilePlotterFn	Pointer to a function that does the actual tile plotting

Each of the following data members is pretty self-explanatory, but let's go over them briefly anyway.

- **IsoMapType.** IsoMapType stores the map type you are using (ISOMAP_SLIDE, ISOMAP_STAGGERED, ISOMAP_DIAMOND, or ISOMAP_RECTANGULAR). It is set by CTilePlotter::SetMapType and retrieved by CTilePlotter::GetMapType. This member is directly related to the value in the IsoHexTilePlotterFn member.

- `iTileWidth/iTileHeight`. These two members are used in the actual calculation of a tile plot. They are sent to the tileplotting function (stored in `IsoHexTilePlotterFn`), along with the map position that is being plotted. These members can be retrieved using `CTilePlotter::GetWidth` and `CTilePlotter::GetHeight`.
- `IsoHexTilePlotterFn`. It is strange to think that the real work done by `CTilePlotter` isn't even done by the class itself, but rather is sent to a function that is outside of it. `IsoHexTilePlotterFn` points to that function. No member functions directly access this member. It is set when a call to `SetMapType` occurs.

Member Functions

Like data members, `CTilePlotter` has a small number of member functions—eight in total. Table 15.3 lists them and briefly explains their purpose.

Table 15.3 CTilePlotter Member Functions

Member Function	Purpose
`CTilePlotter()`	Constructs the object, sets defaults
`~CTilePlotter()`	Destroys the object
`void SetMapType (ISOMAPTYPE IsoMapType)`	Sets the type of map used by the plotter
`ISOMAPTYPE GetMapType()`	Retrieves the type of map used by the plotter
`void SetTileSize (int iTileWidth, int iTileHeight)`	Sets the size of the tile used in tile plot calculations
`int GetTileWidth()`	Retrieves the width of the tile used to calculate tile plots
`int GetTileHeight()`	Retrieves the height of the tile used to calculate tile plots
`POINT PlotTile (POINT ptMap)`	Plots the world space coordinate from a map coordinate

I further subdivide these member functions into four groups: Construction/Destruction, `MapType`, `TileSize`, and Plotting.

Construction/Destruction Functions

The constructor (`CTilePlotter()`) and the destructor (`~CTilePlotter()`) don't do much and aren't really very interesting. In fact, the destructor is completely empty. (I make a habit of making classes with a destructor, just in case I need it later.) The constructor simply sets the map type to ISOMAP_RECTANGULAR and sets the tile size to a width and height of 1. This means that the default behavior of an instance of CTilePlotter plots a point to the exact same coordinate.

```
CTilePlotter::CTilePlotter();
```

This assigns default values to map type and tile size.

```
CTilePlotter::~CTilePlotter();
```

This does nothing.

MapType Functions

Two CTilePlotter functions have to do with the IsoMapType and IsoHexTilePlotterFn data members (indirectly). SetMapType assigns a new map type to the plotter (and selects the proper plotting function for IsoHexTilePlotterFn), and GetMapType returns the plotter's currently assigned map type.

```
void CTilePlotter::SetMapType(ISOMAPTYPE IsoMapType);
```

This sets a new map type for the plotter. It does not return a value.

```
ISOMAPTYPE CTilePlotter::GetMapType();
```

This returns the currently set map type for the potter.

TileSize Functions

There are three of these: one "setter" and two "getters." These functions work with the iTileWidth and iTileHeight data members.

```
void CTilePlotter::SetTileSize(int iTileWidth,int iTileHeight);
```

This sets a new tile width and tile height. It returns no value.

```
int CTilePlotter::GetTileWidth();
```

This returns the currently assigned tile width.

```
int CTilePlotter::GetTileHeight();
```

This returns the currently assigned tile height.

Plotting Function

There is only one of these. The plotting function is the main purpose of the plotter. It uses the data members assigned to the plotter by the various set functions.

```
POINT PlotTile(POINT ptMap);
```

This converts the position in ptMap into an appropriate world space coordinate. It returns the world space coordinate as a POINT.

Using CTilePlotter

There's really not much to this: you declare the plotter, set it up, and you're ready to use it. `CTilePlotter` was intended to be used without dynamic allocation (that is, without the use of `new`), but nothing prevents you from using dynamic allocation to set up your plotter. I certainly don't mind.

The following code shows various snippets that you could use exactly as written (except for adjusting the width and height for your own particular tile size). It shows the setup for all four types of supported maps.

```
//////////////////////////////////////////////////////////////
//declaration (all map types)
CTilePlotter TilePlotter;
//////////////////////////////////////////////////////////////
//setup (slide)
//////////////////////////////////////////////////////////////
TilePlotter.SetMapType(ISOMAP_SLIDE);
TilePlotter.SetTileSize(64,32);//replace numbers with your actual tile sizes
//////////////////////////////////////////////////////////////
//setup (staggered)
TilePlotter.SetMapType(ISOMAP_STAGGERED);
TilePlotter.SetTileSize(64,32);//replace numbers with your actual tile sizes
//////////////////////////////////////////////////////////////
//setup (diamond)
TilePlotter.SetMapType(ISOMAP_DIAMOND);
TilePlotter.SetTileSize(64,32);//replace numbers with your actual tile sizes
//////////////////////////////////////////////////////////////
//setup (rectangular)
TilePlotter.SetMapType(ISOMAP_RECTANGULAR);
TilePlotter.SetTileSize(64,32);//replace numbers with your actual tile sizes
//////////////////////////////////////////////////////////////
//use (all map types)
POINT ptMap;
POINT ptPlot;
//MAPWIDTH/MAPHEIGHT are whatever numbers you are using for the size of your map
for(ptMap.y=0;ptMap.y<MAPHEIGHT;ptMap.y++)
{
      for(ptMap.x=0;ptMap.x<MAPWIDTH;ptMap.x++)
      {
            //plot the tile
            ptPlot=TilePlotter.PlotTile(ptMap);
```

```
            //tile rendering code goes here
        }
}
```

Pretty simple, right? Perhaps it's a little more involved than the little tileplotting functions used in earlier chapters, but the price of flexibility is a bit of complexity.

IsoTileWalker.h/IsoTileWalker.cpp

The files IsoTileWalker.h and IsoTileWalker.cpp contain the declarations and implementation required for the `CTileWalker` class, the declaration of which appears next.

```
//typedef for a function pointer to a tilewalker function
typedef POINT (*ISOHEXTILEWALKERFN)(POINT ptStart,ISODIRECTION IsoDirection);
//tilewalker class
class CTileWalker
{
private:
        //tile walker function pointer
        ISOHEXTILEWALKERFN IsoHexTileWalkerFn;
        //iso map type
        ISOMAPTYPE IsoMapType;
public:
        //constructor
        CTileWalker();
        //destructor
        ~CTileWalker();
        //map type
        void SetMapType(ISOMAPTYPE IsoMapType);
        ISOMAPTYPE GetMapType();
        //tile walking
        POINT TileWalk(POINT ptStart,ISODIRECTION IsoDirection);
};
```

Just like with the TilePlotter earlier, the TileWalker component consists of two parts: a function pointer called `ISOHEXTILEWALKERFN`, and the `CTileWalker` class itself.

ISOHEXTILEWALKERFN

I gave you the big talk about pointer functions during the discussion of the TilePlotter, so I'll spare you the pain of rehashing. All TileWalker functions are required to look very similar to the function declaration shown next. A variable of the type `ISOHEXTILEWALKERFN` points to a function like this:

```
POINT TileWalkerFunction(POINT ptStart,ISODIRECTION IsoDirection);
```

This function works just like the tilewalking functions seen in earlier chapters. Take a starting position (`ptStart`) and a direction (`IsoDirection`, one of the `ISODIRECTION` values defined in IsoHexDefs.h), send them to this function, and it spits out whatever tile lies in that direction. This TileWalker function works only for single steps, just as it did in earlier chapters, mainly because staggered maps make multistep tilewalking more difficult.

IsoTileWalker.cpp declares and implements four tilewalking functions—one for each of the supported map types. It would be a relatively small matter to make a new function that walked through another type of map if you needed one.

```
POINT IsoHex_SlideTileWalk(POINT ptStart,ISODIRECTION IsoDirection);//slide walk-
er
POINT IsoHex_StagTileWalk(POINT ptStart,ISODIRECTION IsoDirection);//staggered
walker
POINT IsoHex_DiamondTileWalk(POINT ptStart,ISODIRECTION IsoDirection);//diamond
walker
POINT IsoHex_RectTileWalk(POINT ptStart,ISODIRECTION IsoDirection);//rectangular
walker
```

The names of the functions state their purposes pretty clearly, so I won't bother with a detailed explanation.

CTileWalker

The other part of IsoTileWalker.h/IsoTileWalker.cpp is the `CTileWalker` class itself. It is by far the simplest class in this engine, with only two data members and five member functions.

Data Members

Table 15.4 lists `CTileWalker`'s data members and briefly describes their purpose. `CTileWalker` has only two data members.

Table 15.4 CTileWalker Data Members

Member	Purpose
`IsoMapType`	Keeps track of the map type currently being used with this TileWalker
`IsoHexTileWalkerFn`	Contains a pointer to the function currently being used by the TileWalker to do its walking

The IsoMapType member is set with a call to CTileWalker::SetMapType and is retrieved with CTileWalker::GetMapType. IsoHexTileWalkerFn is not a directly accessed data member. It is set from within the CTileWalker::SetMapType function and is used by the CTileWalker::TileWalk function.

Member Functions

There are five member functions in CTileWalker's public section. They are listed in Table 15.5, along with a brief statement of their purpose. Each member function is explained further after the table.

Table 15.5 CTileWalker Member Functions

Member Function	Purpose
CTileWalker()	Constructor. Sets defaults.
~CTileWalker()	Destructor
void SetMapType (ISOMAPTYPE IsoMapType)	Assigns a new map type for the walker to work with
ISOMAPTYPE GetMapType()	Retrieves the currently assigned map type for the walker
POINT TileWalker (POINT ptStart, ISODIRECTION IsoDirect)	Performs a tile walk by taking a single step

Each of these member functions deserves a sentence or two explaining how they work and what they do.

```
CTileWalker::CTileWalker();
```

This is CTileWalker's constructor. It takes no parameters and returns no value. Since it is a construction, you never really call it directly anyway. It does only one thing—set the map type to ISOMAP_RECTANGULAR.

```
CTileWalker::~CTileWalker();
```

This is CTileWalker's destructor. It does even less than the constructor. In fact, this function is completely empty.

```
void CTileWalker::SetMapType(ISOMAPTYPE IsoMapType);
```

This function sets up a TileWalker to use a given map type. It also indirectly sets the function used by the TileWalker to tile walk. This takes a parameter of the ISOMAPTYPE and returns no value.

```
ISOMAPTYPE CTileWalker::GetMapType();
```

This returns an ISOMAPTYPE and takes no parameters. The return value contains the ISOMAP_* value assigned in the last call to SetMapType.

```
POINT CTileWalker::TileWalk(POINT ptStart,ISODIRECTION IsoDirection);
```

This function is the main purpose of `CTileWalker`. It takes a `POINT` parameter and an `ISODIRECTION` parameter, calls the function contained in `IsoHexTileWalkFn`, and returns the result of that function call (a `POINT`).

Using CTileWalker

Using `CTileWalker` is sublimely easy. You declare it, set it up, and go. The following code shows you how to perform each of these tasks. You could copy these verbatim into a program that includes IsoTileWalker.h/IsoTileWalker.cpp.

```
/////////////////////////////////////////////////////////////
//Declaration
CTileWalker TileWalker;
/////////////////////////////////////////////////////////////
//Setting Up (Slide)
TileWalker.SetMapType(ISOMAP_SLIDE);
/////////////////////////////////////////////////////////////
//Setting Up (Staggered)
TileWalker.SetMapType(ISOMAP_STAGGERED);
/////////////////////////////////////////////////////////////
//Setting Up (Diamond)
TileWalker.SetMapType(ISOMAP_DIAMOND);
/////////////////////////////////////////////////////////////
//Setting Up (Rectangular)
TileWalker.SetMapType(ISOMAP_RECTANGULAR);
/////////////////////////////////////////////////////////////
//Use
POINT ptStart;//starting point of the tile walker
POINT ptNext;//destination of the tile walker
ISODIRECTION idIsoDir;//direction of movement
ptStart.x=STARTX;//replace STARTX with whatever x starts at
ptStart.y=STARTY;//replace STARTY with whatever y starts at
idIsoDir=ISODIR;//replace ISODIR with a suitable direction of movement
ptNext=TileWalker.TileWalker(ptStart,idIsoDir);//plot the tile
```

And that's about all there is to the `CTileWalker` class. It is used later to help the `CMouseMap` class do its job. This class is the simplest of the bunch, as you probably can tell by the shortness of the section devoted to it.

IsoScroller.h/IsoScroller.cpp

These files contain the declaration and implementation of the `CScroller` class, which is by far our largest class if you count by the number of member functions. Here are the declarations that appear in the header:

```
//wrapping modes for anchors
typedef enum
{
	WRAPMODE_NONE,//no clipping of any kind is done to the anchor
	WRAPMODE_CLIP,
	WRAPMODE_WRAP
} SCROLLERWRAPMODE;
//world space/screen space management class
class CScroller
{
private:
	//screen space
	RECT rcScreenSpace;
	//world space
	RECT rcWorldSpace;
	//anchor space
	RECT rcAnchorSpace;
	//anchor
	POINT ptScreenAnchor;
	//wrapmodes
	SCROLLERWRAPMODE swmHorizontal;
	SCROLLERWRAPMODE swmVertical;
public:
	//constructor
	CScroller();
	//destructor
	~CScroller();
	//screen space
	RECT* GetScreenSpace();
	void SetScreenSpace(RECT* prcNewScreenSpace);
	void AdjustScreenSpace(int iLeftAdjust,int iTopAdjust,int iRightAdjust,
int iBottomAdjust);
	int GetScreenSpaceWidth();
	int GetScreenSpaceHeight();
	//world space
```

```
        RECT* GetWorldSpace();
        void SetWorldSpace(RECT* prcNewWorldSpace);
        void AdjustWorldSpace(int iLeftAdjust,int iTopAdjust,int iRightAdjust, int
iBottomAdjust);
        int GetWorldSpaceWidth();
        int GetWorldSpaceHeight();
              //calculates worldspace based on a tile plotter, a tile extent rec-
        tangle,
              //and a map's height and width
        void CalcWorldSpace(CTilePlotter* TilePlotter,RECT* prcExtent,
              int iMapWidth,int iMapHeight);
        //anchor space
        RECT* GetAnchorSpace();
        void SetAnchorSpace(RECT* prcNewAnchorSpace);
        void AdjustAnchorSpace(int iLeftAdjust,int iTopAdjust,int iRightAdjust,
int iBottomAdjust);
        int GetAnchorSpaceWidth();
        int GetAnchorSpaceHeight();
        void CalcAnchorSpace();//calculates anchor space based on world space and
screen space
        //anchor
        POINT* GetAnchor();
        void SetAnchor(POINT* pptNewAnchor,bool bWrap=true);
        void MoveAnchor(int iXAdjust,int iYAdjust,bool bWrap=true);
        void WrapAnchor();//applies clipping or wrapping to anchor
        //conversion
        POINT ScreenToWorld(POINT ptScreen);
        POINT WorldToScreen(POINT ptWorld);
        //wrap modes
        void SetHWrapMode(SCROLLERWRAPMODE ScrollerWrapMode);
        void SetVWrapMode(SCROLLERWRAPMODE ScrollerWrapMode);
        SCROLLERWRAPMODE SetHWrapMode();
        SCROLLERWRAPMODE SetVWrapMode();
        //validation
        bool IsWorldCoord(POINT ptWorld);
        bool IsScreenCoord(POINT ptScreen);
        bool IsAnchorCoord(POINT ptAnchor);
};
```

I told you it was big. The main thing I'd like to point out about this part of the engine is that it has almost nothing to do with isometric tiles, or even tiles at all. Only a single member function even makes mention of tiles of any sort (`CalcWorldSpace`). Without the `CalcWorldSpace` function, this class would still perform just fine. It can be used wherever scrolling is required. It is placed here amidst an isometric engine simply because scrolling is a very commonly needed component. This part of the engine consists of two parts: SCROLLERWRAPMODE and CScroller.

SCROLLERWRAPMODE

This is a little enumeration containing three values: WRAPMODE_NONE, WRAPMODE_CLIP, and WRAPMODE_WRAP. These values are used by CScroller to control how anchor space works. CScroller has one value for each axis so that they can be controlled separately. Using WRAPMODE_NONE makes the axis unbound, and anchor space has no effect on the anchor. WRAPMODE_CLIP make the axis clipped to a given range. If a value is out of that range, WRAPMODE_CLIP sets it to the maximum or minimum value of that range. WRAPMODE_WRAP is for making cylindrical or torus maps. The anchor moves from one edge to the other.

CScroller

Like my other classes, CScroller is divided into two areas: data members (private) and member functions (public).

Data Members

Table 15.6 lists the CScroller data members and briefly describes their purpose. Each one is explained more thoroughly after the table.

Table 15.6 CScroller Data Members

Member	Purpose
rcScreenSpace	Stores a RECT that describes screen space
rcWorldSpace	Stores a RECT that describes world space
rcAnchorSpace	Stores a RECT that describes anchor space
ptScreenAnchor	A POINT representing the screen anchor
swmHorizontal	Controls the wrapping mode of the x-axis
swmVertical	Controls the wrapping mode of the y-axis

rcScreenSpace

This data member keeps track of where screen space is. It can be set to the same size as the screen itself, but it really has no limitations on what its size can be. It is set with `SetScreenSpace`, retrieved with `GetScreenSpace`, and adjusted with `AdjustScreenSpace`. The width and height can be retrieved with `GetScreenSpaceWidth` and `GetScreenSpaceHeight`.

rcWorldSpace

This data member keeps track of where world space is. Usually, it is calculated based on a tile plotter and a tile extent using `CalcWorldSpace`. It can be set manually using `SetWorldSpace`, retrieved with `GetWorldSpace`, and adjusted with `AdjustWorldSpace`. The width and height can be retrieved with `GetWorldSpaceWidth` and `GetWorldSpaceHeight`.

rcAnchorSpace

This data member keeps track of where anchor space is. Normally, it is calculated from world space and screen space by using `CalcAnchorSpace`, but it can be set manually by `SetAnchorSpace`. It can be retrieved by `GetAnchorSpace` and adjusted by `AdjustAnchorSpace`. The width and height are returned by `GetAnchorSpaceWidth` and `GetAnchorSpaceHeight`.

ptScreenAnchor

This data member holds the screen anchor for the scroller. It can be set by a call to `SetAnchor`. To retrieve it, use `GetAnchor`. Other member functions that work on `ptScreenAnchor` include `MoveAnchor`, which changes the position of the anchor by relative amounts, and `WrapAnchor`, which applies the wrapping modes to x and y.

swmHorizontal/swmVertical

These two data members contain the wrapping modes for the x- and y-axis, respectively. They may be assigned by using `SetHWrapMode`/`SetVWrapMode` and retrieved by `GetHWrapMode`/`GetVWrapMode`.

Member Functions

There are a large number of these. They were all listed a few pages back, and they are so numerous that I don't want to list them all again here. They are divided into several categories: Construction/Destruction, Screen Space, World Space, Anchor Space, Anchor, Conversion, Wrap Mode, and Validation.

Construction/Destruction Member Functions

The constructor (`CScroller()`) doesn't do a whole lot. It sets all the various spaces to empty rectangles, sets the anchor to (0,0), and sets both the vertical and horizontal wrap modes to `WRAPMODE_NONE`. The destructor (~CScroller()) does even less than the constructor. It's there simply because it is my custom to include a destructor, even if it isn't being used. Unless you dynamically allocate your scroller objects, you will not directly call either of these methods.

Screen Space Member Functions

Five screen space member functions perform all the necessary operations on the screen space rectangle (stored in rcScreenSpace). Each of these functions is listed and explained next.

```
RECT* CScroller::GetScreenSpace();
```

This member function takes no parameters and returns a pointer to rcScreenSpace. Since this is a pointer, and not a const pointer or a const reference, you can access (and modify) the members of rcScreenSpace through the use of this function. You might not want to do that, though. I thought it would be fair to warn you.

```
void CScroller::SetScreenSpace(RECT* prcNewScreenSpace);
```

This function takes a pointer to a RECT and returns no value. It copies the RECT pointed to by prcNewScreenSpace and copies it member-for-member into rcScreenSpace. For the most part, you would use this function a single time in a program and never need to call it again.

```
void CScroller::AdjustScreenSpace(int iLeftAdjust,int iTopAdjust,int
iRightAdjust, int iBottomAdjust);
```

If you need to be able to adjust the screen space on-the-fly, this function does that for you. It takes four int parameters and returns no value. When this function is called, it adds the appropriate parameter to the corresponding rcScreenSpace member. For example, iLeftAdjust is added to rcScreenSpace.left.

```
int CScroller::GetScreenSpaceWidth();
```

This function has no parameters and returns an integer. This returned value is the difference between rcScreenSpace's right and left members.

```
int CScroller::GetScreenSpaceHeight();
```

This function has no parameters and returns an integer. This returned value is the difference between rcScreenSpace's bottom and top members.

World Space Member Functions

There are six of these, and the first five of them correspond to a similar function that deals with screen space. These functions all affect rcWorldSpace.

```
RECT* CScroller::GetWorldSpace();
```

This corresponds to GetScreenSpace. It takes no parameter and returns a pointer to rcWorldSpace. This function can be used to change the values within rcWorldSpace.

```
void CScroller::SetWorldSpace(RECT* prcNewWorldSpace);
```

This corresponds to SetScreenSpace. It takes a pointer to a RECT and returns no value. It copies the RECT pointed to by prcNewWorldSpace into rcWorldSpace.

```
void CScroller::AdjustWorldSpace(int iLeftAdjust,int iTopAdjust,int iRightAdjust,
int iBottomAdjust);
```

This corresponds to AdjustScreenSpace. It has no return value and four int parameters. It adds the appropriate parameter to the corresponding member of rcWorldSpace.

```
int CScroller::GetWorldSpaceWidth();
```

This corresponds to GetScreenSpaceWidth. It takes no parameters and returns the difference between rcWorldSpace's right and left members.

```
int CScroller::GetWorldSpaceHeight();
```

This corresponds to GetScreenSpaceHeight. It takes no parameters and returns the difference between rcWorldSpace's bottom and top members.

```
void CScroller::CalcWorldSpace(CTilePlotter* TilePlotter,RECT* prcExtent,int
iMapWidth,int iMapHeight);
```

This member function is unique to the world space category. Given a TilePlotter pointer (TilePlotter), a pointer to a RECT that contains the average tile's extent (prcExtent), and the width and height of the tilemap (iMapWidth and iMapHeight), this function calculates the coordinates that define world space.

Anchor Space

There are six of these. The first five correspond to similar screen space member functions. The last one assists in anchor space calculation.

```
RECT* CScroller::GetAnchorSpace();
```

This corresponds to GetScreenSpace. It returns a pointer to the rcAnchorSpace data member. This function can be used to directly access or modify the members of rcAnchorSpace. It takes no parameters and returns a RECT pointer.

```
void CScroller::SetAnchorSpace(RECT* prcNewAnchorSpace);
```

This corresponds to SetScreenSpace. It copies the RECT pointed to by prcNewAnchorSpace into rcAnchorSpace. It takes a RECT pointer parameter and returns no value.

```
void CScroller::AdjustAnchorSpace(int iLeftAdjust,int iTopAdjust,int
iRightAdjust, int iBottomAdjust);
```

This corresponds to AdjustScreenSpace. It takes four int parameters and returns no value. Each member of rcAnchorSpace is adjusted by the appropriate parameter.

```
int CScroller::GetAnchorSpaceWidth();
```

This corresponds to GetScreenSpaceWidth. It takes no parameters and returns an int. The returned value is the difference between rcAnchorSpace's right and left members.

```
int CScroller::GetAnchorSpaceHeight();
```

This corresponds to GetScreenSpaceHeight. It takes no parameters and returns an int. The returned value is the difference between rcAnchorSpace's bottom and top members.

```
void CScroller::CalcAnchorSpace();
```

This member function is unique to the anchor space functions. Based on the current world space and screen space (and the two wrap modes), the anchor space is calculated. The screen space's width and/or height are subtracted whenever the horizontal and vertical wrap modes are not WRAPMODE_WRAP.

Anchor Member Functions

The four anchor functions deal with the manipulation of the anchor itself. They affect the values of ptScreenAnchor.

```
POINT* CScroller::GetAnchor();
```

This function returns a pointer to ptScreenAnchor. Using this function, you can change the values of your anchor to outside of the valid range. This takes no value and returns a POINT pointer.

```
void CScroller::SetAnchor(POINT* pptNewAnchor,bool bWrap);
```

This function takes a POINT pointer and an optional bool pointer. It returns no value. The ptScreenAnchor data member's x and y are copied from those pointed to by pptNewAnchor. If bWrap is true, the scroller calls WrapAnchor immediately afterward.

```
void CScroller::MoveAnchor(int iXAdjust,int iYAdjust,bool bWrap);
```

This member function takes two int parameters and an optional bool parameter. It returns no value. The iXAdjust and iYAdjust parameters are added to ptScreenAnchor's x and y members. If bWrap is true, WrapAnchor is immediately called afterwards.

```
void CScroller::WrapAnchor();
```

This function takes no parameter and returns no value. Depending on the horizontal and vertical wrap modes, it performs different operations on ptScreenAnchor.

If an axis has WRAPMODE_NONE, no range checking is performed. If an axis has WRAPMODE_CLIP, the anchor is clipped to the nearest point in the range. If the axis has WRAPMODE_WRAP, either the anchor space's width or height are subtracted from or added to the anchor until it lies within the range.

Conversion Member Functions

After you set up the various spaces, these two functions, along with MoveAnchor, are the most commonly used. They translate between coordinate sets (namely, world space and screen space).

```
POINT CScroller::ScreenToWorld(POINT ptScreen);
```

This function takes a POINT and returns a POINT. The ptScreen parameter is a screen coordinate, and the returned value represents the corresponding world space coordinate. This function is helpful to use with a MouseMap, since the first step of mousemapping is the conversion from screen to world.

```
POINT CScroller::WorldToScreen(POINT ptWorld);
```

This function takes a `POINT` and returns a `POINT`. The `ptWorld` parameter is a world coordinate, and the returned value represents the corresponding screen space coordinate. This function is helpful to use with a TilePlotter, because the TilePlotter spits out world coordinates, and those need to be converted into screen coordinates.

Wrap Mode Member Functions

These four functions either get or set the two wrapping modes for the scroller. I abbreviated horizontal and vertical to H and V in these functions—mainly to save myself some typing.

```
void CScroller::SetHWrapMode(SCROLLERWRAPMODE ScrollerWrapMode);
```

This takes a `SCROLLERWRAPMODE` parameter and returns no value. It sets a new value to `swmHorizontal`. This value controls how the x value of the anchor is treated in calls to `WrapAnchor`.

```
void CScroller::SetVWrapMode(SCROLLERWRAPMODE ScrollerWrapMode);
```

This takes a `SCROLLERWRAPMODE` parameter and returns no value. It sets a new value to `swmVertical`. This value controls how the y value of the anchor is treated in calls to `WrapAnchor`.

```
SCROLLERWRAPMODE CScroller::GetHWrapMode();
```

This takes no parameter and returns a `SCROLLERWRAPMODE`. It retrieves the value of `swmHorizontal`.

```
SCROLLERWRAPMODE CScroller::GetVWrapMode();
```

This takes no parameter and returns a `SCROLLERWRAPMODE`. It retrieves the value of `swmVertical`.

Validation Member Functions

These three functions aren't absolutely necessary for the scroller to function. They are provided mainly for utility, because code using the existing member functions and a `RECT` function would be longer. Each of these functions checks to see if a given `POINT` lies within that space's `RECT`.

```
bool CScroller::IsWorldCoord(POINT ptWorld);
```

This takes a `POINT` parameter and returns a `bool`. If `ptWorld` lies within world space, the return value is true. If not, the return value is false.

```
bool CScroller::IsScreenCoord(POINT ptScreen);
```

This takes a `POINT` parameter and returns a `bool`. If `ptScreen` lies within screen space, the return value is true. If not, the return value is false.

```
bool CScroller::IsAnchorCoord(POINT ptAnchor);
```

This takes a `POINT` parameter and returns a `bool`. If `ptAnchor` lies within anchor space, the return value is true. If not, the return value is false.

Using CScroller

The beauty of CScroller is that it doesn't have to be tied to any particular type of map, so it has no ISOMAPTYPE member. However, using it properly with one of your map types requires world space to be calculated (unless, of course, you want to do it on your own). This requires that you set up a TilePlotter prior to setting up your scroller. The following are some snippets of code that demonstrate how to make use of a scroller:

```
//////////////////////////////////////////////////////////////
//declaration
CScroller Scroller;
//////////////////////////////////////////////////////////////
//setup
SetRect(Scroller.GetScreenSpace(),0,0,640,480);//this will set up
                                                //a screen space for the
entire
                                                // screen in a 640x480 dis-
play
Scroller.SetHWrapMode(WRAPMODE_CLIP);//set up clipping for the anchor
Scroller.SetVWrapMode(WRAPMODE_CLIP);
//TilePlotter is a preexisting tile plotter object
//rcExtent is a RECT containing a tile extent, usually from a TileSet
//MAPWIDTH and MAPHEIGHT contain the width and height of the tilemap
Scroller.CalcWorldSpace(&TilePlotter,&rcExtent,MAPWIDTH,MAPHEIGHT);
Scroller.CalcAnchorSpace();//calculate the anchor space
//////////////////////////////////////////////////////////////
//moving the anchor about
Scroller.MoveAnchor(dx,dy);//dx and dy are values you wish to scroll by
```

As you can see, despite the rather large size of the CScroller class, its use is pretty easy. In addition, it makes scrolling a snap. If you were ever trapped on a desert island, and you could have only a single class with you, CScroller would be the best one to pick.

IsoMouseMap.h/IsoMouseMap.cpp

Theses files contain the declarations and implementation required for the CMouseMap class. Of all the components, this one changed the least since its last form. It relies on the use of a TileWalker and a scroller, although this is not an absolute requirement. (I'd be interested to see a solution that didn't require at least one of the other components.)

```
//mousemap directions
typedef enum {
```

```
        MM_CENTER=0,
        MM_NW=1,
        MM_NE=2,
        MM_SW=3,
        MM_SE=4
} MOUSEMAPDIRECTION;
//mousemap class
class CMouseMap
{
private:
        //width and height of lookup
        int iWidth;
        int iHeight;
        //reference point (adjustment for the upper left of tile 0,0)
        POINT ptRef;
        //lookup table
        MOUSEMAPDIRECTION* mmdLookUp;
        //scroller
        CScroller* pScroller;
        //walker
        CTileWalker* pTileWalker;
public:
        //constructor
        CMouseMap();
        //destructor
        ~CMouseMap();
        //load mousemap
        void Load(LPCTSTR lpszFileName);//used with iso and hex maps
        void Create(int iWidth,int iHeight);//used with rectangular maps
        //destroy mousemap
        void Destroy();
        //width/height
        int GetWidth();
        int GetHeight();
        //reference
        POINT* GetReferencePoint();
        void SetReferencePoint(POINT* pptRefPt);
        void CalcReferencePoint(CTilePlotter* pTilePlotter,RECT* prcExtent);
        //map the mouse
        POINT MapMouse(POINT ptMouse);
        //scroller
        CScroller* GetScroller();
```

```
        void SetScroller(CScroller* pScroller);
        //walker
        CTileWalker* GetTileWalker();
        void SetTileWalker(CTileWalker* pTileWalker);
};
```

Much like the rest of the components, IsoMouseMap.h and IsoMouseMap.cpp are divided into two main declarations: `MOUSEMAPDIRECTION` and `CMouseMap` class. I'll explain each.

MOUSEMAPDIRECTION

This enumerated type corresponds exactly to the `MouseMapDirection` enumerated types used in Chapters 12 through 14. The only real difference is that the name is now in all capital letters. The value `MM_CENTER` represents the centered tile of the map. `MM_NE`, `MM_SE`, `MM_NW`, and `MM_SW` represent the corners of the lookup. In case you need a refresher, Figure 15.3 shows what I'm talking about.

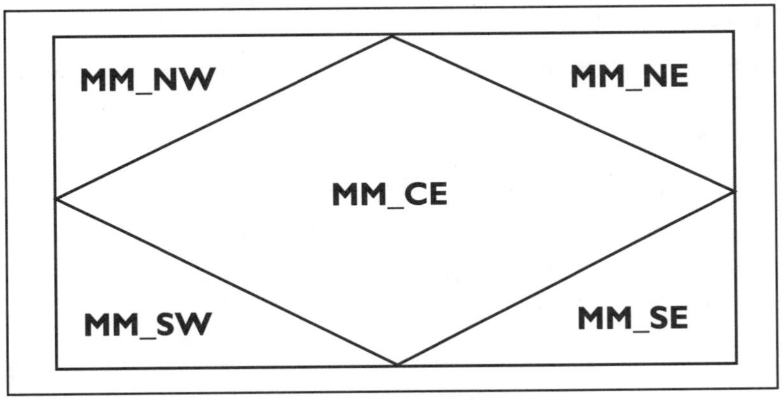

Figure 15.3

A MouseMap and its `MOUSEMAPDIRECTION`s

CMouseMap

Like with all the components so far, I decided to implement the MouseMap as a class. Also, just like all the other classes, it is divided into a private data section and a public member function section. `CMouseMap` is the final piece of the puzzle. Two of the other components—namely, the TileWalker and the scroller—fit nicely into it. Similarly, the MouseMap fits nicely into the TilePlotter, which we will examine later.

Data Members

`CMouseMap` has six data members. They cover a hodgepodge of data, from the size of the map to what scroller and TileWalker to use. Table 15.7 lists and briefly explains these data members.

Table 15.7 CMouseMap Data Members

Data Member	Meaning
`iWidth`	Width of the MouseMap
`iHeight`	Height of the MouseMap
`ptRef`	Reference point for measuring relative to tile (0,0)
`mmdLookUp`	The actual MouseMap lookup array
`pScroller`	A pointer to the scroller to use for converting screen space to world space
`pTileWalker`	A pointer to the TileWalker used for converting MouseMap coordinates to map coordinates

Member Functions

The member functions for CMouseMap are presented in groups of related functions, so that you don't have to look upon them as a big lump.

Construction/Destruction Member Functions

The constructor and destructor don't really do much for the MouseMap. The constructor creates a default 1×1 MouseMap so that if for some reason you use your MouseMap before using `Load` or `Create`, at least you won't get division by 0.

```
CMouseMap::CMouseMap();
```

This creates a default 1×1 tilemap.

```
CMouseMap::~CMouseMap();
```

This destroys whatever MouseMap is currently loaded. (This means you don't have to explicitly call `Destroy` at the end of a program that uses `CMouseMap`.)

Lookup Table Member Functions

I needed to have some way to load bitmaps into my `CMouseMap` class, but I also needed a way to create my own arbitrarily sized MouseMaps that initially are filled with `MM_CENTER` but that can be filled with whatever values I like. These three functions are what I came up with.

```
void CMouseMap::Load(LPCTSTR lpszFileName);
```

This function is used to load the bitmap specified by its `lpszFileName` parameter. The image in question is loaded and parsed into a lookup table. It returns no value.

```
void CMouseMap::Create(int iWidth,int iHeight);
```

This function creates an arbitrarily sized lookup table, the dimensions of which are specified by the `iWidth` and `iHeight` parameters. The lookup table is allocated and filled with the value `MM_CENTER`. Use this function either for a rectangular MouseMap or for some other axonometric MouseMap that needs a user-supplied lookup table.

```
void CMouseMap::Destroy();
```

This function deallocates the lookup table. It is called by the destructor, so you don't ever have to actually call it.

Tile Size Member Functions

Once the mouse map is loaded/created, you need some way to get the size of the MouseMap, so I've provided two functions.

```
int CMouseMap::GetWidth();
```

Returns the width of the MouseMap. It takes no parameters.

```
int CMouseMap::GetHeight();
```

Returns the height of the MouseMap. It takes no parameters.

Reference Point Member Functions

You remember our nice talk about the reference point, right? The one about how you have to match up the corners of the MouseMap with tile (0,0) and how that value isn't necessarily world space (0,0)? That's what these functions help you with.

```
POINT* CMouseMap::GetReferencePoint();
```

This retrieves the reference point. It takes no parameters and returns a pointer to a `POINT`.

```
void CMouseMap::SetReferencePoint(POINT* pptRefPt);
```

This copies a point into the reference point. It takes a `POINT` pointer that points to the `POINT` you want to copy. Returns no value.

```
void CMouseMap::CalcReferencePoint(CTilePlotter* pTilePlotter,RECT* prcExtent);
```

Most of the time, you will use this function to set up your reference point. Based on a tile plotter (pointed to by the `pTilePlotter` parameter) and an extent rectangle (pointed to by `prcExtent`), the reference point is calculated.

Scroller Member Functions

Unless your world space and screen space are the same, which usually isn't so, you'll need to plug a scroller into your MouseMap so that it can do your screen-to-world calculation.

```
CScroller* CMouseMap::GetScroller();
```

This retrieves the scroller that is currently being used by the MouseMap. It takes no parameters and returns a pointer to a CScroller.

```
void CMouseMap::SetScroller(CScroller* pScroller);
```

This sets a new scroller to be used with the MouseMap. It takes a pointer to a CScroller and returns no value.

TileWalker Member Functions

The MouseMap, in addition to a scroller, needs a TileWalker to perform its job properly. These functions get or set a pointer to a TileWalker for the MouseMap to use.

```
CTileWalker* CMouseMap::GetTileWalker();
```

This retrieves the pointer to the TileWalker that the MouseMap is using.

```
void CMouseMap::SetTileWalker(CTileWalker* pTileWalker);
```

This sets a new pointer to a TileWalker for the MouseMap to use.

Mouse Mapping Function

And last, but certainly not least, the main working function of the CMouseMap class. It has fewer parameters than the MouseMaps used in Chapters 12 through 14, since the class itself stores the needed extra information.

```
POINT CMouseMap::MapMouse(POINT ptMouse);
```

This takes the screen coordinate contained by the ptMouse parameter, converts it into a map coordinate, and returns that coordinate.

Using CMouseMap

The CMouseMap class is easy to set up and use. The following code snippets show how the most common tasks, like declaration, setup and use are done.

```
////////////////////////////////////////////////////////////////
//declaration
CMouseMap MouseMap;
////////////////////////////////////////////////////////////////
//setup
MouseMap.Load("mousemap.bmp");//mousemap.bmp contains the proper image.
MouseMap.SetScroller(&Scroller);//Scroller is a CScroller object
MouseMap.SetTileWalker(&TileWalker);//TileWalker is a CTileWalker object
////////////////////////////////////////////////////////////////
```

```
//use
POINT ptMap=MouseMap.MapMouse(ptMouse);//ptMouse is a screen
                                        //coordinate of the mouse
```

IsoHexCore.h

Because each of the four components (TilePlotter, TileWalker, Scroller, and MouseMap) is in a separate header/cpp file, to make use of them you would need to include all the headers into your program. IsoHexCore.h removes that requirement by including all the headers for you in a single header file.

There you have it—a complete isometric engine. Yes, you still have much work to do before it's actually game-worthy, but you have a solid foundation on which you can build.

An IsoHexCore Example

Now that all the explanations for these classes are done, let's make a sample program. Load up IsoHex15_1.cpp. This example demonstrates the true flexibility of the IsoHexCore engine. It can switch from one type of tilemap to another while the application is still running. IsoHex15_1 is based on IsoHex1_1.cpp. It uses most of the files you are accustomed to using—namely, GDICanvas.h/GDICanvas.cpp, DDFuncs.h/DDFuncs.cpp, and TileSet.h/TileSet.cpp. In addition, it brings in the IsoHexCore engine files we've been exploring in this chapter.

Figures 15.4, 15.5, and 15.6 show the three faces of this application. By pressing the 1, 2, or 3 key, you can instantly change what map type is being used, and the scroller will be recalculated so that you can maneuver around just like in some of the earlier chapters' examples. It's like three programs in one!

Figure 15.4

The result of pressing the 1 key

Figure 15.5

The result of pressing the 2 key

Figure 15.6

The result of pressing the 3 key

Globals

Most of the globals listed next are self-explanatory and/or you've used them before. They cover everything from your basic DirectDraw objects, to your tilesets, to your new iso engine components.

```
//directdraw
LPDIRECTDRAW7 lpdd=NULL;
LPDIRECTDRAWSURFACE7 lpddsMain=NULL;
```

```
LPDIRECTDRAWSURFACE7 lpddsBack=NULL;
LPDIRECTDRAWCLIPPER lpddClip=NULL;
//tilesets
CTileSet tsIso;//main tileset
CTileSet tsCursor;//cursor
//isohexcore components
CTilePlotter TilePlotter;//plotter
CTileWalker TileWalker;//walker
CScroller Scroller;//scroller
CMouseMap MouseMap;//mousemap
POINT ptCursor;//keep track of the cursor
POINT ptScroll;//keep track of how quickly we scroll
int iMap[MAPWIDTH][MAPHEIGHT];//map array
```

See? Nothing really new, except for the iso engine components, `TilePlotter`, `TileWalker`, `Scroller`, and `MouseMap`. Is this seeming too easy to you? It sure is to me! (That's not a bad thing, though. Easy is good.)

Initialization and Cleanup

I wanted to cover the beginning and end of the program together, since they are related. The cool thing about IsoHexCore is that none of the components have to be dynamically allocated with `new`, which means you don't have to deallocate them later with `delete`, and they will automatically be destroyed when they go out of scope (when the program ends). This frees you a great deal in your cleanup code.

First, let's take a look inside Prog_Init, where you set everything up. This first part you should already be familiar with, because it sets up your basic DirectDraw objects.

```
//DirectDraw Initialization
//create IDirectDraw object
lpdd=LPDD_Create(hWndMain,DDSCL_EXCLUSIVE |
      DDSCL_FULLSCREEN | DDSCL_ALLOWREBOOT);
//set display mode
lpdd->SetDisplayMode(640,480,16,0,0);
//create primary surface
lpddsMain=LPDDS_CreatePrimary(lpdd,1);
//get back buffer
lpddsBack=LPDDS_GetSecondary(lpddsMain);
//create clipper
lpdd->CreateClipper(0,&lpddClip,NULL);
//associate window with the clipper
lpddClip->SetHWnd(0,hWndMain);
//attach clipper to back buffer
lpddsBack->SetClipper(lpddClip);
```

Nothing too hard, right? Next, you start to initialize your IsoHexCore components. Pay attention to the order in which I'm doing this, because it may seem a little weird.

First, partially initialize the MouseMap by telling it to load the image from which it scans the lookup table.

```
//load in the mousemap
MouseMap.Load("MouseMap.bmp");
```

Next, set up the TilePlotter, even though you aren't yet done setting up the MouseMap. Told you it was weird. Set the TilePlotter's map type (on initially loading, you set it to `ISOMAP_DIAMOND`), and set the width and height for the tileplotting calculations. You get this width and height from the MouseMap. Aha! That's why you load the MouseMap first, and it also explains why you don't just have a single function that you call to initialize your MouseMap.

```
//set up the tile plotter
TilePlotter.SetMapType(ISOMAP_DIAMOND);//diamond mode
TilePlotter.SetTileSize(MouseMap.GetWidth(),
        MouseMap.GetHeight());//grab width and height from mousemap
```

You don't have to touch the TilePlotter again, so move on to the TileWalker. The TileWalker could have been initialized earlier, but this was just the place I chose to do it. Set the map type to `ISOMAP_DIAMOND` and be done with the TileWalker.

```
//set up tile walker to diamond mode
TileWalker.SetMapType(ISOMAP_DIAMOND);
```

Time for the scroller. The scroller's initialization is probably the longest and most involved part of IsoHexCore initialization. First, set up a `RECT` that has the same dimensions as the screen.

```
//set up screeen space
RECT rcTemp;
SetRect(&rcTemp,0,0,640,480);
Scroller.SetScreenSpace(&rcTemp);
```

Now you have to load in your tilesets. What? But you haven't finished setting up the scroller! Well, you need the tile extent to calculate world space, so you need to have the tilesets loaded. In the end, the only thing that matters is that everything gets loaded properly and nothing gets left behind. So, as I was saying, load in the tilesets.

```
//load in tiles and cursor
tsIso.Load(lpdd,"Tiles.bmp");
tsCursor.Load(lpdd,"cursor.bmp");
```

Grab the tile extent RECT from the first tile of tsIso. You could have picked any of the tiles, because they all have the same dimensions. Once you have the extent send it, a pointer to the TilePlotter, and the width and height of the map to calculate the scroller's world space.

```
//grab tile extent from tileset
CopyRect(&rcTemp,&tsIso.GetTileList()[0].rcDstExt);
//calculate the worldspace
Scroller.CalcWorldSpace(&TilePlotter,&rcTemp,MAPWIDTH,MAPHEIGHT);
```

Back to the MouseMap. Use the TilePlotter and the extent RECT to calculate the reference point for the MouseMap. Honestly, you could have waited, but I like having all the code dealing with the tile extent RECT in one area rather than spread out all over the place, making it necessary to scroll up and down to look for it if something went wrong.

```
//calculate the mousemap reference point
MouseMap.CalcReferencePoint(&TilePlotter,&rcTemp);
```

Now finalize the scroller initialization. First, set the horizontal and vertical wrap modes (both of them are WRAPMODE_CLIP). Then calculate the anchor space, and finally set the scroller's anchor to (0,0).

```
//set wrap modes for scroller
Scroller.SetHWrapMode(WRAPMODE_CLIP);
Scroller.SetVWrapMode(WRAPMODE_CLIP);
//calculate anchor space
Scroller.CalcAnchorSpace();
//set scroller anchor to (0,0)
Scroller.GetAnchor()->x=0;
Scroller.GetAnchor()->y=0;
```

At last, finish what you started by attaching the scroller and the TileWalker to the MouseMap, and you have successfully wrapped up your IsoHexCore initialization.

```
//attach scroller and tilewalker to mousemap
MouseMap.SetScroller(&Scroller);
MouseMap.SetTileWalker(&TileWalker);
```

Finally, set up a random map, and return true.

```
//set up the map to a random tilefield
for(int x=0;x<MAPWIDTH;x++)
{
	for(int y=0;y<MAPHEIGHT;y++)
	{
```

```
                iMap[x][y]=rand()%tsIso.GetTileCount();
        }
}
return(true);//return success
```

The Prog_Done function isn't nearly the size of Prog_Init, since you only have to clean up the DirectDraw objects.

```
void Prog_Done()
{
        //release main/back surfaces
        LPDDS_Release(&lpddsMain);
        //release clipper
        LPDDCLIP_Release(&lpddClip);
        //release directdraw
        LPDD_Release(&lpdd);
}
```

Not much to it. It's really cool that you don't have to jump through elaborate hoops in order to get rid of your iso engine components. They practically clean themselves up.

Main Loop

The main loop can be broken into four major steps: clear back buffer, draw tilemap, draw cursor, and flip. All of this code is in Prog_Loop.

This first snippet clears out the back buffer by setting up a DDBLTFX structure. You've seen this before, so I won't say any more.

```
//clear out backbuffer
DDBLTFX ddbltfx;
DDBLTFX_ColorFill(&ddbltfx,0);
lpddsBack->Blt(NULL,NULL,NULL,DDBLT_WAIT | DDBLT_COLORFILL,&ddbltfx);
```

Now, update the scroller's anchor by moving the anchor in accordance with the values stored in ptScroll. The manner in which ptScroll is assigned these values can be found later in the "Event Handling" section.

```
//move the anchor based on scrolling speed
Scroller.MoveAnchor(ptScroll.x,ptScroll.y);
```

Time to plot your tiles. Loop through the map coordinates using a POINT variable ptMap. For each map position, plot the tile using your TilePlotter and then convert that point from world to screen coordinates using the scroller. Always remember that a TilePlotter outputs world coordinates only, and you need the plotter to translate to screen coordinates. After the world-to-screen conversion, simply put the tile with the tileset `tsIso`.

```
//plot our tiles
POINT ptPlot;
POINT ptMap;
for(ptMap.y=0;ptMap.y<MAPHEIGHT;ptMap.y++)
{
	for(ptMap.x=0;ptMap.x<MAPWIDTH;ptMap.x++)
	{
		//plot the tile
		ptPlot=TilePlotter.PlotTile(ptMap);
		//convert from world to screen
		ptPlot=Scroller.WorldToScreen(ptPlot);
		//put the tile
		tsIso.PutTile(lpddsBack,ptPlot.x,ptPlot.y,iMap[ptMap.x][ptMap.y]);
	}
}
```

Next, grab the mouse's current position using the WIN32 function `GetCursorPos`. I haven't covered this function in any of our discussions, but it's pretty simple. Pass a pointer to a `POINT` to be filled with the mouse's current position. Alternatively, I could have stored the value of the current mouse position during the `WindowProc`'s `WM_MOUSEMOVE` message handler, but this way works just as well.

```
//grab the mouse position
POINT ptMouse;
GetCursorPos(&ptMouse);
```

Because you have the mouse position now, you can go ahead and use the MouseMap to figure out what tile you are on and store that position in `ptCursor` (which, if you look back, is your global variable for storing the cursor position).

```
//map the mouse
ptCursor=MouseMap.MapMouse(ptMouse);
```

Naturally, your MouseMap doesn't know how big your map is, so you have to clip it to valid map squares by yourself. That is what this next bit does.

```
//clip the cursor to valid map coordinates
if(ptCursor.x<0) ptCursor.x=0;
if(ptCursor.y<0) ptCursor.y=0;
if(ptCursor.x>(MAPWIDTH-1)) ptCursor.x=MAPWIDTH-1;
```

```
if(ptCursor.y>(MAPHEIGHT-1)) ptCursor.y=MAPHEIGHT-1;
```

So, you've got a mousemapped and validated cursor position. All that is left to do is plot the darn thing. First, you have to use the TilePlotter to calculate its world position, and then the scroller to convert that to a screen position, and finally the tileset to blit the cursor.

```
//plot the cursor
ptPlot=TilePlotter.PlotTile(ptCursor);
//convert world to screen
ptPlot=Scroller.WorldToScreen(ptPlot);
//put the cursor on screen
tsCursor.PutTile(lpddsBack,ptPlot.x,ptPlot.y,0);
```

Oh, yes... and flip the primary surface.

```
//flip to show the back buffer
lpddsMain->Flip(0,DDFLIP_WAIT);
```

This function is a good place to see all the IsoHexCore components in action. All four are used here. (The TileWalker is not explicitly used, but the MouseMap makes use of it.) You'll notice that most of the lines in the `Prog_Loop` function call one of the engine components, and you can see how very little you do yourself.

Event Handling

You're in the home stretch now. IsoHex15_1.cpp responds to two messages (at least as far as user interaction is concerned)—`WM_KEYDOWN` and `WM_MOUSEMOVE`. We'll take `WM_MOUSEMOVE` first, because it's shorter.

The only purpose of the `WM_MOUSEMOVE` handler is to figure out if you intend to scroll and if you do, by how much. You've seen code similar to this in prior chapters' examples. Nothing really new here.

```
case WM_MOUSEMOVE:
	{
		//grab mouse x and y
		int x=LOWORD(lParam);
		int y=HIWORD(lParam);
		//reset scrolling speeds to zero
		ptScroll.x=0;
		ptScroll.y=0;
		//left scroll?
		if(x<8) ptScroll.x=x-8;
		//upward scroll?
		if(y<8) ptScroll.y=y-8;
```

```
            //right scroll?
            if(x>=632) ptScroll.x=x-632;
            //downward scroll?
            if(y>=472) ptScroll.y=y-472;
        }break;
```

In the WM_KEYDOWN handler you do something else entirely—namely, reconfigure the entire IsoHexCore engine to work with another map type. First, the WM_KEYDOWN handler does a switch based on the value of wParam (which contains the virtual key code). If the value is VK_ESCAPE, it tells the main window to close, which then exits the program. If the value is 1, 2, or 3, it goes to short bits of code that reinitialize the iso engine components. I'll only show the code for if 1 is pressed, because 2 and 3 are very similar. (Just replace the instances of ISOMAP_SLIDE with ISOMAP_STAGGERED or ISOMAP_DIAMOND.)

```
case '1':
        {
            //set up the iso engine for slide maps
            TileWalker.SetMapType(ISOMAP_SLIDE);//set walker to slide mapping
            TilePlotter.SetMapType(ISOMAP_SLIDE);//set plotter to slide mapping
            //recalculate the scroller

Scroller.CalcWorldSpace(&TilePlotter,&tsIso.GetTileList()[0].rcDstExt,
                    MAPWIDTH,MAPHEIGHT);
            Scroller.CalcAnchorSpace();
            //set the screen anchor back to zero
            Scroller.GetAnchor()->x=0;
            Scroller.GetAnchor()->y=0;
        }break;
```

As you can see, you don't have to go through all the rigmarole that you had to during Prog_Init, because the main part of the iso engine doesn't change. You simply have to change the map type for the plotter and walker and recalculate the world and anchor spaces for the scroller. Nothing to it! And you can look at the other map types; they have virtually the exact same code.

SUMMARY

Wow. The end of the chapter (and you thought it would never come). Also, the end of the part on isohex basics. You've learned about tiles, about what tile-based means, and about the three isometric map types. You now have a solid engine core to work with. Seems like it's been light-years since Part 1. Of course, at the end of the next part, it'll seem like you've progressed light-years ahead of where you are now. Finally, you're going to get into some real stuff. You've done enough "random tilemap" examples. You're ready for some info that will really make a cool isometric game.

Part III

Isometric Methodology

CHAPTER 16

Layered Maps and Optimized Rendering

- Layered Map Basics
- Layered Map Methods
- Map Scale Layering

It's a brand-new day. The birds are chirping, the sun is shining, and all is right with the world. More importantly, you have survived the first two parts of this book, which means that you are ready to move on to some real stuff. Congratulations!

This chapter covers sort of a hodgepodge of isometric algorithms, and maily deals with layered maps. There will also be some information on how to optimize the rendering of your iso map, and how to update discrete areas of the map. All in all, it should be a fun ride, and you should be saying, "Oh, *that's* how you do that!" before you're done.

As in previous chapters, the methods I will show you will be displayed in a manner that (I hope) is the easiest to understand, which means that the methods aren't necessarily the fastest or don't necessarily perform the best. However, once you have learned the basic idea of how to do something, I have full faith in your ability to find a way to do it faster and better.

Also, you're going to be working with IsoHexCore, which was introduced in Chapter 15, "The IsoHexCore Engine." I'll add components to it, and it will become a more robust engine as time goes on.

Without further ado, let's get started, shall we?

Layered Map Basics

Just so that you and I are both on the same page (figuratively speaking), I want to explain exactly what I mean by a layered map. When I say *layered map,* I just mean that there is potentially more than one tile/sprite blit on a given map location. Figure 16.1 shows a simple layered map. Sometimes, there is no need for a layered map. For example, you can make some board games without layering, although, you'd probably want to use them for most. For example, in a chess game, you might want to have separate images for the board tiles and the piece sprites, although nothing prevents you from making each piece on each board tile and just using a single layer.

What is the main purpose of having layered maps? Generally speaking, layered maps let you make richer worlds (and richer worlds are more immersive) while at the same time decreasing the number of actual tiles/sprites needed. This means you will need to use your artists less, and as a result, your art costs won't be as large.

With a layered map, you can have only a limited number of tiles. For example, if you took three types of terrain (grassland, prairie, and ocean) a few tiles to build coastline (for iso, this can be done with as few as 16 tiles) eight tiles for roads and a few tiles to represent forests, hills, towns, and so on from these 30 or so tiles you could create a world that seems like it was made of hundreds of tiles. In reality, the map only consists of smaller tiles that are put together in different ways.

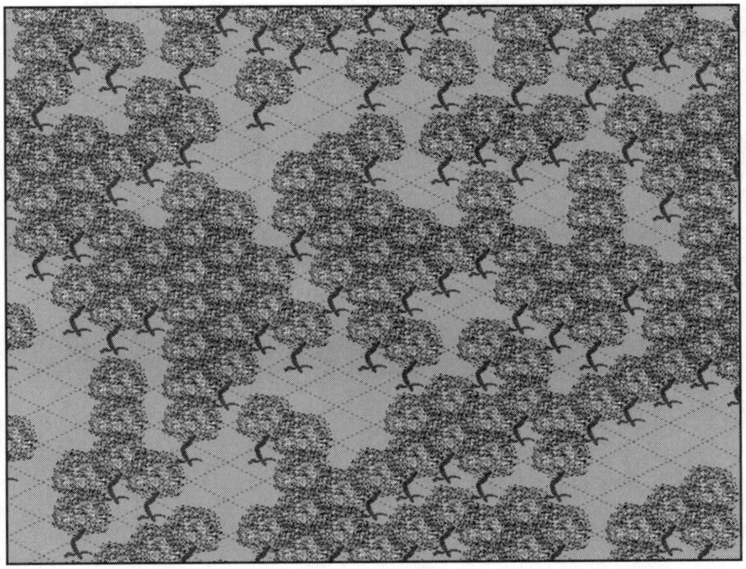

Figure 16.1

A layered iso map

In addition, layering tiles and sprites allows you to convey information about the tile to the user graphically, letting him know where his units, characters, and buildings are, where his enemies are, what resources are available at a given location, and so on.

Layered Map Methods

Now that you've seen the doors that layered maps open for you, you can start to really think about how you'll work with them. Basically, there are two methods: the tile scale method and the map scale method. In most instances either one will work, but there are subtle differences of which you should be aware.

Tile Scale Layering

In tile scale layering, the layering occurs on a per-tile basis. This means that if you have a background of grassland and a tree on a tile, when the map drawing gets to that tile, it blits the grassland, then the tree, and then moves on to the next tile.

Figure 16.2 shows a three-layer map using the tile scale method of layering. The three layers are (from bottom to top) background (a simple green tile), shadow, and foreground.

Figure 16.2

Tile scale layering

Tile Scale Layering Example

Load up IsoHex16_1.cpp. It requires all the standard stuff, including DDFuncs.h/DDFuncs.cpp, TileSet.h/TileSet.cpp, and the IsoHexCore files. This example is responsible for the image shown in Figure 16.2. Mostly, this sample program is the same as IsoHex15_1.cpp, with the map type code taken out and some extra tilesets loaded in. The main changes are in the blitting section of `Prog_Loop`, but the differences aren't limited to that section.

The first change is that instead of a single tileset for your images, you have a separate bitmap for each layer. The background tile is stored in backgroundts.bmp. The tree's shadow is in treeshadowts.bmp, and the tree itself is in treets.bmp. Each of these tilesets has a single image, which might seem like a bit of a waste, but having them separate makes it easier to show how layering works. The background is loaded by a `CTileset` object called `tsBack`. The shadow is loaded into `tsShadow`, and the tree is loaded into `tsTree`. This is all done within `Prog_Init`, in the middle of the IsoHexCore initialization.

The next fundamental change is the manner in which the map is set up. Before, when you had several tiles and only one layer, you had it randomly choose an image to display. In this case, the background is the same for all tiles. The only change from one tile to another is whether or not there is a tree. I picked the value 0 for "no tree" and the value 1 for "tree." Here's the code that sets up the map:

```
//set up the map to a random tilefield
for(int x=0;x<MAPWIDTH;x++)
{
	for(int y=0;y<MAPHEIGHT;y++)
	{
		iMap[x][y]=rand()%2;
	}
}
```

It's really basic. Just assign a map square to `rand()%2`, which gives you either a 0 or 1. No major trickery occurring here! The major change (blitting the map in `Prog_Loop`) is a little more involved. The loop through the map positions is the same as normal; the changes occur in the inner loop. First, blit the background tile, since the background is uniform for all areas. Next, check to see whether the current map position coincides with the cursor. If it does, you blit the cursor onto that position.

Finally, there is a check to see if a tree is at the current position. If there is a tree, blit the shadow and then blit the tree. If no tree exists, skip it. Easy enough, right? Take a look at the code that does it:

```
//plot our tiles
POINT ptPlot;
POINT ptMap;
for(ptMap.y=0;ptMap.y<MAPHEIGHT;ptMap.y++)
{
      for(ptMap.x=0;ptMap.x<MAPWIDTH;ptMap.x++)
      {
            //plot the tile
            ptPlot=TilePlotter.PlotTile(ptMap);
            //convert from world to screen
            ptPlot=Scroller.WorldToScreen(ptPlot);
            //put the background
            tsBack.PutTile(lpddsBack,ptPlot.x,ptPlot.y,0);
            //check for cursor plotting
            if(ptMap.x==ptCursor.x && ptMap.y==ptCursor.y)
            {
                  tsCursor.PutTile(lpddsBack,ptPlot.x,ptPlot.y,0);
            }
            //check for tree
            if(iMap[ptMap.x][ptMap.y]==1)
            {
                  //put shadow
                  tsShadow.PutTile(lpddsBack,ptPlot.x,ptPlot.y,0);
                  //put tree
                  tsTree.PutTile(lpddsBack,ptPlot.x,ptPlot.y,0);
            }
      }
}
```

Nothing to it, right? If you had other foreground objects, like stones, signs, or buildings, you could handle it in pretty much the same way, except that the map position might have 0 to represent nothing, 1 to represent a tree, 2 to represent another object, and so on.

And now I have to apologize. As it turns out, I lied about this example being a three-layer map. Technically, it is not. The cursor can be considered a layer, squeezed between the background layer and the shadow layer. So if you want to be completely accurate about it, this is a four-layer, not a three-layer map. Luckily, I'm not too concerned about the cursor's layer, since I think of the cursor as an almost completely separate system. I just wanted to point out that it was technically a layer. I'll say nothing more on the topic, and we won't consider the cursor layer from here on out.

If you compile and run the example, you'll see something similar to Figure 16.2. By clicking, you can add and remove trees. Moving the mouse to the edge of the screen scrolls in that direction. This is a rather simple example of a map editor, except, of course, that you cannot save or load your map.

In this example, the fact that you are using tile scale layering introduces certain distortions to the images on the map. For example, if a tree is placed to the southwest of another tree, the southwest tree's shadow will cover the lower part of the other tree's trunk. Figure 16.3 zooms in on this effect. In many examples, this would be acceptable, but not when you have a shadow layer.

Figure 16.3

Image distortions for tile scale layering

Map Scale Layering

The other method of layering is to apply layers one at a time to the entire map, rather than applying all the layers to a single tile. Figure 16.4 shows an example of this, using the same tree and tree shadow images you've been using.

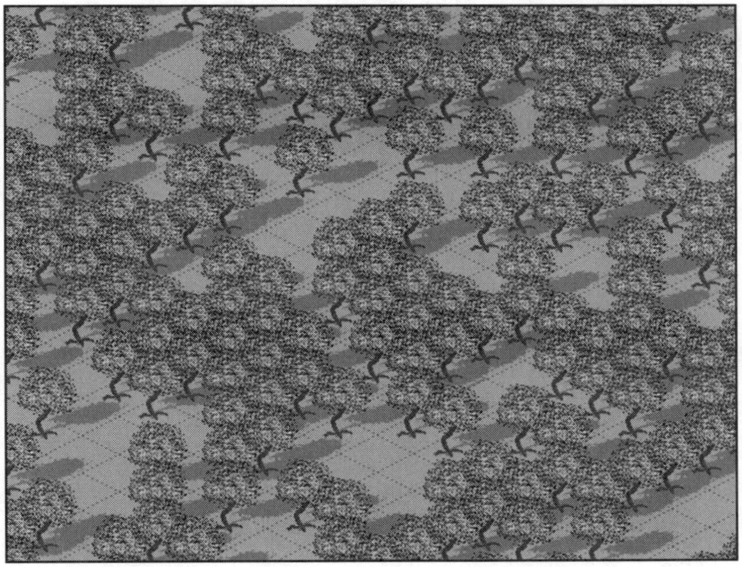

Figure 16.4

Map scale layering

Map Scale Layering Example

IsoHex16_2.cpp is the map scale layering example. The code is almost identical to IsoHex16_1.cpp, with one small, but meaningful, exception. That exception is the main rendering loop. Or, I should say, loops.

In map scale layering, you apply one layer to the entire map and then move on to the next, which means that you have to do your nested mapx, mapy loops as many times as you have layers. You might be thinking that this adds more overhead (because the plotted coordinates have to be calculated several times). True, the example does this, and so yes, you have more overhead than is necessary. However, this does not mean that the map scale type of layering is always less efficient than tile scale layering. Indeed it is not; it is simply less efficient in this case because of the way you set up the loop.

Here is the revised code for the rendering loops:

```
//plot our tiles
POINT ptPlot;
POINT ptMap;
for(ptMap.y=0;ptMap.y<MAPHEIGHT;ptMap.y++)
{
      for(ptMap.x=0;ptMap.x<MAPWIDTH;ptMap.x++)
```

```
        {
                //plot the tile
                ptPlot=TilePlotter.PlotTile(ptMap);
                //convert from world to screen
                ptPlot=Scroller.WorldToScreen(ptPlot);
                //put the background
                tsBack.PutTile(lpddsBack,ptPlot.x,ptPlot.y,0);
                //check for cursor plotting
                if(ptMap.x==ptCursor.x && ptMap.y==ptCursor.y)
                {
                        tsCursor.PutTile(lpddsBack,ptPlot.x,ptPlot.y,0);
                }
        }
}
for(ptMap.y=0;ptMap.y<MAPHEIGHT;ptMap.y++)
{
        for(ptMap.x=0;ptMap.x<MAPWIDTH;ptMap.x++)
        {
                //plot the tile
                ptPlot=TilePlotter.PlotTile(ptMap);
                //convert from world to screen
                ptPlot=Scroller.WorldToScreen(ptPlot);
                //check for tree
                if(iMap[ptMap.x][ptMap.y]==1)
                {
                        //put shadow
                        tsShadow.PutTile(lpddsBack,ptPlot.x,ptPlot.y,0);
                }
        }
}
for(ptMap.y=0;ptMap.y<MAPHEIGHT;ptMap.y++)
{
        for(ptMap.x=0;ptMap.x<MAPWIDTH;ptMap.x++)
        {
                //plot the tile
                ptPlot=TilePlotter.PlotTile(ptMap);
                //convert from world to screen
                ptPlot=Scroller.WorldToScreen(ptPlot);
                //check for tree
                if(iMap[ptMap.x][ptMap.y]==1)
                {
```

```
                //put tree
                tsTree.PutTile(lpddsBack,ptPlot.x,ptPlot.y,0);
            }
        }
}
```

As you can see, there are three sets of nested (x,y) loops, one for each layer. The first set of `for` loops takes care of the background. The next set takes care of the shadow layer, and the final set takes care of the foreground. The cursor is plotted during the background layer (it just looks strange if done otherwise). If you compile and run the example, you'll get something that looks like Figure 16.4.

In Figure 16.5, I've zoomed in on this example to show the subtle difference between tile scale and map scale layering. In the current example, all the shadows are drawn before any of the trees are, so none of the trees are obscured by the shadow like they are in the map scale example. Mostly, this is a matter of personal preference. I prefer the look of the second, but you might prefer the look of the first.

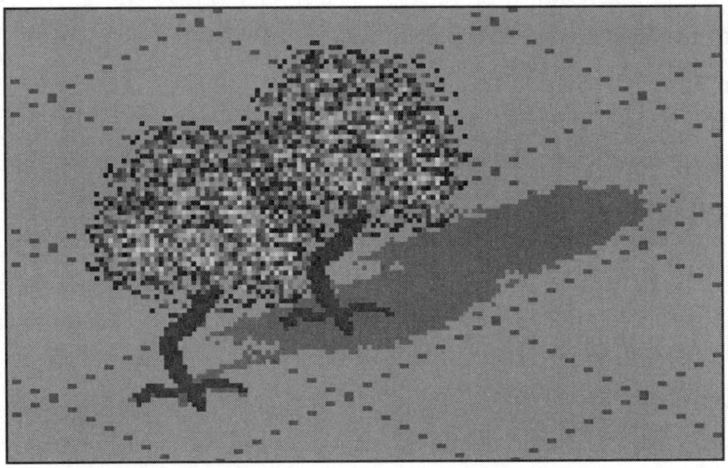

Figure 16.5

Map scale layering close up

What's the Big Deal?

You might have been following along in this chapter wondering, "Well, who cares?" and thinking that I'm the most insane programming book author ever. You may be thinking it shouldn't matter what layering method you use, because it'll turn out OK either way, right? I will conditionally agree with you. If none of your art extends beyond the background tile shape, like it does in most hexagonal strategy games, it doesn't matter, since with either method you will have the same net result.

However, with isometric maps, it is quite rare to have graphics that do not extend outside the basic tile shape, which means that the order of layer rendering does have an impact on the map's final appearance.

A More Efficient Tile Blitting Algorithm

Up until this point, every single isometric application we've written has drawn the entire map every frame. After chapters and chapters of doing this, I'm telling you not to do it anymore. It's fine if you have a small number of tiles, not more than a few hundred. But if you have several thousand tiles, and several layers, you will start to see some performance hits if you blit every tile every time.

An old game programming rule is never to draw anything you don't have to. This is harder to do than it sounds, especially in isometric graphics. So, the problem is how to fill in the screen (or, really, any rectangular area) with isometric tiles and sprites without drawing more tiles than you have to?

The answer lies in the MouseMap. The MouseMap, you remember, converts screen coordinates into map coordinates. Hence, you can determine what map locations are at the corners of the screen, and, based on those map locations, you can blit only map locations that should appear on the screen. (To be honest, you'll include an extra row or two of tiles because of layering. That's an extra 20 or so tiles—a small price to pay in order to *not* blit 10,000 tiles.)

The main problem with using the MouseMap is that you cannot use it in its current configuration. Whatever corner map locations you pick, they have to be in the same row and column as the other corner. As Figure 16.6 shows, that cannot be done with the current MouseMap. In this figure, the lightly shaded section shows the screen rectangle, and the darkly shaded tiles indicate the tiles found at the corners of the screen space. Plainly, deciding what tiles to blit based on these results is a matter of guesswork, and it would be impossible to come up with a solution that would work in all cases. So, you have to abandon using the MouseMap as-is for an isometric map.

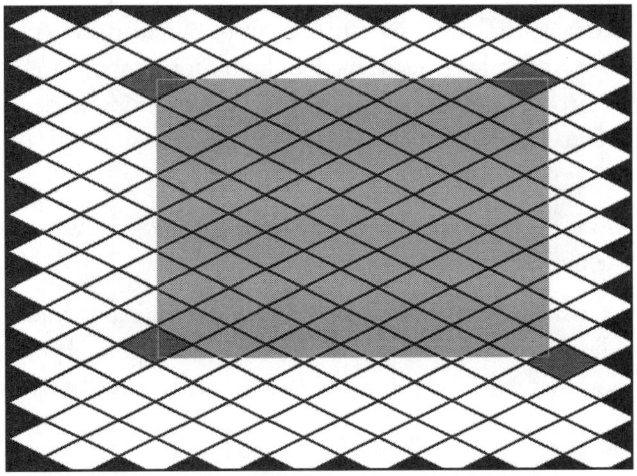

Figure 16.6

Using the MouseMap as-is

However, there is one type of map that can use the MouseMap as is to accomplish this task—the rectangular map. Figure 16.7 shows a rectangular map, with the corner map locations of screen space shown darkly shaded, and the tiles that need to be shown lightly shaded. From this figure, you can see how easy it is to update a rectangular map without writing more tiles than you have to. You simply loop from left to right and top to bottom, blit them, and go.

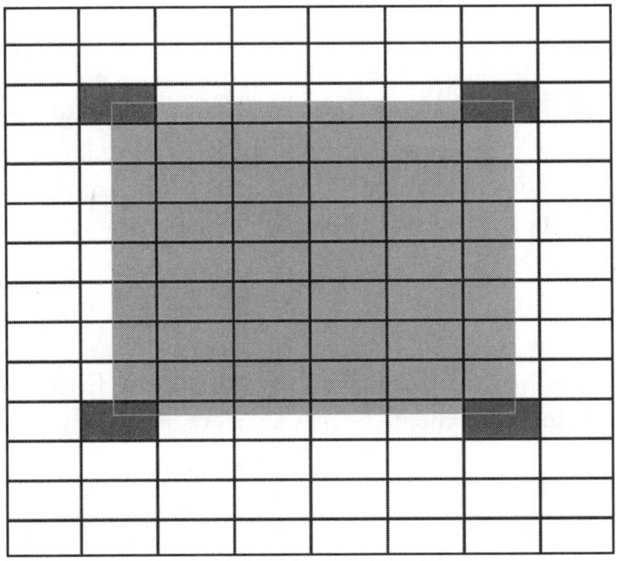

Figure 16.7

Using the MouseMap on a rectangular map

You are dealing with isometric tiles, not rectangular tiles, so this stuff about rectangular tiles can't help you, right? Wrong, of course, or I wouldn't have mentioned it. Think for a moment about how the MouseMap works. First, it takes a screen coordinate and translates it to a world coordinate using a scroller. Next, it changes world coordinates into MouseMap coordinates, both coarse and fine. Now, stop here for a moment.

The phrase *calculate coarse MouseMap coordinates* means nothing more than *divide the area into smaller rectangles.* You need rectangles if you want to limit the number of blits per loop.

Take a look at Figure 16.8, which shows a possible screen space (the inverted rectangular section) amid a number of MouseMap images (which will serve as the rectangular area). It is now quite obvious what tiles you need to blit, but you need a solution that will work no matter where the screen space rectangle is located.

Figure 16.8

MouseMap coordinates

The MouseMap coarse coordinate takes you only halfway to where you want to go, but at least it's a start. You know that if a given rectangular area intersects with the screen space rectangle, at least one of the iso parts that comprise it must be drawn. But, you aren't concerned with the "at least." Instead, you are concerned with "at most." At most, having a given MouseMap rectangle intersecting with your screen space means that you have to redraw five tiles: the central tile and each of the corner tiles. Now you're really getting somewhere.

If you figure out the MouseMap coarse coordinates of each corner, figure out the map location of the center tile, and then move one step in the same direction as the corner (for example, in the northwest corner, move one step northwest), you will have specified a range of tiles that you can draw. Each corner will align with the other corners, and you'll be able to loop through the tiles without a problem. (Well, with only minor problems. You'll have to use the TileWalker quite a bit to make this work right, but I'll get back to that in a minute.)

Figure 16.9 shows a possible screen space, the corner MouseMaps, and the corner isometric tiles. Hopefully, this is a better representation of how this concept works. I know that the wording is a little difficult to understand if you're just reading it. It sounds like a recipe for chocolate chip cookies written in Arabic.

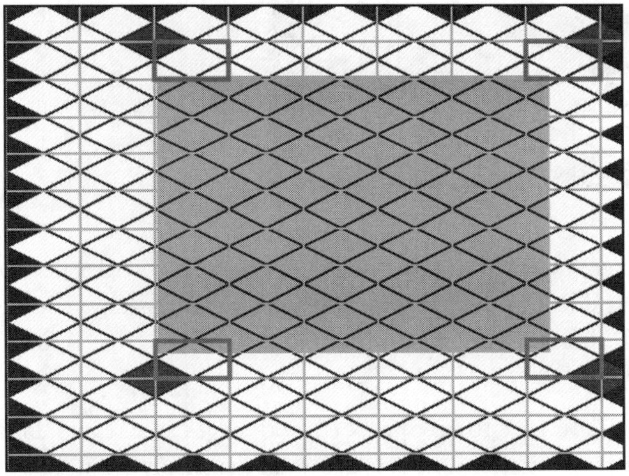

Figure 16.9

Isometric corners

As you can see, the four iso tiles are nicely aligned so that to walk from the northwest corner to the northeast corner, you can simply take eastward steps, as shown in Figure 16.10. So, from a calculated starting location, you simply walk until you hit the other corner.

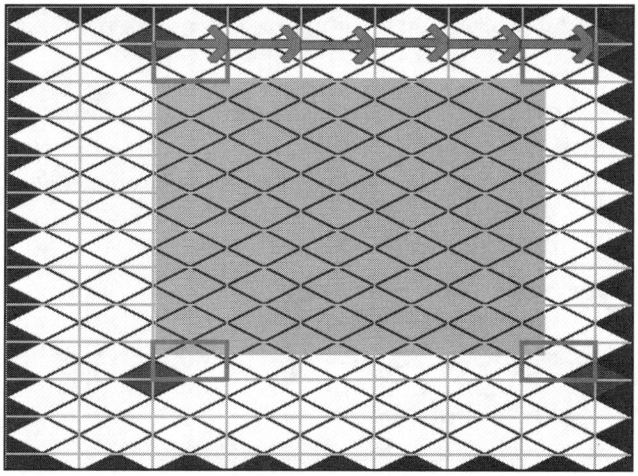

Figure 16.10

Walking left to right

Similarly, you could walk top to bottom, except you would skip alternate rows of tiles that need blitting, so you'll take a zigzag path down each side. On the left side, you will alternately move southeast and southwest. On the right side, you will alternately move southwest and southeast (that is, opposite of the direction you are moving the left edge).

This brings me to an important point. You have to keep track of both edges at all times, because not only do you tilewalk from the left to the right, but afterward you also walk diagonally from that point. In other words, this will involve a whole lot of somewhat messy and hard-to-read code.

I'll show you a programming example soon, but first I want to lay out the algorithm, just in case my explanation up until now has left you wondering.

1. Calculate the coarse MouseMap coordinates for each corner of the screen space.
2. Determine the map location of the central tile of the MouseMap corresponding to the coarse MouseMap coordinate calculated in Step 1 (that is, the map location where the lookup has an `MM_CENTER`).
3. For each of the map locations from Step 2, take one step away from the screen space. This means that the northwest corner takes a step to the northwest, the northeast corner takes a step to the northeast, and so on for southwest and southeast.
4. Set a few control variables: `RowCount` counts the number of rows blitted, starting with 0. `RowStart` and `RowEnd` mark the beginning and end of rows. It starts with the value of the map locations for northwest and northeast, respectively.
5. Start at `RowStart` and blit tiles and move east until `RowEnd` has been blitted.
6. If `RowCount` is even, move `RowStart` to the southeast and `RowEnd` to the southwest. Otherwise, move `RowStart` to the southwest and `RowEnd` to the southeast.
7. Increase `RowCount` by 1.

8. If `RowStart` is at or above the southwest corner, return to Step 4 to blit another row.
9. All the required tile rows have been blitted, but you might want to blit an extra row or two for taller structures that might be on their tiles.

You'll notice something about this method. It doesn't have the words "For Slide Maps," "For Staggered Maps," or "For Diamond Maps," and well it should not. This algorithm is independent of map type, and it will work for any of them. The only issue you should be wary of is nonexistent tiles. The map location found by the MouseMap might not be within the map's range, so you need a "reality check" before going ahead and blitting the tile in question.

Code Example: Reducing the Number of Blits per Frame

Finally, it's time for a programming example. Load up IsoHex16_3.cpp. If you are still a little confused by the explanations so far, this example is a concrete application of what I've been discussing. The first thing I'd like to point out about IsoHex16_3.cpp is that it is rather similar to IsoHex16_1.cpp. It uses tile scale layering, for one, since that makes it easier to show the rendering loop. The second thing I want to point out is that I have increased the map's size from the 20×40 you saw earlier in the chapter to 200×400, a hundred-fold increase in size.

This brings up the question "Why the size increase?" Well, if you were to take one of the other examples from this chapter and increase the map similarly, you would see a drastic reduction in performance. In other words, it would be incredibly slow. Don't take my word for it, though. Go ahead and load up one of the other examples, change the map size to 200×400, and run it. No, really—go ahead. I can wait.

Back? Good. Notice how slow that was? When I did it, it seemed to take ages to scroll even a slight amount. That's because the program is blitting every map location every frame. With 20×40, at an average of two blits per map location, that is 1,600 blits per frame, which most computers today can handle without too much of a problem. However, increasing that to 160,000 blits per frame causes such a performance hit that you might be tempted to go back to your day job.

With the algorithm I've been talking about, you can reduce the number of blits per frame so that only those tiles that need to be blitted to the screen will be blitted. (Actually, for good measure, you throw in a few extras around the edges, but a few extra blits isn't 160,000.)

First, I'm going to show some rough figures. You are currently using a 640×480 display mode and tiles that are 64×32. If your tiles took up the entire 64×32, you would need to blit only 15 rows of 10 columns each. Your tiles overlap, and each row is offset by only half a tile's height, so you really need about 10×30 map locations blitted per frame. For the bordering tiles, you have to expand this by one tile in each direction, so you end up with 12×32 map locations that probably should be blitted per frame. With an average of two blits per map location, this makes for 12×32×2 or 768 blits per frame, which is less than 1 percent of the 160,000 for a 200×400 map, and half of the figure for a 20×40 map.

In conclusion, this is something you *definitely* want to do. So let's do it. Most of IsoHex16_3.cpp is the same as the other examples, as far as how it is initialized, how it is cleaned up, and how it responds to various events. The only real difference is the rendering loop, which takes place during `Prog_Loop`.

The rendering loop has two parts. First is the preparatory stage, in which you use the MouseMap to figure out what map locations bound the area you want to blit. Second is the rendering loop itself, which loops between these calculated locations and draws the images. I should warn you that some of this code is a little on the "evil" side, meaning that it might at first look a little strange and doesn't necessarily follow good programming practice. Don't let that deter you. At least it's fast!

Preparatory Stage

The preparatory stage calculates the corners from which you will be looping in the rendering loop. Each corner is calculated separately and uses calculations in the same way, just with different starting positions. I'll show only the upper-left corner calculation and then tell you what is different for the other corners.

```
//screen point
ptScreen.x=Scroller.GetScreenSpace()->left;
ptScreen.y=Scroller.GetScreenSpace()->top;
```

Here, you start with the screen coordinate that corresponds to the upper-left corner of the screen space. In this case it is (0,0). I could have just used 0s, but I wanted to show that this method can be used for any rectangular area. Hint: this is important information for later in this chapter.

```
//change into world coordinate
ptWorld=Scroller.ScreenToWorld(ptScreen);
//adjust by mousemap reference point
ptWorld.x-=MouseMap.GetReferencePoint()->x;
ptWorld.y-=MouseMap.GetReferencePoint()->y;
```

Next, I translated these coordinates into world space and adjusted them by the MouseMap's reference point. As you can see, I am using a method very similar to the method of mousemapping that I introduced in Part I.

```
//calculate coarse coordinates
ptCoarse.x=ptWorld.x/MouseMap.GetWidth();
ptCoarse.y=ptWorld.y/MouseMap.GetHeight();
```

Next, on to more mousemapping stuff. These are the calculations of the coarse MouseMap coordinates, which you need to find the MouseMap's central tile.

```
//adjust for negative remainders
if(ptWorld.x%MouseMap.GetWidth()<0) ptCoarse.x—;
if(ptWorld.y%MouseMap.GetHeight()<0) ptCoarse.y—;
```

You've seen this before. You have to adjust for negative world coordinates.

```
//set map point to 0,0
ptMap.x=0;
ptMap.y=0;
//do eastward tilewalk
ptMap=TileWalker.TileWalk(ptMap,ISO_EAST);
ptMap.x*=ptCoarse.x;
ptMap.y*=ptCoarse.x;
//assign ptmap to corner point
ptCornerUpperLeft.x=ptMap.x;
ptCornerUpperLeft.y=ptMap.y;
```

Okay, this is where I start to deviate from normal mousemapping algorithms. You start with a map point of (0,0) and retrieve from the TileWalker by how much a step to the east will change it. Then you multiply by the coarse coordinate's x location. This serves the same purpose as doing a loop with single tilewalks to the east. An eastward walk is always consistent, no matter what type of iso map you are using, so this manner of doing a multi-tilewalk is acceptable. However, I still don't suggest using this method for diagonal directions. The results of the multiplication are assigned to the corner point variable.

```
//reset ptmap to 0,0
ptMap.x=0;
ptMap.y=0;
//do southward tilewalk
ptMap=TileWalker.TileWalk(ptMap,ISO_SOUTH);
ptMap.x*=ptCoarse.y;
ptMap.y*=ptCoarse.y;
//add ptmap to corner point
ptCornerUpperLeft.x+=ptMap.x;
ptCornerUpperLeft.y+=ptMap.y;
```

Here, you use a similar idea with the southward tilewalk, after first clearing out the map location. This time you add the value to the corner point variable. South is another direction in which the walker is always consistent.

So, you now have the central tile of the MouseMap that corresponds to the upper-left corner of the screen space. The rest of the corners are calculated in a similar way, just starting with a different screen coordinate at the top. After you've calculated all the corners, walk one step away from the screen space, as shown in the following code snippet:

```
//tilewalk from corners
ptCornerUpperLeft=TileWalker.TileWalk(ptCornerUpperLeft,ISO_NORTHWEST);
ptCornerUpperRight=TileWalker.TileWalk(ptCornerUpperRight,ISO_NORTHEAST);
```

```
ptCornerLowerLeft=TileWalker.TileWalk(ptCornerLowerLeft,ISO_SOUTHWEST);
ptCornerLowerRight=TileWalker.TileWalk(ptCornerLowerRight,ISO_SOUTHEAST);
```

Now you have map locations guaranteed to be at least partially outside the screen space, and your calculations are complete. You're ready to render!

Rendering Loop

The preparatory-stage code wasn't too terrible, right? It's pretty straightforward, I think. It just has a lot of lines. This next bit might not seem nearly as straightforward. Since you have no way of knowing where the corners are, and no way of knowing what map type is being used for the map, this means that you also don't know how many steps to the east the upper-right corner is from the upper-left corner. Nor do you know how many steps south the lower-left corner is from the lower-right corner. Not knowing these things is both good and bad. The good part is that you don't actually have to know in order to render correctly. That means that this method will work with any map type and any screen size, or even any portion of the screen you want. The bad part is that it makes the code kind of strange to look at. Check it out:

```
//set up rows
ptRowStart=ptCornerUpperLeft;
ptRowEnd=ptCornerUpperRight;
//start rendering loops
for(;;)//"infinite" loop
{
      //set current point to rowstart
      ptCurrent=ptRowStart;
      //render a row of tiles
      for(;;)//'infinite' loop
      {
            //check for valid point. if valid, render
            if(ptCurrent.x>=0 && ptCurrent.y>=0 &&
                  ptCurrent.x<MAPWIDTH && ptCurrent.y<MAPHEIGHT)
            {
                  //valid, so render
                  ptScreen=TilePlotter.PlotTile(ptCurrent);//plot tile
                  ptScreen=Scroller.WorldToScreen(ptScreen);//world->screen
                  tsBack.PutTile(lpddsBack,ptScreen.x,
                        ptScreen.y,0);//put background tile
                  if(iMap[ptCurrent.x][ptCurrent.y])//check for tree
                  {
                        tsShadow.PutTile(lpddsBack,ptScreen.x,
                              ptScreen.y,0);//put shadow
                        tsTree.PutTile(lpddsBack,ptScreen.x,ptScreen.y,0);//put
```

```
tree
                    }
                }
                //check if at end of row. if we are, break out of inner loop
                if(ptCurrent.x==ptRowEnd.x && ptCurrent.y==ptRowEnd.y) break;
                //walk east to next tile
                ptCurrent=TileWalker.TileWalk(ptCurrent,ISO_EAST);
        }
        //check to see if we are at the last row. if we are, break out of loop
        if(ptRowStart.x==ptCornerLowerLeft.x && ptRowStart.y==ptCornerLowerLeft.y)
break;
        //move the row start and end points, based on the row number
        if(dwRowCount&1)
        {
                //odd
                //start moves SW, end moves SE
                ptRowStart=TileWalker.TileWalk(ptRowStart,ISO_SOUTHWEST);
                ptRowEnd=TileWalker.TileWalk(ptRowEnd,ISO_SOUTHEAST);
        }
        else
        {
                //even
                //start moves SE, end moves SW
                ptRowStart=TileWalker.TileWalk(ptRowStart,ISO_SOUTHEAST);
                ptRowEnd=TileWalker.TileWalk(ptRowEnd,ISO_SOUTHWEST);
        }
        //increase the row number
        dwRowCount++;
}
```

What might throw you is that there are two nested infinite `for` loops (the `for(;;)`, which does the same thing as a `while(true)`). Now that you've seen it all at once, you're probably saying, "Huh?" and perhaps checking how strong your keyboard is by hitting your head on it a few times. It's weird code, and I didn't have fun debugging it, I can tell you. Trust me, there were plenty of bugs.

I'm going to change the way these loops look so that I can explain them a little better. First, I'll tackle the outer loop:

```
//set up rows
ptRowStart=ptCornerUpperLeft;
ptRowEnd=ptCornerUpperRight;
```

This sets up the two ends of the tile rows. You start at the top and move down. The ptRowStart variable contains the west end of the row, and the ptRowEnd variable contains the east end of the row.

```
//start rendering loops
for(;;)//"infinite" loop
{
```

Oh joy! You've started your outer "infinite" loop. Since the loop has no exit condition, at some point you need to have a method of determining that you are done and use break to get out of it.

```
	//set current point to rowstart
	ptCurrent=ptRowStart;
```

The ptCurrent variable keeps track of the map location that you are currently rendering. With each new row, you set it to ptRowStart and then move eastward from there.

```
	//render a row of tiles
	RenderRow();//this replaces the inner loop
```

RenderRow isn't a real function. It just replaces the inner loop, which renders each tile and then moves eastward until ptRowEnd is reached.

```
	//check to see if we are at the last row. if we are, break out of loop
	if(ptRowStart.x==ptCornerLowerLeft.x && ptRowStart.y==ptCornerLowerLeft.y)
break;
```

This is the exit condition. If the current value of ptRowStart is the same as the lower-left corner of the tile range, you are done. This check is done after the row is rendered to ensure that you get all the rows blitted.

```
	//move the row start and end points, based on the row number
	UpdateRowEnds();//this code replaces the row start and row end movement
code
```

There is also no UpdateRowEnds function. This just replaces the code used to modify the row's start and end variables. I'll explain it in better detail later; it's different depending on whether the dwRowCount variable is odd or even.

```
	//increase the row number
	dwRowCount++;
}
```

Finally, you increase dwRowCount, which affects the behavior of UpdateRowEnds. dwRowCount starts at 0.

So, now the outer loop is demystified. On to the inner loop (the code replaced by `RenderRow()` in the inner loop):

```
//render a row of tiles
for(;;)//'infinite' loop
{
```

Ah, the inner "infinite" loop. You already have `ptCurrent` initialized to `ptRowStart`, so you can work with it from there.

```
	//check for valid point. if valid, render
	if(ptCurrent.x>=0 && ptCurrent.y>=0 &&
		ptCurrent.x<MAPWIDTH && ptCurrent.y<MAPHEIGHT)
	{
		//valid, so render
		RenderTile();//replaces actual tile rendering code
	}
```

The first check you have to do is to make sure that `ptCurrent` is an actual tile in the map, which means it has to be at least 0 and less than the height. If the point falls within the proper range, you can go ahead and render it. The `RenderTile` function is a replacement for the actual tile-rendering code.

```
	//check if at end of row. if we are, break out of inner loop
	if(ptCurrent.x==ptRowEnd.x && ptCurrent.y==ptRowEnd.y) break;
```

Just as you needed an exit condition to get out of the outer loop, you also need one here in the inner loop. In this case, check to see if `ptCurrent` equals `ptRowEnd`. If it does, break out of the loop.

```
	//walk east to next tile
	ptCurrent=TileWalker.TileWalk(ptCurrent,ISO_EAST);
}
```

Last, walk to the next tile, taking a step to the east, and continue the row. This algorithm isn't nearly as bad as it appears, once you start to take it apart and make pseudocode out of it.

The last bit I have to cover is the part of the outer loop that was replaced by `UpdateRowEnds()`. Thankfully, it doesn't include another infinite `for` loop!

```
if(dwRowCount&1)
{
	//odd
	//start moves SW, end moves SE
	ptRowStart=TileWalker.TileWalk(ptRowStart,ISO_SOUTHWEST);
	ptRowEnd=TileWalker.TileWalk(ptRowEnd,ISO_SOUTHEAST);
```

```
}
else
{
        //even
        //start moves SE, end moves SW
        ptRowStart=TileWalker.TileWalk(ptRowStart,ISO_SOUTHEAST);
        ptRowEnd=TileWalker.TileWalk(ptRowEnd,ISO_SOUTHWEST);
}
```

This is probably the most straightforward part of the rendering loop. This bit of code is called after a row has been rendered. If you are on an odd row (`dwRowCount&1!=0`), you have to move the ends of the row outward (`ptRowStart` to the southwest and `ptRowEnd` to the southeast). If you are on an even row, you move inward instead. This gives you a zigzag in the southerly direction, which is what you want.

Now you've got an algorithm that limits the blitting in your rendering loop to a manageable number of tiles. However, it should not satisfy you. Sure, it blits only those tiles that really need it, but ask yourself this question: Frame by frame, how many map locations really change and really need to be redrawn? The answer is just one, unless you're scrolling. When scrolling, you need to update more of the map since everything moves, but there are also ways of limiting that.

In addition, are the calculations in the "preparatory stage" really necessary for all four corners? Couldn't you just calculate an offset for the other four corners based on the upper-left?The fact of the matter is that there are many things you can do to optimize this method and optimize your isometric engine in general. And yes, you will do all of these things before you are done.

There's something I want to point out about IsoHex16_3.cpp before we move on. Next time you run the program, start scrolling to the right slowly, at maybe one or two pixels per frame. While you are scrolling, keep watching the left side of the screen. You will see that as you scroll, certain tree shadows vanish before they are fully off the screen. If you then scroll back to the left, you will see these same shadows suddenly appear (you can see the same thing happen if you scroll up or down and watch the bottom of the screen). This is yet another rendering problem with isometric graphics. Since some of the images extend beyond the tile, you sometimes have to blit for areas that aren't actually on-screen in order to avoid the sudden appearance and disappearance of images. After all, you want the user to think that the screen is just a little camera into this isometric world and have a consistent picture no matter where that camera is located.

So, how can you avoid this problem? Well, to fix the left-right scrolling problem, you could move the upper-left and lower-left corners one tile to the west. Yes, you will have to blit a few more tiles this way, maybe an extra 30 or so, but the cost will be well worth it. Similarly, to solve the up-down scrolling problem, you could move the lower-left and lower-right corners south by one tile. Again, blit a few more tiles for added realism.

If you have exceptionally tall or wide images, you might want to extend the corners farther. This calls for some judgment on your part. Do you use an exceptionally tall image? Or do you split it into two smaller images and place each image to get the illusion of a very tall structure instead? The choice is yours. Either way has its pluses and minuses.

Summary

In this chapter, you broke out of your shell, so to speak. You took the basics from Part I and started to mold them into something real. Your journey is far from over, but hopefully you are starting to see what you can do with this isometric stuff. You've explored layering and optimizing the rendering loop, both of which are fundamental if you ever plan on writing an isometric engine or game that really performs well.

CHAPTER 17

Further Rendering Optimizations

- Get Rid of Blt
- Moving to BltFast
- Whittling Down the Blits er Frame
- Building Crenderer

In the last chapter, I introduced you to the idea that you can render faster by not rendering everything all the time. In this chapter, I'll take this concept even further—in fact, to the very limits of what you can do (at least, within the bounds of using DirectX). You'll add a new component, the map renderer, to your list of isometric components. In any case, it should be an interesting experience, so let's get going!

Get Rid of Blt

You've been using the `CTileSet` class for a while now, and you've gotten some very good mileage out of it. It serves well as a tile/sprite blitter. However, it relies on `IDirectDrawSurface7::Blt` to do the rendering and uses `IDirectDrawClipper` to do the clipping.

This, my friend, is just not acceptable. You have all the information you need to do your own clipping—namely, `rcScreenSpace` in the `CScroller` class. You also have the extent rectangles of all your tiles stored in your `CTileSet`. Surely, by using some simple WIN32 `RECT` functions, you can eliminate the need for a clipper, and also for `Blt`, and replace both of these with the faster `BltFast`.

Take a gander at Figure 17.1. On the left, a source image is being blitted onto a larger image on the right. The dark boxes represent the bounding rectangles. When you blit a partially visible image onto a surface, the clipper is what decides which portion of the image is actually blitted, and which portion is not, based on the clipping area with which you've made your clipper.

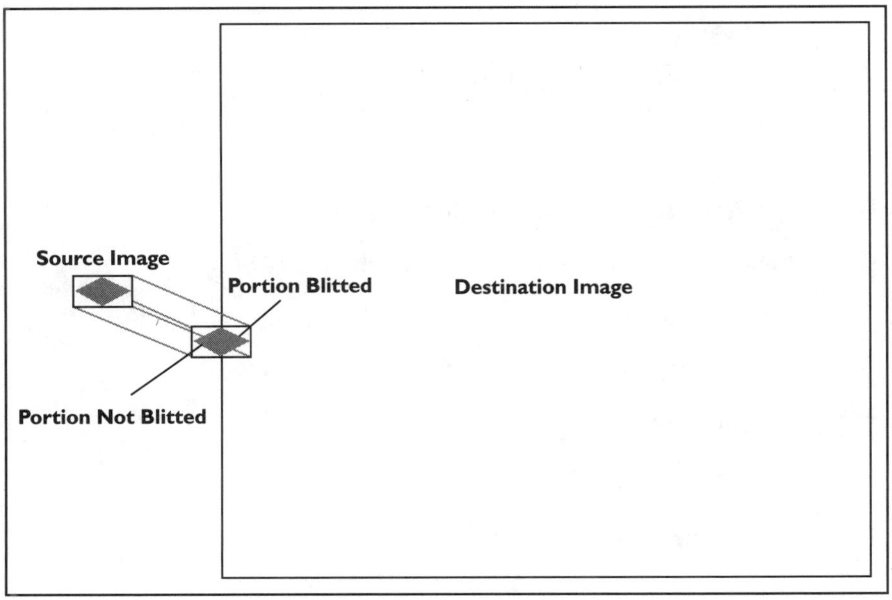

Figure 17.1

The current state of affairs: using `Blt` with a clipper

Consider this: `IDirectDrawClipper` is a general-purpose object, and early on I told you that general-purpose objects are not necessarily good for performance. The example I used at the time was GDI, but the same idea applies here. You have no idea how a clipper works internally; it might be the worst-performing code ever written. I doubt that, but it's possible.

Also, you don't really need a clipper. Your clipping area is a single rectangle. If it were a number of rectangles, you might be justified in using a clipper, but you should be able to work with a single rectangle by yourself. And that is precisely what you will do.

First, take a look at how you will do this. When using `Blt`, you have to specify a source rectangle and a destination rectangle. With `BltFast`, you only have to specify a destination point and a source rectangle. Take a brief look at `BltFast` as a refresher:

```
HRESULT IDirectDrawSurface7::BltFast(
  DWORD dwX,
  DWORD dwY,
  LPDIRECTDRAWSURFACE7 lpDDSrcSurface,
  LPRECT lpSrcRect,
  DWORD dwTrans
);
```

As with all DirectX member functions, `BltFast` returns an `HRESULT`, which contains either `DD_OK`, meaning that no error occurred, or a `DDERR_*` constant, meaning that a problem was encountered. Table 17.1 explains the parameter list.

Table 17.1 BltFast Parameter List

Parameter	Purpose
dwX	The destination coordinate for the left of the image
dwY	The destination coordinate for the top of the image
lpDDSrcSurface	The source surface
lpSrcRect	The source rectangle
dwTrans	Flags specifying how the blit is to occur

The `dwTrans` parameter is one or more of the flags listed in Table 17.2.

Table 17.2 Flags for dwTrans

Flag	Purpose
DDBLTFAST_DESTCOLORKEY	The blit is to use the destination color key
DDBLTFAST_NOCOLORKEY	The blit is not to use any sort of color key
DDBLTFAST_SRCCOLORKEY	The blit is to use the source color key
DDBLTFAST_WAIT	Instructs DirectDraw to wait until the blit is completed

Mainly, you are interested in using DDBLTFAST_SRCCOLORKEY and DDBLTFAST_WAIT, since you have transparent areas in almost all your isometric images.

Moving to BltFast

Now your task is to figure out what to put into these parameters. You already know how to find a destination rectangle for the entire image. Simply take the extent rectangle and add the destination point to it.

```
//dstX,dstY are a destination point
//rcExt is the extent rect for the entire image
//rcSrc is the sourc rect for the entire image
//rcDst is the destination rect for the entire image
CopyRect(&rcDst,&rcExt);//copy the extent rect into the destination rect
OffsetRect(&rcDst,dstX,dstY);//offset the destination rect by the destination
point
```

I'd like to point out something here that will help you a little later. All three RECTs (rcSrc, rcDst, and rcExt) have the same height and width (right-left and bottom-top come up with the same number for each RECT). Hence, there is a number by which you can offset each of these RECTs to change it into the exact same value as another RECT. This little tidbit will help you.

```
//changeX, changeY is the difference between the left and top of rcDst and
rcSrc.
//adding changeX and changeY to any destination pixel will convert it
//to a source pixel
changeX=rcSrc.left-rcDst.left;
changeY=rcSrc.top-rcDst.top;
```

Skeptical? I know I would be. Very well—I'll prove that this will work. The following looks somewhat like code, but it is not.

```
//left
rcDst.left+changeX=
rcDst.left+rcSrc.left-rcDst.left=
rcSrc.left

//right
rcDest.right+changeX=
rcDst.right+rcSrc.left-rcDst.left=
rcSrc.left+(rcDst.right-rcDst.left)=
rcSrc.left+WIDTH=
rcSrc.right
```

Do I need to go on and do top and bottom too? Or do you trust me now?

Your next task is to clip the destination rectangle. To do this, you need a rectangle to clip, which I will conveniently supply in the form of `rcClip`. When you do this for real, this will be `rcScreenSpace` from a `CScroller` object.

```
//determine the clipped destination coordinate
//rcDstClipped will contain the clipped destination
IntersectRect(&rcDstClipped,&rcDst,&rcClip);
```

Now you have your clipped destination `RECT`; you are most of the way there. You just have to figure out the clipped source `RECT` and perform the `BltFast`, and you're done. Of course, you first have to check to make sure that `rcDstClipped` is not an empty rectangle. If it is, there is no reason to proceed.

```
//check to see if clipped destination is empty
if(!IsRectEmpty(&rcDstClipped))
{
	//non-empty rectangle, so calculate clipped source rect
	CopyRect(&rcSrcClipped,&rcDstClipped);//copy clipped destination
	                                       //to clipped source
	OffsetRect(&rcSrcClipped,changeX,changeY);//change to source coords
	//perform the bltfast
	lpddsDst-
>BltFast(rcDstClipped.left,rcDstClipped.top,lpddsSrc,&rcSrcClipped,
	        DDBLTFAST_SRCCOLORKEY | DDBLTFAST_WAIT);
}
```

That's it! You're done! At first glance, this might look like a lot of code, but it really isn't. Mainly, all you're doing is adding integers together and assigning integers, which on any machine is pretty quick, and takes a negligible amount of time. The bottleneck in any graphically intensive application (like all the isometric sample programs) is the rendering, not the calculations.

A BltFast Example

What's next? Well, it's time to put this algorithm into practice by extending the `CTileSet` class. Load up IsoHex17_1.cpp, where I have done just that. This example is based on IsoHex16_3.cpp.

I didn't want to completely redesign the `CTileSet` class; I just wanted to extend it. I chose to do so by adding a member function called `ClipTile`. The declaration is shown here:

```
void CTileSet::ClipTile(
        LPDIRECTDRAWSURFACE7 lpddsDst,
        RECT* prcClip,
        int xDst,
        int yDst,
        int iTileNum
);
```

This member function returns no values. Table 17.3 explains the parameters.

Table 17.3 ClipTile Parameters

Parameter	Purpose
`lpddsDst`	The destination surface to which the `BltFast` will occur
`prcClip`	A pointer to a `RECT` that will be used for clipping
`xDst`	The destination x-coordinate for the tile (used to calculate the destination `RECT`)
`yDst`	The destination y-coordinate for the tile (used to calculate the destination `RECT`)
`iTileNum`	The tile number to be blitted

In a nutshell, `ClipTile` is just like `PutTile`, but with an added parameter, `prcClip`, which is what the function uses to perform its clipping. Now, take a look at the function itself.

```
void CTileSet::ClipTile(LPDIRECTDRAWSURFACE7 lpddsDst,RECT* prcClip,
      int xDst,int yDst,int iTileNum)
{
      //source and dest rects
      RECT rcSrc;
      RECT rcDst;
      //changex and changey
      int changeX;
      int changeY;
      //get the destination rectangle
      CopyRect(&rcDst,&GetTileList()[iTileNum].rcDstExt);
      OffsetRect(&rcDst,xDst,yDst);
      //calculate changex and changey
      changeX=GetTileList()[iTileNum].rcSrc.left-rcDst.left;
      changeY=GetTileList()[iTileNum].rcSrc.top-rcDst.top;
      //clip the destination rect to the clipping rect
      IntersectRect(&rcDst,&rcDst,prcClip);
      //check to see if the destination rectangle is not empty
      if(!IsRectEmpty(&rcDst))
      {
            //copy dest rect to source
            CopyRect(&rcSrc,&rcDst);
            //offset the source rect by changex/y
            OffsetRect(&rcSrc,changeX,changeY);
            //do the bltfast
            lpddsDst->BltFast(rcDst.left, rcDst.top, GetDDS(), &rcSrc,
                  DDBLTFAST_SRCCOLORKEY | DDBLTFAST_WAIT);
      }
}
```

This function uses the exact same algorithm outlined earlier, just with fewer actual `RECT`s. I use only two because... well, that's the fewest I could get away with. Allocating local variables takes time, so I wanted to allocate as few as possible. Admittedly, the allocation doesn't take very much time, but why hurt yourself when you don't have to, right?

There are a few other minor changes in IsoHex17_1.cpp. First, the clipper is gone. In order to use `BltFast`, you cannot use a clipper. That is just the way of things. Your goal was to get rid of the clipper anyway, right? Another change has to do with the rendering loop, and is in the form of replacing the calls to `PutTile` with calls to `ClipTile`. An example is shown here:

```
tsBack.ClipTile(lpddsBack,Scroller.GetScreenSpace(),ptScreen.x,ptScreen.y,0);
//put background tile
```

This line in particular replaces the call to `PutTile` that you previously used to draw the background tile. No big deal; I'm just moving to the new (better) form of tile blitting.

You'll probably see a few other minor changes as well. When scrolling, you no longer have the magically appearing and disappearing images on the left and bottom of the screen. The code responsible for that miracle is as follows:

```
//move left corners to the west by one
ptCornerUpperLeft=TileWalker.TileWalk(ptCornerUpperLeft,ISO_WEST);
ptCornerLowerLeft=TileWalker.TileWalk(ptCornerLowerLeft,ISO_WEST);
//move the lower corners to the south by one
ptCornerLowerLeft=TileWalker.TileWalk(ptCornerLowerLeft,ISO_SOUTH);
ptCornerLowerRight=TileWalker.TileWalk(ptCornerLowerRight,ISO_SOUTH);
```

Actually, I mentioned this concept in the last chapter; we just didn't get around to actually doing it. Simply move the left side one tile to the west and the bottom one tile to the south to give yourself a consistent picture no matter how you scroll.

Last, there is a very, very minor change that ironically is the most noticeable of all. I changed the screen space. Instead of being the entire screen, it is now only 480×480. There was a purpose to this change, of course. I wanted to show just how good our little `ClipTile` function is. Not a single pixel is plotted outside the screen space, which is the `RECT` you supply to your `ClipTile` function. This will have important ramifications later.

Whittling Down the Blits per Frame

So you've successfully passed your first hurdle—eliminating the less-than-optimal `Blt` and replacing it with the more optimal `BltFast`. This is a huge win for our team! (Yay team!) You still have a bit of work ahead, though. Next, I'll show you how to even further reduce your blitting overhead by using off-screen frame buffers. You might be thinking, "But I already have a back buffer." Yes, you do. The back buffer has served you well by allowing you to go smoothly from one frame to another without flicker. As you progress, the back buffer will continue to serve you in this capacity.

However, there is a problem with the back buffer. It has to be completely redrawn for every frame. Well, for any frame in which scrolling has occurred, which, in the examples so far, might as well be every frame. The problem stems from the fact that after the main surface is flipped, the contents of the back buffer are from two frames ago. If you have been scrolling for the last two frames, the back buffer might as well be full of random pixels, because it will do you no good. If there has been no scrolling during the past two frames, the contents of the back buffer should be the same—unless you just clicked to add or remove a tree, in which case it isn't quite the same.

See what I mean? Keeping track of the contents of two frames ago is a logistical nightmare, which is why up until this point you have just been redrawing the whole darn thing. It's just easier. Unfortunately, it is also quite costly. It means that you have to blit all the tiles that are in or partially in the screen space, even if it doesn't need redrawing. As I've said before, the first rule is that you never blit when you don't have to, if you want good performance.

So, concerning the additional frame buffer I've been discussing, as I said earlier, it is an off-screen surface that is the same size as the screen space. Since the frame buffer is off-screen and does not flip, the image data on it remains consistent from frame to frame, which means that you know what's on it at any given time. By knowing what is on the frame buffer, you can then manipulate the image data into the new frame, usually without redrawing the entire thing.

Frame Buffer Scrolling

The first task I'm going to talk about for the frame buffer is scrolling. In any isometric game/engine/utility, scrolling is a must. More than that, scrolling quickly is a must. Have you ever played a game where the scrolling is slow or stuttered? You know what I mean... you move the mouse to the side to scroll, and nothing seems to happen for a moment, and then you are suddenly halfway across the playing field. It's annoying—you don't want to have something like that in your game. You want to have a nice, smooth scroll. Sometimes it's just not possible, especially with outdated video hardware and lower-end machines, but that's no reason not to try!

If you have static data on an off-screen surface, most of your scrolling is very easy. When you scroll, you can simply move a portion of the frame left, right, up, down—however the scroll is occurring. Figure 17.2 depicts the area that is unaffected by a scroll to the right (unaffected meaning that it doesn't need to be totally redrawn). Hence, you can use a large `BltFast` to do the majority of your scroll, rather than the individual tiles. Then you simply need to fill in the left edge of the image with new data to complete the current frame. A similar idea can be applied to left, up, or down scrolls.

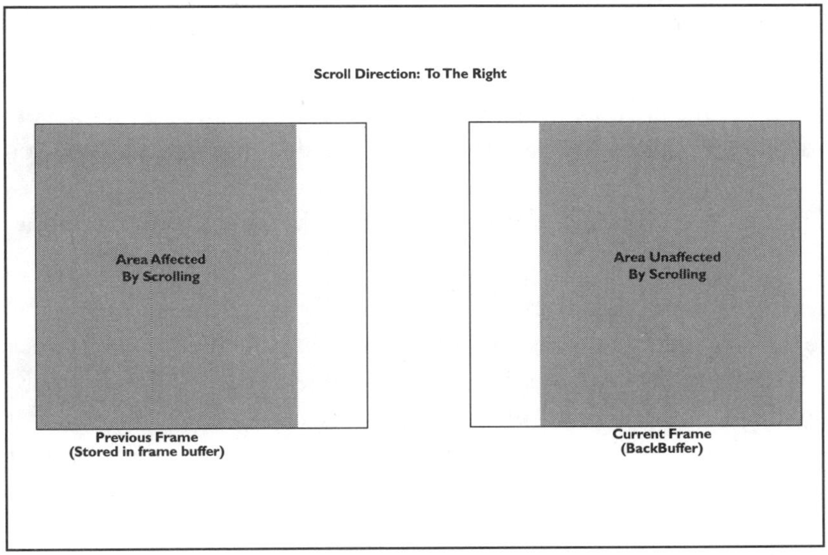

Figure 17.2

Bulk scrolling

Update Rectangles

Ah, if only it were that simple! The fact of the matter is that there very well could be portions of the area that do need to be redrawn. There might be unit movement, animated objects, a tree added or removed, or any number of things. This is not a problem that will keep you from your task, however. You'll just have to get creative.

Say, for instance, that there is a tile smack dab in the middle of that otherwise "unaffected" area that needs to be redrawn. You've worked too hard to go back to redrawing the entire frame. So, you won't. Instead, you will figure out what tiles need to be redrawn using the same method you used to selectively blit the tiles to the screen. You'll just use a smaller clipping rectangle. I told you that algorithm would come in handy!

So, you'll do with this image what you did with the entire screen. You'll determine what rectangle to use for clipping, calculate where the corner tiles of the range are, and blit the tiles in that range. Simple enough, right? But where does that rectangle for clipping come from? You only know what tiles need to be updated. You have no idea how many neighboring tiles will be affected. You can figure it out, though.

The answer stems from the tiles themselves. Each one has its own extent `RECT`, right? Well, you can safely assume that the most complicated thing you might do with all these images is blit every single one of them onto a single tile location. You're looking at me like I'm crazy. I'm not. It's true, in this case, since you have only three tiles—the background, the shadow, and the tree. True, in a more complicated tile map, with hordes of objects, units, people, buildings, and so on, you probably wouldn't blit all of them to a single tile, but I'm just pointing out the most extreme case.

If you blit every single tile/sprite to a single location, what is the smallest RECT that will contain them? Well, it's the union of all the extent RECTs, offset by the screen space coordinates of the map location. Make sense?

So, you can go through all the tiles of all the tilesets and use UnionRect to come up with the largest possible extent for a given map location. Since your tilesets don't change, you can do this once, right after you load them, and just use that extent RECT to figure out your update areas. Now you can update small areas using your enhanced tile-rendering algorithm, and you're doing fewer blits per frame. All is right with the world. Well, almost.

Look at Figure 17.3, where I have placed some random areas for updating. With multiple update areas, you can just go through the list of update rectangles, rendering them as you go. However, you might not want to do that, and here's why. In the figure, rectangle A is fine, and you can just update it. Rectangles B and C, on the other hand, overlap. If you update each rectangle separately, the update for rectangles B and C will update at least one of the same tiles more than once. Rectangles D and E are yet another case. Parts of them lie outside the screen space. So, what to do?

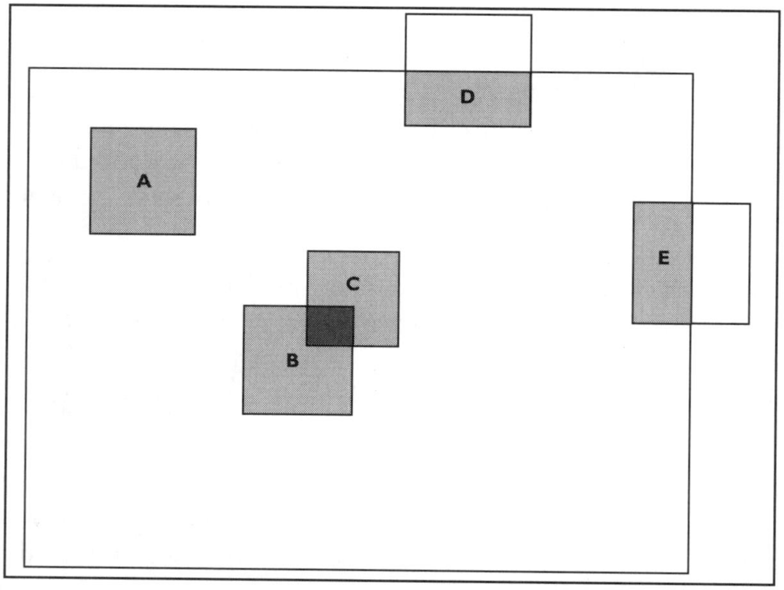

Figure 17.3

Overlapping update areas

In the case of D and E, the answer is simple. Just clip the update rectangles to the screen space, and then update as normal. The answer to B and C is not as simple. One thing you might do is make a union from them. However, that would cause additional tiles to be updated, which means you might as well just be updating the overlapping tiles twice.

The answer to the dilemma is not to immediately update the frame. Instead, somehow mark the map locations for update. The easiest way to do this is to have an array of bools that has the same dimensions as the map array, and to have true indicate that a tile needs updating and false indicate that it does not.

This way, when you add a RECT to be updated, the same tile might be marked several times, but since you aren't blitting yet, you won't be concerned.

After all the update RECTs have been marked in this fashion, you can then scan the entire screen space using your rendering algorithm, but only draw those map locations that are marked for update. This way, a given tile is drawn only once, which is what you want. The way you have it set up now, the frame buffer still has the prior frame on it, and the back buffer has the effects of the scroll on it. When you update the tiles, you should write to the frame buffer, for reasons that will become clear in a moment. After you have updated all the tiles, you then blit each of the update RECTs onto the back buffer so that the back buffer now has the complete current frame. Finally, blit the current frame from the back buffer to the frame buffer, and then go ahead and flip the primary surface.

Do you see why you are updating to the frame buffer rather than the back buffer? It's because when updating, you are using the entire screen space as the clipping RECT instead of the individual update RECTs. Because of this, you will have portions of tiles that spill outside the update rectangle, quite possibly obscuring other tiles. When you then move the update rectangles to the back buffer, you correct this problem.

If you were paying close attention and thinking about overlapping update rectangles, you might have noticed that I just contradicted myself, . When you are blitting the update RECTs from the frame buffer onto the back buffer, you will be blitting the overlapped portion twice. Before you yell "Hypocrite!" and start getting out the pitchfork and torches, give me a chance to explain why I'm allowing this double blitting, but I wouldn't allow drawing the same tile twice. It is a matter of simple arithmetic. Consider two overlapping update RECTs that, for the purposes of this example, have a single map location that needs to be updated for both. If you assume that this map location has a tree and shadow on it, and you update it twice, that is six blits (drawing the background, shadow, and tree each twice). However, if you update the map location only once, that is only three blits. Add to this 2, because the same area is blitted because of the overlap, and that makes 5. This means you've saved yourself one blit! In real situations, the facts become more complicated than what I just showed you here, but it's good enough to show you that I'm not just saying one thing and doing something different.

An Isometric Rendering Class

At last, I'm going to bring all the frame buffer stuff together and create a class that will minimize blitting using a frame buffer for scrolling and update rectangles. First, a decision must be made about what information such a class will need, based on the discussion so far.

Right out in front, you know that a rendering class will need two LPDIRECTDRAWSURFACE7 variables—one for the back buffer and one for the frame buffer. You will supply these two things to the class. For optimal tile updates, you need a CScroller, CMouseMap, CTileWalker, and CTilePlotter to do all the calculations for you. You will also supply these things to the class. You have to set them up anyway, so using pointers to them in another component isn't a big deal. Also, you'll need an extent RECT, which you'll have to calculate based on all the tiles/sprites in the application. This might create a little bit of work for you during initialization, but again, this is not a big deal. Since you'll be using update RECTs, you need some way to store a list of RECTs in the class. Unfortunately, you don't know how many RECTs are needed, so you should probably have some way to allocate a number of RECTs that should be sufficient. Because you will rely on an array of boolean values to check whether to update a given map location, you need such an array in the class itself. The update array isn't needed anywhere but within the rendering class, so doing this is OK. Finally, you need a rendering function. This will not be within the class itself, but rather a function that you create outside of the class and give a pointer to it to the renderer. This will be just like what you do with your TilePlotter and TileWalker, only you must always supply the function rather than having it predefined.

Here's a summary of what you need in the way of members of your rendering class:

- Two pointers to DirectDraw surfaces
- Pointers to one of each IsoHexCore component
- An extent rectangle used for calculating update RECTs
- An update RECT buffer of arbitrary size
- A boolean update array of arbitrary size
- A pointer to a rendering function

While we're at it, I could certainly go for two turtledoves and a partridge in a pear tree!

For member functions, you should have nice friendly functions to set all the members of the class, like the frame buffer, back buffer, IsoHexCore components, and so on. In addition, you should have functions to add update RECTs to the update RECT list, and a function to add a tile to the update RECT list (the function would use the extent RECT and the TilePlotter to figure out what RECT is to be added). Also, you should have a function to do the bulk scroll and a function to update the frame (which blits all the update RECTs and resets the renderer for the next frame).

When using the renderer, you should first call the scrolling member function, then add whatever update RECTs are necessary, and then call the update member function. That makes it pretty simple from your side. Because some of the algorithms you are using are quite complex, you definitely want to wrap them up in an easy-to-use class like this!

Building CRenderer

Without further delay, let's get to it. Go ahead and load up IsoHex17_2.cpp. In this example, I have supplied CRenderer in the files IsoRenderer.h and IsoRenderer.cpp.

The code for CRenderer is the most complicated that I've written so far. This is because there are just so many things that have to be examined and calculated for it to work. The declaration of CRenderer looks like the following:

```
//CRenderer Declaration
class CRenderer
{
```

```
public:
	////////////////////
	//members
	////////////////////
	//surfaces
	LPDIRECTDRAWSURFACE7 lpddsBackBuffer;//back buffer
	LPDIRECTDRAWSURFACE7 lpddsFrameBuffer;//frame buffer
	//isohexcore components
	CTilePlotter* pTilePlotter;//plotter
	CTileWalker* pTileWalker;//walker
	CMouseMap* pMouseMap;//mousemap
	CScroller* pScroller;//scroller
	//update RECT list
	RECT* rcUpdateList;//must be allocated
	int iUpdateRectCount;//number of RECTs in the update list
	int iUpdateRectIndex;//stores the next update RECT in the list
	//update map
	bool* bMap;//will be allocated with enough space for the entire map
	int iMapWidth;//width of the map
	int iMapHeight;//height of the map
	//extent rect
	RECT rcExtent;//extent rect, used when adding tiles to the update list
	//rendering function
	RENDERFN RenderFunction;//function used to render a tile

	/////////////////////
	//member functions
	/////////////////////
	//constructor
	CRenderer();
	virtual ~CRenderer();
	//destructor
	//surfaces
	void SetBackBuffer(LPDIRECTDRAWSURFACE7 lpdds);
	void SetFrameBuffer(LPDIRECTDRAWSURFACE7 lpdds);
	//isohexcore components
	void SetPlotter(CTilePlotter* pPlotter);
	void SetWalker(CTileWalker* pWalker);
	void SetMouseMap(CMouseMap* pMMap);
	void SetScroller(CScroller* pScroll);
	//update list
	void SetUpdateRectCount(int iMaxRects);//sets up the rectangle list
```

```
        //update map
        void SetMapSize(int MapWidth,int MapHeight);//sets up the update map
        //rendering functions
        void SetRenderFunction(RENDERFN RendFunc);
        //extent rect
        void SetExtentRect(RECT* rcExt);
        //add rect to list
        void AddRect(RECT* prcAdd);
        void AddTile(int mapx,int mapy);
        //scroll the frame
        void ScrollFrame(int scrollx,int scrolly);
        //update the frame
        void UpdateFrame();
};
```

You can see that this class has far more members than any other class so far. Every single one of them is needed, too. CRenderer takes from you the task of having to calculate updates yourself. I'm going to briefly go over the parts of CRenderer. The actual implementation is something you can look at on your own. I don't have the space to go over it line by line here.

RENDERFN

There is one typedef for the CRenderer class of which you should be aware. Since the entire operation of the class depends on a user-defined rendering function for individual tiles, you need a function pointer type. This is supplied in the form of RENDERFN. Here is the declaration:

```
//rendering function pointer typedef
typedef void (*RENDERFN)(LPDIRECTDRAWSURFACE7 lpddsDst,RECT* rcClip,
      int xDst,int yDst,int xMap,int yMap);
```

By now, you should be quite familiar with function pointer types. In the case of RENDERFN, there are six parameters. Table 17.4 lists these members and their meanings.

Table 17.4 RENDERFN Parameters

Parameter	Purpose
`lpddsDst`	The destination surface. In all cases, this will be whatever surface is being used as the frame buffer.
`rcClip`	A pointer to a clipping rectangle that will be passed along to whatever tilesets are used as the clipping `RECT` for calls to `ClipTile`.
`xDst`	The tile's screen x-coordinate. It is plotted by the renderer.
`yDst`	The tile's screen y-coordinate. It is plotted by the renderer.
`xMap`	The tilemap x-coordinate.
`yMap`	The tilemap y-coordinate.

Data Members

Table 17.5 lists the data members of `CRenderer` and describes their basic purpose. In almost all cases, these members will be supplied by you—the programmer. In the case of `rcUpdateList` and `bMap`, however, you simply supply dimensions, and `CRenderer` does all the memory management for you.

Table 17.5 CRenderer Data Members

Member	Purpose
`lpddsBackBuffer`	Contains a pointer to the back buffer. Used for rendering.
`lpddsFrameBuffer`	Contains a pointer to the frame buffer. Used for rendering.
`pTilePlotter`	Contains a pointer to a TilePlotter. Used for calculations.
`pTileWalker`	Contains a pointer to a TileWalker. Used for calculations.
`pMouseMap`	Contains a pointer to a MouseMap. Used for calculations.
`pScroller`	Contains a pointer to a scroller. Used for calculations.
`rcUpdateList`	A buffer that contains a list of update `RECT`s.
`iUpdateRectCount`	Contains the total number of `RECT`s that can be stored in the update `RECT` buffer.
`iUpdateRectIndex`	An index into the update `RECT` buffer, indicating the next `RECT` to be assigned.
`bMap`	The update buffer, containing boolean values. It's true if a tile must be redrawn and false if it does not need redrawing.
`iMapWidth`	Width of the update buffer.
`iMapHeight`	Height of the update buffer.
`rcExtent`	An extent rectangle to allow calculations of update `RECT`s based on map locations.
`RenderFunction`	A user-supplied rendering function.

All of these members are public and thus can be examined at any time without the use of member functions. Also, this means that you can change the values of any of these members. While this "open" sort of class design is very flexible and gives the programmer (you) a lot of power, the fact remains that for the most part, you don't want to mess with the member functions except when initializing them. Especially stay away from `rcUpdateList`, `bMap`, and their related members.

Member Functions

The member functions of `CRenderer` fall into two main categories: member access and utilization. The member access functions serve a purpose similar to the initialization functions of the IsoHexCore components, meaning that you use them to set up the data members. Generally, you have to do initialization only once. The utilization members, on the other hand, are used every frame.

Member Access Functions

The member access functions of `CRenderer` are listed in Table 17.6, alongside the data member(s) that they set or help calculate. Most of these member access functions can be used multiple times without any problem, but certain ones cannot. I'll point them out to you so that you will be prepared.

Table 17.6 CRenderer Member Access Functions

Member Function	Purpose
`SetBackBuffer`	Sets the surface to use as the back buffer (`lpddsBackBuffer` data member).
`SetFrameBuffer`	Sets the surface to use as the frame buffer (`lpddsFrameBuffer` data member).
`SetPlotter`	Sets a pointer to a TilePlotter (`pTilePlotter` data member).
`SetWalker`	Sets a pointer to a TileWalker (`pTileWalker` data member).
`SetMouseMap`	Sets a pointer to a MouseMap (`pMouseMap` data member).
`SetScroller`	Sets a pointer to a scroller (`pScroller` data member).
`SetUpdateRectCount`	Allocates the update `RECT` list (`rcUpdateList`) and sets the size of the buffer (`iUpdateRectCount`). Sets `iUpdateRectIndex` to 0.
`SetMapSize`	Allocates the update buffer (`bMap`) and sets the width and height of the update buffer (`iMapWidth` and `iMapHeight`).
`SetRenderFunction`	Sets a pointer to a `RENDERFN` (`RenderFunction`).
`SetExtentRect`	Copies a `RECT` into `rcExtent`.

All but two of these member functions can be called any number of times without detrimental effects. The two oddballs, `SetUpdateRectCount` and `SetMapSize`, should not be called more than once. Why not? Because they deal with memory allocation. If called more than once, they will allocate memory twice, without ever deleting the memory that is no longer used. This means you are leaking memory, which is, on the good-bad scale of things, a bad thing. There is no great secret to using the member access functions.

With the exception of SetMapSize, they all take a single parameter. SetMapSize takes two. These member functions are pretty much common sense.

Utilization Member Functions

After 14 data members and 10 member access functions, you might expect there to be approximately the same number of functions to make use of the class on a frame-by-frame basis. Instead, there are only four, one of which is called only very rarely. Table 17.7 lists these functions and their purpose.

Table 17.7 CRenderer Utilization Functions

Function	Purpose
AddRect	Adds an update RECT to the update list
AddTile	Uses a map location to calculate and add an update RECT
ScrollFrame	Scrolls the frame
UpdateFrame	Updates the frame

It's hard to believe, but that's all there is to the CRenderer class. Here's the basic operation per frame:

1. Scroll the frame using ScrollFrame.
2. Add any necessary update RECTs and update tiles that need it using AddRect or AddTile.
3. Update the frame using UpdateFrame.
4. Flip the primary surface.
5. Go make yourself a sandwich. While you're at it, make me one, too. I'm kind of hungry.

I won't go into the ugly details of CRenderer's implementation here. It would easily take up 50 pages or so, and neither of us has that kind of time. Suffice it to say that CRenderer bases most of its code on the more efficient blitting algorithm that was developed in Chapter 16, "Layered Maps and Optimized Rendering." Every time AddRect is called, that RECT is scanned using that algorithm, and the tiles it encompasses are marked for update. When AddTile is called, the coordinates for the tile are used to offset the extent RECT, and the result is sent to AddRect. ScrollFrame does a bulk scroll and adds two update RECTs to the list: one for the x scroll and one for the y scroll (and no, the update RECTs do *not* overlap). The update frame is what does the real work, scanning the entire screen space for marked tiles and sending the information to the rendering function.

A CRenderer Example

Even though I'm not sharing the nitty-gritty details of how I implemented CRenderer, I will show you how I built an example that uses it. IsoHex17_2.cpp is the example in question. This example uses CRenderer, which requires the addition of some global variables.

One extra global exists in the form of LPDIRECTDRAWSURFACE7. Namely, this is your frame buffer. During Prog_Init, I create an off-screen plain surface that is 640 pixels wide and 480 pixels tall (the same size as the back buffer). The other main extra global is an instance of CRenderer, which I have named, of all things, "Renderer."

Initialization

The main change in IsoHex17_2.cpp from IsoHex17_1.cpp is that you have the extra surface (lpddsFrame) and the CRenderer (Renderer). Initializing the frame buffer is a simple one-line deal:

```
//create the frame buffer
lpddsFrame=LPDDS_CreateOffscreen(lpdd,640,480);
```

Woo hoo! Hooray for the DDFuncs library! It makes surface creation not only easy, but fun, too. However, before you can initialize the renderer, first you need to calculate the extent RECT from all your various tile images. This is a simple application of UnionRect, which is as follows:

```
//calculate the extent rect
RECT rcExtent;
//set to background extent
CopyRect(&rcExtent,&tsBack.GetTileList()[0].rcDstExt);
//union with shadow extent
UnionRect(&rcExtent,&rcExtent,&tsShadow.GetTileList()[0].rcDstExt);
//union with tree extent
UnionRect(&rcExtent,&rcExtent,&tsTree.GetTileList()[0].rcDstExt);
```

Pretty easy, I think. First, copy the extent of the background image into your temporary rcExtent variable, and then use UnionRect to merge this with the extent RECTs from the shadow and tree image. If you had more tiles/sprites, you would just loop through them here. To speed up the process, you might decide to add a new member function to CTileSet that takes a union of all the extents in the set. Just an idea. Finally, you initialize all the data members of Renderer, using the member access functions I spoke of earlier.

```
//set up the renderer
Renderer.SetBackBuffer(lpddsBack);
Renderer.SetExtentRect(&rcExtent);
Renderer.SetFrameBuffer(lpddsFrame);
```

```
Renderer.SetMapSize(MAPWIDTH,MAPHEIGHT);
Renderer.SetMouseMap(&MouseMap);
Renderer.SetPlotter(&TilePlotter);
Renderer.SetRenderFunction(RenderFunc);
Renderer.SetScroller(&Scroller);
Renderer.SetUpdateRectCount(100);
Renderer.SetWalker(&TileWalker);
//update the entire screenspace
Renderer.AddRect(Scroller.GetScreenSpace());
```

This bit of code just goes down the list of member access functions, setting them to appropriate values as you go. I used the Visual C++ 6 Intellisense to go alphabetically. For safety, I set the update rectangle buffer to 100 RECTs, even though with your simple application, you will never have more than a few update rectangles.

A brief note about update RECTs: You will never need a huge number, since the highest number of RECTs that need updating is the number of tiles that make up the entire screen, plus two RECTs for scrolling. Currently, your screen takes up about 12×32 tiles, if you count the border tiles. Hence, you could set the update RECT buffer to 500 RECTs, and you shouldn't have to worry too much about overflow if you're careful.

The final line of the code snippet sends an update RECT for the entire screen. This is important, because initially the frame buffer is empty and needs to be totally redrawn.

Cleanup

There is one extra line in the cleanup section of the program. This line releases the frame buffer surface.

```
//release frame buffer
LPDDS_Release(&lpddsFrame);
```

The renderer cleans up after itself after the program terminates.

Main Loop

Ah, finally the main loop! It's actually quite simple compared to the code found in IsoHex17_1.cpp, since all of the hard stuff has been moved to the CRenderer implementation.

```
void Prog_Loop()
{
	//grab the mouse position
	POINT ptMouse;
	GetCursorPos(&ptMouse);
	//map the mouse
```

```
ptCursor=MouseMap.MapMouse(ptMouse);
//clip the cursor to valid map coordinates
if(ptCursor.x<0) ptCursor.x=0;
if(ptCursor.y<0) ptCursor.y=0;
if(ptCursor.x>(MAPWIDTH-1)) ptCursor.x=MAPWIDTH-1;
if(ptCursor.y>(MAPHEIGHT-1)) ptCursor.y=MAPHEIGHT-1;
```

You've seen this code before. It grabs the position of the mouse and uses the MouseMap to calculate where the cursor is.

```
//scroll the map
Renderer.ScrollFrame(ptScroll.x,ptScroll.y);
```

As you'll recall from earlier examples, `ptScroll` is set during `WM_MOUSEMOVE`, and it indicates how far you are to scroll the map in each frame. Rather than scrolling yourself, as you did in earlier examples, you pass the task of scrolling to Renderer and allow it to do its job.

```
//if a click was registered, add an update tile
if(bClick)
{
	Renderer.AddTile(ptCursor.x,ptCursor.y);
	iMap[ptCursor.x][ptCursor.y]=1-iMap[ptCursor.x][ptCursor.y];
}
//set click to false
bClick=false;
```

This is a change from earlier examples. Before, when responding to `WM_LBUTTONDOWN`, you would change the contents of the map location at the cursor. Using `CRenderer`, you cannot do that, because doing so before the scroll will mess up the update `RECT`, and artifacts will result. To solve this problem, I made a new global variable (`bClick`) that is set during `WM_LBUTTONDOWN`. In this code snippet, I check to see if `bClick` is being set. If it is, only then do I update the map and add an update `RECT` to the renderer. This ensures that what needs to be rendered will be rendered. Then I reset `bClick` to false to await another `WM_LBUTTONDOWN`.

```
//update the frame
Renderer.UpdateFrame();
```

If you've looked at `CRenderer`'s code, you know just how much work is being done by this single line. Here, you update the frame buffer and the back buffer and prepare for the next frame.

```
//plot the cursor
POINT ptPlot;
ptPlot=TilePlotter.PlotTile(ptCursor);
```

```
	ptPlot=Scroller.WorldToScreen(ptPlot);
	tsCursor.ClipTile(lpddsBack, Scroller.GetScreenSpace(), ptPlot.x,
ptPlot.y, 0);
```

You've seen code similar to this in prior examples. This is the "place the cursor on the back buffer" code. Since you only put the cursor on the back buffer, and not on the frame buffer, you don't have to worry about erasing it later.

```
	//flip to show the back buffer
	lpddsMain->Flip(0,DDFLIP_WAIT);
}
```

Finally, you flip the primary surface, and your loop is complete. The only thing left to show is the actual rendering function.

```
void RenderFunc(LPDIRECTDRAWSURFACE7 lpddsDst,RECT* rcClip,int xDst,int yDst,int
xMap,int yMap)
{
	//put background tile
	tsBack.ClipTile(lpddsDst,rcClip,xDst,yDst,0);
	//check for a tree
	if(iMap[xMap][yMap])
	{
		//put shadow
		tsShadow.ClipTile(lpddsDst,rcClip,xDst,yDst,0);
		//put tree
		tsTree.ClipTile(lpddsDst,rcClip,xDst,yDst,0);
	}
}
```

Looks a lot like the inner part of the rendering loop from IsoHex17_1.cpp, doesn't it? It should because it is, with a few minor changes like the removal of code using the TilePlotter and scroller. This is the function you send to Renderer. It is called during `UpdateFrame()` for as many tiles as need redrawing.

So, you have now drastically simplified your life by encapsulating your rendering within `CRenderer`, and it's now faster to boot. How much faster depends on your computer and video card, but I can tell you that on mine, the scrolling certainly became a lot smoother as a result. If your machine or video card is lower-end, you might not notice a difference (it'll be just as choppy either way). Also, if your machine and video card are sufficiently high-end, you won't see much of a difference either (it'll be just as smooth, even if you're using the less-efficient method). That's just hardware for you.

SUMMARY

`CRenderer` will be around for the rest of the book, at least until you start to delve into Direct3D. `Crenderer` is handy, it's fast, and it encapsulates a lot of otherwise very ugly code.

You probably have noticed that as you've built the various components of your isometric engine, you've gotten further away from the raw calculations that make it work. This is a good thing. It means that you have added power and flexibility and that you can adapt your engine to whatever task you can imagine without having to redo anything you hard-coded.

I've taken rendering optimization about as far as DirectX will let me. Sure, there are still optimizations you can do, using `Lock/Unlock` and rendering things yourself, but that's beyond the scope of this book. However, if you do come up with an interesting optimization, be sure to drop me a line and let me know. I'm always interested in increasing performance, and many people I talk to think of things that I might not, and vice versa.

CHAPTER 18

Object Placement and Movement

- Object Placement (COP versus FOP)
- Course Object Placement
- Multiple Objects
- Multiple Units

I'd like to extend to you a hearty congratulations for making it through Chapter 17. There were moments when I thought *I* wasn't going to get through it. Believe it or not, the preceding chapter contained about the most complicated code in the entire book. This isn't to say I'm going to let you coast through the rest! Plenty of challenges await you.

This chapter is about object selection and movement. I'm going to discuss the objects (units, items, obstacles) that inhabit your isometric worlds. You started down this path in Chapters 16 and 17, but I'm pretty sick of looking at that darned tree, and I think that you are too.

Object Placement (COP versus FOP)

This next sentence might sound like common sense, but bear with me. Before you can get into object selection, the objects must first be somewhere. While you cursing me for saying something so idiotic, let me say that I'm not really talking about *where* the objects are placed, but rather *how* they are placed.

Basically, there are two ways to place objects. One way is to say that in a given map location, an object fills the entire map location. So, if map location (15,15) contains a mountain, and you are moving your cavalry unit there, and the rules state that cavalry units cannot move onto mountains, the move is disallowed, and the unit must stay outside map location (15,15). With this type of object placement, all the objects within a given location take up the entire location. Therefore, collision detection is very simple, because all moves can be considered to be from the center of one location to the center of an adjacent location. This type of object placement is common in turn-based strategy games, which by their nature are more abstract. I call this method *coarse object placement*.

The other type of object placement is fuzzier. Objects do not necessarily take up the entire map location, and they might or might not be positioned at the centers of locations. This type involves much more work, and it complicates things. First, you have to do collision detection, through either bounding rectangles or bounding ellipses. Second, the rendering is more complicated, because several different objects might be occupying a location or a portion of a location, so you have to figure out in which order to blit the images. This method adds realism, since it makes it harder to tell whether the world is tile-based, even though the overhead that can be introduced by this method can easily degrade performance. This is the method most commonly used by real-time strategy games. I call it *fine object placement*.

Both methods have their pluses and minuses when used in their pure forms. Generally speaking, you will want to use coarse object placement when making turn-based strategy games and fine object placement when making real-time strategy or role-playing games.

However, most real-time strategy games use a sort of hybrid methodology, perhaps using coarse object placement to place buildings and structures and such and using fine object placement for units. Like most things, there is no one true way. You have to consider the needs of your game before making a decision either way.

Coarse Object Placement

Let's say, for the moment, that you have decided to use coarse object placement in your game. This decision has some far-reaching ramifications for the methods you use within your game for object selection and movement, mainly making both pretty easy, but some extra difficulties with a useful display echo occur. (For example, you have to do some extra work for everything to look OK and to be able to size up your situation at a glance.)

Moving Objects Around

You've already done coarse object placement with the little tree image, so I won't bore you by explaining it again. Suffice it to say that you just need to accommodate each object in the map structure somehow. Inanimate objects, like trees, fortifications, roads, and rivers, should be handled separately from units, since you can have both an inanimate object and a unit on the same tile.

It's example time! Load up IsoHex18_1.cpp. In this example, I've provided a single unit/character that will move around the map (almost the same as the map from Chapter 17). This unit/character is shown in Figure 18.1. IsoHex18_1.cpp is quite a bit like IsoHex17_2.cpp, just with most of the mouse scrolling ripped out and keyboard control placed in.

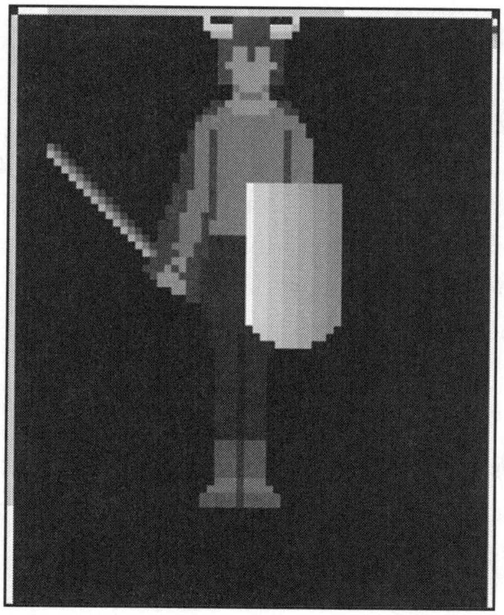

Figure 18.1

An example of a unit/character

Figure 18.2 shows what this example looks like when I run it on my machine. After you press 6 on the numeric keypad (with Num Lock engaged), it looks like Figure 18.3. Finally you have something on your screen that isn't background terrain or a darned tree! Go ahead and move the unit around the map. Right now, the way it works is less than ideal, but at least it's something.

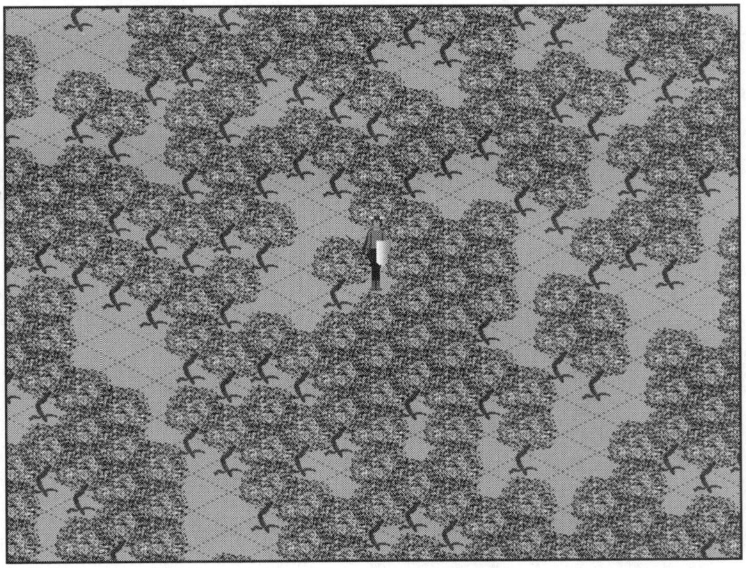

Figure 18.2

IsoHex18_1.cpp on startup

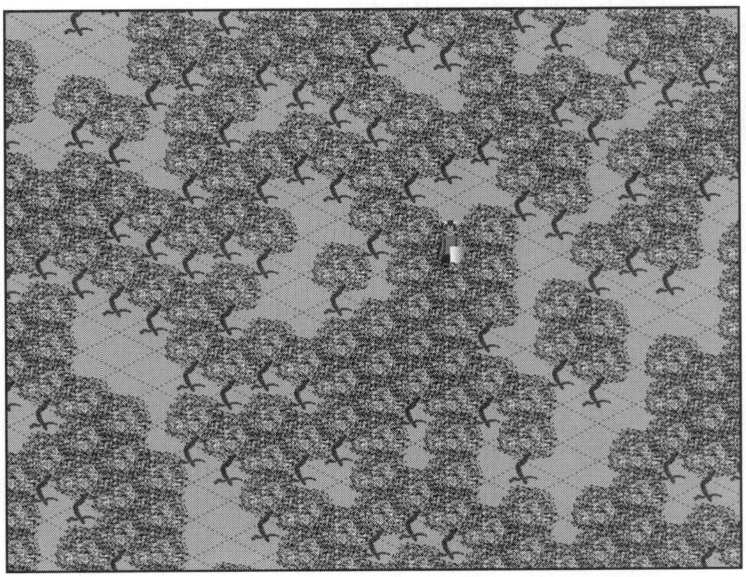

Figure 18.3

IsoHex18_1.cpp after a move to the east (right)

What do I mean by "less than ideal"? Well, for one thing, when the unit moves from one location to another, it just "jumps" suddenly. One moment it's in the original map location, and the next, it's in the new one, like magic. For some games this might be OK, but in most, you don't want to do this, lest the player get vertigo or go into epileptic fits. We'll get to a more smooth movement in a few minutes.

Another aspect of IsoHex18_1.cpp is the manner in which it scrolls. Rather than using the mouse to scroll, the display is scrolled whenever the unit passes the screen boundary (that is, when `x<0`, `y<0`, `x>=SCREENWIDTH` or `y>=SCREENHEIGHT`). When one or more of these thresholds are crossed, the display jumps up/down/left/right by half a screen (320 pixels for left or right and 240 pixels for up or down). Figure 18.4 shows the "before" picture, and Figure 18.5 shows the "after" picture. This isn't the only way I could have done it, and in fact, it wasn't the only way I did it. At first, I had the display centered on the unit at all times. Talk about jumpy and disconcerting!

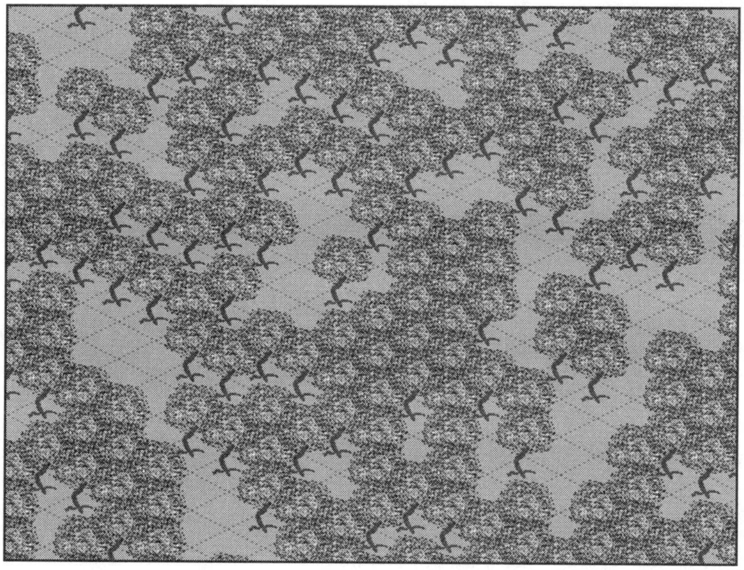

Figure 18.4

Just before a major scroll

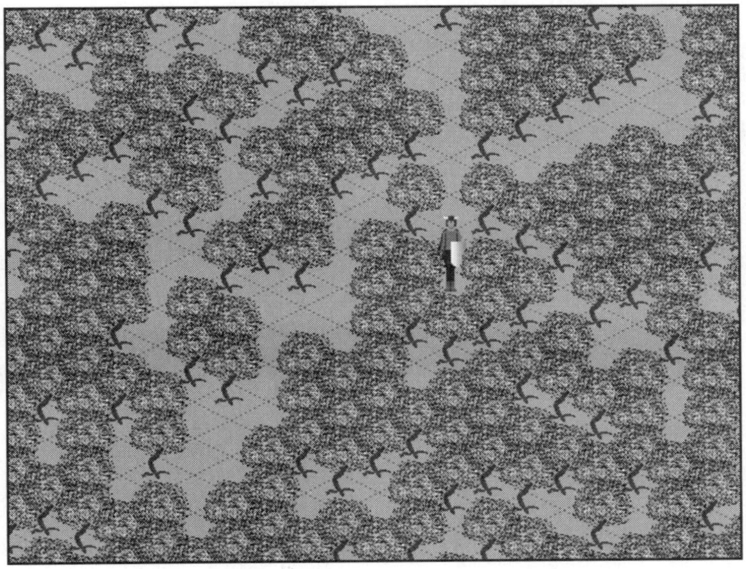

Figure 18.5

Just after a major scroll

Naturally, you'd like me to just shut up and show you the code, right? Of course.

The Code

As I said earlier, IsoHex18_1.cpp is based on IsoHex17_2.cpp, meaning that `CRenderer` is being used. Since the program is quite long, I will just highlight the big changes and leave it at that.

Globals

The first changes occur in the section of code where all the globals are declared. The code doesn't use all the same tilesets (I got rid of the shadow and the cursor), and I added a new tileset with the unit's image. The global tilesets are as follows:

```
//tilesets
CTileSet tsBack;//background
CTileSet tsTree;//tree foreground
CTileSet tsUnit;//unit
```

The `tsBack` and `tsTree` objects contain the tilesets for the background tile and the tree (can't get away from that tree!). The `tsUnit` object contains the image for our nifty new unit. Next is an addition to the global section rather than a change. The following is all of the global variables needed to keep track of our unit's position, direction of movement, and whether or not it is moving.

```
//keep track of unit location
POINT ptUnit;//current position of the unit
POINT ptUnitOld;//last position of the unit
```

```
ISODIRECTION idMoveUnit;//direction of movement
bool bMoveUnit;//the unit should be moved
```

ptUnit keeps track of the unit's current position. ptUnitOld keeps tabs on the unit's last position (since you have to update both where the unit was and where the unit is when the unit is moved). idMoveUnit is an ISODIRECTION specifying in which direction to move the unit. Finally, bMoveUnit is a bool that is true when you move the unit and false when you don't.

The last change to the global section is how the map is represented. As you might recall, in most of the last two chapters' examples, it was a simple two-dimensional array of ints, with 0 being no tree and 1 being a tree. Since a unit has been added to the mix, the map structure gets more complicated, but not overly so, because this is still quite a simple stage.

```
//map location structure
struct MapLocation
{
	bool bTree;//false=no tree; true=tree
	bool bUnit;//false=no unit; true=unit;
};
MapLocation mlMap[MAPWIDTH][MAPHEIGHT];//map array
```

The struct named MapLocation contains two members, bTree and bUnit. They control what is on a given tile. (At this point, all tiles have the same background, so they are not represented in the map structure.) The new array, mlMap, gives you a large-enough map to work with. It's mostly the same as previous sample programs, other than the type.

Initialization

Most of Prog_Init is the same as in previous examples. The images get loaded into their respective tileset variables, and the CRenderer extent RECT is calculated from all tilesets. The initialization of the IsoHexCore components is mainly the same. The first change occurs when you initialize the map.

```
//set up the map to a random tilefield
for(int x=0;x<MAPWIDTH;x++)
{
	for(int y=0;y<MAPHEIGHT;y++)
	{
		mlMap[x][y].bTree=((rand()%2)==1);//random tree
		mlMap[x][y].bUnit=false;//no unit
	}
}
```

I admit it—this isn't a really big change. This change occurred for the simple reason that the map structure changed from being int-based to being MapLocation-based.

Now for something important: the unit's initial placement. I'm going to explain as I go, because it's too long to explain all at once.

```
//set the position of the unit
ptUnit.x=rand()%MAPWIDTH;
ptUnit.y=rand()%MAPHEIGHT;
```

The idea here is that you want the unit to start on a random map location, so take random numbers based on MAPWIDTH and MAPHEIGHT and assign them to ptUnit.

```
ptUnitOld=ptUnit;//set the old position to the same position
mlMap[ptUnit.x][ptUnit.y].bUnit=true;//set the unit on the map
bMoveUnit=false;//set unit movement to false
```

Since you are keeping track of the old unit position, you have to initially assign the old unit position to the current position. Next, place the unit by setting the correct map location's bUnit member to true. Finally, you set bMoveUnit to false so that you won't start out with a moving unit.

```
//plot the position of the unit
POINT ptPos=TilePlotter.PlotTile(ptUnit);
ptPos.x-=(Scroller.GetScreenSpaceWidth()/2);//center the unit horizontally
ptPos.y-=(Scroller.GetScreenSpaceHeight()/2);//center the unit vertically
//set the anchor
Scroller.SetAnchor(&ptPos);
Scroller.WrapAnchor();
```

This is where the code gets a little weird. Initially, I wanted to have the unit centered on the screen, if possible. Since you have the rather spiffy IsoHexCore components to do the work for you, this is a simple matter of setting the anchor location. So, I plotted the position of the unit, and from that location, subtracted half of the screen width from x and half of the screen height from y to give me the position of the upper-left corner, which I then assigned to the anchor. Take a moment and consider what kind of work you would have to do if you didn't have the IsoHexCore components. Makes me shudder just to think about it!

Main Loop

Despite its length, the Prog_Loop is pretty simple. It mainly deals with movement of the unit whenever it occurs. Let's go over it piece by piece.

```
void Prog_Loop()
{
```

```
//set scroll to 0,0
ptScroll.x=0;
ptScroll.y=0;
```

First, you have to make sure that the scrolling is set to 0s. If the unit is being moved, this might be changed a little later on. These two lines of code just ensure that if there was a scroll last frame, there isn't one this frame.

```
//if we are to move the unit
if(bMoveUnit)
{
        //calculate the next position of the unit
        POINT ptNextPos=TileWalker.TileWalk(ptUnit,idMoveUnit);
        //bounds checking
        if(ptNextPos.x<0) bMoveUnit=false;
        if(ptNextPos.y<0) bMoveUnit=false;
        if(ptNextPos.x>=MAPWIDTH) bMoveUnit=false;
        if(ptNextPos.y>=MAPHEIGHT) bMoveUnit=false;
```

As stated earlier, `bMoveUnit` is true when you move the unit and false when you don't. Also, `idMoveUnit` is the direction of movement. In this snippet of code, you calculate the next position for the unit by using the TileWalker. After that is done, the code performs a few checks to make certain that the new position is still within the map. If the new position is not within the bounds of the map, `bMoveUnit` is set to false, thus canceling the move.

```
        //are we still moving the unit?
        if(bMoveUnit)
        {
                //set the unit position to ptnextpos
                ptUnit=ptNextPos;
                //plot the unit's next position
                POINT ptPlot=TilePlotter.PlotTile(ptUnit);
                //translate plot position into screen coordinates
                ptPlot=Scroller.WorldToScreen(ptPlot);
                //check for scrolling
                if(ptPlot.x<0) ptScroll.x=-320;
                if(ptPlot.y<0) ptScroll.y=-240;
                if(ptPlot.x>640) ptScroll.x=320;
                if(ptPlot.y>480) ptScroll.y=240;
        }
}
```

If bMoveUnit is still true after the bounds checking, you set up the unit's movement and any scrolling that might be required. The unit's position (stored in ptUnit) is set to the new calculated position. Then the unit's position is plotted using the TilePlotter and is translated into screen coordinates by the scroller. If the plotted position is outside the screen, ptScroll is set to an appropriate scrolling value.

```
    //scroll the map
    Renderer.ScrollFrame(ptScroll.x,ptScroll.y);
```

This line performs whatever scrolling you might require. Most of the time, this will be none, so it will just copy from the frame buffer to the back buffer the entire image using the renderer.

```
    //if we are still moving the unit
    if(bMoveUnit)
    {
        //reset the old position
        mlMap[ptUnitOld.x][ptUnitOld.y].bUnit=false;
        //set the new position
        mlMap[ptUnit.x][ptUnit.y].bUnit=true;
        //add update tiles to renderer
        Renderer.AddTile(ptUnitOld.x,ptUnitOld.y);
        Renderer.AddTile(ptUnit.x,ptUnit.y);
        //set moveunit to false
        bMoveUnit=false;
        //set old position to current position
        ptUnitOld=ptUnit;
    }
```

Finally, you actually move the unit. Reset the bUnit member of the map location at ptUnitOld and set the bUnit member of the map location at ptUnit. Then send the ptUnitOld and ptUnit positions to the renderer to be updated. Last, set bMoveUnit to false (you are done moving now) and set ptUnitOld to the current unit position, ptUnit.

```
    //update the frame
    Renderer.UpdateFrame();
    //flip to show the back buffer
    lpddsMain->Flip(0,DDFLIP_WAIT);
}
```

Last, tell the renderer to update the frame and then flip the primary surface. Note that there is absolutely no rendering code of any form inside Prog_Loop. All rendering is done through CRenderer, so you can concentrate on just figuring out what changes from frame to frame, and just deal with that. Very liberating, really.

Rendering Function

All the rendering work is done through CRenderer and hence through RenderFunc.

```
void RenderFunc(LPDIRECTDRAWSURFACE7 lpddsDst, RECT* rcClip, int xDst, int yDst,
int xMap, int yMap)
{
	//put background tile
	tsBack.ClipTile(lpddsDst,rcClip,xDst,yDst,0);
	//check for a tree
	if(mlMap[xMap][yMap].bTree)
	{
		//put tree
		tsTree.ClipTile(lpddsDst,rcClip,xDst,yDst,0);
	}
	//check for the unit
	if(mlMap[xMap][yMap].bUnit)
	{
		//put unit
		tsUnit.ClipTile(lpddsDst,rcClip,xDst,yDst,0);
	}
}
```

How simple can you get? First, you render the background tile from tsBack. Next, if bTree is set at (xMap,yMap), you render the tree from tsTree. Finally, if bUnit is true, you render the unit.

Event Handling

Mainly, you are only concerned with WM_KEYDOWN, since you are controlling the unit with the keyboard. You can take a look at the code if you like. Table 18.1 shows the VK_* constants I used and the corresponding ISODIRECTION values.

Table 18.1 Virtual Keycode-to-ISODIRECTION Mapping

Virtual Keycode	Direction
VK_NUMPAD8	ISO_NORTH
VK_NUMPAD9	ISO_NORTHEAST
VK_NUMPAD6	ISO_EAST
VK_NUMPAD3	ISO_SOUTHEAST
VK_NUMPAD2	ISO_SOUTH
VK_NUMPAD1	ISO_SOUTHWEST
VK_NUMPAD4	ISO_WEST
VK_NUMPAD7	ISO_NORTHWEST

SMOOTH SLIDING

Sample program IsoHex18_1 is pretty cool, but it probably leaves you lacking. I agree, but it's just a simple example illustrating basic unit movement; your vision of unit movement probably far exceeds its capabilities. First, it has only a single unit, which is great for illustrating an example, but it has rather limited use. Second, the movement is too... abrupt. It's like the unit is teleporting from one map location to another. On a purely aesthetic bent, the unit is taller than the tree, so it looks unrealistic.

> **NOTE**
>
> **The virtual keycodes listed in Table 18.1 work only when the Num Lock is engaged. If you wanted to respond to the keypad when the Num Lock is off, you would have to respond to the arrow keys (`VK_LEFT`, `VK_RIGHT`, `VK_UP`, `VK_DOWN`) and the document navigation keys (`VK_HOME`, `VK_END`, `VK_PAGEUP`, `VK_PAGEDOWN`). For a simple example like this one, I felt it unnecessary to do this, but in a professionally done game, you'd want to have that feature.**

It would be preferable to have the unit either slide from one map location to the next or go through an animated sequence of images from one tile to another. This will be a bit of work, considering how the `CRenderer` class is set up, and because of the overlapping nature of isometric tiles. Fear not. We are creative, and we shall overcome all obstacles! (A positive attitude will take you far.)

The next example, which will be revealed in just a moment, slides the unit from one tile to the next, making smaller movements per frame. I figure that four frames to make a move is more than adequate to make it look like you are sliding the piece. Plus, 4 goes into 64 (the tile width) and 32 (the tile height) evenly.

For an even smoother slide, you could use eight frames, and for a very quick slide, you could use only two. You'll use four in the example, although adapting this method to use other numbers is a simple matter.

Table 18.2 shows the changes in screen/world coordinates for the various isometric directions, based on the 64×32 tile. It also shows the change in x and the change in y divided by 4. This table is just a rehash of TilePlotter information. It's nothing new.

Table 18.2 Pixel-Scale Movement

Direction	ChangeX	ChangeY	ChangeX/4	ChangeY/4
North	0	–32	0	–8
Northeast	+32	–16	+8	–4
East	+64	0	+16	0
Southeast	+32	+16	+8	+4
South	0	+32	0	+8
Southwest	–32	+16	–8	+4
West	–64	0	–16	0
Northwest	–32	–16	–8	–4

The basic idea here is that when a user presses a key, indicating that the unit is to be moved, the unit's world/screen position will be changed by ChangeX/4 and ChangeY/4 during the next four frames.

Ah, if only it were that simple! Unfortunately, problems ensue because of the tile overlap. For example, let's say that you want to move your unit to the south. If, for the moment, the unit remains in its original map location, and you change x and y each frame by the values in Table 18.2, after the bottom of the unit's image is below the bottom of the background's tile image, it will be partially obscured by other tiles that are "in front" of the original position. Similarly, you cannot move the unit to its new location and offset from that, because in half of the cases, the same thing happens. Of the two positions for the unit, the starting location and the ending location, during the move you want the unit to be associated with the location that is rendered last.

Without further ado, load up IsoHex18_2.cpp. This example, which is based on IsoHex18_1, demonstrates smooth sliding. Figure 18.6 shows one such slide in the middle of making it happen. Because of the method I am using, there are certain visual inconsistencies when an object moves. For example, in Figure 18.6, the unit is shown after the tree that would otherwise be "in front" of it. Of course, you probably wouldn't notice these inconsistencies, because the unit moves too fast for you to notice them.

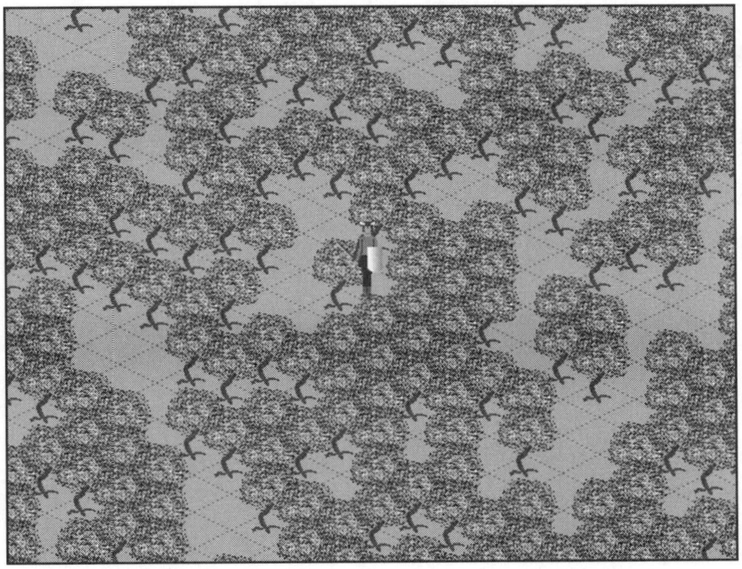

Figure 18.6

Smooth sliding demo

Let's take a look under the hood, shall we?

Globals

Most of the globals in IsoHex18_2 are the same as in IsoHex18_1. A few were added to accommodate the smooth scrolling nature of unit movement.

```
//game state
int iGameState=GS_IDLE;
```

The first of these new globals is `iGameState`. Unfortunately, the smooth scrolling algorithm is just too complicated to do in a single game state. There are four game states, as shown in Table 18.3.

Table 18.3 Game States

State	When It Happens
GS_IDLE	Most of the time (when no movement is happening)
GS_STARTMOVE	When a key is pressed
GS_DOMOVE	During a move
GS_DONEMOVE	When a move has finished

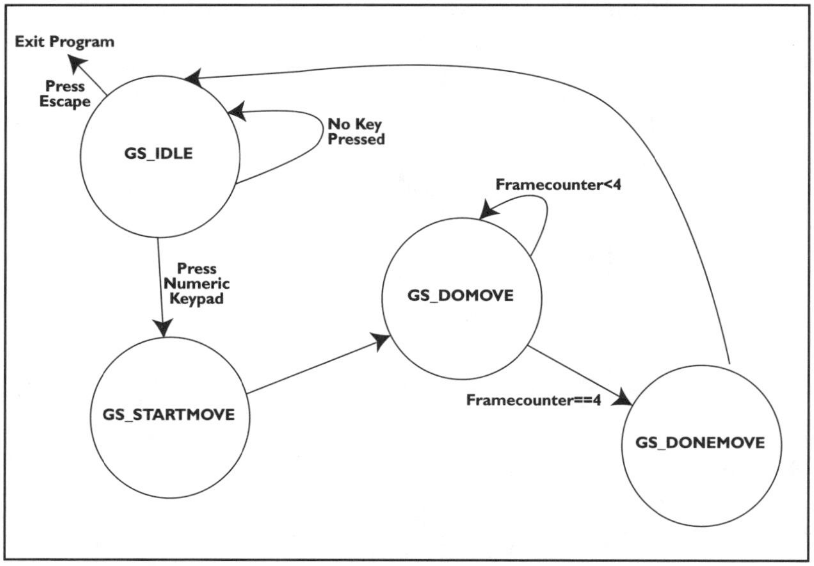

Figure 18.7

IsoHex18_2 game states

Most of the time, the application sits around in `GS_IDLE`, waiting for a key to be pressed. Figure 18.7 shows the flow of the program from game state to game state.

```
//unit offset
POINT ptUnitOffset;
int iUnitFrame=0;
```

These two little variables control how the unit is "slid" across the map. The x and y components of `ptUnitOffset` are added to the unit's plotted position during the `RenderFunc`. The `iUnitFrame` variable keeps count of how many frames of the move have occurred. If it hits four, the move is finished.

Initialization/Cleanup

In this example, the initialization code and cleanup are identical to IsoHex18_1. No changes are necessary.

Main Loop

The main loop, on the other hand, has changed a great deal, especially because of the switch to multiple game states. Let's look at them one at a time.

GS_IDLE.

Most of the time, the application sits in GS_IDLE (sort of like being in neutral for a car). The code for it is rather simple.

```
case GS_IDLE://the game is idling; update the frame, but that's about it.
	{
		//scroll the frame (0,0)
		Renderer.ScrollFrame(0,0);
		//update the frame
		Renderer.UpdateFrame();
		//flip to show the back buffer
		lpddsMain->Flip(0,DDFLIP_WAIT);
	}break;
```

As you can see, not much is going on here. The code shown is the bare minimum required to update the frame and flip the primary surface. No big deal.

GS_STARTMOVE.

At any time during GS_IDLE, if a numeric keypad key is pressed, a direction is placed in idMoveUnit, and the game state is set to GS_STARTMOVE. GS_STARTMOVE does not update the display; it simply sets things up so that the move can be performed.

```
case GS_STARTMOVE:
	{
		//remove the unit from the old position
		mlMap[ptUnitOld.x][ptUnitOld.y].bUnit=false;
```

First, you remove the unit from its old position, even though there is a 50-50 chance that you'll place it right back there.

```
		//calculate new position (virtual new position)
		switch(idMoveUnit)
		{
		case ISO_NORTH:
		case ISO_NORTHEAST:
		case ISO_NORTHWEST:
		case ISO_WEST:
			{
				//move ptUnit
				ptUnit=TileWalker.TileWalk(ptUnit,idMoveUnit);
				//set the offset
				ptUnitOffset.x=0;
				ptUnitOffset.y=0;
				//place unit at old position
				mlMap[ptUnitOld.x][ptUnitOld.y].bUnit=true;
			}break;
```

Depending on the direction stored in idMoveUnit, you set up the ptUnitOffset and place the unit on either the starting or ending location, depending on which location is rendered last. If the direction is north, northwest, northeast, or west, you leave the unit at its old position and set ptUnitOffset to (0,0). Take a look at Figure 18.8, which shows the rendering order of the original tile (the one in the center of the figure) and its eight neighbors. The original tile is shaded darkly, and the neighbors rendered before the center tile are lightly shaded. This is why for the four directions I just listed, you must leave the unit on the original tile—at least for the time being.

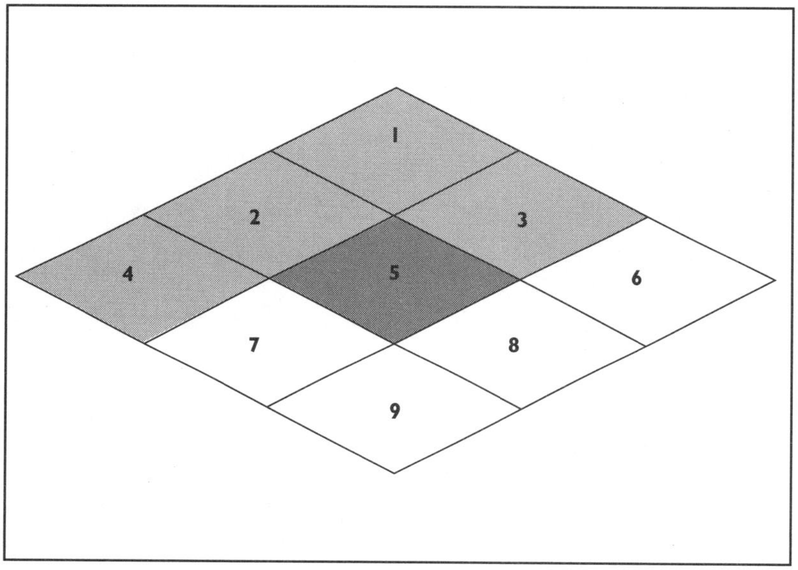

Figure 18.8

Rendering order of neighboring map locations

```
case ISO_EAST:
        {
                //move ptUnit
                ptUnit=TileWalker.TileWalk(ptUnit,idMoveUnit);
                //set the offset
                ptUnitOffset.x=-64;
                ptUnitOffset.y=0;
                //place unit at new position
                mlMap[ptUnit.x][ptUnit.y].bUnit=true;
        }break;
case ISO_SOUTHEAST:
        {
                //move ptUnit
                ptUnit=TileWalker.TileWalk(ptUnit,idMoveUnit);
                //set the offset
                ptUnitOffset.x=-32;
```

```
                    ptUnitOffset.y=-16;
                    //place unit at new position
                    mlMap[ptUnit.x][ptUnit.y].bUnit=true;
                }break;
            case ISO_SOUTHWEST:
                {
                    //move ptUnit
                    ptUnit=TileWalker.TileWalk(ptUnit,idMoveUnit);
                    //set the offset
                    ptUnitOffset.x=32;
                    ptUnitOffset.y=-16;
                    //place unit at new position
                    mlMap[ptUnit.x][ptUnit.y].bUnit=true;
                }break;
            case ISO_SOUTH:
                {
                    //move ptUnit
                    ptUnit=TileWalker.TileWalk(ptUnit,idMoveUnit);
                    //set the offset
                    ptUnitOffset.x=0;
                    ptUnitOffset.y=-32;
                    //place unit at new position
                    mlMap[ptUnit.x][ptUnit.y].bUnit=true;
                }break;
            }
```

The rest of the directions—south, southeast, southwest, and east—are rendered after the center tile, so you have to move the unit to that new tile and set up `ptUnitOffset` so that it appears to remain in the same position.

```
            //set unit frame to 0
            iUnitFrame=0;
            //set the next gamestate
            iGameState=GS_DOMOVE;
        }break;
```

Finally, you set the unit frame counter to 0 and set the game state to `GS_DOMOVE`. At this point, you're done with `GS_STARTMOVE`.

> **NOTE**
>
> You don't have to have a separate game state for starting to move the unit. That's just the way I decided to do it in this case. It seems like kind of a waste, since nothing is rendered during GS_STARTMOVE, so you might want to move this code into the event handler or into a class or something. I'll talk more about this later.

GS_DOMOVE

After the move is set up with GS_STARTMOVE, the next game state to be processed is GS_DOMOVE. This game state is called four times and then yields control to GS_DONEMOVE.

```
case GS_DOMOVE:
	{
		//move the unit offset
		switch(idMoveUnit)
		{
		case ISO_NORTH:
			{
				//change offset
				ptUnitOffset.x+=0;
				ptUnitOffset.y-=8;
			}break;
		case ISO_NORTHEAST:
			{
				//change offset
				ptUnitOffset.x+=8;
				ptUnitOffset.y-=4;
			}break;
		case ISO_EAST:
			{
				//change offset
				ptUnitOffset.x+=16;
				ptUnitOffset.y+=0;
			}break;
		case ISO_SOUTHEAST:
			{
				//change offset
				ptUnitOffset.x+=8;
				ptUnitOffset.y+=4;
			}break;
		case ISO_SOUTH:
```

```
        {
                //change offset
                ptUnitOffset.x+=0;
                ptUnitOffset.y+=8;
        }break;
case ISO_SOUTHWEST:
        {
                //change offset
                ptUnitOffset.x-=8;
                ptUnitOffset.y+=4;
        }break;
case ISO_WEST:
        {
                //change offset
                ptUnitOffset.x-=16;
                ptUnitOffset.y+=0;
        }break;
case ISO_NORTHWEST:
        {
                //change offset
                ptUnitOffset.x-=8;
                ptUnitOffset.y-=4;
        }break;
}
```

The very first thing that `GS_DOMOVE` does is update `ptUnitOffset` based on the value in `idMoveUnit`. The values listed here come from Table 18.2, if you need to check back.

```
//grab the update RECTs
RECT rcUpdate1,rcUpdate2;
CopyRect(&rcUpdate1,&Renderer.rcExtent);
CopyRect(&rcUpdate2,&Renderer.rcExtent);
//plot the unit's old position
POINT ptPlot=TilePlotter.PlotTile(ptUnitOld);
ptPlot=Scroller.WorldToScreen(ptPlot);
OffsetRect(&rcUpdate1,ptPlot.x,ptPlot.y);
//plot the unit's new position
ptPlot=TilePlotter.PlotTile(ptUnit);
ptPlot=Scroller.WorldToScreen(ptPlot);
OffsetRect(&rcUpdate2,ptPlot.x,ptPlot.y);
//merge the two update RECTS
UnionRect(&rcUpdate1,&rcUpdate1,&rcUpdate2);
```

This part might be a little confusing, so I'm going to spend some time on it. What you need to do here is calculate the update RECTs to send to the renderer. Unfortunately, you can't just send the map location, because as the unit is sliding, it might be partially outside of the rectangles that bound the starting and ending map location (which, on the good-bad scale of things, is kind of bad). So, I chose to calculate the RECTs for the tile locations contained in ptUnit and ptUnitOld and then merge those two RECTs into a single update rectangle, thus guaranteeing that the unit will be fully displayed.

```
            //scroll the frame (0,0)
            Renderer.ScrollFrame(0,0);
            //send update rect to the renderer
            Renderer.AddRect(&rcUpdate1);
            //update the frame
            Renderer.UpdateFrame();
            //flip to show the back buffer
            lpddsMain->Flip(0,DDFLIP_WAIT);
```

These are the standard CRenderer calls to scroll the frame (albeit by 0 horizontally and vertically), add the update rectangle that you calculated earlier, update the frame, and flip the primary surface.

```
            //increase the unit frame counter
            iUnitFrame++;
            //check for done with gamestate
            if(iUnitFrame==4)
            {
                //set to the next gamestate
                iGameState=GS_DONEMOVE;
            }
        }break;
```

In the home stretch, I increment iUnitFrame and check to see if it equals 4 yet. When it reaches 4, I set the game state to GS_DONEMOVE. Otherwise, it just continues next frame with GS_DOMOVE.

GS_DONEMOVE

This is the final game state. It finishes up the move, updates the map, and then returns the game to GS_IDLE so that it can wait for another keypress.

```
        case GS_DONEMOVE:
            {
                //finish the move, make sure the unit is positioned correctly
                switch(idMoveUnit)
                {
                case ISO_NORTH:
```

```
case ISO_NORTHEAST:
case ISO_NORTHWEST:
case ISO_WEST:
      {
            //remove from old position
            mlMap[ptUnitOld.x][ptUnitOld.y].bUnit=false;
            //place on new position
            mlMap[ptUnit.x][ptUnit.y].bUnit=true;
      }break;
}
```

If you recall GS_STARTMOVE, you had a special case for a few directions—namely, north, northwest, northeast, and west. This is where you correct for whatever inconsistency you might still have. It's simply a matter of removing the unit from ptUnitOld and placing it on ptUnit.

```
//plot new tile's position
POINT ptPlot=TilePlotter.PlotTile(ptUnit);
ptPlot=Scroller.WorldToScreen(ptPlot);
//set scrolling to 0,0
ptScroll.x=0;
ptScroll.y=0;
//check for scrolling
if(ptPlot.x<0) ptScroll.x=-320;
if(ptPlot.y<0) ptScroll.y=-240;
if(ptPlot.x>=640) ptScroll.x=320;
if(ptPlot.y>=480) ptScroll.y=240;
```

This should look somewhat familiar. After the move has finished, only then does the game scroll. In this snippet, the position of the unit is plotted, and if it is outside of the screen space, ptScroll is set to an appropriate value.

```
//scroll the frame
Renderer.ScrollFrame(ptScroll.x,ptScroll.y);
//add update tiles
Renderer.AddTile(ptUnitOld.x,ptUnitOld.y);
Renderer.AddTile(ptUnit.x,ptUnit.y);
```

Now the frame is scrolled (as needed) and the map locations ptUnitOld and ptUnit are added to the update list.

```
//set ptUnitOffset to (0,0)
ptUnitOffset.x=0;
ptUnitOffset.y=0;
```

```
                        //set the old unit position to the current unit position
                        ptUnitOld=ptUnit;
                        //go to idling gamestate
                        iGameState=GS_IDLE;
```

After the tiles are sent to the update list, ptUnitOld is set to the same value as ptUnit. ptUnitOffset is set to (0,0), and the game state is set to GS_IDLE.

```
                        //update the frame
                        Renderer.UpdateFrame();
                        //flip
                        lpddsMain->Flip(0,DDFLIP_WAIT);
                }break;
```

Finally, the frame is updated by the renderer, the primary surface is flipped, and voila! A unit has successfully slid from one tile to another. Seems like an awful amount of work, doesn't it? Perhaps it is. Maybe your game doesn't need this kind of precision as far as unit movement is concerned. It's just one of those things I thought I'd throw out there, just because.

Multiple Objects

Thus far, you've dealt with only a single unit of a single type all alone on a rather huge playing area. While this is useful for instructional purposes, chances are your game will have dozens of unit types and hundreds of individual units. You, as the programmer, have to find a way to keep track of all these units.

Storage Methods

There are many ways to keep track of units—everything from simple arrays to complex collections. Usually, these methods have one thing in common—they keep track of the unit in at least two places—once in a master list of all units (so that you can loop through the list and have them carry out orders) and once in the map itself. They may also be stored in other places, but for now, you're just concerned with these two.

The first problem you'll run into is developing a way to store all the units. In simple games, you might be able to get away with a simple array. It's a valid technique if the game is small or has a limitation on how many units a player can control. Most games, however, require something more. My personal favorite is the linked list.

If you're already familiar with linked lists and, in particular, the STL list template, feel free to skip the next couple of sections. If you are unfamiliar with linked lists (or dynamic storage structures in general) or have never used the list template, you might want to give these sections a read, at least to get the basics.

What Is a Linked List?

A *linked list* is nothing more than a way to store data when you don't know how many items you will need to store. Consider an array for a moment. When you create your array, you write some code like the following:

```
int MyArray[10];
```

This, as you know, sets aside enough memory to store 10 `int`s which, on modern computers, are 32 bits or 4 bytes long, so the code would set aside 40 bytes of memory which you can then access by using `MyArray` with a subscript elsewhere in code.

Arrays are nice when you have a known number of items in a list. For example, a deck of cards can be contained in an array that has a size of 52, or a chessboard can be stored in an 8×8 array. However, when the number of items might at some time be stored in a list, an array just can't do it—at least, not efficiently.

Following is an alternative way to declare an array of `int`s using C++'s `new` operator to dynamically allocate the space on the heap:

```
int ArrayElements=10;
int* MyArray=new int[ArrayElements];
```

Using this code, you request 10 `int`s to be set aside on the heap, which is also known as the *free store,* meaning just a big hunk o' memory that isn't being used. The key word in the preceding sentence is "requested." There is no guarantee that enough space for 10 `int`s will be available, which means that `MyArray` will be set to 0 (`NULL`). Of course, this is an extreme case. Most of the time, with modern machines, you have to really mess up in order to be out of memory.

Using `new` to make your arrays, if you suddenly determined that you needed an extra element in the list, you could do something like the following:

```
int* TempArray=new int[ArrayElements+1];
for(int count=0;count<ArrayElements;count++)
{
	TempArray[count]=MyArray[count];
}
delete[] MyArray;
MyArray=TempArray;
ArrayElements++;
```

Looks pretty evil, doesn't it? Basically, I allocated a brand-new array, the size of the original plus 1, copied from one to the other, and finally deleted the old array. I know it's a mess. Also, while this method might be fine for small arrays of 10 or 20 elements, doing the same thing for an array that has 10,000 elements is disastrous for performance. Ideally, what you would like to do is to be able to add and remove elements without having to do a lot of recopying. That is what a linked list will do, and here's why.

How Linked Lists Work

The basic building block of a linked list is called a *node*. A node serves the same purpose as an index into an array, like `MyArray[4]`. Keep in mind that "serves the same purpose" is not to be confused with "works the same way." Linked lists and arrays are completely different. The only thing they have in common is that they both store more than one element of data.

The following code is an example of what a typical node structure might look like:

```
struct Node//basic node structure
{
	void* DataPtr;//pointer to the data stored in this node
	Node* next;//pointer to the next node
	Node* prev;//pointer to the previous node
};
```

A node consists of three simple parts. First is the `DataPtr`, which isn't necessarily a `void*`. If you need a linked list of integers, you would have an integer member instead—you get the idea. The other two parts are integral to the way linked lists work. In order to arbitrarily insert nodes, you keep track of the next node in the list (with the `next` member), and you also keep track of the node just prior to the current one (with the `prev` members). Hence, the nodes are linked into a little string of pointers, so they are called *linked lists*. Having both a `next` and `prev` pointer means that it is a "doubly linked list" since you can navigate both ways along the list of nodes.

Heads or Tails

In your linked list, two nodes are special: the head node and the tail node. You might call them "front and back" or "top and bottom" or "first and last," but suffice it to say that the list "starts" at the head node and "ends" at the tail node, even though you can work backwards from the tail node and wind up back at the head node. This is just the convention used. If you want to use other terminology that you feel more comfortable with, you're free to do so.

Figure 18.9 shows how a linked list works. It shows identical rows of nodes, including the head node and tail node. The top row shows how the `next` pointers are assigned to the address of the next node, and the bottom row shows a similar thing for the `prev` pointers. (Showing them both at the same time would be a mess of crisscrossed lines that would be hard to read.)

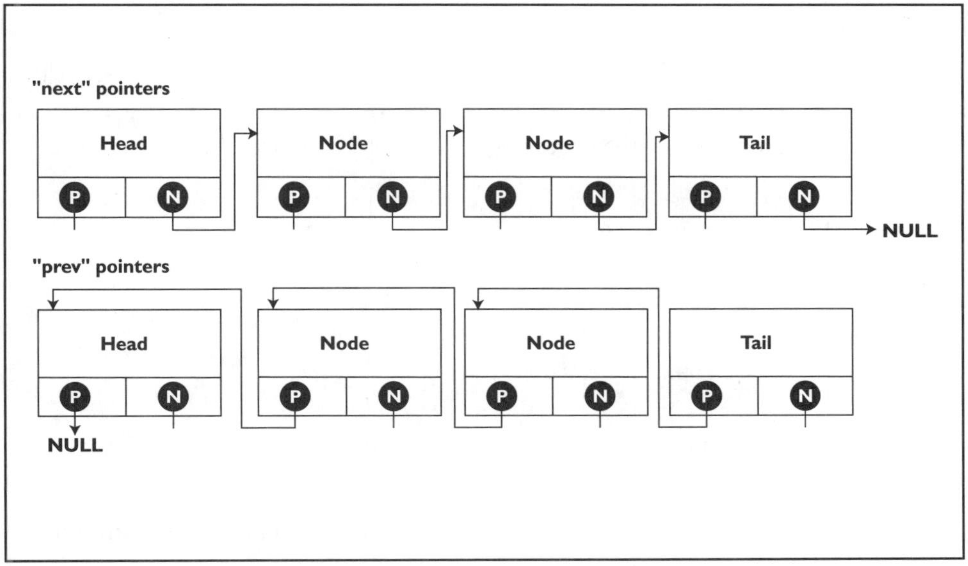

Figure 18.9

Visual representation of a linked list

Rolling Your Own Linked List

Even though I'm going to get to the STL list template in a few moments, no discussion about linked lists is complete without at least showing how to make one on your own. Several methods are used to make linked lists. Some use the same node for head and tail, in reality making a sort of "linked ring." For our purposes, I will have the head and tail nodes as separate nodes, both of which will contain nothing except links to other nodes, so at any given time, our linked list will contain at least two nodes.

```
Node* pHead;//head node
Node* pTail;//tail node
//allocate the head and tail nodes
pHead=new Node;
pTail=new Node;
//point the head and tail nodes to one another and to NULL
pHead->prev=NULL;
pHead->next=pTail;
pTail->prev=pHead;
pTail->next=NULL;
```

This code snippet sets up the head and tail for a linked list. It is important to note that all nodes must be dynamically allocated (by using either `new` or `malloc`). You cannot take a local variable of type `Node` and add it to the list, because that variable disappears as soon as the function returns, which means that your linked list will be broken. It is perfectly fine to use `new` or `malloc` to create new nodes within functions using local `Node*` variables.

Adding to the Linked List

Just having a head and tail node (both of which contain nothing) won't get you anywhere. In order for the list to be useful, you must populate it with data, which means you have to insert nodes. The first insertion I'm going to show you is how to insert a node at the beginning of the list (right after the node pointed to by pHead).

```
Node* pNode=new Node;//allocate a new node
//set up the data in the node here
pNode->next=pHead->next;//copy the next pointer from pHead
pNode->prev=pHead;//set the prev pointer to the top of the list (pHead)
pHead->next=pNode;//point to the new node from pHead
```

As you can see, there's a whole lot of messing around with the next and prev pointers. This is the basis for how linked lists work and is also the source of most of the errors associated with linked lists.

Next, I'm going to show you how to add a node to the end (right before pTail). This code is rather similar to the previous "top of list" code. It just switches next for prev.

```
Node* pNode=new Node;
//set up data in node here
pNode->prev=pTail->prev;//copy prev pointer from tail to new node
pNode->next=pTail;//point to tail from new node
pTail->prev=pNode;//point to new node from tail
```

Like I said, it's about the same code either way. Most of the time, these two insertions are the only ones you'll use. However, fast arbitrary insertions are one of the strengths of linked lists, and the code is almost identical to the code I've already shown, so let's take a look.

In both of the following examples, pCurrent is a node somewhere in the list, and not the head or the tail. First, here is how to insert a node after pCurrent:

```
Node* pNode=new Node;//allocate new node
//set up data within node here
pNode->next=pCurrent->next;//set new node's next pointer
pNode->prev=pCurrent;//set new node's prev pointer
pCurrent->next=pNode;//update pCurrent's next pointer
```

If you're saying "Hey! You can take the 'insert after the head' code and replace all the pHeads with pCurrents!" you are correct, and you get a blue ribbon. In fact, to do the "insert before pCurrent" code, you can just take the "insert before tail" code and replace pTail with pCurrent. It's just that easy.

Deleting from a Linked List

In order to delete a node from a linked list, the list must first have a node that is not the head or the tail. Deleting the head or tail nodes can be disastrous for this style of linked list. For this example, we return to using `pCurrent` as a node somewhere in the list that is neither the head nor the tail.

```
Node* pNextNode=pCurrent->next;//get a pointer to the next node
Node* pPrevNode=pCurrent->prev;//get a pointer to the previous node
pNextNode->prev=pPrevNode;//link next node to previous node
pPrevNode->next=pNextNode;//link previous node to next node
//do whatever needs doing to free up the data used by the node here
delete pCurrent;//delete the current node
pCurrent=pNextNode;//set pCurrent to a valid node
```

Checking for an Empty List

Quite commonly, you will need to check if the list has any node (not the head or tail) in it. With this style of linked list, this is a pretty easy check. You can do it two ways. One, you can see if the next pointer of `pHead` points to `pTail`:

```
if(pHead->next==pTail) {/*the list is empty*/}
```

And two, you can see if the `prev` pointer of `pTail` points to `pHead`:

```
if(pTail->prev==pHead){/*the list is empty*/}
```

It is not always necessary to check if a list is empty before iterating through it, but this is a good idea at many other times.

Iterating Through a List

The word "iterate" might be new to you, even though you are already familiar with the concept. Whenever you do a `for` loop, you are in fact iterating:

```
for(int count=0;count<MAXVALUE;count++)
{
	//do something
}
```

In this piece of code, you "iterate" through a number of values for `count`, which might be used as an index into an array or part of a function that totals the values of `count`, searches for a particular item, or whatever.

The dictionary definition of iteration is "the process of repeating a set of instructions a specified number of times or until a specific result is achieved." This is straight out of the *American Heritage Dictionary of the English Language, Third Edition*. What better way to describe a `for` loop? A simpler definition is that iteration involves repetitive tasks, such as looking at each of the values stored in an array. In a linked list, you iterate through all the nodes in the list, usually performing some action with them.

In order to iterate, you must first have an iterator. In the preceding `for` loop, the variable `count` was the iterator. With your linked lists, you will use a node to step your way through the list.

> **NOTE**
>
> **Another good example of an iterator is how the `CTileWalker` class is used by `CMouseMap` to determine the position of a pixel on-screen.**

Generally speaking, you will want to iterate through a linked list one of two ways: either forward or backward, and usually from head to tail or tail to head. Both methods are very similar. Here's a little look-see at iterating from head to tail:

```
Node* pCurrent=pHead->next;//pHead is NOT the first node in the list; pHead->next
IS
while(pCurrent!=pTail)//while pCurrent does not point to the tail of the list
{
	//do something with the current node
	pCurrent=pCurrent->next;//move to the next node in the list
}
```

Or, if you prefer to use `for` rather than `while` (I know I do, anyway), do this:

```
for(pCurrent=pHead->next;pCurrent!=pTail;pCurrent=pCurrent->next)
{
	//do something with the current node
}
```

During a list iteration, you might perform one of a number of operations, like counting nodes, searching for a particular node, modifying the data stored in the node, and so on. Be careful about deleting or adding nodes, however. If you add a node as a result of an iteration, you might not want it to be part of the current iteration, in which case you probably want to add it to the beginning of the list. However, you might indeed want to have the new item be part of this iteration, in which case you would add it to the end. It's all a matter of what function the iteration performs. Just be sure you design your iterations properly, and everything should be fine.

If you want to loop from tail to head, you just reverse everything, like so:

```
for(pCurrent=pTail->prev;pCurrent!=pHead;pCurrent=pCurrent->prev)
{
```

```
	//do something with pCurrent here
}
```

One of the more common tasks you will use list iteration for is that of searching out a particular node. The way I normally go about this is shown next. For the moment, assume that `Node` contains a member called `Value` that is an `int`, and assume that I am looking for the number 13 in the list.

```
Node* pFound=NULL;//this node will point to a node, if found,
//and NULL if not found
for(pCurrent=pHead->next;pCurrent!=pTail;pCurrent=pCurrent->next)
{
	if(pCurrent->Value==13)//check for a value of 13
	{
		pFound=pCurrent;//set the found node to the current node
		break;//break out of the loop
	}
}
if(pFound)
{
	//found a node!
}
else
{
	//did not find a node!
}
```

At this point, I'm going to point out a major weakness of linked lists. Whenever you want to do anything, like search, count, or whatever, you have to go from one end to the other, one step at a time. This makes accessing a given node (for example, the fifth node) slower than it is in an array. However, most of the time you will use linked lists in places where moving from one end to the other is what you wanted to do in the first place anyway, so this is not a problem. Plus, you gain the ability to arbitrarily insert and delete items quickly, which is not possible in an array.

Another common iteration you will be likely to perform is that of counting nodes. This is a rather simple matter.

```
int Tally=0;//initialize counter to 0
for(pCurrent=pHead->next;pCurrent!=pTail;pCurrent=pCurrent->next) //iterate
	Tally++;//for each node, add one to Tally
```

No big deal, right? How tough can counting things be, really? Unfortunately, counting the nodes does require moving through the entire list each time you want to do so, and since adding nodes is so easy (it can be done anywhere in code), keeping track of a count separately can be a pain.

Fortunately, many times you don't really care how many items are in a list. In a strategy game, for example, you might be concerned with only three values: 0, 1, and more than 1. If a given map location has no units, don't render anything. If the map location has one unit, render it. If the map location has two or more units, you want to render whatever unit is "on top" of the stack (the first node in the list), and you want to render some sort of visual clue to let the player know that there is a stack of units on this location.

I have already shown you how to check if a list has zero nodes—just check to see if it is empty or not. In order to check for a single unit in the list, you just compare `pHead->next` and `pTail->prev`. If these two values are the same, the list contains exactly one unit. In any other case, there is "more than one" unit.

The STL List Template

Now that I've gone over how to create and implement a linked list, let's switch gears and just use Standard Template Library (STL). STL is a library of templates that comes with most if not all C++ compilers, including Visual C++ (hence the S in STL).

If you aren't familiar with templates, they are a way to make a generic function or class that applies to many different types without having to rewrite the code. For example, with a linked list, you have no idea what kind of data you want to store in it, and using `void*` is just kind of messy. The declaration for STL's list looks like the following:

```
template<class T,class A=allocator<T>> class list{/*...*/}
```

The values between the < and the > are similar to function parameters that lie between a (and a), except that now, the parameters are types. In a list, `class T` represents what you want to store in the list. It can be any type—`int`, `void*`, `float`, `double`, or a struct or class that you make yourself. `class A` represents an allocator for an object of `class T`, but you don't worry about that, since it defaults to `allocator<T>`, which is a generic version of an allocator object.

In order to use STL's list template, you only have to do the following:

```
#include <list>//include the header file
std::list<int> MyList;//declare a linked list of ints
//now we can use MyList
```

If the `std` part confuses you, it is because the list template resides in a namespace called `std` (meaning "standard," *of course*). A namespace is simply a mechanism to keep name clashes to a minimum. The word "list" is rather common, especially in programming.

Most of the time, you will use the STL list by first defining a struct or class that will store the information for something. Then you will make a list for that class or struct. (Personally, I like to `typdef` them into more easily readable type aliases.)

```
struct UnitInfo{/*...*/};//unit information structure
typedef UnitInfo *PUNITINFO;//point typedef for unit info struct
typedef std::list<PUNITINFO> UNITLIST;//typedef for unit list
typedef std::list<PUNITINFO>::iterator UNITLISTITER;//typedef for unit list iter-
ator
```

After this code, you can just use `UNITLIST` instead of `std::list<PUNITINFO>` to declare your list and work with that list type. Ah, the power of `typedef` to keep us from hurting ourselves! The last line declares a type alias for the iterator type contained in the list template (the iterator is also a template). We'll use this iterator to walk through the list later. I just wanted to show you how to declare one.

I'm not going to show you the ins and outs of the list template. One, it would take too long, and two, it would be a waste of space, since our use of lists is mainly just to keep track of units. Mainly, I'll just show you how to add, remove, and count items, check for emptiness, and iterate through a list.

For all of these examples, you will assume that the code using `UnitInfo` and `PUNITINFO` is what you're doing, plus the following declaration:

```
UNITLIST MainUnitList;//declare the main unit list
```

Adding Items

Just as when you rolled your own, there are three different ways you might like to add a new item to the list: at the beginning, at the end, or somewhere in the middle. To add an item to the beginning of the list (STL calls this the "front" of the list), you use `push_front`, like so:

```
PUNITINFO pUnitInfo=new UnitInfo;//allocate a new unit
//set up pUnitInfo here
MainUnitList.push_front(pUnitInfo);//put it in at the beginning
```

If instead you would like to place a new item at the end of the list, you use `push_back`:

```
PUNITINFO pUnitInfo=new UnitInfo;//allocate a new unit
//set up pUnitInfo here
MainUnitList.push_back(pUnitInfo);//put it in at the beginning
```

The third method, arbitrary insertion, requires an iterator (in this case, a `UNITLISTITER`), and you use the insert method. The iterator works kind of like `pCurrent` did in the "Rolling Your Own Linked List" section.

```
//assume iter is a valid UNITLISTITER
PUNITINFO pUnitInfo=new UnitInfo;//allocate a new unit
//set up pUnitInfo here
MainUnitList.insert(iter,pUnitInfo);//iter is a valid iterator for this list
```

I'd like to point out that in all cases, the insert method places the new item before (in the direction of the beginning of the list from) the iterator, not after. There are two other overloaded insert methods, but I'm not going to cover them. We can make do with this "single item" insertion.

Removing Items

To remove items, you use the remove method of the list template. If your list is using pointers to a struct, you probably first want to iterate through a list to find out what pointer you want to get rid of, and then use remove:

```
//assume pUnitInfo is a pointer that you want removed from the list
MainUnitList.remove(pUnitInfo);//removes all items that equal pUnitInfo
```

If you instead have an iterator at which you would like the removal to occur, you can use erase instead:

```
//assume iter is a valid iterator
iter=MainUnitList.erase(iter);//remove the item at the iterator, points the
iterator to the item after
```

And, just in case you are interested in removing all the items in the list, I present the clear method:

```
//clear out the list
MainUnitList.clear();
```

If you are dynamically allocating items before placing them in the list, you probably want to iterate through and deallocate all the items in the list prior to using clear, or else you'll have a memory leak. If you want to remove items at the beginning or end of the list, you can use pop_front and pop_back. Neither has any parameters.

Checking for Emptiness

This one is really easy. To do this, you use the empty method:

```
if(MainUnitList.empty())
{
	//empty
}
else
{
	//not empty
}
```

Like I said... not a difficult method to master.

Counting Items

Also not a very complicated method for STL lists. This time, the word is `size`.

```
int ItemCount=MainUnitList.size();//get the number of items in the list
```

While the documentation doesn't say this, you know full well that when `size` is called, it iterates through the entire list. You might not want that to happen. You might only be concerned about whether a list has zero, one, or two items. I'll get to how to do that with an STL list in just a moment.

Iterating Through a List

The final piece of using the STL list is iteration. Rather than going into explanations of the special iterators that are built into the list class, let me just show you the generic iteration loop, and then I'll explain it in terms of the "roll your own" example.

```
PUNITINFO pUnitInfo=NULL;
for(UNITLISTITER iter=MainUnitList.begin();iter!=MainUnitList.end();iter++)
{
	pUnitInfo=*iter;//grab the unit pointer from the iterator
	//do something with pUnitInfo
}
```

`MainUnitList.begin()` works in a manner similar to `pHead->next`. It is the first item in the list if you are iterating forward. `MainUnitList.end()` is similar to `pTail`. `iter++` uses an overloaded operator (++) to move to the next node in the list. Another overloaded operator (*) is used by the iterator to access the data stored there. I've used the preceding code as a basis for my list iterations since I started using them. It hasn't failed me yet. It won't fail you either.

As promised, I'm going to show you a quick function to check for how large a stack of items is using STL and not iterating through the entire list using size.

```
int StackSize(UNITLIST& UnitList)
{
	if(UnitList.empty()) return(0);//check for empty
	UNITLISTITER iter=UnitList.begin();//move to beginning of list
	iter++;//move to the next item (we know there is at least one)
	if(iter==UnitList.end()) return(1);//if we are at the end of the list,
	                                   //there is only one unit in the stack
	return(2);//all other cases, there are at least two units
}
```

This way is a lot more efficient than iterating through the entire list each time you want to see how large a stack of units is, which is a very common task. Got all that? The STL lists will be a lot easier once you've worked with them.

Multiple Units

Now that you've got a handle on linked lists, you can make examples that start to actually resemble strategy games. The first example in this vein is IsoHex18_3.cpp. Before I actually get into how it was built, however, I'd like to take a moment to talk about the general idea of a turn-based strategy game, and how the program will flow (in other words… design).

In turn-based strategy games, two or more players fight against each other, the goal being to either eliminate all the other players or achieve some victory condition known from the start of the game. The players might be actual human beings playing in turn on the same machine (this is called "hot seat multiplayer"), human beings playing over a network or the Internet, or computer-controlled players.

Regardless of who is playing (human or computer), the game takes place in turns. Each player gets a chance to give all his units (and/or bases) orders. In some games, the action is resolved automatically during the player's turn. In other games, the action is resolved only after all players have given their units orders. Most of the time, the "immediate resolution" model is used, unless there is some overwhelming reason not to. During a player's turn, he may order any or all of his units to move, attack, or perform some special action, or just do nothing. Special actions vary from game to game, but they typically include fortifying one's position, "sleeping" until an enemy unit comes into range, boarding a naval vessel, destroying structures (farms, roads, mines) built by enemy players, performing spy functions, or just about anything else you can imagine.

IsoHex18_3.cpp doesn't concern itself with any of the special actions. Rather, it just allows a team of units to be moved around a tilemap. However, this example is a good step toward implementing an honest-to-goodness turn-based strategy game.

Here's a basic rundown of a game turn. A "game turn" is different from a "player turn" in that each player has his player turn before a single game turn elapses.

> **Game Turn #1:**
> Player #1 gives his units orders (orders are carried out immediately)
> Player #2 gives his units orders (orders are carried out immediately)
>
> **Game Turn #2:**
> Player #1 gives his units orders (orders are carried out immediately)
> Player #2 gives his units orders (orders are carried out immediately)
>
> (and so on)

With each player turn, typically the following actions occur:

> **Player Turn:**
> Check to see if player has achieved "victory condition."
> Do whatever "upkeep" is necessary. (There might be maintenance costs for units.)

For each unit:

Wait for a command from the player.

Carry out the command.

Now that you've got the basic flow down, keep it in mind as I discuss the code. There are a number of differences between IsoHex18_3 and prior examples. For one thing, most of `Prog_Loop` has been completely rewritten and the map structure completely changed. I took out the tree (I knew you were getting tired of seeing it; it's rather homely), and I added a new type of unit. Most fundamentally, you are now using linked lists to store your units.

Constants and Globals

Naturally, the constants and globals changed quite a bit. First, I made the map smaller (there's no need to have a huge map for a simple unit example). It is now 40×40 tiles, so at least it's bigger than the screen. I could have had as large a map as I wanted.

```
const int MAPWIDTH=40;
const int MAPHEIGHT=40;
//gamestates
const int GS_IDLE=0;//waits for a keypress
const int GS_STARTTURN=1;//starts a player's turn
const int GS_ENDTURN=2;//ends a player's turn
const int GS_NEXTUNIT=3;//finds the next unit to move
const int GS_STARTMOVE=4;//starts moving the unit
const int GS_DOMOVE=5;//moves the unit
const int GS_ENDMOVE=6;//ends a unit move
const int GS_NULLMOVE=7;//tells a unit to not move
const int GS_SKIPMOVE=8;//temporarily skips the move
```

The second big change to the constants are the game states. The last example had only four. Now, there are nine. Table 18.4 lists these game states and their purposes.

Table 18.4 IsoHex18_3 Game States

Game State	Purpose
GS_IDLE	This game state is "neutral" and is used to wait for keyboard input from the player
GS_STARTTURN	At the beginning of a player's turn, this game state takes care of all details that need to be taken care of at that time
GS_ENDTURN	At the end of a player's turn, this game state cleans up whatever needs cleaning and sets the next player as the new current player
GS_NEXTUNIT	This game state selects the next unit to receive commands from the current player
GS_STARTMOVE	After a move command has been received from the player, GS_STARTMOVE begins the move
GS_DOMOVE	After a move has begun, GS_DOMOVE implements the actual move
GS_ENDMOVE	This game state finalizes a unit's movement
GS_NULLMOVE	If the player chooses not to move a unit during his turn, GS_NULLMOVE takes care of it
GS_SKIPMOVE	If the player does not want to move the current unit, but would like the option to move it this turn, he can skip this unit and come back to it later

Figure 18.10 shows a graphical view of these game states as well as the basic flow from game state to game state. From this figure, it is easy to see that GS_NEXTUNIT and GS_IDLE are the most important. Most of the time, the game will be in GS_IDLE, waiting for keyboard input.

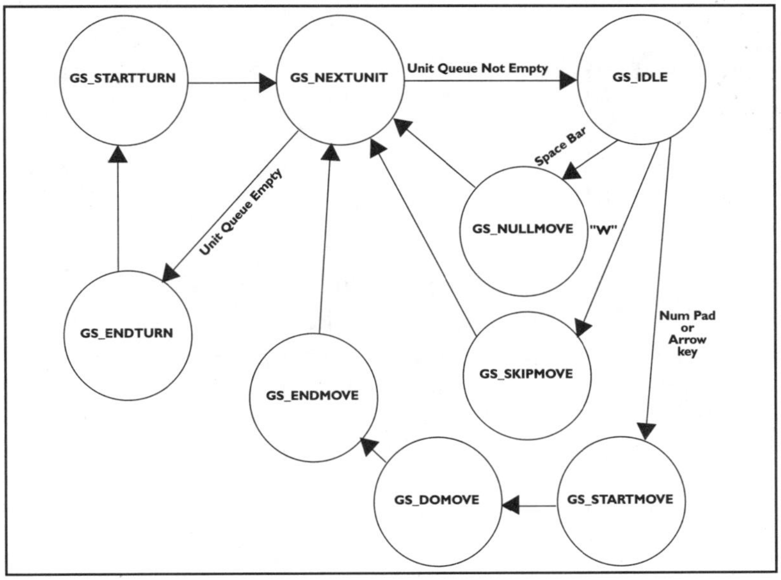

Figure 18.10

Graphical view of game states

We'll talk all about these game states a little later. For now, let's get back to globals.

```
struct UnitInfo//unit information structure
{
	int iType;//type of unit
	int iTeam;//team to which the unit belongs
	POINT ptPosition;//map location of the unit
};
typedef UnitInfo *PUNITINFO;//pointer type alias for unitinfo
typedef std::list<PUNITINFO> UNITLIST;//list of units
typedef std::list<PUNITINFO>::iterator UNITLISTITER;//iterator for unit list
```

I sort of covered this earlier, in the discussion of linked lists. I defined a `UnitInfo` structure to contain all the pertinent information about an individual unit. Table 18.5 lists the members of `UnitInfo` and their meanings.

Table 18.5 UnitInfo Members

Member	Meaning
`iType`	The type of the unit. In `tsUnit`, there are two images, each of which represents a "type" of unit.
`iTeam`	The team or player to whom this unit belongs. A new tileset called `tsShield` has images of shields with differing colors to represent the different teams. Currently there are two teams: blue(0) and red(1).
`ptPosition`	The map location in which this unit can be found.

Besides `UnitInfo`'s definition, a number of `typedef`s are used for the linked lists. `PUNITINFO` is a pointer type alias for `UnitInfo`. `UNITLIST` is an STL list that keeps `PUNITINFO`s. `UNITLISTITER` is an iterator for `UNITLIST`.

```
//map location structure
struct MapLocation
{
      UNITLIST ulUnitList;//list of units on this map location
};
MapLocation mlMap[MAPWIDTH][MAPHEIGHT];//map array
```

The `MapLocation` structure has been completely changed as well. Both `bTree` and `bUnit` have been taken out, and they have been replaced by a `UNITLIST`. Each map location maintains a list of all the units currently occupying that location.

```
UNITLIST MainUnitList;//unit list for all units
UNITLIST TeamUnitList;//unit list for teams (current player's turn)
PUNITINFO pCurrentUnit;//current unit being moved
bool bFlash;//controls the flashing of the current unit
ISODIRECTION idMoveUnit;//direction in which the unit will be moved
```

This stuff is used to manage the units. `MainUnitList` is, to no one's surprise, a master list of all units in the game.

`TeamUnitList` is a list containing all the current player's units. It gets filled during `GS_STARTMOVE` and is slowly emptied from `GS_NEXTUNIT`. `pCurrentUnit` represents the current unit, or the unit that the player is going to give orders to. It is assigned during `GS_NEXTUNIT`. `bFlash` toggles between false and true during `GS_IDLE`. If it's false, the current unit will not be shown during the current frame. If it's true, the current unit will be shown during the current frame. This results in a nice effect of a "blinking unit" to give the player a visual clue that this is the unit he will be moving. idMoveUnit is the same as it was in prior examples. It controls a unit's direction of movement.

There are a few more globals, like iCurrentTeam, which keeps track of which player is having his turn. Also, there is an additional tileset variable, tsShield, which I'll get into more detail about in this example's rendering function.

Main Loop

Now that all the preliminaries are out of the way, we can get to the meat of the program—namely, the game states that Prog_Loop responds to. These are in no particular order, so if you have to refer to Figure 18.10 or Table 18.4 to keep them straight in your head, that's OK.

GS_STARTTURN

Start at the beginning, and when you come to the end, stop. That's good advice, and I'm going to follow it here. The following snippet handles GS_STARTTURN, which occurs at the beginning of a player's turn.

```
case GS_STARTTURN://start the current team's turn
	{
		PUNITINFO pUnitInfo;//variable to check for the team's units
		UNITLISTITER iter;//iterator for the main unit list
		for(iter=MainUnitList.begin();iter!=MainUnitList.end();iter++)
			//iterate through the main unit list
		{
			pUnitInfo=*iter;//grab the unit from the list
			if(pUnitInfo->iTeam==iCurrentTeam)
				//does this unit belong to the current team?
			{
				//add this unit to the team list
				TeamUnitList.push_back(pUnitInfo);
			}
		}
		//set the next gamestate
		iGameState=GS_NEXTUNIT;
	}break;
```

This game state doesn't do much, but what it does is very important. Basically, at the start of the player's turn, all his units (or, at least, pointers to them) are taken from MainUnitList and are added to TeamUnitList. The main work is done by an iteration loop, which is a "search" loop that checks to see if the iTeam member of UnitInfo is the same as iCurrentTeam. If this criteria is met, the unit is added to the team's unit list. After the TeamUnitList has been filled, this game state yields to the next game state, GS_NEXTUNIT.

GS_NEXTUNIT

Other than GS_IDLE, the program spends the most time in GS_NEXTUNIT, which is perhaps the most important game state in the entire program. This one is a big one, so I will "annotate" as I go along.

```
case GS_NEXTUNIT://select the next unit as the current unit
    {
        //set current unit to NULL
        pCurrentUnit=NULL;
        if(TeamUnitList.empty())//if the team unit list is empty
        {
            iGameState=GS_ENDTURN;//end the turn
        }
```

The entire purpose of GS_NEXTUNIT is to set the current unit (pCurrentUnit) to point to whatever the next unit owned by the current player (iCurrentTeam) is to move. Since all the player's units were placed in TeamUnitList during GS_STARTTURN, the task is somewhat simplified. First, you check to see if TeamUnitList is empty. If it is, this player's turn is over, and you yield control to GS_ENDTURN.

```
        else
        {
            //turn is not over
            UNITLISTITER iter=TeamUnitList.begin();
                //get the first unit in the team list
            pCurrentUnit=*iter;//grab the unit from the list
            TeamUnitList.pop_front();//remove the unit from the list
```

If TeamUnitList is not empty, simply take the unit from the top or front of the list (by setting an iterator to the beginning of the list and grabbing the unit pointer from there). After you have this value, remove this unit from TeamUnitList, since presumably the unit will be moved. If it is not moved, you will replace it in the list.

```
            mlMap[pCurrentUnit->ptPosition.x]
                [pCurrentUnit->ptPosition.y].ulUnitList.remove(
                pCurrentUnit);
                //remove the unit from the map location
            mlMap[pCurrentUnit->ptPosition.x]
                [pCurrentUnit->ptPosition.y].ulUnitList.push_front(
                pCurrentUnit);//place unit at the top of the
                                //map locations unit list
```

This part might puzzle you, because the reasons for doing it are not entirely self-evident. I discovered a need to do this while writing the example. The rendering function only renders the image of the unit that is at the top or front of the map location's unit list, which means that if you want the current unit to be seen, it must be at the beginning of the list. That's what the preceding lines of code do. The first line removes the unit from the list, and the second line puts it in the front of the list.

```
                    POINT ptPlot=TilePlotter.PlotTile(pCurrentUnit->ptPosition);
                          //plot the unit's location
                    POINT ptScreen=Scroller.WorldToScreen(ptPlot);
                          //translate into screen coordinates
                    if(!PtInRect(Scroller.GetScreenSpace(),ptScreen))
                    //check to see if point is within screenspace
                    {
                          //not on screen
                          ptPlot.x-=(Scroller.GetScreenSpaceWidth()/2);
                          ptPlot.y-=(Scroller.GetAnchorSpaceHeight()/2);
                          //set the anchor
                          Scroller.SetAnchor(&ptPlot);
                          Renderer.AddRect(Scroller.GetScreenSpace());
                    }
                    iGameState=GS_IDLE;//set to idling gamestate
             }
      }break;
```

Before yielding to GS_IDLE (the final task that takes place in GS_NEXTUNIT), you first must guarantee that the unit can be seen on-screen. I took a rather simple approach to this by plotting the tile, translating to screen coordinates, and checking to see if this point is within the screen space. If it isn't, the scroller's anchor is modified to center on the unit, and the renderer is told to update the entire screen. This method works, but it's less than ideal, especially when a unit is near the edge of the screen space. You might replace the screen space rectangle with some other rectangle that guarantees that the entire unit will be visible on-screen.

GS_ENDTURN

As I said earlier, these game states are in no particular order. (Actually, they are, but explaining how my mind works would take a whole other book.) The next on the list is GS_ENDTURN.

```
case GS_ENDTURN://end of a player's turn
      {
            //clear out team unit list (just to be sure)
            TeamUnitList.clear();
            //change team
            iCurrentTeam=1-iCurrentTeam;
            iGameState=GS_STARTTURN;//set gamestate to start next turn
      }break;
```

This one is pretty short and sweet. First, you clear out the TeamUnitList. It's empty already, of course, because otherwise, GS_NEXTUNIT would not have sent you to GS_ENDTURN, but clearing out an empty list doesn't take up any overhead (at least, not enough to worry about), and being safe is good. After you have ensured that the TeamUnitList is empty, the next player is selected (by changing the value of iCurrentTeam), and you are then sent to GS_STARTTURN to start the cycle over.

GS_IDLE

As stated earlier, most of the time spent in the program is spent in GS_IDLE. Its job is to update the display each frame until keyboard input is processed, at which time you switch to another game state.

```
case GS_IDLE://the game is idling; update the frame, but that's about it.
      {
            DWORD dwTimeStart=GetTickCount();//get the frame start time
            //scroll the frame (0,0)
            Renderer.ScrollFrame(0,0);
            //toggle unit flash
            bFlash=!bFlash;
            //add the tile in which the current unit lives
            Renderer.AddTile(pCurrentUnit->ptPosition.x,pCurrentUnit-
>ptPosition.y);
            //update the frame
            Renderer.UpdateFrame();
            //flip to show the back buffer
            lpddsMain->Flip(0,DDFLIP_WAIT);
            //wait until 200 ms have passed
            while(GetTickCount()-dwTimeStart<200);
      }break;
```

There is nothing earth-shattering here. Mainly, you just tell the renderer to do its job. There's one thing of note, however. Your new global, bFlash, changes value each time GS_IDLE is executed, and the tile occupied by the current unit is updated. Also, a frame limiter ensures that 200 milliseconds pass before another frame is shown. This is what gives you a "flashing unit" effect for whichever unit is the current unit (pCurrentUnit). There will be more about this when I cover the rendering function.

GS_NULLMOVE

This game state is one of three ways to get out of GS_IDLE. To get here, the user presses the spacebar, indicating that he does not want to move this unit this turn.

```
case GS_NULLMOVE://do not move the current unit
      {
            //don't really do anything, just go to the next unit
```

```
            pCurrentUnit=NULL;
            iGameState=GS_NEXTUNIT;
        }break;
```

Not a lot going on here. You set the current unit to NULL and set the game state to GS_NEXTUNIT.

GS_SKIPMOVE

The second option for getting out of GS_IDLE is GS_SKIPMOVE. You can get there by pressing the W key on the keyboard, indicating that you might still want to move this unit a little later, but not right now.

```
case GS_SKIPMOVE://skip this unit for now
        {
            //put unit at end of team unit list
            TeamUnitList.push_back(pCurrentUnit);
            pCurrentUnit=NULL;//set current unit to NULL
            iGameState=GS_NEXTUNIT;//select the next unit
        }break;
```

This game state is only slightly more complicated than GS_NULLMOVE. In fact, it adds only one line. Since the player might want to move the unit later, you replace it back in TeamUnitList before setting the current unit to NULL and moving to GS_NEXTUNIT.

GS_STARTMOVE

This is the third and final way to get out of GS_IDLE. It is accomplished by processing a movement keystroke. The movement keys are the arrow keys, the numeric keypad, and Home, End, Page Up, and Page Down. (The numeric keypad works whether Num Lock is on or off.)

```
case GS_STARTMOVE:
        {
            //remove the unit from the map location
            mlMap[pCurrentUnit->ptPosition.x]
                [pCurrentUnit->ptPosition.y].ulUnitList.remove(
                pCurrentUnit);
            Renderer.AddTile(pCurrentUnit->ptPosition.x,pCurrentUnit-
>ptPosition.y);
            //set next gamestate
            iGameState=GS_DOMOVE;
        }break;
```

This example, as you might have already noticed, does not use the methods I discussed in IsoHex18_2, where you smoothly slid the unit from one tile to another. However, all the appropriate game states already exist in this example, so implementing it wouldn't be that big of a deal. The reason that I did not is because I wanted to showcase the linked list and multiple-unit stuff without cluttering it up with other code.

In GS_STARTMOVE, the current unit is removed from its current map location, and that map location's coordinates are added to the renderer for updating. No rendering is done during GS_STARTMOVE. Next, the game moves to GS_DOMOVE. In essence, GS_STARTMOVE is "picking up" the unit, much in the same way you would pick up a chess piece.

GS_DOMOVE

This game state performs the actual move. If GS_STARTMOVE is picking up the piece, this game state is actually moving it (but not setting it down).

```
case GS_DOMOVE:
	{
		//move the unit
		pCurrentUnit->ptPosition=
			TileWalker.TileWalk(pCurrentUnit->ptPosition,idMoveUnit);
		//set next gamestate
		iGameState=GS_ENDMOVE;
	}break;
```

This is an easy one. Simply use the TileWalker to move the current unit's ptPosition member, and then send the game into GS_ENDMOVE.

> **NOTE**
>
> **It might seem silly to have these very small, overly broken-up game states, but I feel that they illustrate the concept pretty well in bite-sized pieces, rather than dumping a whole bunch of code on you and then saying "Here, figure this out." In reality, you would probably implement it differently, but the same things would still occur.**

GS_ENDMOVE

This is the last game state, where you finally "set the piece down." After this game state, a unit is considered to have made a complete move, and then the next unit is selected.

```
case GS_ENDMOVE:
	{
		//place the unit on its new map location
		mlMap[pCurrentUnit->ptPosition.x]
```

```
                [pCurrentUnit-
            >ptPosition.y].ulUnitList.push_front(pCurrentUnit);
            Renderer.AddTile(pCurrentUnit->ptPosition.x,pCurrentUnit-
>ptPosition.y);
            pCurrentUnit=NULL;
            //set next gamestate
            iGameState=GS_NEXTUNIT;
            DWORD dwTimeStart=GetTickCount();//get the frame start time
            //scroll the frame (0,0)
            Renderer.ScrollFrame(0,0);
            //update the frame
            Renderer.UpdateFrame();
            //flip to show the back buffer
            lpddsMain->Flip(0,DDFLIP_WAIT);
            //wait until 500 ms have passed
            while(GetTickCount()-dwTimeStart<500);
        }break;
```

This game state does sort of the opposite of GS_STARTMOVE by placing the unit onto its new position. Then, a single frame is rendered, and the game waits for 500 milliseconds so that you get at least a half-second to see where your unit has moved. After that, the game moves to GS_NEXTUNIT, where the process starts all over again.

Next, I want to move on to the rendering function, which will bring to light certain details that I have yet to discuss.

Rendering Function

Ah, the rendering function... workhorse of the renderer, which accomplishes all the drawing for the entire application. This time around, the rendering function has changed a great deal, and it has gotten rather large, so I'm going to discuss it bit by bit.

```
void RenderFunc(LPDIRECTDRAWSURFACE7 lpddsDst, RECT* rcClip, int xDst, int yDst,
int xMap, int yMap)
{
        //put background tile
        tsBack.ClipTile(lpddsDst,rcClip,xDst,yDst,0);
```

This part you've seen before. It's the only part that didn't change from prior examples. Naturally, you have to render the background tile before rendering anything else.

```
        //check for an empty list
        if(!mlMap[xMap][yMap].ulUnitList.empty())
        {
```

The remainder of the function is executed if and only if the unit list for the map location (xMap,yMap) is not empty. If it is empty, the rest of this stuff is skipped.

```
//list is not empty
UNITLISTITER iter=mlMap[xMap][yMap].ulUnitList.begin();
      //get iterator to beginning of list
PUNITINFO pUnitInfo=*iter;//grab the item
```

This is your basic "grab the unit pointer" code, which is in this example several times. Simply set an iterator to the beginning of the unit list of the map location in question, and then use the overloaded * operator to gain access to the item stored there.

```
//if this is the current unit
if(pUnitInfo==pCurrentUnit)
{
      //this is the current unit
      if(!bFlash) return;//if flash is "off" don't render
}
```

I mentioned bFlash (one of the new globals) earlier. This is where the "flashing" effect of the current unit is accomplished. If the topmost unit is the current unit (pCurrentUnit), you check if bFlash is false. If it is, return without rendering anything.

```
//place the unit
tsUnit.ClipTile(lpddsDst,rcClip,xDst,yDst,pUnitInfo->iType);
```

I know that this is just a single line, but it's an important one. Based on what is stored in the unit's iType, render the appropriate image from tsUnit.

```
iter++;//move to the next item in the list
if(iter==mlMap[xMap][yMap].ulUnitList.end())
      //if the end of the list, this is a single unit
```

Now that the unit is rendered, you must also render the shield next to it. Which shield image is shown depends on two things. The first is the contents of iTeam, giving you which color to use, and the second is whether this is a single unit or a stack. The preceding code moves the iterator (which previously was at the beginning of the list) and advances it by 1. If the iterator now sits at the end of the list, you know that there is only a single unit here, so the next bit of code is executed.

```
{
      tsShield.ClipTile(lpddsDst,rcClip,xDst+
            ptShieldOffset[pUnitInfo->iType].x,yDst+
            ptShieldOffset[pUnitInfo->iType].y,pUnitInfo->iTeam*2);
```

```
                        //place the shield
            }
```

This code renders a "single unit" shield. The image for the shield contains four images: `Team1-Single(0)`, `Team1-Stack(1)`, `Team2-Single(2)`, and `Team2-Stack(3)`. So, you can use `iTeam*2` for single units.

```
            else//more than one unit...this is a stack
            {
                tsShield.ClipTile(lpddsDst,rcClip,xDst+
                      ptShieldOffset[pUnitInfo->iType].x,yDst+
                      ptShieldOffset[pUnitInfo->iType].y,pUnitInfo-
                >iTeam*2+1);
                            //place the shield
            }
        }
}
```

If the unit is part of a stack, you use `iTeam*2+1` for the image number from the shield tileset.

And that's it for the rendering function. Almost half of it is concerned with rendering the appropriate shield. I could have instead used the `count` method of the list template, but since you don't actually care how many units are in the stack, I felt it was a waste.

Event Handling

Last, but certainly not least, we come to event handling. All input for this example is in the way of keypresses and can be found under `WM_KEYDOWN` in the window procedure. These keypresses are the only way to get out of `GS_IDLE` and into another game state.

VK_SPACE

Whenever the spacebar is pressed during `GS_IDLE`, you must inform the game that the current unit will not be moving this turn.

```
case VK_SPACE://do not move unit
        {
                if(iGameState==GS_IDLE) iGameState=GS_NULLMOVE;
                        //only respond when gamestate is GS_IDLE;
                return(0);
        }break;
```

This is a simple event handler. First, make sure that the game state is `GS_IDLE`. If it is, set it to `GS_NULLMOVE`.

W

The character W is the wait command, telling the game that you might want to move this unit during the current turn, but you do not want to move it just now.

```
case 'W'://wait to move this unit later
      {
            //skip this unit for now
            if(iGameState==GS_IDLE) iGameState=GS_SKIPMOVE;
            return(0);
      }break;
```

Again, this is a very simple handler. Check for GS_IDLE, and set it to GS_SKIPMOVE.

Direction Keys

There are 16 of these in total, but I'm only going to show you two of them, since they are all so similar (the only difference is the direction to which idMoveUnit is set). Table 18.6 shows what keys initiate movement in the various directions.

Table 18.6 Keys and Directions

Main Key	Secondary Key	Direction
VK_NUMPAD8	VK_UP	ISO_NORTH
VK_NUMPAD9	VK_PRIOR	ISO_NORTHEAST
VK_NUMPAD6	VK_RIGHT	ISO_EAST
VK_NUMPAD3	VK_NEXT	ISO_SOUTHEAST
VK_NUMPAD2	VK_DOWN	ISO_SOUTH
VK_NUMPAD1	VK_END	ISO_SOUTHWEST
VK_NUMPAD4	VK_LEFT	ISO_WEST
VK_NUMPAD7	VK_HOME	ISO_NORTHWEST

These keys were chosen so that the example would work regardless of the state of the Num Lock key. With this in mind, let's take a look at the case for northward movement, VK_NUMPAD8 and VK_UP.

```
case VK_NUMPAD8:
case VK_UP:
      {
            if(iGameState==GS_IDLE)//gamestate must be GS_IDLE
            {
```

First and foremost, the game must be in GS_IDLE, or no key processing should be done, and this keypress should be ignored.

```
                  idMoveUnit=ISO_NORTH;//move to the north
                  //check the next position
                  POINT ptNext=TileWalker.TileWalk(
                        pCurrentUnit->ptPosition,idMoveUnit);
```

Next, select the appropriate direction for idMoveUnit (ISO_NORTH in this case), and assign a POINT variable (ptNext) to the next location if this move were allowed by using the TileWalker. Before a move is processed, you must first validate it.

```
                  if(ptNext.x>=0 && ptNext.y>=0 &&
                        ptNext.x<MAPWIDTH && ptNext.y<MAPWIDTH)
                        //bounds checking
                  {
```

The very first thing to check before allowing this move to go forward is whether or not the destination (ptNext) even exists as a map location. If you have moved out of bounds, the following code is skipped:

```
                        if(mlMap[ptNext.x][ptNext.y].ulUnitList.empty())
                              //if the map location is empty
                        {
                              //set the unit in motion
                              iGameState=GS_STARTMOVE;
                        }
```

The second part of validation requires that you eliminate "illegal" map locations. For the purposes of this example, the only illegal map locations are those occupied by units of the opposing team, so if the map location at ptNext is empty, the move can go ahead with no problems, and the game state is set to GS_STARTMOVE.

```
                        else
                        {
                              UNITLISTITER iter=mlMap[ptNext.x]
```

```
                                [ptNext.y].ulUnitList.begin();
                                //get the first entry in the list
                            PUNITINFO pUnitInfo=*iter;
                            //get the unit from the list
                            if(pUnitInfo->iTeam==pCurrentUnit->iTeam)
                                //must be the same team
                            {
                                iGameState=GS_STARTMOVE;
                            }
                        }
                    }
                }
            }break;
```

If the destination map location is not empty, you proceed to the third part of validation. You must determine what team occupies the map location at `ptNext`. If it is your team (`pCurrentUnit->iTeam`), the move can proceed, and the game state can be set to `GS_STARTMOVE`. If not, the movement command is ignored.

You now have full understanding of the thought process behind IsoHex18_3.cpp. I hope I have shown that linked lists aren't as scary as you might first have thought, and that STL isn't as evil as everyone makes it out to be. In our case, it drastically reduces the complexity of the program and also makes it so that you don't have to "roll your own" linked lists.

Oh... you probably want to see what the application looks like, right? Figure 18.11 gives a glimpse. This figure really doesn't do it justice, so you just have to run it and play around with it for a while. I think it's pretty neat, but then again, I wrote it.

Figure 18.11

Output of IsoHex18_3.cpp

SUMMARY

It's been a long journey, but well worth it. We've covered coarse object placement and movement, and the examples are starting to look game-like. We've gone from a single unit to multiple units and linked lists. After a long time in building, you are starting to see some results from all the hard work you've put into these isometric components, and they are serving you well. In the next few chapters, you'll refine and enhance what you've already got, and by the end, you should have enough information to start work on an honest-to-goodness strategy game.

CHAPTER 19

Object Selection

- Simple Object Selection Design
- Simple Object Selection Implementation
- Pixel-Perfect Object Selection
- Minimap, Zones of Control, and the Fog of War

After spending so much time on object placement and movement, object selection might seem almost anticlimactic, since most of the foundation for the tasks ahead has already been taken care of. Nevertheless, a good, solid grasp of object selection will enhance your games immeasurably. If you've ever played a game that had a clunky interface, you know what I mean. Many game developers tend to pay only a passing amount of attention to what matters most—control over your game. I don't mean user interface elements (like buttons, windows, and so on), but rather how you select the objects under your control, and how you give them orders. Also, I'll introduce you to three very common strategy game features: the minimap, zones of control, and the fog of war.

Simple Object Selection

I'm currently using the *turn-based strategy game* paradigm, and I'm going to stay with it for a while, since it makes demonstrating concepts easy. Still, the concepts shown here can be adapted for use in a real-time system as well. The first thing we'll look at is a very simple object selection algorithm.

Chapter 18, "Object Placement and Movement," explored a way to control multiple units in example IsoHex18_3. Although it was a very simplistic example, it got the job done. However, it left the user relatively few options as far as organizing unit movement. You could simply move the unit, not move the unit, or move the unit later, which isn't much as far as control is concerned. Ideally, you might like to select a different unit with the mouse, either by clicking on that unit, or by clicking on the map location containing that unit. You'll start with clicking on the map location, because that is easier, and later you'll move on to "pixel-perfect" unit selection.

Simple Object Selection Design

Before you do any work, you must figure out exactly what you want to accomplish. In the next example, which is based on IsoHex18_3.cpp (it already has the multiple-unit stuff built into it), you want the following features:

- The ability to click on another unit and have it become the current unit
- The ability to tell a unit to "fortify" or "hold current position" indefinitely (it gets annoying to press the spacebar each turn for units you do not want to move)
- The ability to "scout" the map by scrolling the screen space
- The ability to center the screen on the current unit (in case you were scouting and now you want to find your unit again)

Now, let's take these one by one, and explore the benefits and pitfalls of making them happen.

Click-Selecting Units

In IsoHex18_3, you simply looped through all the units, one at a time, moving or not moving them as desired. This method remains a suitable way to do things, so you won't change it. What you want to do, however, requires that you "short-circuit" this loop after clicking on a unit's map location. The benefit gained is that you help achieve one of the main objectives for this example—more choices in controlling units.

The pitfalls aren't too deep—there are just a few things to think about. First, you have to decide whether you are responding to `WM_LBUTTONDOWN` or `WM_LBUTTONUP`. This isn't a tough choice, but it's a significant one. You'll use both, actually, and I'm about to tell you why.

If you've been working with Windows for a while, you probably use an important feature of it without really thinking about it—canceling a button press by moving off it. Whenever you click on a button, it displays its "down" image, indicating to you that yes, you have pressed the left mouse button over that control. However, the action associated with that button does not occur until you release the left mouse button, and, more importantly, you must release the mouse button over that same control, or nothing happens.

That is sort of what I want to accomplish here. If you click the left mouse button, the tile on which the mouse rests is recorded. Later, if the left mouse button is released while over that same tile, a click is registered, and the appropriate action takes place. Later on, you'll change this behavior to include unit dragging, but for now, it will suffice. So, if the left mouse button is pressed and released within the same map location, the program must perform the appropriate action. Depending on what the map location in question contains, the "appropriate action" might differ.

For unit selection, you are concerned with map locations that contain units belonging to the current team. Also, the map location must have a unit that has not moved or received an order earlier in the turn. This will involve some bookkeeping on your part.

Finally, there might be more than one unit on the map location in question, so you have to allow some manner of selecting exactly which unit is to be moved. See? It's getting complicated already, or at least less simple.

Fortification/Holding Position

This item sounds relatively simple, but it has some significant ramifications for the rest of the program. The basic idea here is that you provide some way to tell a unit to stay where it is, indefinitely, until you select it again on some other turn. The benefit is that you will no longer need to press the spacebar every turn for that unit, which in turn lowers the "annoyance" factor. The first issue you need to address in order to make this work is that of indication. You must have some way to visually show the player that the unit is holding position. My personal choice is to make a little H that appears on the shield of that unit.

The impact on your code is that there must be a flag in the `UnitInfo` struct that tells you the unit is holding position, which is a simple enough matter. Also, you have to add art to the shield bitmap (another simple matter), and you need to modify the rendering code.

The next little snag is more subtle. Let me paint you a scenario. During my turn, I tell one of my units to hold position instead of move. This is fine, so I set the little member of `UnitInfo` to true. Now, later in the same turn, I click on this same unit, and I should be able to move it, because it hasn't moved yet. Now, let's say I wait until my next turn to click on it and move it. Again, this isn't much of a problem, because the unit has been holding position since the beginning of the turn.

Now, let's look ahead. I'm rather confident that later you will want units that move more than a single tile per turn. In fact, I'm sure of it. Let's say that the unit I told to hold position has a movement allowance of two squares per turn, and that I moved it one square and then told it to hold position. If I were to click on it and select it later in the turn, I should be allowed to move it only one square.

The concept I'm trying to get across is "movement points." You haven't worried about them, because all your units move only one square per turn, but this won't always be so. So, you should add a member to `UnitInfo` to keep track of how many movement points a unit has, even if for now the number is only one.

There are other issues: What happens when the units holding position come up during the iteration of the team's unit list? Do you just skip that unit's turn? Do you hold off until all the nonholding units have been moved? What if all of a player's units are holding position? Do you just skip his turn, because there is nothing to move? Answering these questions now, instead of when you're in the middle of writing the program, will help you immensely and will avoid problems when you are testing the program.

To answer the question of what to do when a holding unit comes up in rotation, it would be unfair to skip that unit's turn, since the player might still want to move that unit later, and he should be given a chance to do so. To do this, you either have to leave the unit in the team list, which means you'll have to change how `GS_NEXTUNIT` selects its next unit, or you can keep units that are holding position in another list, which means you'll have to change the way you select units with the mouse (which you haven't written yet anyway, so it's no big deal).

To answer the question of what to do if all of a player's unit's are holding position, it would be grossly unfair (and not very fun) to exclude a chance for a player to change his orders. As long as at least one unit has been moved, you can skip the units that are holding position and progress to the other player's turn, since the player had a chance to change orders if he wished. If no unit has been moved, the program should go into a semi-paused state so that the player can change his unit's orders if he wishes, or just click a button or press a key to skip his turn. This will be pretty simple to implement. You'll just need an extra `bool` global that you set to false at the beginning of a player's turn, set to true if a unit is moved (or given an order) during that turn, and check for at the end of the player's turn.

Scouting

Compared to the last two items, this one is pretty simple. You want to be able to look around the map before you decide what you're doing with a unit. This feature is an absolute must for most types of games.

You have two basic methods to choose from. One is the "mouse at the edges" scrolling method (which you've done in previous examples), and the other is the "click on an empty square to move screen space" method. For a change, I want to use the second method (not that there is anything wrong with the first one). This brings to mind the question of what constitutes an empty square. For your purposes, an empty square is any square that does not have a unit belonging to the current player's team. When clicked (you will follow the same rules as for the first item), the screen space will be centered on the map location in question.

That's about it for scouting. It's not tough, it just requires playing with the screen-space anchor.

Centering on the Current Unit

Because you added the ability to scout the surroundings in the preceding item, it is entirely possible that the screen space might move quite far afield, and it's quite likely that you will forget where the heck that unit you were about to move is. This happens to me all the time in the games I play. Almost all games give you the ability to quickly center screen space back on the current unit. (As for those that don't, let's just say those CDs gather a lot of dust in my house.)

In this program, centering is simple. During `GS_IDLE`, if the C key is pressed, you have screen space center on the current unit's position, exactly the same way it does during `GS_NEXTUNIT`.

Simple Object Selection Implementation

Go ahead and load up IsoHex19_1.cpp. In this example, I've implemented all of what was listed during the design discussion. Visually, you won't be able to tell the difference between this example and IsoHex18_3.cpp (the example upon which this one is based), except in a few places.

Game States

Most of the changes in IsoHex19_1 consist of modifications to existing game states and the addition of new game states. The rest of the application is left untouched for the most part. There is a new tileset (`tsPressEnter`) and a few extra globals, but I'll shed light on them as they are used.

Table 19.1 lists the game states for this example. As you can see, most of them are carried over from IsoHex18_3. Because of the new capabilities, most of the game states have been modified, even if very slightly.

Table 19.1 IsoHex19_1 Game States

GS_IDLE	GS_SKIPMOVE
GS_STARTTURN	GS_HOLDPOSITION*
GS_ENDTURN	GS_CLICKSELECT*
GS_NEXTUNIT	GS_CLICKCENTER*
GS_STARTMOVE	GS_CLICKSTACK*
GS_DOMOVE	GS_PICKUNIT*
GS_ENDMOVE	
GS_NULLMOVE	*New game state

As you can see, there are only five new game states, but the functions of a few of the old ones have changed significantly to compensate for the changes. Let's take them one at a time.

GS_IDLE

As in IsoHex18_3, the bulk of the time is spent in GS_IDLE. However, GS_IDLE is now performing double duty. The current unit (pCurrentUnit) can be NULL, indicating that no unit is currently selected, but the player's turn isn't over yet. This happens when all of a player's units are holding position. I'm going to quickly go through this game state's code and annotate the changes I have made.

```
case GS_IDLE://the game is idling; update the frame, but that's about it.
      {
            DWORD dwTimeStart=GetTickCount();//get the frame start time
            //scroll the frame (0,0)
            Renderer.ScrollFrame(0,0);
            //toggle unit flash
            bFlash=!bFlash;
            //if the current unit is not null
            if(pCurrentUnit!=NULL)
            {
                  //add the tile in which the current unit lives
```

```
                        Renderer.AddTile(pCurrentUnit->ptPosition.x, pCurrentUnit-
>ptPosition.y);
                }
```

This is the first change. Before, no matter what, pCurrentUnit was always non-NULL when you were in GS_IDLE. You can no longer make that assumption, so you must check to see if pCurrentUnit is not NULL. If it is, you add its tile position to the renderer for updating.

```
                //update the frame
                Renderer.UpdateFrame();
                //if the current unit IS null
                if(pCurrentUnit==NULL)
                {
                        //show the end of turn marker if bflash is true
                        if(bFlash) tsPressEnter.PutTile(lpddsBack,0,0,iCurrentTeam);
                }
```

This is the flip side of the preceding change. If pCurrentUnit is NULL, the player can choose to select a unit with the mouse or press Enter to indicate that he does not wish to move any of his units. While in this situation, you must somehow clue the user in that he is in this state. I chose to do this by flashing "Press Enter" in the player's color (blue or red) in the upper-left corner of the screen. The images for this text exist in tsPressEnter and come from PressEnter.bmp. In a real situation, you probably want to have actual text, but implementing a font engine for such a small part seemed wasteful to me. Also of note, the text is blitted to the back buffer *after* the renderer has updated the frame, so you don't have to worry about updating it next frame.

```
                //flip to show the back buffer
                lpddsMain->Flip(0,DDFLIP_WAIT);
                //wait until 200 ms have passed
                while(GetTickCount()-dwTimeStart<200);
        }break;
```

GS_IDLE ends as it did before, waiting for 200 milliseconds before returning. The changes to GS_IDLE are small, but they do have important impact as far as how the program looks.

GS_STARTTURN

This game state has also been modified slightly from its older version. IsoHex18_3 had no movement points, but this example does. In fact, just to make things interesting, I made one unit able to move two squares per turn, and the other unit just one.

```
case GS_STARTTURN://start the current team's turn
```

```
	{
		PUNITINFO pUnitInfo;//variable to check for the team's units
		UNITLISTITER iter;//iterator for the main unit list
		for(iter=MainUnitList.begin();iter!=MainUnitList.end();
			iter++)//iterate through the main unit list
		{
			pUnitInfo=*iter;//grab the unit from the list
			if(pUnitInfo->iTeam==iCurrentTeam)
				//does this unit belong to the current team?
			{
				//give the unit a movement point
				pUnitInfo->iMovePoints=1+pUnitInfo->iType;
```

This is one change to GS_STARTTURN, setting each unit's iMovePoints member to iType+1. Since iType is either 0 or 1, iMovePoints will be set to 1 or 2.

```
				//add this unit to the team list
				TeamUnitList.push_back(pUnitInfo);
			}
		}
		//set moved unit flag to false
		bMovedUnit=false;
		//set the next gamestate
		iGameState=GS_NEXTUNIT;
	}break;
```

A few lines from the bottom is another change—setting bMovedUnit to false. The bMovedUnit variable is a new global. It records whether or not a player has given a unit a command during his turn—that is, by going to GS_STARTMOVE, GS_NULLMOVE, or GS_HOLDPOSITION. The GS_SKIPMOVE game state does not set this variable to true, because telling a unit to wait for orders later is not considered an actual order to do something. bMovedUnit comes into play later in GS_NEXTUNIT.

GS_NEXTUNIT

This game state was modified more than most because of its central role in the program. The first factor that I had to take into account was that of units that were holding position (bHolding==true). Another factor was the state of bMovedUnit when there were no units left to move.

```
case GS_NEXTUNIT://select the next unit as the current unit
	{
		//set current unit to NULL
		pCurrentUnit=NULL;
		if(TeamUnitList.empty())//if the team unit list is empty
```

```
        {
                //if a unit has been moved, send to end of turn
                if(bMovedUnit)
                {
                        iGameState=GS_ENDTURN;//end the turn
                }
                else
                {
                        //send to GS_IDLE
                        iGameState=GS_IDLE;//send to idle state
                }
        }
```

This code takes into account the status of bMovedUnit. If bMovedUnit is true, a unit has been given an order during this player's turn, so it is safe to end his turn. If it is false, the player must be given a chance to select a unit with the mouse and give it an order, so the program proceeds into GS_IDLE (with pCurrentUnit==NULL).

```
        else
        {
                //turn is not over
                UNITLISTITER iter=TeamUnitList.begin();
                        //get the first unit in the team list
                pCurrentUnit=*iter;//grab the unit from the list
                TeamUnitList.pop_front();//remove the unit from the list
                //check to see if this unit is holding position
                if(pCurrentUnit->bHolding) return;//go to next unit
                mlMap[pCurrentUnit->ptPosition.x]
                        [pCurrentUnit->ptPosition.y].ulUnitList.remove(
                        pCurrentUnit);//remove the unit from the map location
                mlMap[pCurrentUnit->ptPosition.x]
                        [pCurrentUnit->ptPosition.y].ulUnitList.push_front(
                        pCurrentUnit);//place unit at the top of the map loca-
                tions unit list
                POINT ptPlot=TilePlotter.PlotTile(pCurrentUnit->ptPosition);
                        //plot the unit's location
                POINT ptScreen=Scroller.WorldToScreen(ptPlot);
                        //translate into screen coordinates
                if(!PtInRect(Scroller.GetScreenSpace(),ptScreen))
                        //check to see if point is within screenspace
                {
                        //not on screen
```

```
                    ptPlot.x-=(Scroller.GetScreenSpaceWidth()/2);
                    ptPlot.y-=(Scroller.GetScreenSpaceHeight()/2);
                    //set the anchor
                    Scroller.SetAnchor(&ptPlot);
                    Renderer.AddRect(Scroller.GetScreenSpace());
                }
                iGameState=GS_IDLE;//set to idling gamestate
            }
    }break;
```

The rest of GS_NEXTUNIT remains the same, with one exception. If the first unit in TeamUnitList is holding position, you skip this unit (by simply returning from the function—the unit has already been moved from the list) and wait for GS_NEXTUNIT to be executed again. Otherwise, you process the unit as normal, set pCurrentUnit equal to it, and move into GS_IDLE.

GS_STARTMOVE AND GS_NULLMOVE

These game states change almost imperceptibly, so I'm not going to waste space describing them here. You can check them out in the code if you want. The main change for these game states is that they set bMovedUnit to true in addition to their former roles.

GS_HOLDPOSITION

This is one of the new keyboard commands holding position. This can occur only during GS_IDLE when pCurrentUnit is non-NULL and the H key is pressed. When this happens, the game moves into GS_HOLDPOSITION.

```
case GS_HOLDPOSITION://tell unit to hold position
    {
        //set holding flag
        pCurrentUnit->bHolding=true;
        //show the holding unit
        Renderer.AddTile(pCurrentUnit->ptPosition.x, pCurrentUnit-
>ptPosition.y);
        pCurrentUnit=NULL;
        bFlash=true;
        //set next gamestate
        iGameState=GS_NEXTUNIT;
```

This game state is comprised of two parts. This first part modifies the unit data (setting the bHolding member to true), tells the renderer to update the tile on which the current unit is resting, sets pCurrentUnit to NULL, sets bFlash to false (you don't want flashing right now), and sets the next game state, which is GS_NEXTUNIT.

```
            DWORD dwTimeStart=GetTickCount();//get the frame start time
            //scroll the frame (0,0)
            Renderer.ScrollFrame(0,0);
            //update the frame
            Renderer.UpdateFrame();
            //flip to show the back buffer
            lpddsMain->Flip(0,DDFLIP_WAIT);
            //wait until 500 ms have passed
            while(GetTickCount()-dwTimeStart<500);
        }break;
```

This second half of GS_HOLDPOSITION is taken almost verbatim from GS_ENDMOVE, where the display is updated. You wait for 500 milliseconds before proceeding. This is so that the player can actually see that his unit is now holding position for a split second before proceeding to the next unit.

GS_CLICKSELECT

GS_CLICKSELECT, along with GS_CLICKCENTER, GS_CLICKSTACK, and GS_PICKUNIT, comprises the large addition of functionality in this example. These game states handle all the mouse input once it occurs. See figure 19.1.

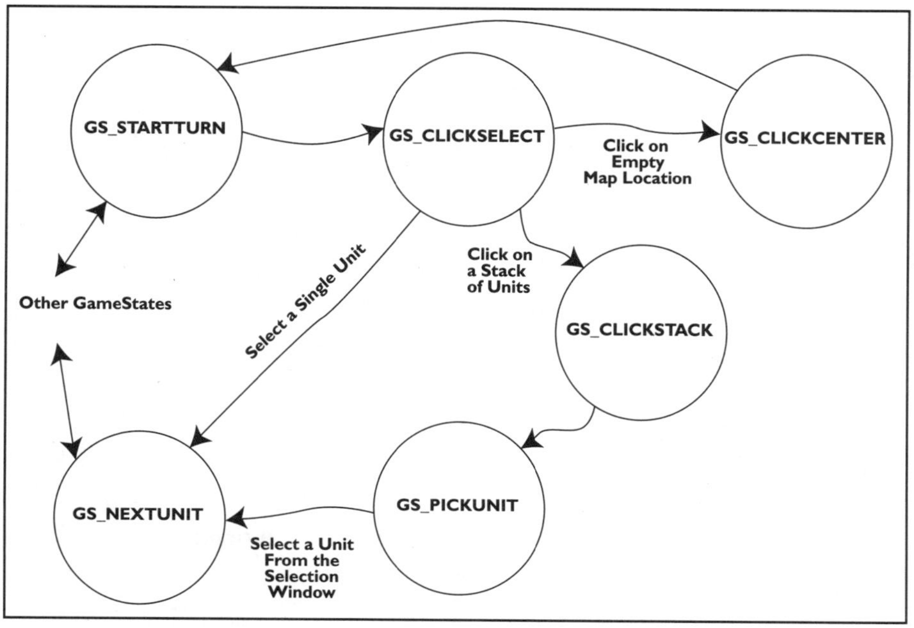

Figure 19.1

Additional Game States

GS_CLICKSELECT acts as a router of sorts. I decided I'd rather do that than put all the conditional code (there's a lot of it) into the handler for WM_LBUTTONDOWN and WM_LBUTTONUP. This game state, despite the appearance, contains a lot of code, mainly because of all the testing that needs to be done in order to decide what action to perform once a map location is clicked.

First, GS_CLICKSELECT checks if the map location in question is empty. If it is, the program gets sent to GS_CLICKCENTER. If not, it then checks to see what team the units within that location belong to. If they belong to the other player, again the program is sent to GS_CLICKCENTER. Otherwise, the current player owns the units within that location. If it is a single unit, GS_CLICKSELECT attempts to make it the current unit (checking if the unit has any movement points before doing so). If it is a stack of units, the program goes into GS_CLICKSTACK.

```
case GS_CLICKSELECT:
        {
                //check map location for emptiness
                if(mlMap[ptClick.x][ptClick.y].ulUnitList.empty())
                {
                        //map location is empty
                        //we want to center on this map location
                        iGameState=GS_CLICKCENTER;
                }
```

First, check the unit list at the map location stored in ptClick for emptiness. If the unit list is empty, send the game into GS_CLICKCENTER.

```
                else
                {
                        //map location is not empty
                        //look at top of list
                        UNITLISTITER
iter=mlMap[ptClick.x][ptClick.y].ulUnitList.begin();
                        PUNITINFO pUnitInfo=*iter;
                        //check if this unit belongs to the current team
```

The unit list is not empty, so the mouse has clicked on an occupied square, and you must determine what team the units there belong to. The preceding code grabs the unit at the beginning of the list.

```
                        if(pUnitInfo->iTeam==iCurrentTeam)
                        {
                                //belongs to current team
                                //one unit?
```

Aha! The units in question belong to the current team! This leaves the question of how many units there are and whether any of them receive orders.

```
if(mlMap[ptClick.x][ptClick.y].ulUnitList.size()==1)
{
        //a single unit (already contained in pUnitInfo)
        //is this the current unit?
        if(pUnitInfo==pCurrentUnit)
        {
                //this is the current unit
                iGameState=GS_IDLE;
                //return to the neutral gamestate
        }
```

This piece of code has detected a single unit belonging to the current team. Before proceeding, you check to see if this unit is the same as `pCurrentUnit`. If it is, you need do nothing, and can just go back to `GS_IDLE`.

```
else
{
        //this is not the current unit
        //does this unit have any movement points left?
        if(pUnitInfo->iMovePoints>0)
        {
                //has movement points left
                //push the current unit to front of team
                if(pCurrentUnit)
                TeamUnitList.push_front(pCurrentUnit);
                pCurrentUnit=NULL;
                //set holding to false for the new unit
                pUnitInfo->bHolding=false;
                //remove new unit from team list
                TeamUnitList.remove(pUnitInfo);
                //put new unit in front of team list
                TeamUnitList.push_front(pUnitInfo);
                //go to gs_nextunit
                iGameState=GS_NEXTUNIT;
        }
```

Now that you have determined that it is not the current unit, the next test is to see whether the unit has any movement points left. If it does, you should set this unit up to be the next selected. The way to do this is to first put pCurrentUnit back into TeamUnitList if pCurrentUnit is non-NULL. Next, you put the new unit at the head of the list and send the program into GS_NEXTUNIT.

```
                        else
                        {
                                //does not have movement points left
                                //go back to gs_idle
                                iGameState=GS_IDLE;
                        }
```

This bit of code is executed when no movement points are left for the unit. It simply returns you to GS_IDLE. Alternatively, you could have it send the program into GS_CENTER.

```
                else
                {
                        //a stack of units
                        iGameState=GS_CLICKSTACK;
                }
```

This bit is run when more than one unit is in the map location clicked on. You are sent into GS_CLICKSTACK, where more processing will occur.

```
                else
                {
                        //does not belong to current team
                        iGameState=GS_CLICKCENTER;
                        //we want to center on this map location
                }
        }
}break;
```

Finally, this code executes when the units within the map location do not belong to the current team. For all intents and purposes, it is treated as though it were an empty square by sending the program into GS_CLICKCENTER. GS_CLICKSELECT might be really long, and perhaps it isn't the best way to accomplish the goals. Indeed, a few more game states could have been added to make the code a bit cleaner. Maybe I'll do that in a future example.

GS_CLICKCENTER

This game state is small and simple. From GS_CLICKSELECT, there are a few places where the program gets sent into this game state. All you have to do here is center the screen on the location clicked.

```
case GS_CLICKCENTER:
        {
                //center on clicked tile
                POINT ptPlot=TilePlotter.PlotTile(ptClick);//plot tile
                //adjust by half screenspace
                ptPlot.x-=(Scroller.GetScreenSpaceWidth()/2);
                ptPlot.y-=(Scroller.GetScreenSpaceHeight()/2);
                Scroller.SetAnchor(&ptPlot);//set anchor
                Renderer.AddRect(Scroller.GetScreenSpace());
                //return to GS_IDLE
                iGameState=GS_IDLE;
        }break;
```

You'll probably notice that this looks a great deal like the centering code of GS_NEXTUNIT. It should, since I mostly cut and pasted it here. In fact, I probably could have just had GS_UNIT go to this game state and eliminate the centering code there.

GS_CLICKSTACK

In order to explain fully what goes on in GS_CLICKSTACK, I must first discuss a few new globals, and a new UI feature I added with this example. As I discussed earlier, you must provide some way of selecting a unit when a stack of units is clicked. Figure 19.2 shows this (the stack of units to the right of the window is the one that I clicked on to bring up this window). If you have ever played strategy games with stackable units, you have undoubtedly seen similar windows.

Figure 19.2

The unit selection window

SELECT

WINDOW GLOBALS

To make this window happen, I added several globals:

```
//unit selection variables (for selecting stacks of units)
RECT rcSelectWindow;//the selection window
POINT ptCellSize;//size of selection cell
PUNITINFO SelectUnitList[20];//unit selection list (max of 20 units)
POINT ptUnitOffset;//offset for placing units in the selection window
DWORD dwSelectWindowColor;//color for the selection window
```

`rcSelectWindow` is a `RECT` that defines where and how big the selection window is. At first, I considered putting it in a corner of the screen, but I wound up putting it in the middle, because it makes the display more balanced.

`ptCellSize` keeps track of how large a cell of the selection window is. A cell can contain one unit, and the selection window is five cells wide by four cells high. This lets you select from up to 20 stacked units (since each player has only 20 units, this will work just fine). If the player could have any number of units, you would have to modify the selection window, either to have more than one page or to have some sort of way to scroll through the units. `ptCellSize` is based on the combined extents of all the units (using `UnionRect`).

`SelectUnitList` is an array, not a linked list, that stores pointers to all the units to be shown within the selection window. A `NULL` specifies that there is no unit in a given cell. `ptUnitOffset` helps place the unit within a cell. Since the images for your units are anchored at the center, you must have a way of centering the unit within the cell. `ptUnitOffset` allows you to do that. After the combined extent for the units is calculated, ptUnitOffset is set to –left and –top of that extent. dwSelectWindowColor just keeps track of what color to fill the window with. I picked a 75% gray since it is a common color in Windows and it doesn't interfere with any of the colors in the units.

Select Window Initialization

All of the following was taken from Prog_Init. This is the only code added to that function this time. You set up all the select window variables before you get started so you won't forget later.

```
//set up the selection window variables
DDPIXELFORMAT ddpf;
DDPF_Clear(&ddpf);
lpddsMain->GetPixelFormat(&ddpf);//grab pixel format
ddpf.dwRBitMask=(ddpf.dwRBitMask*3/4)&(ddpf.dwRBitMask);//calculate 3/4 red
ddpf.dwGBitMask=(ddpf.dwGBitMask*3/4)&(ddpf.dwGBitMask);//calc 3/4 green
ddpf.dwBBitMask=(ddpf.dwBBitMask*3/4)&(ddpf.dwBBitMask);//calc 3/4 blue
//make select window color
dwSelectWindowColor=ddpf.dwBBitMask | ddpf.dwRBitMask | ddpf.dwGBitMask;
```

I did the simplest thing first—namely, calculate the color of the select window. Basically, I just grabbed the pixel format and multiplied the color masks by three-fourths, getting a nice 75% gray tone.

```
//calculate the cell extent
RECT rcCell;
CopyRect(&rcCell,&tsUnit.GetTileList()[0].rcDstExt);
UnionRect(&rcCell,&rcCell,&tsUnit.GetTileList()[1].rcDstExt);
rcCell.right+=(tsShield.GetTileList()[0].rcDstExt.right-
tsShield.GetTileList()[0].rcDstExt.left);
```

Now move on to calculating the cell size; doing so will help you calculate the window size later. The first task is to calculate the combined extents of the units. You have only two unit types right now, but you can see how it would be simple to add others. After the rectangles are combined, you add the width of the shield image so that you can also show a shield in the selection window without overlapping other units.

```
//cell size
ptCellSize.x=rcCell.right-rcCell.left;
ptCellSize.y=rcCell.bottom-rcCell.top;
//unit offset
ptUnitOffset.x=-rcCell.left;
ptUnitOffset.y=-rcCell.top;
```

This is where ptCellSize and ptUnitOffset are initialized. ptCellSize is assigned to the differences between right and left and bottom and top, whereas ptUnitOffset is set to –left and –top (since rcCell contains negative values in `left` and `top` because it is an extent).

```
//calculate select window rect
SetRect(&rcSelectWindow,0,0,ptCellSize.x*5,ptCellSize.y*4);
//center the select window
OffsetRect(&rcSelectWindow, 320-rcSelectWindow.right/2, 240-rcSelectWindow.bot-
tom/2);
```

Finally, you can set up the `RECT` containing the position of the selection window. First, you place it with left and top at 0 and then offset it to a centered position. Now, all the select window stuff is set up and ready to use later.

Back to `GS_CLICKSTACK`. The following code is run after a mouse click has been registered and `GS_CLICK-SELECT` decides that the map location in question contains a stack of units. The job of `GS_CLICKSTACK` is simple: set everything up so that the program has enough information to show the selection window.

```
case GS_CLICKSTACK:
      {
            //prepare the stack
            int count;
            for(count=0;count<20;count++)//clear out the list
                  SelectUnitList[count]=NULL;
            //reset count to 0
            count=0;
```

First and foremost, you must ensure that `SelectUnitList` is empty (all items are `NULL`) so that you don't erroneously have a unit from some other map location shown in the window, which would be bad (or, at least, a bug).

```
            //iterate through the list of units at the current map location
            UNITLISTITER iter;//iterator
            PUNITINFO pUnitInfo;//unit info
            for(iter=mlMap[ptClick.x][ptClick.y].ulUnitList.begin();
                  count<20 &&
            iter!=mlMap[ptClick.x][ptClick.y].ulUnitList.end();
                  iter++)//iterate through list
            {
                  pUnitInfo=*iter;//grab the unit
                  //place unit in list
                  SelectUnitList[count]=pUnitInfo;
                  //add 1 to count
                  count++;
            }
```

This for loop might seem a little weird, since it doesn't follow the usual for loop pattern (I put two conditions in its second part). This is the basic "iterate through a list" loop, with a "don't look at more than 20" part added. The variable count starts at 0 and is used as an index into the SelectUnitList array. For each unit found at this map location, add it to SelectUnitList, and add 1 to count.

```
            //send to next gamestate
            iGameState=GS_PICKUNIT;
    }break;
```

That's it for GS_CLICKSTACK. After it has completed its assigned tasks, it moves to GS_PICKUNIT, which is discussed next.

GS_PICKUNIT

This game state displays the selection window every frame, and that's about it. It's kind of like a specialized render function for the select window. It's important for me to note that the select window is rendered onto the back buffer (lpddsBack) after the screen has been updated. This means it has to be fully redrawn every frame. Sure, there were other ways to do it, but this way was the quickest.

```
case GS_PICKUNIT:
    {
            //no scrolling
            Renderer.ScrollFrame(0,0);
            //update frame
            Renderer.UpdateFrame();
```

You have to update the display before rendering the select window, and that's what these two lines do. The display is scrolled by 0 (a necessary step), and then the frame is updated, even though there is no update list.

```
            //place select window onto display
            DDBLTFX ddbltfx;
            DDBLTFX_Clear(&ddbltfx);
            ddbltfx.dwFillColor=dwSelectWindowColor;
            lpddsBack->Blt(&rcSelectWindow,NULL,NULL,DDBLT_WAIT |
                  DDBLT_COLORFILL,&ddbltfx);
```

Next, you have to clear out the selection window rectangle with the color in dwSelectWindowColor. This is just the basic "color fill a rectangle" code taken from Part 1 of this book.

```
            //show the units
            int cellx,celly;//cell position
```

```
int cellnum;//number of the cell
int pixelx,pixely;//pixel position
for(celly=0;celly<4;celly++)
{
        for(cellx=0;cellx<5;cellx++)
        {
                cellnum=cellx+celly*5;//calculate the cell number
```

Now you get into the fun part, looping through all the units in SelectUnitList. First, you set up a set of nested loops (celly and cellx) and calculate the cell number (cellx+celly*5). Finally, you can check for a unit.

```
                //check that the unit exists
                if(SelectUnitList[cellnum])
                {
```

The bulk of the code happens here, on the inside of the nested loop, and only if there is a unit present in the current cell.

```
                        //calculate pixel position
                        pixelx=rcSelectWindow.left+ptCellSize.x*cellx;
                        pixely=rcSelectWindow.top+ptCellSize.y*celly;
                        //plot the unit's position
                        pixelx+=ptUnitOffset.x;
                        pixely+=ptUnitOffset.y;
                        //put the unit
                        tsUnit.PutTile(lpddsBack,pixelx,pixely,
                                SelectUnitList[cellnum]->iType);
```

First you do the easy part: plotting the cell's location. (It's easy. Because the cells are rectangular, you just multiply by ptCellSize's x and y. After that you offset by ptUnitOffset, which centers the unit in the cell. Finally, you place the unit there, and the unit is rendered!

```
                //move the pixel to place shield
                pixelx+=ptShieldOffset[SelectUnitList[cellnum]->iType].x;
                pixely+=ptShieldOffset[SelectUnitList[cellnum]->iType].y;
```

Now you have to place the shield, which is a bit more conditional. To set it up, you move the pixel position you are plotting at by the ptShieldOffset of the unit you just rendered. Then you are just left with the task of deciding which shield to render with it. For this example, I added a new shield with a check mark in it, indicating that the unit has already been moved this turn. This shield is shown only in the selection window, not anywhere else.

```
                    //place appropriate shield
                    if(SelectUnitList[cellnum]->bHolding)
                    {
                            //unit is holding
                            tsShield.PutTile(lpddsBack,pixelx,pixely,
                                iCurrentTeam*2+4);
```

This is simple enough. If the unit is holding position (`bHolding==true`), you show the "I am holding" shield, which is image numbers 4 and 6, so `iCurrentTeam*2+4`.

```
                    }
                    else
                    {
                            //unit is not holding
                            if(SelectUnitList[cellnum]->iMovePoints)
                            {
```

The unit is not holding, so you check to see if it has any movement points left. If it does, you put the normal shield, which is image 0 or 2.

```
                            //unit has movement points left
                            tsShield.PutTile(lpddsBack,pixelx,pixely,
                                    iCurrentTeam*2);
                    }
                    else
                    {
```

The unit is not holding, nor does it have any movement points left. The images for the "I have moved" shield are 8 and 10.

```
                            //unit does not have move points left
                            tsShield.PutTile(lpddsBack,pixelx,pixely,
                                    iCurrentTeam*2+8);
                    }
                }
            }
        }
    }
```

```
        //flip
        lpddsMain->Flip(0,DDFLIP_WAIT);
    }break;
```

And, for the coup de grace, flip the primary surface so that the user can see the lovely select window you have made!

RenderFunc

The rendering function, too, has undergone some changes, mainly in adding some checks to `pCurrentUnit`, but also in checking the top of a map location's stack to see whether or not the unit is holding position.

```
void RenderFunc(LPDIRECTDRAWSURFACE7 lpddsDst, RECT* rcClip, int xDst, int yDst,
int xMap, int yMap)
{
    //put background tile
    tsBack.ClipTile(lpddsDst,rcClip,xDst,yDst,0);
```

Of course, no matter what, the background tile is always shown.

```
    //check for an empty list
    if(!mlMap[xMap][yMap].ulUnitList.empty())
    {
```

If the unit list at this map location is empty, the rest of the function is skipped. Otherwise, all the unit rendering code shown next is executed.

```
        //list is not empty
        //get iterator to beginning of list
        UNITLISTITER iter=mlMap[xMap][yMap].ulUnitList.begin();
        PUNITINFO pUnitInfo=*iter;//grab the item
        //if this is the current unit
        if(pUnitInfo==pCurrentUnit)
        {
            //this is the current unit
            if(!bFlash) return;//if flash is "off" don't render
        }
```

First, you grab the unit from the top of the stack and check to see if it is the current unit. If it is, and `bFlash` is false, nothing needs to be rendered, so just return. If not, you must render the unit.

```
    tsUnit.ClipTile(lpddsDst,rcClip,xDst,yDst,pUnitInfo->iType);//place the unit
```

```
        iter++;//move to the next item in the list
        if(iter==mlMap[xMap][yMap].ulUnitList.end())//if the end of the
        list, this is a single unit
        {
```

The next thing to check is whether or not this map location contains a single unit, or a stack, by moving to the next unit in the map location's list and checking that against the end of the list. If you have reached the end of the list, you know that this is the only unit at the map location in question.

```
                if(pUnitInfo->bHolding)//if holding position
                {//holding
                        tsShield.ClipTile(lpddsDst,rcClip,
                                xDst+ptShieldOffset[pUnitInfo->iType].x,
                                yDst+ptShieldOffset[pUnitInfo->iType].y,
                                pUnitInfo->iTeam*2+4);//place the shield
```

The shield can be one of two states—holding position or normal. If `bHolding` is true for the unit, render the H shield (either image 4 or 6).

```
                }
                else
                {//not holding
                        tsShield.ClipTile(lpddsDst,rcClip,
                                xDst+ptShieldOffset[pUnitInfo->iType].x,
                                yDst+ptShieldOffset[pUnitInfo->iType].y,
                                pUnitInfo->iTeam*2);//place the shield
                }
        }
```

If it isn't holding position, render the normal shield (image 0 or 2).

```
        else//more than one unit...this is a stack
        {
                if(pUnitInfo->bHolding)//if holding position
                {//holding
                        tsShield.ClipTile(lpddsDst,rcClip,
                                xDst+ptShieldOffset[pUnitInfo->iType].x,
                                yDst+ptShieldOffset[pUnitInfo->iType].y,
                                pUnitInfo->iTeam*2+5);//place the shield
```

In the case of a stack, the holding position images are 5 and 7, but choosing between holding and normal is exactly the same.

```
                }
```

```
			else
			{//not holding
				tsShield.ClipTile(lpddsDst,rcClip,
					xDst+ptShieldOffset[pUnitInfo->iType].x,
					yDst+ptShieldOffset[pUnitInfo->iType].y,
					pUnitInfo->iTeam*2+1);//place the shield
			}
		}
```

Finally, if the top of a stack is not holding position, place the normal shield (image 1 or 3) from the shield tileset.

Handling Input

In this example, most of the keyboard input remains the same, except that now there is a new check for `pCurrentUnit` being `NULL` (which means that keyboard input is being ignored). Also, there are new handlers for the H key and the C key, which respectively bring about the hold position and center on unit commands. These key handlers are very simple (they just move from game state to game state), and you can take a look at them in the `windowproc` if you like.

Mainly, I want to discuss here the mouse input that I incorporated into this example. Only two game states respond to mouse input: `GS_IDLE` and `GS_PICKUNIT`. All other game states are ignored as far as the mouse is concerned.

WM_LBUTTONDOWN

When the left mouse button goes down, only `GS_IDLE` responds to it. This response simply grabs the current map position.

```
	case WM_LBUTTONDOWN://beginning of click-select
		{
			//process differently, depending on gamestate
			switch(iGameState)
			{
			case GS_IDLE:
				{
					//grab the mouse position
					POINT ptCursor;
					ptCursor.x=LOWORD(lParam);
					ptCursor.y=HIWORD(lParam);
					//use the mousemap to get click position
					ptClick=MouseMap.MapMouse(ptCursor);
```

```
                }break;
            }
            return(0);//handled
        }break;
```

There's not much to this code. Mainly, you just grab the cursor position from lParam and use the MouseMap to determine the current map location.

WM_LBUTTONUP

When the mouse button is released, the code is a bit lengthier. Both GS_IDLE and GS_PICKUNIT respond to this input.

```
    case WM_LBUTTONUP://end of click-select
        {
            //process differently, depending on gamestate
            switch(iGameState)
            {
            case GS_IDLE:
                {
                    //grab the mouse position
                    POINT ptCursor;
                    ptCursor.x=LOWORD(lParam);
                    ptCursor.y=HIWORD(lParam);
                    //use the mousemap to get click position
                    POINT ptMap=MouseMap.MapMouse(ptCursor);
                    //check map position against ptClick
                    if(ptMap.x==ptClick.x && ptMap.y==ptClick.y)
                    {
                        //set gamestate to GS_CLICKSELECT
                        iGameState=GS_CLICKSELECT;
                    }
                }break;
```

When the left button is released during GS_IDLE, you again grab the mouse position from lParam. However, you don't stop there. You also check to see that this position is the same one you pressed the left button on. If it is, you proceed to GS_CLICKSELECT. If it isn't, you remain in GS_IDLE.

GS_PICKUNIT is another story. It has to do with the select window and has nothing to do with the map.

```
case GS_PICKUNIT:
    {
        //grab the mouse position
        POINT ptMouse;
```

```
ptMouse.x=LOWORD(lParam);
ptMouse.y=HIWORD(lParam);
```

First, as with all mouse handlers, you must grab the position from `lParam`. Most of the time, you can't get around this... it's just a part of programming.

```
//check to see if the click was within the select window
if(PtInRect(&rcSelectWindow,ptMouse))
{
```

The first check is to see whether the mouse is in the selection window. If it is, the following code is run. If not, you skip a bit.

```
//within the select window
//determine which cell was clicked
ptMouse.x-=rcSelectWindow.left;//subtract top left of the window
ptMouse.y-=rcSelectWindow.top;
ptMouse.x/=ptCellSize.x;//divide by cellsize
ptMouse.y/=ptCellSize.y;
int cellnum=ptMouse.x+5*ptMouse.y;//calc cell number
```

These few lines of code are kind of like a custom rectangular MouseMap. First, you subtract the left and top of the selection window from the mouse's x and y, getting the relative x and y pixel coordinates of the mouse within the window. x will now be from 0 to the width of the selection window (minus 1), and y will now be from 0 to the height of the selection window (again, minus 1). After the subtraction, divide each by the cell's width and height to get the cell's column and row. Finally, based on cell column and row, figure out which cell you are pointing to with the mouse.

```
        //check for a NULL
        if(SelectUnitList[cellnum]==NULL)
        {
                //empty cell
                //do nothing
                return(0);
        }
```

Now that you have the cell number, you check to see if that cell contains `NULL`. If it does, the cell is empty, so you treat it as a disabled button and do nothing.

```
        else
        {
                //non-empty cell
```

```
                    //check if the unit has any movement points left
                    if(SelectUnitList[cellnum]->iMovePoints==0)
                    {
                          //no movement points
                          //do nothing
                          return(0);
                    }
```

The unit here is non-NULL but has no movement points left, so again you do nothing.

```
              else
              {
                    //check for holding position
                    if(SelectUnitList[cellnum]->bHolding)
                    {
                          //set holding to false
                          SelectUnitList[cellnum]->bHolding=false;
                    }
                    //remove this unit from the team list
                    TeamUnitList.remove(SelectUnitList[cellnum]);
                    //re-add this unit to the team list at the beginning
                    TeamUnitList.push_front(SelectUnitList[cellnum]);
                    //select next unit
                    iGameState=GS_NEXTUNIT;
                    //add entire screen to update rect
                    Renderer.AddRect(Scroller.GetScreenSpace());
              }
```

Finally, if the unit in the cell is non-NULL and has movement points left, you activate it, put it at the front of the TeamUnitList, set bHolding to false, and move along to GS_NEXTUNIT, where this unit will be selected.

```
        else
        {
```

If the click was not within the selection window's rectangle, consider that a "cancellation" of the selection window, and pass the program along to GS_NEXTUNIT, where you can resume normal stuff.

```
              //outside of select window
              iGameState=GS_NEXTUNIT;
```

```
        }
    }break;
```

That's about it for simple object selection. Wasn't that fun? These examples are getting longer and more complicated every time we do one. Heck, with IsoHex19_1, if you were to add a simple combat system, it would almost be a game!

Pixel-Perfect Object Selection

Since I spent a great deal of time on simple object selection, I can only really give you an overview of pixel-perfect object selection and nudge you along the correct path to making it work. For turn-based strategy games, you can usually get away with simple object selection, but for real-time strategy games, you need pixel-perfect selection, or something close.

Like many things in life, pixel-perfect object selection is simple for humans to understand but requires a great deal of work for computers to understand. This is because of the human ability to think in the abstract, whereas a computer can only think in rigid terms. I use the word "think" here to mean "process information." We are still some time away from having machines that actually "think" in a way that everyone agrees on.

To start with, let's think about pixel-perfect object selection as human beings and then think about it the way a computer would. From the human perspective, we select a unit by clicking on it. As humans, this is easy to determine, because we see the units as separate from the background. A computer, however, knows no such distinction. As far as a computer is concerned, the display is just covered with a bunch of numbers. It knows nothing of color or shape or units. It just sees (for example) the value 0xFFFF (which to us appears to be pure white). As far as the computer is concerned, this number is meaningless. While we, as human beings, might be able to say "If you click here, this unit should be selected," the computer has a much more involved process to make the same thing happen, since pixel colors are meaningless. However, the computer does have all the information necessary to determine whether or not you have clicked on a unit, or, at least, it can be given this information.

As human beings, we can "eyeball" the display and see if we have clicked on a unit or not. The computer, having no eyeballs (no, that webcam doesn't count), cannot do this. The closest thing to "eyeballing" that a computer has is bounding rectangles, as shown in Figure 19.3. By checking the mouse position against these rectangles, you can easily determine if the mouse is *not* over a unit, but the best result you can get is that the mouse *might* be on a unit, if it is within a bounding `RECT`.

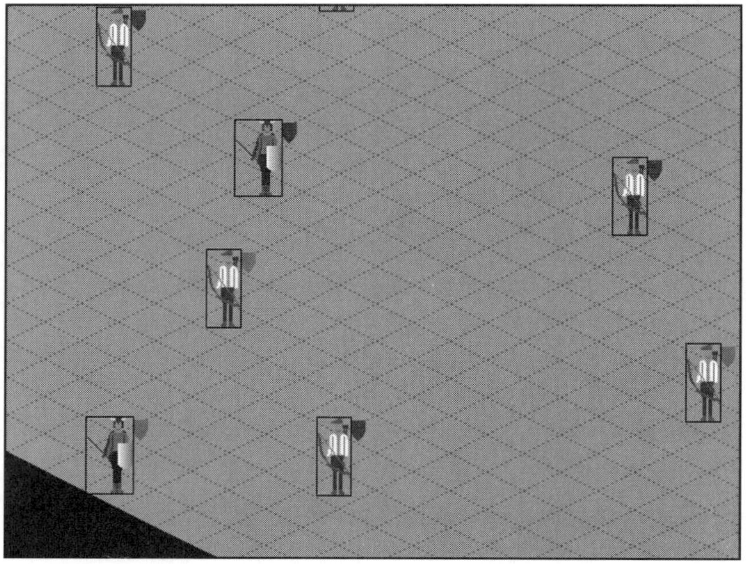

Figure 19.3

Bounding rectangles

Well, something is better than nothing, so you'll take it. If you can eliminate some pixels as "not on a unit," that just shortens your search. Computers do pretty well with deductive reasoning like this.

Next, if the mouse is over one of these bounding rectangles, you can determine where in the rectangle it is by subtracting the left and top of the `RECT` from x and y. From here, you can get a pixel from the image containing the unit, which will be either the transparent color of the unit's tileset (in which case the mouse is not on the unit) or some other color (in which case the mouse is on the unit).

I'm not actually suggesting you start poking around in the tileset image. Instead, right after loading it, you can create a two-dimensional array that is the same size as the unit's bounding `RECT` and fill it with true and false, depending on the pixel's color. Then, it's just a matter of going into this lookup table. Using this method, you have to poke around the image only once (right after loading), and looking up values is then very quick. Of course, this solution isn't quite complete. Sure, you can tell whether or not the mouse is over a given unit, but the goal here is to select a single unit, and because of the isometric overlap, the mouse might be pointing to two units at once.

If the mouse is over multiple units, logic dictates that you select the unit that is the southernmost (the farthest down the display). The easiest way to determine this (without poking around the tilemap structure and doing some lengthy tests and calculations) is to check the value of the unit's anchor point (specified in world coordinates). A higher y value wins. If the y values are the same, a higher x wins.

Making It Happen

I'm not going to do a full-fledged example on pixel-perfect object selection, but I will give you some code fragments that should put you on the right track.

Constructing a Lookup Table

Much of the information needed for pixel-perfect selection can be found in `CTileSet` or calculated from it. The anchor and the extent can be pulled directly out of the tileset for bounding box information. For a lookup table, you have to actually do some calculations and use some GDI.

```
//this pointer will be allocated to contain the lookup table for a unit
bool* bLookUp;
int iWidth;//width of the lookup table
int iHeight;//height of the lookup table
//we are going to take the first unit (index 0) from tsUnit
//get the width
iWidth=tsUnit.GetTileList()[0].rcSrc.right-tsUnit.GetTileList()[0].rcSrc.left;
//get the height
iHeight=tsUnit.GetTileList()[0].rcSrc.bottom-tsUnit.GetTileList()[0].rcSrc.top;
//allocate the lookup table
bLookUp=new bool[iHeight*iWidth];
//grab the dc from the tileset's image
HDC hdc;
tsUnit.GetDDS()->GetDC(&hdc);
//grab the transparent color
COLORREF crTrans=GetPixel(hdc,0,0);
COLORREF crTest;//test pixel
for(int y=0;y<iHeight;y++)
{
	for(int x=0;x<iWidth;x++)
	{
		crTest=GetPixel(hdc,tsUnit.GetTileList()[0].rcSrc.left+x,
			tsUnit.GetTileList()[0].rcSrc.top+y);//grab pixel
		if(crTest==crTrans)//test this pixel for transparency
		{
			bLookUp[x+y*iWidth]=false;//transparent pixel
		}
		else
		{
			bLookUp[x+y*iWidth]=true;//non-transparent
		}
	}
}
//put the dc back
tsUnit.GetDDS()->ReleaseDC(hdc);
```

This is a simple scan conversion that copies the image into a monochrome bitmask. Now, anytime you want to look up a value in this array, you can simply use `bLookUp[x+y*iWidth]`. If the value is true, the pixel is within the unit. If it's false, it isn't. This code is good if you want to create just a single lookup table. If you have more than one unit type (and it's pretty likely that you do), you'll want to have some sort of structure and make an array of that structure, like so:

```
struct ObjectBitMask//structure to contain object bitmask
{
        bool* bLookUp;
        int iWidth;
        int iHeight;
};
typedef ObjectBitMask* POBJECTBITMASK;//pointer type alias
```

From here, creating an array of `ObjectBitMasks` and filling in that array is a simple matter of iterating through all the tiles and filling in the structures.

Creating a Unit Selection List

As I mentioned earlier, there are three steps to pixel-perfect object selection. First is the bounding box, second is the object's bitmask, which I just covered, and third is the object's anchor, in case you are hovering over more than one unit or object. The most convenient thing to do is to make a `struct` that contains this information:

```
struct UnitSelector//unit selection information struct
{
        RECT rcBound;//rectangle bounding the object (world coordinates)
        POINT ptAnchor;//anchor for the object (world coordinates)
        POBJECTBITMASK pobm;//pointer to a bitmask for the object
};
typedef UnitSelector* PUNITSELECTOR;
```

For each object that can be selected in the world, you must fill in one of these structures. This brings up the question, "Which objects can be selected?" For the most part, you only want to fill out a structure for units that belong to the current player, and moreover, only units that are currently on-screen. Some games allow you to select enemy units so that you can see the status of that unit, but you cannot give it orders. Either way, you still only want those objects on-screen to be selectable (it shortens the search time).

Before you get ahead of yourself, you must first know how to fill in this structure.

```
UnitSelector UnitSel;//structure for our unit
//pUnitInfo will be a pointer to a UNITINFO structure
//similar to the one we've been using
//first, copy the destination extent from the tileset
```

```
CopyRect(&UnitSel.rcBound,tsUnit.GetTileList()[pUnitInfo->iType].rcDstExt);
//plot the world position of the unit
UnitSel.ptAnchor=TilePlotter.PlotTile(pUnitInfo->ptPosition);
//assume that OBMList is an array of ObjectBitMasks
//select the proper bitmask for the object
UnitSel.pobm=&OBMList[pUnitInfo->iType];
//offset rcBound by the anchor
OffsetRect(&UnitSel.rcBound,UnitSel.ptAnchor.x,UnitSel.ptAnchor.y);
```

`UnitSel` now contains all the applicable information for a single object in the game. If you did this for all the units and objects in the game, perhaps storing them in a linked list, pixel-perfect selection would be within your grasp.

```
typedef std::list<PUNITSELECTOR> UNITSELLIST;//unit selection list
typedef std::list<PUNITSELECTOR>::iterator UNITSELLISTITER;//iterator
```

However, you don't want to look through the entire list, just those objects that are on-screen or partially on-screen. You can keep a main list of `UnitSelectors` that gets updated whenever a unit is moved, perhaps named `MasterUnitSelList`. This lowers the overhead a little, because you don't have to completely fill in this list each frame.

So, you can keep a separate list that you fill in each frame (or at least whenever the screen-space anchor changes or a unit moves), perhaps calling it `ScreenUnitSelList`. Then all you need to do is fill it in.

```
RECT rcClip;//this will be the rect we clip selectable units by
RECT rcTest;//testing rect
PUNITSELECTOR pUnitSel;//list item
//copy the screenspace rect from the scroller
CopyRect(&rcClip,Scroller.GetScreenSpace());
//translate the screenspace rect into world space
OffsetRect(&rcClip,Scroller.GetAnchor()->x,Scroller.GetAnchor().y);
//clear out the ScreenUnitSelList
ScreenUnitSelList.clear();
//iterate through the master selectionlist
for(UNITSELLISTITER
iter=MasterUnitSelList.begin();iter!=MasterUnitSelList.end();iter++)
{
	pUnitSel=*iter;//grab item from list
	//find intersection
	IntersectRect(&rcTest,&rcClip,&pUnitSel->rcBound);
	if(!IsRectEmpty(&rcTest))//if the intersection rect is non-empty...
	{
```

```
            ScreenUnitSelList.push_back(pUnitSel);// add unit to screen list
        }
}
```

This isn't the optimal way to go about this, and you probably don't want to do this every frame, especially if you have a large number of units, but the preceding code is the main idea. Naturally, you'll want to optimize it so that fewer calculations need to be done.

Finally, the actual selection can take place. You've got all the units and objects filtered into a smaller list. Now you just have to see which units the mouse is over.

```
//ptMouse is the mouse position (translated into world coordinates)
POINT ptTemp;//temp testing point
//the selected unit will be here, or NULL if none found
PUNITSELECTOR pUnitSelFound=NULL;
PUNITSELECTOR pUnitSelTemp;//temporary, for grabbing info out of list
UNITSELLISTITER iter;//iterator
//iterate through the screen list
for(iter=ScreenUnitSelList.begin();iter!=ScreenUnitSelList.end();iter++)
{
        ptTemp=ptMouse;//copy mouse point
        pUnitSelTemp=*iter;//grab the item from list
        //phase one: check bounding rectangle
        if(PtInRect(&pUnitSel->rcBound,ptTemp))
        {
                //point is within bounding rect
                //translate into rcBound coordinates
                ptTemp.x-=pUnitSel->rcBound.left;
                ptTemp.y-=pUnitSel->rcBound.top;
                //check the bitmask
                //phase two: check bitmask
                if(pUnitSelTemp->pobm->bLookUp[ptTemp.x+
                        ptTemp.y*pUnitSelTemp->pobm->iWidth])
                {
                        //this is a "hit"
                        if(pUnitSelFound==NULL)
                        {
                                //this is the first unit found
                                pUnitSelFound=pUnitSelTemp;
                        }
                        else
                        {
                                //phase three: anchor position
```

```
                //this is not the first unit found
                if(pUnitSelTemp->ptAnchor.y>pUnitSelFound->ptAnchor.y)
                {
                        //farther south
                }
                else
                {
                        //not farther south
                        if(pUnitSelTemp->ptAnchor.y==pUnitSelFound-
        >ptAnchor.y)
                        {
                                //same y
                                if(pUnitSelTemp-
        >ptAnchor.x>pUnitSelFound->ptAnchor.x)
                                {
                                        //greater x
                                        pUnitSetFound=pUnitSetTemp;
                                }
}
```

The bold lines mark the beginning of each of the stages of the algorithm so that you can more easily separate them in your mind. This is about all I'm going to say on the matter of pixel-perfect object selection. When you make your own object selection code, you should probably do the pixel-perfect stuff, because your users will expect it.

Minimap, Zones of Control, and the Fog of War

There are a few elements common to most if not all isometric strategy games. These are the minimap, zones of control, and the fog of war. None of these are really very complicated or difficult to implement, but a discussion of isometric games is not complete without discussing these, since they are so prevalent.

Minimaps

A minimap is a smaller version of the game's tilemap that lets a player get the big picture of the game as he is playing. All strategy games, whether real-time or turn-based, use the minimap. It has become a standard feature, so not including it will hurt you.

Since the minimap is just a smaller version of the tilemap, it is quite easy to implement. I usually have my minimap use tiles that are 4×2 pixels in size. In a 4×2 iso tile, the top four pixels are filled in with a color (usually all the same color and representing a full-sized tile), and the bottom four pixels are the transparent color. For example, if you were making a minimap tile for an ocean, the top four pixels would be blue, but if you were making a minimap tile for a grassland, you would probably use a shade of green.

A minimap usually is shown somewhere on-screen, typically in a corner, so it has its own screen space. The minimap tiles, being only 4×2, calculate to a different world space, so in order to use a minimap, you need to make new copies of the isometric components that you will use only with the minimap. However, you won't need all of the components—just the TilePlotter, and maybe the scroller.

The idea is that the minimap is there primarily to show you the status of the entire playing area, but it is also a control that, if clicked, takes you to the area of the map that you clicked in the minimap. I think you've probably got a good understanding of the minimap and its role in games, so I'll just shut up now and get to the example.

Minimap Example

Because you have decided that you want a minimap, you need someplace on-screen to put it. This means you have to sacrifice some of the playing area. Typically, a minimap appears in the upper-right corner of the display, so that's where I decided to place it in IsoHex19_2.cpp, as you can see in Figure 19.4.

Figure 19.4

Minimap example

The minimap code in this example is really just an add-on to the existing code base, so for easy separation, I placed it in a number of functions that take care of all the minimap stuff. Table 19.2 lists these functions, with a brief statement of their role in the example.

Table 19.2 Minimap Functions

Function	Purpose
`SetupMiniMap`	Allocates and sets up the initial state of the minimap
`UpdateMiniMap`	Updates minimap information based on game information
`RedrawMiniMap`	Redraws the minimap
`ShowMiniMap`	Displays the minimap on-screen
`DestroyMiniMap`	Cleans up minimap information and deallocates structures

These five functions take care of most of what you want to do with the minimap, but they are not by any means all-inclusive. Each of these functions is explained in detail in the following sections.

SetupMiniMap

Before I get to the actual code, I need to briefly discuss the new globals that were added because of the minimap. After all, this information has to be stored somewhere, right? Table 19.3 lists the new globals and describes their role in the application.

Table 19.3 Minimap Globals

Variable	Purpose
`lpddsMiniMap`	Off-screen surface on which the minimap's image is stored
`tsMiniMap`	Tileset used by the minimap to plot its mini-tiles
`MiniMap`	A pointer to an `int`, which is allocated to be the same size as the tilemap. Each map location then holds a number that is an index into the `tsMiniMap` tile list.
`MiniTilePlotter`	TilePlotter used by the minimap
`MiniScroller`	Scroller used by the minimap

With the preliminaries out of the way, you can finally get to the code. First on the list is (naturally) `SetupMiniMap`, which does all your minimap initializations.

```
void SetupMiniMap()//does initial setup of the minimap
{
        //create the surface
        lpddsMiniMap=LPDDS_CreateOffscreen(lpdd,160,80);
        //load in the tileset
        tsMiniMap.Load(lpdd,"minimapts.bmp");
```

Before doing anything else, create a new surface 160 pixels wide and 80 pixels tall to contain the entire minimap. This is hardcoded in the example but probably should not be. When you use a diamond map, as you are here, the calculations for width and height required by a minimap are as follows:

```
MiniMapWidth=(MAPWIDTH+MAPHEIGHT)*TILEWIDTH/2;
MiniMapHeight=(MAPWIDTH+MAPHEIGHT)*TILEHEIGHT/2;
```

In this example, `MAPWIDTH` and `MAPHEIGHT` are both 40, `TILEWIDTH` is 4, and `TILEHEIGHT` is 2. If you plug these numbers into the equations just shown, you'll get 160×80, which is what I got. Other tilemap styles have different ways of figuring out the size of the minimap. It's just based on the world space calculations.

```
        //initialize the minimap arrays
        MiniMap=new int[MAPWIDTH*MAPHEIGHT];
        for(int count=0;count<MAPWIDTH*MAPHEIGHT;count++)
        {
                MiniMap[count]=0;
        }
```

Next, you allocate the minimap array by allocating space for the global variable `MiniMap` and initializing the array to all 0s.

```
        //initialize iso components
        //tile plotter
        MiniTilePlotter.SetMapType(ISOMAP_DIAMOND);
        MiniTilePlotter.SetTileSize(4,2);
        //scroller
        //calc worldspace
        MiniScroller.CalcWorldSpace(&MiniTilePlotter,
&tsMiniMap.GetTileList()[0].rcDstExt, MAPWIDTH, MAPHEIGHT);
        //set screen space
        RECT rcMiniScreenSpace;
        SetRect(&rcMiniScreenSpace,0,0,160,80);
        MiniScroller.SetScreenSpace(&rcMiniScreenSpace);
```

```
        //set the anchor
        POINT ptAnchor;
        ptAnchor.x=MiniScroller.GetWorldSpace()->left;
        ptAnchor.y=MiniScroller.GetWorldSpace()->top;
        MiniScroller.SetAnchor(&ptAnchor);
}
```

Last, SetupMiniMap initializes the iso components used by the minimap. This is pretty standard, and you've seen it before. The only weird part might be setting the anchor position. Since the entire minimap must be visible, the anchor is set to the world's left and top.

UpdateMiniMap

Because the tilemap changes throughout the game, so too does the minimap, since it is nothing more than a small reflection of the bigger picture. In this example, a given tile really has only three states. Either the map location is empty, or it contains units from one team or the other. Empty map locations show up green (tile 0 from tsMiniMap), and the blue and red teams each have their own tiles within tsMiniMap.

```
void UpdateMiniMap()//updates the minimap array
{
        //update the minimap array to reflect game status
        for(int y=0;y<MAPHEIGHT;y++)//loop through rows
        {
                for(int x=0;x<MAPWIDTH;x++)//loop through columns
                {
                        MiniMap[y*MAPWIDTH+x]=0;
                        //if empty, place a zero
                        if(mlMap[x][y].ulUnitList.empty())
                        {
                                MiniMap[y*MAPWIDTH+x]=0;
                        }
                        else
                        {
                                //occupied by a player
                                UNITLISTITER iter=mlMap[x][y].ulUnitList.begin();
                                PUNITINFO pUnitInfo=*iter;
                                if(pUnitInfo!=pCurrentUnit || bFlash)
                                        MiniMap[y*MAPWIDTH+x]=
                                        1+pUnitInfo->iTeam;
                                        //put team info into minimap array
                        }
                }
```

```
        }
}
```

This is pretty simple, really. You loop through all the map locations and check for emptiness (in which case you put a 0 in the minimap array). If the location is not empty, place the appropriate colored tile in the array (with a special case if the unit being considered is the current unit, which must be made to blink).

RedrawMiniMap

At some point, you will want to redraw the minimap. Naturally, you'll want to completely draw it during the beginning of the program, to give yourself a starting point. Later, as the map changes or as units move, you will want to redraw the minimap (or portions of it) to reflect changes in the game.

The `RedrawMiniMap` function does a complete redraw of the entire minimap. In a real game, you probably don't want to do this, especially if the map is very large. Instead, you might want to come up with a way of tracking changes on the minimap, and only redraw that which absolutely needs it.

```
void RedrawMiniMap()//redraws the minimap to reflect current gamestate
{
        //redraw the entire minimap
        //in real code, you can keep two arrays
        //one valid this frame and one valid last frame
        //and then only blit the changes from last frame to this one
        //thus reducing the number of blits
        //clear out the minimap surface
        DDBLTFX ddbltfx;
        DDBLTFX_ColorFill(&ddbltfx,0);
        lpddsMiniMap->Blt(NULL,NULL,NULL,DDBLT_WAIT | DDBLT_COLORFILL,&ddbltfx);
```

The first thing, naturally, is to clear out the minimap's surface to black (or whatever your background color is). Do so if you intend to do a complete redraw, which is what I'm doing here.

```
        POINT ptPlot;//plotting point
        for(int y=0;y<MAPHEIGHT;y++)//loop through rows
        {
                for(int x=0;x<MAPWIDTH;x++)//loop through columns
                {
                        //put the mini-tile
                        ptPlot.x=x;
                        ptPlot.y=y;
                        //plot map position
                        ptPlot=MiniTilePlotter.PlotTile(ptPlot);
```

```
                //convert to screen coords
                ptPlot=MiniScroller.WorldToScreen(ptPlot);
                tsMiniMap.PutTile(lpddsMiniMap,
                    ptPlot.x,ptPlot.y,MiniMap[y*MAPWIDTH+x]);
            }
        }
```

Next, loop through the map tiles and plot the appropriate tile image from `tsMiniMap`. To plot the tile position, make use of `MiniTilePlotter` and `MiniScroller`, just like with a real isometric map.

```
        //show a rectangle around viewable area on minimap
        HDC hdc;
        lpddsMiniMap->GetDC(&hdc);//borrow the dc from the minimap surface
        //get the anchor point from the main scroller
        POINT ptAnchor;
        ptAnchor.x=Scroller.GetAnchor()->x;
        ptAnchor.y=Scroller.GetAnchor()->y;
        //scale down by a factor of 16 (to go from a 64x32 tile to 4x2)
        ptAnchor.x/=16;
        ptAnchor.y/=16;
        //subtract the mini-scroller's upper left
        ptAnchor.x-=MiniScroller.GetWorldSpace()->left;
        ptAnchor.y-=MiniScroller.GetWorldSpace()->top;
        //move to position in minimap
        MoveToEx(hdc,ptAnchor.x,ptAnchor.y,NULL);
        //draw box, one line at a time
        LineTo(hdc,ptAnchor.x+30,ptAnchor.y);//30 is 480/16
        LineTo(hdc,ptAnchor.x+30,ptAnchor.y+30);
        LineTo(hdc,ptAnchor.x,ptAnchor.y+30);
        LineTo(hdc,ptAnchor.x,ptAnchor.y);
        lpddsMiniMap->ReleaseDC(hdc);//restore the dc to the minimap
}
```

This final bit is lengthy but doesn't do anything spectacular. When using a minimap, you will no doubt want a rectangle bounding the area visible on-screen, since this gives your player a visible clue as to where in the world he is looking. Most of the calculations convert world space coordinates into minimap pixel coordinates. Since your world uses 64×32 tiles, and the minimap only uses 4×2, you have to scale x and y down by a factor of 16.

ShowMiniMap

This is an easy one. You simply blit the minimap onto the back buffer.

```
void ShowMiniMap()//shows the minimap on-screen
{
	RECT rcSrc;//src blitting rect
	RECT rcDst;//destination blitting rect
	//set src rect
	SetRect(&rcSrc,0,0,160,80);
	//set dest rect
	CopyRect(&rcDst,&rcSrc);
	OffsetRect(&rcDst,480,0);
	//do the blit
	lpddsBack->Blt(&rcDst,lpddsMiniMap,&rcSrc,DDBLT_WAIT,NULL);
}
```

Like I said, not much to it.

DestroyMiniMap

As part of keeping the minimap separate from everything else in the program, I made a separate function to clean up the memory and tileset used by the minimap.

```
void DestroyMiniMap()//cleans up the minimap
{
	//delete minimap array
	delete[] MiniMap;
	//destroy minimap surface
	if(lpddsMiniMap)
	{
		lpddsMiniMap->Release();
		lpddsMiniMap=NULL;
	}
	//destroy minimap tileset
	tsMiniMap.Unload();
}
```

Mainly, this function does three things: it gets rid of the minimap array, it gets rid of the minimap surface, and it unloads the minimap tileset.

Minimap Wrap-up

I've only really scratched the surface of minimaps. There are many ways to optimize what I've discussed here. The main point of this exercise is just to show you that a minimap is nothing more than a regular isometric map that has been reduced in size.

Zones of Control

If you play any turn-based strategy games, whether on computer or with the old-style hex grids with the little pieces of cardboard to represent units, you are probably familiar with the concept of a zone of control. Other genres, like real-time strategy or RPGs, don't include this concept. I include this topic here mainly because it has to do with units, and I couldn't really come up with a better place for it.

There will be no example demonstrating zones of control, since it is relatively simple to implement. I'm just going to describe how to do it, show a few pictures demonstrating the concept, and leave it to you.

Figure 19.5 shows some units and the zones of control they exert. A zone of control includes not only the square that the unit currently occupies, but also all neighboring squares, so determining which map locations are occupied by a given player is pretty simple.

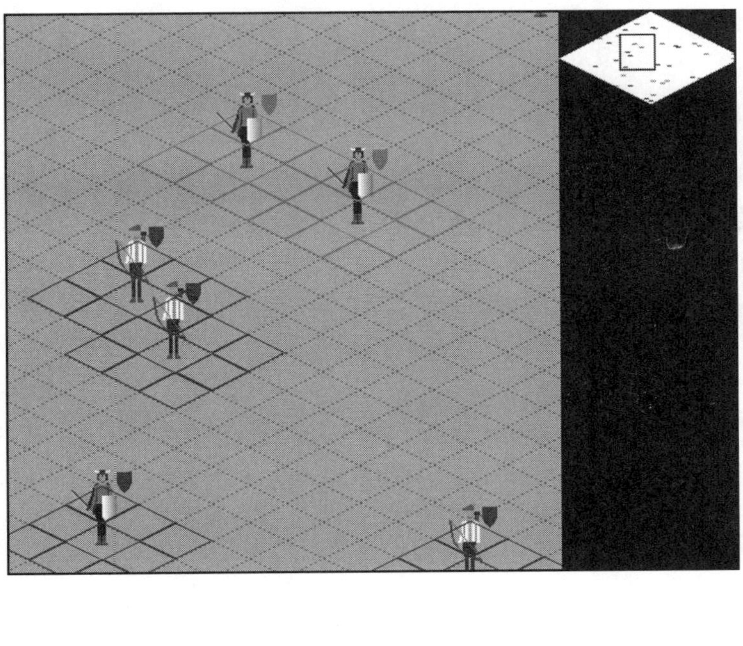

Figure 19.5

Zones of control

The Purpose of Zones of Control

The reason for zones of control goes way back into tabletop strategy game history. The idea is that a unit will not just control a single square, but can help regulate what goes on within one tile of that square. When I say "square," I mean map location, since an isometric game has no squares!

The main purpose of zones of control is to enable a player to get a tactical or strategic advantage with a relatively small number of units. In order to understand how this can happen, you must first examine the rules of zones of control.

Zones of Control Rules

You may move your own units in and out of any zone of control exerted by other units you control. This can also be extended to include "friendly" units with whom you have a diplomatic alliance, and so on. The rules for zones of control only apply to "hostile" units. Hostile units are any units that are not "friendly." It's sort of a circular definition, I know.

Table 19.4 is a subset of possible "diplomatic" relationships that your team of units might have with other teams of units. It also describes whether units belonging to that team are considered friendly or hostile. Keep in mind that even though you might be at peace with another team, it doesn't make their units friendly.

Table 19.4 Diplomatic Situations and Unit Friendliness

Relationship	Unit Friendliness
Self*	Friendly
Allied	Friendly
Peace	Hostile
War	Hostile

*You are always considered to be "allied" with yourself

So, you've established that zones of control are only taken into account with hostile units. Also, certain special units (such as diplomat and spy) might ignore zones of control entirely, and thus are not subject to the effects. These special types of units are usually called "stealth" units and are not typically detectable except by other stealth units.

A unit may move into a hostile unit's zone of control. Once within a zone of control, however, he cannot move from that tile onto another tile that is a zone of control. He can move into a non-zone-of-control tile, or he can attack, and that's about it. This is to simulate how one unit will keep another unit "pinned down" and unable to maneuver in a location.

While you lose some maneuverability when moving into a zone of control, the enemy unit is similarly constrained by your unit's zone of control and so is "pinned down" as well. Obviously, adding more units on either side can completely trap or surround a unit, which will then be completely unable to do anything but attack and try to fight its way out.

Implementing Zones of Control

There are a couple of ways you might do this, but the simplest idea that occurs to me is to use some sort of bit flag within the map location structure. Each bit can mean a different team has a zone of control over that particular map location. If you don't like bit flags, an array of `bools` works just as well. Keeping it within the map structure is much better than calculating it on-the-fly, and is less prone to errors, plus you need to update the zones of control only when a unit is moved or killed.

Fog of War

The fog of war is a feature much more widespread than the zones of control. Most genres that typify isometric games have them, including turn-based strategy, real-time strategy, and RPGs.

I lump two related ideas into the single concept of the fog of war. One idea is to mark which areas of the playing area you have explored, and the other is to mark which areas of the playing area you can actually see at a given point in time.

Units typically have what is called a *sight radius,* which differs in size depending on the unit. For example, a typical infantry unit might have a very small sight radius, but a unit on horseback will have a larger one.

As a unit moves, different parts of the map become actively visible. By "actively visible," I mean that the unit can see any enemy activity happening within that area. Once an area becomes actively visible, it is considered "explored," and explored areas do not disappear from the map once it is no longer actively visible (although when it is not actively visible, no enemy activity is shown). Typically, an explored area that is not actively visible is darkened or grayed out. You can either supply a darkened version of each tile (this looks nice but requires a lot of extra art) or supply a dithered (checkerboard) pattern of dark pixels to write over the top of the explored but not actively visible tiles.

Implementing a Fog of War

Putting together a fog of war is no great feat, once you've got the basics of isometric algorithms down—and you've already got the knowledge. It's just a matter of putting the necessary information into the map structure and keeping that information up-to-date. Then, you just have to modify the rendering function to blit it correctly.

Keep in mind that the fog of war should affect not only the playing area, but also the minimap. I'm not doing a fog of war example for the simple reason that you can figure out how to do it on your own by now, I'm sure.

Summary

We've explored quite a lot in this chapter—everything from object selection to minimaps and the fog of war. Some topics I explored in detail, and others I touched on only briefly. My explanation of isometric algorithms is pretty much complete. The rest of the book is just refinements and applications of those algorithms.

CHAPTER 20

Isometric Art

- Tile Ripping and Slanting
- Extra Graphical Operations

Until now, you've been learning about programming various components of an isometric engine—the plotter, the walker, the scroller, the MouseMap, and the renderer. You've learned about objects and units, and how to get them onto your tilemap. As the creator of isometric worlds, you need to know more than just these things to be effective.

One of the most frequently asked questions I hear—through e-mail, on my message board, and in the chat room—is "How can I make isometric art?" Most of the time, I cannot answer this question in the small space given to me by e-mail or the message board, because the explanations require pictures to make them easy to understand. The chat room you can completely write off, since very little can really be explained in that manner. So, this is my answer to all the people who have ever asked me about isometric art. My techniques are neither all-inclusive nor exhaustive. They are the best I've come up with so far, and they are effective.

However, this chapter is not just about art. I am a programmer first and foremost. My artistic skills (in case you haven't noticed) are somewhat lacking, and I have to fake it quite often. However, you can do some things with textures (you can find textures just about anywhere on the Web) that will make them look like isometric art.

Additionally, this chapter covers a few "how do they do that" kinds of algorithms that primarily have to do with isometric art—things like coastline, terrain fringes (including making the fog of war fuzzier), roads, rivers, and other connecting structures. Also, I have a few tricks up my sleeve to take a texture that is the wrong color and make it the right color.

Tile Ripping and Slanting

I want to start with ripping and slanting. These are the two most fundamental tricks I use to convert a rectangular piece of art into an isometric tile. Both give good-looking results. If you're stuck for terrain tiles, you can use these methods in a pinch to take a texture you found on the Web and turn it into isometric tiles.

Tile Slanting

I've used tile slanting a number of times, mainly for board games, but this is not to say you couldn't use it in other situations. Figure 20.1 shows a snapshot of my game *Knight's Challenge* (you can find it on the CD in the Examples folder). Believe it or not, the entire chessboard was creating using a single 16×16 square tile, but I rotated, slanted, and changed the color of the tile to make it look like more art was required than actually was. In other words, I used tile slanting to fake it, and it turned out looking awesome.

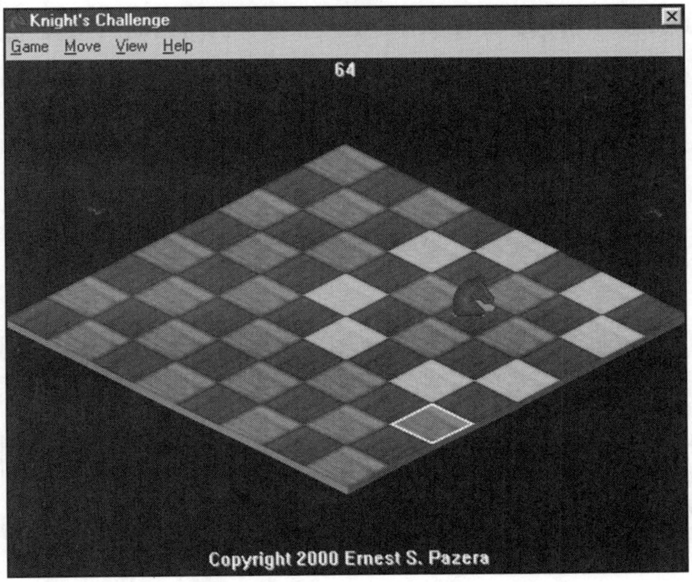

Figure 20.1

Knight's Challenge uses tile slanting

So, how does tile slanting work? If you take a look at Figure 20.2, you will see the simple principle on which it is based. Tile slanting is just texture mapping—extrapolating the pixels within a different shape based on a texture and the vertices of another polygon.

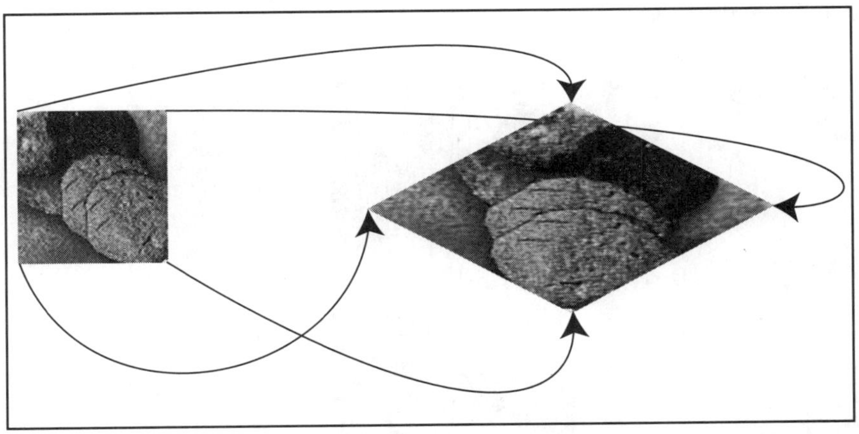

Figure 20.2

Texture mapping

Later, when you get into Direct3D, DirectX will take care of texture mapping for you. Unfortunately you're still in 2D land, so you have to do it yourself. Don't worry, though. You won't be required to do any really complicated math, because changing a square into a diamond is a lot easier than changing it into a different arbitrary shape.

And now, here's the big trick: when tile slanting, you simply treat the isometric tile as if it were a diamond map, and just use really small tiles (4×2 pixels in size, with the bottom pixel row empty), using the rectangular art as a "tilemap" that contains the colors that belong on the diamond map.

For a 64×32 isometric tile (which is my standard), you need a 16×16 square image. From there, you can slant it to look like it was drawn isometrically.

> **CAUTION**
>
> **I've only really gotten tile slanting to work for isometric tiles that have an aspect ration of 2:1 (the width is 2 times the height). If you are working with other sizes and shapes, texture mapping becomes more complicated.**

I've been throwing numbers at you here without really explaining their basis. I plan to rectify that situation now.

Figure 20.3 shows a zoomed-in version of the tile shape I have been using throughout this book. It is no accident that I use this tile shape (and very similar shapes with an aspect ration of 2:1). This shape is by far the easiest to work with, and it looks good.

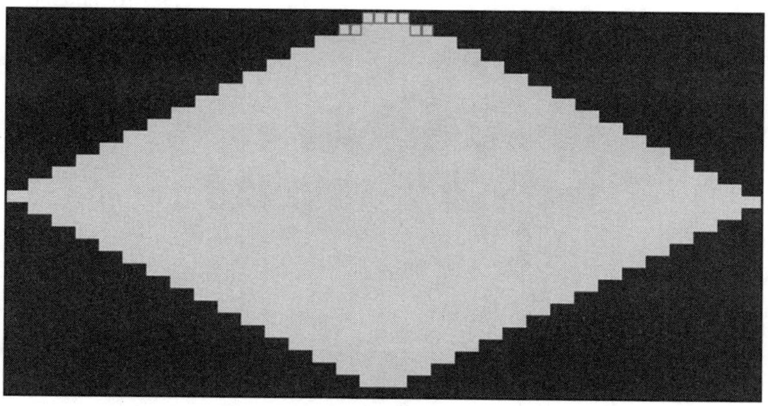

Figure 20.3

Standard iso tile shape, severely magnified

Notice that there are four dark boxes around the topmost pixels of the tile. Also, next to and one row down on either side are two more dark boxes. This is to show you how the tile shape is being converted into a diamond map, to give a basis for all these numbers I've been spouting.

So, the first row of the image has 4 pixels, located at positions (30,0) through (33,0). The next row adds 2 to either side, giving 8 pixels from (28,1) through (35,1). This trend continues until row 16, which extends the width of the image, from (0,15) to (63,15). After that, the number of pixels per row is reduced on each side by 2, until at row 31 there are again only 4 pixels, from (30,30) to (33,30). Row 32 is empty. I'll repeat that: *row 32 is empty*. In all of the 2:1 ratio tiles, the last row is empty. This will be important in a minute.

Now, say that the top pixel row contains map location (0,0) of a diamond map. There are 4 pixels, so use a 2:1 ratio tile that is 4 pixels wide, making a 4×2 tile. The first row of this "micro-tile" is filled with 4 pixels. The second row, which is the last row, is empty. See? I told you that would be important.

The second row has 8 pixels, which can fit two micro-tiles, which, handily enough, will be map locations (0,1) and (1,0) in the diamond map. See how this is shaping up? You keep progressing this way down the map until row 16, which has all 64 pixels set. Dividing by 4, you get 16 micro-tiles across the image, so the diagonal of the square image needs to have 16 pixels, which means you need a 16×16 square image in order to make this work.

To make a more general statement, if you want to break up a 2:1 iso tile into 4×2 micro-tiles, you divide the width by 4 and use that for the width and height of the square source image. However, you might not have a 16×16 image. Instead, you might have a 64×64 or 128×128 or even 256×256 image (these three are by far the most common texture sizes). No problem. Simply divide the image into little 16×16 squares, and slant each one of them. Naturally, you probably want to keep track of which one is which so that you can use the images together without having them look strange.

Tile Slanting Example

Enough talk about tile slanting. Let's go ahead and do it, programmatically. Load IsoHex20_1.cpp. This example is kind of a throwback to Part I, because it operates within a window instead of full-screen, and it doesn't use any of the isometric components you've developed since then.

The program works by loading a square texture into a `CGDICanvas` (`gdicSquare`) and creating a larger GDI canvas to contain the isometric image (`gdicIso`). It is loaded during `Prog_Init`. The isometric tile is created with the following code:

```
//loop through x texture coords
for(tx=0;tx<16;tx++)
{
        //loop through y texture coords
        for(ty=0;ty<16;ty++)
        {
```

```
                //grab the color from the texture
                crColor=GetPixel(gdicSquare,tx,ty);
                //calculate x and y
                x=30+tx*2-ty*2;
                y=tx+ty;
                //loop through four pixel positions
                for(tempx=x;tempx<(x+4);tempx++)
                {
                        SetPixelV(gdicIso,tempx,y,crColor);
                        //set color on iso picture
                }
        }
}
```

This code is all hardcoded, and it will only work to convert a 16×16 square image into a 64×32 isometric image. If you have a different size, though, this method is easily adjusted to accommodate it, as long as the iso tile has a ratio of 2:1.

There isn't much to the operation of this program. It loads the image and shows the isometric tile repeated, as it would be on a tilemap. Pressing 2 takes you to a view of a map of the square tile. Pressing 1 takes you back to the isometric view. Figure 20.4 shows the isometric view, and Figure 20.5 shows the square view.

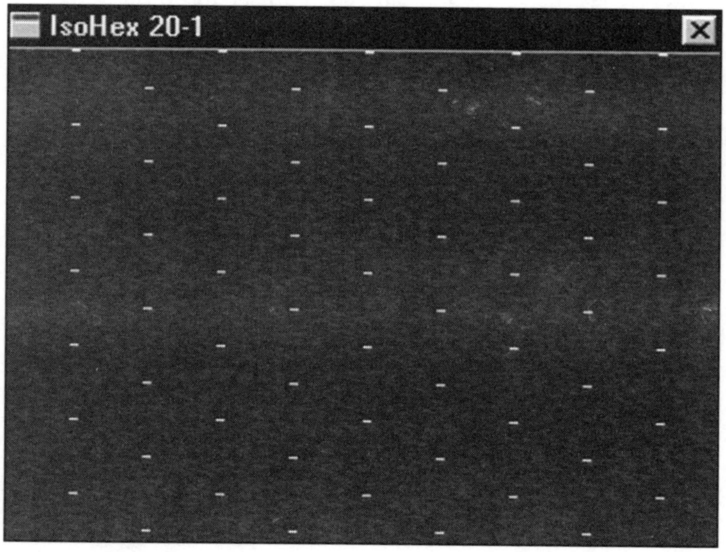

Figure 20.4

IsoHex20_1.cpp in the isometric (default) view

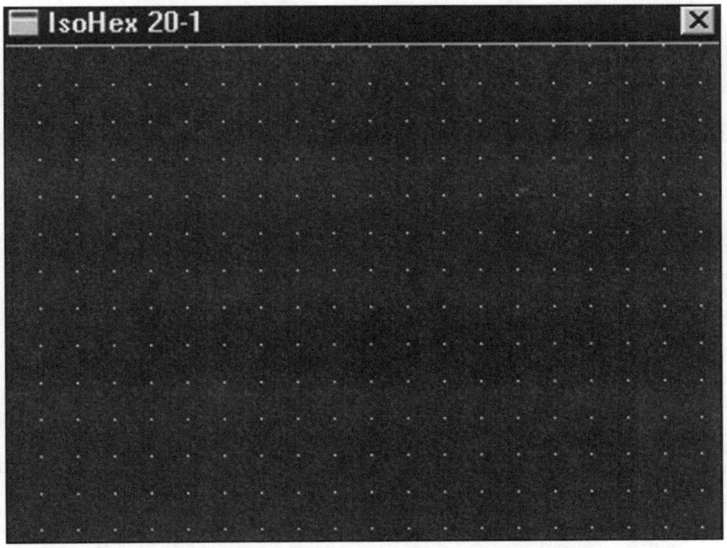

Figure 20.5

IsoHex20_1.cpp in the square view

Before you move on, I want to give you the generic code that will work with any 2:1 ratio isometric tile:

```
//WIDTH is the width of an isometric tile. This must be a multiple of 4.
//HEIGHT is the height of an isometric tile. This must be WIDTH/2.
//TEXTURESIZE is the width and height of the texture. It will be WIDTH/4.
//loop through x texture coords
for(tx=0;tx<TEXTURESIZE;tx++)
{
	//loop through y texture coords
	for(ty=0;ty<TEXTURESIZE;ty++)
	{
		//grab the color from the texture
		crColor=GetPixel(gdicSquare,tx,ty);
		//calculate x and y
		x=WIDTH/2-2+tx*2-ty*2;//see below
		y=tx+ty;
		//loop through four pixel positions
		for(tempx=x;tempx<(x+4);tempx++)
		{
			SetPixelV(gdicIso,tempx,y,crColor);
			//set color on iso picture
		}
	}
}
```

Of the preceding lines of code, one in particular merits some extra discussion: `x=WIDTH/2-2+tx*2-ty*2`. The `tx*2-ty*2` is easily explained, because this is the standard calculation for a diamond map, but where does the `WIDTH/2-2` come from? Well, since a diamond map's (0,0) lies at the topmost map location, you must have some way of centering, so you add `WIDTH/2`. The `-2` part comes in because the micro-tile you are putting onto the image is 4 pixels wide and also must be centered. Hope this clears up any confusion.

Color-Blended Tile Slanting

Tile slanting looks pretty cool, and it can be used to generate decent looking images from square textures. However, the isometric images generated in this manner look a bit more coarse than the square textures from which they were generated. This is a natural result of a pixel's being expanded into a string of 4 pixels.

To minimize this look, you can either not use tile slanting at all, or you can find a way to smooth out the isometric image. The way I'm about to show you is using color blending.

Consider Figure 20.6 for a moment. It's a graphical, zoomed-in schematic of how tile slanting works. Admittedly, it uses a very small 3×3 texture, but the principle is the same. The three highlighted pixels in the texture are stretched to become the highlighted squares in the isometric image.

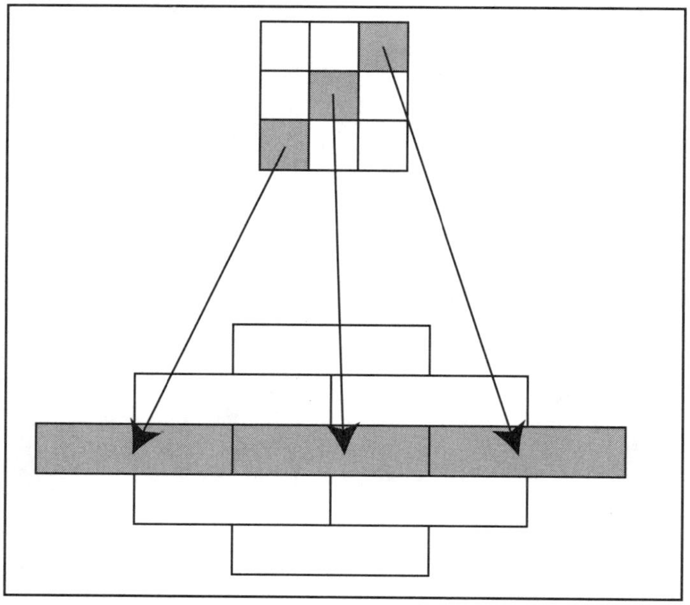

Figure 20.6

Tile slanting (a zoomed-in view)

Now, say you want to make the transition from one 4-pixel micro-tile to another less abrupt. You could put an "in between" color on each of the ends and the main color in the middle two pixels. This would give you something that resembles Figure 20.7. As you can see, the color transitions are smoothed out somewhat for an overall better-looking tile.

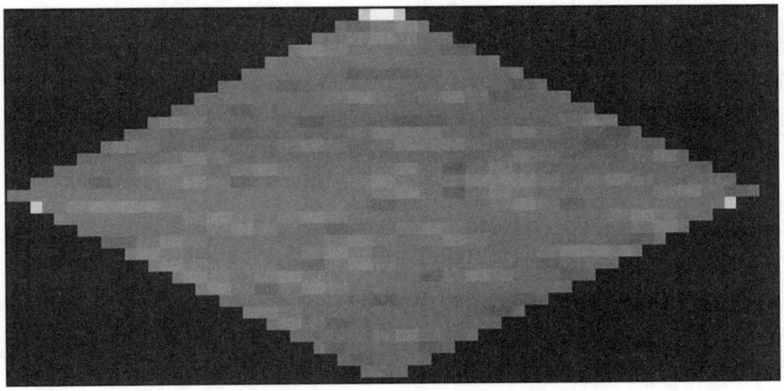

Figure 20.7

Tile slanting with color blending

This color blending is done with just a modification of the scanning loop in IsoHex20_1.cpp. In fact, IsoHex20_2.cpp has the exact modification you need. It's all just a matter of grabbing the diagonal neighbors and using them to calculate the appropriate colors.

Whether or not you color blend with your tile slanting is totally up to you. I'm just here to present the information and give you choices.

Tile Ripping

I like tile ripping. It can make a boring tilemap into an interesting one, because you can texturize a map with a texture that is larger than a single tile, and the texture can be a rectangular piece of art. In addition, you can get some interesting effects from modulating a textured isometric tile onto another texture. I'll cover modulation and what it's all about in a moment.

The first thing you need, of course, is a texture (see Figure 20.8). The texture should be repeating, meaning that when a copy of the texture is put next to another copy, there should be no seam. If you do have a texture with a seam, there are a few methods you can use to make it seamless. I'll get to those methods soon, too.

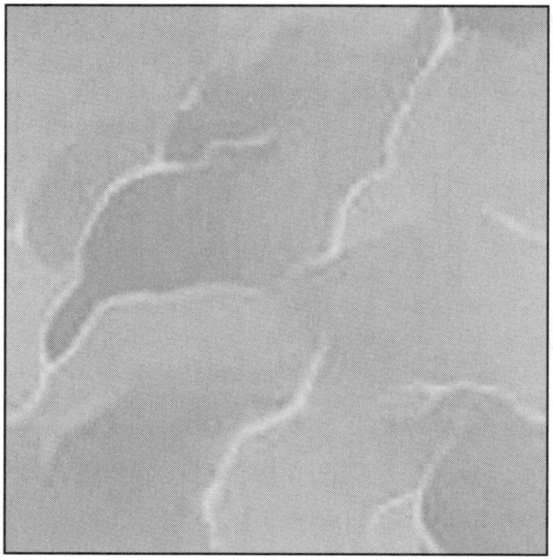

Figure 20.8

A texture

The size of the texture is pretty important. The width has to be a multiple of your iso tile width, and the height has to be a multiple of the iso tile height. Since you are using 64×32 tiles, this won't be a problem, because most textures are 128×128 or 256×256. If you are using a different tile size or an irregular texture, you might need to stretch or squash the texture.

Making a Repeating Texture out of a Nonrepeating Texture

You don't have to worry about the texture I chose for illustration. It repeats seamlessly, as shown in Figure 20.9. However, many of the textures you'll find (there are a lot of them on the Web) don't quite repeat. They're supposed to, but there's usually some sort of seam visible, despite the texture creator's attempts to hide it.

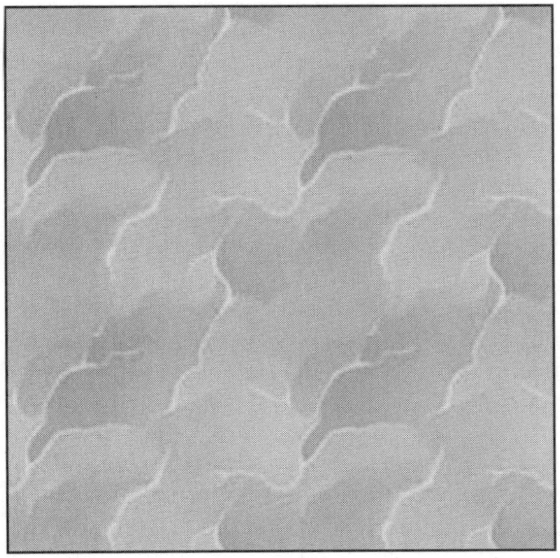

Figure 20.9

A repeating texture

NOTE

By the way, if you can't make textures yourself, be sure to get on the Web, go to your favorite search engine, and type textures. You will find more textures than you'll ever need. Also, because I'll show you how to modulate to change the color, it doesn't matter if the color of the texture doesn't quite match, because you can make it match.

Figure 20.10 shows a texture I found on the Web. It is a repeating texture, but there is a problem with using it for my 64×32 tiles. This texture is 170×170, and neither 64 nor 32 divides evenly into 170.

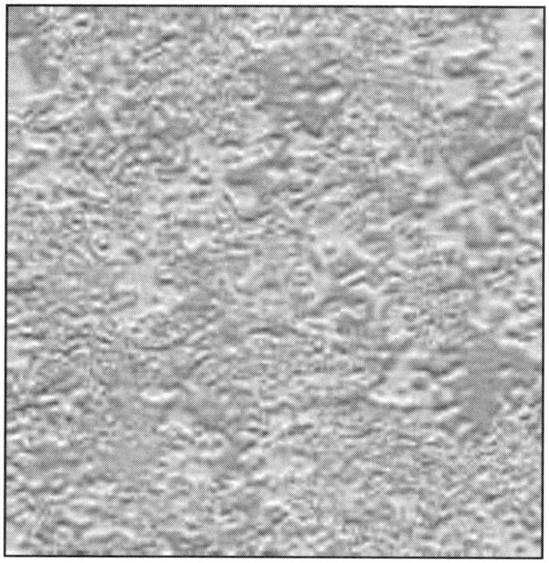

Figure 20.10

Texture 170×170 I found on the Web

So, I have a few choices. I can shrink it to 128×128, expand it to 192×192, or crop it to 128×128. Because cropping to 128×128 gives me a nonrepeating texture, I'll do that, just to illustrate how you can get a repeating texture out of a nonrepeating one.

Figures 20.11 through 20.13 show the process of cropping to 128×128, checking for the repeat, and zooming in on the seams. Figure 20.12 demonstrates that even after being cropped to 128×128, the texture still looks pretty good, and the seam is hardly noticeable. Still, if you zoom in, as shown in Figure 20.13, the seam is indeed there.

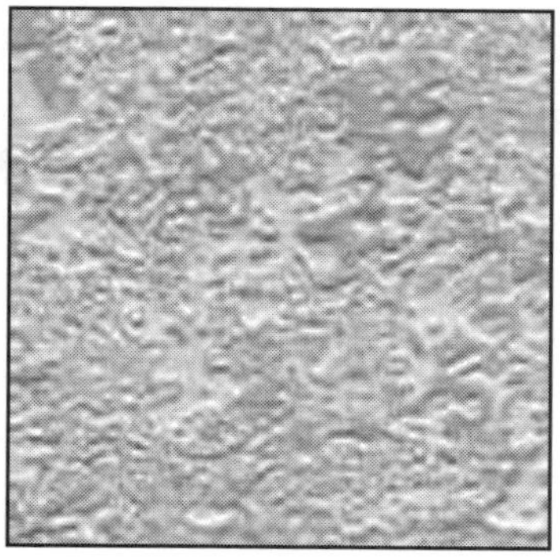

Figure 20.11

The texture cropped to 128×128

Figure 20.12

Checking for the repeat

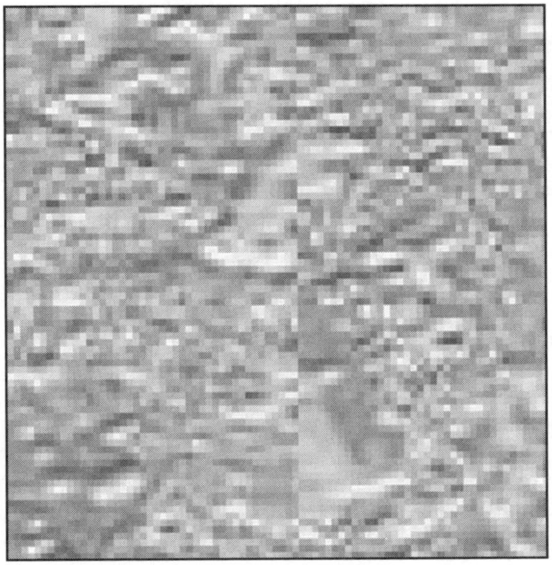

Figure 20.13

Zooming in on the seams

Honestly, this texture can be used without any more work, and that is a credit to the texture's designer. Still, I'm trying to demonstrate making seamless tiles, so that is what you're going to do!

Basically, you make a nonrepeating texture into a repeating one by using the texture four times and flipping some of the copies horizontally or vertically, or both. You first make an image that is twice the width and twice the height of the original texture. Then you place the texture (flipped as needed) in each of the four corners.

In the upper-left corner, do no flipping at all. In the upper-right corner, do a horizontal flip. In the lower-left corner, do a vertical flip, and in the lower-right corner, do a horizontal flip and a vertical flip. This gets rid of the seam but adds a sort of "reflected" pattern to the texture, as shown in Figure 20.14. Also, the texture is now four times larger, so you have to take that into consideration.

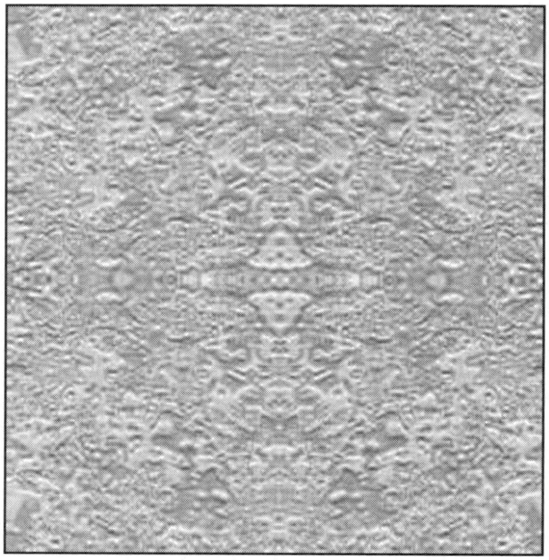

Figure 20.14

Making it seamless

Basically, this is a game of deciding what looks good. You often have to play with a texture, stretching, flipping, rotating, and applying filters until you find what looks good to you. There is no one set method.

Getting Tiles out of a Texture

So, you either found yourself a repeating texture of the appropriate size, or you played with a texture until it was satisfactory in size and repeated. Great! Now what?

Now it's just a matter of getting all the tiles out of it. In order to do that, you need your basic tile shape, which you've got, and the `RECT` extent that will be used for your tiles, which you also have or can determine very easily. You need one other thing: a TilePlotter.

The basic steps for tile plotting are as follows:

1. Make a larger image, and place the texture on it four times in a 2×2 pattern.
2. Determine the number of tiles you need to fully rip this texture.
3. Loop through the tiles that need ripping.
4. Plot the tiles.
5. Rectify the tiles to be within the texture.

6. Copy the rectangular portion of the texture onto a new image.
7. Apply the isometric shape using modulation.

I know at this point the process sounds like a bunch of mumbo jumbo. All in due time.

Step 1: Tile the Texture 2x2

Because of the nature of isometric tiles (the overlapping), you will have some tiles that will be on the edge of the texture. If you didn't tile your texture, you would have partially empty tiles, which is not good.

Step 2: Determine the Number of Tiles

The number of tiles you need depends on texture width and height and tile width and height. Divide texture width by tile width and texture height by tile height. Multiply these two numbers, then multiply the result by 2, and that's the number of tiles.

If you're interested in the basis, here goes: Imagine that you have a 128×128 texture and are using 64×32 tiles. An example of tile ripping for these parameters is shown in Figure 20.15. The tiles in this figure look the most like a staggered map, so you'll deal with this as though it were a staggered map for the time being.

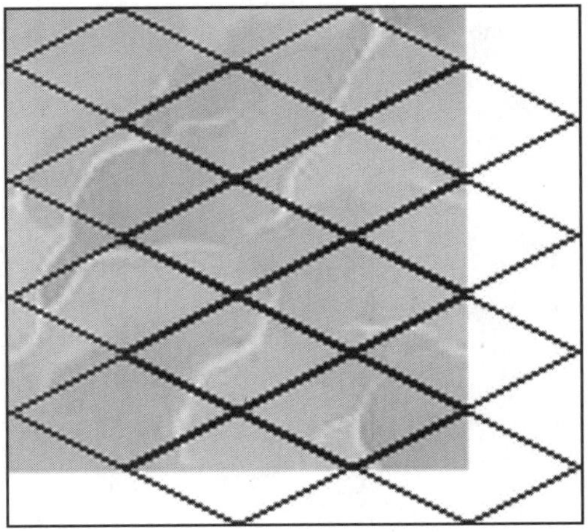

Figure 20.15

Example of tile ripping

There are two columns of tiles and eight rows. Columns=`TextureWidth/TileWidth`. 128/64=2.

Rows are based on texture height, but you have to take into account the overlap between rows, and multiply by 2. Rows=2*`TextureHeight/TileHeight`. 2*128/32=8.

Take the number of rows times the number of columns, and that's the number of tiles. 2*8=16.

Step 3: Loop through the Tiles

This is pretty easy. You loop X from 0 to Columns–1, and you loop Y from 0 to Rows–1. It's important to note here that you can use any sort of tileplotting, and use the same loop, and it will come out fine no matter what. One warning, though: be sure to use the same sort of tileplotting when ripping tiles as you do when placing tiles. Otherwise, putting the tiles back together again is a pain.

```
//calculate columns and rows
int Columns=TEXTUREWIDTH/TILEWIDTH;
int Rows=2*TEXTUREHEIGHT/TILEHEIGHT;
//loop through columns
for(int x=0;x<Columns;x++)
{
	//loop through rows
	for(int y=0;y<Rows;y++)
	{
		//we'll do some plotting and ripping here
	}
}
```

Step 4: Plot the Tiles

You can already do this step. Use `CTilePlotter`, or your own function, or even just a few quicky formulas—whichever makes you happy. The following code does a standard plot for a diamond-shaped tilemap. (This code would go within the column and row loops).

```
//standard diamond-map plot
plotx=(x-y)*TILEWIDTH/2;
ploty=(x+y)*TILEHEIGHT/2;
```

Step 5: Rectify the Tiles

In this case, *rectify* means to validate, or to take a value and bring it into an acceptable range.

The variables `plotx` and `ploty` describe the upper-left corner of the rectangular region from which your tile will be ripped. In order for tile ripping to work, `plotx` and `ploty` have to be within the upper-left quadrant of the 2×2 tiled texture. This guarantees that you will have a full 64×32 image from this portion of the texture.

So, in order to get `plotx` and `ploty` where they need to be, simply take the modulus (`%`) with `TEXTUREWIDTH` and `TEXTUREHEIGHT`, and check for negatives.

```
//find remainder
plotx%=TEXTUREWIDTH;
ploty%=TEXTUREHEIGHT;
//check for negatives
if(plotx<0) plotx+=TEXTUREWIDTH;
if(ploty<0) ploty+=TEXTUREHEIGHT;
```

Now `plotx` and `ploty` are within the acceptable range, and you can continue.

Step 6: Blit the Rectangular Area to Tile

Now you plot the part of the textured image from `(plotx,ploty)-(plotx+TILEWIDTH,ploty+TILE-HEIGHT)` to wherever you are storing the tile image, whether that be an HDC somewhere, a DirectDraw surface, or elsewhere. I'm not putting any code in right now, since rendering is rather API-specific. I'm just trying to get the algorithm across.

Step 7: Modulate with the Tile Shape

Again with the word "modulate?" *Modulate* just means to multiply, although it's a different sort of multiplication, because you are multiplying colors. Essentially, this step can be accomplished with an all-white tile shape and blitting with `SRCAND`. Officially, however, I have to say "modulate" because you can use tile shapes that don't necessarily consist of all-white pixels to do neat tricks.

So, there it is—seven steps to tile ripping. I'm pretty sure, however, that you would like some sort of example to make the concept more concrete. I know I would, so let's do that.

Tile Ripping Example

Go ahead and load up IsoHex20_3.cpp, our tile ripping example du jour. Like IsoHex20_1, this is a very simple application that doesn't use any fancy isometric components, because they are not needed.

The following code is all that is needed to rip a rectangular texture into small isometric bits. It should be easy enough to follow.

```
//load texture canvas
gdicTexture.Load(NULL,"texture.bmp");
//load iso shape
gdicIsoShape.Load(NULL,"IsoShape.bmp");
```

First (of course), you have to load in the two images you are using—the texture and the isometric shape. It's pretty cool, really, that only these two are necessary, and the rest can be generated programmatically. In real-world situations, you'd want to prepare the textured tiles *before* distributing the game.

```
//grab dc from main window
HDC hdc=GetDC(hWndMain);
//calculate rows and columns of tiles
iColumns=gdicTexture.GetWidth()/gdicIsoShape.GetWidth();
iRows=2*gdicTexture.GetHeight()/gdicIsoShape.GetHeight();
//create tiled texture canvas
gdicSource.CreateBlank(hdc,gdicTexture.GetWidth()*2,gdicTexture.GetHeight()*2);
//create tile canvas
gdicTiles.CreateBlank(hdc,gdicIsoShape.GetWidth()*iColumns,gdicIsoShape.GetHeight
()*iRows);
//restore dc to main window
ReleaseDC(hWndMain,hdc);
```

Second, you need a few extra surfaces to work from, the 2×2 texture tiled image, and an image large enough to accommodate all the ripped tiles (which is why the columns and rows are calculated).

```
//create tiled texture image
//upper left
BitBlt(gdicSource,0,0,gdicTexture.GetWidth(),gdicTexture.GetWidth(),gdicTexture,0
,0,SRCCOPY);
//upper right
BitBlt(gdicSource,gdicTexture.GetWidth(),0,gdicTexture.GetWidth(),gdicTexture.Get
Width(),gdicTexture,0,0,SRCCOPY);
//lower left
BitBlt(gdicSource,0,gdicTexture.GetHeight(),gdicTexture.GetWidth(),gdicTexture.Ge
tWidth(),gdicTexture,0,0,SRCCOPY);
//lower right
BitBlt(gdicSource,gdicTexture.GetWidth(),gdicTexture.GetHeight(),gdicTexture.GetW
idth(),gdicTexture.GetWidth(),gdicTexture,0,0,SRCCOPY);
```

Next, you need to fill the source image (the 2×2 tiled texture image) with the image data from the textures. There are four blits, one for each corner.

```
//rip out the tiles
int x;
int y;
int plotx;
int ploty;
//loop through columns
```

```
for(x=0;x<iColumns;x++)
{
//loop through rows
	for(y=0;y<iRows;y++)
	{
		//determine plotx and ploty
		plotx=x*gdicIsoShape.GetWidth()+(y&1)*gdicIsoShape.GetWidth()/2;
		ploty=y*gdicIsoShape.GetHeight()/2;
		//bring plotx and ploty within appropriate range
		plotx%=gdicTexture.GetWidth();
		ploty%=gdicTexture.GetHeight();
		//check for negatives
		if(plotx<0) plotx+=gdicTexture.GetWidth();
		if(ploty<0) ploty+=gdicTexture.GetHeight();
		//grab this part of the source surface, and place it on the tile
surface

BitBlt(gdicTiles,x*gdicIsoShape.GetWidth(),y*gdicIsoShape.GetHeight(),
			gdicIsoShape.GetWidth(),gdicIsoShape.GetHeight(),
			gdicSource,plotx,ploty,SRCCOPY);
		//modulate with the iso shape

BitBlt(gdicTiles,x*gdicIsoShape.GetWidth(),y*gdicIsoShape.GetHeight(),
			gdicIsoShape.GetWidth(),gdicIsoShape.GetHeight(),
			gdicIsoShape,0,0,SRCAND);
	}
}
```

Finally, rip the tiles, and modulate the image data with the isometric shape. That's really all there is to it. Then, all you have to do is make use of the tiles you have created, as demonstrated in `ShowMap`.

```
void ShowMap(HDC hdc)//show sample map
{
	//vars
	int x;
	int y;
	int tilex;
	int tiley;
	int plotx;
	int ploty;
	//clear out dc
	RECT rcFill;
```

```
        GetClientRect(hWndMain,&rcFill);
        //fill rect
        FillRect(hdc,&rcFill,(HBRUSH)GetStockObject(BLACK_BRUSH));
        //loops
        for(x=0;x<10;x++)
        {
                for(y=0;y<20;y++)
                {
                        //calculate plotted positions
                        plotx=x*gdicIsoShape.GetWidth()+
                              (y&1)*gdicIsoShape.GetWidth()/2;
                        ploty=y*gdicIsoShape.GetHeight()/2;
                        //calculate which tile to use
                        tilex=(x%iColumns)*gdicIsoShape.GetWidth();
                        tiley=(y%iRows)*gdicIsoShape.GetHeight();
                        //blit the tile
                        BitBlt(hdc,plotx,ploty,gdicIsoShape.GetWidth(),
                        gdicIsoShape.GetHeight(),gdicTiles,tilex,tiley,
                        SRCPAINT);
                }
        }
}
```

This is pretty basic, with perhaps one exception—the calculation of `tilex` and `tiley`. These numbers are based on the x and y (in a more complex app, they would be `mapx`, `mapy`). The reason is that you need to keep the texture looking right, and any given tile has to have a certain piece of the texture or else the image won't look right. Luckily, you can just find the remainder of `x/column` and `y/row` to find out which one.

Extra Graphical Operations

I promised I'd discuss two very common graphical operations and how you can do them programmatically. These are *grayscaling*—taking an image and converting it to *an* image with 256 shades of gray in it and *modulating,* which you can use to modify an image's colors). You can combine these two operations to change textures to something more to your liking.

Grayscaling

The act of grayscaling is pretty simple and straightforward. You take the red, green, and blue components and combine them, making a single gray component for the image.

Usually, the RGB components are weighted percentage-wise. The human eye is most sensitive to green, so that usually gets the highest percentage weight. The eye is least sensitive to blue, which gets the lowest weight. Red gets whatever is left over. A very good weighting scheme is 30% for red, 59% for green, and 11% for blue.

The following is an example of grayscaling an image that has been loaded onto an HDC:

```
//hdc is the dc of the image
//WIDTH is the width of the image
//HEIGHT is the height of the image
int iRed,iGreen,iBlue,iCombine;
COLORREF crColor;
//loop through rows
for(int y=0;y<HEIGHT;y++)
{
	//loop through columns
	for(int x=0;x<WIDTH;x++)
	{
		//grab the pixel
		crColor=GetPixel(hdc,x,y);
		//extract the RGB components
		//and multiply by percentage
		iRed=GetRValue(crColor)*30;
		iGreen=GetGValue(crColor)*59;
		iBlue=GetBValue(crColor)*11;
		//combine the rgb
		iCombine=(iRed+iGreen+iBlue)/100;
		//reform into a gray image based on iCombine
		crColor=RGB(iCombine,iCombine,iCombine);
		//replace the pixel
		SetPixelV(hdc,x,y,crColor);
	}
}
```

As you can see, grayscaling is pretty easy. You can also change the percentage weights (always make sure they add up to 100) to get some different effects. The effects won't be drastically different, but the appearance will change.

Modulation

Modulation is the act of multiplying colored images to get new colored images. It can be used for a variety of effects; one of these effects is changing a texture's color after it has been grayscaled.

For example, you might find a texture that you really like, but it's the wrong color; maybe it's purple when you want it to be green. No problem. First, grayscale the image, and then modulate it with the color of green that you want, and blammo, you've instantly changed the color of the texture while retaining its detail and the proper variations in tone.

That just leaves you with the question of how to multiply a color by another color. Actually, you don't multiply the colors by one another. Instead, each color's components get multiplied by another color's components. Red multiplies with red, green with green, and blue with blue. However, multiplying colors in their current form (from 0 to 255) can't work, because the final result must also be within that range. So you have to make the components equal a value from 0.0 to 1.0, with 0 being 0.0 and 255 being 1.0. To convert from the 0-to-255 to the 0.0-to-1.0 format, you need only convert to floating-point and divide by 255. So, the following formulae will work for modulating color components:

```
RC/255=R1/255*R2/255
GC/255=G1/255*G2/255
BC/255=B1/255*B2/255
```

R1,G1,B1 and R2,G2,B2 represent the two source colors, and RC,GC,BC is the combined color. Naturally, you'd like a more simplified version of the formula, with RC,GC, and BC alone on the left side so that you can use them in a program. Here they are:

```
RC=R1*R2/255;
GC=G1*G2/255;
BC=B1*B2/255;
```

And there you have it. You can use these lines as-is in a program. Now let's modulate.

```
//hdc1 and hdc2 are source images; hdc3 is the combined
//WIDTH is width of images; HEIGHT is height of images
//all three images are the same dimensions
int r1,g1,b1;//source color 1
int r2,g2,b2;//source color 2
int r3,g3,b3;//destination color
COLORREF crColor1;//source 1
COLORREF crColor2;//source 2
COLORREF crColor3;//dest
//loop through rows
for(int y=0;y<HEIGHT;y++)
{
        //loop through columns
        for(int x=0;x<WIDTH;x++)
        {
                //grab pixels
                crColor1=GetPixel(hdc1,x,y);
```

```
            crColor2=GetPixel(hdc2,x,y);
            //extract components
            r1=GetRValue(crColor1);
            g1=GetGValue(crColor1);
            b1=GetBValue(crColor1);
            r2=GetRValue(crColor2);
            g2=GetGValue(crColor2);
            b2=GetBValue(crColor2);
            //multiply components
            r3=r1*r2/255;
            g3=g1*g2/255;
            b3=b1*b2/255;
            //combine components
            crColor3=RGB(r3,g3,b3);
            //set pixel
            SetPixelV(hdc3,x,y,crColor3);
        }
}
```

And that's modulation. If you want to combine portions of an image with one color and other portions with another color, just make a two-colored image and modulate. Modulation can also be used to make light maps, shadow maps, and a variety of other effects. Play around with it and see what you can create.

Summary

Compared to other chapters, this one was a little short, and not nearly as technologically sophisticated. Art, in general, tends not to be so. Still, looking good is a part of making a game, and it never hurts to have a few tricks up your sleeve (especially if you can't draw very well, like me).

CHAPTER 21

Fringes and Interconnecting Structures

- Art Requirements for Fringes
- Making a Lookup Table
- Making Interconnecting Structures

I had a hard time deciding where to put this chapter. It seemed to belong in several places, and at the same time there was really no perfect place for it. So I tacked it onto the end of Part II, because it was just too important to put into an appendix.

This chapter is concerned with a few topics, mostly dealing with isometric art and how to handle it. I focus on two major areas: fringes and interconnecting structures. By *fringes,* I mean transitions from one sort of terrain to another, like from grassland to plains, but also including coastline (coastline being just a transition from land to ocean). By *interconnecting structures,* I mean roads, railroads, rivers, forests, hills, mountains, walls, and so on.

As you can see, these issues are important both to the artist designing the isometric tiles and objects and to the programmer, who has to make use of the art. The main idea is that you want to make the art as easy to generate as possible, and you want to rely on as few images as possible, thus conserving valuable display memory. However, you still want good performance, so you want to reduce the number of blits necessary to get a tile onto the screen. This is the eternal juggling act that you as a graphics programmer have to face every day.

Fringes

Fringes can be used for several things, the most obvious being coastline, but they can also work for transitions from one terrain to another, or the edge of a fog of war.

The first question out of your mouth will be "Why use fringes?" Figures 21.1 and 21.2 provide a good example of why. This is an old isometric sample program I wrote about a year or so before I started this book. You can find it and the source for it on the CD. In this program, I set out to demonstrate a very simple coastline effect. Figure 21.1 has the coastline effect turned off, and Figure 21.2 has the coastline effect on. Naturally, the coastline on makes a better-looking picture. So, in answer to your question, you should use fringes because they enhance a game's appearance.

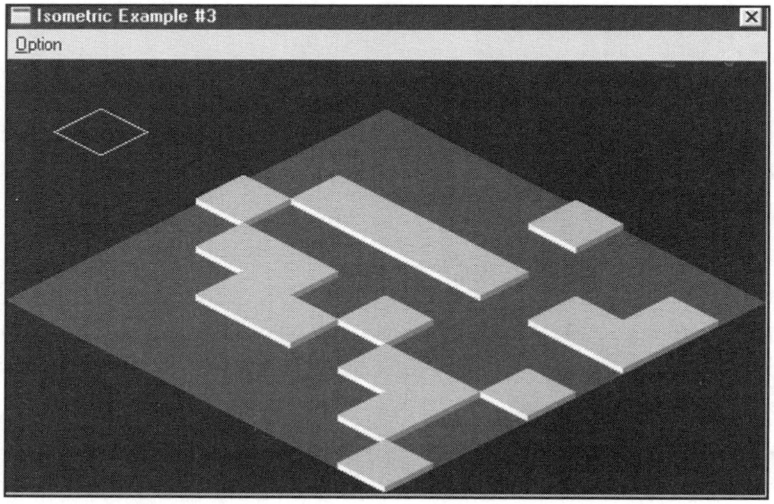

Figure 21.1

No fringe makes for unrealistic-looking games

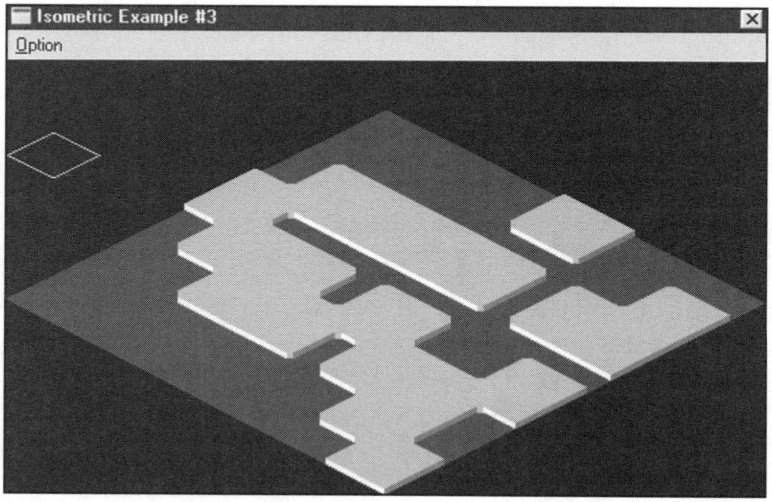

Figure 21.2

A fringe smoothes things out

Just to hammer home the point, I've included Figure 21.3, which I believe looks very good, even though it is very simple. (The graphics were tile ripped using the method presented in the last chapter from 128×128 textures and then modulated with different colors.) The fringes look a lot better than just having the two different terrains placed together with no sort of transition at all.

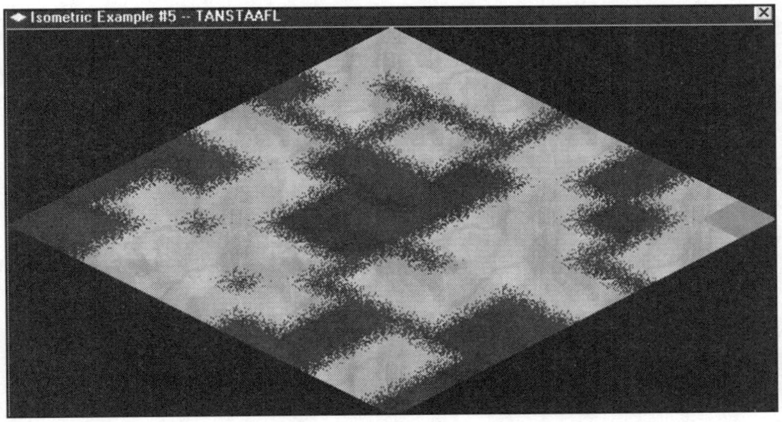

Figure 21.3

Another fringe example showing transition between terrains

Art Requirements for Fringes

Believe it or not, I can do a fringe like the one shown in Figure 21.3 for a 64×32 standard iso tile shape with an image that is 128×64—exactly four tiles worth of information. Of course, this means a lot of on-the-fly modulation of textures with the fringes, which decreases performance by quite a bit.

First, let's take a look at some basic math. For any given tile, the fringe that needs to show within that tile depends on all its neighbors. If you consider a case in which only two types of terrain exist, the neighboring tiles will either be of the same terrain or of the other terrain. Since each tile has eight neighbors, that is 2 to the eighth power, or 64 combinations. If your terrain is ripped from a texture, meaning that you could possibly have 2, 4, 8, 16, or even more different tiles that represent that same terrain, you are looking at anywhere from 128 to 1,024 or even more different images that can appear for a tile.

Since it is very likely that you have more than two types of terrain, the number keeps increasing. The cold, hard fact is that you don't have enough display memory to store the fifty bazillion images for the various fringe pictures, which would be ideal for performance. So, you have to compromise by taking a little away from performance to reduce the requirements of the art to a manageable level. That is what I'm here to show you how to do.

Before going on, let's take a look at what kind of requirements you would have for art if you were to make a distinct image for every possible tile configuration. I'm going to deal only with the fringing for coastline, which is, in my opinion, the best example of using a fringe. First, you must decide which type of terrain (either land or water) is "on top" of the other. The type of terrain "on top" does not get a fringe written on top of it, but the "on the bottom" terrain does. Logically, land is on top of water, but this could go either way. In most games you will see, the fringe/coastline is written onto water tiles and not onto land tiles, but this is a convention, not something that's written in stone.

To illustrate the point, I present Figure 21.4, which shows various representations of a 3×3 tile neighborhood. The lightly shaded tiles represent water, and the darkly shaded tiles represent land. Notice that the central tile of each neighborhood is a water tile, since it is upon the water tiles that you will be placing the fringe/coastline.

Figure 21.4

A tile neighborhood with tiles representing water and land

If you count the neighborhoods in Figure 21.4, there are 256 of them, and each neighborhood configuration is represented exactly once. Ideally, you would provide images for each of these, and if you had such a simplistic map—only water and land—you could probably get away with that. However, you usually cannot spend the display memory required for 256 images when you also need units, the units' animation frames, various types of land terrain, buildings, and so on.

If having 256 distinct images just for coastline is wasteful, what do you do? My own way of getting around the prohibitive art requirement for coastline (and other fringes) is to divide the tile into zones, as shown in Figure 21.5.

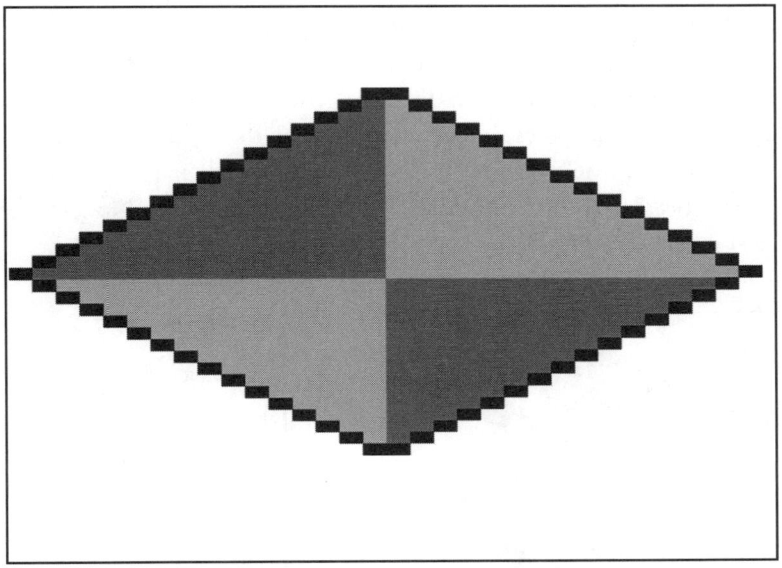

Figure 21.5

A tile divided into zones

With the tile divided into zones, you can just consider a single zone and its neighbors. Figure 21.6 shows an analysis of the possibilities for the upper-left zone. As you can see, there are eight possibilities, so an image that covers just the upper-left zone of the tile shape would need eight images. Do the same thing for each of the other three zones. A total of 32 images is needed, which is already much better than 256, but you aren't done yet!

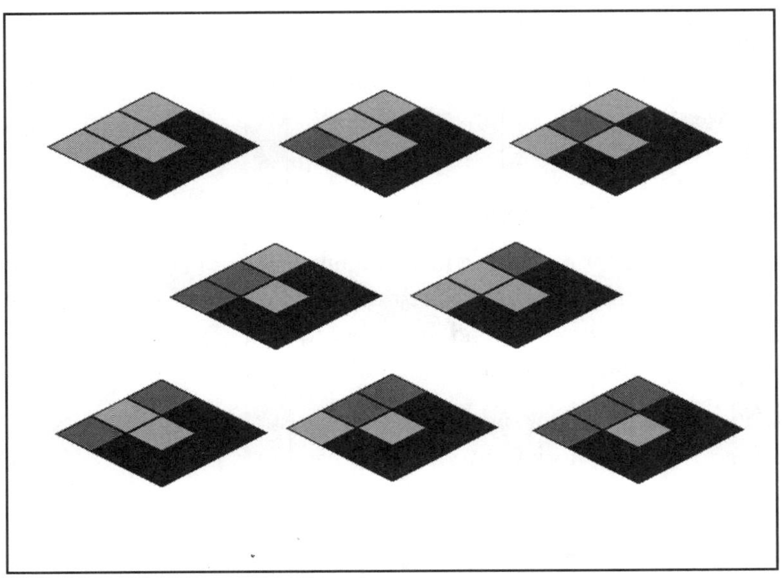

Figure 21.6

Neighbors of a fringe tile zone (upper left)

The last picture I have to show you before we get into a more concrete example is Figure 21.7, which shows the actual fringe for the upper-left tile zone based on the value of its tile neighbors. Eight tile neighborhoods are shown in this figure, but if you look closely, you will see that whenever the northwest tile is land, the same fringe is shown in the central tile. Since this occurs in four of the eight configurations, you can eliminate three of the eight pictures you would otherwise require. Similarly, when all of a water tile's neighbors are also water, no picture is needed, so that eliminates another picture needed. Now you have just four images required per tile zone, for a total of 16 pictures, which is hardly any at all.

Figure 21.7

Actual fringes based on a tile's upper-left zone

I've seen a number of people flounder when trying to get some sort of coastline or fringing working, usually because they try to make an image for every possibility, which is completely unnecessary. I'm here to show you the easy way, if not the fastest.

Making a Lookup Table

For the time being, give each of your images for each tile zone the numbers 0 through 3. The actual images reflected by this number will be arbitrary. Now, the easiest thing to do is to take the values (land = 1, water = 0) of the tile neighborhood for a given zone and map them to the image numbers. (This way, you can do coastline image lookup with a simple array rather than a bizarre set of `if` statements.)

I count my directions clockwise, just as a convention, and I see no need to stop doing so now. For tile zones, I will start with the upper left and move clockwise to hit the other zones.

Upper-Left Tile Zone

The three neighboring tiles are those to the west, the northwest, and the north, in clockwise order. Check out table 21.1.

Table 21.1 Lookup Values for the Upper-Left Corner

West	Northwest	North	Value	Image
Water	Water	Water	0	–1*
Land	Water	Water	1	0
Water	Land	Water	2	1
Land	Land	Water	3	1
Water	Water	Land	4	2
Land	Water	Land	5	3
Water	Land	Land	6	1
Land	Land	Land	7	1

*The number –1 indicates that no fringe exists for this configuration.

Remember that I said earlier that the northwest neighbor dominates the choice of image? That's what is happening here. The image number assignments, as you can see, are completely arbitrary.

Upper-Right Tile Zone, Lower-Right Tile Zone, and Lower-Left Tile Zone

The work is finished, actually. You can use the same table; just use different directions in place of the ones used for the upper-left zone.

- **Upper right.** Use north, northeast, and east.
- **Lower right.** Use east, southeast, and south.
- **Lower left.** Use south, southwest, and west.

Think ahead, keep it simple, and never write a convoluted mess of `if/else` blocks when a perfectly good lookup table can be used in its stead!

NOTE

More than just the three tiles listed for each zone affect that zone. For example, for the upper-left zone, I listed the west, northwest, and north tiles. To this list you should add southwest and northeast. Why didn't I list these earlier? Because the southwest counts the same value as the west tile, and northeast counts the same as north. This would have just made the previous table more confusing. Just keep this in mind during the code example.

A Fringing Example

Blah blah blah! All I seem to do is talk anymore! Well, it's time for another code example. Warm up the isometric components, for you shall be making use of them, although this won't be nearly as complicated as some of the stuff back in Chapter 17!

IsoHex21_1.cpp and associated files make up a very simple editor. They demonstrate my fringing algorithm to make coastline. It's not the most convincing coastline by any means, but it should get the idea across.

Figure 21.8 shows the coastline example. Because of how the fringe was drawn, there is still something of a "blocky" appearance to the map, but the difference is less stark than it would be if green land tiles were laid next to blue water tiles without any sort of transition.

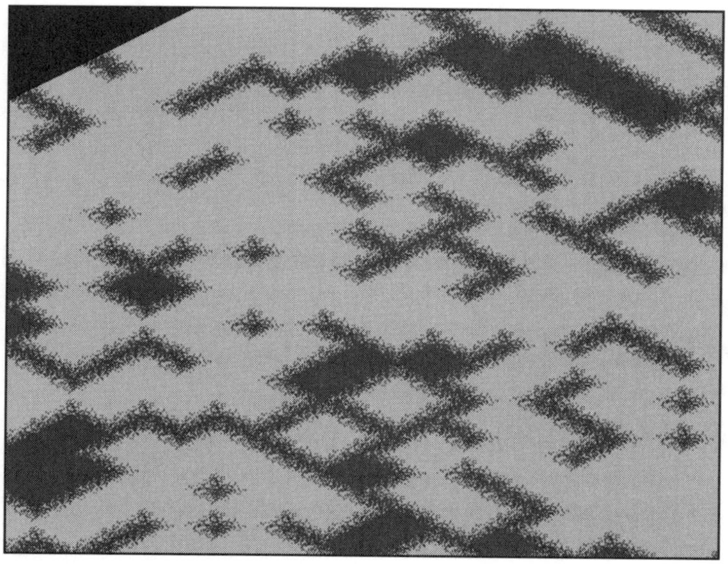

Figure 21.8

Coastline example, IsoHex21_1.cpp

The vast majority of IsoHex21_1.cpp is much the same as the examples in Chapters 17 through 19, using the IsoHexCore components to take care of the details of isometric management. I won't bore you by repeating descriptions of these components. Mainly, I'm going to concentrate on what makes this example unique.

Map Structure

First I changed the way in which the `MapLocation` structure looked, in order to accommodate the fringes. I ripped out all the stuff for managing units so that I could highlight the stuff necessary for fringes. The following is what `MapLocation` looks like:

```
const int UPPERLEFT=0;
const int UPPERRIGHT=1;
const int LOWERRIGHT=2;
const int LOWERLEFT=3;
//map location structure
struct MapLocation
{
	bool bLand;
	int iFringe[4];
};
MapLocation mlMap[MAPWIDTH][MAPHEIGHT];//map array
//fringe lookup table
int FringeLookUp[8]={-1,0,1,1,2,3,1,1};
```

It's still a very basic structure. First, it contains a single `bool` that is true when that location contains land and false when it contains water. In a more complicated example, this would very likely be replaced with an `int`, with 0 representing water, 1 representing grassland, and 2 and up representing different types of terrain. For now, a `bool` suffices.

The next bit is a four-item array called `iFringe`. Each of the items in this array contains a value for whatever fringe exists at that particular map location—one for each of the four tile zones. The four constants in the code snippet give names to the four regions.

Lastly, the `FringeLookUp` table (an eight-item array) contains the lookup values for tile images, which we talked about earlier. A –1 value means no fringe is to be rendered.

Rendering Function

Naturally, the next thing is the rendering function. We'll get to how the `MapLocation` structure array (`mlMap`) gets filled in and calculated in a moment.

Here's a basic rundown of RenderFunc before we get to the actual code. First, if bLand is true, you render land and ignore the values in iFringe. Second, if bLand is false, you render a water tile and then put in each of the appropriate fringes if applicable.

```
void RenderFunc(LPDIRECTDRAWSURFACE7 lpddsDst,RECT* rcClip,int xDst,int yDst,int
xMap,int yMap)
{
        //check land or sea
        if(mlMap[xMap][yMap].bLand)
        {
                //land
                tsBack.ClipTile(lpddsDst,rcClip,xDst,yDst,0);
        }
```

First case: If bLand is true, render the land tile, and that's it. No other activity is required for this map location. Both the land and the sea tiles are stored in tsBack. Land has a tile index of 0, and sea has an index of 1.

```
        else
        {
                //sea
                tsBack.ClipTile(lpddsDst,rcClip,xDst,yDst,1);
```

Case, the second (to emulate my friend Mason's manner of speech): bLand is false, which means you need to render the sea tile (tile index 0 of tsBack) and then render any of the fringe images as appropriate.

```
                //upper-left zone
                if(FringeLookUp[mlMap[xMap][yMap].iFringe[UPPERLEFT]]>=0)
                        tsFringe.ClipTile(lpddsDst,rcClip,xDst,yDst,
                                FringeLookUp[mlMap[xMap][yMap].iFringe[UPPERLEFT]]);
```

A quick heads-up: the items in iFringe contain numbers 0 through 7, indicating land in neighboring tiles. In order to determine which fringe image should be rendered, you first have to plug that number into the FringeLookUp array, which you do here. If it is greater than or equal to 0 (that is, not –1), go ahead and render the image you looked up. If it is –1, skip it.

```
                //upper-right zone
                if(FringeLookUp[mlMap[xMap][yMap].iFringe[UPPERRIGHT]]>=0)
                        tsFringe.ClipTile(lpddsDst,rcClip,xDst,yDst,
                                FringeLookUp[mlMap[xMap][yMap].iFringe[UPPERRIGHT]]+4);
                //lower-right zone
                if(FringeLookUp[mlMap[xMap][yMap].iFringe[LOWERRIGHT]]>=0)
                        tsFringe.ClipTile(lpddsDst,rcClip,xDst,yDst,
```

```
                    FringeLookUp[mlMap[xMap][yMap].iFringe[LOWERRIGHT]]+8);
            //lower-left zone
            if(FringeLookUp[mlMap[xMap][yMap].iFringe[LOWERLEFT]]>=0)
                tsFringe.ClipTile(lpddsDst,rcClip,xDst,yDst,
                    FringeLookUp[mlMap[xMap][yMap].iFringe[LOWERLEFT]]+12);
        }
}
```

You do the same thing for the other three tile zones: upper-right, lower-right, lower-left. I like doing things clockwise. It seems more organized that way.

So, that's it for `RenderFunc`. It seems incredibly simple and, in fact, it is. The hard part was done several pages ago, divvying up the tile shape into zones, and coming up with lookup tables. Thinking ahead pays off!

Calculating the Fringe

Naturally, the numbers in `iFringe` for all the map locations don't just magically appear out of nowhere. They were carefully calculated by several functions. Let's get to them!

The CalcFringe Function (Part 1)

OK, it's not the most original name for a function, I admit (I tend to make up uninteresting function names). This function, to no one's surprise, calculates all the fringes for the entire map.

```
void CalcFringe()
{
        //loop through x
        for(int x=0;x<MAPWIDTH;x++)
        {
                //loop through y
                for(int y=0;y<MAPHEIGHT;y++)
                {
                        //calc the fringe
                        CalcFringe(x,y);
                }
        }
}
```

This is one of the `CalcFringe` functions. There are two, and the other one is next. If any of you C programmers are feeling faint because I have two functions with the same name, just take a deep breath and be a trouper.

This CalcFringe function takes no parameters, returns no values, and simply loops through the entire map, sending each (x,y) location to the other CalcFringe function.

The CalcFringe Function (Part 2)

The second CalcFringe function takes two parameters (an x- and y-coordinate), returns no value, and does most of the fringe calculation (the other functions just pass information along to this one)..

```
void CalcFringe(int x,int y)//calculate for individual map location
{
	//range checking
	if(x<0) return;
	if(y<0) return;
	if(x>=MAPWIDTH) return;
	if(y>=MAPHEIGHT) return;
```

First, check to see if (x,y) corresponds to a valid map coordinate, so if x or y is less than 0 or equal to or greater than MAPWIDTH or MAPHEIGHT, respectively, you return immediately. This means you can call this CalcFringe without fear.

```
	//calculate the tile neighborhood
	bool Neighbor[8];
	//store starting point
	POINT ptStart;
	ptStart.x=x;
	ptStart.y=y;
	//next map location
	POINT ptNext;
```

This next bit gets a little confusing, because of all the conditional code, so let me clue you in to exactly what you're doing. You're storing the values of the tile neighborhood in a temporary array of ints (called Neighborhood). The value of 0 means a water tile, and 1 means a land tile. These values, in turn, will be used to determine the iFringe values for this map location. Got all that? Let's dive in!

```
	for(int dir=0;dir<8;dir++)
	{
		//walk to neighbor
		ptNext=TileWalker.TileWalk(ptStart,(ISODIRECTION)dir);
```

A variable called ptStart contains the current (x,y) position, so use the TileWalker to determine what tile lies in a given direction (loop through them all using the variable dir). Once you have the neighboring map location, you can test it for land or water.

```
            //range check
            if(ptNext.x<0 || ptNext.y<0 || ptNext.x>=MAPWIDTH ||
ptNext.y>=MAPHEIGHT)
            {
                //out of bounds
                Neighbor[dir]=0;
            }
```

The first check, of course, is a bounds check. If `ptNext` does not exist on the map, set this neighbor to 0, meaning water. Really, you could default to 1 or land; it doesn't really matter. Generally, however, it is assumed that outside of the map is open ocean.

```
            else
            {
                //check map location
                if(mlMap[ptNext.x][ptNext.y].bLand)
                {
                    //land
                    Neighbor[dir]=1;
                }
                else
                {
                    //water
                    Neighbor[dir]=0;
                }
            }
        }
```

If `ptNext` is not out of bounds, you can check the value of `bLand` at that map location and assign 1 for true and 0 for false. Then you can loop through the remaining values of `dir`.

```
        //determine zones
        mlMap[ptStart.x][ptStart.y].iFringe[UPPERLEFT]=(Neighbor[6]+2*Neighbor[7]+
            4*Neighbor[0])|(Neighbor[5]+4*Neighbor[1]);
        mlMap[ptStart.x][ptStart.y].iFringe[UPPERRIGHT]=(Neighbor[0]+2*Neighbor[1]+
            4*Neighbor[2])|(Neighbor[7]+4*Neighbor[3]);
        mlMap[ptStart.x][ptStart.y].iFringe[LOWERRIGHT]=(Neighbor[2]+2*Neighbor[3]+
            4*Neighbor[4])|(Neighbor[1]+4*Neighbor[5]);
        mlMap[ptStart.x][ptStart.y].iFringe[LOWERLEFT]=(Neighbor[4]+2*Neighbor[5]+
            4*Neighbor[6])|(Neighbor[3]+4*Neighbor[7]);
}
```

And finally, the end of the function with some crazy-looking equations. I used numbers here instead of the ISO_* constants mainly because not doing so would make all the lines 10 miles long.

To better explain what the heck is going on, I'll convert the first line into the ISO_* constants.

```
mlMap[ptStart.x][ptStart.y].iFringe[UPPERLEFT]=
(
        1*Neighbor[ISO_WEST]+
        2*Neighbor[ISO_NORTHWEST]+
        4*Neighbor[ISO+NORTH]
)|(
        1*Neighbor[ISO_SOUTHWEST]+
        4*Neighbor[ISO_SOUTHEAST]
);
```

This should be a little easier to read. Remember that for the upper-left tile zone, you build a value based on five tiles: West or southwest is 1, northwest is 2, and north or northeast is 4, giving you a value from 0 to 7. That's all you're doing here, in a very concise form.

The CalcFringeNeighborhood Function

The final fringe calculation function is CalcFringeNeighborhood. Supply it with an (x,y) coordinate, and it recalculates not only that map location, but all map locations surrounding it. This function isn't used in this example, but if you were to, say, modify this program so that bLand were changed for whatever map location you clicked on, you would want to recalculate not only that tile, but also all tiles around it.

```
void CalcFringeNeighborhood(int x,int y)//calculate for a tile neighborhood
{
        //send tile (x,y) to calculate fringe function
        CalcFringe(x,y);
        //store center point
        POINT ptCenter;
        ptCenter.x=x;
        ptCenter.y=y;
        POINT ptNeighbor;
        //loop through directions
        for(int dir=0;dir<8;dir++)
        {
                //determine neighbor
                ptNeighbor=TileWalker.TileWalk(ptCenter,(ISODIRECTION)dir);
                //send neighbor to calculation function
                CalcFringe(ptNeighbor.x,ptNeighbor.y);
        }
}
```

This function is no great feat of computer science. I simply use the TileWalker to walk around the center tile and send the (x,y) values to `CalcFringe`. The function is, however, of great use when you're constructing an editor that has to maintain coastlines or fringes.

A Final Note about Fringes

I certainly hope I was able to demystify and simplify fringes and coastline for you. My own first attempts at making them were rather unsuccessful. I would either take up too much space with the images, or something else would go wrong and the resulting pictures looked awful. Eventually I stumbled upon this algorithm, which makes life much easier.

However, it would be arrogant of me to say that my coastline algorithm is the best ever. My coastline algorithm requires anywhere from one to five blits per map location, and if there is a lot of coastline, this can affect performance detrimentally. It won't matter so much once you get to iso-3D later on, but it seems to me that there should be a less-performance-intensive solution that is also not very art-intensive. If you find one, be sure to let me know!

Interconnecting Structures

This is possibly the vaguest heading I've come up with. When I say *interconnecting structures,* I primarily mean two things: rivers and roads. These aren't the only applications of interconnecting structures, of course. You can also make forests, hills, mountains, walls, and so on as interconnecting structures, but rivers and roads are the best examples and are the easiest to use for teaching.

I'm going to show you two basic methods for isometric tiles—one that uses four directions and one that uses eight directions. Generally, the four-direction version is more commonly used for rivers and the eight-direction for roads, but either can be adapted for use in a number of areas. I'm only going to show you roads (because they are easy to draw).

Four-Direction Structures

As I stated, a four-direction connecting structure is commonly used for rivers, but I have also seen it used for forests, hills, mountains, and walls. In all cases, the lines of the connecting structure (the road or river, or the base line of the wall or trees) connect the center of one tile to the center of an adjacent tile.

In the four-direction version, you use the diagonal directions—northeast, southeast, southwest, and northwest. Truth be told, you could use the cardinal directions instead, but the diagonals line up nicely with the faces of the rhombus, and in my opinion, it looks nicer.

A Four-Direction Example

Load up IsoHex21_2.cpp. Figure 21.9 shows this particular example. This program isn't much, but it does do interconnected lines (meant to simulate roads—m y mediocre artistic talent shows again).

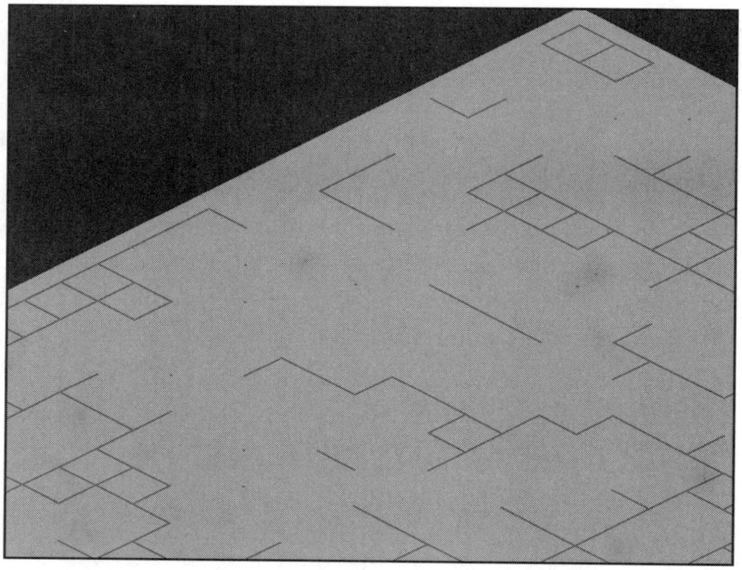

Figure 21.9

Four-direction interconnectedness

This program is an awful lot like IsoHex21_1. In fact, all I had to do was rip out a few variables, change a few function names, rewrite the rendering function, and poof, I had the new example.

Map Structure

The most fundamental change, of course, occured in the structure that contains information for a map location. Dealing with roads is a little less involved than dealing with fringes and the four tile zones.

```
//road flags
const int ROAD_NORTHEAST=1;
const int ROAD_SOUTHEAST=2;
const int ROAD_SOUTHWEST=4;
const int ROAD_NORTHWEST=8;
//map location structure
struct MapLocation
{
	bool bRoad;
	int iRoad;
};
MapLocation mlMap[MAPWIDTH][MAPHEIGHT];//map array
```

First, you have the road flags (all the `ROAD_*` constants at the top). I store road direction information in individual bits rather than in a `bool` array (which is just as good, by the way). These flags, and combinations of them, are stored in the `iRoad` member of `MapLocation`. The other member of `MapLocation`, `bRoad`, indicates whether or not a road runs through this particular tile. In this simple model of reality, a road either runs through an area or it doesn't, period.

When initializing this map during `Prog_Init`, I simply set `bRoad` randomly to true or false, as shown next.

```
//set up the map to a random tilefield
int x;
int y;
for(x=0;x<MAPWIDTH;x++)
{
        for(y=0;y<MAPHEIGHT;y++)
        {
                if(rand()&1)
                {
                        mlMap[x][y].bRoad=true;
                }
                else
                {
                        mlMap[x][y].bRoad=false;
                }
        }
}
//calculate the fringe
CalcRoad();
```

This little bit of code takes no great programming skill, but it's kind of hidden amid the IsoHexCore initialization calls in `Prog_Init`, so I thought I'd point it out for you. In the case of the example, I can get away with this totally random map. In a game, you'd probably load the map from disk, or generate the world (see Chapter 22 for more on world generation).

Rendering a Map Location

Besides the change to `MapLocation`, I also had to completely rewrite `RenderFunc`, but this should come as no surprise to you, since I couldn't possibly use the fringe version to render roads.

```
void RenderFunc(LPDIRECTDRAWSURFACE7 lpddsDst,RECT* rcClip,int xDst,int yDst,int
xMap,int yMap)
{
	//put down a land tile
	tsBack.ClipTile(lpddsDst,rcClip,xDst,yDst,0);
	//check for a road
	if(mlMap[xMap][yMap].bRoad)
	{
		//put the road image
		tsRoad.ClipTile(lpddsDst,rcClip,xDst,yDst,mlMap[xMap][yMap].iRoad);
	}
}
```

This `RenderFunc` is vastly simplified from that of the fringe. You render the background tile for every map location and then render the road on top of it, but only if `bRoad` is true for that map location. Since you're storing road flags in `iRoad`, simply make the number (0 through 15) correspond to numbers within the `tsRoad` tileset.

The CalcRoad Functions

Of course, the values in `iRoad` don't just magically appear—they must be calculated. Thus, I created the `CalcRoad` functions—one with no parameters that performs calculations for the entire map, and another that calculates the value for only a single map location.

```
void CalcRoad()
{
	//loop through x
	for(int x=0;x<MAPWIDTH;x++)
	{
		//loop through y
		for(int y=0;y<MAPHEIGHT;y++)
		{
			//calc the fringe
			CalcRoad(x,y);
		}
	}
}
```

The void parametered `CalcRoad` performs much the same function as the void parametered `CalcFringe`. In fact, it is the same code with "Fringe" taken out and replaced with "Road." Cheap and easy, the way I like it! The second `CalcRoad` function takes two parameters—the x and y map location to calculate. You'll probably note a striking similarity between this function and the `CalcFringe(x,y)` function in the prior example. Again, cheap and easy.

```
void CalcRoad(int x,int y)//calculate for individual map location
{
	//range checking
	if(x<0) return;
	if(y<0) return;
	if(x>=MAPWIDTH) return;
	if(y>=MAPHEIGHT) return;
	//calculate the tile neighborhood
	bool Neighbor[8];
	//store starting point
	POINT ptStart;
	ptStart.x=x;
	ptStart.y=y;
	//next map location
	POINT ptNext;
	for(int dir=0;dir<8;dir++)
	{
		//walk to neighbor
		ptNext=TileWalker.TileWalk(ptStart,(ISODIRECTION)dir);
		//range check
		if(ptNext.x<0 || ptNext.y<0 || ptNext.x>=MAPWIDTH ||
ptNext.y>=MAPHEIGHT)
		{
			//out of bounds
			Neighbor[dir]=0;
		}
		else
		{
			//check map location
			if(mlMap[ptNext.x][ptNext.y].bRoad)
			{
				//road
				Neighbor[dir]=1;
			}
			else
			{
				//no road
				Neighbor[dir]=0;
			}
		}
	}
	//clear road flags
```

```
        mlMap[x][y].iRoad=0;
        //add road flags as appropriate
        if(Neighbor[ISO_NORTHEAST]) mlMap[x][y].iRoad|=ROAD_NORTHEAST;
        if(Neighbor[ISO_SOUTHEAST]) mlMap[x][y].iRoad|=ROAD_SOUTHEAST;
        if(Neighbor[ISO_SOUTHWEST]) mlMap[x][y].iRoad|=ROAD_SOUTHWEST;
        if(Neighbor[ISO_NORTHWEST]) mlMap[x][y].iRoad|=ROAD_NORTHWEST;
}
```

The vast majority of the `CalcRoad` function is unchanged from its former incarnation as the `CalcFringe` function, except when you get to the last few lines. First, you clear out any prior `ROAD_*` flags by setting `iRoad` to 0. Then, you check each of the pertinent directions (the diagonals) and tack on the appropriate `ROAD_*` flag. It's pretty self-explanatory, since I managed to use constant names instead of raw numbers. You wind up with a value from 0 to 15 for `iRoad`, and that gives you the index into the tileset that is used by `RenderFunc`.

Hopefully, you can now see why fringes and interconnecting structures were discussed in the same chapter, since the algorithms used to determine what to show are closely related. Oh, and if you want to see an example of interconnected structures that looks more impressive than the very simple roads, you can go ahead and make `tsRoad` load in a bitmap called wallts.bmp, which replaces the road images with images of walls.

Using the Four-Direction Method

As stated earlier, you can use the four-direction method for roads, rivers, forests, hills, mountains, walls, and a lot of other stuff. There are a few things I want to mention before going on.

First, the four-direction method requires only 16 pictures, which is acceptable. You have to take care, however, to make these pictures line up properly (it took me a good half an hour to make even the simplistic roads look right). The easiest way to do this is to put a few tiles on a bitmap, with the centers marked, and draw images between the centers to the northeast and southeast, and then crop out the images for each direction. It's a painstaking process, but the results are faster than with trial and error.

A note about rivers: undoubtedly, you will want your rivers to empty into oceans or seas of some sort (since real-life rivers tend to do that). Combining rivers and fringes can get a little hairy, since you have to create graphics for the mouths of rivers. This adds only four extra images, but I felt it was worth pointing out. Also, you have to mark the ocean square into which the river empties as a river square, so that the coastal image comes out correctly when you call `CalcRiver` (or whatever you call your river calculation function).

Eight-Direction Structures

The eight-direction structures are usually only used for roads, railroads, and so on. Most other types of structures use only four directions. The eight-direction structure can be a severe liability to video memory or performance, especially if the connecting structures are quite common in the game, as roads tend to be. There are two methods you can use to make eight-direction structres—the high-performance and video-memory-costly solution, or the high-video-memory, low-performance solution.

The high-performance version requires a different image for each possible configuration. Since there are eight directions and two possible values for each direction, the number of pictures required is 2 to the eighth power, or 256. The advantage is that it adds only a single layer to the map, no matter what configuration the road is in. The disadvantage is that it requires 256 images in order to do so.

The low-performance version requires one image for each direction. These images are combined during the rendering to make the composite image. This requires only eight pictures. The advantage is that you have a lower video memory requirement to get it done. The disadvantage is that it adds anywhere from one to eight layers, which can adversely affect performance if there are many roads.

So, which to use? If performance isn't as much of an issue, as with many turn-based strategy games, go ahead and use the lower-performance version. If speed is required, and you have the video memory to spare, go ahead with the higher-performance version.

The calculation of eight directions is much the same as that for four directions, except that you don't ignore any of the directions (duh), so I won't offer a whole extra example of something that I'm confident you can figure out on your own, based on the other examples from this chapter.

Summary

Fringes and interconnecting structures are very important in isometric games, and knowing how to work with them will greatly improve the appearance of your games. Still, there is the specter of video memory versus performance, although with modern video cards, available video memory increases, and the efficiency of blitting increases, and both problems diminish. Still, that's no reason to be sloppy.

This part of the book has been sort of a hodgepodge of stuff, starting with optimization and ending with artistic concerns. I hope it has been an enlightening journey. We've got a few more topics to cover, but with your arsenal of isometric knowledge, you are ready to face the challenges of AI and Iso-3D.

Part IV

Advanced Topics

CHAPTER 22

World Generation

- What is World Generation?
- Using Mazes
- Growing Continents

Welcome to the first part of the final leg of the journey through isometric land. You've mastered quite a few isometric tricks to optimize and enhance the look of your game. However, you've mainly been concerned with rendering, and as you know, being able to blit an image onto the screen does not a game make! Indeed, a game needs more. It needs something to set the stage behind the scenes, before you render even a single pixel. That is what this chapter and the next cover.

In a moment, I'll get into world generation. This is a rather ambitious topic for a single chapter, for a couple of reasons. First, since many types of games make use of the isometric perspective, it is difficult to offer a comprehensive solution for every possible circumstance. Second, there is never a single way to do anything, and world generation is no exception.

As a result, I can only give you some very general world-generation algorithms and some vague hints to head you in the right direction. Decent world generation involves trial and error. The goal is to be reasonably convincing with the finished product; it doesn't have to be perfect.

What Is World Generation?

Naturally, before getting into this topic, you should take a moment to understand exactly what world generation means and what your goals are. Foremost, the goal of world generation is to generate worlds.

And what is a world? If you are playing a strategy game, the world might consist of a single isometric map. A dungeon-crawling game might involve several maps, each with its own unique look and configuration. So, by *world*, I mean all the places in the game that the player might visit. What, then, are your goals when generating worlds?

- **Cohesiveness.** Your worlds need to be cohesive. In other words, they must make sense. This doesn't mean that they have to be accurate representations of the real world, but there should be some sort of internal consistency. For example, if I travel out of a room through a door to the west, I fully expect that when I arrive in the new room, there should be a door on the east, or there should be a logical reason why there isn't a door going back (for example, it might be a magical one-way door, or maybe there was a cave-in after I passed through the door and triggered a trap).

- **Believability**. Again, your world does not have to adhere to the real world, but some sort of "reality check" should be performed. For example, you are not likely to find a desert right next to a swamp, and a good world-generation algorithm will not combine two such unrelated elements. Instead, the algorithm would put something in between, like grassland or plains.

As another example, imagine a room with four walls, a door in each. Each door is about the size of a normal door in the real world (when game scale is taken into account). How, then, would a monster the size of a dragon (dragons being much larger than the doors) get into this room? If there is a decent justification for this apparent conflict, that's fine. Just don't make weak justifications. ("Um, a dark priest, yeah, that's it, a dark priest took the dragon egg and, um, brought it to this room, and he, no, he, um, well, anyway, it hatched, and the dragon grew up, and, um, that's how the 50-foot-long dragon is here in a room with doors it won't fit through.")

- **Playability**. Games, for the most part, are finite in scope. They have a beginning and an end. Usually, the end is brought about either by total defeat or by meeting certain criteria at which point the player is said to have won the game. Not all games have a "win" condition, but almost all of them have a "lose" condition, or at least a "stalemate" of some sort.

  What does this have to do with world generation? Quite simply, if there is a win condition, the world generator must create a world in which reaching that goal is possible. It does not need to make achieving that goal easy, but it should not render it impossible.

- **Replayability**. Separate and distinct from playability, replayability enhances a game's value immensely. Generally speaking, world generation uses some sort of random determination in order to put the pieces of the world together in a coherent, believable, and playable manner. When you go back and start a new game from scratch, you should have before you the same basic elements of the game you played before, but in a different order and in a variation you have not seen already. This keeps a game from getting stale and winding up on someone's shelf after it was played through a single time (I've got a few of these kinds of games).

Using Mazes

"World" is a rather vague term. It can mean anything. Some worlds might be continents and oceans, as in empire-building games. Others might have wilderness locales or underground dungeons. In the latter case, mazes can be utilized to generate unique worlds.

Mazes are not limited to the labyrinth-type structures we think of, or the little cardboard tabletop things that lab mice run through in search of cheese. Mazes can simply tell you a path from one location to another, no matter if the nature of the location is a bunch of forest paths, an underground cave, some sort of building, a river, and so on.

The algorithm I'm about to show you builds a 2D maze of any size and can be extended to create 3D mazes. I've even done 4D mazes, but you shouldn't really think about those unless you want your brain to short out! (Plus, they are extremely difficult to map out.)

Mazes are an integral part of the games you play, whether those mazes are obvious or not. Knowing how to generate a maze and how to use it to build a world will take you far.

What Is a Maze?

It seems like a silly question, I know, but as you have by now figured out, I like defining things so that there aren't any embarrassing questions later. You already know what a maze is, I'm sure.

A *maze* is a series of locations (they could be rooms, clearings in a forest, caves, whatever) connected by passages of some sort (hallways, doors, portals, paths). In a basic maze, with no trickery going on, any location in the maze can be reached from any other position in the maze by navigating the many passages. In English, that means you can get from one end of the maze to another—there *is* a solution. Generally, these passages follow some sort of rule so that the maze can be mapped on a normal piece of paper or graph paper. This is not always so, however, especially if there are portals that teleport you from one location to another.

Creating a Maze

The algorithm I'm going to show you is rather plain. It has locations and passages, but nothing else. No secret doors, no one-way doors, no locked doors, no magic portals. This is intentional. You create a basic, plain maze and then populate it with special features like those I just listed.

To start, you must have some sort of structure into which you can place data for a distinct location in the maze. I usually call these "rooms" even if they aren't used to make rooms in a world.

```
//constants to use for directions
const int MAZE_NORTH=0;
const int MAZE_EAST=1;
const int MAZE_SOUTH=2;
const int MAZE_WEST=3;
//number of doors possible
const int MAZE_DOORCOUNT=4;
//room structure
struct Room
{
	//array of doors leaving this room
	bool Door[MAZE_DOORCOUNT];
};
```

You're looking at this, saying, "You've got whether or not the doors exist, but you don't have where the doors lead!" Well, you're right, but in my defense, I haven't stated the rules for this maze yet. I also call the passages between rooms "doors" even though they might not be doors when I'm finished.

You will place the rooms in a rectangular grid of any size and call it MAZE_WIDTH by MAZE_HEIGHT. So, you'll make an array of rooms.

```
//room array
Room Maze[MAZE_WIDTH][MAZE_HEIGHT];
```

If you are in any given room and you travel in a direction, the x and y coordinate within the grid will change based on the data listed in Table 22.1.

Table 22.1 Maze Direction and Change in Location

Direction	X	Y
MAZE_NORTH	+0	–1
MAZE_EAST	+1	0
MAZE_SOUTH	+0	+1
MAZE_WEST	–1	+0

As usual, I start with north and rotate clockwise from there, as is my habit. To begin the maze, start with a completely blank array of Room structures. It is a completely clean slate, a fresh piece of paper, upon which your maze will be born.

The first time around, you can just pick a room randomly and place a door that will connect two of the rooms. Thereafter, until the maze is complete, you must pick a room with a door already in it and figure out whether or not you can add another door to it. If you can, add one. If not, pick another room.

There's an important concept to point out here. One door connects two rooms. Adding another door connects three, and so on. When you are all done, you will have one door less than the number of rooms. For example, in a maze with MAZE_WIDTH*MAZE_HEIGHT, you will have MAZE_WIDTH*MAZE_HEIGHT-1 doors.

For your purposes, you'll disallow wrapping around the maze, meaning that you can't go west from the westmost rooms and wind up on the eastern side of the map.

Without further ado, here is the maze-generation code. You can find this function in IsoHex22_1.cpp, which is a simple little program that demonstrates a maze being built using the GDI method for drawing.

```
void MakeMaze()
{
	//start making the maze
	//assumes the maze array is clean (i.e. all values are false)
```

```
int doorcount=0;//number of doors we have placed
//x and y position of the room
int x;
int y;
int dir;//direction
//randomize the seed
srand(GetTickCount());
//clear out the maze
for(x=0;x<MAZE_WIDTH;x++)
        for(y=0;y<MAZE_HEIGHT;y++)
                for(dir=0;dir<MAZE_DOORCOUNT;dir++)
                        Maze[x][y].Door[dir]=false;
```

Before you do anything, make sure the data is properly initialized. This means that you must clear the maze so that all doors are false. Failing to do so might cause a garbled maze or might cause the program to hang. Actually, it is very likely that the program will hang indefinitely if you don't clear the maze.

```
while (doorcount<MAZE_WIDTH*MAZE_HEIGHT-1)
{
        DrawMaze();
        //this flag is set if a suitable room is found
        bool found=false;
        //blocks, used a little later
        int blockcount;
        bool block[MAZE_DOORCOUNT];
```

Place each door individually. In order to do so, you must first find a place where a door can go, according to your door placement rules. That is what the `found` variable is for. The `blockcount` and `block` variables are used to test whether a particular room can add a door.

```
        while(!found)
        {
                //if doorcount is 0, just pick a room
                if(doorcount==0)
                {
                        x=rand()%MAZE_WIDTH;
                        y=rand()%MAZE_HEIGHT;
                }
                else
                {
                        //doorcount not zero, pick a room
                        //with a door in it
```

```
            do
            {
                  x=rand()%MAZE_WIDTH;
                  y=rand()%MAZE_HEIGHT;
            } while (CountDoors(&Maze[x][y])==0);
            //CountDoors is pseudocode for
            //a function we'll write later
      }
```

The first part of finding a suitable location for a door is picking a room, since all doors exist within rooms. Depending on the number of doors you have already placed (either none or more than none), you choose a room differently. When you have not placed any doors at all, any old room will do. After the first door, however, you must find a room with a door already in it. Otherwise, your maze will not be navigable.

```
      //so far, so good, we have a room
      //we now must analyze blocked passages
      blockcount=0;
```

Once you have picked a room candidate, verify that this room can add another door. Not all rooms can. For example, a room in the corner of a maze can have only two doors. Also, a direction from one room might lead to a room that has always been created. There are a few conditions for which you call a direction from a room "blocked."

```
      //loop through directions
      for(dir=0;dir<MAZE_DOORCOUNT;dir++)
      {
            //set block to false
            block[dir]=false;
            //if the door in the room for dir is set, set the
block
            if(Maze[x][y].Door[dir])
            {
                  block[dir]=true;
                  blockcount++;
                  continue;
            }
```

The first "blocked" condition is whether a door already exists in that direction. Naturally, you cannot place a door twice, so you mark that direction as blocked and continue with the loop through all the directions.

```
            //calculate the next position based on this direction
            int nx=x,ny=y;//next position
```

```
switch(dir)
{
case MAZE_NORTH:
        {
                ny--;
        }break;
case MAZE_EAST:
        {
                nx++;
        }break;
case MAZE_SOUTH:
        {
                ny++;
        }break;
case MAZE_WEST:
        {
                nx--;
        }break;
}
//bounds checking
if(nx<0 || ny<0 || nx>=MAZE_WIDTH || ny>=MAZE_HEIGHT)
{
        block[dir]=true;
        blockcount++;
        continue;
}
```

The second condition is whether the direction will cause you to leave the bounds of the maze. The big `switch` statement just shown calculates the next position if you start at (x,y) and go in the direction of `dir`. If nx or ny is less than 0 or equal to or greater than `MAZE_WIDTH` or `MAZE_HEIGHT`, mark this direction as blocked and continue with the loop.

```
        //final check, make sure the room at nx,ny has no doors
        if(CountDoors(&Maze[nx][ny])!=0)
        {
                block[dir]=true;
                blockcount++;
                continue;
        }
}
```

The final test is to see whether a suitable destination lies on the other side of the wall, meaning that the room at (nx, ny) cannot have existed prior to this moment. If it has, set a block and continue the loop.

```
                //if blockcount is not the same as MAZE_DOORCOUNT,
                //we can place a door
                if(blockcount!=MAZE_DOORCOUNT) found=true;
        }
```

If you have at least one opening after testing all the directions for blockage, you can place a door.

```
        //found is now true, so we can place a door

        do
        {
                //select a door direction
                dir=rand()%MAZE_DOORCOUNT;
        }while (block[dir]);//make sure that direction is not blocked
        //dir contains a valid direction
        Maze[x][y].Door[dir]=true;
```

To place a door, first pick a nonblocked direction. (This is easy, because you have the block array, and you can just randomly choose until you find one that is false.) Once you have a suitable direction, place the door.

```
        //move to next room
        switch(dir)
        {
        case MAZE_NORTH:
                {
                        y–;
                }break;
        case MAZE_EAST:
                {
                        x++;
                }break;
        case MAZE_SOUTH:
                {
                        y++;
                }break;
        case MAZE_WEST:
                {
                        x–;
                }break;
```

```
            }
            //change direction to opposite direction
            dir=(dir+(MAZE_DOORCOUNT/2)) % MAZE_DOORCOUNT;
            //set door in the next room
            Maze[x][y].Door[dir]=true;
            //increment the doorcount
            doorcount++;
        }
}
```

Next, move the x and y position in the direction specified in `dir`. Reverse the direction and place another door so that the doors match. In this manner, you guarantee that someone in the maze can go back the way he came.

Using a Maze

All right, you've got a maze. Now what to do with it? The mazes generated by IsoHex22_1.cpp are generic and simplistic—practically featureless except for the doors. It's a great starting point, but you will want to do something to make the maze more interesting. A player will quickly get bored with such a simple maze, and boring the player is the last thing you want to do. Now it's time for me to throw out two big words: variegate and populate.

Variegate

Variegation just means "variety," but it's a cool-sounding word and makes me seem smart. The fact is, it just won't do to have a bazillion rooms all the same size and shape, with a wall missing wherever passage between rooms is allowed.

Instead, you might want to make some rooms into chambers and others into hallways. You might want to place locked doors or hidden doors. You might even want to add a few extra nonessential doors just to make it less. . . well, maze-like. If you put in locked doors in, be sure to put keys where the player can get to them. If you put in secret doors, be sure there is a way to detect them. And so on, and so forth.

Or you might implement a maze as something that isn't a dungeon or castle. A maze can just as easily be a bunch of forest paths or roads through mountains. Or a river system, or anything where passage from one area to another can occur.

Populate

The scenery is only part of a world, and you're world-building here. So you need something of interest for the players to do in the maze (in whatever form it takes). This can take the form of items, monsters, traps, NPCs (non-player characters), and so on.

Both variegation and population should follow some sort of rules that you come up with beforehand. For instance, you might decide that all dead ends are locked. Following this rule, you would need to create the locks, create keys for the locks, and be sure not to put a key in a locked room (unless you're sadistic).

A Few Words about Isometric Mazes

When you generated your maze, it was rectangular, not isometric. Thus, the changeover requires some thought. I think that diamond maps are the best suited for mazes, since you simply have to shift the directions a little bit, making `MAZE_NORTH` actually point to the northwest when you create the map. This is just my opinion, though.

When taking a maze and converting it to an isometric map, you might want to use a sort of "tile template." I have not discussed these prior to now. A tile template is just a mini-tilemap representing perhaps a room or corridor. The tile template contains all the information about what background tile goes where and what foreground images go where, but it's set up in such a way that they can be put together like a puzzle and result in a reasonably rich-looking tilemap, even if it's based on a generic maze.

Growing Continents

Mazes are rather on the microscopic end of world building. On the other end of things is growing continents, where you build entire planets full of map information. It's a pretty simple algorithm.

I generally like to begin my continent building by starting with a blank map, which represents unending ocean. I then place a number of "seed" pixels to represent land. From there, I randomly seek out ocean squares that exist next to land squares, and I place new land pixels there until I have as many land areas as I desire (usually, I specify this as a percentage of the map).

Simple enough, right? IsoHex22_2 has an example of code that does this. Here's a simple breakdown of how it works: start with a blank blue (representing ocean) bitmap and place a number of seed dots consisting of pixels and lines in green (representing land). After you place the seeds, randomly select ocean squares next to land squares and make them into land squares. In this manner, you grow continents.

```
//map constants
const int MAPWIDTH=320;
const int MAPHEIGHT=320;
const int MAPSEEDS=100;
const int LANDPERC=30;
```

These are a few constants used for generating the continents. `MAPWIDTH` and `MAPHEIGHT` are self-explanatory. `MAPSEEDS` is the number of seeds with which you start the map. `LANDPERC` is the percentage of the map you want to have as land.

```
int x,y,count;
//pick random location
x=rand()%MAPWIDTH;
y=rand()%MAPHEIGHT;
//move to the location
MoveToEx(gdicMap,x,y,NULL);
```

You start in a random location (x,y) and work from there. The method I came up with for this example uses both single pixels and line segments. If a line segment is chosen first, it needs to have a starting point other than (0,0).

```
//place the seeds
for(count=0;count<MAPSEEDS;count++)
{
        if((rand()%4)==0)
        {
                //pick random location
                x=rand()%MAPWIDTH;
                y=rand()%MAPHEIGHT;
                //move to the location
                MoveToEx(gdicMap,x,y,NULL);
                SetPixelV(gdicMap,x,y,RGB(0,255,0));
        }
```

On a one-in-four chance, the generator will start a new continent with a single pixel. That's what this little bit of code does:

```
        else
        {
                //line to that location
                x=x+rand()%50-25;
                y=y+rand()%50-25;
                LineTo(gdicMap,x,y);
        }
```

On a three-in-four chance, the generator continues with the same continent, drawing a short line segment. Line segments make for better continents than single pixels.

```
}
//place the rest of the land
for(count=0;count<MAPWIDTH*MAPHEIGHT*LANDPERC/100;count++)
{
        //pick a coord next to a land square
        bool found=false;
```

```
        do
        {
                //pick random place
                x=rand()%MAPWIDTH;
                y=rand()%MAPHEIGHT;
                //ensure the area is water
                if(GetPixel(gdicMap,x,y)!=RGB(0,0,255)) continue;
```

Finally, after you have placed all the map seeds, it is time to place the rest of the land. First, choose a random location, and you make sure that this location has a water (blue) pixel there. You don't want to place land pixels twice in the same spot!

```
                //ensure it is next to another land area
                if(x>=0 && GetPixel(gdicMap,x-1,y)==RGB(0,255,0)) found=true;
                if(x<(MAPWIDTH-1) && GetPixel(gdicMap,x+1,y)==RGB(0,255,0))
found=true;
                if(y>=0 && GetPixel(gdicMap,x,y-1)==RGB(0,255,0)) found=true;
                if(y<(MAPHEIGHT-1) && GetPixel(gdicMap,x,y+1)==RGB(0,255,0))
found=true;
```

The second rule is that the pixel in question has to be next to an existing land square (hence, you have the seed pixels to start with). These lines check for a neighbor that is green:

```
        //keep looping until you find an appropriate space
        }while(!found);
        //place pixel
        SetPixelV(gdicMap,x,y,RGB(0,255,0));
        SendMessage(hWndMain,WM_PAINT,0,0);
}
```

Finally, set the pixel, and continue looping until all the pixels are set. This method places `MAPWIDTH*MAPHEIGHT*LANDPERC/100` pixels, plus an insignificant number of pixels that were in the seeds.

After you have grown the continents, you need to variegate and populate them just like a maze. You might want to place rivers, forests, mountain ranges, deserts, and so on. Just try to be coherent, and don't put ocean right next to mountains. Unfortunately, since there are so many different types of games in which you would want to generate continents, it's impossible to give decent advice as to how to populate them.

Summary

There are many more ways to generate worlds besides continent growing and maze generation, but the best method is always the one you come up with on your own. Use the maze generator or the continent grower as a base for your own methods. World generation isn't very scientific; it's very much trial and error.

CHAPTER 23

Pathfinding and AI

- What is AI?
- More Advanced Algorithims
- Making Pathfinding Useful

As you have seen over the course of this book, the graphical aspect of making isometric games is quite easy once you've got the hang of the algorithms behind it. Unfortunately, spiffy graphics, stereo sound, an intuitive user interface, and a shiny box do not a game make.

In this age of multiplayer "death match" and "capture the flag" games, *artificial intelligence* (AI) seems to have gone by the wayside. Many games now ship with only a minimal solo play component, and this, in my opinion, is just wrong. Multiplay is a great thing, and nowadays it is virtually a required feature of games, but it should not be the whole game. A good game should be a challenge, period, whether you're playing against other players or playing against the computer. If this is not the case, you have failed. Harsh words, yes, but I mean them.

This chapter can only touch upon a few relatively minor aspects of AI, since many voluminous books have been written on the topic of AI in general. In the modern day, we cannot hope to put the computer on par with an experienced player. The best we can do is fake it. I'm mainly going to discuss pathfinding, and I'll touch on a couple of other AI topics. The problem is that many different genres of game fall under the isometric umbrella, and I can't sufficiently cover all of them. If you want, go ahead and e-mail me, and I'll give you a few good suggestions for reading about AI.

What Is AI?

AI, as just stated, is artificial intelligence. A good definition cannot be found, because the great thinkers are having a hard time deciding what "intelligence" means. The commonly understood meaning of AI is *making the computer think*, which will do just fine for us.

We do not yet understand the inner workings of the human brain, which means we don't actually know how thinking takes place. So, you aren't really going to make the computer think. Instead, you will make it *look* like the computer is thinking, and if you do a good job, no one will be the wiser.

Really Simple AI Stuff

We'll start out really simple and then get more complicated as we go. That way, you won't have to digest any seriously technical details up front.

Take a look at Figure 23.1, which shows a game board (8×8, much like a checkerboard) with two pieces, each shaded differently to show that the pieces are on different teams.

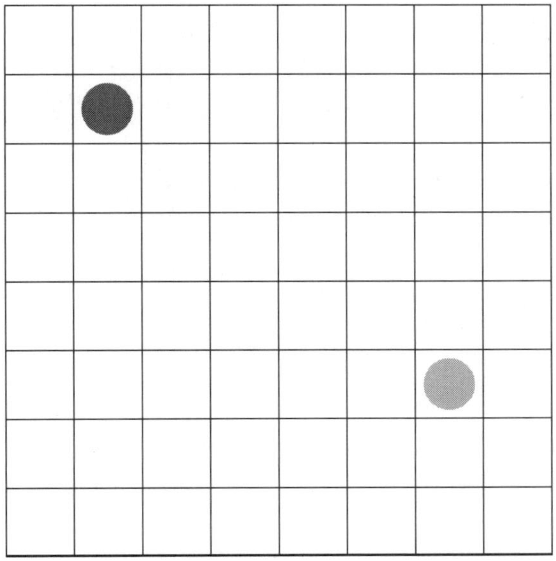

Figure 23.1

A board with tokens

In the absence of obstacles, making the lighter piece move toward the darker piece is simple. As human beings, we can simply eyeball it and move the lighter piece diagonally up and to the left, closing the gap, as shown in Figure 23.2.

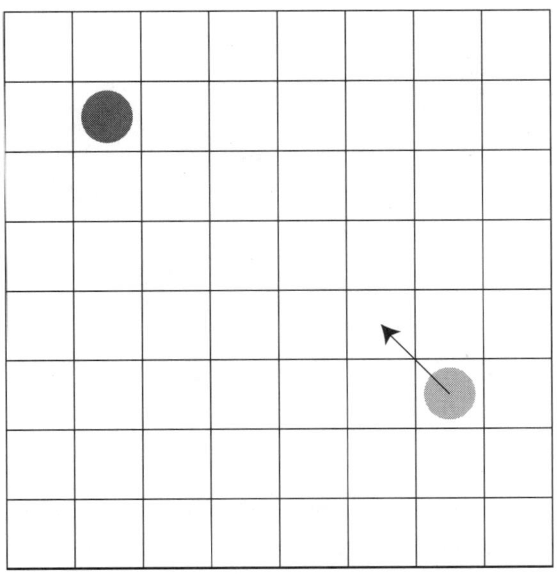

Figure 23.2

Closing the gap

This is a simple matter for us, because we have long been accustomed to such tasks. A computer, on the other hand, has no way of "eyeballing" the situation. It must rely on mathematical calculations. It is your job to teach the machine to do this very simple task.

This example is elementary and very easy to solve, which is why I picked it. Since you can move in any of the eight directions, you know that you can increase or decrease x and/or y by 1, or not change it at all, so that making a move leaves the piece on any one of nine squares (the square it currently occupies and all neighbors).

So, if you assigned numbers to the grid and made the light piece be at (lx,ly) and the dark piece be at (dx,dy), you could use the following code to determine what move to make:

```
//chase algorithm
if(lx!=dx)//check for non-matching x
{
	if(lx>dx)
	{
		//higher x, so decrease it
		lx--;
	}
	else
	{
		//lower x, so increase it
		lx++;
	}
}
if(ly!=dy)//check for non-matching y
{
	if(ly>dy)
	{
		//higher y, so decrease
		ly--;
	}
	else
	{
		//lower y, so increase
		ly++;
	}
}
```

Voila! After a certain number of steps, the light piece would quickly catch the dark piece. This is a really basic *chase* algorithm. It works effectively only in the simplest of cases.

While we're here, let's take a quick look at a really basic *evade* algorithm, which is the exact opposite of the chase algorithm. If you switch around the ++s and - -s of the chase algorithm, you've now got an algorithm that will run away as fast as it can.

```
//chase algorithm
if(lx!=dx)//check for non-matching x
{
	if(lx>dx)
	{
		//higher x, so increase it
		lx++;
	}
	else
	{
		//lower x, so decrease it
		lx—;
	}
}
if(ly!=dy)//check for non-matching y
{
	if(ly>dy)
	{
		//higher y, so increase
		ly++;
	}
	else
	{
		//lower y, so decrease
		ly—;
	}
}
```

Both the chase and evade algorithms are quite simple, so they're only well-suited to very simple situations. So, if the board were made more complicated, to include blocked squares where pieces cannot move, something similar to Figure 23.3 might result.

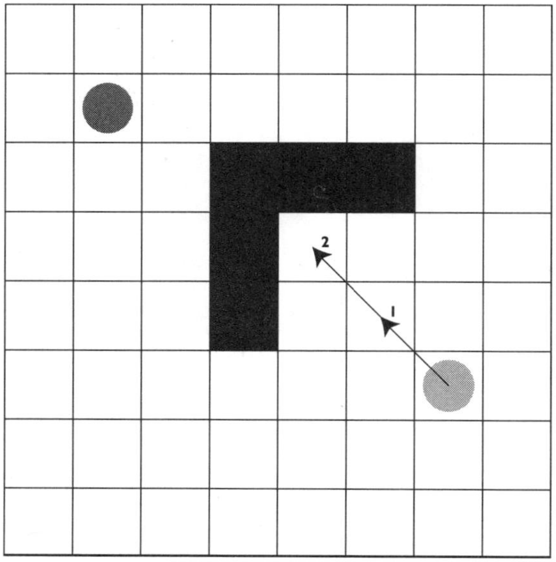

Figure 23.3

Where the simple chase algorithm fails

Figure 23.3 has five blocked squares. If the light piece tries to use the simple chase algorithm, it will be stuck after two moves (assuming, of course, that the dark piece remains stationary).

What the light piece *should* do is go around the obstacle, as shown in Figure 23.4. The path in Figure 23.4 isn't the only one that the light piece could take, but it'll do for now. Naturally, in order to make the light piece catch the dark piece, you need a fancier algorithm than just the simple chase algorithm.

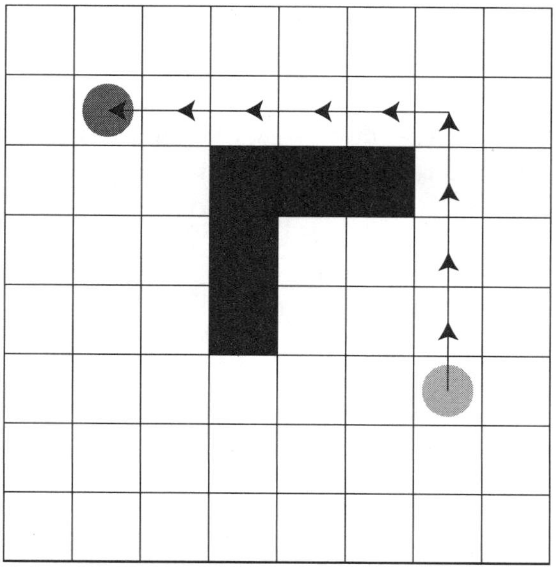

Figure 23.4

Evading the obstacle

More Advanced Pathfinding Algorithm

A lot of AI terms exist that I don't use. The algorithm I'm about to show you is an implementation of what is called *A** (A-star) pathfinding. Rather than cluttering your mind (and these pages) with a lot of AI mumbo-jumbo, I'm just going to show you how to do decent pathfinding without the terminology, which you don't need anyway.

First, you need a 2D array of integers (or any old type, really; it just has to be large enough to contain distance values). The array, of course, has to have the same dimensions as the game board (8×8 in the case of the figures).

To start, set all of the array's cells to a value of –1. –1 means that the square has not been tested yet. For any "blocked" square, put a number so large as to not be a possible distance. In this case, 255 is a good value. Finally, at the destination (meaning the dark piece's location), place a 0. The current board is shown in Figure 23.5.

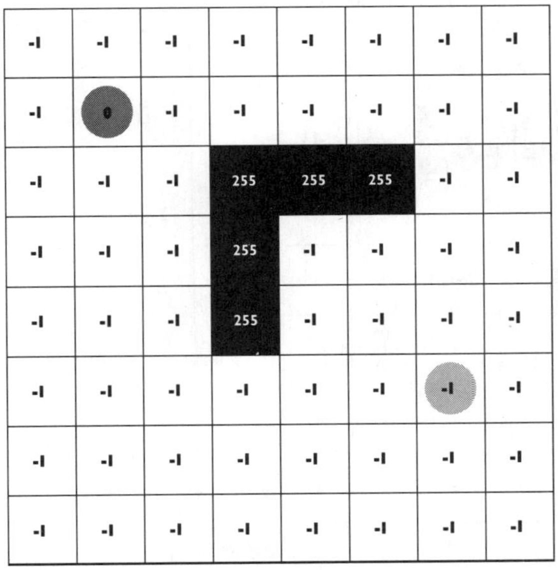

Figure 23.5

Initial state of the array

Next you will perform a number of passes over the array. Each pass will involve a couple of steps.

Step 1: Scan Array for Cells Adjacent to Cells with Known Distances

This step may need a little clarification. You know a few things about the board at this point. The cell containing a 0 is the goal. Naturally, the cell with the goal is no distance from the goal (duh!). This is what I call a *known* distance. Based on this, naturally any of the cells adjacent to the cell with a 0 in it would have a distance of 1. I'm getting slightly ahead here, but it's pretty plain to see.

The goal of Step 1 is to determine the cells next to a "known" distance. This can be stored in a 2D boolean array where *true* means an adjacent cell and *false* means a nonadjacent square. In the figures, I'll just highlight the squares.

After the first step of the first pass, the result looks like Figure 23.6. Note that the 255 squares are not considered known distances, and that only squares with a value of –1 are marked.

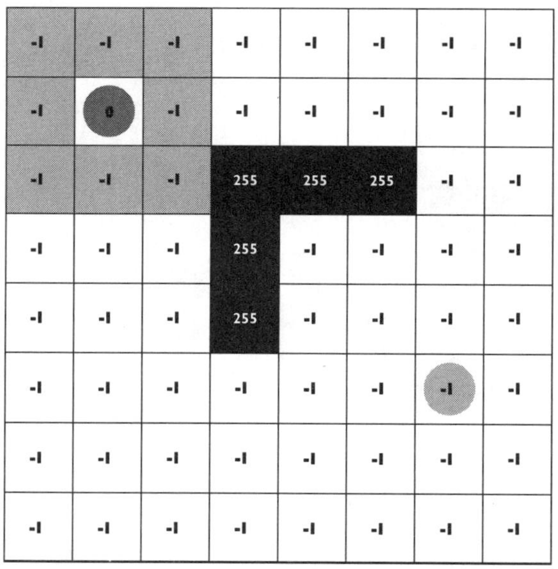

Figure 23.6

Step 1 of the first pass

Now for something important about the first step of a pass: if no squares get marked in the first step, the pathfinding is over, even if there are still values of –1 elsewhere in the array. If no squares were marked, no adjacent squares were found, and a path might be impossible.

Step 2: Give Adjacent Squares a Known Distance Value

Next, you replace all the –1s that have been highlighted with a value. For the first pass, this value is 1, for the second pass, 2, and so on. The first pass would look like Figure 23.7.

1	1	1	-1	-1	-1	-1	-1
1	0	1	-1	-1	-1	-1	-1
1	1	1	255	255	255	-1	-1
-1	-1	-1	255	-1	-1	-1	-1
-1	-1	-1	255	-1	-1	-1	-1
-1	-1	-1	-1	-1	-1	-1	-1
-1	-1	-1	-1	-1	-1	-1	-1
-1	-1	-1	-1	-1	-1	-1	-1

Figure 23.7

Giving values to marked squares

This process is repeated until one of the following occurs:

- Step 1 finds no adjacent squares.
- The cell of origin (the location of the light piece) gets filled in.

I almost added a third condition—when the board is full—but in that condition, Step 1 would find no adjacent squares in the next pass, so it is redundant.

When It's All Done

Figure 23.8 shows the board with a completed pathfinding array. Note that the light piece has a value of 7. In order for the light piece to capture the dark piece, the light piece must move to lower-valued squares—from 7 to 6, 6 to 5, 5 to 4, 4 to 3, 3 to 2, 2 to 1, and finally 1 to 0—until the dark piece has been caught!

1	1	1	2	3	4	5	6
1	0	1	2	3	4	5	6
1	1	1	255	255	255	5	6
2	2	2	255	6	6	6	6
3	3	3	255	5	6	7	7
4	4	4	4	5	6	7	8
5	5	5	5	5	6	7	8
6	6	6	6	6	6	7	8

Figure 23.8

A completed array

All in all, this is a beautiful algorithm. It will always get the piece to where you want it to go, or it will let you know if such a move is impossible.

Now, if I were to tell you that each of the squares in the array is called a *node,* and that you were making links between the nodes into a search tree in order to do pathfinding, and that you have just learned how A* pathfinding works, you'd look at me like I was nuts. It's true, though. This algorithm is an implementation of A*, as I stated earlier, in a more practical form. (Since a grid of tiles is easier to work with than the real world, the nodes become more discrete.)

IsoHex23_1.cpp has an implementation of this pathfinding algorithm. Most of this example is concerned with showing the graphical representation of the map. The actual pathfinding is done in a function called `FindPath`. This is a rather simple example. Two types of areas exist—one that you can walk on, and one that you cannot. In a real application, this would be more complicated, with different types of terrain having different path costs. However, the simplest case (this one) is easiest to understand, and once you understand it, extending it to deal with more complicated maps is pretty easy. Figure 23.9 shows the program output.

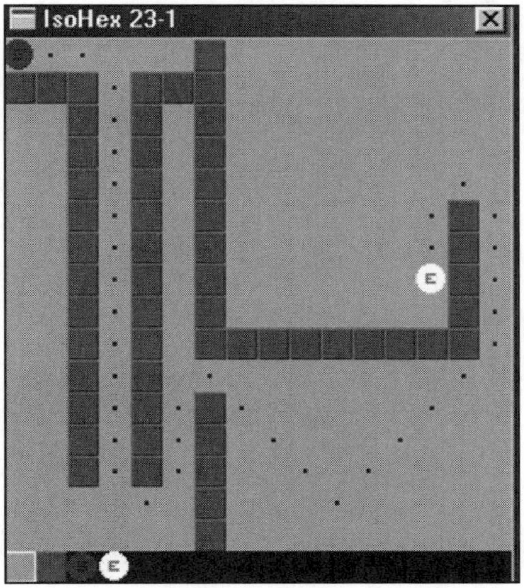

Figure 23.9

Output of IsoHex23_1.cpp

```
void FindPath()//find the path
{
	POINT ptStart;
	POINT ptEnd;
	POINT ptPath;
	ptStart.x=-1;
	ptEnd.x=-1;
	int x;
	int y;
	int nx;
	int ny;
	bool found;
	int lowvalue;
```

First, you need a number of variables to make this work, including starting and ending positions (`ptStart` and `ptEnd`), a few looping variables (x,y), some temporary variables for x,y coordinates (nx,ny), and some testing `vars` (`found` and `lowvalue`). The x part of `ptStart` and `ptEnd` is set to –1, because you first check that a starting point and an ending point exist in the map. If they don't, there is no need to continue with finding the path.

```
	//find the start
	for(x=0;x<MAPWIDTH;x++)
	{
		for(y=0;y<MAPHEIGHT;y++)
```

```
		{
			//check for the start
			if(Map[x][y]==TILESTART)
			{
				ptStart.x=x;
				ptStart.y=y;
			}
		}
	}
```

Lo and behold, this code snippet attempts to find the starting point. If one is found, its position is placed in ptStart.

```
	//find the end
	for(x=0;x<MAPWIDTH;x++)
	{
		for(y=0;y<MAPHEIGHT;y++)
		{
			//check for the end
			if(Map[x][y]==TILEEND)
			{
				ptEnd.x=x;
				ptEnd.y=y;
			}
		}
	}
	//if no start or end, exit function
	if(ptStart.x==-1 || ptEnd.x==-1) return;
```

The following code is the same as the preceding, except that this time you are seeking the ending point. After you have looked for both, you check to see whether they exist (that is, that the x values of the POINTs in which they are stored is not –1).

```
	//fill out the path array
	for(x=0;x<MAPWIDTH;x++)
	{
		for(y=0;y<MAPHEIGHT;y++)
		{
			switch(Map[x][y])
			{
			case TILESTART://place a 0 at the start
				{
					MapPath[x][y]=0;
```

```
                    }break;
                case TILEBLOCK://place a 999 at any blocks
                    {
                        MapPath[x][y]=999;
                    }break;
                case TILEEMPTY://if empty, place a -1
                    {
                        MapPath[x][y]=-1;
                    }break;
                default://anything else, place a -1
                    {
                        MapPath[x][y]=-1;
                    }break;
                }
            }
        }
```

An array called `MapPath` (a global array) is where you build the pathfinding information. You start by replacing everything with a –1 (passable square), a 0 (starting position) , or a 999 (a blocked, unpassable area).

```
        //scan for pathable tiles
        do
        {
            //haven't found one yet
            found=false;
            //scan the map
            for(x=0;x<MAPWIDTH;x++)
            {
                for(y=0;y<MAPHEIGHT;y++)
                {
                    MapMark[x][y]=false;
```

You now check for tiles to which you can determine paths. For this, you use another global array, `MapMark`. This array contains true at a place where you can calculate the path cost and false in a place where you cannot. To start out, set it to false, thus erasing whatever happened before.

```
                    //make sure this is a -1 square
                    if(MapPath[x][y]==-1)
                    {
```

Ensure that the `MapPath` array has a –1 at the position you are checking. If it does not, it is either a blocked square or one whose path has already been calculated (and you don't want to calculate it twice!).

```
                    //scan the neighbors
                    for(nx=x-1;nx<=x+1;nx++)
                    {
                        for(ny=y-1;ny<=y+1;ny++)
                        {
                            //make sure the neighbor
                            //is on the map
                            if(nx>=0 && ny>=0 && nx<MAPWIDTH
                            && ny<MAPHEIGHT &&
                            !(nx==x && ny==y))
                            {
                                //check against negatives
                                //and 999
                                if(MapPath[nx][ny]>=0 &&
                                MapPath[nx][ny]!=999)
                                {
```

Next, you scan the neighbors of this location. You are looking for a nonnegative, non-999 value, indicating that this position is next to a position that has already been calculated, which means that this position can now be calculated.

```
                                    //mark the map
                                    MapMark[x][y]=true;
                                    //mark it as found
                                    found=true;
                                }
                            }
                        }
                    }
                }
            }
        }
```

If you find such a neighbor, you mark it as true in the `MapMark` array and also set the local variable `found` to true, meaning that you have found at least one. (When `found` stops being true, pathfinding is over, whether or not the entire map has been calculated.)

```
        //now scan the marks
        for(x=0;x<MAPWIDTH;x++)
        {
            for(y=0;y<MAPHEIGHT;y++)
            {
```

```
//if this square is marked
if(MapMark[x][y])
{
        //set low value very high
        lowvalue=999;
```

It's time to loop again. This time, you're checking for marked squares. If one is found, you know that you can calculate the path. However, you want to step from this square to the square next to it with the lowest path cost, so you need to loop through all the neighbors and check those path costs.

```
        //loop through neighbors
        for(nx=x-1;nx<=x+1;nx++)
        {
                for(ny=y-1;ny<=y+1;ny++)
                {
                        //make sure the neighbor
                        //is on the map
                        if(nx>=0 && ny>=0 && nx<MAPWIDTH
                        && ny<MAPHEIGHT)
                        {
                                if(MapPath[nx][ny]>=0)
                                //must be a nonnegative
                                //value
                                {
                                        //assign the value
                                        //if it is lower
                                        if(MapPath[nx][ny]<
                                                lowvalue)
                                        lowvalue=MapPath[nx]
                                        [ny];
                                }
                        }
                }
        }
```

This loops through the neighbors and checks their values against `lowvalue`. If the value at that square is lower, `lowvalue` becomes that new value.

```
        //assign the value to the path map
        MapPath[x][y]=lowvalue+1;
    }
}
```

```
            }
        }
        while(found);
```

Because you have found the lowest-valued neighbor, assign that value +1 to the `MapPath` array at the position in question, and continue looping. The last line, `while(found)`, concerns the state of the `found` variable, which I discussed briefly earlier.

Now you have as complete a picture of the board as you can. All squares that can be reached from the starting point have been assigned values. What you need to do now is start at the ending point, make sure that it has a path value, and work backwards.

```
        //done with pathfinding
        //check to see that ptEnd has found a path
        if(MapPath[ptEnd.x][ptEnd.y]!=-1)
        {
                //start the path
                ptPath=ptEnd;
                //take the value from the map
                lowvalue=MapPath[ptEnd.x][ptEnd.y];
```

You recycle the `lowvalue` variable here, this time keeping track of the current position's path cost. With each iteration, continue to seek a lower value.

```
                while(lowvalue>0)
                {
                        found=false;
                        do
                        {
                                do
                                {
                                        //pick a random neighbor
                                        nx=rand()%3-1;
                                        ny=rand()%3-1;
                                }while((nx==0 && ny==0) || (ptPath.x+nx)<0 ||
                                (ptPath.x+nx)>=MAPWIDTH || (ptPath.y+ny)<0 ||
                                (ptPath.y+ny)>=MAPHEIGHT);
```

This bit of code picks a random direction of movement, making sure that the movement is not 0 and that it does not go outside the map's boundaries. Set `found` to false again, because you might need to check several directions before you find one that has a lower pathing cost.

```
                                //check to see if the value is lower
                                if(MapPath[ptPath.x+nx][ptPath.y+ny]<lowvalue)
```

```
                    {
                            //found!
                            found=true;
                            //set tile to path tile
                            Map[ptPath.x][ptPath.y]=TILEPATH;
                            //move the path
                            ptPath.x+=nx;
                            ptPath.y+=ny;
                            lowvalue=MapPath[ptPath.x][ptPath.y];
                    }
            }
            while(!found);
```

If you have indeed struck gold, `found` is set to true, place a little marker for the path, move in that direction, and decrease the value of `lowvalue`. If you have not found a suitable move, continue checking until you do.

```
        }
        //replace the end tile
        Map[ptEnd.x][ptEnd.y]=TILEEND;
    }
}
```

Because of the method I used to place markers on the path, I needed to replace the end marker when I was done. That's all that this final line does. And that's all there is to a pathfinding function. If I weren't actually marking the path, it wouldn't be quite as long.

Making Pathfinding Useful

Although the algorithm for finding a path can become quite complicated (much more complicated than it has been in the simple case I've shown here), it is by far the easiest part of AI. It is easy to figure out how to get from point A to point B in the shortest path possible. The hard part is deciding to which point B you want to go. That is the "true" AI aspect. By comparison, finding a path is child's play.

For example, let's say you're writing an RPG of some sort (with monsters and the player characters, treasure, swords, magic spells, the whole bit). You can go the simple route and have all the monsters head for the player characters, but that's not much of an AI. You might as well be playing *Gauntlet*.

Instead, you want to make your monsters work as a team. You might have some monsters maneuver around so that the player's escape is blocked, and you might place others in a position to fire arrows or cast spells at the player. Also, if this is a party-based RPG in which the player controls a group of characters instead of just one, you want your monsters to intelligently decide on targets, meaning that you want them to take out the archers and spell casters first and then slug it out toe to toe with the rest. A pathfinding algorithm can help with a lot of this. It can figure out how to get a monster from one place to another, but it can't decide where to send them. In addition, you need your monsters to be able to deal with the unforeseen, such as when one of their comrades is killed and the plan has to be changed. This is the real AI.

Here's another example, for turn-based strategy. The players (both human and computer) have a number of units at their disposal. However, different units are better suited to different roles, such as attack, defense, scouting, transporting, and so on.

Fast-moving horse units are good for exploring new territory, so you use the pathfinding algorithm to find a square next to a previously unexplored square and send the explorer in that direction. Attack units need to be able to find their way to enemy cities or move to ward off invaders. The uses of pathfinding here are quite clear. Transport units need to be able to meet up with the units they will be transporting and then get those units where they need to go.

As you can see, even after you can find the path from A to B, the work is anything but done. There is a lot to AI besides algorithms.

Summary

Unfortunately, I can only vaguely touch on artificial intelligence, with emphasis on pathfinding, since its need is so common in isometric games. Please forgive me. Many brilliant people have written entire volumes on the nature of AI and the methodology for achieving a semblance of intellect. I am mainly a graphics programmer. I'm not on par with people who make AI their life study.

Still, I hope this chapter at least got you thinking. Artificial intelligence is definitely an area that is not written in stone. New theories are coming to the front all the time. As Andre LaMothe says, the next great leap forward in computer technology will come from studies in AI, and nowhere else.

CHAPTER 24

Introduction to Direct3D

- Direct 3D as a 2D Renderer
- Direct 3D Basics
- Textures

Throughout this book, one detail may have been gnawing at you. Up until now, I've been using DirectDraw to do all of the rendering. Admittedly, we've wrapped it up pretty well with the `CTileSet` class and the IsoHexCore components, but the fact is that it's still DirectDraw, and it is from DirectX 7.0, not DirectX 8.0, which was the latest version of DirectX at the time of this book's publication.

Why am I using the (obviously inferior) version 7.0 rather than the new and spiffy 8.0? The answer is a bit involved and comes in two flavors. I have actual reasons for using 7.0 rather than 8.0, and I also have some cop-outs. I'll give you the cop-outs first:

- **Cop-out #1.** It's easier to learn a 2D API like DirectDraw, which DirectX 8.0 doesn't have (8.0 incorporates DirectDraw and Direct3D (D3D) into a single part of the API).
- **Cop-out #2.** When DirectX 8.0 came out, I had less than two months until the book had to be complete, which is insufficient time to update all the text and code adequately.
- **Cop-out #3.** DirectX is backward-compatible.
- **Cop-out #4.** The book is mainly concerned with algorithms, not 2D or 3D APIs, and the techniques apply no matter what you are using to render.

How true or false are these cop-outs? Well, #1 is true to an extent. Learning a 3D API is a bit more involved than learning a 2D API, and isometric algorithms are primarily 2D in nature, and the extra math is unnecessary. Also, DirectDraw and D3D were merged in DirectX 8.0.

Similarly, cop-out #2 is true, sort of. I was not on the DirectX 8.0 beta program, so 8.0 became available to me at the same moment it became available to all of the other developers in the world. When DX8 came out, I had two choices: Either stick with 7, or update everything (dozens of sample programs and hundreds of pages of text).

Cop-out #3 is also true. DirectX is backward-compatible and promises to be so forever (forever meaning until Microsoft doesn't feel like it anymore). You can still use the old version 7 interfaces.

The final cop-out comes closest to the truth. The isometric algorithms in this book can be applied to any platform and any API. I've done isometric games that use GDI, DirectDraw, Direct3D, and even some old DOS stuff. The methodology is the same no matter what.

Now the truth: My reason for using DirectX 7.0 instead of DirectX 8.0 is that in DirectX 8.0, there is no real support for traditional 2D graphics. You can still do 2D graphics with DirectX 8.0, as you will see in a moment, but not in the traditional manner, and doing graphics the way you have been doing them thus far is a pain in the butt in DX8 and would be highly confusing (for both of us).

Now that I have admitted this, let's move on. This chapter is an introduction to D3D (version 7.0). Because of the nature of isometric games and the algorithms behind them, you won't be exploring most of the D3D API, because most of it is useless to you. Instead, you will use D3D as a 2D renderer, and these algorithms, with only slight modification, can be applied with ease.

Direct3D as a 2D Renderer

It might seem strange to read this heading. The word "3D" is right at the end of "Direct3D," and to use it as a 2D renderer seems far-fetched and a gross misuse of power. Far-fetched, no, but a gross misuse, yes! However, that is a good thing. I will explain.

3D Games (and 3D APIs) Are Still Only 2D

Yes, they look 3D. There is perspective correction for distance. There is the illusion of lighting, and various other factors that make the image appear as though it were 3D. Your screen, however, is still flat (or slightly curved, if you're using a CRT and want to get technical about it) and is, for all intents and purposes, strictly 2D. Hence, anything drawn on the screen can be nothing other than 2D, at least until science invents some sort of holographic projector that will allow true 3D.

So, the image on your screen as you play a 3D game is merely a projection of that scene in 2D, giving the illusion of 3D.

How Direct3D Works

This is probably going to be the most simplistic explanation of the workings of Direct3D ever written, but at its core, it is true: Direct3D does nothing more than render triangles on the screen.

Naturally, it's a little more involved than that. The triangles can be textured with a pattern of bits stored in a DirectDraw surface, and the triangles can be given the illusion of lighting and can be blended translucently. Even multiple textures can be used, merged by different means to give a different look. Direct3D can also take care of the complex math required to project a 3D scene onto your 2D screen, but it doesn't require that you make use of that ability.

So, you're still just drawing triangles on the screen, and two-dimensional triangles at that (triangles, by their nature, being 2D). If all you are doing is rendering triangles, doing 2D graphics is very easy. To make a rectangle, you need only two triangles, as shown in Figure 24.1. Similarly, you can split an isometric tile in half (either lengthwise or widthwise), and you again have two triangles.

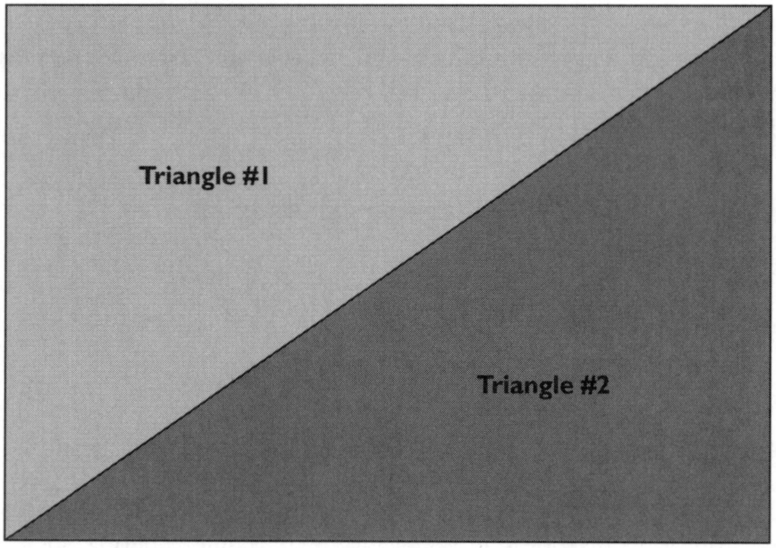

Figure 24.1

Using triangles to make a rectangle

Direct3D Basics

This next section will seem like a "back to basics" section, because I'll discuss the innards of DirectX, which you haven't really dealt with since the creation of `CTileSet` many chapters ago.

In Direct3D (version 7.0, at least), you will be primarily concerned with two new objects—`IDirect3D7` (which is akin to the `IDirectDraw7` object) and `IDirect3DDevice7` (similar in function to `IDirectDrawSurface7`).

First, in order to have your applications use Direct3D, you must add a new library file and a new header. The library is named d3dim.lib, and you add it to your project in the same manner as you have added ddraw.lib and dxguid.lib all along. The header is named d3d.h, and you simply include it in any file that needs to use Direct3D.

Icky COM Stuff

Before you do anything else related to Direct3D, you must first have an `IDirect3D7` object and store a pointer to it in an `LPDIRECT3D7` variable. In order to get this pointer you must do icky COM stuff.

Every DirectX component has three member functions: `AddRef`, `QueryInterface`, and `Release`. You're already familiar with `Release`, since you use it all the time to clean up objects. `AddRef` is a way to manually add a reference to an object so that it does not get deleted at an inappropriate time (`AddRef` remains largely unused). `QueryInterface`, however, is a little trickier to explain, and it just so happens to be the member function you need to get started with Direct3D.

I won't go into the subtleties of the COM interface stuff. It takes a lot of explanation, it's really boring, and you probably don't care. You just want to make use of Direct3D, and and you want to do it *now*. I understand and will comply.

Here's the magic line that will give you a pointer to an `IDirect3D7` object:

```
//lpdd is an LPDIRECTDRAW7 variable
//lpd3d is an LPDIRECT3D7 variable
lpdd->QueryInterface(IID_IDirect3D7,(void**)&lpd3d);
```

I suppose a little explanation couldn't hurt. The first parameter of `QueryInterface` is a `REFIID`, or a reference to an interface identifier. Use a different one in `DirectDrawCreateEx` to make your `IDirectDraw7` object.

The software component that you are used to thinking of as an `IDirectDraw7` object is more than it seems. Hidden within it is an `IDirect3D7` object. The best analogy would be the layers of an onion. You simply use `QueryInterface` to bring the other layers to light.

Once you've got your `IDirect3D7` object, all you need to do is store it in a variable somewhere, and don't forget to release it later. This is all the icky COM stuff you need to do for now.

Surface Creation

Since you're now using Direct3D, you have to make some subtle modifications to the way in which your rendering surfaces (the primary surface and the back buffer) are created. You have to let DirectX know that you intend to render using 3D methods onto these surfaces. The manner in which you do this involves a slight change to the `DDSURFACEDESC2` structure.

The following code was taken from DDFuncs.cpp. It sets up a primary surface with a given number of back buffers.

```
//set up a DDSD for a primary surface, with any number of back buffers
void DDSD_PrimarySurfaceWBackBuffer(DDSURFACEDESC2* pddsd, DWORD
dwBackBufferCount)
{
	//clean out the ddsd
	DDSD_Clear(pddsd);
	//set flags
	pddsd->dwFlags=DDSD_CAPS | DDSD_BACKBUFFERCOUNT;
	//set caps
	pddsd->ddsCaps.dwCaps=DDSCAPS_PRIMARYSURFACE | DDSCAPS_COMPLEX |
		DDSCAPS_FLIP;
	//set back buffer count
	pddsd->dwBackBufferCount=dwBackBufferCount;
}
```

And now here's the same function, rewritten so that the primary surface can be used with Direct3D.

```
//set up a DDSD for a primary surface, with any number of back buffers
void DDSD_3DPrimarySurfaceWBackBuffer(DDSURFACEDESC2* pddsd, DWORD
dwBackBufferCount)
{
	//clean out the ddsd
	DDSD_Clear(pddsd);
	//set flags
	pddsd->dwFlags=DDSD_CAPS | DDSD_BACKBUFFERCOUNT;
	//set caps
	pddsd->ddsCaps.dwCaps=DDSCAPS_PRIMARYSURFACE | DDSCAPS_COMPLEX |
		DDSCAPS_FLIP | DDSCAPS_3DDEVICE;
	//set back buffer count
	pddsd->dwBackBufferCount=dwBackBufferCount;
}
```

Since the change is not obvious, I made it bold. All you need to do is add an extra flag to the surface's ddsCaps.dwCaps, and you are ready to use it as a 3D device. It's just that simple.

Similarly, if you intend to render onto the back buffer, you need to place the same flag into its `DDSCAPS2` structure, as you did with the primary surface. Don't worry too much. You'll make a small set of functions to help you out in this regard.

Creating a Device

Once you've got your `IDirect3D7` object, and you've set up a surface to be used as the rendering target, it's time to make the `IDirect3DDevice7` object. To do so, use `IDirect3D7`'s `CreateDevice` member function.

```
HRESULT IDirect3D7::CreateDevice(
  REFCLSID rclsid,
  LPDIRECTDRAWSURFACE7 lpDDS,
  LPDIRECT3DDEVICE7 *  lplpD3DDevice,
);
```

The `rclsid` parameter is a `REFCLSID`, which is like a `REFIID`, which is in turn a GUID. Don't ask me why Microsoft felt it needed so many names for the same thing! More about this parameter a little later. The `lpDDS` parameter is the surface you want to use as the rendering target for this device. Finally, `lplpD3DDevice` is a pointer to a pointer to the device to be created. Devices are created in this way, much like DirectDraw surfaces are.

So, what of `rclsid`? Well, this is a class identifier (GUID) telling Direct3D which 3D device to use. Depending on your video card, you might have several flavors available to you. In DirectX 7.0, there are four flavors of device: `IID_IDirect3DTnLHalDevice`, `IID_IDirect3DHALDevice`, `IID_IDirect3DMMXDevice`, and `IID_IDirect3DRGBDevice`. These are listed in decreasing order of desirability and speed.

Ideally, you have a TnLHal device, which is super fast. It handles texturing and lighting in hardware and tends to have the best hardware capabilities. Next is the HAL device, which is usually pretty good, but not nearly as good as the TnLHal. This is followed by the MMX device, which has multimedia extensions, etc., etc. And last and certainly least is the RGB device, which is software emulation and can always be used. It is there mainly for maximum compatibility, and it is darned slow!

So, which one to pick? It would be nice to make use of the TnL, but not all machines have one. Same thing for HAL and MMX. You could use the RGB device, but that would be an insult to the machines that have a much greater 3D acceleration capability. What you must do, then, is use the best device of the machine on which that the program is running, defaulting to the RGB device only when nothing else is available.

How do you do that? There are two ways—the "professional" way, which enumerates devices, and the "hack" way, which is simpler, shorter, and does the exact same thing as the professional way.

So, here's the hack function to give you a 3D device for D3D:

```
LPDIRECT3DDEVICE7 CreateD3DDevice(LPDIRECT3D7 lpd3d,LPDIRECTDRAWSURFACE7 lpdds)
{
	LPDIRECT3DDEVICE7 lpd3ddev;
	//try to make a TnL device
	if(FAILED(lpd3d->CreateDevice(IID_IDirect3DTnLHalDevice,lpdds,&lpd3ddev)))
	{
		//no TnL; try for HAL
		if(FAILED(lpd3d-
	>CreateDevice(IID_IDirect3DHALDevice,lpdds,&lpd3ddev)))
		{
			//no HAL; try for MMX
			if(FAILED(lpd3d->CreateDevice(IID_IDirect3DMMXDevice,
				lpdds,&lpd3ddev)))
			{
				//no MMX; try for RGB
				if(FAILED(lpd3d->CreateDevice(IID_IDirect3DRGBDevice,
					lpdds,&lpd3ddev)))
				{
					//no RGB; so return NULL
					lpd3ddev=NULL;
				}
```

```
                    }
            }
        }
        //return the new device
        return(lpd3ddev);
}
```

This is a pretty simple function. You try to make the best device you can, and failing that, you fall back to an inferior device, finally falling to an RGB. If you can't even get an RGB, something else is probably wrong, so the function returns `NULL`. Later, during program cleanup, you release the device just like any other DirectX object.

Making a Viewport

You've got the `IDirect3D7` object, and you've created your `IDirect3DDevice`. You're most of the way set up to start rendering. One last thing stands in your way: the viewport.

In D3D, you don't have to render to the entire target surface. You can instead render to only a portion of it, and you can choose which portion. To do so, fill out a `D3DVIEWPORT7` structure.

```
typedef struct _D3DVIEWPORT7{
    DWORD       dwX;
    DWORD       dwY;
    DWORD       dwWidth;
    DWORD       dwHeight;
    D3DVALUE    dvMinZ;
    D3DVALUE    dvMaxZ;
} D3DVIEWPORT7, *LPD3DVIEWPORT7
```

Table 24.1 explains the members of `D3DVIEWPORT7` and their purposes.

Table 24.1 Members of D3DVIEWPORT7

Member	Purpose
dwX	The left edge pixel coordinate of the viewport
dwY	The top edge pixel coordinate of the viewport
dwWidth	Width of the viewport in pixels
dwHeight	Height of the viewport in pixels
dvMinZ	Minimum z value (see the next paragraph)
dvMaxZ	Maximum z value (see the next paragraph)

You might get a little hung up on D3DVALUE and dvMinZ and dvMaxZ. I'll explain, briefly. A D3DVALUE is a float, plain and simple. Since D3D is a 3D API, it takes into account a z value along with an x and a y to do rendering. Since you're just using x and y, you don't really care about z, so you'll use 0.0 for dvMinZ and 1.0 for dvMaxZ (these are the normal values for these members) and forget about it.

Once you've got a D3DVIEWPORT7 filled out, set your device's viewport to it using IDirect3DDevice7::SetViewport.

```
HRESULT IDirect3DDevice7::SetViewport(
  LPD3DVIEWPORT7 lpViewport
);
```

This function returns D3D_OK if successful and an error value if not. The lpViewport parameter is just a pointer to a D3DVIEWPORT7. The following code is what you might use to set a device's viewport, assuming you are at a 640×480 resolution and want to use the entire screen.

```
D3DVIEWPORT7 vp;//vp stands for viewport
vp.dwX=0;
vp.dwY=0;
vp.dwWidth=640;
vp.dwHeight=480;
vp.dvMinZ=0.0;
vp.dvMaxZ=1.0;
lpd3ddev->SetViewport(&vp);
```

Not too rough, right? This is mostly like telling DirectX twice what you want to use—once when you set the mode and once when you set the viewport. Most of the time, you'll want to use the entire surface for the viewport, but there are times when you might not, such as when you have a frame around the playing area.

Rendering

The stage is set, and your objects are initialized. You're ready to start drawing. Unfortunately, drawing objects in D3D is absolutely nothing like drawing objects in DirectDraw. In D3D, you generally adhere to the following steps:

1. Clear out the viewport using `IDirect3DDevice7::Clear`.
2. Tell D3D you want to begin drawing by calling `IDirect3DDevice7::BeginScene`.
3. Do your drawing using `IDirect3D7Device7::DrawPrimitive`.
4. Tell D3D you are done drawing by calling `IDirect3DDevice7::EndScene`.
5. Flip the surfaces (assuming that you are writing to the back buffer).

All of this is done each time `Prog_Loop` is executed.

IDirect3DDevice7::Clear

In almost all cases, you will want to clear out the entire rendering surface each frame. This differs from what you did in DirectDraw, where you used update rectangles and attempted to do as little blitting as possible.

Why the difference? Well, assuming you have any hardware acceleration at all on your video card (and chances are you do have a little), using Direct3D to render is just so much faster than doing the same thing with DirectDraw, because of the hardware acceleration. So, to clear out the buffer, you use `IDirect3DDevice7::Clear`.

```
HRESULT IDirect3DDevice7::Clear(
  DWORD      dwCount,
  LPD3DRECT lpRects,
  DWORD      dwFlags,
  DWORD      dwColor,
  D3DVALUE   dvZ,
  DWORD      dwStencil
);
```

There are lots of parameters here, most of which you don't care about. Like all DirectX functions, this function returns an `HRESULT`, which contains `D3D_OK` if successful or something else if not. Table 24.2 explains the parameter list.

Table 24.2 IDirect3DDevice7::Clear Parameters

Parameter	Purpose
dwCount	The number of RECTs pointed to by lpRects. May be 0 if lpRects is NULL.
lpRects	A pointer to a list of RECTs that will be cleared by this function. May be NULL to clear the entire viewport.
dwFlags	Flags specifying how the clear is to be performed (see Table 24.3).
dwColor	A color value to clear the target (discussed in a moment).
dvZ	A z value to assign on the z buffer. (Don't worry about it; you don't use z buffers.)
dwStencil	A stencil value to assign the stencil buffer. (You don't use stencil buffers.)

I need to add some explanation to the dwFlags and dwColor parameters. I'll start with dwFlags. Table 24.3 lists and describes the various flags that can be used in this parameter.

Table 24.3 Flags for Clear

Flag	Meaning
D3DCLEAR_TARGET	Clear out the target surface, so dwColor is valid.
D3DCLEAR_STENCIL	Clear out the stencil buffer, so dwStencil is valid. (You aren't using stencil buffers, so you don't care.)
D3DCLEAR_ZBUFFER	Clear out the z buffer, so dvZ is valid. (You aren't using z buffers, so you don't care.)

So, dwFlags tells you which of the dwColor, dwStencil, and dvZ parameters are valid. For your purposes, you will only be using D3DCLEAR_TARGET.

That brings us to dwColor. If you recall from the discussion of DirectDraw, you had to deal with calculations involving members of the DDPIXELFORMAT structure. In D3D, that need is gone. There is a simple macro you use to determine the color—D3DRGB. It takes three parameters—a red value, a green value, and a blue value, each in the range from 0.0 to 1.0. Treat 0.0 the same as 0, and 1.0 the same as 255 in the

GDI RGB macro. So, if you wanted to clear the viewport to white, you would do the following.

```
//clear viewport to white
lpd3ddev->Clear(0,NULL,D3DCLEAR_TARGET,D3DRGB(1.0,1.0,1.0),0,0);
```

Normally, of course, you'll use D3DRGB (0.0,0.0,0.0) to clear out the target surface so that you have a nice, fresh black surface to work with. But clearing out the viewport is not the only use of IDirect3DDevice7::Clear. You can also use this function to perform color fills, just as you did with Blt. The mechanism changes just a little bit. Like the DirectDraw method, you still fill out a RECT with information about the area you want to fill, and you pick a color using the D3DRGB macro and then call Clear.

```
//rcFill contains information about the area to fill
//dwColor contains a color constructed with the D3DRGB macro
lpd3ddev->Clear(1,&rcFill,D3DCLEAR_TARGET,dwColor,0,0);
```

Additionally, if you have several rectangles you need filled with the same color, you can make an array, pass the number of RECTs in the first parm and a pointer to the first RECT in the second parm, and do it.

IDirect3DDevice7::BeginScene and IDirect3DDevice7::EndScene

Because of the intimate relationship between these two functions, I thought it best to discuss them at the same time. You are about to make a rendering sandwich, and these functions are the slices of bread.

```
HRESULT IDirect3DDevice7::BeginScene();
HRESULT IDirect3DDevice7::EndScene();
```

Neither takes a parameter, and both return the usual HRESULT value, with success indicated by D3D_OK. BeginScene tells D3D that you are ready to draw. EndScene tells D3D that you are done drawing.

IDirect3DDevice7::DrawPrimitive

Now, and finally, comes the actual rendering of primitives. A *primitive* is just a generic term for a geometric object. There are several types, including points, lines, and triangles. You are concerned mainly with triangles, but once you can draw one of them, you can draw the others without difficulty.

The DrawPrimitive function of IDirect3DDevice7 is probably the most complex DirectX function I will cover in this book.

```
HRESULT IDirect3DDevice7::DrawPrimitive(
  D3DPRIMITIVETYPE dptPrimitiveType,
  DWORD  dwVertexTypeDesc,
  LPVOID lpvVertices,
  DWORD  dwVertexCount,
```

```
  DWORD   dwFlags
);
```

DrawPrimitive takes a number of parameters (explained in Table 24.4 and in the following text) and returns the standard HRESULT, with D3D_OK indicating success.

Table 24.4 DrawPrimitive Parameters

Parameter	Purpose
dptPrimitiveType	The type of primitive to be drawn (discussed in the next section).
dwVertexTypeDesc	The format of the vertices to be drawn (discussed in a moment).
lpvVertices	A pointer to a list of vertices (discussed in a moment).
dwVertexCount	The number of vertices pointed to by lpvVertices.
dwFlags	Either 0 or D3DDP_WAIT. You'll be using 0.

I look at that table and think back to when I first looked at Direct3D and felt my stomach drop because it seemed so complicated. It's really not so bad, as long as it's explained correctly.

dptPrimitiveType

dptPrimitiveType is of type D3DPRIMITIVETYPE, an enumeration. Table 24.5 lists the possible values and their meanings. Some of them are a little vague and need extra explanation, but we'll have picture time in a moment.

Table 24.5 D3DPRIMITIVETYPE Values

Value	Meaning
D3DPT_POINTLIST	Used to draw a series of points. This is useful for making a star field.
D3DPT_LINELIST	Used to draw a series of lines.
D3DPT_LINESTRIP	Used to draw a series of lines connected end to end.
D3DPT_TRIANGLELIST	Used to draw a series of triangles.
D3DPT_TRIANGLESTRIP	Used to draw a series of triangles that are linked (more on this later).
D3DPT_TRIANGLEFAN	Used to draw a series of triangles in a fan shape (more on this later).

The first four should be pretty self-explanatory. D3DPT_TRIANGLESTRIP and D3DPT_TRIANGLEFAN are a little fuzzier, so I'll show you pictures to give you a better idea of what I mean.

Figure 24.2 shows a triangle strip using six vertices. V0 through V5 are the end points, or vertices, and they define triangles 1 through 4. Triangle 1 is defined by V0, V1, V2; Triangle 2 is defined by V1, V2, V3; Triangle 3 is defined by V2, V3, V4; and Triangle 4 is defined by V3, V4, V5. In all cases, triangles next to one another on the strip share one side.

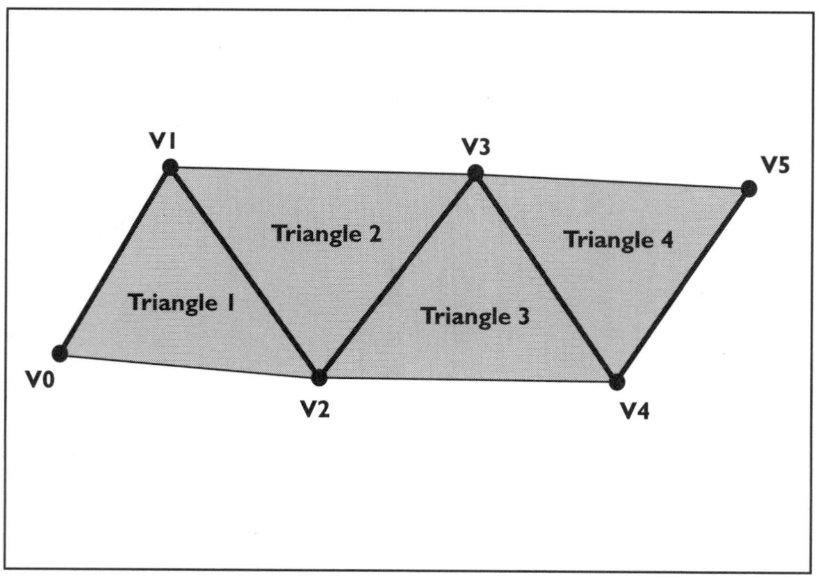

Figure 24.2

A triangle strip

Figure 24.3 shows a triangle fan. The difference between a fan and a strip is obvious once you see what they look like. A triangle fan uses the first vertex (V0) in all the triangles and uses the other two vertices to complete the triangle. Again, adjacent triangles end up sharing a side, and additionally, all triangles share a single vertex.

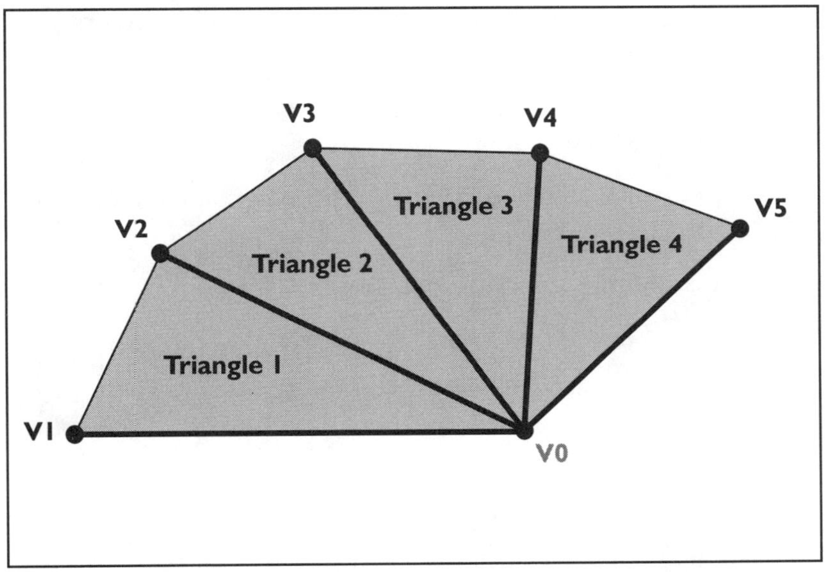

Figure 24.3

A triangle fan

dwVertexTypeDesc and lpvVertices

These two parameters are joined intimately, so by discussing one, you must discuss the other. There is actually a great deal of information regarding these two parameters, but because you are just using D3D as a 2D rasterizer, you will only be touching the tip of the iceberg.

The `dwVertexTypeDesc` parameter contains a combination of flags describing what kind of vertices you are using. There are many ways you can represent a vertex, and to accommodate that, Microsoft came up with the Flexible Vertex Format (FVF) to allow you to express the many types of vertices you might be inclined to use. Table 24.6 lists and describes the various FVF flags.

Table 24.6 Flexible Vertex Format Flags

Flag	Meaning
D3DFVF_DIFFUSE	The vertex contains a diffuse color (we'll get to diffuse colors a bit later).
D3DFVF_NORMAL	The vertex contains a surface normal (this is vector stuff, and you won't be using vectors).
D3DFVF_SPECULAR	The vertex contains a specular color (you won't be using specular highlights, either).
D3DFVF_XYZ	The vertex contains untransformed position data.
D3DFVF_XYZRHW	The vertex contains transformed position data.
D3DFVF_XYZB*n*	This is for vertex blending, which you won't be doing. *n* is a value 1 through 5.
D3DFVF_TEX*n*	This specifies how many sets of texture coordinates the vertex has. *n* is a value 0 through 8.
D3DFVF_TEXTUREFORMAT*n*	This specifies in what format the texture coordinates are. *n* is a value 1 through 4.

Sound complicated? It is. Luckily, Microsoft knew that people like us would exist, and they did a nice thing for us by making a vertex type that we can use for our purposes and by making a D3DFVF_* constant to use it with DrawPrimitive. Be sure to send Microsoft a thank you note.

The vertex type is called D3DTLVERTEX, and the FVF constant associated with it is D3DFVF_TLVERTEX. Actually, this type has more information than you really need, but you can just ignore what you don't use. The TL part stands for "transformed and lit." You won't be making use of D3D transformation and lighting. You'll specify all the information pertinent to the primitive yourself.

```
typedef struct _D3DTLVERTEX {
    D3DVALUE sx;
    D3DVALUE sy;
    D3DVALUE sz;
    D3DVALUE rhw;
    D3DCOLOR color;
    D3DCOLOR specular;
    D3DVALUE tu;
    D3DVALUE tv;
} D3DTLVERTEX, *LPD3DTLVERTEX;
```

This isn't the actual declaration for D3DTLVERTEX, so don't be surprised if you see something bizarre when looking it up in the help files. There are anonymous unions for each of the members. Table 24.7 lists the members and their meanings.

Table 24.7 D3DTLVERTEX Members

Member	Purpose
sx	x-coordinate of the vertex
sy	y-coordinate of the vertex
sz	z-coordinate of the vertex
rhw	Reciprocal of the homogenous w-coordinate
color	Diffuse color
specular	Specular color
tu	First texture u-coordinate
tv	First texture v-coordinate

The sx, sy, and sz members are intuitive enough. They are the coordinates at which the vertex exists. The rhw explanation has to do with matrix multiplication and homogenous coordinates, and you *really* don't want to hear about it, so just trust me and put a 1.0 in your rhw. Color and specular are your two colors, diffuse and specular. You don't need to worry about specular—it's just added baggage. tu and tv are texture coordinates. I'll get to texture a little later, because it is a discussion in its own right.

The lpVertices parameter of DrawPrimitive is just a pointer to an array of whatever type of vertex you specify using dwVertexTypeDesc, which in this case will always be D3DTLVERTEX.

A Simple Direct3D Example

This section is subtitled "The Spinning Technicolor Nacho of Death." Just like you did when you got into GDI by plotting single pixels, you will similarly immerse yourself in Direct3D by drawing its most common primitive—the triangle.

CAUTION

In order to compile a Direct3D program, your application needs to include d3d.h, *not* d3d8.h, because you are using version 7 of the API, not version 8. However, the library file required is still d3d8.lib, no matter what version you use.

Traditionally, the "hello world" program for a 3D API is a triangle spinning in three dimensions. Because you are not using the third dimension, you will instead have a slight variation on this simple example. The triangle will rotate in two dimensions instead of three.

Load up IsoHex24_1.cpp and run it, because Figure 24.4 doesn't do it justice. You really need to see it in color. It shows a shaded triangle with one red corner, one blue corner, and one green corner, slowly rotating around the center of the screen.

Figure 24.4

Spinning Technicolor Nacho of Death

This program is about as simple as you can get with Direct3D. It is even simpler than any example using actual 3D math with matrices, because you don't have to set up any transformations. Take a look at how this example was built so that you can move on to bigger and better things.

Globals

IsoHex24_1 is based on IsoHex1_1, with DirectDraw stuff added. Globals include the normal `LPDIRECTDRAW7`, `LPDIRECTDRAWSURFACE7` for the primary surface and the back buffer, and also a few globals you have not yet seen—mainly the stuff to set up Direct3D.

```
//IDirect3D7
LPDIRECT3D7 lpd3d=NULL;
//IDirect3DDevice
LPDIRECT3DDEVICE7 lpd3ddev=NULL;
//vertices
D3DTLVERTEX vert[3];//three vertices
//angle, used for vertex calculations
double angle=0.0;
```

lpd3d is a pointer to your IDirect3D7 object, which you have to QueryInterface from out lpdd. lpd3ddev is your 3D device, which you create from lpd3d. vert is an array of D3DTLVERTEX, and you use it for drawing. angle is used to calculate the positions of the vertices stored in the vert array.

Initialization and Cleanup

Most of this will be familiar, except that the surface creation is no longer from DDFuncs.h/DDFuncs.cpp, because you need to add a capability to the surface. The rest involves setting up Direct3D and initializing the parts of your vertex array (vert) that will not change throughout the course of the application. And so, for your perusal, here is the Prog_Init function:

```
bool Prog_Init()
{
      lpdd=LPDD_Create(hWndMain,DDSCL_EXCLUSIVE |
            DDSCL_FULLSCREEN | DDSCL_ALLOWREBOOT);
      //set the display mode
      lpdd->SetDisplayMode(SCREENWIDTH,SCREENHEIGHT,SCREENBPP,0,0);
```

This bit has not changed since you first started using DDFuncs.h/DDFuncs.cpp. You create your IDirectDraw7 object, and you still set the display mode. There's nothing new here.

```
      //create primary surface
      DDSURFACEDESC2 ddsd;
      memset(&ddsd,0,sizeof(DDSURFACEDESC2));
      ddsd.dwSize=sizeof(DDSURFACEDESC2);
      ddsd.dwFlags=DDSD_CAPS | DDSD_BACKBUFFERCOUNT;
      ddsd.dwBackBufferCount=1;
      ddsd.ddsCaps.dwCaps=DDSCAPS_PRIMARYSURFACE |
            DDSCAPS_FLIP | DDSCAPS_COMPLEX | DDSCAPS_3DDEVICE;
      lpdd->CreateSurface(&ddsd,&lpddsPrime,NULL);
```

Earlier in this chapter, I told you about DDSCAPS_3DDEVICE, which allows you to use a surface as a rendering target for a D3D device. Hence, the way you create your primary surface has changed subtly, which means that you can no longer use DDFuncs.h/DDFuncs.cpp to create your primary surface. (Don't worry. You'll make a D3DFuncs.h/D3DFuncs.cpp in the next chapter.)

You probably will never set your primary surface as the rendering target, but for debugging purposes, you might want to use it in a limited way, so that it doesn't really hurt anything.

```
//create back buffer
DDSCAPS2 ddscaps;
memset(&ddscaps,0,sizeof(DDSCAPS2));
ddscaps.dwCaps=DDSCAPS_BACKBUFFER | DDSCAPS_3DDEVICE;
lpddsPrime->GetAttachedSurface(&ddscaps,&lpddsBack);
```

Just as the primary surface is now a D3D rendering target, so must the back buffer be. Setting this up is less involved than creating the primary surface, but it is necessary, because the back buffer is the surface to which you want D3D to render.

```
//get the idirect3d pointer
lpdd->QueryInterface(IID_IDirect3D7,(void**)&lpd3d);//ICKY COM STUFF!
```

Next on the list is to get your IDirect3D7 pointer by using the evil COM QueryInterface method of your IDirectDraw7 object. Now you're ready to make your 3D device.

```
    //create the idirect3ddevice (hack method)
    if(FAILED(lpd3d-
>CreateDevice(IID_IDirect3DTnLHalDevice,lpddsBack,&lpd3ddev)))//try tnl
            if(FAILED(lpd3d->CreateDevice(IID_IDirect3DHALDevice,
                    lpddsBack,&lpd3ddev)))//no tnl; try hal
                    if(FAILED(lpd3d->CreateDevice(IID_IDirect3DMMXDevice,
                            lpddsBack,&lpd3ddev)))//no hal; try mmp
                            if(FAILED(lpd3d->CreateDevice(IID_IDirect3DRGBDevice,
                                    lpddsBack,&lpd3ddev)))//no mmx; resort to
                            rgb
                            return(false);//problem; return false
```

This is the hack method. You use it to create your 3D device, using the back buffer as the rendering target. I took out all the brackets in order to take up less space, but this remains the exact same method I showed you earlier. Try the most advanced device first, and gradually settle for less and less capability.

```
//set up viewport
D3DVIEWPORT7 vp;
vp.dwX=0;
```

```
        vp.dwY=0;
        vp.dwWidth=SCREENWIDTH;
        vp.dwHeight=SCREENHEIGHT;
        vp.dvMinZ=0.0;
        vp.dvMaxZ=1.0;
        //set viewport for device
        lpd3ddev->SetViewport(&vp);
```

Now that you have a 3D device, you must set up the viewport for it. You'll be using the entire screen, so dwX, dwY, dwWidth, and dwHeight are set appropriately. Set the z values to their "usual" values, even though you don't care at all about z.

```
        //initialize the vertices (partially, anyway)
        vert[0].color=D3DRGB(0.0,1.0,0.0);//set the color for this vertex
        vert[0].specular=0;//zero for specular
        vert[0].rhw=1.0;//rhw is 1.0
        vert[0].tu=0.0;//0.0 for both texture coordinates
        vert[0].tv=0.0;
        vert[0].sz=0.5;//static z value
```

Finally, set up the static parts of your vertex array. During this example, the only values that will change are sx and sy, so you can safely fill in the rest of the values. For vertex 0, you have a diffuse color of pure green, no specular color, and an rhw of 1.0 (you need this to make it look right). You need a texture coordinate of (0.0,0.0) since you aren't using textures yet, and to top it off, you need an sz value of 0.5. The sz value doesn't really matter.

```
        vert[1].color=D3DRGB(0.0,0.0,1.0);//set the color for this vertex
        vert[1].specular=0;//zero for specular
        vert[1].rhw=1.0;//rhw is 1.0
        vert[1].tu=0.0;//0.0 for both texture coordinates
        vert[1].tv=0.0;
        vert[1].sz=0.5;//static z value
        vert[2].color=D3DRGB(1.0,0.0,0.0);//set the color for this vertex
        vert[2].specular=0;//zero for specular
        vert[2].rhw=1.0;//rhw is 1.0
        vert[2].tu=0.0;//0.0 for both texture coordinates
        vert[2].tv=0.0;
        vert[2].sz=0.5;//static z value
        return(true);//return success
}
```

Then set up the other two vertices, mostly with the same values, except for color. Vertex 1 is bright blue, and vertex 2 is bright red.

On the other end of the program, Prog_Done, simply do a safe release of all your DirectX objects, which you should be accustomed to by now.

Main Loop

The really sick part of this example is that the initialization takes longer than the main loop. I'm not kidding. Take a look:

```
void Prog_Loop()
{
        //set up the vertex positions
        vert[0].sx=cos(angle)*240.0+320.0;
        vert[0].sy=sin(angle)*240.0+240.0;
        vert[1].sx=cos(angle+2*PI/3)*240.0+320.0;
        vert[1].sy=sin(angle+2*PI/3)*240.0+240.0;
        vert[2].sx=cos(angle-2*PI/3)*240.0+320.0;
        vert[2].sy=sin(angle-2*PI/3)*240.0+240.0;
        //add to the angle for next time
        angle+=PI/180;
```

These six lines calculate the sx and sy values for each of the vertices based on the value of the global variable angle. If you aren't familiar with trigonometry, don't worry about it, because this is the only time I use it in this book, and only to make the nacho spin.

After the vertex positions are calculated, the angle is increased by pi/180, which is the same as turning the triangle 1 degree.

```
        //clear the viewport to black
        lpd3ddev->Clear(0,NULL,D3DCLEAR_TARGET,0,0,0);
        //start the scene
        lpd3ddev->BeginScene();
```

Next, clear out the entire viewport and tell D3D you are ready to begin the scene.

```
        //draw the triangle
        lpd3ddev->DrawPrimitive(D3DPT_TRIANGLELIST,
                D3DFVF_TLVERTEX,vert,3,0);
```

After all that setup and all those calculations, the entire functionality of this program boils down to this single line, a DrawPrimitive call. This is what draws the triangle on the screen. All the rest just sets everything up so that you can do so.

```
        //end the scene
        lpd3ddev->EndScene();
        //flip
        lpddsPrime->Flip(NULL,DDFLIP_WAIT);
}
```

Finally, end the scene, and flip so that the back buffer is now visible. Then return so that you can process input and draw another frame.

You're probably disappointed, I know. Direct3D should be so much more complicated than what I've just shown you. Actually, it *is* more complicated. You're just using a limited subset with no 3D math involved. However, even if you included everything else in Direct3D, you're still just drawing triangles.

This wraps up the Direct3D basics. If you can draw one triangle, you can draw a billion of them. I have a bit more to cover in Direct3D, because colored triangles won't get you where you need to go. What you need is a way to do textures, and then you're good to go for ISO 3D.

Textures

Nifty colored triangles are neat, and they are the basis of all other 3D graphics, but you want more, right? You want the ability to place images on the screen much as you did in DirectDraw, while making use of the hardware acceleration you can get from Direct3D.

Of course, you can still use DirectDraw's `Blt` to copy rectangles from surface to surface, much as you have been doing all along. After all, these are still just surfaces, at least in DirectX7.0 (this isn't so in DirectX8.0, which has no `Blt` to speak of).

The other road you can take is to use textures. After all, the rectangles you've been blitting throughout this book are nothing more than two triangles with a common line between them.

What Is a Texture?

In DirectX 7.0, a texture is just a special kind of surface. It has the capabilities of `DDSCAPS_TEXTURE` to indicate that it is a texture surface, and the width and height each have to be a power of 2, although they need not be the same power of 2. With that in mind, 64×64, 128×64, 64×128, and 128×128 are all valid measurements for a texture, whereas something like 65×21 is not.

Depending on hardware, support for nonsquare textures (like 128×64) can be limited to allow only a single power difference (so, 128×64 is allowed, but 128×32 is not). Also, a texture's maximum size is limited by hardware, but just about all hardware supports sizes up to 256×256, which is more than sufficient for your needs.

For maximum compatibility, you need to follow a few rules. First, always use a square texture. Second, don't use a texture greater than 256×256. Third, use only a single texture at a time.

The "single texture at a time" rule exists because some cards support multitexturing—that is, combining up to eight textures on a single polygon (triangle). Many cards still do not support this, so you'll use just a single texture at any given time. You don't really need multitexturing anyway.

This is how you create a texture:

```
//lpdd is a pointer to an IDirectDraw7 object
//lpddsTex is a LPDIRECTDRAWSURFACE7 variable
//TEXTUREWIDTH and TEXTUREHEIGHT specify the size of the texture
DDSURFACEDESC2 ddsd;
memset(&ddsd,0,sizeof(DDSURFACEDESC2));
ddsd.dwSize=sizeof(DDSURFACEDESC2);
ddsd.dwFlags=DDSD_WIDTH | DDSD_HEIGHT | DDSD_CAPS;
ddsd.dwWidth=TEXTUREWIDTH;
ddsd.dwHeight=TEXTUREHEIGHT;
ddsd.ddsCaps.dwCaps=DDSCAPS_TEXTURE;
lpdd->CreateSurface(&ddsd,&lpddsTex,NULL);//create the surface
```

It's just like creating an off-screen surface, with the exception of the size requirements and the `DDSCAPS_TEXTURE` instead of `DDSCAPS_OFFSCREENPLAIN`.

Texture Mapping and Texture Coordinates

After you've created a texture, your next task is using it. In order to use it, you must first know something about how texture mapping works, at least on a conceptual level, and you must be able to specify texture coordinates.

If you think back to Chapter 20, "Isometric Art," when you did tile slanting, it was very much like texture mapping. You took a square texture and stretched and slanted it into a rhombus shape. This is not true texture mapping, but it has similarities.

You don't have to go into the intricacies of how texture mapping works on a pixel-by-pixel level. That part has been done for you by the people who programmed Direct3D. You just have to know what information to send Direct3D so that it all comes out looking right. Figure 24.5 shows a texture and a texture-mapped polygon. The texture (on the left) shows its four corners with the coordinates that correspond to them. Likewise, the polygon (on the right) has its four corners (vertices) marked with their coordinates (no actual numbers, of course). Table 24.8 shows how the texture's coordinates correspond to the vertices.

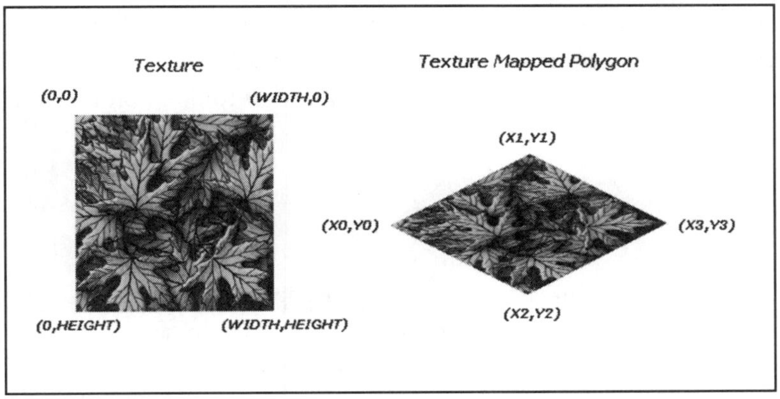

Figure 24.5

A texture and a texture-mapped polygon

Table 24.8 Texture Coordinates to Vertices

Texture Coordinate	Vertex Coordinate
`(0,0)`	`(X0,Y0)`
`(WIDTH,0)`	`(X1,Y1)`
`(0,HEIGHT)`	`(X2,Y2)`
`(WIDTH,HEIGHT)`	`(X3,Y3)`

Based on these coordinate matchups, you can do a whole lot of linear algebra and figure out that a particular pixel in a particular polygon matches up with such-and-such a pixel within the texture. Or, you can just rely on Direct3D to do it for you. That is Direct3D's entire purpose—to make fancy triangles.

However, you have to take it just one small step further, since texture coordinates are not specified between 0 and `WIDTH` and 0 and `HEIGHT`, but rather in the range of 0.0 to 1.0, where 0.0 corresponds to the 0 coordinate on the texture surface (duh!) and 1.0 corresponds to `WIDTH` (or `HEIGHT`, depending on the texture coordinate).

The horizontal coordinate is called U by Direct3D, and the vertical coordinate is called V. The reasons for these letters? X, Y, and Z were already taken, and W is for homogenous coordinates, so they decided to work their way backward through the alphabet. In other words, I don't really know, but that's my guess.

The various U and V coordinates are stored in the tu and tv members of D3DTLVERTEX. Pretty simple, eh? After setting up the appropriate texture coordinates for each vertex (there will be a lot more about this in Chapter 25, "The Much Anticipated ISO3D"), you have only one thing left to do in order to make use of your texture.

```
//set tells Direct3D what texture we wish to use
lpd3ddev->SetTexture(0,lpddsTex);
```

The first parameter of IDirect3DDevice::SetTexture is a number that specifies the texture stage. There are eight stages, numbered 0 through 7. You aren't multitexturing, so you only care about the first texture stage (0). After a call to SetTexture, rendering a texture-mapped triangle is as simple as a call to DrawPrimitive.

Texture Mapping Example

This example is called "The Spinning Texture-Mapped Saltine of Death" (see Figure 24.6), and other than a few lines, it is identical to IsoHex24_1.cpp. Following are the changes:

- There are four vertices instead of just three (hence a Saltine and not a nacho).
- The texture surface is created and is loaded with a texture.
- The vertices now have texture coordinates.
- Because you are rendering a square and not a triangle, the call to DrawPrimitive uses a triangle strip, not a triangle list.
- I changed the colors of the vertices to give the illusion that one corner is lit and the opposite corner is in shadow.

The changes are so minor I'm not even going to show the code, because I've already shown the snippets that do it. It would be like listing IsoHex24_1.cpp twice. Just be sure to take a look at the code before moving on to the next chapter, where you will use texture mapping (a lot).

Figure 24.6

IsoHex24_2.cpp output

Summary

One thing this chapter should demonstrate is that Direct3D is not nearly as hard as everyone makes it out. I admit, you haven't used a lot of its functionality, such as vectors, matrices, depth buffers, and lighting. You don't need all of those things where you're going. Already, you can render a textured square onto the screen (and rotate it to boot! Try doing *that* in DirectDraw), and that is the fundamental way in which you will be using Direct3D as a 2D renderer.

Indeed, once you strip down D3D to its bare functionality, it's not so intimidating at all. At the same time, it does a lot for you. The texture mapping is superb, and you have only two polygons per object, unlike a "real" 3D game, in which an object can consist of thousands of polygons.

Next up, we'll take the knowledge in this chapter and adapt it to the unique needs of an isometric game. I'll show you a few tricks, too, that'll make life a lot easier (for one thing, we're going to get rid of the MouseMap). The really good stuff, the stuff you've been waiting for, is next.

CHAPTER 25

The Much-Anticipated IsO3D

- D3DFuncs.h/D3DFuncs.cpp
- 2D Sprites Using Direct3D
- Tile Selection/Mousemapping

This is what you have been waiting for. Over hill and dale you've trudged through 2D isometric algorithms with the promise that using 3D was just around the corner. You have finally rounded that corner.

Using an API like Direct3D to do an isometric display is called "ISO3D" even though all of the drawing is still 2D-based. Such is life.

The first thing you'll do here is put together a group of functions in a header and cpp file, much like you did in DirectDraw with DDFuncs. Then we will discuss what changes occur when you move from a 2D API to a 3D API. All in all, it should be great fun.

D3DFuncs.h/D3DFuncs.cpp

Much as you have relied on DDFuncs.h/DDFuncs.cpp throughout most of the book, so shall you come to rely on D3DFuncs.h/D3DFuncs.cpp to help you create and manage the D3D pointers you will be using in this chapter. Table 25.1 lists the functions in the D3DFuncs minilibrary.

Table 25.1 Functions from D3DFuncs.h/cpp

Function	Purpose
LPD3D_Create	Creates an IDirect3D7 object using an LPDIRECT-DRAW7 pointer.
LPD3D_Release	Cleans up an IDirect3D7 object.
LPD3DDEV_Create	Creates an IDirect3DDevice7 object using an LPDIRECT3D7 pointer.
LPD3DDEV_SetViewport	Sets a viewport for an IDirect3DDevice7.
LPD3DDEV_Clear	Clears a viewport.
LPD3DDEV_DrawTriangleList	Draws a triangle list using a D3DTLVERTEX array/pointer.
LPD3DDEV_DrawTriangleStrip	Draws a triangle strip using a D3DTLVERTEX array/pointer.
LPD3DDEV_Release	Cleans up an IDirect3DDevice7.
LPDDS_CreatePrimary3D	Creates a primary surface that can be used as a 3D device's rendering target.
LPDDS_GetSecondary3D	Gets a back buffer that can be used as a 3D device's rendering target.
LPDDS_CreateTexture	Creates a texture surface.
LPDDS_CreateTexturePixelFormat	Creates a texture surface and specifies what pixel format it will have (more on this a bit later).
VERTEX_Set	Sets up the values in a D3DTLVERTEX.

This is a pretty sparse little library of functions, really, but if you look back, so was DDFuncs.h/DDFuncs.cpp, and you've done plenty of stuff using that simple little set of functions. And so shall it be with D3DFuncs.h/D3DFuncs.cpp.

LPD3D Functions

There are two of these. One creates the `IDirect3D7` object (`LPD3D_Create`), and the other cleans it up afterwards (`LPD3D_Release`).

```
//create the IDirect3D7 interface
LPDIRECT3D7 LPD3D_Create(LPDIRECTDRAW7 lpdd);
```

`LPD3D_Create` takes a single parameter (`lpdd`). It uses `QueryInterface` to call the proper interface to use for D3D stuff and then returns the newly gotten `LPDIRECT3D7` pointer. Typically, this function is called during `Prog_Init`.

```
//clean up an IDirect3D7
void LPD3D_Release(LPDIRECT3D7* lpd3d);
```

During `Prog_Done`, you need to clean up all the DirectX stuff you've used. To clean up the `LPDIRECT3D7` pointer, you need only call `LPD3D_Release` and send a pointer to the `LPDIRECT3D7` variable.

LPD3DDEV Functions

In spite of the many tasks that an `IDirect3DDevice7` object can be called on to do (and believe me, in a "normal" type of 3D program, there are plenty of diverse tasks), we are concerned with only six functions.

```
//create the device
LPDIRECT3DDEVICE7 LPD3DDEV_Create(LPDIRECT3D7 lpd3d,LPDIRECTDRAWSURFACE7 lpdds);
```

Naturally, after you've called `LPD3D_Create`, your next task (after creating the appropriate surfaces) is to create the 3D device itself. To do this, you call `LPD3DDEV_Create` and pass an `LPDIRECT3D7` pointer (used to create the device) and an `LPDIRECTDRAWSURFACE7` pointer (used as the rendering target). The return value is a pointer to the new device, which you can begin to use immediately. This function uses the "hack" method of creating a 3D device.

```
//set up the viewport
void LPD3DDEV_SetViewport(LPDIRECT3DDEVICE7 lpd3ddev,DWORD x,DWORD y,DWORD
width,DWORD height);
```

After your device is created, you need to set up the viewport parameters. Because you ignore the z-coordinate, you need only specify the upper-left corner (x and y) and the width and height of the viewport. This function returns no value but does fill in a `D3DVIEWPORT7` structure and sets the device to use that viewport.

```
//clear out the viewport
void LPD3DDEV_Clear(LPDIRECT3DDEVICE7 lpd3ddev,D3DCOLOR color);
```

I didn't bother making functions for BeginScene or EndScene, because these functions would take up more typing time than just calling them in the first place. However, since you are using only one part of the IDirect3DDevice7::Clear member function, and you're only interested in clearing out the entire viewport, making a special function for it seemed appropriate. Calling LPD3DDEV_Clear with the pointer to the device and a color causes the entire viewport to be filled with that color.

```
//draw triangle list
void LPD3DDEV_DrawTriangleList(LPDIRECT3DDEVICE7 lpd3ddev,D3DTLVERTEX* pver-
tices,DWORD dwvertexcount);
//draw triangle strip
void LPD3DDEV_DrawTriangleStrip(LPDIRECT3DDEVICE7 lpd3ddev,D3DTLVERTEX* pver-
tices,DWORD dwvertexcount);
```

These functions are so similar that I thought it best to discuss them together. The first draws a triangle list, and the second draws a triangle strip. They take as parameters a pointer to the device and a pointer to an array of D3DTLVERTEXs, along with a count of how many vertices are in the array. It's pretty simple, really, and it beats the heck out of typing D3DFVF_TLVERTEX every time you want to call DrawPrimitive.

```
//clean up a device
void LPD3DDEV_Release(LPDIRECT3DDEVICE7* lpd3ddev);
```

This is the ubiquitous "cleanup" function, much the same as all the other functions used to clean up the various components of DirectX. When you're done with a device, usually at the end of a program, call this function.

LPDDS Functions

Since there is a change in the way you have to set up surfaces to be rendering targets, I needed to add a couple of functions to create primary surfaces and back buffers. These two functions, described next, work about the same as their DDFuncs.h/DDFuncs.cpp versions, just with a "3D" appended to the end.

```
//primary surface as a 3D rendering target
LPDIRECTDRAWSURFACE7 LPDDS_CreatePrimary3D(LPDIRECTDRAW7 lpdd,DWORD
dwBackBufferCount);
//back buffer as a 3D rendering target
LPDIRECTDRAWSURFACE7 LPDDS_GetSecondary3D(LPDIRECTDRAWSURFACE7 lpdds);
```

Now, instead of LPDDS_CreatePrimary, you use LPDDS_CreatePrimary3D, and instead of LPDDS_GetSecondary, you use LPDDS_GetSecondary3D. You still use LPDDS_Release to clean up at the end of the program, however.

Texture Functions

I've spoken only briefly about textures and texture surfaces. I'll talk about them a great deal more as this chapter progresses (since just about everything in ISO3D relies on the use of textures).

```
//create a texture
LPDIRECTDRAWSURFACE7 LPDDS_CreateTexture(LPDIRECTDRAW7 lpdd,DWORD dwWidth,DWORD
dwHeight);
//create a texture with a particular pixel format
LPDIRECTDRAWSURFACE7 LPDDS_CreateTexturePixelFormat(LPDIRECTDRAW7 lpdd,DWORD
dwWidth,DWORD dwHeight,LPDDPIXELFORMAT lpddpf);
```

These two functions are quite similar. The first, `LPDDS_CreateTexture`, creates a texture surface with the given width and height (remember, these must be powers of 2!) with the same pixel format as the primary surface. The second function allows you to supply a pixel format different from that of the primary surface. The reasons for having this function may not be clear now, but they will be soon; I didn't want to add to D3DFuncs.h/D3DFuncs.cpp in the middle of the chapter.

Vector Function

This is just a single function, but it is pretty important and will save you a great deal of work.

```
//set vertex data
void VERTEX_Set(D3DTLVERTEX* pVert,D3DVALUE x,D3DVALUE y, D3DCOLOR color, D3DVAL-
UE tu, D3DVALUE tv);
```

`VERTEX_Set` allows you to fill out a `D3DTLVERTEX` structure without having to type the variable name a billion times. Instead, you can do this concisely in a single line.

The D3D Shell Application

If you load IsoHex25_1.cpp you'll see all the basic functionality necessary for a D3D application. I admit, the program doesn't really *do* anything, but it definitely sets you up nicely so that you *can* start doing things.

The applications in this chapter rely on IsoHex25_1.cpp as the code base.

Plotting Tiles in ISO3D

Naturally, the first thing you'll want to be able to do is plot tiles, just as you did in 2D. To do so, you need an isometric plotting equation (any one will do), some vertices, and some textures.

Figure 25.1 shows a standard isometric tile with some coordinates. In ISO3D, you will base everything on the middle of the tile, just to make things easy. If you're like me, you like things easy (please try not to read anything into that).

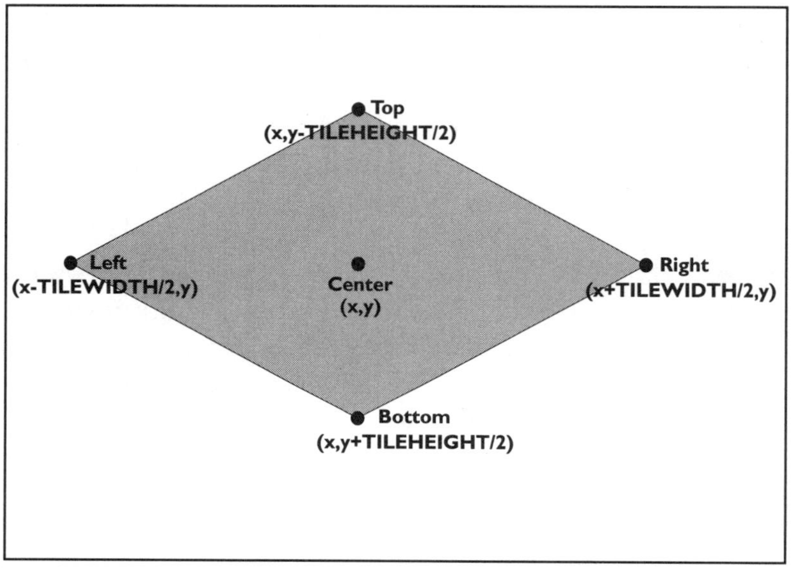

Figure 25.1

A standard isometric tile with coordinates

So, you have a four-pointed figure, but D3D draws only triangles. Luckily, this four-pointed figure splits nicely into two triangles, as shown in Figure 25.2. The vertices are numbered V1 through V4 and are in order of how you must make a triangle strip out of them. Poly1 (really, TRIANGLE 1) is defined by V1 through V3, and Poly2 is defined by V2 through V4.

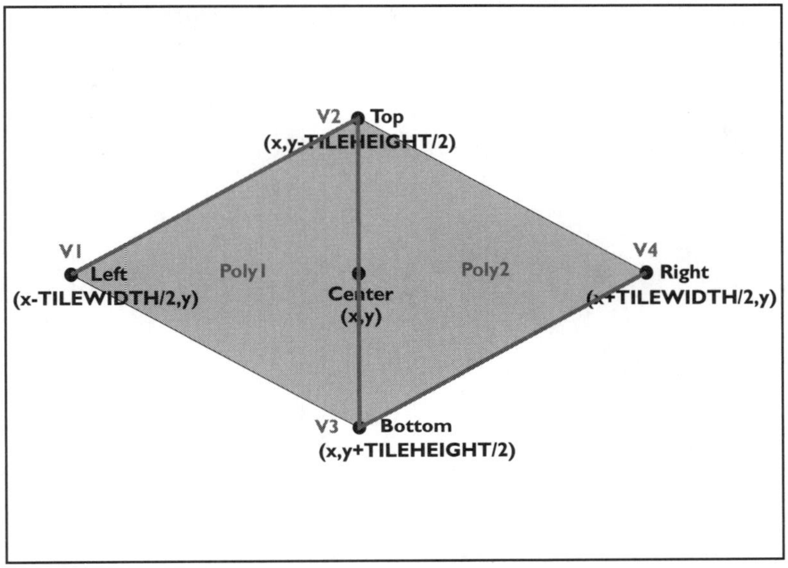

Figure 25.2

An isometric tile split into triangles

Using an isometric plotting equation (for example, for staggered maps), filling out an array of vertices is quite easy.

```
//mapx,mapy are map coordinates
//TILEWIDTH and TILEHEIGHT are dimensions of a tile
//vert is an array of D3DTLVERTEX
//calculate center point (staggered calculation)
D3DVALUE CenterX=(float)((mapx*TILEWIDTH)+(mapy&1)*(TILEWIDTH/2));
D3DVALUE CenterY=(float)(mapy*(TILEHEIGHT/2));
//v1
VERTEX_Set(&vert[0],CenterX-TILEWIDTH/2,CenterY,D3DRGB(1.0,1.0,1.0),0.0,0.0);
//v2
VERTEX_Set(&vert[1],CenterX,CenterY-TILEHEIGHT/2,D3DRGB(1.0,1.0,1.0),0.0,0.0);
//v3
VERTEX_Set(&vert[0],CenterX,CenterY+TILEHEIGHT/2,D3DRGB(1.0,1.0,1.0),0.0,0.0);
//v4
VERTEX_Set(&vert[0],CenterX+TILEWIDTH/2,CenterY,D3DRGB(1.0,1.0,1.0),0.0,0.0);
```

With this code, you could then progress to a call to `LPD3DDEV_DrawTriangleStrip`, and you would see a white isometric tile (since you have no texture yet).

But that's not quite good enough. You want a textured isometric tile, which means you need texture coordinates and a suitable texture. Figure 25.3 has a possible set of texture coordinates for your tile. This is not the only configuration, of course. Also, it assumes you are using the entire texture, which you most likely will.

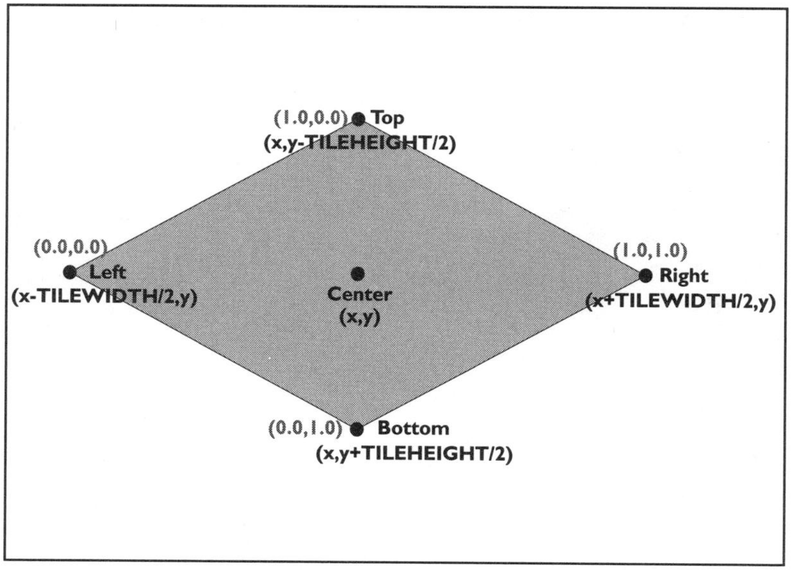

Figure 25.3

Texture coordinates for an isometric tile

With the addition of texture coordinates, your code for loading a triangle strip becomes as follows:

```
//mapx,mapy are map coordinates
//TILEWIDTH and TILEHEIGHT are dimensions of a tile
//vert is an array of D3DTLVERTEX
//calculate center point (staggered calculation)
D3DVALUE CenterX=(float)((mapx*TILEWIDTH)+(mapy&1)*(TILEWIDTH/2));
D3DVALUE CenterY=(float)(mapy*(TILEHEIGHT/2));
//v1
VERTEX_Set(&vert[0],CenterX-TILEWIDTH/2,CenterY,D3DRGB(1.0,1.0,1.0),0.0,0.0);
//v2
VERTEX_Set(&vert[1],CenterX,CenterY-TILEHEIGHT/2,D3DRGB(1.0,1.0,1.0),1.0,0.0);
//v3
VERTEX_Set(&vert[0],CenterX,CenterY+TILEHEIGHT/2,D3DRGB(1.0,1.0,1.0),0.0,1.0);
//v4
VERTEX_Set(&vert[0],CenterX+TILEWIDTH/2,CenterY,D3DRGB(1.0,1.0,1.0),1.0,1.0);
```

After this, you would set the texture and draw the triangle strip. This isn't as hard or as daunting as it might have seemed. So, let's do it!

Go ahead and load IsoHex25_2.cpp. In this example, I use almost line-for-line the earlier code for setting vertices, and I added a line for drawing the triangle strip. This is what the `Prog_Loop` function looks like:

```
void Prog_Loop()
{
	//clear the viewport to black
	lpd3ddev->Clear(0,NULL,D3DCLEAR_TARGET,0,0,0);
	//start the scene
	lpd3ddev->BeginScene();
	//center positions
	D3DVALUE CenterX,CenterY;
	//loop through map
	for(int y=0;y<MAPHEIGHT;y++)
	{
		for(int x=0;x<MAPWIDTH;x++)
		{
			//calculate world coordinates for center of tile
			CenterX=(float)(x*TILEWIDTH+(y&1)*(TILEWIDTH/2));
			CenterY=(float)(y*(TILEHEIGHT/2));
			//set up the vertex
			//v1
			VERTEX_Set(&vert[0],CenterX-TILEWIDTH/2,
				CenterY,D3DRGB(1.0,1.0,1.0),0.0,0.0);
			//v2
			VERTEX_Set(&vert[1],CenterX,
				CenterY-TILEHEIGHT/2,D3DRGB(1.0,1.0,1.0),1.0,0.0);
			//v3
			VERTEX_Set(&vert[2],CenterX,
				CenterY+TILEHEIGHT/2,D3DRGB(1.0,1.0,1.0),0.0,1.0);
			//v4
			VERTEX_Set(&vert[3],CenterX+TILEWIDTH/2,
				CenterY,D3DRGB(1.0,1.0,1.0),1.0,1.0);
			//render the triangle strip
			LPD3DDEV_DrawTriangleStrip(lpd3ddev,vert,4);
		}
	}
	//end the scene
	lpd3ddev->EndScene();
	//flip
	lpddsPrime->Flip(NULL,DDFLIP_WAIT);
}
```

As you can see, this is the same as the preceding code, just nested within two loops. If you take a look at texture.bmp (the graphic for this example), you will find that it is a 128×128 bitmap, and yet D3D does a marvelous job of shrinking and rotating it into your isometric tile shape.

With this example in mind, it is easy enough to extend it to allow for more than one type of tile. You would simply make an array of texture surfaces and set the device to use the appropriate one for each tile.

2D Sprites Using Direct3D

Although it would be nice if every graphic in your game were the same size and shape as an isometric tile, unfortunately this is just not the case. Your units, objects, trees, mountains, roads, and so on are oddly shaped, so you need to do the 3D equivalent of a color key in order for everything to look right.

Direct3D does have some support for the type of color keys you have used in your 2D programs. However, using this support is not suggested. I was reading a newsgroup post about it, and the answerer (whose name eludes me) said there are other ways to do it.

At the time, I didn't know what the "other ways" were, but knowing that I would have to use a technique for doing this, and also tell others how to do it, and not wanting to do it "the wrong way," I asked around.

A friend of mine told me what I had to do. It's a little bizarre, but not too hard. In order to do it, you have to use some of Direct3D's alpha functionality. If you haven't heard of alpha before, don't worry about it too much. It is used to blend colors to make objects look partially transparent (translucent) for things like ghosts, pieces of glass, and water. In addition, it can be used to simulate a color key.

In order to make use of this functionality, you must make a texture that has alpha information. You don't need a whole lot of alpha information (just a single bit will suffice), but you do need some. In 16bpp mode, with the normal format being 5:6:5 for RGB, giving up a bunch of bits for alpha is the last thing you want to do. Luckily, most graphics cards support a 1:5:5:5 ARGB format, so you have to give up only 1 bit of green.

Enumerating Texture Formats

So, how do you figure out what texture formats are available to use? You use `IDirect3DDevice7::EnumTextureFormats` and a callback function.

```
HRESULT IDirect3DDevice7::EnumTextureFormats(
  LPD3DENUMPIXELFORMATSCALLBACK lpd3dEnumPixelProc,
  LPVOID lpArg
);
```

This function returns an `HRESULT`, which is `D3D_OK` if successful and some `D3DERR_*` value if it fails. The first parameter is the address of your callback function (which I will get to in a moment), and the second parameter (`lpArg`) is a pointer used to retrieve information from the callback.

TEXTURE FORMAT CALLBACK

In order to make use of `IDirect3DDevice7::EnumTextureFormats`, you must create a callback for it to use. Because you are simply looking for a format with alpha information, retrieving this information is quite easy. Here's an example of what a texture format callback function looks like:

```
HRESULT CALLBACK D3DEnumPixelFormatsCallback(
  LPDDPIXELFORMAT lpDDPixFmt,
  LPVOID          lpContext
);
```

You can name the function whatever you want, actually. It returns an `HRESULT`, which is `D3DENUMRET_OK` if you want to continue enumerating, or `D3DENUMRET_CANCEL` if you want enumeration to end. After you've found what you're looking for, you don't need to enumerate any further. The first parameter is a pointer to a `DDPIXELFORMAT`, which contains the various masks for red, blue, green, and alpha. The second parameter, `lpContext`, is the same pointer you send to `EnumTextureFormats` in the `lpArg parameter`.

This is the texture format callback you'll be using:

```
HRESULT CALLBACK TextureFormatCallback(LPDDPIXELFORMAT lpDDPF,LPVOID lpContext)
{
      //check the alpha bitmask of the pixel format
      if(lpDDPF->dwRGBAlphaBitMask)
      {
            //alpha
            //copy to context
            memcpy(lpContext,lpDDPF,sizeof(DDPIXELFORMAT));
            //stop enumeration
            return(D3DENUMRET_CANCEL);
      }
      //no alpha found
      //continue enumeration
      return(D3DENUMRET_OK);
}
```

In the case of this callback, you aren't being picky about the pixel format. It just has to have alpha in it, and you'll take the first one. It copies the `DDPIXELFORMAT` information into the context pointer, so you need to send a `DDPIXELFORMAT` pointer to the enumeration function, like so:

```
//enumerate texture formats
DDPIXELFORMAT ddpf;
memset(&ddpf,0,sizeof(DDPIXELFORMAT);
lpd3ddev->EnumTextureFormats(TextureFormatCallback,&ddpf);
```

```
//check if we found a texture format with alpha in it
if(ddpf.dwSize==0)
{
      //no texture format with alpha
}
```

What do you do if there is no texture format with an alpha in it? Well, there isn't much you can do, but I don't think this issue will come up, so don't worry about it.

Creating the Texture Surface

The next step is to create the texture surface using the `LPDDS_CreateTexturePixelFormat` function from D3DFuncs.h/D3DFuncs.cpp.

```
//create a 64x64 texture surface
lpddsTex=LPDDS_CreateTexturePixelFormat(lpdd,64,64,&ddpf);
```

Now you've got the new texture surface, and the only thing left is to fill it with the graphical information from a bitmap.

Lock and Unlock Review

Unfortunately, using `GetDC` and `ReleaseDC` won't work in this case (I've tried). Apparently GDI doesn't like alpha, so this time, you have to do it manually, which means you have to use `IDirectDrawSurface7::Lock` and `IDirectDrawSurface7::Unlock`. We covered these earlier in the book, but here's a quick refresher.

```
HRESULT IDirectDrawSurface7::Lock(
  LPRECT lpDestRect,
  LPDDSURFACEDESC2 lpDDSurfaceDesc,
  DWORD dwFlags,
  HANDLE hEvent
);
```

The return value, as with almost all DirectX function calls, is an `HRESULT`, which returns `DD_OK` if successful or some `DDERR_*` value if it fails.

Of the parameters, `lpDestRect` is a pointer to a `RECT` that describes the area you are locking. If you want to lock the entire surface (and that is what you will do), use `NULL` in this parameter. `lpDDSurfaceDesc` is a pointer to a `DDSURFACEDESC2`, which you send in to retrieve the locking information. `dwFlags` tells DirectDraw exactly how you want to lock the surface. `hEvent` isn't supported, so put `NULL`.

```
HRESULT IDirectDrawSurface7::Unlock(
  LPRECT lpRect
);
```

Unlock is a lot simpler than Lock. The return value is an HRESULT again, so check for DD_OK. The lpRect parameter is a pointer to the RECT you want to unlock. The RECT has to be the same as the RECT you used to lock, so if you use NULL to lock, use NULL to unlock.

Now that your memory has been refreshed on Lock/Unlock, let's explore how you'll use them to write to your surface. Here is the basic breakdown of the code, minus the actual writing of the pixels:

```
//set up the surface desc
DDSURFACEDESC2 ddsd;
DDSD_Clear(&ddsd);
//lock the surface (lpddsTex is the texture surface)
lpddsTex->Lock(NULL,&ddsd,DDLOCK_WAIT,NULL);
//retrieve the pitch and the pointer to surface memory
LONG lPitch=ddsd.lPitch/sizeof(WORD);
WORD* pSurface=(WORD*)ddsd.lpSurface;
////////////////////////////////
//do whatever drawing here
////////////////////////////////
//unlock surface
lpddsTex->Unlock(NULL);
```

A brief note about lPitch and pSurface: these correspond to the lPitch and lpSurface members of DDSURFACEDESC2, and they let you write directly to a surface's memory buffer. pSurface is the pointer itself, and it's a void*, because Lock works on all manner of surfaces, which might have different bits per pixel. lPitch is the length of a scan line, in bytes. It might or might not be the actual width of the surface, so always use lPitch instead of the width.

You'll notice that I cast pSurface to WORD* (WORD is the same as unsigned short). I did so because you are primarily working in 16-bit color, and a WORD has 16 bits, which makes it really easy to use pSurface as an array.

I also divided lPitch by sizeof(WORD) (which is 2) so that lPitch now measures the size of a horizontal row of pixels in WORDs rather than bytes. This has some important ramifications. For example, this is how to read and write a pixel:

```
//read pixel
WORD pel=pSurface[x+y*lPitch];//retrieve pixel at x,y
//write pixel
pSurface[x+y*lPitch]=0;//set pixel at x,y to 0 (black)
```

Pretty simple, right? Now you can read and write pixels on the lowest level DirectX allows, and you can now load your image onto a texture surface, even with the alpha information.

Loading Pixel Data

You will load pixel data by loading the image into a `CGDICanvas` object (which you can't `BitBlt` directly, but it's good at loading graphics anyway), determining which color to use as the transparent color (black is easiest), locking the surface, and converting the pixels in the `GDICanvas` to the format of the surface using `ConvertColorRef` from DDFuncs. You have to add just a little bit of code, because of the alpha information.

Therefore, the code for converting information on a `CGDICanvas` onto a texture surface looks something like the following:

```
//variables
COLORREF crColor;
COLORREF crTransparent;
int x,y;
DWORD ddColor;
CGDICanvas gdic;
//load the image
gdic.load("texture.bmp");
for(y=0;y<TEXHEIGHT;y++)
{
	for(x=0;x<TEXWIDTH;x++)
	{
		//grab color
		crColor=GetPixel(gdic,x,y);
		//convert color
		ddColor=ConvertColorRef(crColor,&ddpf);
		//check for transparency
		if(crColor!=crTransparent)
		{
			//add non-transparent alpha value
			ddColor|=ddpf.dwRGBAlphaBitMask;
		}
		//set pixel on surface
		pSurface[x+y*lPitch]=(WORD)ddColor;
	}
}
```

Place this code (or something very similar) between the surface's Lock and Unlock. The texture will be properly loaded onto the surface, and you will be nearly ready to start rendering it.

Render States

You have one last stop to make before you actually can do transparency in D3D, and that is letting Direct3D know what you are doing—namely, that you want to use its alpha testing capabilities. For you to do so I must introduce a new method of IDirect3DDevice7—SetRenderState.

```
HRESULT IDirect3DDevice7::SetRenderState(
  D3DRENDERSTATETYPE dwRenderStateType,
  DWORD dwRenderState
);
```

This function returns D3D_OK on success and D3DERR_* values on failure. dwRenderStateType specifies which render state you want to set, and dwRenderState specifies what you want to change the render state to. Confused? I'm not surprised. It's a pretty vague explanation for a pretty vague concept.

Direct3D is a state machine, which is sort of like being a big struct with a whole bunch of members, where the value to which any of these members are set changes the way in which it operates. For example, one member might control what type of lighting or shading to use, or whether to use shading at all. This is what render states are—just little values stored who-knows-where that affect the behavior of Direct3D.

Up until now, you've been using the default values of all the render states. This was fine for what you were doing, but it's no longer sufficient, because you want to make use of alpha stuff as transparency. You need to change three render states: D3DRENDERSTATE_ALPHATESTENABLE, D3DRENDERSTATE_ALPHAREF, and D3DRENDERSTATE_ALPHAFUNC.

The first, D3DRENDERSTATE_ALPHATESTENABLE, is a BOOL that specifies whether or not alpha testing is used. The default value is FALSE, so you must set it to TRUE. Make sure you use capital letters, since the BOOL is not the same as bool.

Next, D3DRENDERSTATE_ALPHAREF contains a reference alpha value (from 0 to 0xFF) against which you will be testing the texture's alpha values. To this render state, you will assign 0x7F. This value is of particular importance because of the 1:5:5:5 format, which has only a single bit for alpha. If the alpha bit is 0, the actual alpha (in the 0 to 0xFF range) is 0. If the alpha bit is 1, the actual alpha is 0x80, which is greater than your alpha test value.

Last, D3DRENDERSTATE_ALPHAFUNC needs an enumerated type called D3DCMP, which contains values like D3DCMP_NEVER, D3DCMP_ALWAYS, and D3DCMP_GREATER. The default value is D3DCMP_ALWAYS, so you need to change it to D3DCMP_GREATER.

The following is the code to set all your render states for alpha testing:

```
lpd3ddev->SetRenderState(D3DRENDERSTATE_ALPHATESTENABLE,TRUE);
lpd3ddev->SetRenderState(D3DRENDERSTATE_ALPHAREF,0x7F);
lpd3ddev->SetRenderState(D3DRENDERSTATE_ALPHAFUNC,D3DCMP_GREATER);
```

With the render states set, Direct3D is ready for your alpha test rendering. Now just supply a triangle strip with the proper vertices and set `IDirect3DDevice7`'s texture, and you can blit a partially transparent sprite, just like you did in DirectDraw (except that using Direct3D is a ton faster).

Setting Up Vertices

Since you are basing the rendering of a tile on its center, you want to be able to do something similar for your sprites—that is, you want to have anchors of a sort. Figure 25.4 shows the basic layout of the bounding rectangle. You can easily supply this information within the image itself by adding an extra column on the right and an extra row on the bottom and placing some sort of control pixel for centering there, just as you did for `CTileSet`. When rendering, you use the entire texture, so there is no need to have the width and height indicated with these control pixels. Figure 25.5 shows what I mean.

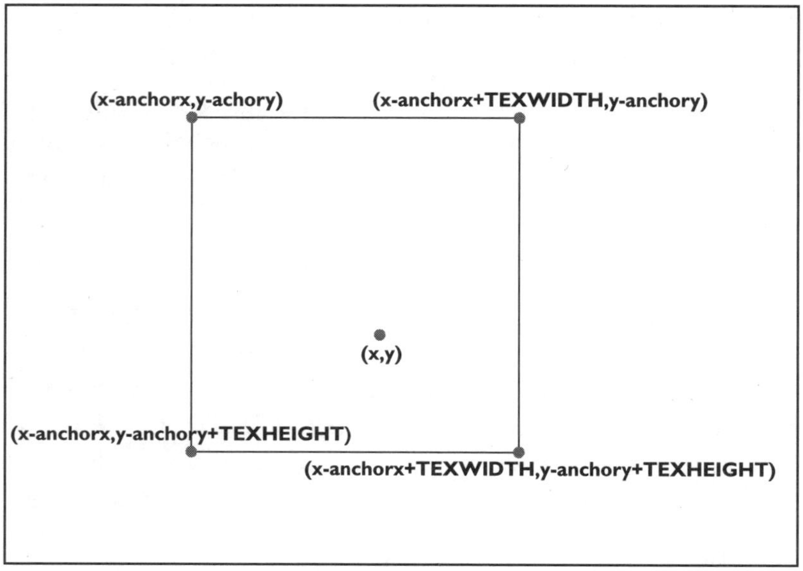

Figure 25.4

Vertex information for a sprite

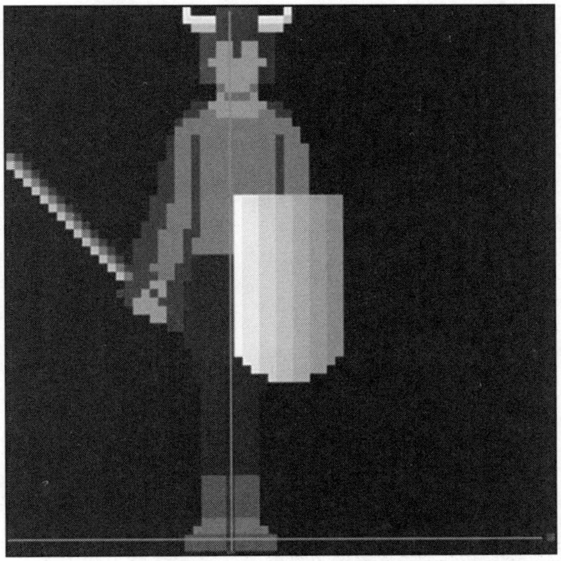

Figure 25.5

Anchor information for sprite

Figure 25.6 shows the four vertices and two polygons that make up the triangle strip needed to make up the sprite, and Figure 25.7 shows the texture coordinates corresponding to these points. You will use all this information to display the sprite on-screen.

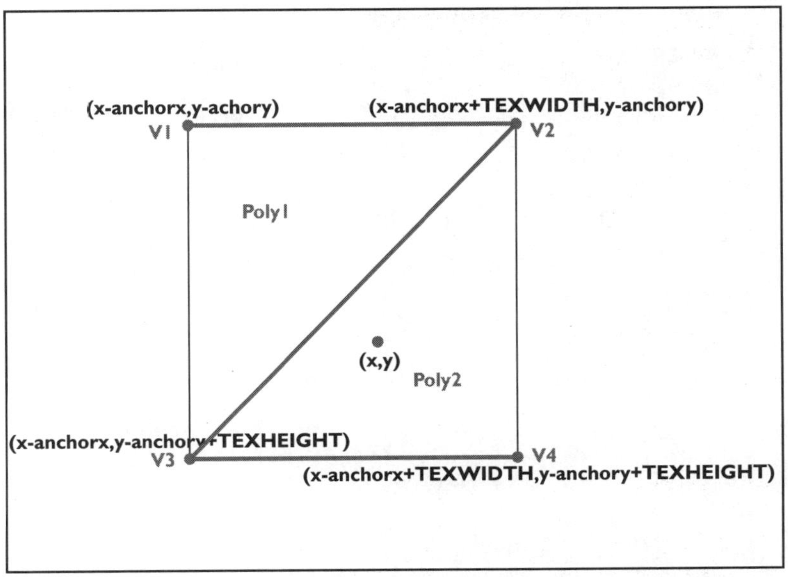

Figure 25.6

Triangle strip for a sprite

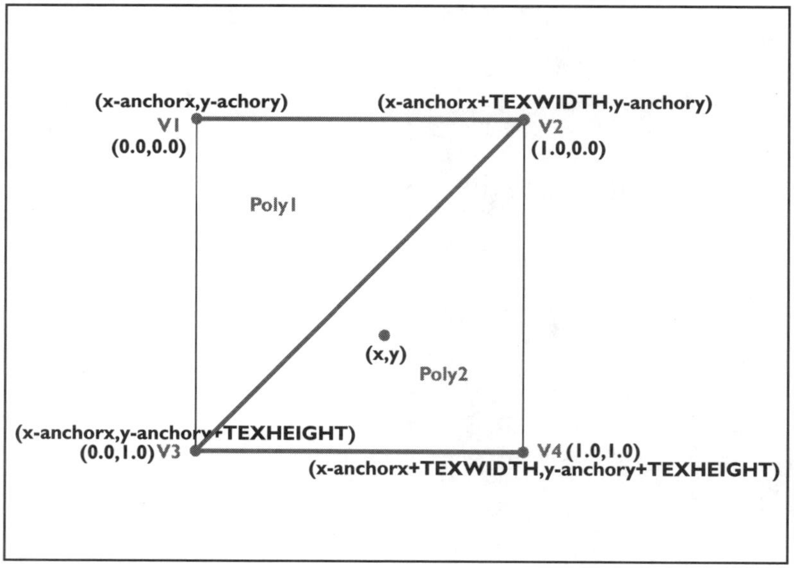

Figure 25.7

Texture coordinates for a sprite

3D Transparency Example

IsoHex25_3.cpp is the 3D transparency sample program (see Figure 25.8). It is based on IsoHex25_2.cpp, with the addition of some code that loads a sprite texture and shows a scene of isometric tiles with the sprite in the center of the screen, so you can see that it is indeed a partially transparent texture. All of the code in this example has been shown before, so I won't repeat it here.

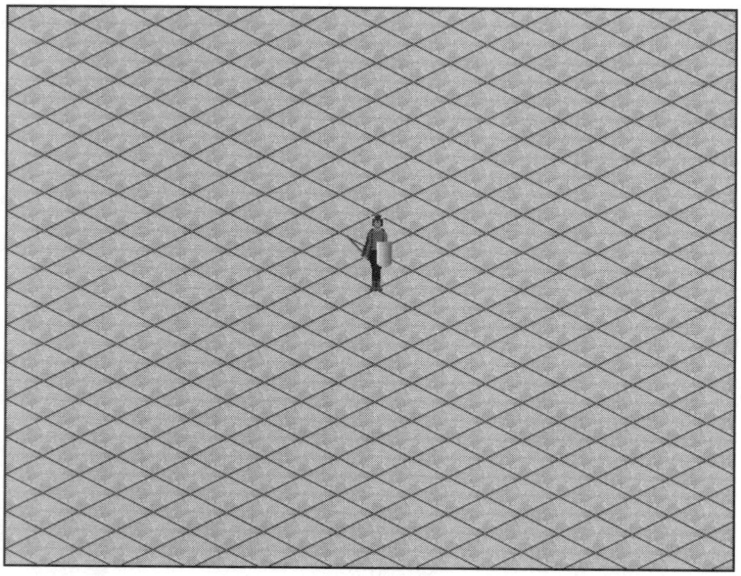

Figure 25.8

IsoHex25_3.cpp, the 3D transparency sample program.

Now you have the ability to do in Direct3D all that you have done in DirectDraw. You can blit tiles and sprites. In DirectDraw, you would have been totally happy with just this. However, this is 3D, and there are a lot more options available to you now, and you have a new set of difficulties to overcome.

DYNAMIC LIGHTING

One feature you can add to something rendered with Direct3D is dynamic lighting. You won't actually be using the Direct3D lighting mechanism (you'll be doing it yourself), but since you can change the colors of a vertex and have portions of a texture appear brighter or dimmer, you can certainly do some cool "lighting" effects.

The only thing you need to change is the color of the vertex, so in your calls to `VERTEX_Set`, you can just vary the intensity of the color attributes. Go ahead and load IsoHex25_4.cpp. This example is based on IsoHex25_2.cpp, with only minor modifications to `Prog_Loop`.

```
void Prog_Loop()
{
        //clear the viewport to black
        lpd3ddev->Clear(0,NULL,D3DCLEAR_TARGET,0,0,0);
        //grab the mouse position
        POINT ptMouse;
        GetCursorPos(&ptMouse);
        //convert mouse position to floating point values
        D3DVALUE MouseX=(D3DVALUE)ptMouse.x;
        D3DVALUE MouseY=(D3DVALUE)ptMouse.y;
```

The area around the mouse pointer will appear lit up compared to the rest of the screen. In order to make that happen, though, I first needed the mouse position—hence the call to `GetCursorPos`. Since D3D deals with floating-point values, I converted the mouse position into `D3DVALUE`'s `MouseX` and `MouseY`.

```
        //declare vector x and y for lighting calculations
        D3DVALUE VertexX;
        D3DVALUE VertexY;
        //distance
        float distance;
        //start the scene
        lpd3ddev->BeginScene();
```

Also, I'm using a few extra variables for lighting calculations. The calculations are based on the distance of a vertex from the mouse. `VertexX` and `VertexY` contain the coordinate of the vertex, and `distance` is used to calculate the distance (in pixels) from the mouse pointer to the vertex.

```
//center positions
D3DVALUE CenterX,CenterY;
//loop through map
for(int y=0;y<MAPHEIGHT;y++)
{
        for(int x=0;x<MAPWIDTH;x++)
        {
                //calculate world coordinates for center of tile
                CenterX=(float)(x*TILEWIDTH+(y&1)*(TILEWIDTH/2));
                CenterY=(float)(y*(TILEHEIGHT/2));
```

This is the normal stuff that plots the tiles using the staggered plotting equation. It doesn't change a bit.

```
                //set up the vertex
                //v1
                VERTEX_Set(&vert[0],CenterX-TILEWIDTH/2,
                        CenterY,D3DRGB(1.0,1.0,1.0),0.0,0.0);
                //distance calculation
                VertexX=vert[0].sx;
                VertexY=vert[0].sy;
                distance=sqrt((VertexX-MouseX)*(VertexX-MouseX)+
                        (VertexY-MouseY)*(VertexY-MouseY))+1.0;
                //max distance of 128
                if(distance>128.0) distance=128.0;
                //convert distance to 0.0 to 0.5
                distance/=256.0;
                //change color
                vert[0].color=D3DRGB(1.0-distance,1.0-distance,1.0-distance);
```

And here's the lighting calculation for the first vertex. First grab the x- and y-coordinates of `vert[0]`, and then do the distance calculation with the mouse position. Next, make sure that you clamp the distance to a maximum value (in this case, I picked 128 as the maximum distance). So, a vertex can have a "distance" of anywhere between 0.0 and 128.0 from the mouse. Next, convert this number to a number between 0.0 and 0.5 by dividing by 256. Since you specify color as being between 0.0 and 1.0, this is necessary if you intend to use some sort of lighting. Finally, set the color of the vertex, all components set to `1.0-distance`, so that a vertex at distance 0 will have a color of `D3DRGB(1.0,1.0,1.0)`, or pure white, and a vertex at or beyond the maximum distance will be at `D3DRGB(0.5,0.5,0.5)`, or dark gray.

```
                //v2
                VERTEX_Set(&vert[1],CenterX,
                        CenterY-TILEHEIGHT/2,D3DRGB(1.0,1.0,1.0),1.0,0.0);
```

```
//distance calculation
VertexX=vert[1].sx;
VertexY=vert[1].sy;
distance=sqrt((VertexX-MouseX)*(VertexX-MouseX)+
      (VertexY-MouseY)*(VertexY-MouseY))+1.0;
//max distance of 128
if(distance>128.0) distance=128.0;
//convert distance to 0.0 to 0.5
distance/=256.0;
//change color
vert[1].color=D3DRGB(1.0-distance,1.0-distance,1.0-distance);
//v3
VERTEX_Set(&vert[2],CenterX,CenterY+TILEHEIGHT/2,
      D3DRGB(1.0,1.0,1.0),0.0,1.0);
//distance calculation
VertexX=vert[2].sx;
VertexY=vert[2].sy;
distance=sqrt((VertexX-MouseX)*(VertexX-MouseX)+
      (VertexY-MouseY)*(VertexY-MouseY))+1.0;
//max distance of 128
if(distance>128.0) distance=128.0;
//convert distance to 0.0 to 0.5
distance/=256.0;
//change color
vert[2].color=D3DRGB(1.0-distance,1.0-distance,1.0-distance);
//v4
VERTEX_Set(&vert[3],CenterX+TILEWIDTH/2,
      CenterY,D3DRGB(1.0,1.0,1.0),1.0,1.0);
//distance calculation
VertexX=vert[3].sx;
VertexY=vert[3].sy;
distance=sqrt((VertexX-MouseX)*(VertexX-MouseX)+
      (VertexY-MouseY)*(VertexY-MouseY));
//max distance of 128
if(distance>128.0) distance=128.0;
//convert distance to 0.0 to 0.5
distance/=256.0;
//change color
vert[3].color=D3DRGB(1.0-distance,1.0-distance,1.0-distance);
//render the triangle strip
LPD3DDEV_DrawTriangleStrip(lpd3ddev,vert,4);
```

```
                }
        }
        //end the scene
        lpd3ddev->EndScene();
        //flip
        lpddsPrime->Flip(NULL,DDFLIP_WAIT);
}
```

Do the same lighting calculations for the other vertices and then draw the triangle strip as normal. The end result looks like Figure 25.9. You can put a light just about anywhere, or even have multiple lights like this (perhaps torches or something). You can even vary their intensity to make them flicker, and get some really neat lighting effects. Don't be afraid to experiment.

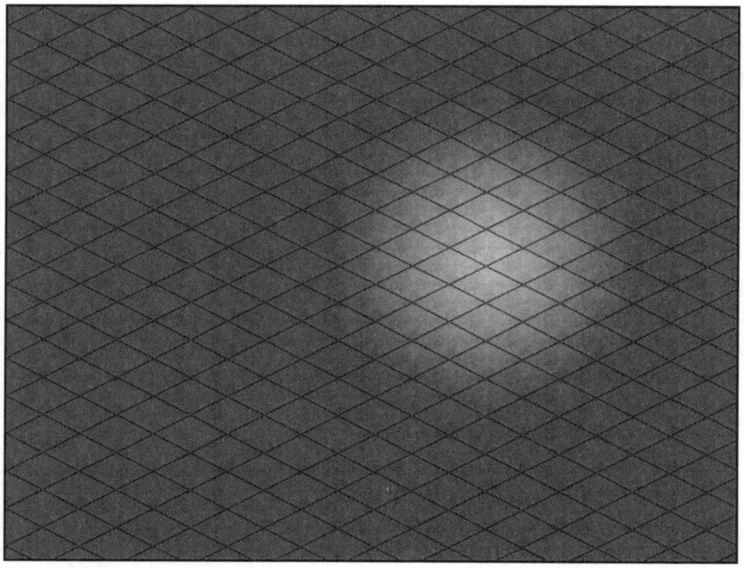

Figure 25.9

IsoHex25_4.cpp; some light is shed.

Height Mapping

In 2D, your isometric worlds have been horribly flat. Sure, there may be trees or units or other things that "stick up" out of the map, but the terrain itself is flat and boring.

Direct3D's entire job is to make things that look 3D. So, it's only fitting that you can use it to give your isometric maps an illusion of depth, even within an isometric projection. This method is called *height mapping*. It takes information from a grid of heights and applies it to the vertices of your tiles. In ISO3D, this is very easy, since "up" goes in the same direction as "north." For example, if a vertex is 32 pixels "up," you just subtract 32 from its y-coordinate. If it's 32 pixels down, you add 32 to y.

Of course, in order to make the height map look right, you need to make neighboring tiles share vertices with their neighbors. The easiest way to do so is to use a diamond map (since it is so similar to a rectangular grid) and place another grid on top of it that keeps track of the lines between the tiles and the intersections of those lines. If you're using another type of map, you just have to be more careful about keeping heights matched between tile vertices.

NOTE

A 20×20 diamond map has 21×21 lines, because there is an extra line at the end of the map as well as before each tile row/column.

Having said that, go ahead and load IsoHex25_5.cpp, shown in Figure 25.10. It is based on IsoHex25_2 and shows a random height map. This example combines a small amount of lighting (higher vertices are more lit than lower vertices) and has a variable-height terrain. Normally, you wouldn't have such rugged terrain, but I wanted to accentuate what you can do with height mapping.

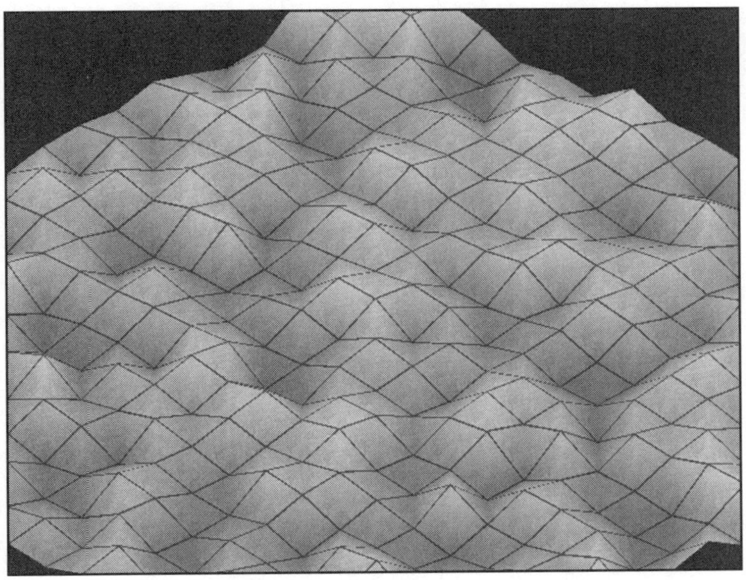

Figure 25.10

IsoHex25_5.cpp

The following code sets up the height map. The height map itself is an array with a first dimension size of `MAPWIDTH+1` and a second dimension size of `MAPHEIGHT+1`.

```
//set up the height map
int x;
int y;
//loop through x
for(x=0;x<=MAPWIDTH;x++)
{
	//loop through y
	for(y=0;y<=MAPHEIGHT;y++)
	{
		//assign random value
		HeightMap[x][y]=(float)(rand()%32);
	}
}
```

This is a simple-enough bit of code. Loop through all the positions in the height map, and assign them a random value of 0 through 31. After the map is initialized, the only other major change to this program is in `Prog_Loop`, during the actual rendering.

```
//loop through map
for(int y=0;y<MAPHEIGHT;y++)
{
	for(int x=0;x<MAPWIDTH;x++)
	{
		//calculate world coordinates for center of tile
		CenterX=(float)((x-y)*(TILEWIDTH/2)+320);
		CenterY=(float)((x+y)*(TILEHEIGHT/2));
		//set up the vertex
		//v1
		VERTEX_Set(&vert[0],CenterX-TILEWIDTH/2,CenterY
			-HeightMap[x][y+1],D3DRGB(1.0,1.0,1.0),0.0,0.0);
		vert[0].color=D3DRGB(0.5+HeightMap[x][y+1]/64.0,
			0.5+HeightMap[x][y+1]/64.0,0.5+HeightMap[x][y+1]/64.0);
		//v2
		VERTEX_Set(&vert[1],CenterX,CenterY-TILEHEIGHT/2
			-HeightMap[x][y],D3DRGB(1.0,1.0,1.0),1.0,0.0);
		vert[1].color=D3DRGB(0.5+HeightMap[x][y]/64.0,
			0.5+HeightMap[x][y]/64.0,0.5+HeightMap[x][y]/64.0);
		//v3
		VERTEX_Set(&vert[2],CenterX,CenterY+TILEHEIGHT/2
			-HeightMap[x+1][y+1],D3DRGB(1.0,1.0,1.0),0.0,1.0);
		vert[2].color=D3DRGB(0.5+HeightMap[x+1][y+1]/64.0,
			0.5+HeightMap[x+1][y+1]/64.0,0.5+HeightMap[x+1][y+1]/64.0);
```

```
            //v4
            VERTEX_Set(&vert[3],CenterX+TILEWIDTH/2,
                  CenterY-HeightMap[x+1][y],D3DRGB(1.0,1.0,1.0),1.0,1.0);
            vert[3].color=D3DRGB(0.5+HeightMap[x+1][y]/64.0,
                  0.5+HeightMap[x+1][y]/64.0,0.5+HeightMap[x+1][y]/64.0);
            //render the triangle strip
            LPD3DDEV_DrawTriangleStrip(lpd3ddev,vert,4);
      }
}
```

There is a change to each call to `VERTEX_Set` to incorporate the appropriate `HeightMap` value, subtracted from the y-coordinate. After each vertex is set up, a calculation is done based on the height of the vertex to determine the color of that vertex. All in all, it's a pretty simple example, but it looks pretty sweet. Play around with it.

Tile Selection/Mousemapping

So, now that you've seen what Direct3D makes very easy, it's time for the other shoe to drop. You may have looked at the height map example and wondered, "How the heck do I use a MouseMap on this?" The short answer is, you don't use a MouseMap in ISO3D. The long answer is, you do use a MouseMap, just not one like you are used to. Instead of using a small MouseMap that is repeated across the tilemap, you will be constructing a full-screen MouseMap. Why? Because with ISO3D—and especially when you use a height map—no set area is taken up by a tile's pixels. You will counteract this situation by having an extra surface that Direct3D will write your MouseMap onto.

One of the properties of isometric maps is that the x-coordinates align perfectly, even when you use a height map, since the z-coordinate affects only the y and leaves the x alone (see Figure 25.11). You can use this property to your advantage, because it divides the map into horizontal strips. This makes part of mousemapping easy, because you can narrow down which tiles the mouse is on, depending on the mouse's x position.

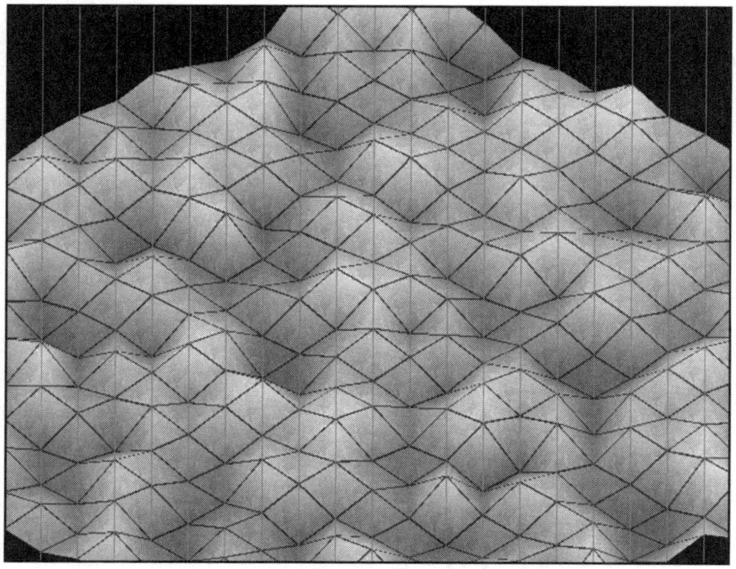

Figure 25.11

Alignment of x-coordinates

Unfortunately, the same cannot be said for the y position, because in a height map, it can vary widely. This is the part you have to do. The simplest solution that I have found is to assign a number to each row, starting with the number 1 for the first row (0 means "off the map"), and keep adding 1 to this number for additional rows.

I should point out that these are horizontal rows, not the diagonal rows you find on a diamond map. For slide and staggered maps, calculating which row a tile is on is easy, since it is just `MapY+1`. For diamond maps, it is `MapX+MapY+1`.

So, why not give each tile its own color? Well, you can do that, too, but it limits your map's size. In 16bpp, you have 65535 colors (not counting 0). This allows a map no larger than 255×255 if you are using the map colors strictly for tiles and not for object selection. In the one-color-per-row solution, you can have as many as 65535 rows. In a diamond map, this means that up to a 32767×32767 map is supported, and in other styles of map, up to 65534 rows are supported. Since you are unlikely to even come close to these limits, I'd say that one color per row is a good long-term solution.

You are left with only one problem: converting a row number into a color. Since Direct3D uses the `D3DRGB` macro to construct colors, you'll have something of a hard time converting. As luck would have it, the `D3DCOLOR` type is just a `DWORD` with 8 bits set aside for each of alpha, red, green, and blue. So, you can construct a color manually and guarantee that it will be unique for the row. In order to do that, however, you need to do some bit shifting.

You are in 16-bit mode, meaning either 5:6:5 or 5:5:5, and `D3DCOLOR` is 8:8:8, so you must ignore the 2 to 3 bits of each color component when constructing your colors from row numbers. This isn't really a big deal.

```
//5:6:5
//dwRow is row number
DWORD dwColor;
DWORD dwBlue=(dwRow & 0x1F)<<3;//and with mask, shift right by 3
DWORD dwGreen=((dwRow>>5)&0x3F)<<2;//and with mask, shift right by 2
DWORD dwRed=((dwRow>>11)&0x1f)<<3;//and with mask, shift right by 3
//construct the color
dwColor=(0xFF<<24)+(dwRed<<16)+(dwGreen<<8)+dwBlue;
```

Here's the equivalent code if you're unlucky enough to still have a 5:5:5 card (there's no shame in having an old computer):

```
//5:5:5
//dwRow is row number
DWORD dwColor;
DWORD dwBlue=(dwRow & 0x1F)<<3;//and with mask, shift right by 3
DWORD dwGreen=((dwRow>>5)&0x1F)<<3;//and with mask, shift right by 3
DWORD dwRed=((dwRow>>10)&0x1f)<<3;//and with mask, shift right by 3
//construct the color
dwColor=(0xFF<<24)+(dwRed<<16)+(dwGreen<<8)+dwBlue;
```

It seems silly, really. You take a number and convert it to a `D3DCOLOR`, which Direct3D converts into the surface's pixel format (it winds up as the same number you encoded in the first place).

So, how do you read this number? Simply lock the surface you are using for the MouseMap, and read the color at `MouseX`, `MouseY`. It's just that easy. From here, you can use the vertical strip that `MouseX` is in, and use the row number, and figure out which tile you are on. I'll let you figure out how on your own.

If you want to include object selection in your MouseMap, you must do only a few things. First, you must have a monochrome version of the sprite's texture (white where the image exists and black where it does not), which you load just like any other sprite texture (that is, alpha information). Next, you set aside one of the color bits as an indicator of an "object" (usually, this will be the highest red bit). Finally, you draw this texture on your additional rendering target. This makes object selection a cinch! It does limit the number of objects, but if you have more than 32,000 objects, there's really nothing I can do to help you make it fast!

Summary

We've touched on many subjects in this chapter without going deeply into any, because the information found herein relies entirely on the foundation of earlier chapters. For example, I didn't discuss how to do coastlines or roads on an ISO3D map because you're smart enough to be able to translate the 2D version to the 3D version, and I don't want to insult your intelligence or unnecessarily repeat subject matter.

Everything is moving to 3D now. For a while, isometric graphics were holding out in 2D land. As time progresses, doing so will be harder and harder, so it's best to accept the inevitable and just go to ISO3D—but not before you have mastered the fundamentals of ISO2D.

CHAPTER 26

The Road Ahead

- Current Trends
- What Lies Ahead

It looks like we've reached the end of the book. I hope I haven't left you hanging too much; I tried my best to cover all the bases adequately. If I haven't, I sincerely apologize, and I promise to make it up to you.

I started out easy, with basic WIN32 coding. It was by no means a comprehensive lesson in WIN32. I didn't talk about a whole bunch of stuff, including multithreaded programming, using controls such as buttons and textboxes, and so on. Then I moved into DirectX—namely, `DirectDraw` and `DirectSound`. I purposely didn't cover `DirectInput`, `DirectShow`, `DirectPlay`, `DirectMusic`, and any other `DirectSomethings`. I just put in what I thought was important. You might want to get a more well-rounded DirectX education. Also, I used DirectX 7 instead of 8, so you'll probably want to update to a newer version at some point.

With a firm foundation in place in WIN32 and DirectX, I got into the nuts and bolts of isometric graphics, the various types of maps, how to scroll, and object placement and selection. All of this stuff works mostly the same no matter what platform you're programming for or what type of game you're making.

Next, it was time for a bit of optimization, containing some of the wackiest code I've ever written. As a side note, I don't actually write code like what you've seen in this book. My usual approach to coding is a lot more object-oriented, but I was trying to write code that was pretty easy to read (I know my normal code takes an interpreter to decipher).

I touched on isometric art issues, tile slanting, and tile ripping. I also touched on world building and artificial intelligence. I truly wish I could have done more with AI, but I am not exactly a master of it (my skills lie mainly with graphics), and besides, there are entire volumes written about AI that cover it much better than I could.

Finally, I gave you a taste of Direct3D and showed you a few neat things you can do with 3D graphics to simulate 2D graphics while not overly complicating the rendering. You may be alarmed that I covered it in only two chapters. Well, in my defense, I can say that all the rest of the knowledge about isometric engines is in the chapters leading up to the Direct3D chapters.

If I didn't answer all your questions, or if I brought up more, come find me. I've got a Web site dedicated to support of this book (http://www.isohex.net). You can also e-mail me at tanstaafl@gamedev.net. I'll either try to answer your concern myself or refer you to a Web page that answers your question.

And hey, you can always come find me at the GDC or XGDC. I'm the fat guy with a crew cut wearing a GameDev.net t-shirt.

Current Trends

The entire world, it seems, is programming 3D games, although the isometric perspective is still quite popular, mainly for strategy and role-playing games. These games too are moving into 3D, even if that just means using 3D acceleration to render in 2D.

Why is this so? There are a number of factors. First, publishers won't put out any more 2D games except as value titles (things like "1,000 Games" packages that you see on the rack in department stores and electronics stores). Even in value titles, they are usually bundled with a bunch of other 2D games.

Second, technology is continuing to grow by leaps and bounds. At the beginning of 2000, I had a K6-2 300MHz computer with a lousy video card. By the end of the year, I was using an Athlon 700MHz with a Geforce 2 GTS, which still isn't top of the line. (If you're reading this any significant amount of time in the future—that is, 2002 or later—please try not to snicker at my puny computer.) The theory is that a big-title game should make use of the most modern technology available. If you're anything like me, you understand that not all games *need* to be 3D. Unfortunately, the rest of the world disagrees—or, at least, it seems to.

Third, gamers are like drug addicts; they need something new and better with each game they buy in order to get their high. This is especially true of first- and third-person shooter gamers. Gamers who are into strategy games and RPGs usually don't require that all the graphics be top-notch. The trick is to reach this group with your product. Since a publisher won't publish a 2D game, this makes it a little bit tougher, but that's where the Web comes in.

What Lies Ahead

Why are you still reading, when you should be coding a game? There's no time like the present, you know. I don't exactly have a crystal ball to look into the future and anticipate all the problems that are coming.

What I think is ahead: a more complete move to 3D. If DirectX 8.0 is any indicator, traditional 2D will, for the most part, be dead. Why blit partially transparent rectangles when you can texture map while using dynamic lighting and height mapping? The stuff that is currently new in video card technology will become commonplace (if the feature is used a lot) or will go away (if no one uses it). This is the way of things in technology.

What's ahead for you is totally up to you. Following are just a few bits of wisdom to ponder:

- **It doesn't happen overnight.** It takes a certain mind-set that not everyone has to be a solid game programmer. You must be creatively logical and logically creative. Both hemispheres of your brain must be fully engaged.
- **Programming is programming.** The rest is just syntax. Currently, I program in C++ using Microsoft Visual C++ 6.0 and make use of the DirectX API. This has not always been so and will not always be so. I have no particular loyalty to any operating system, compiler, or API. I used to program in BASIC and Pascal. I only moved to C++ in 1998. Lately, I've been learning to program for the Cybiko, so as of this moment, I am a cross-platform programmer. Here's the point: you don't want to be a "Windows programmer" or a "DirectX programmer"—you want to be a *programmer*. Programmers solve the problems of the day using the tools of the day, and they create the problems of tomorrow (job security, you know).
- **Games are supposed to be fun.** You probably already know that, but some people forget and they need to be reminded. Also, if you're just doing this as a hobby, game programming should also be fun. If neither the game nor making it is fun, stop and move on to something else. You can always take up gardening.
- **Start small.** I've seen it a thousand times: some young dude gets a compiler and a book and gets it into his head that he can program the greatest game ever with full 3D graphics, multiplayer, surround sound, and so on. This just doesn't happen. Beware of "feature creep," where you start adding ideas to the program in the middle of making it, thus guaranteeing it will never be done.
- **Finish what you start.** This goes along with the previous item. When you start small, finishing is easier, provided that you keep feature creep in check. Also, by finishing a project, you boost your morale a great deal, which makes finishing other projects easier. Oh, and by "finished," I don't mean "playable" or "fully functional." I mean a game that has been polished to publishable or near-publishable quality.
- **Don't be afraid to fail.** This is really important. If something is unfamiliar to you, try it out. Attempt to muddle through it. Leave a long trail of runtime errors and page faults and blue screens of death in your wake. Be patient.
- **Don't be afraid to get help.** Buy books. Buy lots of books. Read them. Do the sample programs. Modify the sample programs until they break (that's what they're for). Go to Web sites and look for articles, post your questions on message boards, go to game programming chat rooms, find the game programmers on ICQ and AIM. No matter what your programming level, there are programmers better than you are (apologies if this book happens to get into the hands of the best programmer in the world).

"Never give up; never surrender!" "Do, or do not. There is no try." (Insert words of encouragement here.) All right...enough is enough. Stop reading and go make a game or something. Shoo!

Part V

Appendices

APPENDIX A

Loading Sample Projects into the IDE

In this appendix, I'll show you how to load the examples into your compiler so that you can build them and run them. I wrote all the examples for this book using VC++ version 6. This isn't to say that they won't work on other versions of VC++ or that you can't get them to work on other compilers.

To demonstrate the loading of an example, I will use IsoHex1_1.cpp. I have chosen this example because it contains only one file. At the top of the main file (the only file in this case), you can see a number of commented lines.

```
/*********************************************
IsoHex1_1.cpp
Ernest S. Pazera
08APR2000
Start a WIN32 Application Workspace, add in this file
No other libs are required
*********************************************/
```

Within this area, I have placed applicable information about the example: the name of the file, the name of the author (me!), when I wrote it, how to start a project for it, and what other files or libraries are required to make the program work. As you get further along, you'll have more than just a single file in your projects. You'll never quite get to the level of a real-world project, which can contain hundreds of source files, but expect at some point to reach at least half a dozen.

To load an example into your compiler, do the following:

1. Start your compiler and select the menu option File, New, as shown in Figure A.1. This brings up the dialog box shown in Figure A.2.

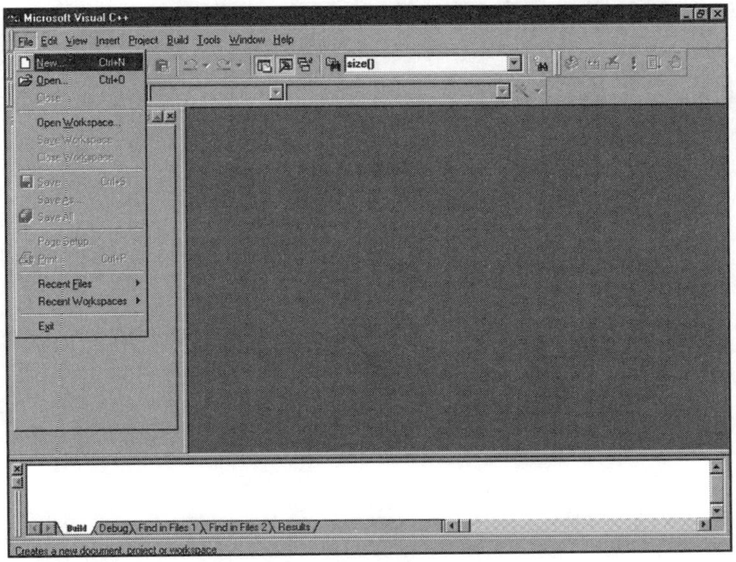

Figure A.1

Selecting File, New from the IDE

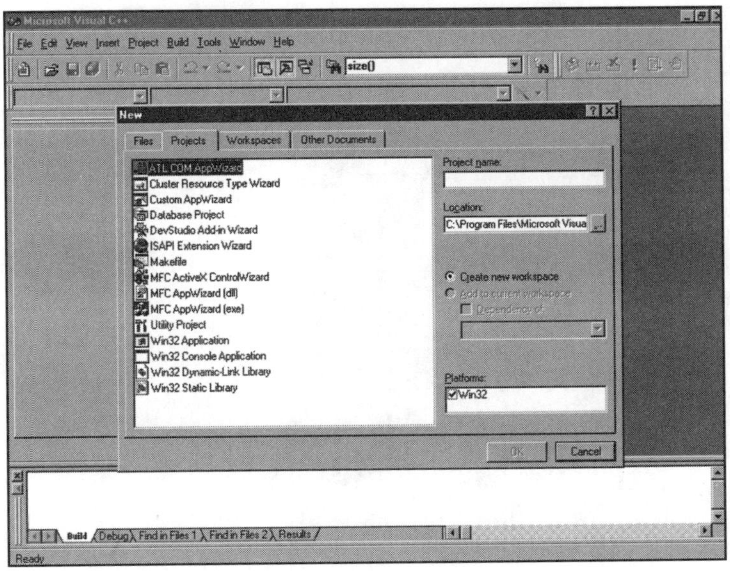

Figure A.2

The new project dialog box

2. Make certain you are on the Projects tab.
3. You can create many different types of projects. My examples are all WIN32 applications, so click on the line that says Win32 Application, and enter a project name in the Project name textbox at the top right (see Figure A.3).

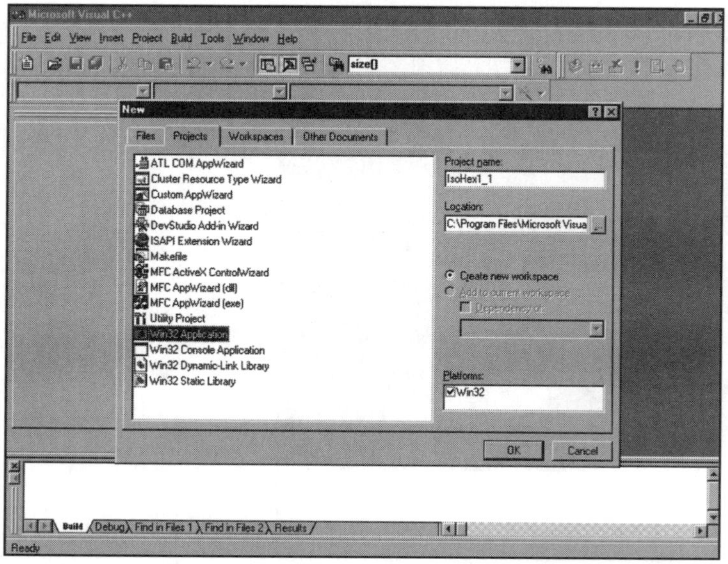

Figure A.3

Giving a project a name (always be sure to select WIN32 Application)

4. Click on the OK button. You'll see the dialog box shown in Figure A.4.

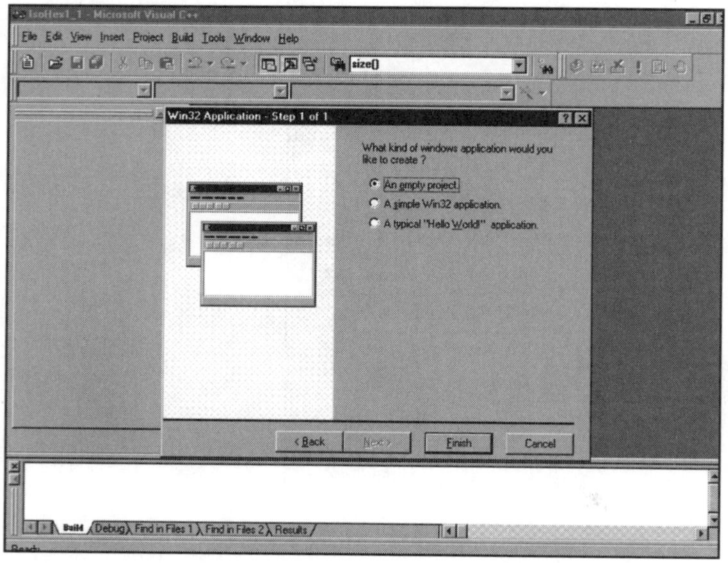

Figure A.4

The WIN32 Application Wizard

5. Make certain that the "An empty project." option is selected, and click on the Finish button.

You will be taken to your new, empty workspace. Now, copy any of the needed files into the project's folder. (The default location when you install VC++ is C:\Program Files\Microsoft Visual Studio\MyProjects*ProjectName*\, where *ProjectName* is whatever name you gave your project.)

After you have copied the applicable files, you must add them to your project by doing the following:

1. Select Project, Add To Project, Files, as shown in Figure A.5. The dialog box shown in Figure A.6 will open.

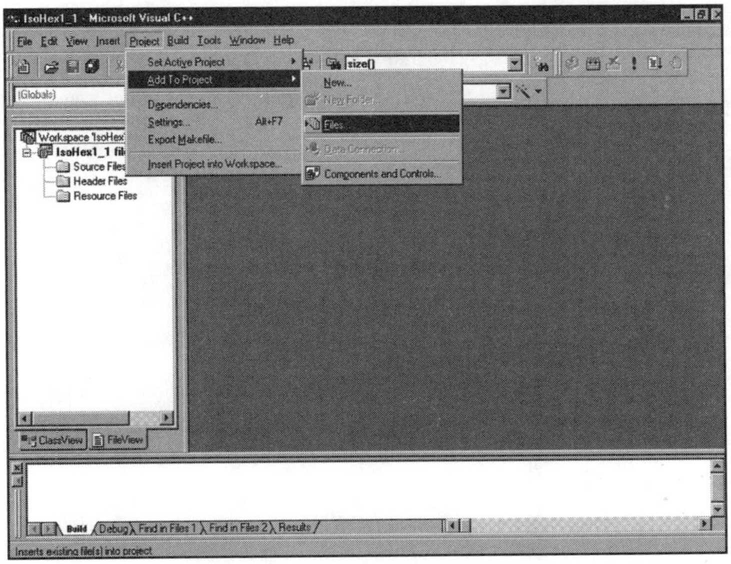

Figure A.5

Adding files to a project

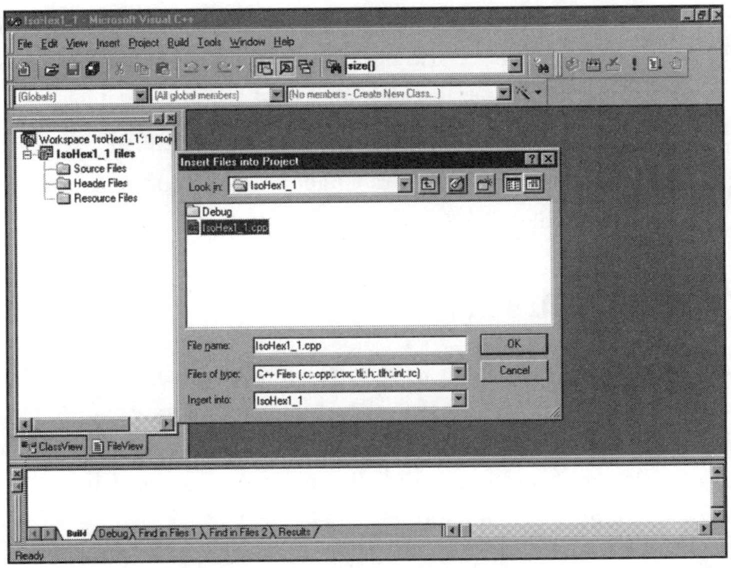

Figure A.6

The standard file open dialog

2. Select whatever .cpp or .h files the example requires, and click on OK.

You can now examine the files from the File View tab in the compiler's leftmost pane by manipulating the tree view (see Figure A.7).

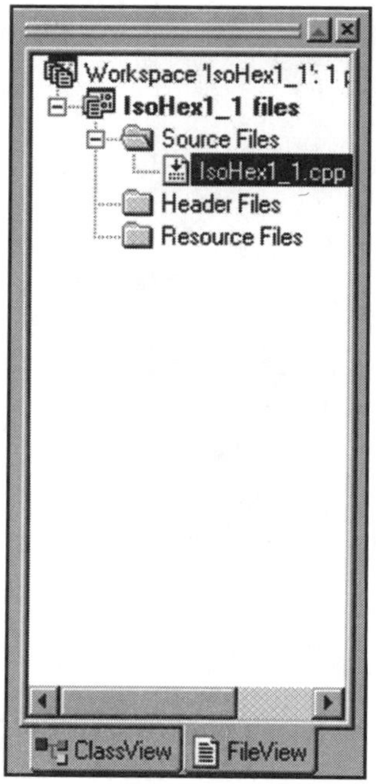

Figure A.7

The tree view of files, in which double-clicking on a file displays the file's contents in the main viewing pane

You can build the executable by pressing F7 or by selecting Build, Build. After it is built, you can run it by pressing Ctrl+F5 or by selecting Build, Execute. There are also buttons on the toolbar for these tasks. If you run before you have rebuilt, the compiler will ask you if you want things rebuilt (compilers are getting smarter and smarter).

That's really all there is to it, at least until you get into DirectX in Chapter 4 (I'll show you what you need to do then).

Coding Conventions

After you spend any amount of time looking at code I have written, you'll notice that I precede the names of variables with letters such as "dw" and "lp" and "n." This is called Hungarian notation. I don't follow all the convention to the letter, but I've tried to be consistent for the book's sake. Table 0.1 lists some of the most common prefixes I commonly use. Knowing these will help you when you read Microsoft documentation, because all Microsoft code uses Hungarian notation.

Table A.1 Common Prefixes in Hungarian Notation

Data Type	Prefix
`bool`	b
`char`	c or ch
`unsigned char` (`BYTE`)	uc or by
`short int`	n
`unsigned short` (`WORD`)	w
`int`	n or i
`unsigned int` (`DWORD`)	dw
Flags	f (usually combined with w or dw)
`char*` (pointer to a string)	lpsz
Pointer	p
Long pointer	lp

My indentation style is pretty normal. The contents between a `{` and a `}` are indented. The initial `{` is on a new line, as shown here:

```
for(int x=0;x<10;x++)
{
      //code here is indented
}
```

This might be a slight change if you're used to indenting in the more traditional C style:

```
for(int x=0;x<10;x++){
      //code here is indented
}
```

I was never very fond of this style (I used to program in Pascal), because I like to see the `{` and `}` line up vertically. This is just a matter of taste.

APPENDIX B

Hexagonal Tile-Based Games

In my original articles on the topic of isometric graphics, I also spoke of hexagonal graphics, because they were so similar. In this book, I have primarily concentrated on isometric graphics, but I didn't want to leave out people who are into hex (and you know who you are). I also wanted all the hex-specific stuff to be in one place, where I could just show what differs from iso, for those who are just interested in the iso stuff (and I imagine most people are interested in iso rather than hex).

Iso versus Hex

Depending on the game you're making, there are plenty of good reasons to choose iso over hex, or hex over iso. Some games make more sense one way and seem kind of weird when using the other. This mainly boils down to a judgment call on your part. If something isn't working as well using hex, switch to iso to see if it's any better. If something just doesn't seem right in iso, give hex a try.

If you've played tabletop strategy games (many of these games are from Avalon Hill, the ones with little cardboard counters to keep track of units), and you like these games, and you want to make a video game that is similar, hex is probably your best bet.

Another reason to use hex rather than iso is that hex is different. All kinds of games use iso, but not many use hex. If you want your game to stand out, hex is a way to do it.

What's the Difference?

The vast majority of the algorithms for iso can be used for hex, with no change or very little change. Generally, about the only thing you'll need to change is the MouseMap. Figure B.1 shows what a hex MouseMap might look like.

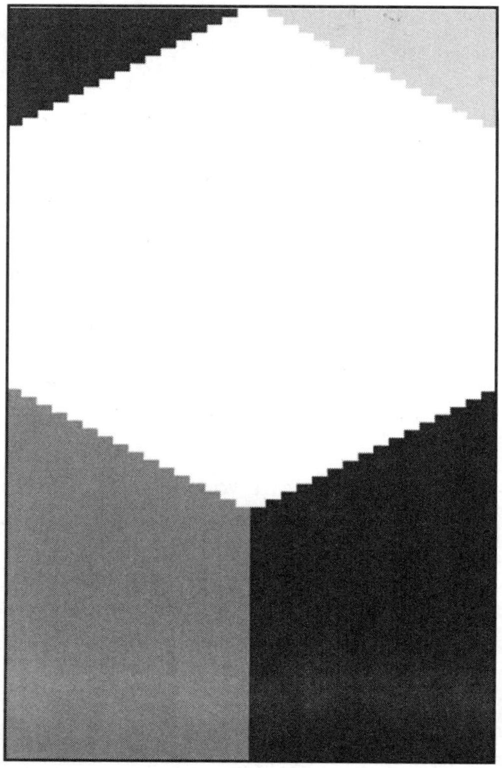

Figure B.1

Hexagonal MouseMap

Take a look at IsoHexB_1.cpp and its associated files (shown in figure B.2). This example is the exact same code as IsoHex15_1.cpp, except with different, hexagonal graphics. This example shows you exactly how easy it is to switch between iso and hex. It also shows that there is nothing you don't already know about the rendering of the hexagonal engine. Almost everything is the same. I do suggest that you primarily stick to staggered maps for hex, unless you have a good reason not to.

Moving around the hex map is slightly different than in iso, but it simply involves the removal of two directions (in the case of this tile shape, north and south are those directions). So if you don't move in those directions, everything will be OK.

Summary

Hexagonal graphics and hexagonal engines are nothing but an isometric graphical engine with a rectangular block inserted in the middle. I don't mean to belittle hexagonal engines, but this is what they really boil down to. This book's support site (http://www.isohex.net) has a section dedicated to hex games.

APPENDIX C

IsoHex Resources

A book about game programming is not complete without a list of other resources you can turn to for help. This appendix mainly lists Web pages, but I've also included a few books on general game programming and other general programming topics. As luck would have it, this book is the only book (that I know of) that specifically covers the topic of isometric graphics in games, so I really have no competition to speak of.

See the Sites

The following is a list of Web sites/pages that might be of interest to you. You've probably already been to several of these in search of knowledge.

IsoHex.net

http://www.isohex.net

This is my own site, specifically for the support of this book. If you are having trouble with some of my code, or are looking for errata, or have a neat isometric game or tutorial or new technique you've written, come on by. The purpose of IsoHex.net is to build upon the content in the book, and you can contribute if you like.

I will also keep a list of good sites for isometric information at this site.

GameDev.net

http://www.gamedev.net/gamedev.asp

Apologies to Dave, Kevin, John, and Mike for not listing this page first. GameDev.net is the best game programming Web site ever created. I know this because I am one of the members of the company that maintains this site.

http://www.gamedev.net/reference/list.asp?categoryid=44

This specific GameDev link is for the list of isometric and other tile-based programming articles on the site. A few old ones are by me. There's lots of good stuff there.

XTreme Games

http://www.xgames3d.com/

This is Andre LaMothe's site. If you don't know who Andre LaMothe is, well, you should. He's the series editor for this book and series; his name is on the cover. He's the guy who wrote *Tricks of the Windows Game Programming Gurus,* as well as a number of other books about game programming. And he plays Metallica MIDIs on his page.

Isometrix

http://www.isometrix.org/

Comprehensive resources on isometric algorithms and graphics are few and far between. Before I created IsoHex.net, this site, run by Yanni Deliyannis, was really the only one. Isometrix is an iso engine based on an older DOS engine by Jim Adams. If you don't know who Jim Adams is, just wait. He has a book in this series that should be coming out soon.

Hit the Books

It would be great if you only needed the information in this book and never needed to go to another. Unfortunately, it doesn't work like that. And yes, I know that these books are expensive. Here are a few selections from my own library I'd like to share.

LaMothe, Andre. *Windows Game Programming for Dummies* Indianapolis: IDG Books, 1998

This is a great book for learning DirectX and WIN32 programming (it goes into greater detail than I was able to).

LaMothe, Andre. *Tricks of the Windows Game Programming Gurus* Indianapolis: Sams Publishing, 1999

Although much of the subject matter in this book and the *Dummies* book is the same or similar, there is much more detail in this one. Also, the second edition will cover more 3D graphics.

Drop Me a Line

Web sites come and go, as do Internet service providers. If you want to get in touch with me, your best bet is probably to e-mail me. For the conceivable future, my e-mail address is tanstaafl@gamedev.net. I also hang out in IRC on afternet, in the #gamedev channel. My nick is TANSTAAFL.

And before you feel the need to ask, TANSTAAFL stands for "There ain't no such thing as a free lunch."

Index

D

E

F

G

H

I

N

O

T

U

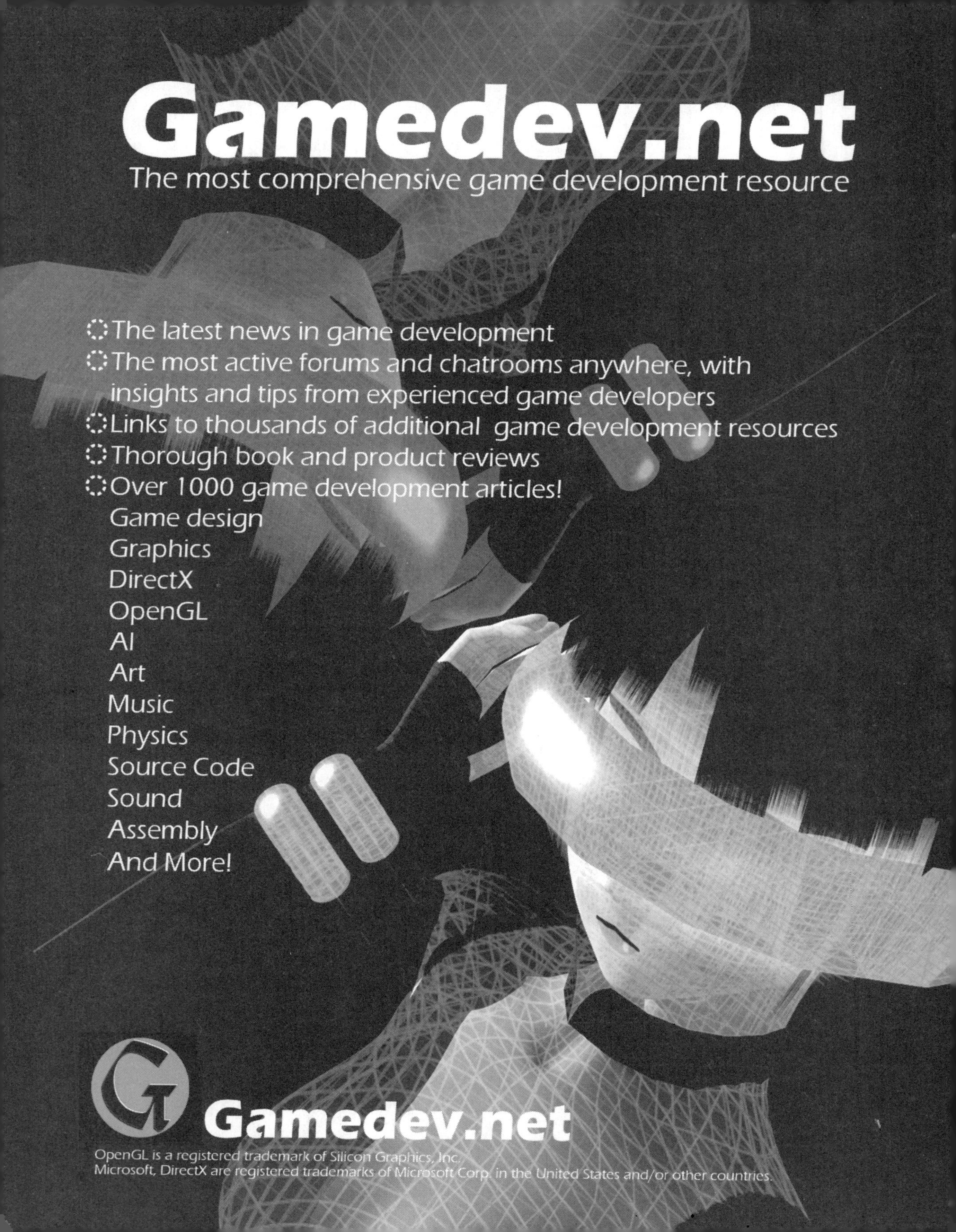
Gamedev.net
The most comprehensive game development resource
The latest news in game development
The most active forums and chatrooms anywhere, with insights and tips from experienced game developers
Links to thousands of additional game development resources
Thorough book and product reviews
Over 1000 game development articles!
Game design
Graphics
DirectX
OpenGL
AI
Art
Music
Physics
Source Code
Sound
Assembly
And More!
Gamedev.net
OpenGL is a registered trademark of Silicon Graphics, Inc.
Microsoft, DirectX are registered trademarks of Microsoft Corp. in the United States and/or other countries.

TAKE YOUR GAME TO THE
XTREME!
Xtreme Games LLC was founded to help small game developers around the world create and publish their games on the commercial market. Xtreme Games helps younger developers break into the field of game programming by insulating them from complex legal and business issues. Xtreme Games has hundreds of developers around the world, if you're interested in becoming one of them, then visit us at www.xgames3d.com.
www.xgames3d.com
XTREME GAMES LLC

License Agreement/Notice of Limited Warranty

By opening the sealed disc container in this book, you agree to the following terms and conditions. If, upon reading the following license agreement and notice of limited warranty, you cannot agree to the terms and conditions set forth, return the unused book with unopened disc to the place where you purchased it for a refund.

License:
The enclosed software is copyrighted by the copyright holder(s) indicated on the software disc. You are licensed to copy the software onto a single computer for use by a single concurrent user and to a backup disk. You may not reproduce, make copies, or distribute copies or rent or lease the software in whole or in part, except with written permission of the copyright holder(s). You may transfer the enclosed disc only together with this license, and only if you destroy all other copies of the software and the transferee agrees to the terms of the license. You may not decompile, reverse assemble, or reverse engineer the software.

Notice of Limited Warranty:
The enclosed disc is warranted by Prima Publishing to be free of physical defects in materials and workmanship for a period of sixty (60) days from end user's purchase of the book/disc combination. During the sixty-day term of the limited warranty, Prima will provide a replacement disc upon the return of a defective disc.

Limited Liability:
THE SOLE REMEDY FOR BREACH OF THIS LIMITED WARRANTY SHALL CONSIST ENTIRELY OF REPLACEMENT OF THE DEFECTIVE DISC. IN NO EVENT SHALL PRIMA OR THE AUTHORS BE LIABLE FOR ANY OTHER DAMAGES, INCLUDING LOSS OR CORRUPTION OF DATA, CHANGES IN THE FUNCTIONAL CHARACTERISTICS OF THE HARDWARE OR OPERATING SYSTEM, DELETERIOUS INTERACTION WITH OTHER SOFTWARE, OR ANY OTHER SPECIAL, INCIDENTAL, OR CONSEQUENTIAL DAMAGES THAT MAY ARISE, EVEN IF PRIMA AND/OR THE AUTHOR HAVE PREVIOUSLY BEEN NOTIFIED THAT THE POSSIBILITY OF SUCH DAMAGES EXISTS.

Disclaimer of Warranties:
PRIMA AND THE AUTHORS SPECIFICALLY DISCLAIM ANY AND ALL OTHER WARRANTIES, EITHER EXPRESS OR IMPLIED, INCLUDING WARRANTIES OF MERCHANTABILITY, SUITABILITY TO A PARTICULAR TASK OR PURPOSE, OR FREEDOM FROM ERRORS. SOME STATES DO NOT ALLOW FOR EXCLUSION OF IMPLIED WARRANTIES OR LIMITATION OF INCIDENTAL OR CONSEQUENTIAL DAMAGES, SO THESE LIMITATIONS MAY NOT APPLY TO YOU.

Other:
This Agreement is governed by the laws of the State of California without regard to choice of law principles. The United Convention of Contracts for the International Sale of Goods is specifically disclaimed. This Agreement constitutes the entire agreement